THE BUSINESS STUDENT'S GUIDE TO STUDY AND EMPLOYABILITY

Sara Miller McCune founded SAGE Publishing in 1965 to support the dissemination of usable knowledge and educate a global community. SAGE publishes more than 1000 journals and over 800 new books each year, spanning a wide range of subject areas. Our growing selection of library products includes archives, data, case studies and video. SAGE remains majority owned by our founder and after her lifetime will become owned by a charitable trust that secures the company's continued independence.

Los Angeles | London | New Delhi | Singapore | Washington DC | Melbourne

SECOND EDITION

THE BUSINESS STUDENT'S GUIDE TO STUDY AND EMPLOYABILITY

PETER MORGAN

$SAGE

Los Angeles | London | New Delhi
Singapore | Washington DC | Melbourne

Los Angeles | London | New Delhi
Singapore | Washington DC | Melbourne

SAGE Publications Ltd
1 Oliver's Yard
55 City Road
London EC1Y 1SP

SAGE Publications Inc.
2455 Teller Road
Thousand Oaks, California 91320

SAGE Publications India Pvt Ltd
B 1/I 1 Mohan Cooperative Industrial Area
Mathura Road
New Delhi 110 044

SAGE Publications Asia-Pacific Pte Ltd
3 Church Street
#10-04 Samsung Hub
Singapore 049483

Editor: Kirsty Smy
Assistant editor: Jessica Moran
Associate content development editor: Sunita Patel
Production editor: Nicola Carrier
Copyeditor: Gemma Marren
Proofreader: Tom Bedford
Indexer: Elske Janssen
Marketing manager: Abigail Sparks
Cover design: Naomi Robinson
Typeset by: C&M Digitals (P) Ltd, Chennai, India
Printed in the UK

Library of Congress Control Number: 2020936916

British Library Cataloguing in Publication data

A catalogue record for this book is available from
the British Library

ISBN 978-1-5264-9338-5
ISBN 978-1-5264-9337-8 (pbk)

At SAGE we take sustainability seriously. Most of our products are printed in the UK using responsibly sourced
papers and boards. When we print overseas we ensure sustainable papers are used as measured by the PREPS
grading system. We undertake an annual audit to monitor our sustainability.

CONTENTS

ABOUT THE AUTHOR

 **Dr Peter Morgan** is currently Associate Dean – Education and Student Experience, at the Nottingham University Business School in China. He qualified as a teacher of English as a Foreign Language in 1992, and began his academic career in 1996, first graduating with a PhD in Occupational Psychology from – and subsequently working at – the University of Bradford School of Management. He led the development of the School's learning and teaching strategy as Learning and Teaching Coordinator, had responsibility for the development of academic staff as Faculty Development Coordinator and was on interviewing panels for administrative, academic and senior institutional appointments as a member of the senate. He moved to China in September 2012, taking up the role of Associate Dean at the Business School in June 2013, and was the Director of Teaching for the Faculty of Social Sciences between October 2013 and March 2019. He is also Inter-Campus Quality Officer for the University of Nottingham, has worked on projects relating to interactive teaching and student transition and established the University of Nottingham Ningbo China's Teaching and Learning Conference in 2015.

As a passionate believer in the student experience and the importance of personal development, Dr Morgan has been developing and delivering skill development modules for undergraduate, postgraduate (including MBA) and doctoral students since beginning his academic career. He has delivered interactive and engaging workshops on study skills, personal transferable skills and employer selection methods to students in the UK, Singapore, India, China, the Netherlands, Malaysia and Israel; trained academic staff in Poland, China, India and Singapore on issues of educational pedagogy; presented at the Academy of Management and provided workshop sessions organised through the Higher Education Academy; and received institutional awards for his teaching work at both the University of Bradford and the University of Nottingham.

ACKNOWLEDGEMENTS

Writing a text like this has not been easy. It has taken a long time and, in the middle of a very busy role in China, has taken determination. That has needed a great deal of patience from the publishers and a great deal of encouragement from a number of others.

So, my sincere thanks go to my many colleagues, friends, critics and publishers who have helped with this book in so many ways. To my colleagues who have taught and worked with me in the UK and helped to develop and steer my teaching in this area in order to support several thousand students, I am deeply appreciative. I am particularly grateful to my father, who has given me more support and resources than I could have expected to help me get this far in life – and with this book. I am also grateful to my family and friends who have not seen me for some time.

I would also like to thank those colleagues and friends who have contributed so freely to the final chapter of this text, giving insights and learning developed over the course of their careers to date. On behalf of those who will read and benefit from what they have written, many thanks indeed.

I would also like to thank those who have contributed to the content through their comments or their editorial input. My thanks go to the anonymous reviewers who have been extremely encouraging and helpful – without their input, this text would not have been what it is. Most of all, I would like to thank all those at SAGE with whom I have worked, and who have encouraged me with this book over the many months that it has taken to get this far: to Kirsty Smy, Sarah Turpie and all the editorial and production teams who had faith in me at the start, provided encouragement even when little was arriving in their inbox, and who have guided the production of this text so smoothly.

And finally … to all my students over the years, my deepest and sincere thanks for engaging with me and helping me to improve what I do. Without you, there would be no book. Thanks, indeed.

PUBLISHER'S ACKNOWLEDGEMENTS

The publisher would like to extend their warmest thanks to the following individuals for their invaluable feedback on the proposal and the draft material for this book.

LECTURER REVIEWERS

Aarti Vyas-Brannick, Manchester Metropolitan University

Anni Hollings, Staffordshire University

Aron Truss, University of Portsmouth

Edward Thompson, De Montfort University

Geetha Karunanayake, University of Hull

Izabela Robinson, University of Northampton

Jela Webb, University of Brighton

Kathy Daniels, Aston University

Keith Pond, Loughborough University

Maria McCabe, University of Leeds

Moira Hughes, Edinburgh Napier University

Peter Naudé, University of Manchester

Silvia Szilagyiova, York St. John University

Stephen Robinson, University of Kent

Sunrita Dhar-Bhattacharjee, Anglia Ruskin University

Tracy McAteer, Oxford Brookes University

STUDENT REVIEWERS

Ben Summerton, De Montfort University

Carrie Stevens, De Montfort University

Chen Dong, University of Leeds

Daniel Pallas, Aston University

Emma Wilson, Aston University

Hannah Derry, Aston University

Karen Stringer, Aston University

Michaela Maginnis, De Montfort University

Moondy Zheng, University of Leeds

Saif Javed, Aston University

Weiwei Lin, University of Leeds

Every effort has been made to trace the copyright holders and we apologise in advance for any unintentional omissions. We would be pleased to insert the appropriate acknowledgement in any subsequent edition of this publication.

GUIDED TOUR OF YOUR BOOK

WHEN SHOULD YOU READ THIS CHAPTER?

Provides an indication of when – in a typical undergraduate's academic career – the chapter would be most useful.

SKILLS SELF-ASSESSMENT TABLES

List tasks that help you to evaluate your own skills, attitudes and behaviours, before studying each topic. Answers or guidance can be found on the companion website for the book.

KEY LEARNING POINT

A useful stop-point to help make sure you have understood the key concepts and issues.

'BUT I HAVE A QUESTION ...'

Offers common FAQs and helpful advice on the topic you are studying.

FOR YOU TO DO

Short exercises to help you to apply the learning that has been given elsewhere in the chapter.

REFLECTION POINT

Encourages you to pause from your reading and think further about key topics that have been presented.

BOXES

Offer key points of interest or examples of real-life situations to help explain the content of the chapter or relate pieces of research to real-life experiences.

DEFINITIONS

Clear explanations of key concepts.

CHAPTER TASK

Tasks designed to help you put into practice what you have learned in that chapter.

INTERVIEW QUESTIONS

In Parts I–IV, each chapter concludes with a list of possible interview questions that an employer might ask around the topic. Discussion of these questions is provided on the companion website.

ADDITIONAL RESOURCES

Each chapter ends with a list of key additional resources to help you broaden your understanding of the topic.

Web Icons

Indicate when you will find exciting and relevant additional content on the companion website at **https://study.sagepub.com/morgan2e**

COMPANION WEBSITE

Head online to **https://study.sagepub.com/morgan2e** to access a range of online resources that will aid study and support teaching. The second edition of *The Business Student's Guide to Study and Employability* is accompanied by:

Lecturer resources:

Video introduction to the book for lecturers by the author.

Instructor's manual providing a useful referencing tool to help lecturers navigate the textbook.

PowerPoint slides that can be downloaded and customised to suit teaching needs.

One author video per chapter ideal for use in class to spark discussion and debate.

Student resources:

Video introduction to the book for students by the author.

Interactive self-testing activities to assess knowledge and aid exam preparation.

Group and individual tasks designed to enhance learning both online and in the classroom.

Further readings and templates that expand on knowledge of key concepts discussed in the book.

Two additional online chapters 'Psychometric Tests and Assessment Centres' and 'Alternative Options After Graduation', with accompanying author videos for extra support.

When you see the this means go to the companion website **https://study.sagepub.com/morgan2e** to do a quiz, complete a task, read further or download a template.

INTRODUCTION

Welcome to this book … and the start of your time at university. This text has been written to help you move from pre-university studies to completing those studies successfully and then to move into employment by performing well in employer selection events. There is no other text which does this at this level of detail.

MY OWN BACKGROUND

I would like to tell you something about myself – it might help you to learn more about how I have recognised and learnt the things written in this book. I studied at a university some 300 miles (480 km) away from my home: I moved from a seaside resort to a very diverse inner city to join about 170 other students on a four-year management course. I had particular reasons for choosing the university and the course – it was the only course at a university (we had academic universities and the more applied 'polytechnics' in the UK at that time) I could do that gave me a year in industry. I was aiming for a career in human resources management, and chose a course that gave me a sufficient mix of HR and psychology to enable me to enter that career.

Despite my understanding of employee selection issues, I graduated without a job, an experience I would never want to repeat, nor would I want anyone else to do so. I had a place on a PhD programme, but no funding, so I trained for a month as a teacher of English as a Foreign Language, became a teacher in a local language school and eventually received the funding I had sought to begin a PhD a year after graduating.

After I completed my PhD, I started using the interactive teaching techniques I had picked up while teaching English to deliver skills workshops to undergraduate students for two hours once a week – first interpersonal employability skills, and then study skills support as the need became apparent. Some of that teaching involved asking students to develop ideas to raise money for well-known charities, while other ideas included bringing in managers from a local business to mentor or assess student presentations.

I moved from the UK to work in China in 2012 and became Associate Dean at Nottingham University Business School (and Faculty Director of Teaching for the Faculty of the Social Sciences) the following summer.

All this has not been particularly planned, I have to confess. While most of my family are or were teachers in some form or another, it was not my intention to follow them, although that is what happened. As I have moved through my 20+ years in academia, I have picked up some ideas about what university education is really about and how it works – and many of those are written here for you.

The world has changed a great deal since I studied at university. That was a time before mobile phones and when the internet and email did not exist (which makes me sound very old!), when plagiarism was not a concern, when a BlackBerry was a fruit from the garden, and when we picked up how to do citations through some magic process of mimicking what we saw when we read journal articles. Student numbers were much lower then and we could access our lecturers far easier than seems to happen in some places nowadays. Some of the luxuries I grew up with at university are not quite so apparent now, yet studying at university is one of the most fantastic and challenging experiences any individual can have. This book is intended to support your experience, so please use it wisely and get any additional advice from your lecturers.

PART I
LIFE AT UNIVERSITY

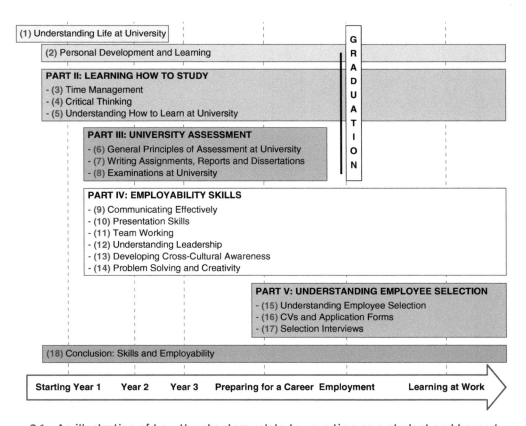

Figure O.1   An illustration of how the chapters relate to your time as a student and beyond

This book is intended to take you from your first weeks as a university student (or returning student, if you are studying a postgraduate course), through your university years and into employment. As such, it is fairly unique. In fact, if I had included everything I wanted to write, this book would have been a lot larger than it already is, so there is additional information on the companion website.

As shown in Figure 0.1, the text is broken down into parts, broadly following the various stages of your university studies. For undergraduate students, these will last for three or four years, and for most UK postgraduate courses, between one year and 18 months. The first part is intended to provide a supplement to any induction you might be given at university and to help provide some explanation of what universities do and how they do it: having this understanding means that this text can be most useful to you. Part II is about learning at university and includes chapters on time management, teaching methods, and the nature and importance of critical thinking. Part III covers assessment at university. The chapters here can never cover every method of assessment used, but they provide some broad principles and apply them to written coursework assessment and examinations.

Part IV provides an overlap between the skills that you will develop during your time at university as a student and those you will almost certainly use in the workplace. University is intended to be a period in your life that will prepare you for what some people call the 'real world', where what you do will have a very real impact on others' lives; that preparation is often more about the skills you develop than the knowledge you gain.

To really benefit from Parts II to IV, it is helpful to have an understanding of how skill development and personal learning takes place, and to feel comfortable in this new world of 'university'. To that end, the first part of the book covers two areas: a brief initial chapter outlining life at university, which is intended to help you make sense of the new world in which you now find yourself, and a chapter that discusses the processes of personal development and the acquisition of personal transferable skills. The content of this second chapter gives a foundation to your development of the skills covered in Parts II, III and IV – skills that will be crucial in your moving through the employee selection processes outlined in Part V.

1 UNDERSTANDING LIFE AT UNIVERSITY

Learning is the only thing the mind never exhausts, never fears and never regrets. (Leonardo Da Vinci)

CHAPTER STRUCTURE

Figure 1.1

When you see the this means go to the companion website https://study.sagepub.com/morgan2e to do a quiz, complete a task, read further or download a template.

AIMS OF THE CHAPTER

By the end of this chapter, you should be able to:

- Describe what it is that universities do, and start some thinking about how they do it.
- Understand how university may differ from previous learning environments you might have come across.
- Understand why differences between university and other forms of education exist.
- Find your way around the university bureaucracy and systems so that your time at university will be enjoyable, rather than stressful.

WHEN SHOULD YOU READ THIS CHAPTER?

This chapter provides an introduction to university life, and so it is best to read this during your first three weeks at university.

INTRODUCTION

This chapter is intended to act as a 'knowledgeable friend' to guide you through the world of study. This may be as a mature student, an undergraduate or postgraduate student, an international or domestic student – studying for a variety of reasons and in a variety of circumstances.

It is intended to provide a welcome to university and sets out to clarify what universities are about and how they do what they do. Before we go too far, it is important to say that different universities will do things differently: terminology might vary, the methods and facilities used to support students will vary, and the course structures and regulations will also vary.

We will begin by giving you a chance to develop your own expectations regarding university life. We will also provide a welcome to university life and help you to answer questions such as 'What is university all about?' and 'How can I access any help I might need?' The chapter will then give some ideas as to why the non-academic side of life at university can be as important as the academic side, before providing some analysis of university culture, university processes and student culture. We will conclude by giving you the chance to consider and recognise some differences between your previous education and education at university.

Let's start by finding out how much you know.

SKILLS SELF-ASSESSMENT

How much do you know about university? Please indicate whether you think that the following statements are true or false.

Item		True?	False?
1.	University is just about attending lectures, getting to tutorials and passing your modules		
2.	I am excited about starting university		
3.	I do not think my university experience is going to be very different from my previous school or college experience		
4.	Personal development is something that I do not really need to think about very much		
5.	I do not really have much of an idea what I will do after I finish university		
6.	I want to do as much paid work as I can during university		
7.	Lectures are where all my learning will take place		
8.	I am committed to getting the best grades I can; I do not want 'just to pass'		
9.	I expect that most of my assessment will be by examination at the end of the module		
10.	If I can, I would prefer to live outside of the university and study as much as I can		
11.	Universities exist solely to teach students		
12.	I do not really need to think about getting a job or starting a career yet, I need to focus on my studies		
13.	My parents are really interested in my university studies, so I am likely to talk to them about my progress		

Item		True?	False?
14.	My learning will depend on my own effort and the work I put in		
15.	I think I am going to find it easy to manage my budget		
16.	I know how to use the internet well and am comfortable with using it for my learning		
17.	Study skills are simply skills that teach me how to study; when I finish university, I will have no need for such skills		
18.	I intend to use my time at university to have as much fun as possible		
19.	I will always ask my lecturers if I have some questions about university		
20.	Lecturers will always be available for me when I want		
21.	My university will always understand that I need to pay for university by working, rather than attend classes – if there is ever a clash		
22.	If I have domestic duties (e.g. looking after children), then I will need to give these up in order to develop myself		
23.	Every employer will be looking for the same skills from the university graduates they take on		

An interactive version of this test, along with answers, comments and thoughts about these questions can be found on the companion website for this book at https://study.sagepub.com/morgan2e.

INTERACTIVE
TEST

UNDERSTANDING THE ACADEMIC SIDE OF UNIVERSITY LIFE

What is the 'university experience'? The next few years of living and studying at university will give you a range of experiences. Some of these will arise from your degree course (or 'academic') experiences. Others will be social. Some parts of this experience will be compulsory for you, and some parts will be entirely optional. Your choice has been to take up a university place with all the enjoyment (and challenges) that being a university student involves. It can be a scary experience, but the variety of opportunities is generally unrivalled in life and, for many, the impact of making mistakes is much smaller than it would be after graduation.

The academic staff – your tutors, lecturers, professors and associated administrative staff based in the various departments of the university – have responsibility for managing your academic experience. That means they have responsibility for ensuring that you are being given a teaching, learning and assessment experience which encourages and facilitates your learning and personal development. One of the key things you need to be aware of is the following: *everything else* – the content of lectures, the ways that you are taught and assessed, the organisation of social activities, living independently – *arises from this key goal*.

Studying at university is generally seen as a good idea. Some argue that university is artificial, that it is not 'real life'. Some suggest that you can learn better from being in a work environment, or even that you can study all the videos and materials available online, or use your Kindle/e-reader and learn that way. There are courses and programmes available online from universities where you have the option of reading through academic materials and using/watching online resources (grouped together around certain topics), before undertaking some assessment on a voluntary basis with the payment of a fee. These are called 'MOOCs' (Massive Open Online Courses).

The question then arises, 'Why study at university?' To answer this, we need to look at some principles that are widely accepted as important as part of any good and credible academic experience:

1. Face-to-face contact time is crucial in developing your ability to think through issues.
2. Feedback on your ideas and opinions is vital in ensuring that you are developing a correct understanding of the course material.
3. Interacting with others develops your ability to defend and debate your ideas.
4. Accessing resources outside of the classroom extends your awareness of the way that different researchers deal with different ideas.

It is around these four 'pillars' (and sometimes others, depending on the nature and subject of a university course) that nearly all university education is constructed, including most good online courses. To return to the question 'Why study at university?', or rather 'Why not learn in a different environment?', the answer is fairly straightforward: actually, it is *only* university that fully offers these four aspects for your learning (see Chapter 4, 'Critical Thinking').

 'BUT I HAVE A QUESTION ...'

... What do I need to do to graduate?

The answer is in some ways simple and in other ways more complex. Basically, in most UK universities, you need to pass your subjects. Each module you pass will give you some credits – think of this like a currency. You have to obtain enough credits to pass the degree (360 'credits', over three years in the UK system). If you fail a subject, then you might not get the credits you need.

Some modules might be 10 credits, some might be 15 or 30, or even 60. The higher the number of credits given for a module or subject, the higher the number of hours you will probably have to put into the subject. The number of credits is usually related to the amount of work involved in attending classes, doing the independent studying (reading etc.) and preparing for and undertaking the assessment.

This does not sound too complex until you realise that universities can have very different rules about giving you credits when you do not do well. Some universities, for example, will give you a pass if (let's say) you are taking 60 credits and you pass at least 40 of them with an average of more than 50%. In other universities or degree programmes, you will not be able to continue to your second year without passing all of your courses, and so on.

In most cases, undergraduate students will graduate with a first-class honours degree (usually above 70% average in the UK), an upper second-class or 2:1 (60-70% average), a lower second-class or 2:2 (usually 50-60%) or what is known as a 'pass' or third-class degree (40-50%). For Master's degrees (which will usually include a dissertation), a 'Distinction' is given for work with an average above 70%, a 'Merit' for 60-70% and a 'Pass' for work with an average of 50-60%, though institutions will vary on how they give these awards.

This should give you an idea of the purposes of this large organisation in which you have just registered, particularly in relation to learning. Of course, there are other stakeholders and other roles that universities fulfil. Those benefits – relating to research, training and consultancy – for businesses, public and charity sector organisations (locally and nationally), and for other individuals and groups, are very important but are less relevant for us here. At the start of your time at university, it is helpful to look at *how* universities do what they claim to do, so you might want to take a careful look at Chapter 5, 'Understanding How to Learn at University'.

Remember that, in terms of your experience, universities seek to prepare you for the start of your career and the rest of your life – extending your knowledge, your skills and your view of 'how the world works'.

━━━━━ REFLECTION POINT ━━━━━

Take some time to think about the following questions and write down some answers.
List three reasons why you have come to university:

1.

2.

3.

What excites you about being at university? What scares you? You can keep these answers as personal as you wish.

Understanding Other Students

It is likely that there are going to be a range of different students on your programme, and some of those will be unlike others that you have met. A lot depends on the university you have joined, but those going to university are not solely individuals who have just left school after A levels (or some kind of entrance examination). There may be older students who are returning to study after a long time away from the classroom. There may be individuals who are studying full time, but who are also looking after relatives or brothers or sisters, or children somewhere. There may be international students from all over the world and there may be folk who are studying part-time while developing their own business. The values, personalities and situations of the individuals sitting next to you in the lecture theatre will vary just as much as their appearances.

Starting a conversation with those who are like you is not always difficult – people who behave or think the same way as you can be easier to get along with and often you find you will have things in common. The challenge is to get to know people who are different from you. This can appear daunting and difficult sometimes, of course, but there are so many benefits in getting to know people who are from different backgrounds to yourself. After all, they may have similar ambitions, and maybe have chosen the university or course for the same reason as you. In times to come, you may be working with others different from you on group projects and assignments, and so the more you learn about others, the more able you will be to work with those you would not naturally associate with.

Being an International Student

If you are an international student, the very strong temptation is to find other international students from the same country and background as yourself. To some extent this will reduce the feelings of loneliness and emotional struggle that people may experience when they go to another country, and it is quite a natural thing to do. After all, you will speak the same language, may eat and enjoy the same food, use the same apps and have things in common to discuss; but it is not usually the most beneficial thing to do. If you just stick with those from your own country, then you will be unlikely to increase your confidence or vocabulary in English, and will not learn about the ways that others think (or will make a lot of incorrect assumptions because you won't be asking questions to find out if your assumptions are correct). You will discover far more if you break out from your familiar group.

Induction for international students tends to involve a lot of activities aimed at helping you to get to know the local culture and the area. This might involve a visit to register with the local police, day trips out or visits to local homes, or sessions where you can try your hand at local cooking or enjoying local specialities. In many cities, there will be a friendly local café run especially for international students and aimed at encouraging your confidence in speaking the native language, or a language corner where you can share your own language with other students from other countries. If these sorts of activities are not available, then see if you can work with some native-speaking students to set something up. Regardless, it might be good to consider something about UK culture and life in a foreign culture, especially because seeing your home country from another country's perspective can give you a great insight into your own culture.

The issue of language is a big one. You have probably entered university with a suitable English language qualification such as IELTS, and this will help to a certain extent, but there is always a need to improve on your listening, speaking, reading, writing or grammar, so then the question is about how to improve. The best way to learn and develop English language skills is to spend time with people who speak the language. But that very thing brings with it a number of anxieties and fears: 'How will I cope if they use language I don't understand?', 'What if they think I am being rude?' or 'What if they have an accent and I can't make out the words they are using?' These fears are usually not real, and most people will be happy to help. If you are an international student, making English-speaking friends is the best thing you can possibly do to improve your English, and it might just help you get to know a little more about your new country.

Being an international student is a huge challenge on so many levels – emotionally, practically, educationally and physically. However, although being an international student in an unfamiliar country can be challenging, it can also be an immensely rewarding experience, and something that many UK students might not have done.

 KEY LEARNING POINT

Getting to know other students who are different from you will broaden your perspectives and is an important part of your personal and academic development.

UNDERSTANDING THE NON-ACADEMIC SIDE OF UNIVERSITY LIFE

Universities are about far more than just studying: they provide a process of education, but also structures to support you through and beyond that educational experience. When you arrived at university, you were probably given lots of information about many different activities provided by the university.

The information may have been too much or insufficient, but it is up to you to review and understand (or ask about) what you are being given.

Universities are also places where individuals mature and become independent adults – if they were not already. This means developing and maintaining skills around three areas: cooking, laundry and managing your money. Cooking and laundry aside, learning to manage your money is an important life skill that will have a significant impact on your future well-being.

=== **BOX 1.1** ===

Learning to Manage Your Money

In Chapter 3 we cover managing your time. In many ways the principles that apply there also apply to managing your money. You have a finite resource and you need to consider your priorities in deciding how to spend that resource. There are a number of stages to go through here, and decisions about the allocation of whatever funds you have access to. If you are wholly dependent on a student loan and are paying fees, then the way you apply these ideas will have an impact well beyond your graduation: the mental issue here is that graduation seems so far off, and the next party or student activity seems so close, that the student activities often take priority. Above all, learning how to manage your money will reduce your stress and anxiety but will also show an employer that you are able to budget and use your resources effectively.

The principles of money management:

1. **Understand your priorities**: eating and maintaining your health need to come above everything else. After that, you are at the university to study, so consider what comes next. You also need to explicitly recognise areas of spending which are not priorities at all. Alcohol may be a part of life at your university, but (ignoring any potential for humour for a moment) alcohol will not help you to do well in your studies. The same is true for some other social student activities, though not all.
2. **Identify your sources of funds**: funds come into your bank account (income) and go out of your bank account (spending, or outgoings). Typically, funds come from family members, employment, scholarships, the sale of property, grants and loans. That's not difficult to understand, but some funds are more regular than others and, in some cases, the timing of your income can be crucial.
3. **Identify your foreseeable outgoings**: you will have items on which you need to spend money, and you should list these according to the priorities you identified in point 1. Your course fees will need to be paid, and then your priorities might be paying for accommodation and food, unless you are staying at home. For your university work, you might need to spend money on a laptop/tablet, and textbooks, and in some cases, those can be expensive. Your university will probably let you have access to free software under its own software licences. You may also need funds for travel to and from the university, or perhaps to/from part-time work. Most of your larger outgoings (accommodation, course fees, for example) will be payable in advance, and if you are renting a property, you will probably need to pay a deposit. There are expenses that we cannot predict. Some of these will be small (e.g. irregular taxi fares, printing of work, etc.) and some of these (e.g. library fines) will be within your control, but it is a good idea to consider unpredictable items, just as we should when we are considering time management.
4. **Make a budget**: thinking about your outgoings, you need to ensure that you are balancing your budget, so it makes sense to develop a table, such as the one below:

(Continued)

Expected Income		Expected Spending		
Sources of funding:	Amount	Item of expenditure:	Amount:	
Loan	£3,200	Food	£2,200	
Parents	£1,500	Books	£300	
Employment	£2,500	Accommodation	£4,700	
TOTAL:	£7,200	TOTAL:	£7,200	
		TOTAL Surplus/(Debt):	£0	

The amounts listed under sources of funding and items of expenditure should equal each other and you will have budgeted well. Where the total figure under expected spending is greater than expected income, then you will have a shortfall (debt), which will need to be filled in some way. However, should the reverse be true, then you will have some resources that have not been spent (surplus).

5. **Check the budget regularly**: it is a good idea to keep an eye on what you are spending and where your money is going. Understanding what you are spending your money on is crucial to managing your budget: if you are spending money on items which are not a priority then you may need to change where you spend your money.

Sources of Practical Student Support

Being a student in an unknown setting – whether international or domestic, whether mature student in work on a part-time course or a full-time undergraduate fresh from college or school – you will probably need some support at some time or another. This may come from a Personal Tutor, who will have a role in overseeing and advising on your academic progress, or merely another student on your course. But there will also be a wide network of others you might like to consider, such as those dealing with disability, counsellors and mental health advisers for emotional support, study support centres to assist you with academic skills, careers advisers for assistance in determining what you will do after university, among other services. There will also be officers who advise on international student exchanges and who may organise local trips to other cities, for those visiting the country.

FURTHER READING

If you are a postgraduate student, then you may be familiar with some of these issues, but bear in mind that different universities work in different ways and your previous experience may not reflect the reality of your current university. The advice you would seek from the careers services may also be somewhat different.

 ━ KEY LEARNING POINT ━━━━━━

Managing your resources is a key skill to develop, which will benefit your future employment.

UNIVERSITY CULTURE

If the right support systems are there for you, how you interact with them can have some impact on whether you obtain all that you hope for. An understanding of university culture will help you understand how to do this. If the services and systems (personal tutoring, careers, etc.) are the visible signs of 'what' the organisation does, then the culture will reflect 'how' those things are done.

Language is a key aspect of the culture for any organisation, including universities. By using particular words, universities tend to signal to the rest of society that they have a different purpose, go about things in a different way and have a different culture. For those reasons, universities tend to use language that is very different from that in most organisations. Some of this language can make you feel uncomfortable and uncertain, but in many cases you will be familiar with what things really mean in practice. It may be useful to consider making a list of the words you hear and read, but which are new to you. See the 'For You to Do' section below.

 WHAT IS 'CULTURE'?

Culture is famously defined as: 'The way we do things around here'. It is used to describe how 'friendly', 'supportive', 'bureaucratic', and so on, any organisation is.

 FOR YOU TO DO

During your first three weeks at university, watch out for any words that you have not come across before and try to guess what you think they mean. Different cultures will have different languages. If you are an overseas student, this list may be large, but even if you have studied at a university before, there will be some words that could be new or, importantly, words that get used in a different way.

Write them down and guess what you think they mean.

Once again, a cautionary note for postgraduate students is in order: the language used by one institution may be similar to that used at your previous university, but it is wise not to make that assumption and to check your understanding.

UNIVERSITY PROCESSES

Universities are very diverse in their nature. They can be small or large, new or old, rich or poor, have great diversity in their student population or focus on one particular type of student. They can be very focused and specialise in a small number of areas or be very broad in the subjects they teach, and they can do a lot of research or focus mainly on teaching. You have probably chosen to study at your university because of three or four factors – the grades required, whether there was a course you were interested in, the cost (course fees and maybe living expenses) and whether your friends were going there – rather than the culture of the university.

However, one thing that UK universities do share is a need to comply with a number of UK government requirements, and this includes providing information, ensuring that degrees of similar subjects achieve similar goals and cover similar topics, ensuring that a degree develops your thinking and skills, and ensuring that decisions about qualifications are similar to those made at other universities. There is actually a lot of monitoring that goes on within your university to ensure that there is innovation and improvement where needed.

All of this means that there is a lot of compliance with government requirements, which can make the organisation seem very bureaucratic with its large number of committees and administrative processes – and also seem apparently very slow to deal with issues sometimes, or even unhelpful on rare occasions.

Your Voice at the University

All of this can make a university seem like a large, impersonal organisation that operates in an unhelpful way by implementing rules about what it can and cannot do for you as an individual student; this can appear very disappointing. The good news for you is that there is also a need to involve students in nearly everything the university does and how they do it. For example, you will almost certainly be asked to complete questionnaires regularly on how effectively the different subjects and modules are taught. Universities are accountable for how they use this information and what they do with it and need to demonstrate that they are changing to take account of your views as a student.

STUDENT CULTURE

Of course, from a student's perspective university can be a very rewarding and enjoyable experience. The lectures can be entertaining, the learning should be interesting, and the social side can be fun in the short term (while you are at university) and useful in the longer term (as you meet other people who will become friends for life).

The various forms of entertainment you might experience at university may or may not be attractive and some students will prefer to study hard rather than socialise. It is a personal choice, of course, though social activities are a great way to develop your interpersonal skills and it is by studying that you will develop your thinking skills and make the most of the complex life at university, which will develop your planning and organisational skills. It is often said that the years at university are the best years of your life: you can make it what *you* would like it to be. Being part of a university community – whether postgraduate or undergraduate, domestic or international student – is preparation for the rest of your life in a much larger community.

 ━━━ KEY LEARNING POINT ━━━━━━━━━━━━━━━━━

Understanding and engaging with the non-academic side of university life, such as university and student culture, will help support your academic and personal development.

UNIVERSITY EDUCATION AND YOUR PREVIOUS EDUCATION

If you have already experienced university, then you may think you know what to expect. Of course, the reality (as this chapter has tried to note) is that every university will do things in slightly different ways so the issue is then learning to make sense of why those differences exist and how to adjust to them (see Chapter 5 for more details on how teaching and learning take place at university, and Chapter 6 for information on assessment of academic work at university).

REFLECTION POINT

Take some time to think about the following questions and write down some answers.

How do you think university is similar to – and different from – the experiences you might have had in your earlier education?

What do you think are going to be some of the challenges you might face in coping with university life in general during your first three weeks?

What do you think you need to do in order to make the most of your life at university?

THE START OF THE REST OF YOUR LIFE: EMPLOYABILITY

This chapter has outlined a range of experiences and issues faced by universities and has tried to enable you to make sense of what you have entered into. There is, however, a very important aspect of what universities do through their degree programmes, and this is to enhance you as an individual by developing your interpersonal skills, your ability to think critically and analytically, and your knowledge so that you can leave university and contribute to society.

Your ability to do so will be determined by what happens in the weeks and months leading up to and shortly after your graduation. You will need to determine a future for yourself, and that will be determined by the opportunities you see for yourself, and those you create. The later chapters of this text cover ideas around how to find and obtain a first job and begin your career, but the online chapter – 'Alternative Ideas After Graduation' – gives some alternative ideas.

The employment market is always changing. The internet started to become widely available in the mid to late 1990s: before that, there was no Android or Google, and many things needed to be done manually. The first smartphones were available in the early 2000s: before that, there were no apps. And now businesses are talking about the application of ideas such as 'artificial intelligence', 'big data' (the use of technology to determine trends from huge amounts of data gathered from online activities) and students are developing apps before they leave their university courses. Of course, these alternatives are only made possible through previous technologies – and the kinds of jobs available in these areas have changed. But it is not just technology that has brought change. The numbers of students graduating has increased steadily over the years and that number now includes a lot more international and postgraduate students seeking international careers. In a well-known text, Steven Covey (1989) noted that one of the 'habits' effective people possess is that of beginning 'with the end in mind'. The last part of this book is about life towards the end of your studies and being able to start the career that you want. The introduction to Part V (which you might like to read now) states the following:

Academic success in your degree is going to be a very significant factor in your being able to get the future you want, but it is not the only factor. To an employer, a student who has a first-class degree in Philosophy but no leadership or work experience or no involvement in social activities is more likely to be overlooked for a graduate role than one who has a lesser degree (e.g. 2:1 or 2:2, more rarely a 3rd class), but leadership experience in a student society and some work experience. It is about balance, and employers are looking for competent and able individuals who are critical thinkers, analytical and able to use their communication and inter-personal skills to work well with others. This means that your working career starts on day one of your university studies – and your choices made during the start of your time at university *can have* a significant impact on your employability at the end of it.

In effect, the rest of your life *after* your university studies begins during your early days *at* university. Make a decision not to get involved in student clubs and societies, or make a choice to spend nearly all your time socialising or at your part-time job, and you may find that there are consequences to those choices some significant time later. The kinds of jobs available for you in five to ten years, the economic environment, the ability for you to work internationally and the competition for first jobs is likely to change. The implication of this is that the most important skills you can ever develop are the ability to learn, to be determined in what you wish to do, to identify your own goals and to develop the interpersonal and other skills which will enable you to work with others to achieve what you would like to achieve during your life. Your goals and intentions will change as you go through your life, but studying at university is the beginning of this process.

CONCLUSION

This chapter set out to ensure that you would be able to achieve the following:

- Describe what it is that universities do, and start thinking about how they do it.
- Understand how university may differ from previous learning environments you might have come across.
- Understand why differences exist between university and other forms of education.
- Find your way around the university bureaucracy and systems so that your time at university will be enjoyable, rather than stressful.

It is probably a good idea to get more details on the final bullet point by reading Chapters 6 to 8, which will give you more of an introduction to university life and an understanding of the ways that learning at university takes place, and discusses assessment, respectively.

This chapter has looked at the various processes which make universities run as they do and the activities that you may be involved in at the beginning of your time as a university student. It has also tried to give some indication of how you might be able to manage your first days as a university student. It is for you to determine how you will make the most of them.

 CHAPTER TASK

This chapter has focused on helping you to adjust to life at university. No two universities are the same, so each part of what has been discussed may be slightly different from that presented here, but all universities try to help their students understand how university works and provide inductions, documents and websites to help students to come prepared.

The task for this chapter is to answer the following 10 questions, so that you can have a better understanding of what you need to know about how your university works.

1. Who can you talk to if you are feeling upset?
2. How many library books can you borrow at any one time?
3. Where is the careers service located?
4. How can you learn more about writing assignments at your university?
5. How many subjects can you choose this year?
6. How many nationalities are there in your class?
7. What apps are the most popular and important among your classmates?
8. If you fall sick before an examination, what should you do?
9. What are the penalties and regulations about cheating in examinations and assignments?

━━━━━ INTERVIEW QUESTIONS ━━━

This text – as indicated above – has several aims, but one of the most important is to prepare you to enter what is usually referred to as 'the workplace'. This is done in a number of ways: helping you to pass your studies (Part I), developing your thinking and interpersonal skills (Parts II–IV) and guiding you through the selection process (Part V). However, as many management writers point out, having a goal to achieve and thinking about that goal at the very start are vital in order to plan effectively.

With that in mind, each chapter will contain two or three interview questions for you to think about. These are questions which might be used when you have a graduate selection interview after university, but it is worth thinking about them at the start of your university studies so that you know what you need to achieve as you move through life at university.

Think about the following questions. What might your answers be?

1. Why did you choose the university and the course you have been studying?
2. How successful have you been at achieving the goals you set out to achieve by studying at university?

Chapter 17 gives a lot more information on selection interviews and the online content gives some guidance on these questions.

ADDITIONAL RESOURCES

Want to learn more? Visit https://study.sagepub.com/morgan2e to gain access to a wide range of online resources, including interactive tests, tasks, further reading and downloads.

Website Resources

The following websites offer useful advice on starting at university.

Evening Standard – national newspaper article providing some reassurance to those who might be nervous: www.standard.co.uk/lifestyle/health/how-to-combat-stress-and-anxiety-as-you-start-university-a3637421.html

Student Minds: www.studentminds.org.uk/startinguniversity.html

Studential.com: www.studential.com/university/guides/5-important-ways-prepare-university-life

Top Universities: www.topuniversities.com/student-info/health-and-support/starting-university-what-expect

YoungMinds: https://youngminds.org.uk/blog/coping-with-anxiety-at-university/

Textbook Resources

Burns, T. and Sinfield, S. (2016) *Essential Study Skills* (4th edition). London: Sage (particularly Chapter 3).

Cameron, S. (2016) *The Business Student's Handbook: Skills for Study and Employment* (6th edition). Harlow: Pearson (particularly Chapter 1).

Cottrell, S. (2013) *The Study Skills Handbook* (4th edition). New York: Palgrave (particularly Chapter 1).

Courtney, M. and Du, X. (2014) 'Introduction: Living and Studying in the UK', in *Study Skills for Chinese Students*. London: Sage (offers essential information to Chinese students coming to the UK to study).

Denicolo, P. and Reeves, J. (2014) *Developing Transferable Skills*. London: Sage (particularly aimed at researchers).

Horn, R. (2012) *The Business Skills Handbook*. London: CIPD (particularly Chapter 4).

McMillan, K. and Weyers, J. (2012) *The Study Skills Book* (3rd edition). Harlow: Pearson (particularly Chapters 3, 5, 10 and 11).

Smale, B. and Fowlie, J. (2009) *How to Succeed at University: An Essential Guide to Academic Skills, Personal Development & Employability*. London: Sage (particularly Chapter 1).

2

PERSONAL DEVELOPMENT AND LEARNING

Tell me and I forget. Teach me and I remember. Involve me and I learn. (Benjamin Franklin)

CHAPTER STRUCTURE

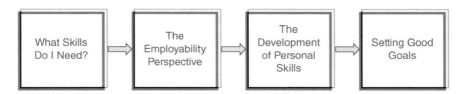

Figure 2.1

When you see the this means go to the companion website https://study.sagepub.com/morgan2e to do a quiz, complete a task, read further or download a template.

▬ AIMS OF THE CHAPTER ▬

By the end of this chapter, you should be able to:

- Discuss how academic and interpersonal skills are developed during a degree.
- Analyse some of your own strengths and weaknesses as they relate to your immediate, medium-term and longer-term development needs.
- Develop some ideas for working on your weaknesses and enhancing your strengths.

WHEN SHOULD YOU READ THIS CHAPTER?

This chapter provides details of how we develop our skills, and so it is best to read this during your first semester at university, but it has strong application throughout your time at university - and beyond, into your first role at work.

INTRODUCTION

The contents of this chapter provide a foundation for Part II – enhancing your study skills – and Part IV – enhancing your employability skills. Learning a skill can sometimes take a matter of hours or sometimes take years – it depends on a range of factors, such as how quickly you learn, how you learn, what opportunities you have to practise those skills and the availability of any objective feedback. Failing to develop your study skills quickly enough has consequences for your academic success and failing to develop the skills required for 'the workplace' has consequences for your career. At university, failing to develop the appropriate skills means performing below potential and possibly failing modules. In the world of management, those who fail to develop the skills they need find that their promotional prospects become less and less.

In this chapter, we will spend a little time examining the skills needed for successful study at university as well as those sought by employers (commonly but perhaps incorrectly called 'employability skills'). We will provide you with a way of evaluating yourself against those skills and give you some guidance on how you might go about developing all of your skills while at university. The reality is that there are very few skills which are entirely 'study skills' and there are very few skills which are entirely 'employability skills': there is a significant amount of overlap – as we shall see at the end of the chapter (see Figure 2.7). If there weren't, then university would solely be about giving you knowledge, and it would be irrelevant to wider society if that knowledge had no use. Instead, university is as much (if not more) about skill development as it is about giving you knowledge.

If you are currently in work and studying part-time, then the content here applies to your working life as much as to your study life. Being able to budget your time and money, being able to manage information and demonstrating interpersonal skills are skills that you may develop in a variety of different situations.

SKILLS SELF-ASSESSMENT

Complete the questionnaire below to see how well you think you know the items covered in this chapter. Give each item a score between 1 and 5, where 1 is 'strongly disagree' and 5 is 'strongly agree'. Answer each item quickly, but take a little time to think about why you give the answers that you do. This thinking may reveal something about yourself (and perhaps the way you relate to others) that you had not thought about before.

Item	Statement	Score
1.	I am confident that I understand what university education is all about	
2.	I know what makes the difference between good work at school and good work at university	
3.	I think the skills I have developed during my earlier education will be important to me at university	
4.	I am confident that I will do well in my university career	
5.	I have high expectations of myself and of the grades I will eventually obtain	

Item	Statement	Score
6.	I have a good understanding of how the skills I develop at university will relate to those I will need for my future career	
7.	I am clear about what my future career will be	
8.	I want to achieve the very best I can for me, my family and those I will work with	
9.	I have the capacity to lead others and enjoy leadership roles	
10.	I am competitive and will do nearly anything to ensure that I win	
11.	I think competition among students is a good thing, so I will use this to motivate myself	
12.	My motivation comes from seeing others benefit from the advice I give them	
13.	I enjoy achieving something good when working with others	
14.	I prefer to do academic work on my own	
15.	At university, I will try to focus only on my studies rather than on student clubs and societies	
16.	There is nothing more important than academic grades to get a good career	
17.	All the skills I will need for a good career will be developed through the activities I do during my studies	
18.	I am good at developing my skills and can now do things that I could not do before	
19.	I am very clear in my mind about the skills I will develop during my degree	
20.	I know how to develop my skills	
21.	I think it is easy for me to be aware of my own strengths and weaknesses	
22.	I think I know myself better than other people know me	
23.	My parents can tell me what my skills are and can help me find a career	
24.	I find it very easy to change who I am	
25.	I think university is about developing knowledge, rather than skills	

An interactive version of this test along with comments and thoughts about these questions can be found on the companion website for this book at https://study.sagepub.com/morgan2e. However, there are no right or wrong answers for most of the questions above; they are really about how we see ourselves – a common theme through this chapter and others. Nevertheless, certain issues suggested above may help or hinder you when working through your life at university.

INTERACTIVE
TEXT

'BUT I HAVE A QUESTION ...'

... Why put effort into developing my skills, if they will develop 'naturally'?

We said earlier that failing to develop your skills quickly enough has consequences, and that one of the issues that can affect *how quickly* you develop your skills is *how much effort you put into doing so*. There is an impact on the development of academic skills if the development of the relevant skills is not fast enough

(Continued)

(i.e. you will not do as well as you could do in your studies) and an impact on the development of your 'employability skills' if other students from other universities have put effort into developing their skills (or have them at a higher level already) and you have not done so; they will then be more successful at their employer interviews than you.

· During your degree, you will grow and develop these skills anyway, as you mature as an individual. The more effort you put into your own development, however, the faster you will grow and develop these skills.

We will look at the processes involved in skill development in more detail later in the chapter, but, for now, it is important to realise that developing skills is never an easy thing to do and can often be challenging. If you are an athlete or if you enjoy undertaking a challenge, then there is nothing new to add that will motivate you, but if you are not used to 'being stretched', then it can be a difficult and perhaps painful experience. The long-term benefit will be immense if the short-term challenges can be seen in a positive light – that is, *challenges to be overcome, rather than avoided*.

WHAT SKILLS DO I NEED?

We start by looking at the skills required for academic success. Each university programme will develop specific skills through the exercises you undertake during your course.

 ■■■ FOR YOU TO DO ■■■■■■■■■■■

Have a look at the websites for your university, your department, your course/degree programme and a couple of your modules. You might also want to look at the website for your university careers service. What skills do your modules, your course, your department and your university develop during your studies?

You may have to search a little and take some time, but the information about these skills will be available somewhere on your university website.

TIP: You might like to search for 'Programme specifications' or 'Module specifications' or something similar.

The skills listed below are those frequently seen as being important in a managerial role.

Table 2.1 Subjects typically classified under the heading of 'study skills' and usually important for enabling you to study well

• Time management and being able to work independently • Critical thinking and reading • Essay and report writing • Research and library skills • Quantitative skills • Proactive attitude	• Team working • Active reading • Listening skills • Self-reflection • Business awareness	• Presentation skills • IT skills • Problem solving • Communication skills (written/oral) • Influencing skills

The chapters that follow will provide a great deal more detail on good practice in most of these skills, but before we get to those chapters, it would be good for you to try to define briefly what each one is and why it is important. Ideas on how you might go about developing these skills can be found in Table 2.3 at the end of this chapter.

In developing an accurate view of our abilities, we need to gather evidence. Our brain is very good at telling us we are good at things that we are, in reality, not very good at. Look at the next 'For You to Do' section below, remembering that the more evidence you gather, the more accurate your response will be. (We look at this further when we discuss critical thinking in Chapter 4.)

━━━━━━━━━━ **FOR YOU TO DO** ━━━━━━━━━━

Work with a partner to complete this exercise, which should take a maximum of 20 minutes to do.

1. Have a look at the list in Table 2.1: are there any skills that you think are missing?
2. Take two skills from each of the columns. Try to choose different skills from each other, if you can.
3. On your own, try to identify: (a) what you think each one means in practice; and (b) the implications of not being good at this skill.
4. Compare your answers with those of your partner. Do they match?
5. With your partner try to rank all the skills listed in terms of their importance to your studies.
6. Now try to determine how good you think you are at the six skills you have selected.
7. How much evidence do you currently have for evaluating how good you actually are at this?
8. Do you believe that the skills you have chosen are more important for your studies, or for the workplace, or equally important for both?

Answering questions 6 and 7 will enable you to start looking at what you are good at and where you need to refine what you do or how you behave.

You can download this template grid on the companion website for this book at **https://study.sagepub. com/morgan2e**.

TEMPLATE

THE EMPLOYABILITY PERSPECTIVE

Imagine that at 2.30 pm tomorrow, you have an appointment for an interview with the regional manager for an international UK-based organisation. The manager will want to find out about what motivates you, what skills you have and whether you will be the sort of person the organisation will want as a future manager.

The idea of imagining someone sitting in front of you asking some questions might be a little unrealistic right now. But in a few years' time, employers (if you choose to seek a job rather than take other options) will generally want to know that you *can and will* do two things:

1. Perform well in the role that they have given you. This means many different things in different organisations, but it certainly means adding 'value' to the organisation.
2. Learn, grow and develop yourself. Technology and knowledge are increasing all the time and the way businesses used to find success does not necessarily bring success today. The same is true for the individuals within that business.

Employers typically look for individuals who have a number of qualities. Employees should have the appropriate personal transferable skills, motivation, specific skills and abilities required for a particular role (if there are any) and personality (e.g. attitude towards risk, conscientiousness, willingness to learn) in order to do well. These qualities will be different from organisation to organisation, but there are some characteristics that are seen as important, whatever the organisation.

PERSONAL TRANSFERABLE SKILLS

Behaviours that can be used and developed in a variety of different situations in order to perform well. Examples include time management, critical thinking and communication skills.

Graduate employers usually look for motivated self-starters: confident individuals who are independent, who can lead and work with others, and who can add value to their business (and there are few better places to demonstrate how much of a self-starter you are than by taking the initiative and getting involved in university life).

In more detail, the following skills typically get listed (this list is from the Quality Assurance Agency, 2015):

- People management: to include communications, team building, leadership and motivating others.
- Problem solving and critical analysis: analysing facts and circumstances to determine the cause of a problem and identifying and selecting appropriate solutions.
- Research: the ability to analyse and evaluate a range of business data, sources of information and appropriate methodologies, which includes the need for strong digital literacy, and to use that research for evidence-based decision making.
- Commercial acumen: based on an awareness of the key drivers for business success, causes of failure and the importance of providing customer satisfaction and building customer loyalty.
- Innovation, creativity and enterprise: the ability to act entrepreneurially to generate, develop and communicate ideas, manage and exploit intellectual property, gain support, and deliver successful outcomes.
- Numeracy: the use of quantitative skills to manipulate data, evaluate, estimate and model business problems, functions and phenomena.
- Networking: an awareness of the interpersonal skills of effective listening, negotiating, persuasion and presentation and their use in generating business contacts.
- Ability to work collaboratively both internally and with external customers and an awareness of mutual interdependence.
- Ability to work with people from a range of cultures.
- Articulating and effectively explaining information.
- Building and maintaining relationships.
- Communication and listening, including the ability to produce clear, structured business communications in a variety of media.
- Emotional intelligence and empathy.
- Conceptual and critical thinking, analysis, synthesis and evaluation.
- Self-management: a readiness to accept responsibility and flexibility, to be resilient, self-starting and appropriately assertive, to plan, organise and manage time.
- Self-reflection: self-analysis and an awareness/sensitivity to diversity in terms of people and cultures. This includes a continuing appetite for development.

This long list gives government guidance to universities on what you – as students – should be able to do by the end of your course. Other lists come from research with employers carried out by careers advisory services and HR professionals across the UK. The CBI-Pearson skills report (2017) indicated that business was looking for the following (in order of importance) from their graduates:

- Use of IT
- Numeracy skills
- Technical skills
- Basic literacy/use of English
- Analytical skills
- Team working
- Problem solving
- Positive attitude to work
- Communication skills
- Knowledge about the job
- Relevant work experience*
- Attitude/resilience*
- Intercultural awareness*
- Customer awareness*
- Foreign language skills*

(*The CBI-Pearson report indicated a lack of satisfaction on the part of employers with the presence of these work-related skills from their graduate recruits.)

The Institute of Student Employers (2020) indicated that the following were commonly sought from graduates (in order of percentage of employers seeking the skill):

- Teamwork (91%)
- Interpersonal skills (98%)
- Listening (78%)
- Problem solving (77%)
- Taking responsibility (73%)
- Time management (73%)

With the exception of 'Taking responsibility', all the above are covered in the following chapters. It is interesting to note that Presentation and Leadership skills were rated as important by only 41% and 21% respectively of those employing graduates.

The Prospects website (2019) (which is used extensively throughout UK higher education to help graduates prepare for and find graduate jobs) lists the following:

- Interpersonal skills
- Communication and motivation
- Organisation and delegation
- Forward planning and strategic thinking
- Problem solving and decision making
- Commercial awareness
- Mentoring

FOR YOU TO DO

Covid-19 has been a global phenomenon which has increased pressures on economies worldwide. Some countries have faced complete lockdown situations while others have taken a less restrictive approach, but economies globally have struggled. Have a look at the following questions:

1. Do you think the Covid-19 situation might have much of an impact on the qualities that employers need? If so, what kind of an impact might that be – medium to long term?
2. What personal qualities do you think the Covid-19 situation might enhance, or reduce?
3. Do you think working from home is going to become more or less common than it was prior to Covid-19? If so, what additional qualities might be needed for individuals who work at home to be successful in their work roles?

BOX 2.1

International Employability: What Is the Picture Like Elsewhere?

Research on global and internationally local employability trends indicates some similarity with these kinds of skills, though English language abilities tend to be far more important. Even then, there are specific cultural issues that can affect the skills sought by business.

Researchers in India (Wheebox/Confederation of Indian Industry, 2019) have identified that Indian businesses look for learning agility, adaptability and English language abilities as the top three, but also seek interpersonal skills, emotional intelligence, conflict resolution, self-determination and communication skills.

Employers in New Zealand (Hodges and Burchell, 2003) noted that the most important skills included ability and willingness to learn, working in teams, good interpersonal relations, providing excellent service to clients, and being accurate, organised, and maintaining excellent standards.

In Malaysia, a study of online advertisements (Omar et al., 2012) indicated that management science graduates should possess communication/interpersonal skills, ICT skills, foreign language skills, team work and other personal qualities (good attitudes to work, etc.). In comparison, a more recent Malaysian study (Azmi, Hashim and Yusoff, 2018) found that attitude was more important than anything else, with the ranking of the top five qualities being: discipline, responsible nature, positivity, good time management and team working.

In South Africa, graduates need to demonstrate management attributes, critical thinking, systems thinking, literacy and numeracy, interpersonal skills, leadership, work ethics and IT (Shivoro, Shalyefu and Kadhila, 2018). A small-scale study (Adebakin, Ajadi and Tayo, 2015) in Nigeria found that analytical/problem-solving skills, team working, English language, ICT skills and leadership were important.

Finally, from a global perspective, the World Economic Forum (2016) looked at changes in the skill sets needed in all jobs – those needing graduates as well as others. Against a world that was changing rapidly, they noted that a third of all jobs would require complex problem-solving abilities, but that the relative importance of social skills, process skills, systems skills, HR skills, technical and then content skills would vary according to industry, and that nearly all industries were expecting to see cognitive abilities being more important than they were in 2016.

Whatever the ranking, there does seem to be a global consensus around the need for interpersonal skills, attitudes/work ethics, language skills, team working and leadership.

There is always an argument about the comparability of similarly sounding skills, and different surveys sometimes use different or vague categorisations (soft skills, interpersonal skills, transferable skills, etc.).

Many pieces of academic research seem to omit national or government employers or skills surveys, so while academic research might pick up issues such as literacy and time-keeping as important in the UK (Martin et al., 2008), there are discrepancies between this and the findings of other larger scale national surveys that show attitude being most important.

It is worth noting that these are lists of skills, not knowledge. The information you gather from lectures and seminars (i.e. your 'learning') will need to be there as well, which is why many employers seek individuals who reach a particular degree grade. However, without many or all of the skills listed above, you might find it tough competing in the job market in the months and years to come.

It is the application of skills that sometimes makes the apparent difference, not the skills themselves.

══════════ KEY LEARNING POINT ══════════

The distinction between what we might refer to as 'study skills' and 'employability skills' is somewhat artificial. The overlap between the two helps universities to be sure that they are developing skills which will enable you to do well in future employment.

We have examined the nature of the skills we are covering in this book, and if you have done the exercises above, you will have developed a definition of what you think these skills mean. We will present more academic and employer-focused definitions as we move through the book, so do not be too concerned about whether those definitions are correct just yet. What we are now going to do in the remainder of this chapter is to explore how you can develop such skills, both by understanding the skill development process itself and by understanding what opportunities you might have to develop these skills.

THE DEVELOPMENT OF PERSONAL SKILLS

There are two steps required for the development of any skills: identifying the skill desired and developing strategies to acquire it. We will look at each step in turn and try to make this process as clear as possible.

Step 1: Decide What Skills You Need to Develop

Imagine the following dialogue between Cindy, an international student studying in the UK, and her tutor.

Tutor: Which skill would you like to improve, Cindy?

Cindy: I think I'd like to improve my presentation skills.

Tutor: OK. So, why do you want to improve your presentations skills, rather than, for example, your team-working skills?

Cindy: Well, maybe I should improve those as well. What do you think?

Tutor: Well, it is for you to decide. Perhaps there are certain skills that your course director or dean need you to demonstrate. But presentation skills are often something that students do choose to work on. How would you rate your presentation skills?

Cindy: Hmmm, I don't feel very confident or able to do good presentations – they were something we never had to do when I have studied before.

Tutor: What do other people think about your presentation skills?

Cindy: You mean I should ask them? [Embarrassed smile.] Hmmm, I don't know. I have never asked my classmates what they think.

Tutor: Well, you could think of them as friends rather than classmates and maybe that might make it easier to ask them.

Cindy: OK, I will do that …

Tutor: Good. Do that and then let's discuss further when we know whether there is really a need to develop this set of skills.

Cindy: OK. Thank you for your time. And I will arrange the appointment soon.

In the example above, Cindy was starting to decide what she was good and bad at. This is one of the reasons why we did the second exercise earlier in this chapter. To decide what we need to develop is always a personal decision, and in some ways it needs to be. Having someone else tell us what we need to develop does not usually inspire us to go away with much enthusiasm for doing so. In business life, however, we often have to think about 'core skills', which are those essential for the continuation of the culture and processes of the organisation, and peripheral skills, which could be either those essential for certain roles or, more likely, those that are helpful but not essential.

Planning for anything is often about finding a gap between where you are and where you want or need to be. Personal development is no different. So, whether you are looking at skills which will assist you in your studies or those which will help you in your career (or both), the question is: 'In thinking about the important skills I need to develop, what skill do I need to develop the most? Where is the gap largest?'

That is easier said than done, but there are ways to do this. Some of what is written here overlaps with some of what we will examine when it comes to research skills.

Key to identifying this gap is *information* (see Figure 2.2). The more information we gather from various sources on many occasions, the more we can be sure that such information is accurate and useful to us.

Subjective Information

We could ask a number of different kinds of people one of two questions: 'What do you think I am good (and bad) at?' or 'How good do you think I am at X …?' The follow-up question should always be, 'Why do you think that?' As we will see in Chapter 17, employers will frequently use these questions when carrying out a job interview.

 FOR YOU TO DO

Look at the list of people below who can provide information about your skills. Who do you think can provide the most accurate information for you?

- Your mother
- Your father

- Your brothers and sisters, and other family members
- Other students
- A past employer
- A past schoolteacher
- A current employer
- Your personal tutor
- Other university tutors
- A university careers adviser.

So, how about asking some of these people for their views?

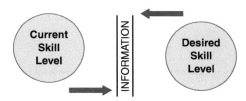

Figure 2.2 Identifying the gap between your current skills and your desired skill level

There is one (or maybe two, depending on how you see it) more group of people missing from this list, namely *friends* and *partners*. If you are going to obtain accurate information, then it needs to be impartial (or objective) and the closer you are to someone emotionally (either positively or negatively), the less accurate that information is likely to be. This might also apply to parents, so it is up to you to make a judgement.

The Johari Window

There is a problem here: sometimes, we hide what we do not like about ourselves – and, sometimes, people do not tell us what we are really like because they do not want to offend us. These ideas led Joseph Luft and Harry Ingham to develop what became known as the Johari Window (Luft and Ingham, 1955). The model is outlined in Figure 2.3 and uses and categorises information according to what we know about ourselves and what other people know about us.

═══════ PANEL 1: ═══════

What We Know about Ourselves and What Others Know about Us: The 'Arena'

When someone goes to fight in a boxing match or compete on a tennis court, everything that they do is public – their anxieties, their abilities and how they react when things are going well or badly.

The same is true when we talk about our day-to-day skills as well: people can see what we struggle with and what we excel at, hence the name of this conceptual place.

(Continued)

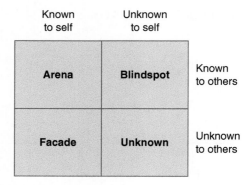

Figure 2.3   The Johari Window

━━━━━━━━ **PANEL 2:** ━━━━━━━━

What We Know about Ourselves but What Others Do Not Know about Us: The 'Facade' or 'Mask'

There are certain times – or certain activities – that can make us behave in ways that we might consider embarrassing or wrong, and there are times when we do things we probably should not. In both contexts, we keep such behaviour hidden from others. For example, people at work might see us quite differently from our family and friends, so we typically keep some parts of who we are hidden, or masked.

These activities would come under the panel labelled 'Facade'.

━━━━━━━━ **PANEL 3:** ━━━━━━━━

What We Do Not Know about Ourselves but What Others Believe about Us: The 'Blindspot'

In terms of vision, everyone has a blindspot: an area of vision that is momentarily obscured. If you drive, you might have a number of mirrors to enable you to see around the car, but there are places which may be missed and you will need to move your head to see. In these situations, we talk about the 'blindspot'.

In terms of personal development, the blindspot consists of those skills which you have but are not aware you have them, or those skills you think you have, but have never been told that you were poor at them.

━━━━━━━━ **PANEL 4:** ━━━━━━━━

What We Do Not Know about Ourselves and What Others Do Not Know about Us: The 'Unknown'

If you have never been skiing, ice-skating or jumped out of an aircraft to go skydiving, then you will not know whether you are any good at it – and the same applies to any skill we might need to demonstrate. In addition, no one else will know whether you are any good at it either, and in such situations we would say that we are operating in 'the unknown', or – to put it more simply – we are exploring our skills.

When we are children, we do this all the time. Can I climb? Walk? Count from 1 to 100, and so on. But as adults, we start to slow down our development and often concentrate on things that we are good at. There is really nothing wrong with this, as long as we have all the skills we need to do everything we need to do both now and in the future. However, life rarely stays the same: we change jobs, change our plans, get married, start to use technologies we have never used before, become parents, and so on, and thus there will nearly always be something we need to develop.

═══ 'BUT I HAVE A QUESTION ...' ═══

... I've heard some people say that we should focus on our strengths and develop those rather than work on our weaknesses. After all, we're never going to be perfect are we?

It is often the case that people can be very successful in their careers but then only get so far because of a lack of certain important skills that are needed for more senior positions.

Working on your weaknesses is important to enable you to become a balanced individual. Over time, and as your life takes you in various directions, you might realise that certain skills are more important than others, but imagine for a moment your life now – as a university student.

Let's say that you are really good at essay writing. That is great, as long as the assessments you have to do are essays. As soon as they become calculations or presentations, you have a problem. Right?

The same is true in work: you can be great at some things, but as soon as something changes in your work, your lack of skills in some areas can become a real issue.

Gathering information can be problematic, of course. It is fine in theory to say that we can ask others to tell us what they think, but some may be very general in the feedback they give or some may not wish to give it at all. There may be also be cultural factors or stereotyping, which could influence feedback.

═══ KEY LEARNING POINT ═══

Gathering as much information as possible from others is crucial for understanding how good we are at certain skills. The information needs to be accurate and so the more we gather, the more accurate our skills assessment becomes.

Objective Information

Objective information is often seen as being more definite and factual: for example, if you sell three pairs of shoes in a shop, then you sell three pairs of shoes and there really is not much debate about it. In reality, badly collected objective information can be more unhelpful than subjective information: for example, perhaps you sell three pairs of shoes but make a financial loss on each one.

The question is, 'What kind of objective information can you gather about your skills?' In reality, the answer is not easy to find. It is true to say that if you are good at something, you will achieve more success, but measuring that success factually is not easy. After all, it is perfectly possible to sell more shoes, for example, but maybe you have to press customers to buy them and actually do the business more harm than good.

 REFLECTION POINT

Take some time to think about the following questions and write down some answers.

If someone were to ask you right now what your two strengths and two weaknesses were, what would you say? Why would you choose those?

STRENGTHS

1.
2.

WEAKNESSES

1.
2.

Step 2: Identify Strategies to Develop New Skills

Identifying strategies to develop new skills requires an understanding of how the process of skill development works. We will look briefly at two models of learning and skill development, and examine the role of additional resources – including people – in our development. The first is known commonly as Kolb's 'Learning Cycle', first devised in 1984 (Kolb, 2015) and details some ideas about how we learn through an ongoing cycle of activities. The second is entitled 'The Four Stages of Learning a New Skill' (Robinson, 1974) and could be applied to both motor and cognitive skills.

Model 1: Kolb's Experiential Learning Cycle

David Kolb's experiential model of learning (Kolb, 2015) is based on individuals having, and thinking about, their experiences, rather than simply absorbing and trying to apply theory. The basic principle of the model is that, in learning a new skill, we go through four activities in a cycle (see Figure 2.4).

It is important to say that we could start our skill development at any place on the cycle and that 'stage 1' is numbered that way just because it makes understanding the theory easier, but most applications of the model work as described in Figure 2.4.

Stage 1: Experience

Imagine for a moment that one of your modules requires you to take an examination. So, you do what you think you need to do in order to pass: the reading, organising your notes, searching on the internet, and so on. After a while you receive your examination timetable and take the exam. The task or activity is completed and your work is sent for marking by the tutor.

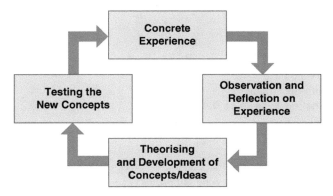

Figure 2.4   Kolb's Learning Cycle (2015)

Kolb, David A. (2015) *Experiential Learning: Experience as the Source of Learning and Development* (2nd edn). © 2015. Reprinted by permission of Pearson Education, Inc., New York.

Stage 2: Reflection

Reflection was mentioned earlier in Chapter 1. It was defined as the process of considering what we do and how we do it, with a view to seeing if there is a way to improve.

After the exam, you might spend time discussing your ideas with other students – what theories you included, what you thought was relevant, what examples you gave and so on – and comparing your answers, or maybe you simply go back to your notes and compare your answers with the information you tried to revise. Doing something active – e.g. going for a walk – while you are reflecting can enhance the brain's ability to identify areas for development as well as strategies for improvement. When you do either of these things, you are reflecting on your performance. Or, to put it another way, you are evaluating how well you think you have done.

Reflection produces deep learning and thinking, and should move us on to consider which practical steps to take in order to improve what we do.

Some time later, you get your marks. Sadly, you have not done as well as you wanted to do; let's assume that this has come as a bit of a shock. You think about what you could have done better, why you did so poorly and, importantly, develop your own thinking about where you need to improve. Again, you are reflecting.

To get the most out of any opportunity to demonstrate and improve on a particular skill, reflection involves thinking about a number of key questions, either individually or with a tutor/coach (see Box 2.2 below).

━━━━━━━━ BOX 2.2 ━━━━━━━━

Reflection on Specific Incidents

Gallagher (2016) notes that it is generally good to reflect on specific events, and ask some or all of the following questions:

(Continued)

- What was the critical incident?
- What happened?
- What were my initial thoughts?
- What were my initial feelings?
- What skills/behaviours did I use?
- How well did I deal with the situation?
- How confident am I that my behaviours were appropriate?
- What have I learnt?
- What will I do differently next time?

Think about a time when something you did turned out not as you planned. Thinking about the questions above, was there anything you would have done differently?

Your lecturers and tutors might add more questions to these, but they go right to the heart of any *reflective* activity.

Of course, reflection without any information to guide you is simply 'thinking', and the biggest mistake after an examination that many students make is that they reflect *without* gathering extra information from their tutors, who will know more. You will almost certainly get feedback on your coursework but less often on an examination. It might not be comfortable to speak to a tutor who has given you a mark you do not feel you deserve, but it is vital, otherwise how will you know what to change?

 KEY LEARNING POINT ━━━━

In reflecting on the marks you get for your examinations, it is vital to get feedback from your lecturers. Not doing so means that you are relying on guesswork.

Stage 3: Theorising

The present situation is that you have taken your exam, you have reflected on what you could have done differently, and you now start to become more analytical and think about why you did what you did, or why it was successful. In other words, you will start to develop a 'theory' of what happened and why.

This stage should also involve some input from experts and other tutors to help understand how you should have answered the exam. In our example, you might have found out that you needed to manage time better, structure the answers in a different way or include more references. Your university lecturers should also be able and willing to give you feedback – either in oral or written form – and may well publish a report for you to look at. If you do not get any response to a request for feedback, then be persistent: it is your degree which might be at stake.

Stage 4: Planning

If you have gone through the three stages listed above, then there is just one major question left unanswered:

What am I going to do differently next time?

Nearly a whole semester has passed by and you are about to sit some more examinations. This time, you want to do better, so you go back to your reflections, think about the changes you need to make in what you did and how you did it, and actually implement those changes. This time, you know what you need to do and you are ready to achieve better results, which is exactly what you want.

Answering this final question – and importantly implementing your own thoughts – should enable you to do better in the next examination.

Thus, you complete the learning cycle (Figure 2.5). Or rather you have been through the cycle once.

If you are going to become very good at a particular skill, then you need to go through this cycle a number of times: you do not learn how to ride a bicycle or a horse or motorbike by riding, falling off and then simply thinking about what to do differently – you have to get back on and try again. The same applies to learning to drive, swimming, giving a presentation, communicating with others in a group, persuading team members or customers of something, learning to email your tutors, carrying out a selection interview, and so on.

It is the application of theory that makes it useful, so have a look at the exercise in the next 'For You to Do' section, which asks you to apply the learning styles to the development of writing skills (though it could apply to any skill).

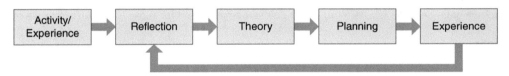

Figure 2.5 Repeating Kolb's Experiential Learning Cycle (2015)

FOR YOU TO DO

Think through the information above regarding Kolb's (2015) ideas. Check your understanding of how each component of the learning cycle might work by applying the model to the development of your writing skills.

Stage of the learning cycle	In order to develop my writing skills at this stage of the learning cycle, I should ...
Concrete experience	
Observation and reflection	
Developing ideas and theory	
Testing new concepts	

There are no right and wrong answers for this exercise, but thinking through the 'For You to Do' exercise above will give you an understanding of how well you understand how Kolb's Learning Cycle works. We tend to think that experience on its own is sufficient to become 'perfect', though in reality we usually need more than just practice, as Box 2.3 illustrates.

━━━ **BOX 2.3** ━━━

A Common Saying ... and a Recipe for Improvement

There is a saying that most people seem to accept as common sense, and most people believe, and you will have probably have heard it, too:

'Practice makes perfect'

Think about this. Maybe you can drive: does doing more driving make you better? Or maybe you can give presentations: does giving more presentations make you better at them?

Possibly; but for most people, practice – on its own – does not make someone better or perfect at something. Just doing something does not make you better at it: you just develop habits or behaviours that you do instinctively. For many people, simply practising something makes inappropriate or ineffective behaviour become a bad habit, so additional input is needed.

The first thing to add to this mixture is *feedback*. If we think about the driving example, we can get feedback from passengers (if they are scared after being in the car with you, then something is probably wrong), other drivers (even if they are sometimes not polite), from the police, perhaps, from reflection on our own driving and as a result of any accidents that we might be unlucky enough to have.

The second item to add is *motivation to change*. If we do not care about how many speeding fines we have, or whether people want to be our passengers, then we are unlikely to actually do anything about the feedback we get. The same is true for any of the skills we have – and for those we seek to improve on.

Questions

1. In thinking about the skills you want to improve on, what sources of feedback could you use to see how much improvement you have made?
2. What is your motivation for changing and improving these skills? Is it strong enough to keep you focused until you are good enough at them?

Model 2: The Four Stages of Learning a New Skill

A very different model of learning was developed in the late 1960s and early 1970s. The exact origin of the model is not known, but a claim of authorship was noted in 1974 (Robinson, 1974). The model consists of four relatively simple stages in becoming skilled, and we will use presentation skills as an example to illustrate how the model works.

Unconscious Incompetence: We have no idea whether we can or cannot do something. It is simply a question we have never thought about or received any feedback on. For example, 'I have never done a presentation and I have no idea whether I am good or not. I think I might be, but ...'

Conscious Incompetence: We are aware that we are not as good as we could be and have a desire to get better at this skill. For example, '*I have done* a presentation and the audience seemed confused because I did not explain myself well and some people could not hear me. I now know that I am not as good as I want to be.'

Conscious Competence: We have developed our skills and now know that we are good. We still have to try out certain things because they do not come naturally, but we are performing at a level where others can see that we can demonstrate this skill well. In relation to the example we are using here, 'I have regularly received feedback that my audience enjoys my presentations and finds them informative. I have to try to appear confident because I still have lots of nerves and I work hard to hide them, but my presentations go down well.'

Unconscious Competence: The classic goal of any skill development activity or strategy is this one, where individuals are skilled without needing to put any effort into what they do. Everything seems to be done – and is done – naturally or effortlessly. The final stage in our example would be where: 'I feel good about what I do and can give a good and entertaining presentation without really thinking about it. My nerves don't affect me, and my confidence is there. In fact, I really don't need to think very much about what I am doing.'

Once again (as with Kolb's Learning Cycle above), there are obvious applications to nearly all the skills we are considering in this text and a range of others we are not looking at here.

KEY LEARNING POINT

All good personal development activities – based on the theories identified above – require some formal input and some forms of practice. In that sense, practice + feedback + motivation can help to 'make perfect' (see Box 2.3), but without practice, there will be very little skill development.

SETTING GOOD GOALS

Knowing how to plan is essential to a busy work life, and the same is no less true for life as a student. The very beginning of the chapter noted that 'managing' time is something we cannot do, but learning how to plan gives us a significantly greater sense of control over what we do.

If you can learn to plan during your time as a student, then you will achieve three things very easily: 1) you will be able to do much better in your coursework; 2) you will finish your coursework before others and will be able to relax more; and 3) you will be able to demonstrate good 'time management' and planning skills to future employers. Of course, you cannot plan what to do unless you know what is important, and that is where goal setting comes in.

In his influential book *The 7 Habits of Highly Effective People*, Covey (1989) outlines two 'habits' that have some place in this chapter: firstly, 'Begin with the end in mind'; and secondly, 'First things first'. The first relates to setting goals and the second to effective planning and prioritisation. It is worth reading and thinking about what Covey has to say on the subject, but for us, looking at studying, we need to get down to basics with some fundamental questions.

FOR YOU TO DO

Have a look at the following questions. How easy are they for you to answer?

1. When you woke up this morning, how clear were you on what you wanted to achieve?
2. What do you want to achieve/complete/have done in the next three hours?
3. Was reading this chapter of the book something you intended to do today, or are you surprised you are doing this?
4. Why are you reading this chapter?

Let's look at the second question above: do you know what you want to have completed in the next three hours? If we can answer this question clearly, then it means we have set a goal: 'Within the next three hours, I will have completed X, finished Y and discussed the topic with Z …'. We will look at what makes a good goal in a little while, but it is important to understand *why* we need goals in the first place. Some goals can relate to careers, and some will relate to the much more mundane activities involved in daily life (see Figure 2.6).

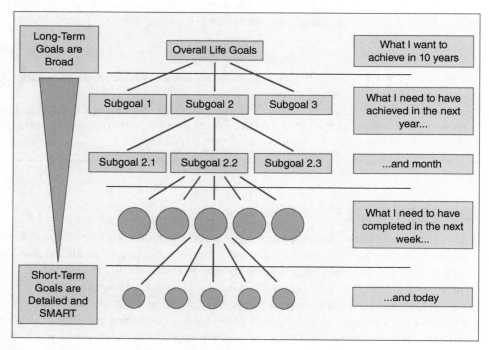

Figure 2.6 Relationship between career achievement and shorter-term goals

Of course, the longer-term goals can change a great deal, and we need to ensure we are not totally inflexible in what we seek, but as we look towards shorter-term goals, we need to ensure that they are SMART.

The Nature of Good Goals: SMART Goal Setting

Good goals, as nearly any management website or textbook on the subject will tell you, should be SMART, although the meaning of each letter varies depending on who you read. This acronym is usually defined thus:

Specific: What exactly do you want to have completed?

Measurable: How will you know whether or not you have completed it?

Achievable: Are you likely to be able to achieve this goal/complete this work …?

Realistic: … in the timescale you have allocated? Or **Resourced**: Do you have sufficient resources available to you?

Time-based: By when do you want to have completed this? The shorter the timescale, the more precise you should be.

So, taking the three-hour example, we could write that the goal is SMART in the following ways:

Specific: It says, 'I will have completed X'. X could be 'read two chapters' or 'complete Exercise 2 which was set as homework'. Both are specific. If we wrote, 'I will have done some of the reading from one of my textbooks,' then the example is not specific. How much reading? From which textbook? Can you see the difference?

Measurable: It says, 'I will have completed X'. It is much better to have a goal which can be measured, because then you (and other people) know whether you have completed it. The key question here is, 'How will you know whether or not you have achieved the goal?' If your goal is 'to graduate with the best degree you can', then that is a great broad intention, but it is not measurable. How will you know whether or not you have achieved it?

Achievable and **R**ealistic relate to the likelihood of your achieving the measure you set out, bearing in mind the resources at your disposal. This includes time, but also includes people, facilities, other commitments that you might have made, data and information, and so on.

Time-based: Have you given a very clear date (i.e. month and day, and perhaps even a time) by which you will have achieved what you have stated? 'Within the next three hours' is very clear; 'Within the next week' is not.

━━━━━━ FOR YOU TO DO ━━━━━━

Have a quick look at the goals below:

'I intend to be a good hard-working student during the next semester. I hope that I can write my assignments to the best of my ability and submit them on time. I want to pass this semester of study with only a couple of retake examinations.'

Questions

1. How SMART do the goals appear to be?
2. If you came back after the time period given, would you be able to see clearly whether this individual had achieved their goals?

INTEGRATION AND APPLICATION

If we look at the information above, we end up with two stages:

1. Evaluation of our strengths and weaknesses.
2. Development of a plan to improve our weaknesses.

Table 2.2 Example of a personal development plan

Skill/ behaviour	Action needed	Resources needed (incl. people)	Date(s) for action	Date for review (i.e. next opportunity to practise and demonstrate skill)	Aspirational goal (SMART)	Met?
Giving regular eye contact in presentations	Rehearse presentation in mirror and in front of friends Gather feedback from friends	Friends Books on presentation skills Online resources Computer	Rehearse every Friday afternoon Read presentation every Thursday	Complete presentation in front of friends every Saturday morning: 18th, 25th, 2nd	I want to be hitting 5/5 for eye contact each time I do the practice presentation. I'll use the evaluation form to collect evaluations from friends	
Develop encouraging attitude towards others in coursework group	Refrain from being overly critical Ask for evaluation from others in the group Read up on having a positive approach towards group members	Friends to evaluate my progress Books on team-working skills Online resources	Group meeting on Thursday and Saturday to do accounting coursework	Discuss feedback from friends immediately after the group meeting on Thursday and Saturday for the next two weeks	I want to collect evidence of statements from my friends showing that I have encouraged others in the group I want to have at least five such statements each meeting	

There are some weaknesses that we will struggle to develop – I am not really able to play a musical instrument, for example – but there are weaknesses that we can improve on, and where we might have some potential, so the second stage becomes really important.

Remember the conversation between the tutor and Cindy (see page 27/28)? Assuming for a moment that we have identified that we wish to develop our presentation skills, and in particular our ability to present in a confident manner (see Chapter 9 for more details on oral presentation skills) and also to work on our team-working skills (see Chapter 11), our personal development plan might look something like that in Table 2.2 on the previous page.

This example gives a clear indication of what this individual will do, how they will evaluate what they will do, how good they intend to be, and whether the goal is met. In real life, they would then go on and give additional comments to indicate what they intend to do or to work on next. They are very clear on exactly when they will take these actions and the goal is very clear.

Some skills are not easy to develop (e.g. presentation skills, critical thinking skills), so consider the ideas in Table 2.3.

Table 2.3 Ideas for skill development

Skill	Ideas for development
Time management and being able to work independently (see Chapter 3)	Reflect on why you might find this skill difficult. Is it prioritising? Is it planning? Is it about identifying personal goals? • Write down daily goals somewhere where you can see them. • If you have a smartphone, then set reminders on your phone indicating what you have to do and when. • Buy and use an alarm clock, and set it for a time in line with the tasks you have to get done that day. • Review your use of time as regularly as possible and see how much improvement you are making. • Look at your next task. Are you able to plan your time to do what you need to do? If not, is the issue that your plan is too ambitious, or that you need to develop the motivation to do what is needed?
Critical thinking and reading (see Chapter 4)	• Have a look through Chapter 4 to identify what is meant by critical thinking. • Arrange to discuss an issue with a friend: give them the chance to say whether they agree or disagree with a particular point of view and then take the opposite viewpoint – the role of 'devil's advocate' – in order to develop your ability to think of counter-arguments. • Identify where what is written in the example essay in Chapter 5 is different (more analytical) than what you might naturally write. • When the results from another essay are available, find someone who has a better mark than you and ask to see their assignment to see what they did differently. • Active reading means to engage your brain while reading articles and textbooks. Take an article that you find easy to read, and take time to ask questions. Do you believe what it is telling you? Are there any reasons why the conclusions may not be valid? What are the implications of the article you are reading? Write down your thoughts, so that you can think about them later and use them in your writing. • Discuss what you have been reading with a friend: do they think it makes sense? Is there anything they notice about what you have been reading that you have missed? • Join a debating club, to develop your abilities to identify and give the strongest arguments. • Listen to debates and interviews on the media: as you listen, critique the arguments you hear. Was any evidence presented? Was the point of view accurate?

(Continued)

Table 2.3   (Continued)

Skill	Ideas for development
Developing your writing skills – both timed examination essays and coursework (see Chapters 6, 7 and 8)	• Try to write an essay plan about a particular question and get some feedback on it from a tutor or adviser. • Write an essay under timed conditions and review your work, preferably with a lecturer: did you finish it in time? Was it sufficiently well structured? How analytical was it? (Do you understand what 'analytical' means?) Did it include everything that it should have included? Was the evidence there to support your argument? • When the results from another essay are available, find someone who has a better mark than you and ask to see their assignment to see what they did differently. • Review Chapters 6 and 7 to identify whether there is something you have missed in your written work.
Research and library skills	• Most academic libraries will have staff whose role it is to assist students to find what they need to find, so visit the library and learn what online and offline facilities are on offer. • Check that you know what information databases and search tools are available for online journals and how you can obtain articles or items not on the shelves of your particular library.
Quantitative skills	• Get hold of some books – either from the library or from an academic skills unit in your university – that match your level of mathematics and work your way through. Can you understand the meanings of 'p' value? What is a 't' test? Can you differentiate between mode, mean and median? What are positively and negatively skewed distributions? You will need to understand these and other mathematical concepts to understand the journal articles you are reading. • Seek some assistance from older students or search for online resources which match your level and style of learning.
Communication skills (Chapter 9), team-working skills (Chapter 11), leading others (Chapter 12)	• Identify which aspect(s) of communicating and working with others/leading that you struggle with; working in a team requires a great number of different skills. • Gather feedback from other team members and then work together to improve on whatever specific areas require development. • Consider teams that you have enjoyed working with and those which you have not enjoyed working with: what made the difference? Was it the people in the team, or the task, or the leadership? The answer will then give you an idea as to whether you are learning from what you see others do, from what you do or from what you prefer to do as a task. You cannot always change the task but you can change how the team interacts. • What did the leader do that helped you to follow/hindered you from following them? What can you learn from what they did? If the relationships were challenging, then how might people have communicated around issues differently? Did there seem to be respect? Were any negative aspects of communication deliberate, or the result of misinterpretation or misunderstanding by others? What might have been done differently? • Work with others to organise a charity event (or some other event that you are not required to do as part of your course). Removing the pressure means that you can enjoy it and relax a little more, and then let your real abilities and personality show. • Imagine yourself in different kinds of relationships with your current team members than those you have now (which could be unhelpful, very constructive, destructive, aggressive, etc.): what would need to happen in order for you to change your behaviour? View any issues from the others' perspective: could they be seeing the problem in a different way from you? What would need to happen for *them* to change *their* behaviour? • Read some material on what it means to work well as a team – share it with others in an uncritical, objective manner. Is there anything the team can learn? • Take some time to review how the team is working. Listen well and gather accurate feedback with specific evidence. • Write down and review some sentences that you said: was there any other way that they could have been interpreted? Ask a friend to help you answer this question. • Watch others working in teams on TV: what do they do well? What might they be doing which isn't working? What should they do differently?

Skill	Ideas for development
Self-reflection	• When you try to do something to develop your skills, ask yourself some important questions. How well did you do what you hoped to do? What might you have done differently? What else could you do to enhance your performance?
Presentation skills (see Chapter 10)	• Identify which aspect(s) of giving presentations you struggle with, since different areas may require very different actions. • Preparation: if you never give yourself sufficient time to prepare, then set yourself specific goals for preparation. By when will you have visual aids ready? By when will you have rehearsed? By when will you have found out about the presentation facilities? • Develop a presentation preparation checklist (based on Chapter 10), and use it. • Delivery: practise and rehearse, preferably in front of others who can give you some feedback, but in front of a mirror if needed. Undertake some structured reflection/evaluation – be systematic and ask others to give you feedback on the same criteria each time. Get feedback on your para-linguistic and non-verbal behaviour (see Chapter 9) as well as your content. • Watch how others present (e.g. on TV, on videos of TED talks, at your lectures). • Join a TEDx or University Toastmasters Club to practise giving presentations and getting/giving feedback. • Evaluate what your lecturers do that is good and bad, in terms of presenting and engaging their audience • Join and practise speaking at a debating club, to develop your ability to speak confidently.
Business awareness	• Spend time talking to those you know who have set up a small business. Read a bibliography of a well-known business leader. Ask yourself: what does it take to make a business profitable? How does a business obtain customers? How does a business balance its costs?
IT skills	• Try using relevant software (including using search engines) to complete your work. If there are things you cannot do, seek advice from other students and technical staff. • Post requests onto social media to seek help as you feel appropriate. • Search for assistance online: there will usually be someone somewhere who can explain what you need to do. There may be a document or a help guide from the software provider.
Problem-solving skills (see Chapter 14)	• Is there anything that is stopping you – or someone else – from doing what you would like to do: how might you solve that problem? What creative ideas can you develop? • Ask your lecturers to provide business case studies for you to 'solve'. • Read the news to see what problems businesses are solving. Get together with some other students to find solutions to these problems.
Influencing skills	• Start with small activities to build confidence if you need to. • Review how good you seem to be at persuading others to undertake a social activity. • Try to persuade others to meet up for a discussion around a topic covered in a lecture. Lead the meeting and ask someone to write some notes of the discussion. Was this successful? • Look at the needs of your local community. Is there an obvious need for something to change? Arrange a meeting with some other students to develop plans to meet such needs. Identify actions and delegate tasks to others to implement the plans. • Before a group discussion, gather evidence to support a particular point of view. What might others disagree with? During the discussion, respectfully see if you can present and use that evidence to persuade others of your point of view.
Developing cross-cultural awareness (Chapter 13) and problem solving and creativity (Chapter 14)	• Both these chapters include specific ideas for developing your skills.

CONCLUSION

By now, you should be able to:

- Discuss how academic and interpersonal skills are developed during a degree.
- Analyse some of your own strengths and weaknesses as they relate to your immediate, medium-term and longer-term development needs.
- Develop some ideas for working on your weaknesses and enhancing your strengths.

This chapter has aimed to give you an idea of how personal development and learning works in practice, at least as far as skill development is concerned. Some of the more detailed aspects of planning for personal development (especially in terms of how you might use opportunities to develop your skills) is given in the online content.

Each of the chapters which follow will relate to the development of your skills in some way or another. Some will only relate to your short-term situation – as a student. Others will be important for you in the short term and in the longer term – to help you become successful in a career after employment. Depending on the role you take after employment, there may also be knowledge gaps which employers will often help you to fill through professional qualifications. The key issue here is that nearly all the skills that you will use and develop during your degree will be important for personal success in the workplace as well, as shown in Figure 2.7.

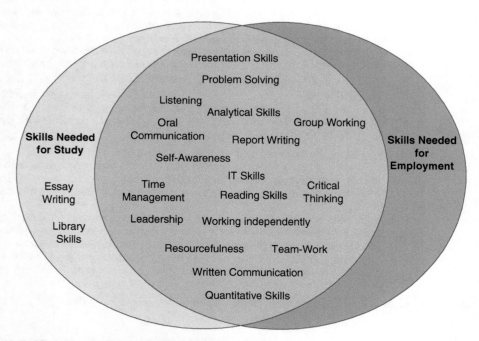

Figure 2.7 Overlap of 'study skills' and 'employability skills'

CHAPTER TASK

Based on the content of this chapter, what do you now know about personal learning that you did not know before?

What key learning point had the most impact? Why?

Do your answers to either of the above questions have the potential to change your attitude to studies at university? If so, why?

Have a look at Donald Clark's webpage on learning and learning styles: www.nwlink.com/~donclark/hrd/styles.html. What does this teach you about the way you prefer to learn and the theory covered above?

INTERVIEW QUESTIONS

Think about the following questions which might be asked at a job interview. What might your answers be?

1. How have you changed or tried to develop yourself while at university?
2. What were the most useful and least useful parts of your studies at university?
3. What are your personal strengths and weaknesses in relation to this role?

Chapter 17 gives a lot more information on selection interviews and the online content gives some guidance on these questions.

ADDITIONAL RESOURCES

Want to learn more? Visit https://study.sagepub.com/morgan2e to gain access to a wide range of online resources, including interactive tests, tasks, further reading and downloads.

Website Resources

The following websites offer useful advice on personal development planning:

The Open University: https://help.open.ac.uk/pdp

University of Bath: www.bath.ac.uk/learningandteaching/enhance-learning-experiences/personal-development-planning.html

University of Bristol: www.bristol.ac.uk/arts/skills/self-evaluation/pdp/

University of Manchester: www.humanities.manchester.ac.uk/studyskills/progress/career_planning/PDP.html

Textbook Resources

Burns, T. and Sinfield, S. (2016) *Essential Study Skills* (4th edition). London: Sage (particularly Chapter 8).

Cameron, S. (2016) *The Business Student's Handbook: Skills for Study and Employment* (6th edition). Harlow: Pearson (particularly Chapter 3).

Cottrell, S. (2010) *Skills for Success* (2nd edition). New York: Palgrave (particularly Chapter 8).

Cottrell, S. (2013) *The Study Skills Handbook* (4th edition). New York: Palgrave (particularly Chapter 2).

Gallagher, K. (2016) *Essential Study and Employment Skills for Business and Management Students* (3rd edition). Oxford: Oxford University Press (particularly Chapter 2).

Hind, D. and Moss, S. (2011) *Employability Skills*. Houghton-le-Spring: Business Education Publishers (particularly Chapters 2 and 14).

Horn, R. (2012) *The Business Skills Handbook*. London: CIPD (particularly Chapter 3).

McMillan, K. and Weyers, J. (2012) *The Study Skills Book* (3rd edition). Harlow: Pearson (particularly Chapter 7).

Smale, B. and Fowlie, J. (2009) *How to Succeed at University: An Essential Guide to Academic Skills, Personal Development & Employability*. London: Sage (particularly Chapter 2).

PART II
LEARNING HOW TO STUDY

This part of the book looks at your immediate short-term needs – that is, how to study successfully in order to achieve the best grades you can.

In order to make the most of the opportunities for learning that universities give us, a number of skills are needed and these form the basis of the next few chapters. Chapter 3 examines what is seen by some to be the most important skill to possess while being a student – that of time management. Chapter 4 provides some insight into what academics call critical thinking. We have already said something about the teaching and learning methods used at universities, but we will discuss those in more detail in Chapter 5.

Each chapter will outline why a skill is important and the potential consequences of demonstrating a particular skill – or understanding a particular aspect of university study – poorly.

3   TIME MANAGEMENT

The key is in not spending time, but in investing it. (Stephen R. Covey)

CHAPTER STRUCTURE

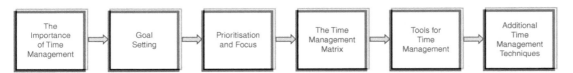

Figure 3.1

When you see the this means go to the companion website https://study.sagepub.com/morgan2e to do a quiz, complete a task, read further or download a template.

━━ AIMS OF THE CHAPTER ━━

By the end of this chapter, you should be able to:

- Assess your time management skills.
- Understand the expectations universities have of the time you spend studying.
- Waste less time and use more of your time productively.

WHEN SHOULD YOU READ THIS CHAPTER?

This chapter gives you some useful tips on managing your time - a skill that you need to develop from the very first week at university when you receive your timetable, and so it is best to read this during your first three weeks at university, but to keep this close to you throughout your life as a student.

INTRODUCTION

In reality, there is no such thing as 'time management'. It is not really something that can be managed or controlled – time is there regardless of what we do, and it ticks away regardless of whether we think we can really 'manage' it or not. We cannot add to it or take away from it – it is a finite resource. What we are really talking about here is *our ability to use our time effectively*.

As we noted in Chapter 2, there is a variety of skills needed for making the most of the academic opportunities you have been given by university study, but this skill is probably the most fundamental – which is why we are looking at this before anything else. Some suggest that the importance of time management increases significantly as we progress through our studies: to some extent that is true, but failing to understand how we can manage our time early on in our studies can mean that we fail to make it through our modules.

Being a student involves undertaking various tasks: from reading to attending lectures, thinking about subject matter, taking exams, and so on. Successful completion of those tasks requires time – usually a considerable amount of time. Failing to manage our time well could mean that we really do not perform well. We give ourselves insufficient time for reading (if we do any at all), do not do any of the seminar exercises, miss a load of lectures and then find that we are really stressed at assignment or examination time because we suddenly realise that we do not know half of what we probably should know (and are perhaps confused about a lot of the lecture slides). The worst situation is where we 'are forced' to go without sleep simply to catch up on work we should have done earlier on the day before an important exam – or we download something from the internet and submit that because we have not given ourselves enough time. In other words, failing to manage time well will mean that you end up behaving in all sorts of ways that you suspect are wrong – or you continue to do what you have always done, and maybe just about pass your degree.

We will begin the chapter by giving you the opportunity to analyse your skills, and then take some time to examine the role that others' expectations play in the way we use our time. We will then spend some time looking at goal setting – a major influence on what we do in relation to time management – and apply this to how individuals set goals in relation to their careers. We will spend some time looking at the impact of motivation on time usage and finally conclude the chapter with some principles and tools which could improve your use of time.

SKILLS SELF-ASSESSMENT

It is helpful to note down your reflections on your own abilities (reflection, remember, should be honest and open). It is private, so there is no need to deceive anyone or make yourself out to be better than you really are.

Read carefully each of the following descriptions and say how typical you think each statement is of your behaviour or attitude by giving it a score between 1 and 5, where 1 is 'strongly disagree' and 5 is 'strongly agree'.

Item number	Item	Score
1.	I get my things ready for the next day's study or work the night before	
2.	I get stressed if I am late	

Item number	Item	Score
3.	I rarely plan anything and would prefer just to deal with whatever comes along at the time	
4.	I get annoyed when I have to wait for others to come to pre-arranged meetings	
5.	I find doing many things at the same time very easy	
6.	I think I need someone else to help organise my life: I always forget what I should be doing or who I should be meeting	
7.	I have been known to lose my keys or my bags quite regularly	
8.	I have and use a diary	
9.	I find waiting for others or waiting for events to start really frustrating: why should I waste time waiting?	
10.	I often plan ahead and think through carefully every possible outcome	
11.	I know what I am doing tomorrow	
12.	I find there is nothing wrong with the excitement of doing everything at the last minute	
13.	If I find something hard, I will try and overcome the difficulties myself rather than ask for help	
14.	I 'live for the moment': tomorrow is another day which will take care of itself	
15.	I am not good at motivating myself over a long time for long projects	
16.	I need others to help me know where I should be and when	
17.	I find it easy to say 'no' to people who invite me for a meal when I have something more important to do	
18.	I probably spend too much time watching TV, playing computer games or chatting to friends online	
19.	I am used to using electronic 'tools' (smartphone, tablet, laptop, etc.) to organise my life	
20.	I keep a record of things I need to do each day, and tick them off as they get completed	
21.	I believe that only the very best work will do: I need to be proud of what I have done	
22.	I find it easy to begin assignments and essays	
23.	I have all my lecture notes in a pile on my desk or on the floor (or similar)	
24.	I am clear about my goals for this year of study	
25.	I think that studying does not usually take that much time: I have got just a few hours of lectures and tutorials each week	
26.	I have never had two appointments clashing at the same time	

An interactive version of this test along with comments and thoughts about these questions can be found on the companion website for this book at https://study.sagepub.com/morgan2e.

INTERACTIVE TEST

THE IMPORTANCE OF TIME MANAGEMENT

It is not just for your studies that time management is important. In the workplace, arrive late at an important sales meeting without letting anyone know and you will lose the sale, or miss a deadline for your work and you will probably either be unprepared for a scheduled meeting or cause others real issues with their work. The implication is that you will be seen as unreliable, a perception that is hard to shake off. It is possible that people will not want to work with you and you might struggle to lead by example (which sometimes means that you will not get the leadership roles you might want in the future).

Being good at time management is important in lots of different ways. In fact, research such as that by George et al. (2008) shows a correlation between a student's ability to manage time and their academic success – and in some cases good time management is the most significant predictor. The important questions here are: What does 'being good' mean? How do we measure our skills in this?

 KEY LEARNING POINT ━━━━━━━━━━━

Learning to manage your ability to use time well will not automatically give you success as a student, but failing to do so well will make passing your courses difficult, if not impossible, to achieve.

Defining 'Good' Time Management

Being 'good' can mean a number of things, and our personal values will have some part to play in deciding which definition suits us best. Have a look at those below and see which you like the best:

- Working for as long as possible, every day.
- Ensuring that you have enough time for leisure as well as study.
- Being able to do everything you need to do.
- Working in a way that gives an adrenalin rush, by doing things at the last minute.
- Being able to boast to others about how far in advance you have completed your work.
- A combination of the above.

Whichever definition you prefer, your reaction to some of the others might be one of surprise – 'how could anyone live their life that way?!' But we need to think carefully about the definition we choose. The way we view 'good' time management is going to have a clear impact on what we do, and this will have a definite impact on how others perceive and work with us. A suggested definition of 'good' time management is provided below.

What we can be sure of is that there are few models about how to manage our time. There are a large number of good ideas and practices, and one or two frameworks, but little which actually provides an overarching framework on why we go about managing time in the way we do, and that is the reason why the content below may seem a little unstructured.

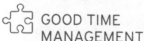 GOOD TIME MANAGEMENT

Good time management is the ability to control our use of time to such an extent that we are able to plan and manage what we do without undue stress or tension.

Either directly or indirectly, everything you do in your studies – and later in your professional and managerial life – will depend to some extent on how good you are at managing your time. Even the way you interact with others will depend on how frustrated and impatient you are, so it is important to get this right, *now*.

GOAL SETTING

We looked at goal setting earlier in Chapter 2 so we should know how to set our own development goals by now, but in order to set realistic goals around the management of our time, we need to understand how we are currently using our time, and how we should be using our time. In many cases, defining how we *should* manage our time comes down to our own personal priorities, but as a student, some expectations are already put on us.

Understanding What Students Do – and What We Should Do

There are two possible ways to bring some order into our lives: either to control our lives, or to control what places demands on our lives. As we have already noted, controlling time is not really possible – it continues to move regardless of what we might like – so the only other possibility is that we control our lives. To do this requires that we know what our lives really consist of – and this requires that we develop some kind of job description.

━━━━━ **FOR YOU TO DO** ━━━━━

Before looking at Box 3.1, try the following.

Make a list of everything you think you will need to do in order to study successfully. In other words, write a kind of job description.

Using the list you have developed above, write down the following *for each activity*:

1. How much time do you think *you are spending* on these activities?
2. How much time do you think *you should be spending* on these activities?
3. What do you *actually* spend your time on?

Using the Time Management Log supplied on the companion website at https://study.sagepub.com/morgan2e use the next seven days to list everything that you do. You can be as detailed or as general as you wish, but remember that you should be trying to answer question 3 from the exercise above, so make it as detailed as you need to. TEMPLATE

So, how well do you manage your time? Does it match the expectations that others might have?

How do you think *your* 'job' as a student compares with the 'job description' in Box 3.1? Is there anything missing?

If we look at the job description of a university student, we find a range of activities which need to be undertaken.

━━━━━ **BOX 3.1** ━━━━━

Typical Job Description of a University Student

- Download course notes put online by your tutors.
- Download and read material in advance of your lectures.
- Attend and make notes of your lectures.
- Attend and contribute to seminars and tutorials.
- Complete relevant 'homework' and coursework.
- Contribute to online discussions.

(Continued)

- Compare lecture content with other reading on the same subject/topics.
- Complete and make notes on the essential reading.
- Meet other students to discuss group work.
- Find and make notes on journal and book reading from the library.
- Revise for examinations.
- Communicate and meet with your tutor(s) as required.
- Organise your notes so that they are easy to find and use.

These may be similar to the tasks you listed for the exercise above. Therefore, the two challenging questions are, firstly, how many of these things have you been doing regularly since you started your studies? And, secondly, how much time have you been spending on each of them?

Personality does have a part to play here. Your figures for the above may be close and you may consider yourself 'totally sorted' as a human being; or you may see differences and suffer from a huge explosion of guilt. Neither are perhaps reflective of reality, so let's have something of a reality check.

The importance of keeping a record of how you are using your time (a Time Log) cannot be understated: it is one thing to have the idea that you cannot control time, but it is another thing entirely to be unaware of how you are spending your time – which is why the last exercise is so important. Understanding how you use your time is critical to knowing how much your behaviour needs to change, and understanding what is expected of you will give you some way of knowing how far away from those expectations you are, and how much you might need to change.

Here is some broad guidance. It tends to shock the students I have taught.

You will be studying a number of modules and, as stated in Chapter 1, each one is allocated a number of 'credits' usually depending on how heavy the workload is for the module. Generally speaking, across a number of universities 10 credits would be roughly equal to 100 hours of study (15 credits equal to around 150 hours and so on). Semesters tend to be around 12–14 weeks in length, and each year of your degree will have approximately 120 credits allocated to it, so that means the calculation works out as follows:

- Each year = 120 credits = 1200 hours of studying
- Each year = 28 weeks of teaching and examinations
- 1200 hours over 28 weeks = **42.8 hours a week**

What is that in percentage terms? If a week has 168 hours (7 × 24), then if we are studying we should be spending around 25% of our time on our studies. That is, 25% of *all* our time, including sleeping, eating, relaxing and travelling.

This is similar to the figures that others have come up with. For example, in asking students how they spend their time, Payne and Whittaker (2006) suggested that students spent 27% of their time on study-related activities. (Sleep was calculated at around 33% of students' time.)

This calculation is slightly flawed, however. For example, it assumes that you do no studying at all during the Christmas or Easter vacations (if each is two weeks long, then the figure goes down to 37.5 hours a week) and the notional figure of 100 hours per 10 credits will vary significantly from individual to individual, and from module to module, so the real figure may be less than the 42.8 hours a week given above. What it does mean, however, is that you should be spending something around this figure on your studies each week. If you do not, you might need to think seriously about increasing the amount of time you give to your studies.

Looking at your time log, is that figure of 42 hours a week (roughly 25% of your time) anywhere near the amount of time you spend studying? Or rather, *is the amount of time you spend studying anywhere near 42 hours?*

'BUT I HAVE A QUESTION …'

… I have 12 hours of lectures and tutorials each week and I can do the reading etc. in another four hours or so. I think I am learning and I have a fairly clear understanding of the lecture material once I have read the book as well, so is there something else I should be doing?

Not necessarily, and some people work faster and harder than others. I know that some international students, for example, struggle a lot with the reading and sometimes, it takes them longer than it would take a native speaker. But think about how many notes you take when you are doing the reading.

It is a good idea to take notes, otherwise you will forget what you have read. It also reinforces or strengthens the learning as well. Spending time thinking about what you read is a great habit to get into.

If any of the above points have surprised or alarmed you, you might need to do something about improving the way you use your time. One way to improve yourself (as we suggested in Chapter 2) in relation to any skill is to evaluate yourself and your progress against some goals. This requires a good understanding of how goal setting should be undertaken and an ability to clearly identify our goals.

REFLECTION POINT

Take some time to think about the following questions and write down some answers.

How often do you set goals for your own activities? Or do you just do things because they 'come along'?

If you do not really set goals, why is that?

If you do set goals, do you achieve them? Would you advise someone else to set some goals for themselves?

PRIORITISATION AND FOCUS

Prioritisation

Identifying our goals is an important first step, but this is still only part of the process. These goals may become more or less important to us as time goes by, so it becomes important to prioritise those things which are important against those which are not. Our priorities can relate as much to our careers as to what we choose to do on a Saturday afternoon.

The issue of prioritisation is as important here as it is for our longer-term career goals. In order to complete an essay due next week, for example, we might decide that it is more important to read an extra book chapter than it is to enjoy a meal out with friends. Whenever we use the words 'more important', we are prioritising, whether we realise it or not.

PRIORITISATION

Prioritisation is the act of deciding which activities to undertake or which goals to aim for at the expense of less important goals and activities.

FOR YOU TO DO

Prioritisation

Look at the activities listed below. Some of them are taken from the 'student job description' and others are taken from anecdotes of typical student life.

For the next seven days, decide: 1) which of these are important priorities for you; 2) which you need to leave alone; and 3) which are not priorities but you would like to undertake if you had the time. Label each activity appropriately:

1. Go to your tutorials.
2. Enjoy a meal out with friends.
3. Go to the local supermarket for food shopping.
4. Complete relevant 'homework'.
5. Go to the bank.
6. Complete the essential reading.
7. Meet with other students to discuss group work.
8. Play some computer games.
9. Go to a meeting of a student club or society.
10. Meet a careers adviser.
11. Make notes on journal and book reading from the library.
12. Complete required coursework.
13. Do your laundry.
14. Revise for examinations.
15. Pre-read lecture material.
16. Get a haircut.
17. Play sport for an hour or two.
18. Download and read course notes put online by your tutors.
19. Contribute to online discussions.
20. Watch soap operas on TV.
21. Go for a drink in the student bar.
22. Spend time in the library.
23. Compare the lecture content with other reading on the same subject/topics.
24. Communicate and meet with your tutor.
25. Go shopping for clothes.
26. Chat to friends on social media.
27. Organise your notes so that they are easy to find and use.

Now make a list of the things you need to do today, and prioritise them according to their importance and how complex the task is (how long it will take to do, how many others it will involve, how many extra resources you will need, and so on).

TIP: If an activity involves another person (e.g. tutor) or limited resources (e.g. library book), you might need to arrange this before actually having the discussion or obtaining the resources.

Developing Focus

Understanding our own priorities is hugely important, but understanding alone will be unlikely to enable us to achieve them: we need to apply some effort as well. So if we understand our priorities (the direction of our effort), then 'focus' describes how much effort we apply.

The more focused we are in our career goals, the more likely we will be to achieve them simply because we will have directed our efforts towards those things in particular (and being focused is seen as a strength by most graduate recruiters). However, one of the challenges is in understanding what is meant by being focused.

When we talk about people being 'focused', we usually mean that they are very clear about what they want and *the goals they want to achieve*. They probably have some good reasons for wanting to achieve those goals and some good ideas about how to achieve them (strategies). These strategies probably include some activities people *do not* want to undertake as much as the ones they do.

By definition, therefore, 'focus' requires that some activities are not undertaken as much as others are. This brings into play the second of the three time management activities we are looking at here, namely 'prioritisation'.

The argument is that focus is important: Li Na or Roger Federer must have had a strong sense of focus (some call it determination, others persistence) in order to become great tennis players. The same is true for some of the world's most successful business entrepreneurs. It takes focus, determination and a huge amount of persistence to achieve tough goals.

Focus is important for the achievement of tough goals, but it carries some risk. Keeping focused on a particular goal when technology and circumstances around you are changing rapidly and making the achievement of that goal impossible is not clever, and some people cannot see the changes in the external environment because they are *too focused*.

KEY LEARNING POINT

To establish personal career goals - or maybe goals related to our daily lives or over the next year - and identify what we want to achieve.

The two issues we have discussed above – goal setting and prioritisation – go together. We cannot determine what is important to us without understanding our goals. If we could not define our goals, we would need to decide what we need to do based on other reasons:

- Others (and typically those who are influential in our lives, including managers and parents, sometimes) want us to do these things.
- We want to do these things because we enjoy doing them.
- We do not have anything more important to do.
- There is a crisis and we need to solve it.
- We are bored and we just waste time.

KEY LEARNING POINT

In identifying our own actions and goals, we need to set priorities. These may change over time as our goals change.

THE TIME MANAGEMENT MATRIX

Both students and managers struggle with goal setting and prioritisation. In 1989, Stephen Covey developed the 'Time Management Matrix' (Figure 3.2), a tool which illustrated how individuals tend to go about managing their time, using two broad categories – importance and urgency – as a way to differentiate between tasks and categorise their priorities.

The use of the ideas here has a lot to do with the issue of prioritisation, but makes clear certain other ideas we mentioned above as well. The two dimensions of urgency and importance are described by Covey as follows:

Urgency: '*Urgent* means it requires immediate attention. It's "Now!" Urgent things act on us' (1989: 150).

Importance: '*Importance* … has to do with results. If something is important, it contributes to your mission, your values, your high priority goals' (1989: 151).

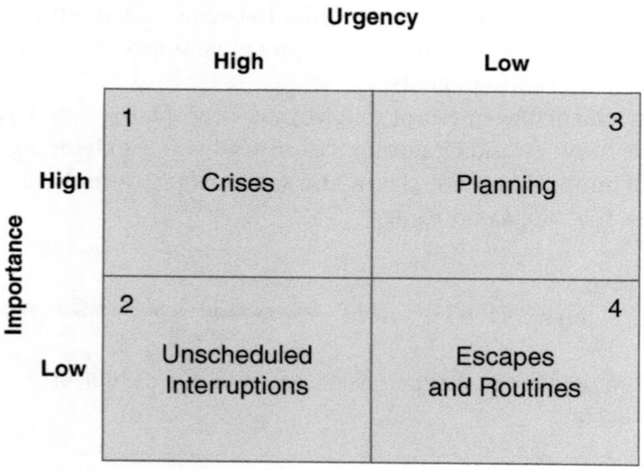

Figure 3.2   Time Management Matrix (Covey, 1989)

The broad idea here is that managers tend to spend their time doing things which fit into one of the four quadrants in Figure 3.2.

1. **Crises**: Some individuals constantly live their lives dealing with the urgent and important things. The word 'constantly' is deliberate here, since if you are fighting a crisis, you can be fairly sure that you will not have much – if any – time to do the long-term planning that can help to settle things down. Life constantly seems 'on edge' and while the occasional thrill can excite some people, dealing with crises on a constant basis over the long term is not the same as an occasional thrill. It is rare for anyone to never have a crisis in their life, and completely eliminating crises in your life will be very unlikely. For most people, crises will come no matter what.

2. **Unscheduled Interruptions**: The nature of such interruptions might vary, but if you are paying attention to urgent and not important things then, by definition, it is the urgent things that will get done and the important things will not (perhaps until a crisis occurs). In terms of an application to student life, some students love interruptions, and it is the interruptions that add variety to a dull life as a student, where 'boring' activities just seem to continue for ever and ever, without any apparent end in sight. However much you might *want* them, though, a continuous stream of friends calling by and distracting you when you have an essay due the next day is probably the last thing you *need*. On a slightly different scale, text messages, social media chats and other similar apps on your smartphone or tablet can act in a similar way.

3. **Planning**: The third of the four quadrants in the model proposed by Covey is that of planning and scheduling. Unlike the other quadrants – which reflect *types of activities* – planning and scheduling are activities in themselves. Managers would consider their goals for the day or week, identify the activities they need to do (i.e. develop a 'to do' list) and prioritise in the way we have seen above. The benefits are that there are few crises since things have been planned for and do not surprise anyone, and that relaxation does not need to be found through unintentional escapes: since life is calmer, there is less time wastage.

4. **Escapes and Routines**: Ironically (or maybe not), there is a point of view which says that managers who spend their time fighting crises tend also to be the ones who use 'escapes' more than others. 'Escapes' are those unimportant and non-urgent activities that managers and individuals undertake, such as having a cigarette, sitting in a park, or watching something unrelated to work (or study) on TV – and they *can* be very big drains on time, even if they do not need to be. Escape activities are those which typically use up very little energy and are not seen in the same way as purposeful leisure activities such as playing sport or hiking to a countryside beauty spot. Of course, 'escapes' can be a great way to recharge your batteries following a long period of stress, or a way to give yourself breathing space when you need a bit of time to think. The question therefore is: 'Why might those who have crises tend to seek escapes?' Put simply, constant 'firefighting' tends to take energy; it is tiring. Thus, the time spent on 'escape' activities tends to be longer, more noticeable and more relaxing than it might be for other individuals. The problem is that 'escape' activities are not always relaxing, as Box 3.2 demonstrates.

===== **BOX 3.2** =====

Are Holidays a Type of 'Escape'?

For many busy managers, finding time to take a holiday can be seen as difficult – and if managers have a family, then the issue can become even more challenging.

Taking a holiday can also require a significant amount of coordination. A holiday is usually taken somewhere away from home, so there is at least travel and accommodation to sort out. For travel abroad, there would be currency, visas, flights, what to do/see, suitable diets, and so on. For families, there is a need to arrange specific types of travel and activities for children.

So, the question is: 'Are holidays relaxing and really a kind of escape?'

Covey makes the astute observation that, in reality, few managers really spend their time planning and scheduling, and most time is spent dealing with interruptions or crises. Of course, how many interruptions there are will depend on various factors such as whether or not the manager has a personal assistant and the nature of potential interruptions, and whether there are any crises will depend on the way a manager delegates (if at all), how well any delegation is monitored and the extent to which the nature of the work – and workload – is predictable.

Considering Covey's observation above – that little time is spent planning and scheduling, while most time is spent dealing with interruptions or crises – the question should be: 'Why is this the case?' We usually have a view of managerial life where managers are intelligent individuals who work in well-resourced offices and have people who behave professionally and get their work done in a calm and logical manner. So, why do they not sit down and plan, if it is such a good idea?

The answer is simple: managerial life is rarely as described above. It can be, but that is not the normal situation. Managers are not always calm, rational human beings who work together in a cooperative manner in well-resourced workplaces, so not everyone will have time to sit down and plan what they will do on any given day or week. Even if they do have time, they will not always think about planning, and there are some who would prefer to escape from a crisis than calmly consider and plan how to avoid the next one (i.e. they do not like to plan). Do they need to work on their time management skills? Yes – and probably other skills as well.

To come back to 'important' and 'urgent' for a moment, what Covey is recommending is that we start to rebalance things so that we spend time looking at and planning for the 'important' activities: if they are well planned, then they should never become 'urgent'.

 ══════ REFLECTION POINT ═══════════════════

Take some time to think about the following questions and write down some answers.

Consider what you might typically do on a day-to-day basis. How much time would you typically spend in each of the four quadrants Covey identified?

What is preventing you from spending time planning and scheduling your week or day more than you currently do?

What could you do to overcome the issue(s) identified in answer to the previous question?

Think about the tasks you need to do over the next three days. Prioritise them according to their importance. What do you see as being important or urgent?

The above exercise should have helped you to identify and prioritise what you need to do to become more effective at time management. Box 3.3 seeks to address the extent to which over-planning can also cause problems.

══════ BOX 3.3 ════════════════════════

Dangerous for Your Health: Too Much Focus, Prioritisation and Planning

Asia is enjoying – or suffering from (whichever way you see it) – a housing boom. Housing developments and apartment blocks are appearing everywhere. In Hong Kong and China, it is common to see scaffolding made from bamboo rather than steel. Why? Hong Kong, China and the South China Sea generally suffer from typhoons and when the wind becomes dangerous, the last thing you want is something that is likely to be hit by the wind and collapse because it is too inflexible. (Bamboo is also significantly cheaper which may also play a part.)

The point being made here is that setting goals, establishing priorities and planning 'with the end in mind' can mean that we are so inflexible that when something unexpected comes along it causes a problem, we are not well equipped to handle it, and we end up missing all our deadlines. Here is a simple example.

A colleague of mine can get to his workplace in seven minutes by car from his driveway to the car park. How long in advance should he leave his home?

If he leaves seven minutes early, he can probably guarantee that he will be late. Why?

There is one simple word there that we need to examine, and another one which is missing. The first word is 'can'. Being able to do something is no guarantee that he 'will' do so. The missing word is 'usually': there can be all sorts of obstacles or problems (e.g. car accidents, traffic lights, heavy rush hour traffic, diversions, road closures, slow-moving cars and buses) which affect his journey on any one particular day.

That is why any plan we make *must* include some contingency time and be sufficiently flexible that we have the time to adapt what we do if we need to. We will look at this further when we come to examine the use of a diary.

TOOLS FOR TIME MANAGEMENT

Once we have decided on our goals and priorities, the next step is to commit ourselves to doing what we have indicated as important. There are a number of tools – digital and/or otherwise – that we can use to do this.

════════════════ KEY LEARNING POINT ════════════════

As a student, your goal should be to do as well as you can in your studies - this is your priority and should come before other activities.

However, you may be someone with a child, or a part-time employee or with other responsibilities. Your challenge is to decide which of the activities/roles you have are your own personal priorities in the long and short term.

Using A Diary

One tool we can look at is a diary, or calendar. When asked whether they have a diary; most students seem to say 'no'. The next question is whether they use a smartphone, and most say 'yes'. If you have a smartphone then (by default) you have a calendar app on it, but even if you do not, there will be a calendar within Microsoft Outlook and on appropriate websites. The third question is then whether they use it; most do not. Therefore, it is important to understand how a diary can assist. Trying to manage your time without using a diary is like trying to cut grass with a butter knife – it is difficult, if not impossible.

Keeping a diary is remarkably simple – and powerful. There are two issues here: identifying what activities we have to do; and prioritising them. It works like this. First of all, make a note of the tasks you need to do (e.g. attend lectures, do your reading) and, second, put into your diary the activities you have to do and have no control over (e.g. your lectures or seminar schedules; if you are going to do well in your studies, these two should be non-negotiable). These two steps mean that you have now blocked out the time taken for class. Next, follow the same idea but for activities over which you have more control (e.g. your reading, group discussions, preparing for seminars) and keep on doing this as you identify activities which become less important to your degree.

Three principles are important here: 1) being clear about how much time projects and activities will take; 2) ensuring that there is flexibility in your schedule; and 3) ensuring that you use your plan and stick to it. If you do not know how long the activities will take, you will find them overrunning or taking less time.

If the things you need to do are based around attending lectures and seminars, having group meetings for coursework, completing assignments, and doing appropriate textbook and journal reading, then your diary may look something like the diagrams in Figure 3.3.

When we have entered the things we have to do and the things we want to do, we need to build in some contingency time – there will always be a need for some flexibility.

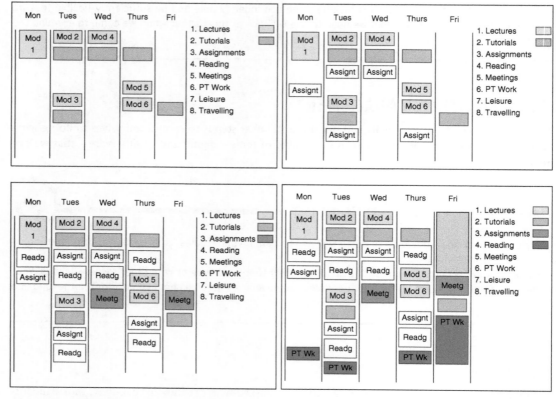

Figure 3.3   Development of a weekly diary

We mentioned that a diary can be a powerful tool. It helps us to understand what we are doing from day to day, and hour to hour, and if we schedule things well and build in some flexibility, then we will find we meet our deadlines and have a more relaxed life. We will feel more in control. A diary is also powerful because it can help us to know when and where there is space for more unusual activities (such as visiting the bank or the dentist).

 'BUT I HAVE A QUESTION ...'

... You say that a diary 'can be a powerful tool', but why not say 'it is a powerful tool'?

Because it is about whether we use it, and then how we do so. It is no good developing a really useful diary and then never using it. Managers use a diary all the time for both short- and long-term activities, but it takes practice and discipline to get used to doing so.

Of course, procrastination can be a huge issue, regardless of how much information is put into a diary. If you put off doing an essay until it becomes essential, then a diary will be of no use and you will find that you are joining between 30% and 60% of undergraduate university students (Rabin, Fogel and Nutter-Upham, 2011) who somehow are able to hit deadlines and manage to avoid printer queues and traffic jams without any forward planning.

We talked earlier about being able to control time. We cannot, but it is much better to be able to manage ourselves than to be controlled by time.

Digital Time Management Tools

There are a large number of tools online designed to assist you to use your time more effectively. Some of these require a subscription, but others are free:

Doodle.com – is a great way to arrange a meeting. The tool allows you to invite a specific number of people to indicate which of several pre-selected times they are free for a meeting. A similar tool is Calendly.com, which can sync with your diary on Outlook®.

Rememberthemilk.com – is a free app which enables you to develop and track progress on your 'to do' lists. Very similar apps are: Mylifeorganised.net, todoist.com and wunderlist.com. The Pro version of wunderlist also facilitates the sharing of to do lists across teams.

Trello.com – is a very visual task/project management tool, which displays projects and tasks across the screen, according to whether they are to 'Be done' are 'Being done' or are 'Done'. You can use this for project management across a number of people (great for a group assignment) by inviting others to the project. (The 'Done' list can be very motivating by showing you what you have already finished. Timetree (timetreeapp.com) is a similar app, but is designed for families and allows the sharing of documents.

Focusatwill.com – is a musical tool based on brain research, designed to improve an individual's focus beyond the standard 100 mins and removes distractions.

Toggl.com – is a tracking tool, which helps you determine how you use your time, and allows you to add other group/team members. RescueTime.com is another app doing the same thing, and Timely (timelyapp.com – there is a subscription charge) allows the same tracking, but has the facility to compare predictions around the use of time with actual time taken.

Of course, the most frequently used tool for self-management is arguably Outlook® which integrates a calendar (allowing you to see others' availability and arrange meetings easily), email communication, the ability to plan tasks – and then get reminders, progress flags and so on. Some of the above tools integrate well with Outlook and Microsoft also owns Wunderlist, referred to above.

━━━━━ TIME MANAGEMENT AT WORK: MULTI-TASKING ━━━━━

Learning how to manage your time as a student – doing what you need to do by the deadline you need to do it, is going to give you a real advantage when seeking work, but in many situations as a student, you will be in control of what you do and when. You will be given tasks to do, but often those tasks will either have deadlines which are some time away (where there is the danger of procrastination) or will be seen as optional (e.g. doing the pre-reading before a lecture), even if they are not.

But when we get into work, we can often find that life becomes a lot more intense. Taking on a management or administrative role can mean that we end up needing to undertake several activities either at the same time, or with very tight deadlines, with an intensity that we rarely experience when studying. The same is true for individuals who have young children or who are undertaking a degree while holding down a full-time job. Dealing with several tasks apparently 'at the same time' is called multi-tasking. This can include undertaking several projects in a similar period of time, but most commonly refers to activities such as answering email or sending a text while in a meeting (both of which mean you probably aren't listening to the discussion in the meeting sufficiently well), or walking somewhere and answering email on your phone

(Continued)

as you do so – something which can be potentially dangerous, of course. The reality is that we rarely do several things at the same time: our brain cannot cope with doing so, but we can sometimes alternate what we do.

Dealing with several tasks at one time can be complex – and sometimes stressful – but the main things to bear in mind are to:

1. Make sure you maintain a list of the activities that need to be done.
2. Track progress carefully on those tasks, perhaps using some of the tools referred to above.
3. Say no, or delegate to someone else where possible *and* where an activity is not a priority for you, if you do not have the time and resources to do what you are being asked to do. (NB: You must establish your own personal priorities before doing so, but some people like to do everything themselves because they don't trust others to do a good job – which will always defeat the purpose of delegation.)
4. Communicate regularly with those giving you the tasks to ensure that they are aware of any progress (or delays) and updates – and communicate clearly with those to whom you might have delegated tasks.
5. Prioritise what you have to do and when, based on the urgency of any task, and the time any task will take – bearing in mind any additional resources needed.
6. Choose what to multi-task: some things will require concentration and cannot simply be done at the same time as being in a meeting with the boss or colleagues.

ADDITIONAL TIME MANAGEMENT TECHNIQUES

FURTHER READING AND TEMPLATES

To give a comprehensive overview in a short chapter like this is really hard, simply because there are so many issues which could be covered. You can find additional online content on the companion website at https://study.sagepub.com/morgan2e, providing a great deal more information and ideas relating to motivation and tips for managing your time. There are tips, templates and further online content regarding:

- Planning.
- Setting career goals.
- Goal setting in daily life.
- Gantt charts.
- Motivation and time management.
- Procrastination.
- Additional and practical tips for managing your time (including multi-tasking, using waiting time usefully, etc.).

Above all, however, keeping a diary and keeping track of how you use time are really at the heart of improvement in your time management skills.

INTEGRATION AND APPLICATION

Learning how to use time most effectively is a skill that takes some time, but we have now looked at some areas we can think about:

Step 1: Analyse how you use your time. There is a time log available online which you can download and use to analyse how much time you spend on different items. If you keep a diary, then analysing how you use your time should probably be fairly straightforward, but if not, then it might be a good idea to think about the last 24 hours.

Step 2: Identify your current priorities. What is important and urgent to you at the present time?

Step 3: Looking at the results of steps 1 and 2, determine whether your time is really being used according to the priorities you currently have. If not, what needs to change?

Step 4: Set yourself some SMART objectives relating to time management to ensure that you have a benchmark against which you can measure your success.

Step 5: Repeat steps 1 to 4 on a regular basis to ensure that you are doing what you need to do.

There are a number of ways we can improve our 'time management' abilities:

- Identify how much better life would be if you were able to control what you do.
- Write down daily goals somewhere where you can see them.
- Reflect on why you might find this skill difficult. Is it prioritising? Is it planning? Is it about identifying personal goals?
- Set reminders on your phone indicating what you have to do and when.
- Buy and use an alarm clock, and set it for a time in line with the tasks you have to get done that day.
- Review your use of time as regularly as possible and see how much improvement you are making.

REFLECTION POINT

Take some time to think about the following questions and write down some answers.

Based on the content of this chapter, what do you now know about time management that you did not know before?

What key learning point had the most impact? Why?

Do your answers to either of the above questions have the potential to change your attitude to studies at university? If so, why?

What will you now do differently? (Write this down and put it somewhere where you can see it regularly.)

Give yourself *two weeks* and complete the skills assessment exercise on pages 5–51. Has your score improved? What else do you need to work on?

CONCLUSION

By now, you should be able to:

- Assess your time management skills.
- Understand the expectations universities have of the time you spend studying.
- Waste less time and use your time more productively.

There is a great deal more that could be written on this topic. We have only just scratched the surface here. We could talk so much more about the psychology of how personality affects how we engage with tasks in ways that may or may not help us to manage time, and we could talk more about other tools and how to deal with some of the key time wasters. Typing 'managing time' into the UK Amazon site yields more than 660 results, and a similar Google search yields more than 750,000 websites, so there is a wealth of advice and expertise available – some of it useful, some undoubtedly less so. But it is one of the most important skills, for both your studies and your future life. As mentioned at the start of this chapter, be clear with yourself: be determined *not* to leave assignments to the last minute and to plan carefully within examinations.

CHAPTER TASK

Find a friend who needs some help with their time management. Find out what they are struggling with - i.e. why time management seems to be a challenge for them - and research/suggest some solutions.
    Watch them as they implement those ideas: how has their time management changed?
    How many of those solutions might also help you?

INTERVIEW QUESTIONS

Think about the following questions: what might your answers be?

1. Give an example of a time when you had to balance conflicting priorities. How did you do so? How successful were you?
2. How have you gone about establishing goals and objectives?

Chapter 17 gives a lot more information on selection interviews and the online content gives some guidance on these questions.

ADDITIONAL RESOURCES

Want to learn more? Visit https://study.sagepub.com/morgan2e to gain access to a wide range of online resources, including interactive tests, tasks, further reading and downloads.

Website Resources

The following websites offer useful advice on time management.

Learnhigher – Centre of Excellence in Teaching and Learning, based on research carried out at the University of Reading in 2005–10, has a good number of additional resources: www.learnhigher.ac.uk/learning-at-university/time-management/

MindTools – the MindTools website has lots of practical tools and resources for time management for you to download and use: www.mindtools.com/pages/main/newMN_HTE.htm

Open University: www2.open.ac.uk/students/skillsforstudy/time-management-skills.php

Skillsyouneed: www.skillsyouneed.com/learn/study-time.html

University of Leeds: https://library.leeds.ac.uk/info/1401/academic_skills/84/time_management

University of the West of England (UWE): www1.uwe.ac.uk/students/studysupport/studyskills/timemanagement/timemanagementtutorial.aspx

Textbook Resources

Cameron, S. (2016) *The Business Student's Handbook: Skills for Study and Employment* (6th edition). Harlow: Pearson (particularly Chapter 2).

Cottrell, S. (2013) *The Study Skills Handbook* (4th edition). New York: Palgrave (particularly Chapter 5).

Gallagher, K. (2016) *Essential Study and Employment Skills for Business and Management Students* (3rd edition). Oxford: Oxford University Press (particularly Chapter 3).

Horn, R. (2012) *The Business Skills Handbook*. London: CIPD (particularly Chapter 1).

Pauk, W. and Owens, R. J. Q. (2014) *How to Study in College* (11th edition). Boston, MA: Cengage (particularly Chapter 2).

Tissington, P. and Orthodoxou, C. (2014) *Study Skills for Business and Management*. London: Sage (particularly Chapter 1 'Planning and Goal Setting' and Chapter 6 'Making Time Work').

Wong, L. (2012) *Essential Study Skills* (7th edition). Boston, MA: Cengage (particularly Chapters 4 and 5).

4 CRITICAL THINKING

It is the mark of an educated mind to be able to entertain a thought without accepting it. (Aristotle)

CHAPTER STRUCTURE

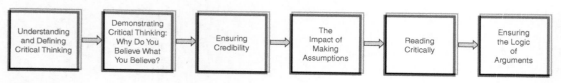

Figure 4.1

 When you see the 🌐 this means go to the companion website https://study.sagepub.com/morgan2e to do a quiz, complete a task, read further or download a template.

━━ AIMS OF THE CHAPTER ━━

By the end of this chapter, you should be able to:

- Know what lecturers mean when they talk about 'critical thinking'.
- Understand what constitutes a strong and a weak argument.
- Evaluate the arguments that others present to you.
- Evaluate the sources of evidence used to support arguments that you see and hear.

INTRODUCTION

Chapter 1 mentioned that one of the great benefits of having the experience of studying at a university was that university helps you to learn how 'to think'. You may well hear your lecturers talking about the need for 'more critical thinking' in your assignments, examinations or presentations, but what does it really mean? And how do you show that you are 'thinking critically'?

This chapter is going to look at these questions, and others, so that you can develop what is arguably the most important set of skills for your life and career. You may already be used to thinking critically but do not know it, or you might be wondering how lecturers and tutors give higher marks for students' academic work. We will be examining what makes the differences that lead to work graded at 50% becoming work that is graded at closer to 70%. Developing critical thinking abilities is the main reason why employers value university-educated employees.

We will start by defining what we mean by critical thinking, but, as we do so, we will discuss what critical thinking really means in terms of creating strong arguments. We will look at how we can ensure that sources of information are credible, how we can avoid making assumptions, how we can ensure that our arguments are logical, how we can avoid interpreting information (for example, X causes Y) incorrectly, and finally, how we can ensure that we read critically – including understanding the impact of the language that we and others use in their writing.

We will provide some details of a model of skill demonstration which will likely be used by your lecturers in assessing your work. We will apply this model to a standard topic in many business studies degrees. We then look at logic, the qualities of a strong argument, and provide some thoughts on how the sources of information can influence the academic credibility of your work. Some ideas on how you might develop these skills were given in Chapter 2.

WHEN SHOULD YOU READ THIS CHAPTER?

This chapter examines one of *the* most important skills needed for doing well at university and beyond. The earlier we begin to examine and analyse information that we read and hear, the better our chances of becoming habitually good, at it so start to develop critical thinking as soon as you begin your course reading - early in the first semester of your university studies.

SKILLS SELF-ASSESSMENT

There are various ways of considering your critical thinking abilities. The first way is to consider a piece of information and then answer some questions on it (*assessing your thinking*), but an easier method is to look at how often you do certain things with the information you have (*assessing your behaviour*). Let's do each in turn.

Assessing Your Thinking

Understanding the logic and truth of what we read or are told is part of what we mean when it comes to critical thinking, so let's see how easily we can detect logical conclusions from very short passages of text.

Think about the following three sentences which examine issues of logic and how well we can identify our assumptions, two elements of critical thinking:

'I went on holiday to another country. I generally don't like holidays by the beach. This was a good holiday, though.'

Now consider the following statements, and decide which of these statements are:

DT = Definitely true, based on the information provided?

PT = Probably true, based on the information provided?

UK = Unknown, the information given does not tell you?

UT = Probably untrue, based on the information provided?

DU = Definitely untrue, based on the information provided?

Statements:

1. This was a holiday by the beach.
2. I enjoyed this holiday.
3. I travelled on an airliner.
4. I don't like beach holidays because my skin gets burnt.
5. I needed my passport to get to my holiday.
6. I travelled with my family.
7. I really enjoy holidays away from the beach.
8. I regularly travel to other countries.
9. I needed to change money when I went on holiday.
10. I did not expect this to be a good holiday.

INTERACTIVE TEST

An interactive version of this test along with the answers can be found on the companion website at https://study.sagepub.com/morgan2e, but it is important to think about what we read, hear and see in relation to the assumptions that we make and the extent to which information is as it first appears.

Assessing Your Behaviour

TEMPLATE

We can examine how good we are at critical thinking (or any skill for that matter) by how likely we are to do certain things. So, look at the statements given below and, for each one, determine whether you agree or disagree with any of the behaviours in terms of your typical behaviour. You can find a template of this task to download and use on the companion website at https://study.sagepub.com/morgan2e.

	Item	Strongly agree (SA)	Agree (A)	Neutral/ not sure (N)	Disagree (D)	Strongly disagree (SD)
1.	I think about whether the lecturer's comments and ideas match my experience					
2.	I consider whether information from others around me is true					
3.	I listen to gossip and generally believe what others tell me					
4.	Whenever I read something I find myself questioning whether it is true					

	Item	Strongly agree (SA)	Agree (A)	Neutral/ not sure (N)	Disagree (D)	Strongly disagree (SD)
5.	I find it easy to identify weaknesses in others' arguments					
6.	In discussions with others, I identify issues that no one else has thought about					
7.	When I listen to a lecture, I try to find examples which support or contradict what the lecturer is saying					
8.	If I am reading a book, I tend to make notes which just summarise what is in the chapter					
9.	I rarely think about 'why' something works as it does					
10.	I am used to questioning information that others give me					
11.	I make sure that everything I say to other people is backed up by factual evidence					
12.	I generally believe that all information is unreliable					
13.	One or two examples are enough to prove my point					
14.	I believe that if something is said often enough by lots of people, then it is probably true					
15.	My own experience tells me more about the world than textbooks or others' experiences					
16.	When others give me new information, I try to relate it to information I have obtained from other sources on the same issue					
17.	If I am studying a topic for an exam, then I probably won't think about anything except that topic					
18.	If I read the research of two authors who come to different conclusions about the same issue, then one of them has to be wrong					

(Continued)

(Continued)

Item	Strongly agree (SA)	Agree (A)	Neutral/ not sure (N)	Disagree (D)	Strongly disagree (SD)
19. I can know how good I am at a particular skill by asking my one closest friend					
20. I know that everything my lecturer tells me is true					

Now, transfer your scores into the scoring key below. Some of the ideas and beliefs/assumptions listed in the exercise above are examples of what we might call critical thinking and others are an example of a lack of critical thinking.

Set A	Please tick if you answered SA or A	Set B	Please tick if you answered SA or A	
1.		3.		
2.		8.		
4.		9.		
5.		13.		
6.		14.		
7.		15.		
10.		17.		
11.		18.		
12.		19.		
16.		20.		
TOTAL		TOTAL		

By counting the number of answers in each set, your personal score is: Set A minus Set B. The further away your score is from 0, then the more room for improvement there will be. However, we can all improve our ability to think critically.

UNDERSTANDING AND DEFINING CRITICAL THINKING

 CRITICAL THINKING

Critical thinking is thinking about your thinking while you're thinking in order to make your thinking better. (www.criticalthinking.org)

'Critical' is usually taken to mean something that is negative and painful to receive, rather than something that is helpful or revealing. In reality, 'critical thinking' means both of these things, but it is far more than that. A much better name, perhaps, would be 'insightful thinking'. A broad definition is given here.

Your lecturers will know that someone is demonstrating critical thinking when they: 1) can identify gaps, errors, assumptions and weaknesses in others' work; 2) can provide a strong argument for a particular view and taking a particular course of action; and 3) provide a clear and sometimes detailed interpretation of situations and events.

It is reasonable to expect your academic tutors to ask, 'Why do you believe what you believe?', 'What evidence do you have?' and 'Why do you believe that evidence?', and in large part, they will assess your work on how well you answer these three simple questions.

Let me give you a very quick example. In looking for quotes to open this chapter, the following quotation from South African statesman Desmond Tutu seemed appropriate: 'My father used to say "Don't raise your voice, improve your argument."' A great quotation and one that really summarises some of the thinking here, but before I give any quote in the main chapter text, I need to think carefully: what is the evidence that Desmond Tutu really did say that? It is quoted commonly, but all that this tells me is that a lot of people think he said it, and probably, that a lot of other people believe a lot of other people. But that does not mean that he really said it. It is, however, referenced to him during the second Nelson Mandela Annual Lecture Address in November 2004, where he went on to say that 'an unthinking, uncritical, party line-toeing is fatal' to the kind of society he wanted to create. So we can be reasonably sure that he did actually say this, and that this is not 'fake news'.

DEMONSTRATING CRITICAL THINKING: WHY DO YOU BELIEVE WHAT YOU BELIEVE?

We will start by looking at the ways in which we need to gather, analyse and use information in order to make sure that any decisions we take or want others to take will result in successful outcomes. To do so, we and others need to be persuaded of our arguments – which means they need to be strong. Some of this can stretch our thinking abilities, so beware.

═══ BOX 4.1 ═══

In a TED talk published in 2017, Professor Philip Fernbach from the University of Colorado at Boulder outlined a number of reasons why the things we believe may not actually be true. He claimed that 'most of what we believe is not based on what is in our heads … and that as human beings, we are not made to store information'. Looking at memory experiments, he argued that others' research has calculated that the information we store comes to around 1GB. He noted that because so much learning is social, we can combine the knowledge that we hold to get things done, and that helps us get amazing things done.

However, that sharing of knowledge produces problems. The access we have to information makes us feel as if we know a lot more than we actually do.

Dr John van Wyhe from the National University of Singapore outlines some historical myths that we still believe: we are taught to believe that before Christopher Columbus, people believed that the earth was flat. That was despite the fact that the globe was developed in 1492 (or in the first century in ancient Greece if you believe others). Or that Isaac Newton discovered gravity because of an apple falling on his head, when it is much more likely that he found gravity through observations around the travel of a comet. We are told that, in the Bible story around Christmas, Mary rode to Bethlehem on a donkey, yet there is no mention of a donkey anywhere in the story. Darwin was not the author of the idea that finches on the Galapagos islands were the inspiration for the theory of evolution, but rather a scientist known as David Lack who published a text called 'Darwin's finches'.

So, why do we believe what we believe? It seems strange that, in an era of so much information on the internet, we still tend to rely on others that we trust more than on scientific research and historical truth. Social psychologists give a variety of reasons, but it seems that a lack of checking information that others give us and a preference for believing what others tell us is a lot easier than checking for ourselves and discovering the true facts.

A Strong Argument

What do we mean by having a 'strong' argument? The answer has three components:

- The extent to which evidence supporting the argument is provided.
- The quality of that evidence.
- The ease with which contradictory evidence can be provided.

An argument is strong when it is difficult to find any weakness in the comment being given. To take a very simple example, we might suggest that 'Tall people are more intelligent than short people', and we might support this idea by giving examples of a few tall people who are indeed very intelligent, but it would not be difficult to find many tall people who are not intelligent or to find short people who are intelligent.

Being able to evaluate the strength of an argument (or theory or piece of research) is crucial to academic essays and assignments. For example, let's assume that someone has been set an essay for a module on 'quantitative methods' (i.e. statistics) and is deciding which investigative method to address the following research question: 'What do people eat at home on a Monday evening?'

An individual addressing this question needs to be very clear on why they are choosing a particular method to find the answer. If they are not clear or if they have a weak reason for choosing the research method to find the answer, then their essay will likely get a poor mark. In our example, the individual undertaking the research might have decided to interview people and so will need to give a number of reasons (see the next exercise below) as to why they are doing interviews.

 ━━━━ FOR YOU TO DO ━━━━

Interviews for Food Research

In writing up the work, a student gives the following reasons for using interviews. Which reasons are strong and which are weak? Which are valid (true) and not valid (false)? Rate each of them on a scale of 0 to 10, where 0 is a 'very weak argument' and 10 is a 'very strong argument'. You might like to compare your answers with those of other students.

1. Asking questions is easy.
2. There are very few other ways of doing this research accurately.
3. Any other way will cost too much.
4. I can't send out any questionnaires; I don't have enough time.
5. Going through rubbish bags on a Monday night is disgusting and dirty.
6. Going to watch what other people eat so that I can write it down is silly.
7. By conducting interviews, I can get lots of information quickly.
8. I can triangulate the results of the interviews with other data later, but I need to start somewhere.
9. Interviews are quick to do, so I shall do them.
10. I enjoy talking to people.
11. Interviews gather information that is more accurate than questionnaires.
12. Everyone likes to talk, so I can just ask people and get lots of information quickly.

INTERACTIVE
TEST

An interactive version of this test along with the answers can be found on the companion website at **https://study.sagepub.com/morgan2e**.

What we find here is that some of these so-called 'reasons' have no basis in fact. Simply because someone enjoys talking to others or because interviews are quick to do (which is not always true anyway), for example, does not mean that this is the right thing to do.

The more you know about the topic, the easier it will be for you to evaluate the arguments being used. For example, if you are unclear what an interview is, then you will struggle to identify whether some of the above ideas (e.g. 'Asking questions is easy') are true or false. Similarly, you will not be able to identify contradictory evidence unless you understand what evidence you are looking for.

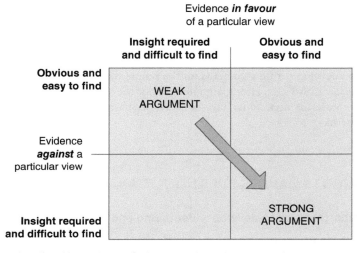

Figure 4.2 Understanding the nature of strong and weak arguments

Figure 4.2 provides a summary of how supporting evidence and contradictory evidence interact with each other to suggest whether an argument is strong or weak. If evidence contradicting a particular point of view (or 'argument' or 'hypothesis') is easy to find or does not require a lot of thinking, then the argument is seen as a weak one. Alternatively, if there is no evidence to contradict the argument being made (and the evidence has been gathered in a valid way), then the argument is seen as being strong. This is why giving examples and presenting evidence become crucial when writing your academic work. Politicians, however, often take advantage of a lack of critical thinking to make relevant points to the media, as shown in Box 4.2 below.

━━━━━━ BOX 4.2 ━━━━━━

Communication, the Media and Politicians

In the UK, it is very common for journalists to question politicians on behalf of the general public. They do so because the public rarely get access to political leaders to challenge the arguments given by them. Government departments (and their civil servants) are very good at producing succinct reports into important issues which would logically lead the reader towards a particular point of view.

Those same reports can also be written in a way to make the reader believe that there is no contradictory evidence to the view being given. It is either discounted on the grounds that the evidence was not sufficiently

(Continued)

strong or simply ignored altogether. The same is true with the use of anecdote (a specific example, and thus a form of evidence, though typically seen as very weak), which can be overplayed in order to 'get emotional buy-in' for a particular point of view, especially when people might already believe that same point of view themselves.

No one can argue with a specific example (other than to say that it was misinterpreted), but for every specific example there may be 200 other examples which show the exact opposite. So, politicians might ignore the 200 and focus on the 1 which supports the view they wish to discuss.

Question

Do you agree with what is written here? Why, or why not? What evidence have I presented?

Ensuring that you develop strong arguments for the points you raise in your coursework and in your examinations is crucial. However, a strong argument is not the same as an emotionally powerful argument: emotionally powerful arguments can be very persuasive, but the evidence presented may sometimes be very weak.

 ── 'BUT I HAVE A QUESTION ...' ━━━━━━

... So is this an important skill to develop – identifying and evaluating arguments?

These are probably the most important skills you will develop. For assignments, this will enable you to get the higher-level marks and demonstrate your ability to evaluate and analyse.

When you get into work, you will need to be a member of a team, taking part in team discussions, leading others, deciding on ways to solve particular problems. If you are unable to evaluate the arguments that others come up with, then you could easily be misled or, worse, be encouraged to do something that is morally wrong or even illegal.

Even if we think we know what is right and wrong, working life can make things more complex.

Imagine that you are very open and honest, and prefer to play by the rules.

Someone comes up to you and says, 'I've found a way of motivating the staff: we can give our team an extra day off', and you say, 'But HR says that we can't do that: it would open the floodgates to others wanting the same thing and would go against the contract we have with them'. Then the person says, 'But nobody would find out and it would create a really good atmosphere. Besides, you know how people feel about HR: you could blame HR for being inflexible and it would reduce their popularity even further'.

What would you do? Would you argue with the person on the grounds that it is wrong (in which case they would accuse you of being inflexible and say that you were not very popular), or would you accept their argument and gain popularity with your own team? The answer would depend on whether we think their arguments are strong or weak

Of course, management is not about being popular – it is about doing the right thing at the right time in the right way. So, we could say that their argument is a weak one.

If so, then we can dismiss them and make our own decisions, but unless we take time to think about the arguments and gather the evidence, then we might simply accept what others tell us. A great deal of management and achieving results is about developing your thinking.

This brings us back to the three areas noted earlier in the chapter: 1) the provision of evidence which supports the argument; 2) the quality of that evidence; and 3) the provision of evidence contradicting the argument. An argument that has no evidence to support or contradict it simply becomes little more than gossip, so we need to ensure that we use some credible sources of information on which to base our arguments.

ENSURING CREDIBILITY

Few people would like to be labelled as 'discredited': the term is only rarely used to refer to folk who have believed something that later turned out not to be true, and the reason we know about it was because that mistake had significant consequences. However, individuals often put forward arguments that are not true – even though they passionately believe them to be fact.

Research tends to show that learning is a social activity. We share information and learn from what others tell us, or share with us on social media, far more than we should, and we do not have time to check it. That means that a lot of what we believe may actually not be true, since we have picked it up from others who have heard it from others and so our knowledge base grows – as Box 4.3 shows. Of course, that is reasonable and not a difficulty in some parts of life, but it is not going to get you a good grade or develop your skills.

Arguably, the most important aspect of providing credible evidence is determining the credibility of the sources that have been used. Using sources of information that have little credibility is going to weaken your own argument.

The next question arising from this is, 'What makes a source of information credible from an academic viewpoint?' This question is central to what we mean by 'critical thinking': we have to get used to making sure that our sources are credible.

CREDIBILITY

'Credibility' refers to how believable a source of information (or the person delivering that information) appears to be, based on how easy it is to identify opposing arguments.

═══ BOX 4.3 ═══

Beyond 'Correct' and 'Incorrect'

You are going to be studying a number of different subjects and modules within your degree. These modules will require different skills, and some may emphasise concepts or ideas (e.g. economics, psychology, accounting) while others will want to make sure that you can apply particular methods (accounting, operations management, statistics) to various situations.

But many of your modules will be looking for you to justify the actions you have taken and to give a reason why you have done things the way you have done them. It is this justification that enables your lecturers to see how you are developing and using your critical thinking skills.

The implication of this is that your mark is going to have a lot more to do with whether you can provide good evidence to justify your viewpoint than with whether you give the lecturer what you think might be the correct answer.

This is particularly hard for some students who come to the UK from certain overseas educational backgrounds. In some countries, students can receive marks easily for giving back to the lecturer the information that the lecturer has given them (i.e. knowledge) without a great deal of that information being processed or thought about.

It can be a shock when a piece of coursework comes back with a mark of 50% when the student has given everything back to the lecturer that was provided in the lectures and expected to receive a mark of 70%. In the lecturer's mind, the assignment may not have given sufficient evidence to support the arguments being made or may not have added any value to the lecturer's material by doing any outside reading. Academic work is about demonstrating your own thinking and argument, it is not just about being 'correct' or 'incorrect'.

The C.R.A.P. Model

We can outline four issues that determine how credible the sources of information we use are. They can be summarised in a strangely appropriate word, using the acronym C.R.A.P. The idea is often used to discuss websites, but the principles can apply to any source of information. Identifying what is a 'fact' and what is an 'opinion' is not straightforward: facts – even if numerical – can be misinterpreted or attempts can be made to discredit statistics. People can give their own interpretation of facts based on personal desires.

C is for Currency

Your lecturers will use a number of references to support their assertions in lecture slides and in their teaching. It is important to understand that knowledge is not static – it moves, it changes, conclusions and methodologies change, and as a result, it is important to understand what the current thinking might be. Your lecturers will engage with current research in different ways but where any ideas are based on outdated thinking or on dated publications, then you would be right to at least question that research. For websites, it might be useful to check whether links from the website are still active, or to check the dates on websites.

However, currency is not the same as 'modern': if you are looking for factual information around a particular event, then it is a good idea to look for articles written or published close to the date of that event – and not many years later.

R is for Reliability

The issue here is around 'How factual is this information?' If a source is written in the first person ('I think …' etc.) then it is personal opinion and should not be included in your work. Similarly, it is worth considering the extent to which the information source provides data or evidence for what it says (in the same way that you should for your essays and work). If there are no sources or references given, then you might want to question the validity of the conclusions of the information source.

R is also seen as relating to **Relevance**. Whether you are reading a textbook, reviewing a website or listening to a lecture, you need to make sure that you are using information that is relevant to the title or subject of the work that you are producing.

A is for Authority

It is important to understand who has put the information together and for what purpose. Information presented as fact may or may not be as valid as you think: people have all kinds of reasons for posting information, and it is not always that they want to share facts. Most people share opinions, and in many cases, we believe information that supports what we already believe, but that does not make that information true. It is not a bad idea to check out the author – maybe on LinkedIn or, if they are well known, on Wikipedia or Google. Whenever we give evidence to support our arguments, we must give a citation and bibliographic reference in order to indicate that the source has authority.

A can also refer to **Accuracy**, another angle on the point made above about authority. If the source of information has little authority in what they are saying, then we would probably assume that the information has a greater chance of being inaccurate. But even with an authoritative source, the information can 1) be incorrect, or 2) be misinterpreted.

Presenting incorrect or inaccurate information will damage the credibility of any argument – whether in an essay, an important speech or at a presentation – even if it might have been accurate previously. If I claimed that the population of the UK was 60 million, then I would have been absolutely correct, but only if I was talking at some stage in 2004. It is now more than 66 million. To be accurate, information needs to be up to date, hence the comment above around **Currency**.

Another issue concerns interpretation: information can be accurate, but can be misused or misinterpreted – i.e. the interpretation is inaccurate. For example, consider the sentence below:

In 2011, around 500,000 people from Wales could speak Welsh (about 19% of the population at the time).

This could be interpreted in two ways. We could say:

Only 19% of people from Wales could speak Welsh.

Or we could say:

An amazing 19% of people from Wales could speak Welsh.

The fact has not changed, but the interpretation could change considerably. In reality, the interpretation means nothing without any context to the facts – i.e. if the proportion in 2001 had previously been 3%, then we might consider the second of the two statements to be more accurate, but if the same figure had actually been 25%, then the first of the two sentences would be understood to be more accurate. The context can change the meaning of the facts.

When we are looking for accuracy, we should look to see whether the information has been critiqued or analysed by others, and if it has, what conclusion they came to, and is that the same as the one you would come to? Can the information be verified by others?

There is one final issue to consider: how emotional is the language used in the source? If the information is presented with words like '*only*' or '*amazing*', then it is more likely to be trying to persuade you of something.

It is true that the more sources of information that say the same thing, the more likely it is that the information is accurate. If seven newspapers all report the same quotation from the same person at the same event, then it is almost certainly the case that the individual did actually say what they are reported to have said. However, when information is circulated on social media, there is a good chance that the same information will appear on several sites within a short space of time – one site reporting it, and others following to keep up with what is seen as important and current. That does not mean that the information is accurate, since the one source has merely been circulated around – hence the importance of giving the *original* source (citations, references) when you give information to others, and the importance of actually *looking at the original* source of information, rather than relying on second-hand accounts of what others have said.

P is for Purpose

The question here is around what the source of information is designed to do. It may be there to entertain or to persuade us of something. Alternatively, the source of the information might be simply trying to inform us of something (as is the case for research articles) or sell us something – in which case there will usually be a way for the supplier of the information to get in touch with you (or you to get in touch with them).

Of course, the best way of getting to see the purpose and the context in which the information was given is by looking at the original (as mentioned above). In doing so, you get to see what has not been more widely reported – and that can reveal far more about the purpose of giving the information than a selected quotation. Identifying what was *not* said or reported by others can reveal any bias or favouritism – and thus any inaccuracy in interpretation.

The four letters C.R.A.P. can help us to determine whether the sources we are using are appropriate. Anything that fails on any one of these requirements might present us with a problem when we are trying to make a convincing argument. In a world of social media and online news where any rumour or comment can be picked up and can spread quickly regardless of its truth, judging the accuracy of the information we are given is becoming a far more important skill than it has needed to be in the past. That means that in your academic work, you will need to be careful about the evidence that you present, and where it has come from.

 FOR YOU TO DO

Look at the various sources of information listed below. Rank them in terms of how strongly you would believe information which appears in these sources. Which ones are the most credible and which are the least credible? You might want to use the C.R.A.P. framework to evaluate each, and give each source a score of 1 (very poor) to 10 (very strong) on each of the four components.

Item	Score for C	Score for R	Score for A	Score for P	TOTAL
Wikipedia					
Textbooks					
Study guides (i.e. short booklets about the essentials you need to know, typically brief and with bullet points)					
Discussions with tutors					
Journal articles					
TV - 'factual'/documentary/news					
Rumours and opinions					
Lectures					
Discussions with other students					
Common sense					
Popular magazines					
Discussions with business leaders					
Blogs					
TV - 'popular' programmes					
Comments from others on social media					

FURTHER READING

We can develop a ranking from most credible to least credible, which should probably look something like Table 4.1. More detail on why the ranking is given in this way is provided on the companion website at https://study.sagepub.com/morgan2e.

Table 4.1 Ranking of credible sources

Ranking	Item	Ranking	Item
1 (most credible)	Journal articles	9	Wikipedia
2	Textbooks	10	Common sense
3	Lectures	11	Popular magazines
4	Discussions with tutors	12	TV – 'popular' programmes
5	Discussions with business leaders	13	Blogs
6	TV – 'factual'/documentary/ news	14	Comments on Facebook, Weibo, etc.
7	Study guides (i.e. short booklets about the essentials you need to know, typically brief and with bullet points)	15 (least credible)	Rumours and opinions
8	Discussions with other students		

KEY LEARNING POINT

Gathering credible information from a number of sources is key to building up a body of evidence which suggests that some idea or theory is 'true'.

FURTHER READING

As a future manager, you will be expected to make a judgement about what is credible and what is not, which takes us back to the above 'For You to Do' exercise. Some thoughts are given on the companion website, but even with the most credible sources and detailed statistics, there is always room for a little uncertainty. So, in the face of all of this, how can you be 100% sure that the sources you are using are definitive and factually correct? The simple answer is that you cannot.

REFLECTION POINT

Take some time to think about the following questions and write down some answers.

Which sources of information (including friends) do you use each day? How accurate is that information likely to be? Are there any reasons why you think the information may not be accurate or necessarily true?

Think about the last interview you watched (online or on TV). Do you think the interviewee was telling the truth? Why or why not?

How might the information in this chapter help you when you are writing essays or submitting coursework?

THE IMPACT OF MAKING ASSUMPTIONS

We like to think that our brain is one of the most complex organs around – that it can cope with a great deal of information and that we can rely on the information that we are given. However, as Philip Fernbach (2017) indicated, our brain is not as competent at analysing information as we might think, and that shows itself most evidently through our propensity to stereotype individuals according to those we have been familiar with in the past.

Critical thinking takes time and, in a fast-moving world where decisions sometimes need to be made quickly, we can sometimes fail to ask relevant questions. So, imagine the following set of statements:

> The car was stationary on the road having been brought to a sudden stop. The passengers had been able to get out of the vehicle but could not be seen. The police had arrived at the scene in order to manage the traffic.

The natural picture that comes into our minds probably reflects an image we have seen of an accident involving a car and maybe a lamp post or another car. Unless we do some thinking, it is natural to make some assumptions about this short passage:

1. The car had been physically damaged.
2. The passengers had experienced some difficulty in getting out of the car.
3. The car had been stolen.
4. The passengers had absconded and run away.
5. A crime had been committed.
6. Other drivers were inconvenienced by the accident.

If we look at the passage carefully, we might find the following regarding each of these assumptions:

The car had been physically damaged: This is never stated. The comment 'The car was stationary on the road having been brought to a sudden stop' suggests that the car had hit something else ('had been brought' – by something else), which usually means that the car was scratched, dented or worse, but could mean that the driver stopped suddenly and avoided hitting something. The evidence for the car needing to stop suddenly might come from tyre tracks, rather than physical damage.

The passengers had experienced some difficulty in getting out of the car: We might ask why the writer includes reference to the passengers getting out of the car if it had not been difficult, but the fact that the reference is there does not necessarily mean that it had been difficult.

The car had been stolen: We might reach this assumption from the fact that the passengers could not be seen and that the police were there: putting those two things together may not be unreasonable, but would not be correct (see below for the issue around the passengers). While the most common reason for the police to be called to the location of a car might be for an accident or because it was stolen, it could be for any number of reasons.

The passengers had absconded and run away: We read that the passengers could not be seen; that does not necessarily imply that they had run away, or even that they were not there. The statement is that they could not be seen, so they could be in an ambulance, or being taken away in a police car, or be being comforted in a police car, or … The person writing the article simply says that they could not be seen.

A crime had been committed: There is no evidence for this, and as indicated above, the police can be called for a variety of reasons – including a risk to others' safety – and the passage does state that the police were there to manage the traffic, rather than to collect evidence of a crime.

Other drivers were inconvenienced by the accident: The image of the police managing the traffic implies – but does not state – that there was a lot of traffic, but there is no evidence for this. We could argue that the police would not be needed if there was no traffic, but that is because of the image we have in our mind rather than what is stated in the passage. 'Manage the traffic' could simply mean putting a couple of warning signs on the road and staying at the scene in order to keep an eye on things.

This incident might have taken place on a quiet road, or on a motorway, at night or during the day. Just putting a few words together can mean that we each develop an idea of what has happened when the reality might be quite different. But the way that this works with our brains is that the conclusions we reach may be false because we interpret the information to arrive at a particular conclusion in a particular way without questioning it. This can apply to any kind of information – including comments made in meetings, the conclusions of a written report or comments made during a presentation. Such information usually goes well beyond the three sentences given in the example above, so the number of assumptions might be much larger.

What Kinds of Information Might We Need to Consider Carefully?

There is no limit to the kinds of information you might assume, but here are some questions your lecturers and mangers in the workplace might typically ask when analysing information presented in a report designed to solve a problem.

1. The sources of this information: who is reported to have said what? How many people said XXX? Are the sources of information really credible? Are there any better sources of information?
2. Is the information current, reliable, accurate and relevant/purposeful?
3. Are the implications of the problem outlined here as serious/less serious/more serious than the report or comments indicate? Are any implications left out of the report?
4. Is the proposed course of action really the best alternative? Are there any alternatives left out of the report?
5. Where a report claims to have found a relationship between X and Y, does that relationship really work in the way outlined in the report?
6. Do the solutions really solve the problem? Is the problem that is stated in the report really the problem, or is there evidence of a different cause to the problem?
7. Is there any evidence of bias in the way the report has been put together? Could there be a reason why this report might not present things in a truthful manner? How might the availability of finances and resources limit what is included in the report?

This list is not exhaustive, but might serve as a checklist to use when looking at a business report. When examining research articles, your lecturers might ask questions around the methodology (can/does it produce the conclusions given), the sample used in a study (nature of the sample, numbers of people/companies/data items involved), the statistics used (method of statistical analysis compared with the methodology), the literature discussed (the currency of that literature, relevance, any major omissions) and the extent to which any explanations for the findings make sense when compared to other relevant literature.

Your lecturers will likely have more experience and expertise in this field, but there is no reason at all why you should not be able to question research findings that you read – and raise those questions in your written work. Published research – especially in good quality journals – tends to go through a lot of editing and 'polishing' before appearing in a journal, a process that can take up to two years, so we can be reasonably sure that, most of the time, the findings of published research can be relied on. But that does not mean that all published research is of a high standard and your lecturers will almost certainly be able to point to an article that they regard as poor quality work. Keep your eyes open – and read with a critical approach.

 KEY LEARNING POINT

Recognising and questioning assumptions is an important part of learning to think critically. It takes time to think through whether the ideas or conclusions are valid, but it is an important skill in many situations.

Watching for Language

We can often make assumptions because of others' use of language: the words used can sometimes try to deflect us from questioning what someone does not want us to question, or can lead us to question something that is, in reality, true. Have a look at the passage below. We are 'taught' to think that where a piece of information contains no emotion, it is likely to be more accurate. That is not always the case: emotional language can be manipulative in a way that 'calmer language' might not be – it tends to have a more explicit impact – yet any form of wording can mislead. Individuals are different: some people are more emotional and passionate in their language than others.

 FOR YOU TO DO

Have a look at the following phrases. Which do you see as being potentially misleading, and which do you see as being believable and which are you sceptical about? Try not to think about whether you would *naturally* agree with these comments, but consider whether someone with no previous view would be likely to do so.

1. Individuals are different: some are more emotional than others. 2. Above anything you have tried to do before, studying at university is going to present a significant challenge to you. 3. Of course, understanding individuals' motivations is not easy.	4. Everyone needs to have a comprehensive understanding of economics. 5. It is abundantly clear that those found guilty of knife crime should be in prison for at least 10 years. 6. Most people believe that the earth revolves around a star at something like 20,000mph. In fact, the true speed is closer to 70,000mph.	7. It seems unbelievable that employers are getting away with not paying pension contributions for some of their workers. 8. The best way of growing food on Mars would be to start growing vegetables. 9. We will eventually find alien life somewhere in the galaxy. 10. Of course we will find life on an alien planet sometime. It is simply inevitable.

The above 'For You to Do' exercise attempted to put a series of statements in front of you, some more emotional than others. In reality (another potentially misleading phrase), we find that emotion really comes through in oral speeches and presentations when we neither have the time nor the immediate availability of evidence to confirm or deny the statements being given. We can get swept along with emotion sometimes: arguing with someone who begins a sentence with some of the phrases used above might be seen as unnecessary by some, but not doing so might mean that we do not question something that is factually incorrect. We can be misled by someone using the words or phrases:

- 'In fact'… when something is not factually correct.
- 'Of course', 'clearly' or 'obviously' … when something is not clear or obvious (and it is intended that no one will question them).
- 'It is simply', 'it seems unbelievable that …' or 'it is abundantly clear'… when questions should be asked about some assumptions or weak logic.
- 'Surprisingly …' when something should not be surprising bearing in mind known facts.
- 'Most …' or 'best …' when it is unclear what the specific facts are and no data is presented.

When we communicate orally, the non-verbal signals (tone of voice, facial expressions, etc.) add to the impact that the words have. Language can have an impact in other ways as well. People can use analogies in their arguments which are not appropriate for the topic being discussed, and which might raise emotions unnecessarily. For example, on 4 July 2019, Brexit politician Anne Widdecombe compared 1) the exit of the UK from the EU to 2) slaves rising up against their owners. Although she stood by her comments, they were many who believed her comparison was inappropriate: slaves had no input into their future and decision making – many argued that the UK has not been in the same position – and that the comparison was invalid.

READING CRITICALLY

When preparing arguments, it is very important to engage in what many authors call 'critical reading'. Critical reading is what it claims to be – the act of reading in a way that asks questions about what is being presented and which records any concerns you may have – thinking about issues of evidence, of logic, of language, and checking for assumptions that others might make.

The extent to which you do this – rather than just accept everything that you read – should train your mind to be able to not only transfer this skill to your reading, but also to question the presentations you see, to challenge the comments you hear at work and to ensure that the information you obtain presents as strong an argument as possible. So, when you read you should ask the following:

1. Are the key arguments logical, bearing in mind the evidence presented?
2. Are there any issues where contradictory evidence is either more recent than what you are reading, is not presented or is brushed away as 'irrelevant' or 'insignificant'?
3. Does the information ignore any assumptions?
4. Are there any pieces of evidence which seem to be misunderstood, or any correlations which are misinterpreted?
5. Are there places where the language seems to lead readers towards a particular view? Is that view valid?
6. Are there any comparisons made in the source which are not appropriate?
7. Is the argument clear and presented well?

Taking notes as you ask these questions will enable you to write your essay with clear references, a logical and credible discussion and a questioning attitude, which will give those who assess your work the impression that you are a critical thinker.

ENSURING THE LOGIC OF ARGUMENTS

Arguments (in essays, reports, presentations, etc.) can have strong evidence, objective language and few assumptions, but can still fail – this time in their logic. Take the following example:

> The rate of increase of certain types of cancer means that we need to spend more money on reducing fatty foods in our diet. Science clearly shows that health, diet and exercise have a significant impact on the numbers of times individuals are admitted into hospital, and since we now have hospital beds nearly full with cases of different types of cancer, we need to attend to our diet more carefully.

This short passage starts by suggesting that fatty foods can cause cancer. However, the passage starts suggesting that there is a link between health, diet and exercise and the number of times we are admitted into hospital. It then goes on to claim that 1) cancer is linked to the number of full beds in hospitals *and* that 2) diet is linked to the number of times we visit hospital. The suggestion is that diet and cancer are related – because they both relate to the number of available beds in hospital.

There are several problems with this suggestion: 1) just because these two things (diet and cancer) cause the same outcome (fewer hospital beds), it does not mean that they are linked; 2) there could be something else that influences both of these; 3) a correlation does not mean that A *causes* B, which we call 'causality' – there are times when the link is random; and 4) there are factors – we call them 'variables' in statistics – mentioned in the passage but not mentioned later on, such as 'general health' and 'exercise', which could also be worthy of study.

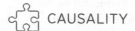 CAUSALITY

The establishment of a link between two items, such that one (Input - A) causes the other (Outcome - B). This link does not mean that one will always cause the other, but when it does there is a clear direction ('directionality') of that influence: item B does not cause item A.

The issue of causality (which item causes the other) is very important in research. Even when two items seem to be linked, there is a need to prove that one causes the other.

Statistical correlations are intended to be mathematical calculations which show us how two items (or more in the case of more complex statistics) might be related. Each correlation has two numerical measures – the strength of a correlation measured from –1.0 to +1.0 – and a p statistic (in published scientific research, usually between 0.01 and 0.001, and indicated by means of *** in research papers), indicating how likely it is that this correlation is down to pure chance.

A correlation of –1.0 means that the two items are perfectly correlated and vary together, but in opposite directions – to take an obvious example: height (cm) and time to run 100 metres. The taller someone is, the less time they will take to run 100 metres. A correlation of +1.0 means that the two items are perfectly correlated and vary together in the same direction. To take another example, the heavier someone is (i.e. increase in kg), the longer (i.e. increase in time) they will take to run 100 metres. The second measure – p-value – can be interpreted thus: a p-value of 0.5 means that this will occur 50% of the time regardless of other factors, 0.1 = 10% of the time, 0.01 = 1% of the time by chance and so on. Researchers in business subjects usually look for a p-value of 0.001 (i.e. that the correlation would only be likely to occur by chance 1/10,000th of the time) as a good indicator that there is a significant correlation, though the exact p-value will depend on the sample size used for the research.

Correlations are powerful, but we need to be careful how we use them. Since at least 2013, Tyler Vigan has been putting together what he calls 'Spurious Correlations' – statistically valid correlations between two factors which have no logical connection. His website (www.tylervigen.com/spurious-correlations) lists some bizarre matches, such as:

- Number of people who drowned in a pool in any one year with the number of films starring Nicholas Cage.
- Per capita cheese consumption with the number of people who died by getting tied up in their bed linen.
- Total revenue generated by amusement arcades with the number of computer science doctorates awarded in the US.

Making links between ideas is at the heart of what we call 'logical argument'. In all of these cases of spurious correlations, it is highly unlikely that there is an actual link, yet we use similar mathematics to argue that one thing causes – or is linked to – another, when clearly that would not always seem to be the case.

There are some key words – like 'Therefore' or 'As a result' – that we can look out for when checking whether an argument has a sense of logic (and to use in work to ensure that we are clearly stating our conclusions). These phrases tell the reader that you are making a link. Consider the following:

The house was sold for a profit. As a result, the captain turned the ship to the left at midday.

As first glance, this argument (that there is a link between the two sentences) makes no logical sense at all. How can the first issue affect the second? It is not dissimilar to the spurious correlations given above. In order to give the argument (made up of the two sentences) some logic, we would need to:

- Know much more information about any potential link – was the captain the house owner? Had he/she made a promise to change the direction of their ship depending on whether there was a loss or a profit? Without this information, the statement makes no sense.
- Be sure that the evidence for the first two sentences *and* the link between the two was credible.

If we assume that the information below is correct, then we have a much more logical argument.

The house owner was the captain of a ship. Depressed at his need to sell the house, he got into his boat and sailed out to sea. To the left was the coast and a return home to a new, larger house. To his right was the start of a poorer life in another place. At the correct time, he received the phone call which settled the matter. *The house was sold for a profit. As a result, the captain turned the ship to the left at midday.*

With this extra information, the argument makes sense. It is an extreme example and often sentences will be more subtle about the weaknesses of their logic (see the 'For You to Do' exercise below), meaning that it is up to the reader to make assumptions. That is not unusual in most social writing, but in academic work, you will need to be explicit. For a logical argument, we need to:

1. State clearly the argument on which our logic is based.
2. Be sure about the credibility of the evidence.

Having a logical argument is insufficient to demonstrate your critical thinking: we need to present the evidence.

FOR YOU TO DO

Have a look at the two passages below. For each, 1) consider whether you think the conclusions seem logical, and if not, then 2) consider whether you think there are any circumstances in which the statements might make logical sense. This will require you to consider any assumptions you are making, identify whether there is an implicit link between the sentences, whether there is clear evidence of the direction for that link and whether the evidence provided is convincing.

1. Cited and published research tells us that there is a clear link between intelligence and confidence. The reasons for this are obvious. Intelligence causes confidence: an intelligent person will be more outgoing, more articulate and more able to get their views across. We see this on a regular basis from political leaders around the world.
2. The key aim of marketing is to sell items to consumers that they would not otherwise need. This is obvious. When we look at how Apple has sold smartphones to customers who did not ask for a smartphone, or iPads to individuals who were not looking for an iPad, we can see that this is what marketeers do all the time. Products can create their own demand, and this is morally wrong.

 KEY LEARNING POINT

The logic of your argument needs to be clear, explicit and factually correct. People can sometimes reach different conclusions based on the same evidence, but an argument made without logic will always fail.

In addition to a lack of factual errors, there is a need to ensure that there are no incorrect assumptions and that the logic of the argument is not contradicted by other parts of the assignment or report. This is more likely in a longer piece of work, where the structure can get confusing at times for the writer, as well as for the reader.

 KEY LEARNING POINT

The extent to which you engage in critical thinking will be based upon the extent to which you actually think about what you read, and then present that thinking in a way which creates a strong and logical argument.

INTEGRATION AND APPLICATION

As suggested at the start of this chapter, being able to think critically is essential to ensuring that you can do well in your degree, but also in your career and life. The above sections have given you some idea of what critical thinking is and some exercises to start assessing and developing those skills.

However, the real development of these skills comes through practice and debate. So, below are some ideas that you might like to think about using:

- Join a debating society (or begin one if there is none at your department or university). You will be forced to think through and evaluate your arguments and ideas in order to win the debates. Debates are important for developing thinking and testing out arguments.
- Watch or listen to the news and try to evaluate whether the views of the journalists or those they are interviewing (e.g. politicians, organisational leaders) actually reflect reality. Is there any evidence they are missing, any assumptions they are making or any information they are misinterpreting?
- When you meet with classmates for a group assignment, think about the comments they are making in order to complete the assignment. Are they correct in their assumptions about what the tutor is looking for? Do they have evidence to support the arguments and ideas that they give?
- Take some articles from different newspapers about a recent national news issue and discuss it with some other students. Take some time to check whether the evidence is good or whether there are other explanations for what has been reported. Do the articles agree? If not, how do they disagree? And why might they disagree?
- Ask a tutor if you can have 30 minutes of their time to discuss something you have covered in their module. See if you can have a good discussion about that subject and prepare by reading two or three relevant journal articles on the subject first. Does your tutor have the same views as those of the authors whose work you have read on the subject?
- Take one popular topic that you hear others talking about (or read others' comments on Facebook or another social networking source). What do you think about that topic? Is your thinking based upon any evidence or just an uninformed opinion?
- As you read, take notes about what you are reading, but make sure you: 1) think carefully about what you are reading by asking questions about why an author is writing what they are writing and whether it makes sense; and 2) write down your thoughts so that you can think about them later and use them in your writing.
- Discuss what you have been reading with friends. Do they think it makes sense? Is there anything they notice about what you have been reading that you have missed?

Critical thinking is one of the most important sets of skills that you can develop, which is why it is given so much importance in terms of your degree.

CONCLUSION

By now, you should be able to:

- Know what lecturers mean when they talk about 'critical thinking'.
- Understand what constitutes a strong and a weak argument.
- Evaluate the arguments that others present to you.
- Evaluate the sources of evidence used to support arguments that you see and hear.

This chapter has given you some illustrations of what critical thinking means in practice. We have looked at what makes strong and weaker arguments, presented the C.R.A.P. framework in relation to sourcing and using credible information, discussed the assumptions that we make and the language that individuals use to make their arguments clear. The chapter has also discussed critical reading and suggested questions that we should ask in order to determine how logical others' arguments may be. Finally, the chapter has identified some actions which can be taken in order to develop this set of skills.

CHAPTER TASK

Based on the content of this chapter, what do you now know about critical thinking that you did not know before?

What key learning point had the most impact? Why?

Do your answers to either of the above questions have the potential to change your attitude to studies at university? If so, why?

What will you now do differently? (Write this down and put it where you can see it regularly.)

Give yourself *two weeks* and complete the skills assessment exercises on pages 70–72 . Have your scores improved? What else do you need to work on?

INTERVIEW QUESTIONS

Because of the nature of critical thinking, the ability to think carefully and quickly can be determined by any question. For example, if we take the answer to one of the questions in Chapter 1, 'Why did you choose the university and the course you have been studying?', we can imagine that clarity of thought, the use of information and the ability to evaluate information quickly all combine to produce a reasonable answer. However, if an employer thought that additional questions were needed, they might develop the questions below.

What might your answers be?

1. Imagine that you are in charge of a government department. The employees in that department want you to achieve one thing, the public want you to achieve something else, and you personally believe that the right thing to do is one that neither group have thought about. What would you do?
2. What do you think are the most challenging problems facing society today? Do you think there are any ways to solve them?*

(* Or an interviewer could ask a very similar question, based around one specific problem, i.e. 'Thinking about [a current affairs issue], how would you go about proposing a solution?')

Chapter 17 gives a lot more information on selection interviews, though employers would be more interested in how you deal with these questions and present your answer than with the actual answer you give.

ADDITIONAL RESOURCES

Want to learn more? Visit https://study.sagepub.com/morgan2e to gain access to a wide range of online resources, including interactive tests, tasks, further reading and downloads.

Website Resources

The following websites offer useful advice on critical thinking.

How to Study: www.how-to-study.com/study-skills-articles/critical-thinking.asp

University of Edinburgh: www.ed.ac.uk/institute-academic-development/study-hub/learning-resources/critical

University of Sussex: www.sussex.ac.uk/skillshub/?id=277

University of Worcester: www.worcester.ac.uk/studyskills/645.htm

Textbook Resources

Bailey, S. (2011) *Academic Writing for International Students of Business.* Abingdon: Routledge (particularly Part 1.2).

Burns, T. and Sinfield, S. (2016) *Essential Study Skills* (4th edition). London: Sage (particularly Chapter 7).

Cottrell, S. (2013) *The Study Skills Handbook* (4th edition). New York: Palgrave (particularly Chapter 7).

Fisher, A. (2011) *Critical Thinking: An Introduction* (2nd edition). Cambridge: Cambridge University Press.

Horn, R. (2012) *The Business Skills Handbook.* London: CIPD (particularly Chapters 10 and 11).

Kaye, S. M. (2012) *Critical Thinking.* Oxford: Oneworld.

McMillan, K. and Weyers, J. (2013) *How to Improve Your Critical Thinking and Reflective Skills.* Harlow: Pearson.

Tanna, M. (2011) *Think You Can Think?* London: Oxbridge Applications.

5 UNDERSTANDING HOW TO LEARN AT UNIVERSITY

Learning is more than absorbing facts, it is acquiring understanding. (William Arthur Ward)

CHAPTER STRUCTURE

Figure 5.1

 When you see the 🌐 this means go to the companion website https://study.sagepub.com/morgan2e to do a quiz, complete a task, read further or download a template.

▬ AIMS OF THE CHAPTER ▬

By the end of this chapter, you should be able to:

- Describe the ways in which your lecturers and professors will help and expect you to learn at university.
- Understand what is meant by 'independent learning'.
- Use time outside of the classroom to study effectively.

INTRODUCTION

The chapter will begin by giving you an opportunity to consider your own understanding of how learning at university works, before providing and applying three models of adult learning which impact on practices at university and affect how activities are scheduled and timetabled. The chapter will then examine how learning can occur through more informal, unscheduled activities. The final exercise in the chapter will ask you to consider how you might apply the ideas covered to your own learning.

We will spend some time looking at the ways in which universities provide opportunities for you to learn and give some suggestions on how best to use those opportunities. We will use the words 'learning opportunity' to refer to any activity or event that can be used for learning – a list that is nearly infinite.

The methods used to help you learn at your university may be different from those you have come across before. If they are, then that has implications for what you do and the extent to which you will succeed in your studies. Chapter 3 on time management showed you that there are various activities which can occupy your time, but the question is always how to balance social activities with your academic responsibilities. This chapter will try to help you with that. It will also try to help you 'see into the mind' of your lecturers, so that you can understand what their expectations might be and examine what is meant by 'independent study'.

It is important to note that this chapter (on learning) and those in Part III (on assessment) are linked: the feedback you get from the assessment of one module or piece of work should get you to think about what you did well and not so well – and every occasion for assessing your thinking is an occasion for developing your work. This applies to everything we might do in class, from giving a presentation to making a verbal contribution during a class discussion, so it is difficult to separate opportunities for learning from those for assessment. The link between receiving feedback and learning may not always be clear to you as a student completing a number of what often appear to be separate modules, but it will be there in the mind of your lecturers and they will expect you to develop your skills based upon the feedback from assessed work.

There is just one additional comment to make about terminology before we get into the chapter: 'teaching' is about 'information transfer' together with a touch of inspiration. It is usually passive from your perspective, as a student, and is something that is *done to you*. 'Learning', covered in Chapter 2, is the result of your engagement with that information. Some academics would rather call themselves 'facilitators of learning' than 'teachers'. This emphasises their role as someone who 'helps you to learn' rather than just teaches. That can occur through their feedback, through giving you things to read and through asking you questions.

WHEN SHOULD YOU READ THIS CHAPTER?

This chapter discusses how learning takes place on university courses, and so it is best to read this during your first three weeks at university in order to make sense of what is happening around you and benefit from your scheduled learning activities.

TEACHING

Teaching is what a lecturer or teacher or professor *does to you* as a student or learner by giving you information. A lecturer teaches. A lecture is one situation where that information is given to you.

SKILLS SELF-ASSESSMENT

Since this chapter is largely about learning at university, the self-assessment exercise here is more about your *knowledge* (what you *know*, rather than what you can *do*).

Have a look at the various learning opportunities listed below. Which of these have you experienced before?

- Lectures
- Seminars or tutorials
- Written coursework assignments
- Reading academic journals
- Receiving feedback on your work
- Discussing your learning with other students
- Doing some practical research
- Thinking through a case study

- Completing a group project
- Developing a presentation
- Being asked to reflect on your own experiences of a topic in a module
- Reading a chapter of a textbook
- Completing questionnaires about yourself
- Using a course or textbook website
- Asking a lecturer for help

Now rank each one in terms of their importance to your learning, with 1 being what you think is the most important and 10 the least important.

TASK

Comments and thoughts about these questions can be found on the companion website for this book at https://study.sagepub.com/morgan2e. The exercise above should start to get you thinking about the many activities which can help your learning while at university. There is no such thing as a complete list: anything which stimulates your thinking – especially your reflection – can help you to learn. However, let's look at some of the most common aspects of learning at university, and how you can use and engage with each of them in ways that will really help your learning.

HOW DO ADULTS LEARN?

We covered issues of skill development in Chapter 2 and critical thinking in Chapter 4, and as we saw, learning has many different components and levels. We start this chapter by examining how individuals at university learn, and we do that in different ways.

It is worth noting that there are differences between the ways that adults learn and children at school learn, and educationalists typically talk about two processes of learning – one describing educational approaches *before* university and the other describing a process where adults are expected to engage in their own learning. The first is referred to as 'pedagogy', where the teacher is seen as the 'expert' and the learner is there to take in information and then use it. The second is known as 'andragogy' and is a process whereby adult learners are expected to engage more in their own learning and where the prior experience and thinking of the adult is used to refine, evaluate and analyse information given to them by a 'facilitator of learning'. It is this second approach – andragogy – that is most relevant and useful for helping adults learn at university.

We will look at three models – all of which are based around andragogy: the first developed by Peter Honey and Alan Mumford, based on Kolb's learning cycle; the second looking at how we take in information; and a third based on research into study behaviour.

━━━━━━━━━━ BOX 5.1 ━━━━━━━━━━

Definitions of Learning

There are various definitions of learning, each with a slightly different context or emphasis. Lexico.com - a collaboration between Oxford University Press and Dictionary.com - states that learning is:

> The acquisition of knowledge or skills through study, experience, or being taught. (www.lexico.com/en/definition/learning, accessed 9 July 2019).

As a psychologist, Sheldon Lachman (1997) recognised that 'learning' was commonly defined as 'a relatively permanent change in behavior brought about by practice or experience' but went on to suggest that a better definition would be: 'Learning is the process by which a relatively stable modification in stimulus–response relations is developed as a consequence of functional environmental interaction via the senses'.

Some definitions focus on 'how' learning takes place (e.g. through the senses, through prior experience, or through study) while others talk about 'what' is learned (e.g. knowledge, behaviours, skills and values) or how it is evidenced (e.g. a change in behaviour). The Wikipedia page on learning includes commentary on machine learning, and we could argue whether any of the above definitions might apply to Artificial Intelligence. In academic life, definitions are rarely simple to develop, though the simplest definitions tend to be the ones that stick: they are easy to remember and easy to understand. The challenge with simplicity is that life is often more complex than we like to recognise.

REFLECTION POINT

Last week, you probably learnt a lot: which celebrity is dating which other celebrity, which of your class-mates has the best taste in clothes or shares your interests, which of your lecturers is the most inter-esting, how much you need to pay for a meal on campus and so on. Our brain is taking in information all the time. Some of your learning would have come from university classes, but the majority of that learning would have come from the way your brain interprets what it takes in from all the experiences you have.

Take some time to think about the following questions and write down some answers.

What has been the main source of your academic learning this week: university classes? Books and read-ing? Discussions with others? Thinking about what you hear and read?

How much time do you give to your learning outside of class – especially your reading? Do you think it is enough?

How good are you at making notes of what you read or hear? What tools does your phone have or tablet have for this purpose?

From Box 5.1, which definition of learning do you prefer? Why?

Honey and Mumford's Learning Styles

Honey and Mumford (1992) identified that different people have innate learning preferences, and their model of learning styles relates closely to each of the four stages noted in Chapter 2 in relation to Kolb's thinking, though with slightly different labels (see Figure 5.2).

Research conducted by Honey and Mumford suggests that some people are better at learning from experience (Activists), others better at learning by reflection (Reflectors), others by developing their own ideas about how the world works and preferring theoretical input (Theorists), and finally some individ-uals prefer to take information, plan for the future and ask 'what if?' (Pragmatists). The authors argue, though, that few individuals are definitely one or another and that in reality we learn in a variety of ways depending on the learning opportunities we are offered.

The 'typical' characteristics possessed by each of the four learner 'types' are as follows – though because most of us possess a main preference (it is very rare for anyone to be *only* one 'type'!), our overall engagement in learning is dependent upon a mixture of the four preferences (as well as the way that any tutor tries to engage you):

Activists will tend to thrive on the immediate. They will be reluctant to spend a great deal of time thinking about what they do and will rarely take time to think through how well they did and why.

Reflectors will tend to be cautious and careful in what they do. They will collect a great deal of information before arriving at any decisions or making judgements, and in a group discussion they will prefer to listen to others' contributions before making their own views known.

Theorists will tend to be highly logical and systematic in what they do. There will be evidence of a perfectionist attitude and they like to use information to build logical models of the world around them that they will defend rigorously when challenged.

Pragmatists will tend to be as energetic as activists, but will prefer to test already formulated ideas. Their keyword might be experimentation, and, typically, pragmatists will jump at the chance to try out ideas in the real world.

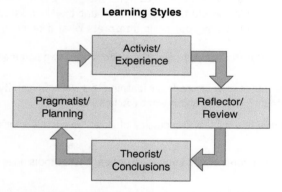

Figure 5.2 Learning styles as developed by Honey and Mumford (1992)

VA(R)K Learning Styles

This model of learning styles was developed in the early 1990s by Fleming and Mills (1992). The basic idea is that the way we take in information can differ from individual to individual, with some learning through hearing (Auditory), others through what they see (Visual, Verbal), some through reading (Reading/Writing) and others through actively touching and experiencing or using information (Kinaesthetic).

Fleming and Baume (2006) argue that it is not strictly a learning styles questionnaire but more a communications questionnaire, which should be used for learning rather than solely recreation. The model itself has more to do with whether you, as a student, can engage with the way you are taught and whether you learn most from your lectures and tutorials than through your own personal reading and thinking, but common sense might suggest that trying to learn skills without any input (whether auditory, visual, read/write or kinaesthetic) is unlikely to succeed.

━━━━━ **BOX 5.2** ━━━━━

'Right-Brained' and 'Left-Brained'

Until recently, it was a common belief that our educational achievements and processing of information depended strongly on whether we were 'right-brained' or 'left-brained'. The idea became a popular and simple way to understand why some people had more of an artistic side than others, and why some seemed to be more analytical than others. It was suggested that right-brained individuals would be better able to show creativity and lateral thinking, while those who were left-brained were seen as more analytical.

The ideas translated into behaviours such as note taking: those who were left-brained would be more likely to write their notes as bullet points and remember mnemonics, while those who were right-brained might use colour and draw mind-maps.

However, research by Nielsen, Anderson and colleagues at the University of Utah (Nielsen et al., 2013) seems to cast significant doubt over this model. It appears that the brain is much more complex than simply dividing it by hemisphere, and that some brain functions are associated with certain sides of the brain – e.g. with language on the left and attention on the right – but, according to Anderson, 'people don't tend to have a stronger left- or right-sided brain network' (cited in Novotney, 2013).

On a more philosophical basis, the idea does find a willing audience with those who are seeking a simple way of understanding how the world operates, regardless of what research actually indicates about the complexity of reality.

Which would you – as a student or as a future manager – prefer to use: a simple model that may not actually be proven through research, or a more complex model that is difficult to apply but bears a stronger reflection of reality?

Deep and Surface Learning

While some have examined learning styles (which deal with the psychological factors affecting our preferences for learning, in the same way that our psychology often affects how emotional we are as human beings), others have taken an approach which looks much more widely at the impact that both our psychology and sociological factors have on how students engage with their learning in academic settings. The latter has led to the powerful concept of an 'approach to learning'.

In the mid-1970s, Marton and Säljö (1976) identified two major approaches that individuals took to their learning. Rather than being a purely psychological analysis, this model suggested that there were two broad approaches that students at university were taking to their studies – either a surface approach or a deep approach. A surface approach might describe a set of behaviours and attitudes where an individual would not necessarily be interested in what they are learning, would focus on memorisation and would principally do what was needed to pass a course and little more. A deep approach, on the other hand, would show itself through a student who was doing extra reading, really seeking to understand what they were being asked to learn and would think critically about the information they were taking in. Their motivation will be much stronger than that of the surface learner and they will usually learn for the enjoyment of learning. In a way, there are parallels between what psychologists call 'intrinsic motivation' where people are motivated by internal factors, and 'extrinsic motivation' where individuals are motivated by money or promotion or some external factors. In terms of the amount of time spent on studies, therefore, a student adopting a surface approach would probably get the work done as quickly as possible, while the student adopting a deep approach would spend a great deal of time – and perhaps more than was expected – examining the research on a particular topic.

The outcomes of these two approaches are quite different, and you might wish to review the Maslow essay given in Chapter 6 to see these differences clearly. The student adopting a surface approach is likely to produce an essay that is 'OK', contains the basic information, but does not show a detailed grasp of the reading or an understanding of how additional factors may influence how successful individuals are in business (for example). If you examine the information regarding Bloom's taxonomy given in Chapter 6 you will see that such an essay probably demonstrates the main facts (knowledge), some understanding of the main concepts (understanding) and perhaps some examples (application).

The student adopting a deep approach to learning is likely to produce something which shows a great deal more thinking, as you might expect. The amount of reading that has been undertaken will be greater, the understanding will be significantly deeper and, as the reading has been done, the student will have taken time to develop questions in their mind about what they are reading. When it comes to assessment, this will enable the student to demonstrate much more analysis (why things are happening), to evaluate what they are reading (Bloom's 'evaluation' level – after all, how can you demonstrate evaluation if you are not actually doing any reading?) and to understand how this theory fits into a wider picture (synthesis). As a result, the marks are typically higher.

There is a third approach that some educational researchers have referred to: the 'strategic approach'. Here the behaviour is similar to that of the deep learner, but the motivational drivers are different. The strategic learner will study hard, do a significant amount of reading over and above expectations, and seem interested in the subject, but the motivation here is to do well in assessment rather than learning simply because learning is a great thing to do. For examinations, strategic learners will spend a great deal of time question spotting and preparing for a limited number of topics. Similarly, in assignments, a strategic learner will concentrate on the particular topic at hand and demonstrate the higher levels of Bloom's taxonomy in their work. Their understanding and thinking around the entire subject will likely be limited, but they may nonetheless do well if their focus is the right one (the risk in an examination is that it will not be, of course.)

Many of your lecturers will think that a surface approach to learning is less helpful than deep learning. Some individuals will take either one approach or the other for all their subjects and all their years of study, but rarely will the lecturing style of your lecturers (or assessment approach of your modules) have no impact on your motivation. In addition, there are some rare occasions where a surface approach can be useful (e.g. when there is a lot to read and some of that reading may be less useful than other parts) but, in general, a deeper approach does tend to lead to higher marks.

LEARNING OPPORTUNITIES AT UNIVERSITY

How Does the University Help You to Learn? What Do You Need to Do Yourself?

There are many answers to the first question. You have probably had your first lecture and some kind of student induction. You will almost certainly have had a student handbook and you might have been given some work to do before you arrived at university, but what are the other ways that universities facilitate your learning and development? We will provide a very brief outline here which covers some of the teaching and learning methods used, and then discuss how best to engage with those opportunities.

Teaching and Learning Tools

There is a variety of mechanisms by which you will be learning at university (see Table 5.1). Some of them are inductive and some are deductive (information on this can be found online on the companion website, but deductive learning usually occurs when you learn from what someone has told you, and inductive learning takes place when you discover something for yourself by making conclusions based on what you see).

Table 5.1 Teaching and learning opportunities commonly given at university

Opportunity	Typical description	Potential relationship to your learning and development
Lectures (deductive)	One-way presentations around an hour in length. Could include examples of how ideas have been used, theoretical models, concepts which are important for the course. Could include online live streamed lectures and video lectures.	Good for introducing you to relevant knowledge.
Small group teaching (partially deductive, partially inductive)	Small to medium-sized groups (maybe 20-30 students) discussing the application of course material with a tutor for around an hour. Usually includes discussion, interaction, maybe student presentations and requires some reading and preparation on the part of the student. Could be virtual/online as well as physically face-to-face.	Good for ensuring your understanding of key ideas. Checks your ability to apply theories introduced elsewhere. Develops your communication/ discussion skills.
Tutorials (partially deductive, partially inductive)	Very small group (maybe 1-6 students) opportunity to discuss specific learning and research with others and a tutor, through examining personal reading and thinking. Has more widely been used at universities as a means of supporting students pastorally.	Develops ability to debate and defend your ideas. Develops your own thinking. Forces students to read and engage with relevant theories/literature. Where used pastorally, ensures that skill development and career planning are taking place.
Independent reading and research (largely deductive, partially inductive; depends on what you are reading)	Lists of relevant reading – books, journal articles, online resources, handouts, etc. – are produced at the start of modules and some reading materials may be posted online. Generally, students not doing any reading would be in danger of not knowing enough to pass the course assessment.	Develops time management skills. Develops understanding of a broader knowledge base than given in a lecture. Enables the development of thinking skills.
Virtual learning environment (largely deductive, unless using blogs)	A collection of materials, announcements, often some interactive resources and other tools to enhance your learning. The idea is that you regularly (weekly as a minimum) review what is there and engage in the learning opportunities given to you.	Develops time management skills. Develops understanding of a broader knowledge base than given in a lecture. Enables the development of thinking skills.

This is not an exhaustive list. There are some combinations that academic staff use, including an idea called the 'flipped classroom', which we will look at later. Different lecturers and different universities will have different practices and activities to enhance your learning.

There are two broad categories of learning opportunities provided by universities. Firstly, there is the face-to-face contact teaching time listed usually as seminars or tutorials, and lectures or laboratory workshops. Of course, face-to-face can mean online as well as physically in the same room. Secondly, the vast majority of the timetable for students is unstructured and is intended for students to undertake their own work to learn independently, as guided by their lecturers. The challenge is that one of the most frequent reasons that academics give for students failing to do well in their studies is that they have a mindset that learning only takes place through lectures. The outcome of this thinking – or perhaps the driver of this, for some – is that the fees that students pay are for the face-to-face teaching that students receive.

 'BUT I HAVE A QUESTION...'

... Shouldn't I get more lectures? After all, I am paying for my degree, and that means I should get more teaching? My lectures should be enough to help me pass, right?

Well, the question of what students (or parents) pay for in their fees is one that is often misunderstood – just as the nature of learning at university is misunderstood – but what is always clear is that no one pays for a degree; instead, you will be paying for the *opportunity to obtain* your degree. If you paid for your degree, then you could actually leave the day after you paid, right? Using the analogy of a gym; you pay to have the opportunity to get fit and perhaps lose weight, but the gym cannot guarantee that this will happen – it is up to you and the effort you put in. The same is true at university: no university will guarantee to award you a degree, it is up to you and the effort you put in.

So what is included in the fee? Well, lectures and seminars, obviously, but also library books, internet access, time with tutors outside of the classroom, welfare support, student societies, computers, access to IT systems, facilities, grounds and rooms, opportunities to undertake research with university professors, careers services, and so on. And above all, the opportunity to learn knowledge related to your discipline of study, and the opportunities to grow as an individual and to develop skills, attitudes and abilities which will help you in future life. It is important, therefore, to know how to use these opportunities for your benefit and learning. If you are taking a course online, then – by definition – the majority of your time will be spent away from a physical university, but technology can easily facilitate the provision of seminars and video lectures online.

A great deal of your time – as we saw in Chapter 3 on time management and as we shall see in this chapter – is given over to you for your independent learning, and what we call 'non-timetabled activities'. Your fees cover these as well, and their value comes from the preparation for life after university, when you will need to learn without lectures and guidance. University is about helping you to do that preparation.

In looking at the second question here, the chapter on assessment (Chapter 6) gives you some ideas about how well you will do if you rely solely on the information given in lectures. The general idea is that you might pass if that is all you do, but your result may be a minimal pass, or a fail.

 KEY LEARNING POINT

You cannot expect to pass your courses well without spending time doing the reading, thinking and other independent activities expected of you.

BOX 5.3

Being an Online Student

Studying a course online can bring significant benefits: the flexibility that such a programme offers and, sometimes, the ability to take a smaller number of subjects to fit around a particular work or personal situation can be a particular advantage to many individuals, but the qualities required to complete an online programme have some differences from those in a full-time setting. Many courses will still give you opportunities for face-to-face contact – perhaps physically by attending an occasional workshop hosted by a tutor, or virtually through online meeting software. Both will give you the chance to 'meet' and get to know other students in your situation. However, the lack of a frequent physical interaction with others does make the learning experience different and requires some different skills:

- **Self-disciplined with good time management**: Studying on a 'distance learning' course without others around usually means that you have to be a lot more organised and disciplined about what you do (e.g. about creating a timetable which fits around your own circumstances and location) than full-time students (who will have other students around them discussing their academic work – 'What did you think of that assignment? How much progress have you made?' etc.) might need to be.
- **Independently minded**: You have to be able to engage with the material (readings, video lectures, etc.) without needing to interact regularly with other students. The lack of a physical community – and the student societies that go with that community – can be a challenge for some.
- **Patient**: Your online tutor may be in a different time zone from you and you might need to wait a while before getting a reply to a query – or be willing to have an online workshop late at night or early in the morning for the same reason.
- **Cross-culturally aware**: Other students in an online workshop might come from places that you have not been to (or sometimes heard of). This *can* create a very dynamic atmosphere where interesting differences of opinion can be raised – and a good tutor will enable discussion in a managed way. More information on cross-cultural awareness is given in Chapter 13
- **Clear in communication**: Much communication on an online course will be in written form – i.e. emails checking on your progress, queries from you to the lecturer. That requires a clarity in expression that is above that needed in a two way conversation, and means that emails etc. might need to be thought through more carefully.
- **Determination and persistence**: The fact that you are studying away from other students means that you will need to be committed to your course of study in a way that enables you to complete your studies. It might be much easier to fall behind when you do not have other students and your tutors around you.

The one area that might be surprisingly missing are skills related to the use of technology. For some, using certain websites might seem to be a daunting process, but universities offering online courses usually provide a significant amount of guidance on how such tools (e.g. 'Zoom' meetings or 'Starleaf' and others associated with Virtual Learning Environments – see page 109) can be used to enhance your learning.

So, do you have these qualities? What difficulties do you think you might have in completing an online programme? What advantages might you experience in undertaking such a programme?

LEARNING OPPORTUNITIES INSIDE THE TIMETABLE

We will start with the most common situation, that of the lecture.

Lectures

Let's assume you have been through induction and are 'enjoying' your first week of lectures. Have a look at the next exercise below. Do any of these ideas relate to actions you have been taking before your lectures?

FOR YOU TO DO

Preparing for a lecture

Which of the following actions do you usually take before attending a lecture?

- Read the relevant chapter from the textbook.
- Download and/or print out the lecture slides.
- Look through any lecture slides.
- Ensure that you know how the lecture topic fits into other topics that you have studied.
- Discuss any lecture slides with other students.
- Look for some additional reading on the same subject.
- Check that you understand the meanings of any technical terms.
- Check that you have some way to take notes of what was said.

Some people enjoy lectures, others find them boring, and there will likely be a lot of variation between the styles of different lecturers. But whatever your own reaction to them, it is certainly true that attending a lecture is unlike many other situations outside of academic life (the exception might be attending church or a formal speech).

Lecturers may have different styles. They will usually display information on a screen and may use videos, quizzes and other media to enable you to remember and understand the information they present in an active way. Some lecturers may use multiple choice answer pads (commonly known as 'clickers') to enable you to answer questions during the lecture. This does not mean that a lecture will be just one way, or that a lecturer will not engage in some kind of discussion or ask you some questions to consider.

 WHAT IS A LECTURE?

A lecture is a class where a tutor will give information regarding an academic subject. Often this will be a one-way delivery of information, lasting about an hour.

The best lecturers will be those who really try to engage with you, to inspire and excite you, and this makes attending the lecture an enjoyable experience. Of course, some lecturers are better at it than others (we are not all good at everything) but, hopefully, most of those you have to listen to will have been lecturing for some time and will have some good examples and stories to tell.

We have already said that the lecturing styles of different lecturers can be very different. Sometimes this is dependent on the lecturer's personality and sometimes it is dependent on the size of the class. It is a lot easier to have a discussion and learn from other students in a smaller class, but the purpose of a lecture is often a little different from that of a small class. At a minimum, a lecture is intended *to give you information*, and can engage, excite and motivate you in your studies, and get you thinking about the subjects you are studying. A lecture will probably also help you to set some boundaries to the limits of your reading and enable you to get a quick overview of the subject matter.

'BUT I HAVE A QUESTION ...'

... Does attendance at lectures really matter?

Yes. Attendance is the easy part, even though some students do not consider it necessary to attend lectures (and they are wrong about that). Most universities will have rules about attendance, and these can particularly impact on students from overseas, who will have requirements about attendance given to them as part of their UK study visa. You can get notes from your friends, of course, but then you are relying on the quality of those notes, and how easy they are to read or understand, and you could miss out on the emphasis given by the lecturer to certain issues and words.

The key point is that you 'engage with' information provided by your lecturers. 'Engage with' means to consider, to think, to get involved. If you engage with lecture content, for example, you will be considering it, reading around it, deciding whether you agree with it, and looking for evidence that confirms or denies what your lecturer was telling you.

Does that mean you have the right to disagree with your lecturers? Yes, of course – but politely. Start a debate with your lecturer and discuss the evidence. That is what active learning is all about. It makes learning much more interesting and gives you a much wider viewpoint than just the view of your lecturer.

As you develop your critical thinking skills, you will need to get used to evaluating what your lecturers are telling you: apply the information, analyse it, compare it with other issues you have covered on a course. That is what university studies are all about. It is a bit like the difference between taking some nice food and quickly swallowing it, and taking the same food, chewing it, enjoying its flavour and then swallowing it. The second is far more rewarding and better reflects what you should be doing with the content of your lectures.

Benefitting from a Lecture

How should you engage with a lecture? This is an important question. There are the obvious things you can do: for example, take a printout of lecture slides with you or a copy on your laptop or tablet; make sure you make some notes you can read some weeks after the lecture has finished; do not talk unless the lecturer asks you to do so and do not look at Facebook or other websites when the lecture is taking place; and turn off your phone. There are, however, some slightly less obvious and more subtle issues to consider. Table 5.2 lists some of these additional issues.

Table 5.2 Getting the maximum benefit from your lectures

1. Make sure you do the appropriate reading both before and after the lecture. This will help to ensure you understand any technical terms used during the lecture.
2. Do not write down everything that your lecturer says – most of the key points will be on a PowerPoint or similar. Do write down examples or ideas that are not written on the slides.
3. Find a way of abbreviating frequently used words (in business studies, these might be words like 'organisation' or 'consumer demand').
4. Review the slides from the previous week before going into the next lecture. Some subjects (especially mathematical ones or languages) are cumulative, i.e. if you did not understand the earlier week, you will find it even more difficult to understand the next week.
5. Contact the tutor as soon as possible if there was something you did not understand.
6. Use what was covered in the lecture as a framework for additional reading.

It may sound somewhat surprising, but a lecturer cannot give you all the information you need about a particular topic during the lecture. An hour or even two are insufficient for most lecturers to tell you everything that you should know. There may be a seminar for every lecture, but the purpose of the seminar – as we will see – is to give you and your tutor the chance to check your understanding and application of what has been studied, not to cover new material.

The question then is how can you ensure that you do get all the information you need? The answer is simple: by doing the reading prescribed for you. The online material covers reading in much more depth, but the impact of that reading will depend on the quality of your note taking during the lecture and then the time you take to consider and evaluate what the lecturer was telling you.

Of course, it is not just in lectures that you need to be good at taking notes. Notes should also be taken from any reading you do, from group discussions or meetings you have, from seminars and from discussions with course tutors. Any situation where learning can occur is a situation where notes need to be taken.

KEY LEARNING POINT

It is helpful to understand how important note taking is during lectures. Without taking notes, we will miss a great deal of what is said during the lecture.

Seminars and Tutorials

While seminars and tutorials are listed separately, the reality is that, in many universities, these two words are used interchangeably. Originally (when there were few universities and few university students), tutorials were occasions for a tutor (professor or lecturer) and maybe no more than six students to meet to discuss a topic or a piece of research, or to review a piece of work that one or more of the students had done. As such, tutorials are fantastic opportunities to receive almost personal coaching in how to think and how to conduct research.

These small tutorials do take place in some environments where there are few students, but many universities do not have the small numbers of students required to run such tutorials, and departments offer their students seminars alongside the subject-based lectures.

If the lecture is the place where you learn information (perhaps for the first time, if you have not done the reading ahead of the lecture), then the seminar is the place where you (and your lecturers) can check whether you understand the ideas presented and can *apply that learning* to examples. Typically, a seminar will run with between 20 and 30 students and so should be a lot more interactive than a much larger lecture. It will be expected that you have done the reading and any exercises you have been set, and you may well be asked to show your work or give a presentation about your work or something which relates to the topic of previous lectures.

Benefitting from a Seminar

Seminars are intended to be interactive so that you have a chance to get feedback on your thinking, that is you can receive some evaluation on whether your ideas are correct. Do not be frightened, then, of contributing your ideas, even if culturally that may seem strange (see Box 5.4); you need to check that your understanding is correct. Saying nothing may leave you with the impression that you *do understand* something when actually your understanding is incorrect, and in an exam this can be disastrous.

BOX 5.4

Culture and Interaction

When discussing culture, it is very dangerous to stereotype, since there will always be an exception to the rule, but classrooms in some countries are often one-way experiences – even at school. Middle and high school students in China, for example, are usually expected to stand up and give an answer to a question only when the teacher asks them.

The culture often enforces this. Such cultures – often called 'Confucian Heritage' – are frequently hierarchical, with a strong degree of what some call 'power-distance'. In the past this meant that the teacher is at the top of the hierarchy and cannot be questioned.

When students from such cultures enter university, there may be little change and those previous experiences impact on students' behaviour in the university. Students are sometimes nervous about contributing their own ideas and this is even more difficult for those studying in an English-speaking environment where they are required to speak or present in a second language. Many UK students struggle to do this!

Some international students might have the ability, but not the confidence, to write, speak, listen and/or read English, and might also be unsure of how to interact with a tutor in an unfamiliar setting, so there are issues of both culture and language which affect some international students.

Some universities – such as Nottingham University in China – assess the contributions that students make in their classrooms and use that as part of students' course marks. This, it is said, encourages preparation before class and enables classrooms to be more interactive.

Participating and interacting in a classroom is not easy, but is vital if everyone is going to get some feedback on their ideas to ensure that their learning is progressing well. Interaction, of course, also makes sure that students can learn from each other. See Chapter 13 for more information on cultural differences.

LEARNING OPPORTUNITIES AND TOOLS OUTSIDE OF THE TIMETABLE

The following are learning opportunities provided by universities, but which are not going to feature in your scheduled timetable, or even in your time for independent study. However, since the majority of your study time is going to involve reading and studying outside of the classroom, they are vitally important.

Independent Reading

Doing your reading is vital to your performance: the importance of doing the required reading – and other reading if you have time – has already been mentioned several times, particularly in relation to deep learning, and cannot be understated. Reading can be of various sources but the most common ones are textbooks, academic research journals and credible information online. There is more information on reading on the companion website at https://study.sagepub.com/morgan2e.

FURTHER
READING

Many journals and textbooks can be challenging to read: the ease of reading is sometimes dependent on our vocabulary and language abilities. Authors of journal articles – i.e. the academics who teach you – tend to have a very high level of academic language, which can make reading journal articles challenging, especially if you are a student whose first language is not English. Sentences tend to be short and sometimes the technical terms used can be new to you. If so, consider reading the 'abstract' of the journal article first to find out if it is relevant to your learning, and then the 'conclusion' and 'discussion': just because something appears difficult does not mean that it really is, or that it will always be difficult.

Completing your degree without undertaking your reading is like going to the cinema to watch a film but falling asleep or leaving the cinema every five minutes: you get the main plot of the film, but you miss out on the details – and that will significantly damage your chances of academic success. As stated elsewhere, your lecturers cannot cover everything you need to know in the few hours they spend with you in lectures.

KEY LEARNING POINT

You cannot expect to successfully complete your degree in the way you want unless you read around the subjects covered in your lectures.

Active Reading

Regardless of our previous experience with reading textbooks or our motivation or interest in doing so, reading is a vital component of study at university, so much so that students used to say that they were 'reading for a degree in … [Business Studies, for example]'. But the value is not in reading alone, since what we read can easily be forgotten in the same way that what we hear can easily be forgotten. There are some ideas around this in the section on critical reading in Chapter 4

 **ACTIVE READING**

Active reading describes a process where we are actively engaged in our reading, usually by thinking about what we read.

The value in reading is gained when we think about what we have read, so we need to learn to 'read actively'.

Our thinking can easily be forgotten, so it is a good idea to write notes in the margin or on the pages, and e-books often come with similar capabilities, but key to this is the idea that we use our reading in the same way that we would use any other source of information, such as lectures, seminars, information online, discussions with other students, and so on.

KEY LEARNING POINT

Engaging actively with your course reading is as important for your learning as attending lectures. It helps you to do well, and the benefits are greater than simply reading the book's content.

Keeping a Record of What You Read

When you come to write up what you have read as an assignment, you will need to compile a bibliography. To do so, you *must* keep a record of what you read and how it could be useful. In times gone past, students and researchers tended to do this through a card filing system, but computer software has developed since then and one of the best tools available now is called EndNote.

Expressed simply, the details of any journal articles you find online (via a library database such as Emerald or ProQuest Direct) can be imported directly into EndNote so you then have a reference which EndNote can use to compile a bibliography. This makes the process of keeping a record of what you have read extremely easy.

You can also use EndNote to keep notes of that reading, so you can make notes about any article you read – content, research methods, conclusions, etc. – within EndNote. If you do not have access to EndNote, then a database tool or Microsoft Excel can be used for similar purposes, but keeping an accurate record is vital if your bibliography is going to be complete and accurate. There is more on referencing and giving citations in Chapter 6 on assessment.

================ REFLECTION POINT ================

Take some time to think about the following questions and write down some answers.

Do you enjoy reading, or do you find it hard to motivate yourself to read? If it is hard for you, what can you do to make it more interesting?

Which of these makes you think the most: listening to a lecture, doing a group exercise in a seminar, or reading the chapter of a book? Why?

Which are you supposed to spend more time on at university: reading the materials given to you, or attending your classes? Why do you think this is the case? Give two or three reasons which come to mind:

1.

2.

3.

================ BOX 5.5 ================

Making Notes and Mind-Maps

Taking notes in lectures was mentioned above, when we looked at lectures (see page 117), but taking notes when we are listening to discussions and when we are reading is also important – it can provide a summary

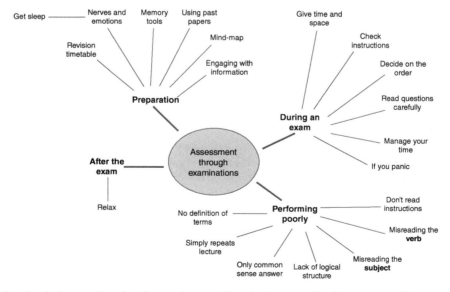

Figure 5.3   A mind-map showing issues to consider during examination preparation

(Continued)

of something that is longer and in turn can help us to remember what we have read. One way to do this that is commonly used – e.g. when writing or compiling longer pieces of work – is to develop a 'mind-map' – see Figure 5.3.

This particular mind-map gives ideas around issues to consider during examination preparation. Such visualisations can be powerful summaries of what you have learnt. All it takes is:

- A clear sheet of paper.
- A clear understanding of the content of the module or a particular topic within a module: what you were taught.
- Some thought about what you have *learned*. NB: This is not the same as what you were 'taught': what you have learned reflects your own independent reading and thinking.
- An understanding of how the ideas in the module relate to each other.
- Some colour and the ability to draw in a way that is clear to you.

Key to a good mind-map is clarity and simplicity: clarity in terms of keeping your writing very limited, and simplicity in terms of making sure that it is easy to visualise.

Making a mind-map with different coloured pens etc. can be useful, but there are also software tools which can assist with producing something that is visually attractive: mindmup.com, mindmeister.com, freemind.sourceforge.net, mindjet.com, xmind.net and others are all available for use, some are free but some need a subscription.

Using and Understanding Feedback

Another crucial source of information for your learning and academic success is the feedback you get from your assignments. It might seem strange to be discussing feedback when we have not yet discussed assessment, and we will look at some aspects of feedback when we look at assessment in Chapter 6, but we first need to be very clear in our definitions and understanding of what we mean by 'feedback'. Have a look at the next exercise below.

 **FOR YOU TO DO**

Look at the views given below and decide for yourself whether they are **True** or **False**.

1. I get feedback on my ideas every time I give my views in a seminar.
2. Feedback is not nice to receive, and it makes me nervous.
3. Other students can give me feedback in group discussions.
4. Feedback is something I would prefer to hear than to see written down.
5. Feedback is something I only get for my assignments.
6. I enjoy getting feedback; it helps me know where to improve next time.
7. Feedback is useful in my learning.
8. The mark is the only thing that counts; the feedback is not important.
9. I find my feedback is very impersonal.
10. I am sure my feedback will come very quickly after I submit my assignment.

This exercise gives 10 ideas on feedback, but it is helpful to understand what feedback really is.

Feedback is far more than simply the written feedback that you might receive on your coursework: it includes the following.

- Comments given to you and others in seminars in response to something you say.
- Something that is emailed to you in respect of work that you have done or a comment that you have made.
- A comment from a classmate responding to something you have said.
- Something said in a one-to-one discussion between you and a member of academic staff.
- A surprised look from another student in response to something you have said.

Feedback is *any* comment or information given to you by anyone at any time in any place relating to anything that you have done (or not done) or something that you have said, and which evaluates those comments you have made or the work you have done. As you can probably deduce from the ideas above, feedback is *not* just about your coursework grade.

Your grade will tell you broadly how well you did, but the feedback is the detailed information that tells you what you did well and what you should think about improving. It is very common to want the grade or mark and not really bother about anything else – and bearing in mind that this is how your lecturers will evaluate your degree, it is understandable. However, the mark is only a very small part of the complete story. As a lecturer, I would never re-mark work (regardless of what my students might ask me to do), but I am generally happy to discuss and explain the feedback if it does not make sense. The feedback in the mind of many of your lecturers will be more important than the mark.

ACADEMIC FEEDBACK

Feedback is any comment or information given to an individual which provides them with some idea of the value of their work.

Feedback given on class contributions or on any work that does not count towards a course grade is vital to learning. Not giving or seeking such feedback will very likely lead to your receiving poorer grades on future work than you otherwise would have received.

If you want to do better, *this information is vital*. How can you do better when you are not sure where you went wrong before? This becomes particularly relevant when examined in conjunction with other aspects of the learning process.

KEY LEARNING POINT

Reading the feedback given to you on your work is highly important. Doing your next academic assignment without reading the feedback you were given on previous work is similar to trying to play tennis with one hand tied behind your back: you are denying yourself the chance to use resources (information) that could help you succeed.

Virtual Learning Environment

Some of your lecturers will have completed their university studies before email and the internet existed, but the internet is now as important a source of learning as the lectures, if not more so. It is highly likely that the internet will have formed a big part of your learning at school and you will have used it to demonstrate your ability to gather information. At university, the internet is also used to give you information and provide you with support for your learning via a VLE (Virtual Learning Environment). This might be Moodle™ or Blackboard™ or another online platform.

VIRTUAL LEARNING ENVIRONMENT (VLE)

A virtual learning environment is an online portal for providing materials, information and interaction for students for their studies.

The VLE may or may not be used for a variety of purposes, and you may or may not have come across one before. The UK's Open University uses its own OpenLearn platform, a tool which it has now made available to other universities.

Universities typically put a variety of information online and you will be expected to look at these very regularly, probably *at least once a week for each module*. The elements listed in Table 5.3 will probably appear for each module each week, though universities and university departments will vary in what they will make available to you online.

Table 5.3 Content typically posted via a VLE

• Contact details for all module teachers • Copy of the module handbook • Class timetable • Details of coursework assignments including submission dates • Marking criteria for assignments	• Relevant lecture slides/notes/materials used in the classroom • Previous examination papers • Feedback on at least the last examination/coursework performance • Reading/resource list

Some additional elements might also be apparent from module to module. You might also find multiple choice questions there, blogs, assignment submission processes and a variety of other tools to support your learning and build the relationships between you and your lecturers.

Massive Open Online Courses

More recently, there has been a move in university education across the world to establish Massive Open Online Courses (MOOCs). MOOCs are open access courses, where anyone in the world can enrol in an online module from a large number of universities, usually without needing to pay any kind of fee. The UK's Open University has a long history of providing online courses (preceded by postal materials and late-night televised lectures in the 1960s) and has developed a platform for its own MOOCs, as Box 5.6 notes. MOOC modules are fully online and are taken by hundreds, or in some cases thousands, of students around the world at any one time. There are no direct, face-to-face interactions between lecturers and students, but the materials posted can give students an opportunity to find out more about specific topics of interest to them. As a resource for learning, they can be fantastic: you can access resources and lectures from some of the most important people in the world in a particular discipline, and get to see a view of a particular topic presented by someone other than your lecturer.

═══════ BOX 5.6 ═══════

MOOCs and Learning

In a 2012 edition of the online journal *Information Age* (Rossi, 2012) noted that the Open University had launched a company called FutureLearn, which had developed a learning platform for other institutions to use. A number of other universities had already signed up to use the platform to support their own MOOCs, some of which are themselves developed across universities, and some further developed across continents.

Whether this proves to be the way that most universities choose to go still remains to be seen. While MOOCs are an innovative concept, most of them do not provide any free assessment or free tutoring, but the resources are usually provided free of charge and are available for anyone to access, whether they wish to get a degree from a particular university providing those resources or not. Payment is usually only needed when an individual decides to undertake some assessment.

As noted in the magazine article:

The Open University (OU) is the most advanced provider of online learning materials in the UK, as its courses are all based on distance learning. The OU's OpenLearn platform, launched in 2006, contains around 11,000 hours of learning materials in over 600 study units, and attracts an average 400,000 unique users per month. (Rossi, 2012)

Education online is not only becoming big business, but is potentially going to transform how learning takes place and how degrees are given. It may be possible to get credits for one module at one institution that can be used as the basis for part of a degree at another university. We are not there yet, but it is likely that this will come sooner or later.

Would you ever think of enrolling in a MOOC? What might put you off, or encourage you?

===== BOX 5.7 =====

The 'Flipped Classroom'

The structure of how these learning opportunities are put together can vary from university to university, but the traditional model for teaching at university often works as follows: students are given some reading to do in preparation for a lecture, the lecture takes place and students are given the information, and then there is a tutorial or seminar where students are given the opportunity to apply and check their learning to a case or by analysing a journal paper. As suggested, this model varies: some university courses will use 'the case method' where the traditional one-way lecture is replaced with a discussion of a company situation and the learning comes out from that discussion – and the extensive thinking and preparation that has been done by students beforehand.

However, a number of universities are now using learning opportunities in a very different way, whereby students are not given a lecture but instead are expected to do reading and watch lectures and other video resources online before coming to a small class where there is discussion of a case. This is called the 'flipped classroom'. The emphasis is on pre-class activities, and the classroom is a place for you to show or test that learning.

Is this a method of learning that would work for you? Why do you think the learning is seen as more powerful here? How would you need to change your behaviour to make this work for you?

APPLYING LEARNING STYLES TO YOUR UNIVERSITY EXPERIENCE

If we take the ideas identified and apply them to the learning opportunities given through the typical university experience, then we will find that people with different and varied learning preferences find different activities *more or less* interesting (see Figure 5.4). This does not mean, of course, that we do not or cannot learn from the other activities given in Figure 5.4.

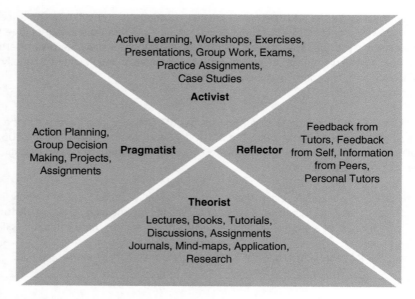

Figure 5.4 An application of learning styles to learn at university

The challenge, therefore, is to learn how to develop the different learning styles and use each learning opportunity as well as you can.

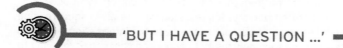

'BUT I HAVE A QUESTION ...'

... If my learning style is 'Activist', but my university uses only one-way lectures and tutorials, does that mean that I am not going to learn very much?

No, not at all. What it means is that you might find other activities more engaging, so there are three questions for you:

1. How could you 'interact' with non-interactive lectures?
2. How could you supplement the lectures and tutorials with other ways of learning which are more 'activist' oriented?
3. How could you encourage the lecturer to be more interactive?

The answer to the first is not that different from what you might be doing when you read (i.e. thinking about what you are reading and making notes), so when you are in your lectures (probably with the lecture slides in front of you), take a bit of time to think about what is being presented. Do you agree with what is being said? Are there any problems with it? In other words, engage in some critical thinking as you listen to what is being said – in the same way that you do when you are reading. Write down the questions that occur to you as you listen.

The answer to the second question is to look at all the various ideas mentioned in Figure 5.4 and use them to supplement what you experienced in the lecture. This may mean forming a group to discuss what you have learnt, or finding a friend to debate the content, or, if you have a job, talking to a manager to find out if they have a different point of view. The lecture is not the only way to learn and, as we saw in Chapter 3, a great deal of your time should be spent studying independently.

Thirdly, lecturers need to have feedback. This is not an excuse to go to the lecturer and be aggressive towards them (see the section on giving feedback in Chapter 9), but *a gentle comment* to your lecturer after class might help them understand your reactions.

The question above might be asked by any individual with any particular learning style. Of course, it is rare that any individual will have a single learning style: the methods you prefer to use for your learning will be a combination of all four styles, though some learners will have more of a particular preference than others. But even where there is a strong preference for using any specific style which differs from the methods typically emphasised, university will still be a fantastic place to learn.

KEY LEARNING POINT

Adults learn in a variety of ways and, as a result, universities provide a variety of learning opportunities for you in the classroom. There are various learning opportunities and tools provided inside and outside of timetabled lectures and seminars, and taking advantage of them all is important.

Visit the companion website for this book at https://study.sagepub.com/morgan2e for more information, tips and guidance on active reading, note taking in lectures, the use of cases and study groups, and different learning styles which may be useful for your learning.

FURTHER
READING

FOR YOU TO DO

Your learning will be made up of a variety of situations. How you use them is going to be crucial to their effectiveness in assisting you to learn to think. There are some questions which might help you to bring the various opportunities together:

1. Which of the learning opportunities will be easiest for you to undertake? Why?
2. Thinking about the descriptions of learning styles given above, which learning style appears to match your preference best? How might it affect your motivation to be involved in other opportunities for learning?
3. Which of the learning opportunities will be the most difficult for you to undertake? Why? Is it because of motivation or your own self-confidence, or both, or something else?
4. Given that lecturers cannot cover all that they need to cover in the depth they expect from you in your work, there is a need for you to do the reading. So, what will you do to ensure that you undertake the reading you need to do for your subjects?
5. How can the internet help or hinder your learning?
6. Would a study group work for you? Why, or why not?
7. How can you seek and receive feedback on your thinking? What can you do to get feedback to see whether you really understand the subjects you are studying?
8. What do you need to happen or to do in order to increase your motivation to use these learning opportunities?

Thinking about the answers to these questions at the start of your university career will give you some helpful ideas on how you might use them and other opportunities most effectively.

INTEGRATION AND APPLICATION

Understanding the match between the way we learn and the learning opportunities offered to us at university is seen as crucial in helping you to learn as much as possible during your university studies. We have spent time looking at three theoretical models of learning:

1. Honey and Mumford's (1992) Learning Styles – Activists, Reflectors, Theorists and Pragmatists.
2. VA(R)K Learning Styles – based around whether we take in information using Visual, Auditory or Kinaesthetic senses and/or through information we read.
3. Our approach to learning – whether it is surface, deep or strategic.

We then looked at the learning opportunities offered to us by universities: both formal and structured – lectures, tutorials/seminars – as well as less structured and more independent opportunities – active reading, using feedback, online learning through the VLE. The more we engage with the above opportunities, the better – even if we are not excited about doing so. When we are not interested in a subject we are likely to take a more 'surface approach' to learning and use fewer of the tools noted above, but when we find a subject interesting, we are more likely to adopt a 'deep approach' and engage in more of these tools.

There are various outcomes to all our learning, whichever approach is adopted. Academic grades is one outcome, changed thinking and behaviour is another, increased motivation is a third and then of course we gain increased knowledge. But of course, as the title of this section 'Integration and Application' implies, it is not until we apply those outcomes to our various situations that we can understand how learning really can affect our lives, and those of others.

CONCLUSION

By the end of this chapter, you should be able to:

•   Describe the ways that your lecturers and professors will help and expect you to learn at university.
•   Understand what is meant by 'independent learning'.
•   Use time outside of the classroom to study effectively.

This chapter has been about helping you to cope with the learning opportunities provided by your university. Studying at university requires the use of different study skills from those typically developed at schools and colleges (see Chapters 3, 4 and the next chapter, Chapter 6, for more information).

Understanding how these opportunities work together to enable you to be an independent learner is vital. University requires you to find and use the opportunities given to you, it does not give you everything you need on a plate. At school, you might have been able to take in information given to you, remember it and give it back to your teacher – and pass your subject. At university, you will do poorly if you do only this, so the understanding you develop of how university works and what your tutors are looking for will be key to doing well and ensuring that the money and time invested in your studies are well spent.

Learning should not be a finite process: learning – as we looked at in Chapter 2 – takes place in a large number of situations and over most of our life. Although students often make a distinction between learning (the process) and assessment (the outcomes and evaluation of that process), the two are very closely linked. The feedback you get from the assessment of one module or piece of work should get you to think about what you did well and not so well. That thinking (or reflection) should then lead on to what you do for your next piece of work, so learning cannot be easily separated out from assessment. The next chapter contains more details about the ways in which your lecturers will be assessing your work.

REFLECTION POINT

Take some time to think about the following questions and write down some answers.

Based on the content of this chapter, what do you now know about learning at university that you did not know before?

What key learning point had the most impact? Why?

Do your answers to either of the above questions have the potential to change your attitude to studies at university? If so, why?

What will you now do differently? (Write this down and put it somewhere where you can see it regularly.)

CHAPTER TASK

There are three exercises for this chapter.

During the next week, take time to identify and evaluate the learning opportunities on your course offered by your university. When you think about your learning style and those opportunities, which learning opportunities (both in the timetable and outside of the timetable) are actually the most useful to you?

Talk to one of your lecturers about how you use the learning opportunities: they might not realise how you are learning.

Finally, think about something you have learnt this week. If you were going to teach this to someone else, how would you help them to learn the same thing? Would you create opportunities for them to discover it for themselves, or would you present what you have learnt to them in a presentation? Or put something about it online? How would you make this decision?

INTERVIEW QUESTIONS

It is unlikely that you will be asked any direct questions about teaching methods in a selection interview – no one is going to ask how many hours you spent in lectures and tutorials, unless they think you might have missed most of them – but they might ask you questions to find out about your ability to think critically or adapt to new situations.

Consider the following questions: what might your answers be?

1. Thinking about your learning at university, which parts of your course (lectures, tutorials, presentations, assignments, etc.) taught you the most?
2. How easy did you find it to adjust to studies at university after school or college?

Chapter 17 contains a lot more information on selection interviews and the online content also gives some guidance on these questions.

ADDITIONAL RESOURCES

Want to learn more? Visit https://study.sagepub.com/morgan2e to gain access to a wide range of online resources, including interactive tests, tasks, further reading and downloads.

Website Resources

The following websites offer useful advice on learning skills.

Sheffield Hallam University: www.shu.ac.uk/study-here/why-choose-us/flexible-learning

University of Nottingham: www.nottingham.ac.uk/studyingeffectively/studying/independent.aspx

York University (Ontario, Canada): https://lss.info.yorku.ca/resources/10-secrets-of-university-success/

Textbook Resources

Burns, T. and Sinfield, S. (2016) *Essential Study Skills* (4th edition). London: Sage (particularly Chapter 2).
Cameron, S. (2010) *The Business Student's Handbook: Skills for Study and Employment* (5th edition). Harlow: Pearson (particularly Chapter 4).
Christopher, E. (2012) *Communication Across Cultures*. Basingstoke: Palgrave (particularly Chapter 6).
Horn, R. (2012) *The Business Skills Handbook*. London: CIPD (particularly Chapter 2).
McMillan, K. and Weyers, J. (2012) *The Study Skills Book* (3rd edition). Harlow: Pearson (particularly Chapters 4 and 5).
Pauk, W. and Owens, R. J. Q. (2014) *How to Study in College*. Boston, MA: Cengage (particularly Chapters 5, 6, 10, 11 and 13).
Smale, R. and Fowlie, J. (2009) *How to Succeed at University*. London: Sage (particularly Chapter 5).
Wong, L. (2012) *Essential Study Skills*. Boston, MA: Cengage (particularly Chapters 7, 8, 9 and 10).

PART III
UNIVERSITY ASSESSMENT

As we have seen, learning at university occurs differently from education that you might have had elsewhere. Lectures, tutorials, discussion and critical thinking are all part of the learning process at university because 1) you are an adult and 2) the number of universities is smaller than that of schools and colleges, so you tend to be taught in larger groups. We have also seen that you are expected to study for around 100 hours for each 10-credit block you study (or 150 for 15 credits, etc.), time which includes all those activities covered above, but which should also include time given for assessment.

Assessment is part of the learning process in two ways. Firstly, it provides evidence of what you are able to do and, secondly, it provides the motivation to learn. It would be wonderful to think that everyone learnt because they really enjoyed it and wanted to learn – and that is true of many – but the assessment does provide a push in many cases.

In reality, you will find that learning can become really exciting and interesting if you learn in order to discover things for yourself, rather than focusing on questions which might come up in an examination or on research for a single question in a presentation or assignment. Assessment has to be there, but your tutors will hope that you will put your efforts into learning anyway, *as if there was no assessment*.

Therefore, the three chapters which follow will cover the aspects of assessment commonly used at university. Chapter 6 will give some general guidance on the principles for assessment and relates closely to some ideas on critical thinking noted in Chapter 4. Chapter 7 will look at assignments, reports and dissertations. Chapter 8 will cover issues related to assessment by examinations and will provide some ideas to assist your revision.

Two other chapters included in Part IV (Employability Skills): Chapter 10 ('Presentation Skills') and Chapter 11 ('Team Working') are highly relevant for both employability and assessment at university. This should not be a surprise, since your studies are intended to prepare you for employment, of course.

6 GENERAL PRINCIPLES OF ASSESSMENT AT UNIVERSITY

Measure what you value instead of valuing only what you measure. (Andy Hargreaves)

CHAPTER STRUCTURE

Figure 6.1

When you see the this means go to the companion website https://study.sagepub.com/morgan2e to do a quiz, complete a task, read further or download a template.

━━ AIMS OF THE CHAPTER ━━

By the end of this chapter, you should be able to:

- Understand some of the assessment methods and criteria used by academics in universities.
- Get a broad insight into what to do – and what not to do – in order to do well in your studies on a variety of forms of assessment.
- Ensure that you avoid any allegations of academic misconduct (commonly known as 'plagiarism') in your work.
- Develop your thinking regarding the criteria for 'good' assessed work.

WHEN SHOULD YOU READ THIS CHAPTER?

This chapter gives you an overview into general principles of assessment at university, and so it is best to read this before you start to prepare your first piece of assessed university work.

INTRODUCTION

This chapter will analyse the requirements that lecturers will have for different forms of assessment, examine some of the key issues when completing group-based assessment, and present some detailed thinking about 'academic misconduct' (or what is more commonly called 'cheating') in assessment, along with some ideas on how to avoid this and how to ensure that citations, quotations and bibliographies can assist.

Whatever forms of assessment are used on your courses, they should all help to assess the criteria referred to in Chapter 4 on critical thinking. Of course, some methods of assessment will seem more amenable to you than others: some people prefer examinations to coursework, others prefer group work to individual work, and so on. But whichever form(s) of assessment are used, most will seem stressful and challenging in some way.

We will begin by giving you the opportunity to identify how much you know about assessment at university and then discuss the nature of what academics call formative and summative assessment.

SKILLS SELF-ASSESSMENT

Complete the brief questionnaire below to see how much you know about assessment at university. Read carefully each of the following descriptions and say how typical you think each statement is of your behaviour or attitude by giving it a score between 1 and 5, where 1 is 'strongly disagree' and 5 is 'strongly agree'. Answer each item quickly. There are right and wrong answers to *some of these items*, so be sure to compare your answers with those on the companion website.

Item	Statement	Score	
1.	I know how my modules are going to be assessed		
2.	Assessment at my university is going to be stressful		
3.	If I remember what my lecturers have told me in lectures, then I should be OK when I have to do exams		
4.	The more content I put into an examination essay, the higher the mark I will receive		
5.	Multiple choice questions are easy, compared with essay answers		
6.	I can use ideas from anyone else (including other students) in my work		
7.	I understand very clearly what is meant by a bibliography		
8.	I can use quotations from other people in my work		
9.	I must use at least 20 citations in my coursework		
10.	If I do well in one year of study, then I should do well in every year of study because the standards don't change		
11.	If I do well in one module, then I should do well in every module because the standards don't change		
12.	Essays and presentations are harder to do than examinations		
13.	In an examination, I won't have to refer to theory		
14.	I must have a good memory if I am going to do well in my modules		
15.	I would never cheat in an assignment		

Item	Statement	Score
16.	Plagiarism is something which only affects coursework assignments	
17.	I'm not allowed to put others' words into my assignments or examinations	
18.	I will only get one form of assessment in each of my modules	
19.	I expect that students who put less effort into their coursework will receive a lower mark	
20.	The amount of effort I put into a piece of work will relate directly to the mark I receive	

There will be some slight variation across universities, but in most aspects of assessment the regulations and practice will be very similar, so remember to check your answers against those available on the companion website via the interactive version of this test at https://study.sagepub.com/morgan2e.

INTERACTIVE TEST

THE GENERAL NATURE OF ASSESSMENT

There are two forms of assessment: formative and summative. There is some difference in how these two terms are used across different international systems, but, broadly speaking, in the UK, formative assessment refers to any form of work that you give to your lecturer that does not count towards your degree, while summative assessment refers to any work that you do that does count towards your degree.

Formative assessment is an input into the learning process and takes place whenever you accept the comments that a lecturer gives you in class, in a one-to-one discussion or in an email. It is spontaneous, rarely written down and involves getting feedback in any way, prior to submitting work which is part of a module assessment. As such it is invaluable, and formative feedback on your work and ideas is one of the most powerful sources of information for your learning that you will find during your time as a student.

Summative assessment is an outcome of the learning process. In other words, submitting a piece of work for a mark or a grade is intended – from your perspective as a student – to show your lecturers what you have learned and what you are able to do with what you have learned. From the lecturer's perspective, such work is required from you in order for them to ensure that you have achieved the 'outcomes' of the module (i.e. that you have learned what they intended you to learn through all the learning opportunities covered in Chapter 5) or at least to assess the extent to which you have done so.

Most of this chapter deals with summative assessment; formative assessment was covered in the section on feedback in the previous chapter.

FORMATIVE AND SUMMATIVE ASSESSMENT OF LEARNING

Formative assessment of learning:
This takes place when you receive some comment on your thinking or on some work that you submit that contributes solely to your own personal learning.

Summative assessment of learning:
This occurs when you submit work as part of the requirements for your modules and degree programme.

DIFFERENT TYPES OF ASSESSMENT

Assessment can take many forms. The ones we might commonly think of include essay or calculation-based examinations, assignments which ask you to analyse a particular situation faced by a company (case study) or to answer an essay question around a particular theory, but this is not an exhaustive list and some lecturers will use other forms of assessment.

Multiple Choice Questions (MCQs): These can seem very easy and straightforward to complete. However, your lecturers usually take some time to construct questions which can challenge not just your understanding, but your ability to analyse the application of information. Some MCQs carry negative marking – where incorrect answers can affect the score obtained – and these ensure that answers are more than guesses.

Presentations: Presentations are used to assess your ability to do something which you will need to do in the workplace: communicate a message orally. We will look at presentations in detail in Chapter 10.

Research into company practice: You may be asked to interview a business leader or find out what an organisation is really doing around a particular issue covered in one of your modules. This is good for the development of your research skills, but will also give you an idea of what is really happening in companies that you may or may not be familiar with.

Organising an event: Some practical modules or those around project or event planning topics might ask you to organise an event for a particular purpose. You would need to show how you can plan and communicate effectively with others, including professionals from the business world, and maybe to lead a team. Such assessment is very powerful when it comes to giving examples of the skills you have demonstrated in an interview, rather than simply possessing academic knowledge.

Developing a practical project: There are modules that ask you to make something – e.g. a video or a poster – and these will be assessed in the usual way. Again, practical assessments reflect activities that might be undertaken in the professional workplace.

Class participation: In some universities, your assessment might include an element of the extent to which you participate in class. This is designed to increase your ability to think on your feet and to communicate (maybe in a language which is not your own) and to build your confidence. The classroom should be a place for you to test your thinking and to understand whether your understanding of the course material is the same as that of the lecturer, and the best way to do that is to speak up in class.

Whatever the nature of the summative assessment, your work will be assessed according to the criteria listed in your course materials, and you should be able to get feedback on your work.

 — KEY LEARNING POINT ━━━━━━━━━━━━━

There are various forms of assessment, but whatever form your assessment might take, understanding the criteria being used for your assessment and applying that understanding to your work is essential for doing well at university.

WHAT DO LECTURERS LOOK FOR IN ASSESSED WORK?

Developing an understanding of what your lecturers look for is one of the most important things you will do as a student. Ultimately, there is absolutely nothing better than asking your lecturer directly and getting some detail from them, but your tutor will almost certainly have made some information about this available to you already, so please check it before asking. Busy academics can get quite frustrated by requests to provide information that they have already provided in some other way. It is helpful to give some general guidelines, firstly, relating to quantitative subjects and, secondly, relating to more discursive subjects such as marketing or HRM.

Quantitative or numerical subjects will traditionally be assessed on the basis of calculations, but it is rarely the case that the right answer will get all the marks. More usually, the marks will be given on the basis of both the answer and the working out. Put simply, this is because lecturers will not simply want to know your conclusion, but rather how you got there. In some ways, this is actually little different from the expectations of those who teach more discursive and 'essay-based' subjects, where the quality of the discussion is as important as the conclusion. Figure 6.2 shows how this works.

In the figure, there are two axes: 'Content' and 'Argument'. Content is self-explanatory, but when lecturers refer to argument, they are referring to the way in which content has been examined using your critical thinking skills – and while we covered that in some detail in Chapter 4, it is a good idea to give some examples of what that looks like in an essay, so read the section below on 'Blooms Taxonomy'. Including a lot of content without any signs of thinking about that content is no different from simply giving back to the lecturer everything they have told you. You also risk including content that is irrelevant. Similarly, giving a strong argument about only one part of the content that a tutor will expect you to cover is also insufficient, so there needs to be both.

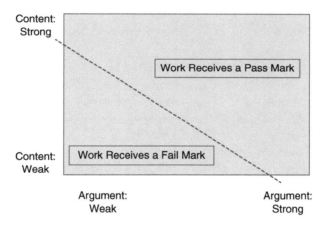

Figure 6.2   What do your lecturers look for in assessed work?

The dashed line across the diagram indicates a theoretical 'pass-mark line': too far below this line and you may be in danger of failing your module; the further you are above the line, the more chance you have of passing.

There are two important issues here:

1. The line might be steep for some pieces of work and gently sloping for other pieces of work (which is why talking to the lecturer is extremely useful).
2. The line might shift left or right depending on which year of study the module is designed for. The expectations of students on a module in the first year will usually be easier when compared with those in the final year, and producing work of identical quality in both years of study will sometimes result in the mark in the final year being lower.

The two axes tend to represent the way that many lecturers will assess work, especially work of a discursive nature.

Whatever the nature of the work, there is considerable overlap between the criteria used for assessing essays and those used for other forms of assessment (e.g. presentations and examinations). We will cover some of these issues in Chapter 7 (assignments and reports), Chapter 8 (examinations) and Chapter 10 (presentations) for the assessment methods noted below, but the commonalities and differences are given here in Table 6.1.

Table 6.1   Overlap and differences in expectations for different methods of assessment

Criterion	Essays	Presentations	Examination assessment
Demonstration of critical thinking skills	Yes, needed	Yes, needed	Yes, needed
Relevance	Yes, needed	Yes, needed	Yes, needed
Use of examples	Yes, needed	Yes, needed	Yes, needed
Support provided by citations and theory	Yes, needed	Yes, needed	If possible, yes
Grammar and spelling	Yes, needed	On slides, definitely. In oral delivery, yes, needed	Yes, though not the most important criterion
Structure	Yes, needed	Yes, needed	Yes, needed
Taking account of the audience	Yes, needed	Yes, definitely!	Yes, though while this is not the most important criterion, doing so may waste time on more important issues to be covered
Academic style	Yes, needed	Yes, to some extent	Yes, to some extent
Good memory	Not really needed	Yes, needed for coherent delivery	Yes, needed
Oral delivery skills	Not really needed	Yes, definitely!	Not needed at all
Delivering work in response to unseen questions	Not really needed	Not usually	Yes, needed
Avoiding plagiarism	Yes, needed	Yes, needed	Yes, though not really an issue in most unseen examinations

This overlap, of course, is not unexpected: if universities are expected to produce critical thinkers who learn independently, then all assessment methods should go some way to producing and assessing those qualities.

Most courses will include a criteria sheet or clear information explaining exactly what your work will be assessed on – see the course handbook or online materials for your module to see what these criteria would be. It is likely that they are going to be something similar to the above list, but there may be some explanation of how the work relates to the criteria set. One point to note here is that not all criteria are weighted equally so the feedback sheet will require some interpretation.

━━━━━ **BOX 6.1** ━━━━━

What Do Your Lecturers Think About When Marking Work?

The reality is almost certainly that very few people like being assessed. It implies judgement, criticism and evaluation of some kind. Maybe we do not always realise it, but often we can think of our work as an extension of who we are, and believe that the effort we put in should relate to what we get back out. Therefore, when someone assesses your work, you might think that they are evaluating you as a person, but this is not what goes through the mind of a lecturer or professor when they assess your work. They will not be making a judgement about who you are, but just about that piece of work.

When a lecturer assesses your work, they will be looking for examples of your thinking, seeking certain content and components and ideas that will make your thinking clear, and comparing that with the way that they operationalise the critical thinking skills covered in Chapter 4. Depending on how many students are in your class, they may or may not have a great deal of time to give you feedback; and depending on whether they know who it is that has written the assignment, the feedback might be tailored to you, or not.

Lecturers love to mark good work. Lecturers are also human beings who sometimes get emotional about what they read. If they know that the student who has written a poor piece of work can do much better, then it is as disappointing for the lecturer to read and assess that piece of work. Equally, it is surprising for them to read a fantastic piece of work from a student whose classroom contributions have been few or poor. One of the best compliments that you can get from a lecturer is, 'Oh, I hadn't thought about that!', so your task is to show that you understand the content you need to understand and can think about it with insight, critical thinking and clarity.

=== KEY LEARNING POINT

The best source of information about what your lecturers are looking for are the lecturers themselves. They are the best placed individuals to explain how they will expect you to demonstrate what they are looking for.

CRITICAL THINKING IN YOUR ACADEMIC WORK: BLOOM'S TAXONOMY

The first item in Table 6.1 above is critical thinking. It is helpful to see what this really looks like, and to give a framework to reflect the marks that critical thinking might help you to obtain.

Most – if not all – of your lecturers will have been trained to think critically (or insightfully). Some of that training will have occurred during their own university education, either as part of their PhD training or before, and some will have developed the skills needed as part of writing their own research papers for academic journals. We will look at the development of these skills, but however your lecturers have developed these skills, they will be expecting you to demonstrate the skills as well – and will be marking your work against them.

Perhaps the most often cited work on critical thinking was developed by Benjamin Bloom and colleagues, and is known by lecturers as 'Bloom's taxonomy' (Bloom et al., 1956). The framework has been used for educational training for many years, and outlines a hierarchy of qualities (nouns) outlining different levels of thinking. At one end, an insightful piece of work would be expected to show some evaluation – whereby the thinker would be able to evaluate the knowledge they had been exposed to – and at the other end, the work would simply be a description of that knowledge. The model was updated by Anderson and Krathwohl (2001) – both of whom worked with Benjamin Bloom – to 1) refer to verbs rather than nouns, and 2) to recognise that there are different forms of knowledge processed in different ways across the framework. The important issue is not so much that there are different forms of knowledge, but that we interact with those forms in different ways across the taxonomy.

The original and updated hierarchical views are represented in Figure 6.3.

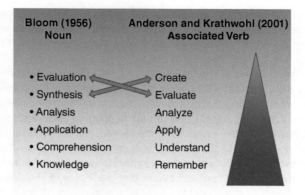

Figure 6.3 Bloom's taxonomy of academic skills, including 2001 revisions

The essential thinking here is that students who demonstrate the skills at the lower end of the hierarchy will tend to do poorly in their assignments.

For example, reproducing knowledge does not require a high level of skill or any understanding of what is being presented, it simply requires a good memory. At the other end of the scale, it is impossible to evaluate ideas unless you can understand them.

There is some appreciation of the value of the model, though there is some discussion as to whether analysis, synthesis and evaluation are quite as hierarchical as has been suggested (Anderson and Krathwohl, 2001). This latter point will be explored below, but the pyramid given in Figure 6.3 implies that fewer students will be receiving marks at the higher end of the hierarchy and, broadly speaking, this does reflect the smaller number of students who typically graduate with a first-class honours degree.

'BUT I HAVE A QUESTION ...'

... Does that mean that if we demonstrate the higher levels of skill, then we will do well in our work? Or is length of work important as well?

Actually, length is no guarantee of any academic success. Your tutors may have marked essays that are one page long and have passed – admittedly only a slight pass – but perhaps also marked essays six sides long and which basically said the same thing over and over again, and received a fail mark. Having said that, an essay which is too short will usually contain insufficient detail and comment to do well. So, while length is not directly assessed, it does play a part.

The language we use plays a part and we have to get the content right, of course. But critical thinking skills are more important than content. In fact, if you reproduce in your essay all the relevant content from your lecture *and* your reading, then perhaps the maximum you can expect will be around the 50% mark in many places. It is evidence of the critical thinking which then lifts that 50% to a higher mark – and the amount and depth/level of that thinking which takes it beyond 60%.

An Example of Applied Critical Thinking

Your academic tutors will usually provide you with details of what they will be assessing, but within that list is likely to be something involving critical thinking. Below, there is a description of the different levels of Bloom's model followed by an example of how that might be demonstrated in an essay on a well-known theory of motivation devised by Abraham Maslow (1943). If you are not familiar with Maslow's Hierarchy of Needs, then a simple internet search will take you to a basic introduction of the model. A practical word of caution about the essay below. Portions of the essay have been written with just one purpose in mind: to give you, as a student, an illustration of what the different skills look like when written in an essay. The essay title is: **'To what extent does Maslow's theory of human needs explain individuals' motivation?'**

Whenever you see an essay entitled 'To what extent …', the expected answer is likely to be 'In some ways … because (and present the evidence) … But in other ways, the theory does not … (and present the evidence)'. The information contained in the essay is partially made up – that is, in parts, the content is not true or accurate. Due to this inaccurate content, do *not* reproduce any of what is written below in any essay you write.

Level 1: Knowledge/Remember

The first level of Bloom's taxonomy is demonstrated by reproducing knowledge. There are some cultures and environments where the reproduction of knowledge is what defines educational success (and which might include certain results for pre-university exams), but that is not what will help you get good marks at university. The reproduction of knowledge simply takes a good memory – you do not even have to understand what you are talking about in an essay to show 'knowledge'.

So, in Box 6.2 is a portion of an essay which shows just basic knowledge.

============ BOX 6.2 ============

Maslow's Theory of Needs – Knowledge/Remember

'To what extent does Maslow's theory of human needs explain individuals' motivation?'

Maslow (1943) developed a theory about human motivation following research done in the United States. His theory – known as the Hierarchy of Needs – gives a number of hierarchical levels to explain motivation. This essay will outline those needs and will show how his model helps to explain why people want to do what they want to do.

Firstly, there are physiological needs, for example food and drink and physical health. Secondly, there is safety and security, but Maslow said we are only motivated to fulfil all our safety needs when we have fulfilled our physiological ones. Thirdly, there is a sense of belonging with other people. Fourthly, we have esteem needs and then, finally, we are motivated to achieve our self-actualisation needs.

Typically, lecturers at university level will rarely expect you solely to demonstrate your ability to remember or reproduce knowledge; the exceptions might be some or all of your first-year modules. Questions at this level tend to be in the form 'Who did this?' or 'List the main factors …' Often, demonstrating solely the recall of knowledge might enable a student to receive a maximum percentage in the mid-40s to low 50s when it comes to grades.

Level 2: Comprehension/Understand

The second hierarchical level relates to an ability to explain something to another person, in other words to understand the ideas. There is a fairly clear hierarchical link here with level 1: it is impossible to explain something unless you know what you are explaining.

The relevant portion of the Maslow essay might go something like that shown in Box 6.3. The additional content showing understanding has been put into bold text.

================= BOX 6.3 =================

Maslow's Theory of Needs – Understanding

'To what extent does Maslow's theory of human needs explain individuals' motivation?'

Maslow (1943) developed a theory about human motivation following research done in the United States. His theory – known as the Hierarchy of Needs – gives a number of hierarchical levels to explain motivation. This essay will outline those needs and will show how his model helps to explain why people want to do what they want to do.

The basic concept that Maslow had was to indicate that in order to reach the next level of motivation, the previous level would need to be satisfied.

The first level relates to physiological needs. These are needs of food and drink and physical health **as well as sex and sleep. They are put at the bottom of the hierarchy because everyone will want to have these needs met**. The second level relates to safety and security – **which means we are secure in our situation,** but we are only motivated to fulfil all our safety needs when we have fulfilled our physiological ones. [Continued ...].

(The remainder of the essay would be changed in a similar way.)

There is some explanation here, and the student has clearly understood something of what they have been taught. Questions at this level will ask students to explain an idea or summarise a theory. Again, marks will not necessarily be particularly high at university simply for understanding the ideas, nor will these questions usually be used on their own for courses much beyond first-year degree studies, but marks will typically be higher than for students who merely reproduce what they have been given.

Level 3: Application/Apply

If you know what you are writing about and are sure that you have understood the main ideas, then the next step is to do what your lecturers do during classes. That is, provide and use examples to show that not only do you have a solid understanding of the concepts and ideas covered, but also you can provide examples of their working. Box 6.4 takes us back to the Maslow essay. Again, additional content demonstrating 'Application' is in bold text.

================= BOX 6.4 =================

Maslow's Theory of Needs – Application

'To what extent does Maslow's theory of human needs explain individuals' motivation?'

Maslow (1943) developed a theory about human motivation following research done in the United States. His theory – known as the Hierarchy of Needs – gives a number of hierarchical levels to explain motivation. This essay will outline those needs and will show how his model helps to explain why people want to do what they want to do.

The basic concept that Maslow had was to indicate that in order to reach the next level of motivation, the previous level would need to be satisfied. **Some examples are given below.**

The first level relates to physiological needs. These are needs of food and drink and physical health as well as sex and sleep, **so, for example, when someone is struggling to find food, they will look hard for it.** The second level relates to safety and security – which means we are secure in our situation, but we are only motivated to fulfil all our safety needs when we have fulfilled our physiological ones, **so, for example, someone will search for a safe place to live, once they are sure they have enough food to eat. Workers at Foxconn are strongly motivated by this, according to Purcell (2001).** [Continued ...].

(The remainder of the essay would be changed in a similar way.)

You can see that most of the additional content here relates to examples, which is essentially what we mean by application: you demonstrate your ability to apply your understanding (i.e. knowledge + understanding) by providing examples of how the ideas work in practice.

It is worth noting that the Maslow essay is getting longer as we put more information into it, but the information we have added has not mentioned any new theories, it has simply applied Maslow's ideas to workplace practice. If we kept the length the same and just added more theories, then the depth would suffer and each extra sentence would give us diminishing returns.

The marks given to an essay demonstrating 'Application' in many institutions may reach the mid-60s and questions expecting the demonstration of 'application skills' would often be found for assignments across all three or four years of a degree.

Level 4: Analysis/Analyse

As indicated earlier (see page 126) in relation to 'Analysis' and the remaining two 'higher level skills', there is some debate as to whether they are seen as hierarchical or equal (in terms of cognitive or thinking skills). In any event, we are talking about three different kinds of skills. Analysis asks the question, 'Why do things happen as they do?'

==================== 'BUT I HAVE A QUESTION ...' ====================

... You mean that analysis is all about asking 'why'? For example, why do leaders sometimes have success and at other times, don't?

Yes, that's exactly what analysis is. Asking why means that we have to have a pretty decent understanding of how the ideas work. You can't ask 'why' until you know the 'how'.

If we start to ask questions about why things work the way they do (and children can sometimes be very good at asking those kinds of questions!), then we can start to consider what might happen if we change things and see if we can do things a little more creatively. This goes beyond 'Analysis' and starts getting us into skills of synthesis. Box 6.5 gives a portion of the essay on Maslow's Theory of Motivation.

━━━━━━━━ ■ BOX 6.5 ■ ━━━━━━━━

Maslow's Theory of Needs – Analysis

'To what extent does Maslow's theory of human needs explain individuals' motivation?'

Maslow (1943) developed a theory about human motivation following research done in the United States. His theory – known as the Hierarchy of Needs – gives a number of hierarchical levels to explain motivation. This essay will outline those needs and will show how his model helps to explain why people want to do what they want to do.

The basic concept that Maslow had was to indicate that in order to reach the next level of motivation, the previous level would need to be satisfied. Some examples are given below.

The first level relates to physiological needs. These are needs of food and drink and physical health as well as sex and sleep, so, for example, when someone is struggling to find food, they will look hard for it. **This level was seen by Maslow as the most basic because without such biological needs being fulfilled, there would be no individual to motivate anyway (Johnson, 2003).** The second level relates to safety and security – which means we are secure in our situation, but we are only motivated to fulfil all our safety needs when we have fulfilled our physiological ones, so, for example, someone will search for a safe place to live, once they are sure they have enough food to eat. Workers at Foxconn are strongly motivated by this, according to Purcell (2001). **This is because a feeling of contentment and personal security is seen by most employees at work as being less important than the search for food, or need for sleep or drink, etc. (McKenna, 2002).** [Continued ...].

(The remainder of the essay would be changed in a similar way.)

─────────────────────────────────

The emboldened sections of the text above represent answers to the question, 'Why is this important?' or 'Why does something work in this way?' and that is at the core of this skill we call 'Analysis'.

I hope that you can see the differences in this essay as we start to show higher levels of thinking about the ideas, rather than simply reproducing them. Work demonstrating such skills could receive marks in the low to high 60s, depending on whether the relevant content was there, whether the citations were accurately done and whether the structure was clear and made sense.

Level 5: Evaluation/Evaluate

In an academic context, 'to evaluate' means 'to identify whether arguments, facts and information are true, untrue or unclear', and this is seen as one of the most important – if not the most important – skill to demonstrate.

Whether or not this item is equal in standing to those of synthesis and analysis, the original hierarchy had this at the top and it was thus seen as the most worthwhile skill to demonstrate. It is at this level that we demonstrate the ability to comment on the research work that others have done and identify areas of argument that others might have missed. To do so takes an insightful mind which has a deep understanding of the issues and has spent time thinking about what the research evidence really says. That is why students who demonstrate this skill are seen as 'first-class' students. The task is clear: to know and identify why certain research says one thing and similar pieces of research carried out in other situations come to different conclusions. The realisation of this, however, is not so easy.

Let's go back to the Maslow essay again to see what this looks like in practice (Box 6.6).

SAGE Publications, Ltd.

1 Oliver's Yard

55 City Road

London, EC1Y 1SP

VAT Registration Number GB 232 6001 16

Telephone: +44 (0) 20 7324 8500

Fax: +44 (0) 20 7324 8600

E-Mail: uk.customerservices@sagepub.co.uk

Website: www.sagepub.co.uk

Company Registration 01017514

UK VAT Registration GB 232 6001 16

⑨ SAGE | CORWIN | ▦ CQPRESS

Invoice

Bill to: **VAT Number:**

1000730944

CRM-Greenwich University

Park Row

London SE10 9LS

Customer:

1000730944

Mazia Yassim

56 Beresford Road

Cheam SM2 6ER

Page Number: 1

Invoice Date	Invoice Number	Customer Reference	Account Number	Due Date
22-DEC-20	715309HN	ORD-1451039-T0G0S6	1000730944	21-JAN-21

Description	Customer Reference	Qty Ord / Supp	Unit Price	Discount %	Line Total
	The following item(s) are supplied free of charge				
Eus Students Guide Study Empl 2E	ORD-1451039-T0G0S6	1/1	36.99		
9781526493378	Tariff Code 49019900				

Tax Breakdown

Classification	Taxable Amount	Tax Rate	Tax Amount	Tax Amount (Local Currency)

Subtotal	
Shipping & Handling	
Tax	
Payments	
Total	

Remittance Advices Email: remits@sagepub.co.uk

Invoice #:
Customer Name:

Account #:
Total Due:

Payment Methods:

Cheque: Cheque # _____ made payable to SAGE Publications, Ltd. in the amount of £ _____

Direct Bank Credit Transfer:
National Westminster Bank Plc
1 Cavendish Square, London W1A 4NU

For GBP Payments
Account #: 24815837
Sort Code: 60-40-02

IBAN #: GB46NWBK60400224815837
BIC Swift Code: NWBKGB2L

Credit Card: [ ] Visa   [ ] MasterCard   [ ] American Express

Name on card: _____

Card #: _____

Valid from Date: _____   Exp Date: _____

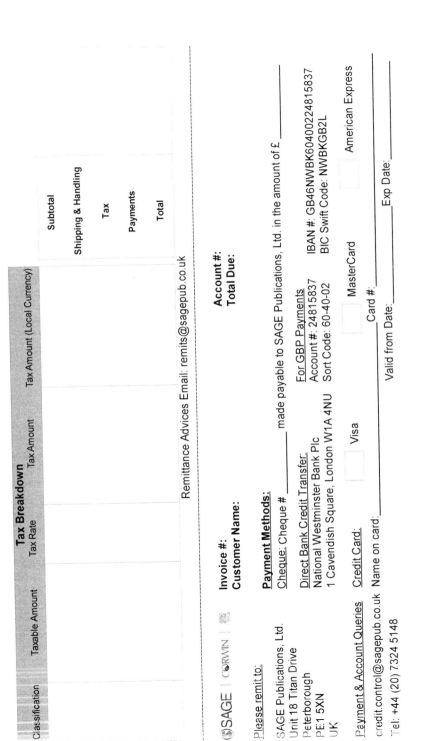

⊕SAGE | CORWIN

Please remit to:

SAGE Publications, Ltd.
Unit 18 Titan Drive
Peterborough
PE1 5XN
UK

Payment & Account Queries
credit.control@sagepub.co.uk
Tel: +44 (20) 7324 5148

━━━━━ BOX 6.6 ━━━━━

Maslow's Theory of Needs - Evaluation

'To what extent does Maslow's theory of human needs explain individuals' motivation?'

Maslow (1943) developed a theory about human motivation following research done in the United States. His theory – known as the Hierarchy of Needs - gives a number of hierarchical levels to explain motivation. This essay will outline those needs and will show how his model helps to explain why people want to do what they want to do.

The basic concept that Maslow had was to indicate that in order to reach the next level of motivation, the previous level would need to be satisfied. Some examples are given below.

The first level relates to physiological needs. These are needs of food and drink and physical health as well as sex and sleep, so, for example, when someone is struggling to find food, they will look hard for it. This level was seen by Maslow as the most basic because without such biological needs being fulfilled, there would be no individual to motivate anyway (Johnson, 2003). **It could be possible that certain physiological needs may be more important at different times as some individuals seem to be able to need less sleep than others, of course, and some may wish to abstain from fulfilling certain physiological needs from time to time (e.g. Ramadan).**

The second level relates to safety and security – which means we are secure in our situation, but, according to Maslow, we are only motivated to fulfil all our safety needs when we have fulfilled our physiological ones, so, for example, someone will search for a safe place to live, once they are sure they have enough food to eat. Workers at Foxconn are strongly motivated by this, according to Purcell (2001). This is because a feeling of contentment and personal security is seen by most employees at work as being less important than the search for food, or need for sleep or drink etc. (McKenna, 2002). **The value of such ideas is enhanced by recognising that findings from Herzberg, Mausner and Mandan (1982) include some similar ideas. Of course, there has been criticism of Herzberg's model in the same way that there has been criticism of Maslow's ideas, but the fact that safety – and even the naming by Herzberg of such ideas as 'hygiene' factors – goes some way to showing that such factors do indeed have an impact on motivation. It is possible to then argue that organisational cultures which seem to place less emphasis on safety might be seen as struggling to motivate their employees.**

Of course, cross-cultural research into collectivism (Nywatt, 1976) casts some doubt over the extent to which Maslow's findings regarding the first two layers of the hierarchy can be seen as valid. There are some concerns about the extent to which his research was separated from the time and place where the research has been done. Such research suggests, for example, that in certain collectivist societies, the needs of the country might come before the needs of any one particular individual (Thompson, 2008). Certain professions (e.g. army, fire) clearly ask individuals to put themselves into potentially dangerous situations, so while Maslow's ideas seem to have some relevance in certain places, there are times and situations where other factors seem to be at work. [Continued …].

(The remainder of the essay would be changed in a similar way.)

We can see here that the additional text presents some insightful and detailed comments which assist us to evaluate whether Maslow's ideas have some validity. Evaluation is – as is noted above – a complex and high-level skill, requiring a detailed understanding of the literature on a particular subject. That is why those demonstrating this skill get very high marks.

Level 6: Synthesis/Create

We will keep the idea of a hierarchy – and the 1956 hierarchy of skill – for the moment as we examine the final skill, namely that of synthesis. The verb attached to this skill is called 'create', so it may seem a little strange that the skill is not called 'creativity'. Hopefully you will understand why after reading this section.

'Synthesis' is the ability to understand how one topic that is studied in a module fits into a much larger picture and, by doing so, you demonstrate that you understand not only how this one topic works and why it works as it does, but also how it influences and is influenced by other issues. From an HRM or organisational behaviour viewpoint, we might look at human behaviour and motivation but then seek to understand how these issues are affected by organisational culture and structure as well as by other factors which might have been studied throughout the course.

The reason why 'create' is there as the associated verb is that once we can see relationships between ideas and why things happen as they do, then we can see what happens when such relationships between business practices, for example, change; it is through this kind of analysis that we can then start to be much more creative. There are many ways of representing such relationships when you are preparing for assignments or trying to solve organisational issues, the most obvious (for note-taking purposes) being the mind-map, where central themes are separated out into smaller and smaller ideas. In management development, however, some trainers use practical tools such as Lego® to enable participants to represent physically how their organisation is structured and functions (see Chapter 14, on creativity and problem solving).

Let's add some synthesis to our essay on Maslow (Box 6.7).

■ BOX 6.7 ■

Maslow's Theory of Needs – Synthesis

'To what extent does Maslow's theory of human needs explain individuals' motivation?'

Maslow (1943) developed a theory about human motivation following research done in the United States. His theory – known as the Hierarchy of Needs – gives a number of hierarchical levels to explain motivation. This essay will outline those needs and will show how his model helps to explain why people want to do what they want to do.

The basic concept that Maslow had was to indicate that in order to reach the next level of motivation, the previous level would need to be satisfied. Some examples are given below.

The first level relates to physiological needs. These are needs of food and drink and physical health as well as sex and sleep, so, for example, when someone is struggling to find food, they will look hard for it. This level was seen by Maslow as the most basic because without such biological needs being fulfilled, there would be no individual to motivate anyway (Johnson, 2003). It could be possible that certain physiological needs may be more important at different times as some individuals seem to need less sleep than others, of course, and some may wish to abstain from fulfilling certain physiological needs from time to time (e.g. Ramadan).

The second level relates to safety and security – which means we are secure in our situation, but, according to Maslow, we are only motivated to fulfil all our safety needs when we have fulfilled our physiological ones, so, for example, someone will search for a safe place to live, once they are sure they have enough food to eat. Workers at Foxconn are strongly motivated by this, according to Purcell (2001). This is because a feeling of contentment and personal security is seen by most employees at work as being less important than the search for food, or need for sleep or drink etc. (McKenna, 2002).

The importance or nature of this need may vary in the same way that physiological needs may vary: job security may be seen as irrelevant to someone whose need for a place to stay is as much of an

issue. It is also possible that individuals may feel content in certain aspects of their lives (e.g. at home) but insecure in other situations (e.g. at work): in such a situation, the individual might seek another job, perhaps, but this issue also applies to the third need – that of belonging.

The value of such ideas is enhanced by recognising that findings from Herzberg, Mausner and Mandan (1982) include some similar ideas. The fact that safety is included in Herzberg's model – and even the naming by Herzberg of such ideas as 'hygiene' factors – goes some way to showing that such factors do indeed have an impact on motivation. It is possible to then argue that organisational cultures which seem to place less emphasis on safety might be seen as struggling to motivate their employees. [Continued ...].

(The remainder of the essay would be changed in a similar way.)

You can see here how the ideas have been developed and how additional concepts have now been brought into the debate. An additional theory (Herzberg) has been introduced to the reader and has been compared with Maslow's ideas. The question did not ask about this additional theory, but the student writing the answer has gone beyond the ideas of Maslow and has shown how additional theories have relevance.

The second thing that has happened is that additional concepts have been introduced, namely organisational culture and personality theory. The student has shown how these issues also have relevance here and, by doing this, has demonstrated that they have not only a good understanding of the question, but also an ability to understand how additional topics studied throughout the course are also relevant.

This does not mean that a student can talk at length about these additional topics, though. One mistake that students make at examination time is to write about a topic that is only slightly relevant, perhaps because they have studied that particular topic.

If a student demonstrated the ability to synthesise information and wrote well (with good structure, appropriate evidence, good academic style and examples), then marks could well extend into the 70s.

KEY LEARNING POINT

The presentation of relevant content and the demonstration of critical thinking in academic work are crucial to performing well in academic assessment.

REFLECTION POINT

Take some time to think about the following questions and write down some answers.

What evidence will your lecturer look for in your work to determine how deeply you are thinking about the subject?

A mark is never going to be necessarily about the number of references to research you provide, but why is it better to have read a good number of journal articles and research papers?

UNDERSTANDING AND AVOIDING ACADEMIC MISCONDUCT

Attempting to demonstrate the criteria for assessment is vitally important in developing written work – you will not be able get marks without doing so. But there is an issue which becomes more important at university than it might be in other settings, namely 'academic misconduct'. We need to explain more about this here since it has relevance to both written and oral forms of assessment.

Read the information below carefully and in conjunction with other materials you have been given by your own university.

Academic Misconduct and Plagiarism

If you have committed plagiarism, then you have pretended that other people's work is your own, which is why this is considered so serious.

 PLAGIARISM

Plagiarism is the use of other people's work and ideas without any kind of acknowledgement that you have done so.

Plagiarism is not an easy offence to explain technically, but the information in the definition here goes a long way towards explaining what it is and why it is a problem. It is an offence because you are misleading the reader into believing that the content of your essay is yours when it is not, so you receive marks for ideas and work that are not your own. Disciplinary offences like this are usually kept on a student's official record.

Plagiarism can take a number of forms. The list in Box 6.8 is not complete but it does contain the most common forms.

====== BOX 6.8 ======

Forms of Plagiarism

- Copying and pasting any information from the Web without acknowledging that you have done so.
- Getting someone else to write your work (with or without payment) without acknowledging their input.
- Working together with another student and submitting nearly identical work.
- Failing to use quotation marks when you are quoting from someone else's work.
- Copying someone else's assignment from a computer and submitting it as your own.
- Downloading an assignment already available online.

Put simply, *you cannot do anything which falls under the definition of plagiarism.* Universities typically have powers to ask students to leave their courses, to retake modules, to pay fines, to move to a lower qualification, and so on. Finally, committing plagiarism will not increase the respect your lecturers have of you.

FURTHER READING   Your university will have a plagiarism policy. Search on your university website under 'Academic Misconduct' to see what the policy is on the issue.

 ====== FOR YOU TO DO ======

Search on your university website under 'Academic Misconduct' (which you will probably find in a document called the 'Quality Handbook' or something similar) and then answer the following questions:

1. What definition does your university use for the terms 'plagiarism' and/or 'academic misconduct'?
2. Does it give any examples of 'academic misconduct'? If so, do any of those surprise you?
3. From what you can read there, do you believe that your university sees plagiarism as a less important offence than cheating in an examination?

Avoiding Committing Plagiarism

As indicated above, plagiarism is an offence that most universities take very seriously, but there are some simple steps that we can take to ensure that you do not commit this offence. There is evidence to suggest that many accused of academic misconduct indicate that they have not intentionally done anything that they believed was wrong. The challenge is that intention does not usually matter in determining whether someone is found 'guilty' – mainly because it is difficult to prove or disprove intention. But to find out how we can avoid plagiarism, we need to revisit the definition given above: 'Plagiarism is the use of other people's work and ideas without any kind of acknowledgement that you have done so'.

It is important to note the following:

- The definition does not say that you cannot use others' work or ideas as part of your assignment.
- The definition does not say that you cannot source your information from the internet.
- The definition does not say that you have to use your own ideas.

However:

- The definition does say that where you use others' work and ideas, you *must* state that they are other people's work and ideas.

━━━━━━━━━ 'BUT I HAVE A QUESTION ...' ━━━━━━━━━

... Does that mean that I can completely fill my assignment with other people's work as long as I say that the ideas are from their work?

The question here covers the situation where a student finds a really good article or book which answers the question well and then submits the article as their answer, acknowledging it as someone else's work.

Put simply, if you want to receive a zero mark, then go ahead.

There are two issues here. Firstly, a student could do so and would not be committing plagiarism. But if all a student does is submit a piece of work stating throughout that it is from another source, and there is nothing from them in the assignment, then they would get no marks.

This would be because they have added nothing to the work that someone else has done. It is not possible simply to copy and paste or quote from other people throughout your whole assignment and get a good mark because there is basically none of your work or ideas or thinking in the assignment. This is called 'poor academic practice'.

The issue, therefore, is *how we show that we are using someone else's ideas*. Some lecturers are very keen that you do this correctly – and you should. It is also worth noting that universities may have different views on how to represent information from others, but the general conventions are used in most cases.

Citations and Quotations

Expressing others' ideas and work in assignments and essays is normally done in one of two ways:

- Other people's *ideas*, usually expressed in your own words, and acknowledged using what is known as a 'citation'.
- Other people's words, usually expressed in the form of a quotation, with a citation.

We will look at each in turn.

Giving Citations

Citations are used throughout journal articles and most texts will give them as well, indicating that the ideas do not come from the author, but from someone else's work.

 CITATION

A 'citation' is a short note in a piece of text - usually the author and date - indicating that an idea or material comes from someone else.

There are a number of different styles for citations. The most common in business journals is what is known as the 'Harvard style' of referencing (although, in reality, this, too, has a number of forms). However, it is not the only style used in academic writing and you *must* check what expectations your lecturers have in terms of the referencing styles they want you to use.

 KEY LEARNING POINT

You *must* use the citation style requested by your lecturer. You need to check which style is required.

The following citations are taken from a fictional article on student learning. By looking at these, you should be able to deduce the following:

- When you use another person's ideas but do not use their name in your essay, then both surname and year of publication of their idea or theory should be put in brackets separated by a comma: (Watson, 2003). *(Surname, year)*
- When you use someone's name in the main text along with their idea or theory, then you simply put the date of the publication of their idea or their research in brackets after their name: Blade (2002) or Price (2003). *Surname (year of publication)*
- When you refer to ideas or theories that have been developed by a number of individuals, then you give the ideas or theories and then put the names and dates of each author in turn, separating each with a semicolon: (Watson, 2003; Paulson, 2012). *(Surname, year; Surname, year)*

In certain instances in your reading, you may find mention of something with the words 'et al.', for example: (Smith et al., 2004). There is variation in practice from publisher to publisher, but this type of citation refers to an instance where there are several authors and, sometimes, where the full list of authors has already been cited in the text. Second and subsequent mentions of the same piece of work usually just list the first author and then use 'et al.' to indicate 'and others'.

━━━━━ KEY LEARNING POINT ━━━━━

Any information that we have obtained from someone or somewhere else (e.g. websites) needs to be indicated with a citation.

Using Quotations

Different lecturers will have different attitudes as to whether a quotation in an essay is acceptable, but if there is no way to summarise what an author is trying to say other than to quote them precisely, then doing so is often acceptable. However:

1. Keep your quotations short: one sentence is usually seen as the maximum acceptable length.
2. Use them sparingly: this is supposed to be your piece of work, not a collection of quotations.
3. Cite them correctly.

On the third issue, the correct way to provide a citation *for a quotation* under the Harvard system usually takes one of two forms:

- Where the name is given in the text before the quotation:

  o Give the quotation in quotation marks (' and ') so that your lecturer can clearly see where the quotation begins and ends.
  o Then give the citation in brackets at the end of the quotation. The citation should be: (year: page from which the quotation is taken).
  o For example: As stated by Scott (2004), 'These basic issues are key to doing well in academic work' (2004: p. 112).

- Where the name is *not* given in the text before the quotation:

  o Give the quotation in quotation marks (' and ') so that your lecturer can clearly see where the quotation begins and ends.
  o Then give the citation in brackets at the end of the quotation. The citation should be: (surname, year: page from which the quotation is taken).
  o For example: As one researcher has stated, 'These basic issues are key to doing well in academic work' (Scott, 2004: p. 112).

Any writing without quotation marks will be assessed as if it was your own writing and/or your ideas. Therefore, if you are using quotations, then clearly show that they are quotations. If you do not use quotation marks and are copying from someone else's work, then you are likely to be accused of plagiarism.

   There are few better ways of learning this than by following the style used in the best research journals in your discipline.

Bibliographies

We have covered how you refer within the text to a piece of research that someone else has completed, and how you show when you are quoting, but there are two other items you need to think about as well. Imagine that I am reading a journal article, a student's essay or a textbook and I find a reference to something that I would like to follow up and read for myself. How can I find that article? The answer is to look in the bibliography to find details of the piece of work – and every piece of work which references information obtained from another source should have one (including presentations, reflective writing, case studies, etc.).

REFERENCE LIST AND BIBLIOGRAPHY

A reference list is the list of sources cited in the document.

A bibliography is a list of all the sources used in developing a piece of work, regardless of whether they were cited in the text or not.

Your bibliography should include all the sources in alphabetical (and then date) order, according to the surname of the first author of a piece of work.

Compiling a bibliography manually takes some considerable time, which is why we have referred to EndNote in Chapter 5, but it is a hierarchical task and once you understand the order in which the details of your sources are put, it becomes relatively straightforward.

However, just as there are different criteria depending on the lecturer and the university you are studying at, so too there are different styles of referencing – and referencing properly is a lot more complex than saying 'this is how you do it'. Many journals in business will use the style required for academic article submissions to journals published by the American Psychological Association (APA) and in most cases, it is this style that you will need to follow, but you should check the style required by you own lecturers. The information below uses the styles used by the APA. EndNote software can automatically format references to this style, and information on the specifics of the APA reference style can be found widely online (e.g. Purdue Online Writing Lab, 2020). It is a good idea, though, to check with your lecturers as to whether this is the style that they wish to see. Some academic subjects (e.g. law and physical/natural sciences) take a different approach.

BUT I HAVE A QUESTION...

... I have heard something about Turnitin and plagiarism. What is Turnitin?

Turnitin.com is a system for picking up information in assignments that seems to be similar to either webpages or assignments from other students' work submitted through the website (which is usually linked through a module's VLE). In doing so, it can compare your work to any other work submitted around the world to the same system, and so it can be useful for checking whether you have: 1) colluded with another student to submit a similar piece of work when it should be an individual piece of work, or 2) copied material from websites or journal articles online, or 3) other forms of unacceptable behaviour, such as purchasing an essay online or asking a friend to write it. As a system, it can be powerful: your lecturers can link directly to the original articles and can limit the system to check without looking at a bibliography or ignoring correctly cited quotations.

Turnitin is something that your lecturers use to check for similarity, and you might be offered the chance to 'pre-test' your assignments before submitting them, in order to see whether you have included any inappropriate content, but it does need careful interpretation – by both you and your lecturers. The percentage of similarity is just that: 'similarity'. It does not always give conclusive proof of plagiarism, but in certain circumstances can be sufficient to prove a case. If you are able to use a 'pre-test' before submission, you should talk to your tutors about what the resulting report means if the percentage is higher than you expected.

Some universities may give a threshold percentage where anything above that level would be unacceptable and could cause you trouble. You might find this helpful – especially if this information is not given by your lecturers – but it is often difficult to say categorically what percentage is and is not acceptable. Your lecturers will need to make a judgement based on the detail of the Turnitin report.

Formatting Each Reference

As mentioned in Chapter 5, EndNote can format and compile a bibliography automatically, but if you wish to do it manually, then the conventions are given below (the articles are real, so see if you can find them from the information given below).

There is further online content on the companion website at https://study.sagepub.com/morgan2e, which includes information about citing webpages, but in Chapter 4 we noted that websites (including Wikipedia) are perhaps one of the least credible sources of information, so they must not be your main source of information in writing and compiling essays.

FURTHER
READING

Journal Articles

Format: Surname, Initial (year). Title of Article, *Title of Journal*, *volume* (issue number): pages.
For example:
Liang, N. and Lin, S. (2008) 'Erroneous Learning from the West? A Narrative Analysis of Chinese MBA Cases Published in 1992, 1999 and 2003', *Management International Review*, 5 (5): 603–36.

Books

Format: Surname, Initial (year) *Title of Book*. Location (city) of publication: name of publisher.
For example:
Arnold, J., Silvester, J., Patterson, F., Robertson, I., Cooper, C. and Burnes, B. (2005) *Work Psychology: Understanding Human Behaviour in the Workplace*. Harlow: FT/Prentice Hall International.

Chapters in Books

Format: Surname, Initial (year) 'Title of chapter'. 'In' surname of book author, initial of book author ('ed.'), *Title of Book*, page numbers. Location (city) of publication: name of publisher.
For example:
Greenberg, J. and Folger, R. (1983) 'Procedural justice, participation, and the fair process effect in groups and organizations'. In Paulus, P. (ed.), *Basic Group Process* (pp. 235–56). New York: Springer-Verlag.

 **'BUT I HAVE A QUESTION ...'**

... I need to ensure that every single thing is done in such correct detail. I have better things to do with my time, surely?

This is an understandable point of view. The reason for referencing everything so thoroughly is so that readers can be very clear about where and how to find the items being referred to. If you imagine that one article includes several different types of source (e.g. a website, other journal articles, book chapters, books, and so on), then you would be unclear exactly how to find a particular source if one entry in the bibliography was not consistent. Take a journal – any journal – and look at the very back of it. There, the journal will be very clear about the style of referencing it expects from anyone wanting to publish research in it.

Your lecturers will expect the same precision from you that they have to show themselves, regardless of whether you pursue an academic career. Getting your bibliography correct is little different from ensuring you use a reasonable academic style or structure your work appropriately or fulfil any other requirement of your lecturers. It is simply another aspect of writing work at university.

(Continued)

To get access to EndNote, the best thing to do is probably to ask your librarian. They may or may not have the answer directly, but they should almost certainly know who to ask.

Citations and DOI

Most articles now come with a Digital Object Identifier – labelled as 'doi: …'. This enables readers to link straight to the article. The correct way to cite an article that includes a DOI is illustrated in Figure 6.4 below: it features as a link after the main details.

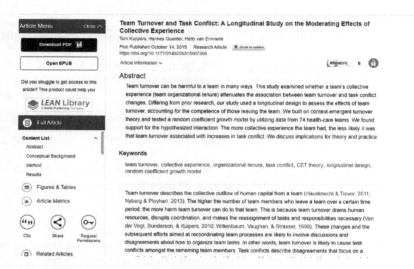

Figure 6.4   Using doi to cite articles correctly under APA referencing conventions

 **FOR YOU TO DO**

There are some useful online resources and quizzes to find out if you really understand plagiarism. Many of them will take you less than five minutes to complete, so you might like to look at one or all of the following:

https://academicintegrity.uoguelph.ca/plagiarism/quiz-plagiarism - plagiarism quiz from the University of Guelph in Ontario.

http://en.writecheck.com/plagiarism-quiz - a very good quiz which gives you feedback and a score for each question as you go along, as well as an interpretation of your score.

www.turnitin.com/static/plagiarism-quiz/ - a quiz from the guys that academics use to indicate plagiarism. This quiz only gives your score after you have completed it and does not give you specific feedback for each question unless you download the answer guide.

https://avoidingplagiarism.uts.edu.au/#quiz - a good 10 question quiz which in many cases, provides you with comparisons between the original texts and how students might cite, paraphrase or summarise that original text.

How did you do? Some of these quizzes indicate whether you are a 'Master' or whether you have a lot still to learn. There are many others, though some refer more to specific university policy than to general principles that apply across institutions.

=== KEY LEARNING POINT ===

Allegations of plagiarism can be avoided by making it clear where others' work and ideas are used by correctly citing them in your essay.

Chapter 7 includes information on how to make it clear when a comment is a personal view. This is often something that students are nervous about doing simply because they are concerned that they will be assumed to be plagiarising. The reality is very different. A student's evaluation of an argument or a piece of research based on the evidence *is exactly what lecturers look for,* so knowing how to do this well is crucial to getting a good mark.

Other Forms of Academic Misconduct

The idea of cheating in your work – examinations, presentations, assignments and so on – appears a silly one when you think that if you don't have the knowledge from your degree that you claim to have, then you will perform poorly in your work. Companies can suffer significant fines where they copy, without permission, ideas and work undertaken by others: international intellectual property law and patents govern permission to use and access others' ideas.

Table 6.2 lists some of the activities which will be considered academic misconduct in most universities.

Table 6.2   Other forms of academic misconduct

Behaviour	Is this academic misconduct?
Sharing your individual assignment with another student who then copies it and submits it as their own. This results in two, almost identical assignments being submitted.	This *is* seen as plagiarism - technically collusion - and may result in both students being investigated for academic misconduct. It is widely understood that students will discuss and share ideas when they are preparing their work, but the assignments must be different. If you use another student's ideas in the work that you submit, then you should acknowledge that. Students should never make their work available to others online.
Purchasing an assignment online.	This is *fraudulent* and will be picked up by the lecturers either through software available to them, or through a discussion with you as a student. It will be penalised heavily.
Copying an assignment that is available online, or from another university.	As with the above, this is not permitted and is easy to track. Assignments translated from foreign languages are also fairly easy to find.
Reading a page from the internet or using a slide from one of your lectures in a different module during an oral presentation.	Most lecturers will be able to pick this up fairly easily. The lecturer will be able to find this themselves without too much trouble.

(Continued)

Table 6.2   (Continued)

Behaviour	Is this academic misconduct?
Taking unauthorised material into an examination.	*Beware*: The issue is not the *use* of any authorised material, it is the *possession* of such material when you are clearly not permitted to have it. That includes written material, mobile phones and other internet-enabled devices. This also applies to notes that should not have been taken into the examination; whether they are used or are relevant is not important. It is the *possession of such notes* that is the offence.
Copying material from the internet, referencing it appropriately, but not adding any personal comment.	This is *not* actually an academic offence, but if there is no work written by the student, then the work will get a zero mark. You cannot get marks by producing no work.

REFLECTION POINT

Take some time to think about the following questions and write down some answers.

How different are issues of plagiarism at university from guidance that you might have had at school or college?

What are the disciplinary processes that your university operates for dealing with instances of plagiarism?

Why do you think plagiarism is taken so seriously?

BOX 6.9

Seeking Help to Do Your Work

You are now clear on what you need to do for your assessment: you have been told that you need to write an essay of 2500 words, analysing the application of a business theory to a real business. You have been given a deadline and have some information about the criteria on which your work will be assessed. So, what do you do next?

You might review your lecture notes to work out what area to look at, start to put down some kind of structure which will form the backbone of your assignment, and get hold of relevant journal articles and books. That would be a logical set of things to do, having already planned out some time to do the work.

But what do you do if you have never done anything like this before? The obvious place to get some help would be from your course or module lecturer: they have probably set the assignment and should be able to give you some clarity and explain the information given in the module materials. But there are other areas of support that can give you a starting point.

Some students seek advice from senior students. This is a risky thing to do: assignments change regularly and – if a senior student gives you their assignment to look at – you *must not* use their work in yours. By giving you their assignment, that student may be committing academic misconduct (it is called 'collusion') since what you then submit would not be your own work. But can you use their advice? Maybe, but the best source of advice would be university staff.

Many universities have a central support service: a series of trained and expert advisors who can help you to start your work, and in many cases, can give you some feedback on what you have done so far.

They are often easier to access than your module lecturers and can give you more support. They will be very familiar with the kinds of issues covered in this book and can support you to complete your work in time. If you are unsure about what you have to do, then make sure you manage your time so that you have time to get that advice, and make appointments early.

Do you know whether your university offers such a service? If so, do you know where it is, what they do, and how to make an appointment?

INTEGRATION AND APPLICATION

Ensuring that you have a good understanding of what you need to do to perform well in your modules is essential to actually translating that understanding into action. This chapter has been about understanding the broad principles underlying academic assessment, so before you start any assessment, it would be worthwhile to answer the following questions:

1. Do I feel confident about what I am being taught? Are there any areas about which I am not clear? Am I seeking clarification of them?
2. Have I done the necessary work to find the relevant examples and research to support the arguments I want to make?
3. Have I taken time to evaluate the strength of those arguments that I want to make in the assignment? Is there evidence to support those points of view?
4. Are there any topics I need to include but have not looked into yet? Are there any arguments I need to make, but where I do not have the appropriate research evidence or examples?
5. Have I cited correctly all the quotations I have used? Have I included page numbers where I needed to within the essay itself? Is everything I have cited included in my bibliography? Is there *anything that I have read and used in my essay* that I have not cited in the essay or included in the bibliography?
6. Do I know how to use EndNote correctly in order to keep a good record of my reading and to produce a bibliography in the appropriate style?

Assuming that you understand and follow the guidance in this and subsequent chapters, you should be ready to produce a good piece of academic work.

CONCLUSION

By now, you should be able to:

- Understand some of the assessment methods and criteria used by academics in universities.
- Get a broad insight into what to do – and what not to do – in order to do well in your studies in a variety of forms of assessment.
- Ensure that you avoid any allegations of academic misconduct (commonly known as plagiarism) in your work.
- Develop your thinking regarding the criteria for 'good' assessed work.

This chapter has covered some of the general principles relating to all forms of assessment. We have looked at the criteria for assessment in academic assessed work and the balance between content and critical thinking skills. Clearly, issues of plagiarism will be more relevant in written essays and dissertations, and issues of cheating will become important during an examination.

More details on specific forms of assessment are given in Chapter 7 on written coursework-based assessment, in Chapter 8 on examinations and revision, and in Chapter 10 on presentation skills.

CHAPTER TASK

The chapter has covered two main areas – the application of critical thinking and academic misconduct.

Find out what your institution defines as academic misconduct when it comes to assignments and examinations. What processes does your institution have to manage such inappropriate behaviour, and what penalties can it apply?

Maybe your university uses Turnitin or something similar as a tool for checking for academic misconduct. When you submit your first coursework assessment (or if you are able to do a test submission before you submit your actual coursework), ask to have a look at your report. What does it show you?

Talk to three of your lecturers about what they expect when they mark written work. Find out what kinds of grades they would give for the different levels in the taxonomy developed by Bloom (Anderson and Krathwohl, 2001) and described here.

INTERVIEW QUESTIONS

In Chapter 5, it was suggested that there would be few interview questions regarding university studies specifically, but that interviewers might ask questions about the topic to find out about your ability to make decisions or think critically – or to find out more about the way you behave or react to certain situations. The same is true for issues around assessment.

Think about the following questions. What might your answers be?

1.   What was the most stressful experience you have had?
2.   Can you give an example of a time when you used feedback to improve your performance?

Chapter 17 contains a lot more information on selection interviews and the online content gives some guidance on these questions.

ADDITIONAL RESOURCES

Want to learn more? Visit https://study.sagepub.com/morgan2e to gain access to a wide range of online resources, including interactive tests, tasks, further reading and downloads.

Website Resources

The following websites offer useful advice on assessment at university.

Aston University: www.aston.ac.uk/current-students/academic-support/ldc/get-ahead/podcasts/assessment-at-university/

Business Balls – information about Bloom's taxonomy: www.businessballs.com/self-awareness/blooms-taxonomy/

University of Reading: www.reading.ac.uk/engageinassessment/peer-and-self-assessment/self-assessment/eia-self-assessment.aspx

Textbook Resources

Bailey, S. (2011) *Academic Writing for International Students of Business*. Abingdon: Routledge (particularly Part 1.8).

Burns, T. and Sinfield, S. (2016) *Essential Study Skills* (4th edition). London: Sage (particularly Chapter 11.4).

Cameron, S. (2016) *The Business Student's Handbook: Skills for Study and Employment* (6th edition). Harlow: Pearson (particularly Chapters 6 and 7).

Courtney, M. and Du, X. (2014) *Study Skills for Chinese Students*. London: Sage (see Chapter 4: 'Assignments, Assessment and Feedback').

Deane, M. (2010) *Academic Research, Writing and Referencing*. Harlow: Pearson.

Fisher, A. (2011) *Critical Thinking: An Introduction* (2nd edition). Cambridge: Cambridge University Press.

Horn, R. (2012) *The Business Skills Handbook*. London: CIPD (particularly Chapters 10 and 11).

Kaye, S. M. (2012) *Critical Thinking*. Oxford: Oneworld.

McMillan, K. and Weyers, J. (2012) *The Study Skills Book* (3rd edition). Harlow: Pearson (particularly Chapters 32, 36 and 45).

McMillan, K. and Weyers, J. (2013) *How to Improve Your Critical Thinking and Reflective Skills*. Harlow: Pearson.

Smale, R. and Fowlie, J. (2009) *How to Succeed at University*. London: Sage (particularly Chapter 7).

Tanna, M. (2011) *Think You Can Think?* London: Oxbridge Applications.

7

WRITING ASSIGNMENTS, REPORTS AND DISSERTATIONS

Either write something worth reading or do something worth writing. (Benjamin Franklin)

CHAPTER STRUCTURE

Figure 7.1

 When you see the 🌐 this means go to the companion website https://study.sagepub.com/morgan2e to do a quiz, complete a task, read further or download a template.

AIMS OF THE CHAPTER

By the end of this chapter, you should be able to:

- Develop your own academic style for writing essays and assignments.
- Understand what your tutor means by the questions they set.
- Evaluate how good your English grammar and spelling are.
- Understand the differences between academic essays and reports.
- Understand clearly how a tutor approaches the assessment for a piece of written work.
- Express the difference between an essay receiving a pass and one receiving a high mark.

INTRODUCTION

Writing an assessed piece of work is arguably one of the most stressful things a student has to do. It is more difficult when trying to complete those pieces under timed conditions without anything to assist you (as is the case of examinations covered in the next chapter), but writing assessed assignments can be stressful in a number of other ways, sometimes because of confusion over what is being sought and sometimes because the demands of the task seem excessive. This chapter seeks to remove some of the mystery and give you some helpful tips in terms of completing the written assignments you need to do.

WHEN SHOULD YOU READ THIS CHAPTER?

This chapter discusses three particular forms of coursework assessment, and so it is best to read this before you start to prepare any reports, essays or dissertations during your degree.

We begin the chapter by giving you the opportunity to see how much you know and to develop your own thinking about your own abilities in terms of written assessment. We will then examine three significant forms of assessment: written essays, reports and dissertations. In addition to content on critical thinking (see Chapter 4) and the general principles of assessment (see Chapter 6), we will spend some time here looking at the specific thinking and criteria used when lecturers assess written essays and the need to find your own academic style. There is also a great deal more on the companion website at https://study.sagepub.com/morgan2e, including information on writing for case study assessment and writing reflectively.

FURTHER READING

As will be clear at the end of this part and in other chapters, there is a great deal of overlap between the criteria for assessment of essay-based assignments and those for examinations, oral presentations and some other forms of assessment. Therefore, the content of this chapter also has relevance to Chapter 10 in the next part of this book.

SKILLS SELF-ASSESSMENT

Read carefully each of the following descriptions and say how typical you think each statement is of your behaviour or attitude by giving it a score between 1 and 5, where 1 is 'strongly disagree' and 5 is 'strongly agree'.

Item	Statement	Score
1.	I prefer writing assignments to presentations or taking exams	
2.	I am used to getting high marks for my written assignments	
3.	I do not need much time to plan my written work; I can develop a structure as I go along	
4.	The most difficult assignment question (i.e. the one worth the highest mark) is probably one which asks me to describe something	
5.	If an assignment question asks me to analyse something, then it is probably the same as asking me to evaluate something	
6.	It is easy to structure essays	
7.	The conclusion to my essays will probably have nearly the same wording as the introduction	
8.	I do not really pay much attention to my spelling and grammar: it is the content that really counts	
9.	If my essay seems too short, I might get penalised for not writing enough	
10.	When I am writing an essay, I am very clear about who my audience is	

(Continued)

(Continued)

Item	Statement	Score
11.	I understand how a report should be structured	
12.	I am clear about the differences between academic essays and reports	
13.	I am clear about requirements for academic written style	
14.	I find it easy to express my own thinking when I am writing an assignment	
15.	I am clear on what makes the difference between pieces of work receiving high and low marks	
16.	I know what a case study is	
17.	I enjoy writing assignments based around case studies	
18.	I think that case studies typically have a clear solution	
19.	I know how to write a good dissertation	
20.	I understand research methodology and can argue for a particular methodology when writing a dissertation	
21.	When I am writing a dissertation, the supervisor is there to help me express myself clearly, and with good spelling and grammar	
22.	Reflective writing means that I simply write down my thoughts	
23.	I really enjoy reflective writing	

The ideas given in the questions above are detailed in the content below.

Some assignments need to be written as pieces of coursework done in groups. When it comes to the assessment of group work, the criteria for assessment are the same as those for individual pieces of work, even if the work has to be longer (which may not always be the case). We will look at group working throughout this chapter, as appropriate, but all the questionnaires and interactive exercises could be done both by an individual and as a basis for group discussion. The main items of focus in this chapter will be essays, reports and dissertations.

WRITING ESSAYS

The methods used to assess students have progressed a great deal over the past 30 years in the UK. Most assessment used to be by examination and then there was a move towards essays, which remains the case in some institutions. However, more recently, assignments have become more personal and practical. For this section, however, we will be dealing with a traditional essay, where you will be expected to examine the theories that you have been taught and to show your critical thinking skills by analysing, applying or evaluating the theories in some way.

 ESSAY

An essay is a piece of writing that applies your critical thinking skills to an area of theory relevant to the course in response to a question set by your lecturer.

It is important to note that everything that relates to essays will also relate to a number of other forms of assessment, including those examinations where you are required to write an essay in order to answer a question, presentations and dissertations. More of a comparison is given in Chapter 6, see Table 6.1.

The Mechanics of Writing Essays

Before we go too far into the discussion of what your tutors look for, it is helpful to provide some guidance on the mechanics of essay writing (i.e. how to go about writing an essay), from a practical point of view. Different people have very different strategies for this, and there is no one definite right way, but there are a number of ideas that people find useful. However, there is one thing to say here: writing your essay the day before the deadline is not going to give you the time you need if you suddenly find you need to talk to the lecturer or recognise that you do not really understand the question. Give yourself time to do this properly!

1. **Do some reading around the subject and make some notes**: For the moment, we will assume that you have done some reading and made some notes. An essay which shows no signs of reading will have lots of signs of personal opinion and 'common sense' – those kinds of essays tend to do very poorly when it comes to academic assessment. Of course, 'common sense' is a value-judgement, made often according to a wider view from society. Different societies will have different understandings of what is 'sensible'. Yet, as the saying goes, 'common sense' is not always so common, and engaging our brain in what we call 'critical analysis' is important.
2. Practically, **prepare yourself and your writing area**: You are preparing to write a draft, so you do not need to get too stressed about doing this; however, you do need to have all the relevant information available to you as you write.
3. **Consider the question carefully**: Try to rewrite the question in your own words two or three times. Try to understand what the question is really asking. If you need to, check your understanding of the question with the lecturer. There is no penalty for asking questions, but *answering the question in the wrong way or answering the wrong question carries a large penalty indeed*. It is dangerous to underestimate the impact of this. Some lecturers make the analogy that a train might be moving quickly, be comfortable and the ticket might be value for money, but if the train arrives in the wrong destination, then everything will have been wasted. It is the same with an essay that does not answer the question: it might have a lot of detailed and well-researched arguments with credible evidence and excellent structure, but if it does not answer the specific question, it will receive a fail mark.

There are a number of verbs used regularly in questions for assessment and it is probably helpful to examine what these verbs mean in terms of the requirements of the essay. Table 7.1 gives the verbs for essays requiring you to discuss different points of views and those which require you to present an argument. Look at the verbs used below and the explanations of what the tutor expects from you. Some – like compare and contrast – regularly appear together in essay questions.

Table 7.1 Expectations for different kinds of essay questions (from Marshall and Rowland, 1998)

Verb	Expectation
QUESTIONS WHICH ASK YOU TO EXPOSE DIFFERENT POINTS OF VIEW	
Compare	Look for and explain similarities between differing points of view
Contrast	Look for and explain differences between differing points of view
Define	Set down the precise meaning of the word or phrase. Show that the distinctions implied in the definition are necessary

(Continued)

Table 7.1   (Continued)

Verb	Expectation
Describe	Give a detailed or graphic account of
Enumerate	List or specify and describe
Examine	Present in depth and investigate the implications
Explain	Make plain, interpret and account for in detail
Illustrate	Explain and make clear by the use of concrete examples, or by the use of a figure or diagram
Outline	Give the main features or principles of a subject, omitting minor details and emphasising structure and relationship
Relate	Narrate/show how things are connected to each other, and to what extent they are alike or affect each other
State	Specify fully and clearly
Summarise	Give a concise account of the chief points or substance of a matter, omitting details and examples
Trace	Identify and describe the development or history of a topic from some point in time
QUESTIONS WHICH ASK YOU TO PRESENT AN ARGUMENT	
Analyse	Show the essence of something by breaking it down into its component parts and examining each part in detail
Argue	Present the case for and against a particular point of view
Criticise	Give your judgement about the merit of theories or opinions about the truth of facts and back your judgement through a discussion of the evidence
Discuss	Investigate or examine by argument, sift and debate, giving reasons for and against
Evaluate	Make an appraisal of the worth of something, in the light of its apparent truth or utility; include your personal opinion
Interpret	Bring out the meaning of, and make clear and explicit, usually also giving your own opinion
Justify	Show adequate grounds for decisions or conclusions
Prove	Demonstrate truth or falsehood by presenting evidence
Review	Make a survey of, examining the subject critically

Source: Marshall, L. A. and Rowland, F. (1998) *A Guide to Learning Independently*. Reproduced with permission of Open University Press in the format 'Republish in a book' via Copyright Clearance Center.

4. **Draw up a rough structure of what you might cover in the essay**: You will then need to confirm the order of what you are covering and ensure that there is some logical flow to what you are writing, but having a structure often makes it easier to begin the essay – and starting the essay can be the biggest struggle sometimes.

5. **Make a note of the references and the content you will use for each section**: Start making notes of what pieces of reading you have done and in which section of your essay they will feature. You might wish to copy some of your notes into the relevant sections or paragraphs, but *do not* insert direct quotations unless you are sure you will use (and cite) them in your final essay. (We examined the reasons for this in the section on avoiding plagiarism in Chapter 6.)

6. **Start writing**: This is often seen as the toughest part of essay writing: there are some benefits that come with procrastination, such as the pressure that sharpens your thinking or the emotional thrill of doing the essay at the last minute! However, working under such pressure has an increased likelihood of submitting a poor – or even plagiarised – piece of work. Many people start with the introduction, which is a good thing if you have a good idea of your final structure, but if the structure should change, then starting with the introduction might not be the right thing to do (unless you have a reminder to change the introduction as well). If you are clear on the structure of your work, then writing the introduction can focus your mind and make the essay structure clearer to you.

7. **There is no need to write in a linear order**, starting with the introduction and working through to the conclusion. If you decide to write in the order that you think, then you will need to revisit what you have written and add phrases to link your thinking together and enable the reader to see clearly how you have reached your conclusions.

8. **Review what you have written**: Ask yourself whether the structure makes sense for any argument you are presenting, whether the evidence you have is strong enough and whether your point of view comes through clearly in the conclusion (see Chapter 4 on critical thinking). Have a look at the next section on what a tutor looks for in an essay. Does your essay fulfil the criteria listed? You should also check any alternative or additional criteria that your lecturer has posted online or given you in some other way. *If not, then go back and rewrite the relevant sections.*

9. Above all, **make sure that you cannot be accused of plagiarism** by what you write and how you have presented the information.

10. **Check the formatting and bibliography** to ensure that all is as it should be. This generally takes a bit of time, so make sure you plan for it. In a long assignment, make sure that sections are numbered correctly.

All the above take time, so careful planning is needed. Go back to Chapter 3 on time management, particularly in terms of using a diary, and review what is written there, if you need to.

What Does a Tutor Look for in an Academic Essay?

Part of this is answered in Chapter 6, but there are some issues that go beyond simple critical thinking and content. Essays are just one form of assessment used in qualitative or discursive subjects, but in many universities they are arguably the most common.

A lecturer will expect you to provide an essay that is:

- **Insightful** and demonstrates your critical thinking skills (see Chapter 4).
- **Relevant** to the question(s) which has been set.
- **Supported by examples** to illustrate the ideas outlined in the essay and strengthen the arguments.
- **Supported by citations and theory** to give those ideas credibility (see Chapter 6).
- Written using **good grammar and spelling**, so that it looks as if effort has been put into the piece of work.
- **Structured well**, so as to have a beginning, middle and an end.
- **Mindful of the audience**, in terms of what it says and the knowledge it expects the audience to possess.
- **Written in appropriate academic style** in order to give you the chance to show your own thinking and give a summary of others' research.

── FOR YOU TO DO ────

Into the Mind of the Assessor

Have a go at putting some thoughts down on paper and thinking about what you would expect to see from an answer to this question. It appeared in a study skills module at a UK university.

What makes the difference between an essay receiving a fail and one receiving a mark of 75%?

1. How would you answer this question? What would you include?
2. How you would structure your answer?
3. What sources might you need to refer to for information?

TASK AND TEMPLATES

The companion website https://study.sagepub.com/morgan2e contains three essays which answered the examination question above. These were real-life essays completed under examination conditions, and many of the thoughts that you might have written down were probably the same as those from the tutor reading and marking the essays. Now we need to examine what the tutor might have written and see if our comments agree.

── 'BUT I HAVE A QUESTION ...?' ────

... I was asking my friends about the criteria used for assessment and what I should do for my assignment, and they seemed a bit vague. One thing they said, though, was that I should just write everything relevant to the module, maybe based on what the students did last year. Is that a good thing to do?

Well, in Chapter 6, the text referred to the following as important in any written work:

1) Insight/critical thinking
2) Use of examples
3) Support from citations and theory

However, the most important criterion is always going to be **relevance** - i.e. did you answer the question? You can use wonderful theory, have a well-structured piece of work and make some wonderful arguments, but *if you do not answer the question*, then it will be to no effect.

With that in mind, writing down everything that you know about a subject is not going to work, and you may well fail your work.

Citations, Plagiarism and Paraphrasing

Giving citations was covered earlier in this text (see Chapter 6) but it is important to distinguish between plagiarism and trying to avoid the need for citations through paraphrasing. Plagiarism – as we saw earlier – is the use of other people's ideas and thinking without referring to them, and so putting in their ideas as if they were your own.

It is important to note that paraphrasing – changing others' words into your own words – does not overcome this. If you are putting another person's ideas into an essay, then you need to indicate that this is what you are doing: changing someone else's words does not change the fact that they are someone else's ideas.

Grammar and Spelling

You might think that any work developed on the computer should have good grammar and spelling – after all, there are now tools such as Grammarly, and the widely used Microsoft Office software has spell-checking and grammar-checking tools. These tools are not always used well and work can be submitted using incorrect words (such as there and their, or pair and pear), which appear fine but are not correct.

There is no real substitute for being able to spell well, and students expecting to work in the UK should have good grammar and spelling – regardless of nationality (and there are occasions when the spelling and grammar of international students is better than that of some UK students). It is the expectations of employers that make these two areas important for assessment. However, it is not always the case that lecturers will provide feedback on your spelling and grammar, though they may say that they do not understand parts of your work. Some take the view that their role is to comment on your thinking, not your English. Of course, if they cannot understand your essay because of bad English, then you will not receive any marks for your critical thinking either.

 FOR YOU TO DO

How Good Is Your English?

The following exercises are intended for both international and UK students: poor English can be found everywhere. They offer a quick check on how good your English grammar and spelling are. This book is not aimed at improving your English, but if you score badly, then you might like to seek some support from your university.

The first test was developed from mistakes that were noticed regularly in academic essays.

Circle the correct word in each of the statements below:

1. They took *there/their/they're* dog with them on the walk.
2. In order to improve *morale/moral*, the company decided to increase pay.
3. The most *relevant/relative* ideas were those which helped solve the problem.
4. 'It is *defiantly/definitely/definately* the correct answer!', he shouted.
5. He was unsure *whether/weather* to choose the black or brown shoes.
6. Of course, the main question is *which/witch* road to choose.
7. The biggest *affect/effect* he had was to cause the company to close down.
8. *You're/your* clearly the tallest person here.
9. I didn't want to take his *advice/advise*.
10. It was common *practice/practise* to plagiarise work.

Choose the correct spelling in each of the statements below:

1. accommodation, accomodation, acommodation
2. conscus, conscious, conscous
3. embaras, embarrass, emmbaras
4. immediatly, immediately, imediately

(Continued)

5. ocasion, occasion, occassion
6. preferred, prefered, prefferd
7. separat, separete, separate
8. necesary, nesessary, necessary
9. devided, divided, dividid
10. benefited, benefitted, bennefited
11. disappeared, disapeared, disappered
12. ocured, occurred, otcured
13. comitted, committed, comited
14. questionare, questionnaire, questionaire
15. posess, posses, possess

Indicate which of the following sentences use the apostrophe (') correctly:

1. The students' had always liked the lecturer.
2. The students had always liked the lecturer's.
3. Sometimes the lecturer's liked the students.
4. The lecturer's books were on the shelf.
5. The students usually kept their books' on the floor.
6. The parents were worried about their children's studies.
7. The students and lecturers always got on well with each other.
8. It was nice of the lecturers to care about their student's.
9. It was nice of the lecturer's to care about their students.
10. It was nice of the lecturers' to care about their students'.

INTERACTIVE TEST

An interactive version of this task along with answers are on the companion website at **https://study.sagepub.com/morgan2e**. Be aware that there are some differences between US and UK English spellings.

Structure

Other than the critical thinking and content areas for assessment detailed in Chapter 6, this is one of the most important criteria for assessing the work. Giving your essay a clear structure enables the reader to follow your line of thought really clearly, and it ensures that your work has a clear 'beginning', a solid 'middle' and an 'end' which gives some clear thought as to the answer to the question asked. It makes sense to spend some time looking at these three elements of essay structure to ensure that you have a clear understanding of what you mean.

The Introduction

An introduction to an essay should set out the aim of the piece of work and the main issues that will be discussed, and do the following:

- Get the reader's interest.
- Indicate the central idea running through the work.
- Give the reader a brief understanding of why the issue is important.
- Explain any information that is needed before the main body of the essay begins.

If you look at the introductions to each of the chapters here, you will find that each one clearly sets out what will be discussed and in what order. Setting out this information clearly enables the reader to feel confident that they can follow the content of the chapter and know where the chapter will 'take them'.

A good introduction will usually have these kinds of phrases:

- 'This chapter aims to …'
- 'This essay will begin by discussing …'
- 'It will also discuss …'
- 'This topic is important because …'
- 'Finally, the essay will show that …'

If your reader does not really understand what your essay is about and is going to cover by the end of the introduction, then it is probably not doing a good job and needs rewriting.

FOR YOU TO DO

Part A

If you have written an essay or started a draft essay, then try the following. Take a look at one of your essays. What do you think of the introduction? Does your essay have an introduction? Does it do what an introduction should really do?

Part B

Have a look at the final essay on Maslow (Box 6.7). Does it have a good introduction? If you were giving feedback on this work, what would you say about it? How would you rewrite it?

The Middle

The middle of the essay provides the main arguments, gives the evidence and enables the reader to feel confident that you – as the writer – understand what you are talking about. If the introduction (and conclusion) are written well, then this part of the essay is where you will demonstrate your critical thinking, show the tutor the reading you have done that you believe to be relevant, and present evidence which helps to answer the question.

Many essay questions from your tutors will require you to debate an issue; that is, to present both sides of an argument and/or discuss why you agree or disagree with a particular point of view.

Many questions set by your tutors will expect you to present the evidence in favour of opposing opinions.

Such essays will require you to use phrases which indicate to the reader that you are linking or contrasting two or more ideas or pieces of research. The companion website at https://study.sagepub.com/morgan2e gives you some phrases which may be useful.

In a long essay (or even in a text like this), you will need to include 'signposts' to tell your tutor/reader what has been covered and what is going to come next. These are important because they help your tutor/reader follow the arguments that you are making.

ARGUMENT

An academic argument is a statement of a particular view or opinion, followed by the evidence to support that opinion.

SIGNPOST

A signpost is a simple statement of what has been covered before a particular point in an essay, followed by a statement of what will come next.

An example of a signpost might be: 'So far, this essay has looked at ... However, we also need to consider ... so the next section will focus on ...'

 **FOR YOU TO DO**

Understanding Sentences and Paragraphs

The middle part of your essay will be a series of paragraphs grouped together to make an appropriate point of view. Each paragraph will have a number of sentences, but each one should discuss only *one* aspect of your particular argument. You should be able to give each paragraph a simple title, summarising the content. It is a good idea to look visually at the page you are writing: when you look at it, does it appear to be neatly broken up with maybe two or three paragraphs on the page? Have a look at the following brief passage written on the subject of motivation, and identify where you think the author should create a new paragraph. What titles would you give each paragraph?

> The evidence regarding intrinsic motivation is clear. Intrinsic motivation describes how people are motivated through their interests and passions. Typically, theories of intrinsic motivation might relate to a sense of responsibility or autonomy. Responsibility motivates because individuals feel they have a contribution to make, and that contribution will be recognised. Autonomy motivates for a different reason – that individuals have a sense of ownership over the tasks they are doing, and a sense of freedom to make decisions. Both these assist in motivating individuals intrinsically. However, many theorists – and working individuals – claim that increased salary or bonuses will help them to work harder. The research seems to suggest that money does not increase motivation but actually a lack of money suggests that people will develop a sense of unfairness around the workplace. This relates to a third area of motivation theory – namely equity theory – where individuals will regulate their own behaviour according to how fairly they feel they have been treated. They might compare their own inputs and outputs with those of others and see others receiving rewards when they do not. As a result of this, they may start to decrease their own effort (as they do not believe that it is valued) or some other behavioural response. Of course, they may change the individuals to whom they are comparing their own performance and maintain their own motivation, rather than change their own behaviour.

Here are some questions to consider:

1. How easy was it to identify where the passage should split into another paragraph?
2. How easy was it to give each paragraph a title?

The Conclusion

When you finish your essay, you will be expected to summarise clearly what you have said previously as a way of enabling the tutor to know what your view is. A conclusion is a summary, a clear statement of your view, bearing in mind the evidence you have presented. An essay without a conclusion will be incomplete, and will lose you marks.

A good conclusion will usually have one or two of these kinds of phrases:

- 'This essay set out to examine ...'
- 'In summary ...'
- 'The questions outlined in the introduction were ... and this essay has covered those by ...'

There is one comment left to make: in the social sciences (i.e. in the more discursive subjects such as business studies, politics, sociology and similar subjects which are neither clearly arts nor clearly sciences), there are rarely right and wrong answers, so students with very different conclusions can get identical grades. As we saw above, it is the quality of debate and the strength and quality of arguments that really enable a lecturer to give marks to a student. This may be different from school or your previous educational experience where getting the right or wrong answer is important.

KEY LEARNING POINT

In degrees in social science subjects, there are rarely right and wrong answers. What matters more is the quality of the debate.

REFLECTION POINT

Take some time to think about the following questions and write down some answers.

How might the information given above change the way that you write your essays at university?

How good were your spelling and grammar? What will you do to improve here?

How will you ensure that your written work has a beginning, a middle and an end?

Understanding the Audience

A question often asked is: 'I have a tight word limit. I want to include as much information as I can to show my critical thinking skills, but how can I do so when I need to explain several theories in the first place?'

It is a fair question, and while you may not think that this has a lot to do with your audience, understanding your audience makes answering this question much easier.

FOR YOU TO DO

Glance through the following list of individuals. There are two questions: 1) which one(s) do you think most closely resemble the audience for your work? And 2) who out of this list might be likely to understand the following terms: a) 'econometrics' – the scientific and mathematical theories underlying economic models; b) 'depreciation' – an accounting term, used to account for the decrease in value of machinery and other fixed assets; c) 'stratified sampling' – a term describing the development of a sample used to investigate particular topics; d) 'occupational psychology' – a subject analysing why people think and act at work in the way that they do; and e) 'plagiarism' – a term defined elsewhere, where others' ideas are not recognised as such.

Your parents

The intelligent man doing a professional job

(Continued)

Another student

The local councillor or Member of Parliament

Your best friend

A well-known professor at another university

A PhD student

A younger brother or sister

An individual who struggles with English

Your (future) husband or wife

The list above is not mutually exclusive (the intelligent man doing a professional job could also be your parent or the local councillor), but it is designed to get you to think about: 1) the level at which you write (your vocabulary or 'register'), and 2) the amount of detail you include.

You need to be writing for an individual who is intelligent and who can pick up ideas quickly if they are written clearly. This means that you do not have to give all the details of every idea or theory you are discussing, but that you should allocate more space in the essay to the areas where the potential for getting higher marks is greater – that is, on demonstrating your critical thinking rather than simply describing theory.

 KEY LEARNING POINT

In an essay where word limits are tight, you should allocate more space to the areas where the potential for getting higher marks is greater – that is, on demonstrating your critical thinking rather than simply describing theory.

Academic Style

There is no one academic style for writing a traditional essay and many lecturers will expect you to develop your own style as you go through university. Even your lecturers will have different styles, since they will be required by their work to write journal articles based on research and theory, and each journal will have different styles. In addition, academics may ask you to write reports (see section 'Writing Reports' below) and you may be asked to produce some reflective writing, and some comments are made about this below.

FURTHER READING

Your own style will develop, but look at the ideas in Box 7.1 below. There are some notable exceptions to these rules. A piece of reflective writing, for example, will expect you to write about what you have done – but the ideas here should help you find your own way to write. You can find more information about this on the companion website at https://study.sagepub.com/morgan2e.

BOX 7.1

'Academic' and 'Non-Academic' Style

There are some important rules to follow when it comes to writing academic work. You need to remember that you are writing for an academic audience. That means:

- You should be making an argument **based on evidence** obtained by research – either from primary or from secondary sources – and not based on emotion.
- Your own experience can count, but **evidence from a large body of research** involving hundreds or thousands of people tends to carry more weight. Use research evidence as the basis for your argument and supplement it with additional examples and anecdotes if you need to.
- **Use the 'passive voice'** wherever possible: instead of writing 'I did this', talk about 'what was done'.
- **Avoid long, complicated sentences**: keep them short and focused on just one issue.
- **Avoid using 'colloquial' language**: for example, writing 'employees' is better than writing 'people'; 'in subsequent research' is better than 'after that'; and '10 out of 12 employees' is better than writing 'a lot of employees'. You need to keep it formal.
- **Try not to use the same nouns or verbs more than once** in one short sentence or in immediately adjacent sentences. For example, 'A number of ideas were proposed at the meeting. One idea was to ...' might be better phrased as, 'A number of ideas were proposed at the meeting. One suggestion was to ...'.
- **Try to be succinct**: is there a way of cutting down on words and yet keeping the same meaning? This usually requires a reasonable vocabulary, but writing succinctly is something that is as important in academic life as it is in professional life.

When writing an essay, it is usually better to avoid definitive statements of truth, phrases such as: 'There is no research into ...' or 'Employees never ...' may well result in a comment from a lecturer arguing that there is some research into something; or instead of 'How can you say that no one will ever ...?' it is better to say: 'It appears that ...' or 'It seems that ...'. However, when you are analysing a case study, you can repeat the facts given to you in the case study material itself, but be sure that you are interpreting such material correctly.

Developing your own voice and style is not an easy thing to do, and comes with practice and time, but it develops a lot quicker *if you do more reading*.

Expressing Your Own View

Some students struggle to write in an academic style (and there is not just one) yet want to express their own opinion. This is a really important issue, especially when critical thinking is such an important part of assessment, so how does it get done? Look at the following exercise and see if you can identify the phrases that are used to express the author's opinions, rather than those of other people.

=== FOR YOU TO DO ===

The following is a fictional passage from an essay which summarises the views of others as well as expresses the author's own views. Underline those sentences or phrases which you think are the opinions of the author, and circle those phrases which you think simply summarise what others have said:

Understanding essay writing seems to be a challenging task for many students (Watson, 2003). Research has suggested that students particularly struggle with giving their work structure and with understanding the criteria that lecturers use (Watson, 2003; Paulson, 2012). Of course, there are other areas that some students seem to struggle with as well: providing sufficient references to research is something that many academics note as an issue (e.g. Scott, 2004) and – as noted by Blade (2002) – understanding whether evidence from personal experience is better than evidence from the literature is also a difficulty for many students. As stated by Scott, 'These basic issues are key to doing well in academic work' (2004: p. 112).

(Continued)

However, what this debate misses is how lecturers and academics can enable students to understand how academics think. Students need to be given examples and be given the chance to assess others' work.

Some work has already begun in this area. Work by Price (2003) has shown that assessment feedback and engaging students in peer-to-peer learning has some benefit, but of course the effectiveness of this rests on how well the students can understand what the criteria mean. What may be of some considerable interest is some research work into how academics develop those skills themselves, and studies in this area may provide some clue as to how to help students understand and recognise these skills also.

In conclusion, we can argue that we are making progress. It is not easy and there will be challenges along the way, but if we can develop students' understanding of how to demonstrate their critical thinking skills, then we will have gone some way to fulfilling our aim as facilitators of learning.

1. How easy was it for you to identify the two different sources of view: those from research and those from the author?
2. Write down some of the phrases and wording used by the author to express the author's own view. (Some ideas are given on the companion website.)
3. Rewrite this passage in your own academic style. Think about how you might change the language and sentence structure to make the passage one that reflects your own academic style.
4. Is there anything else that you can learn from the passage above about academic writing?

DOWNLOAD

When you were completing this exercise, you would have listed a number of phrases which could be useful to you. Learning to express your own view in an academic style is vital if you are going to demonstrate your own opinion, and showing your own opinion is going to push you towards those higher grades. There is a list of useful phrases that you could use to express yourself on the companion website at https://study.sagepub.com/morgan2e.

As a student, you will need to find your own style. Some lecturers might be happier with your using a less conventional academic style and, as we have said before here, the best source of information is always going to be *your tutor*.

 'BUT I HAVE A QUESTION ...'

... My tutor has asked me to produce some reflective writing about the development of my skills. How should I do that?

Well, it is a good question. Reflective writing is a style of writing usually required when an element of thinking or personal development is requested, and relates to the process of reflection detailed in Chapter 2. A tutor will ask students to write a piece which details their own thinking about a particular topic or skill, and in doing so, will be able to see their critical thinking abilities. In some ways, a piece of reflective writing can be similar to a blog or vlog, but there are some significant differences when it comes to writing a reflective piece of work at university – most importantly, academic reflection asks students to think about specific issues or topics, and so it is more than a stream of thoughts. Academic reflection should:

- Be written in the first person: 'I learnt that ...' or 'Because of what I have experienced and read, I believe ...'.
- Be academic in nature: your tutors will expect you to include reference to some theory and the application (and maybe evaluation) of that theory in some way. It will therefore include citations and references just as any other essay or assignment will do.

- Be detailed and give evidence for why you believe what you do: in this way, it is little different from other academic assignments.

Being asked to use reflective writing for a module focused on personal development is quite common. Students are often asked to write something reflective in relation to the development of a personal development plan or the specific development of a prescribed skill. You have been asked to detail how you have developed a skill and in your reflection, you will need to give evidence of how you have progressed towards or achieved your goals. But this should be an assignment written around you, not about 'other people'.

WRITING REPORTS

Essays are important because preparing for and writing an essay will teach you how to collect and use information to develop a clear argument for the point you wish to make, and for this purpose, they are a powerful method of assessment when it comes to assessing critical thinking. However, few businesses – if any – will ever ask you to write an essay, but will instead ask for a report, so it makes sense to take time to look at these as well. There are differences between reports and essays in terms of structure and appearance, style, length and the way that evidence is presented.

Structure and Appearance

Other than structure, the clearest difference is that an essay will often be a continuous piece of writing, while a report will have *headings* – and those headings will indicate a structure to a report that may be quite different. If there is such a thing as a 'typical report', then it might be structured in the following way:

1. **Executive Summary**: This is a succinct summary of the issues covered in the remainder of the report. It is intended to enable busy managers and others to have an overview of the key issues without reading a lot of detailed thinking – and the rest of the report will provide the detailed evidence. In more academic settings and journal articles, the word 'Abstract' is usually given for this section.
2. **Introduction**: This sets out the issues that the report is due to address and the structure of the remainder of the report. It might also identify the key sources used by the report and, having briefly laid out the reason for the report (in business: a report would usually address a problem that the business is experiencing), the important questions to be covered.
3. **Investigation**: This section will usually set out what was done (and why it was done in that way) in order to develop the later sections of the report. This may be split into subsections.

   o **Literature Review**: There will usually be some discussion of what others have already found that is relevant, which sets out the background to your own investigation. This review may comment on the strengths, weaknesses and relevance of the sources you have used.
   o **Personal Investigation**: You will need to determine the answers to the questions set out in the introduction to the report, and you will need to detail how you did this. You might look at secondary data – information that is already publicly available such as company reports, accounting information, press releases, etc. – as well as carry out your own investigation and collect primary data through interviews, discussion/focus groups or questionnaires. Collecting and using primary data will usually require some kind of ethical approval and you will need to indicate something about the nature of those involved in your research – how many individuals you talked to and their relevance for the investigation.

4. **Findings**: You will need to show what you found in relation to the questions set out at the start of the report and what the possible options are. If you were unable to gather sufficient information (e.g. your sample was inappropriate, or you were unable to find the information you were seeking), then this needs to be stated here as well, as you outline the strengths and weaknesses of the investigation you undertook. You will need to be succinct and focused in your writing, but comprehensive and honest in relation to the relevant information you were given. Your findings should give you and the reader a clear idea of the different ways in which the problems set out in the early stages of your report might be solved, and why certain solutions might work when implemented and others might not.

5. **Proposal and Recommendations**: In a business setting, this is what your readers really want to read: you are going beyond setting out the options and are pinpointing what ideas you think will work and could be implemented. You need to set out clearly what action could be taken to help address the relevant issues – usually in bullet point form (because you have already spent some time in the findings section addressing why certain ideas might work) – and maybe, depending on the requirements of your lecturer, give ideas about how the proposal(s) might be implemented through an action plan.

Report Style

For traditional essays, issues around developing your voice are covered in the earlier section 'Academic Style', but in the business world, a report is intended to be read as a summary of work undertaken by others, and that requires a certain style – which means writing a report is not always easy. In terms of style, a good report is going to be succinct – using as few words as possible to express particular ideas – and focused – giving answers to the key questions set as clearly as possible.

A report does not need to give lots of background information – individuals in business can ask further questions if needed, and for students, extra information should be put into appendices.

 KEY LEARNING POINT

Writing a report requires a different approach and style from traditional essays. Realising this is the first step to fulfilling your lecturers' expectations.

DISSERTATIONS

If you are a postgraduate student, then you will almost certainly need to complete a dissertation, probably around 15,000–20,000 words, but many undergraduate students need to do dissertations as well. This might sound scary. You have probably never written anything of that size before, but it is easy to think of dissertations as large essays and, in some ways, that is what they are. However, there are three significant differences between essays and dissertations:

- Their size.
- The usual requirement to undertake some form of research.
- The process for completion.

Of course, dissertations are solely individual pieces of work, so we will not look at group working in connection with dissertations.

Size and Structure

If an essay is usually around 3000 words, then a dissertation could be five or six times as long. On the surface of it, the criteria for assessment are probably the same, but the expectations for depth of analysis may well be greater. However, the size makes issues of structure far more important.

In a large piece of work, a reader needs to be reminded of what they are reading and how it fits into the overall work. This means that the dissertation needs to be split into chapters, and each chapter needs to have an introduction and conclusion.

A typical *conclusion* to one chapter might read: 'This chapter has examined ... It has outlined the theory regarding ... and has shown that ... The following chapter will extend this investigation by ...'.

The *introduction* to the following chapter might then read: 'The dissertation has so far discovered that ... It has shown ... It is now important to examine ... by ... Therefore, this chapter will begin with ...'.

In effect, then, the dissertation becomes a series of essays which *together* introduce the reader to some issues relevant to your degree programme, identify some research questions, investigate those questions and present some answers in a credible way. The dissertation effectively takes the reader on a story revolving around some research questions.

A dissertation based on primary research will usually have a structure similar to that in Box 7.2.

═══════ BOX 7.2 ═══════

Typical Structure of a Research Dissertation

There is no one definitive way of structuring every dissertation, but most research-based pieces of work follow a similar structure to a research journal article. This results in a chapter structure similar to that set out below.

Chapter 1: Introduction and Overview

This chapter provides an oversight of the contents and objectives of the dissertation, establishes the reader's interest and tells the reader how the work is structured. Many supervisors recommend making this the last chapter that you write because, by then, you will know what each chapter has covered.

Chapter 2 (or maybe two chapters): Literature - Secondary Sources

What are you investigating and why?

This chapter provides the theoretical background to the research questions and displays your critical thinking skills. If there is a particular issue to be addressed at a particular company, then there needs to be some background to the company. This may be given in Chapter 1 or in a separate third chapter, but needs to be given before the research questions are set out, which usually happens before the research methodology is given.

With the exception of MBA (Master of Business Administration) projects (which are usually very practical in nature and are more like a report), the literature review will likely form nearly *half* of your dissertation. It has to be evaluative and critical (see Chapter 4), comprehensive in covering the topic, up to date, and should inform both the questions you intend to ask as part of your research and the discussion chapter, where you will be comparing the results of the research with the literature that you have found. As such, the literature review forms probably the largest part of the dissertation.

Chapter 3: Methodology

How will you investigate this?

(Continued)

This chapter establishes the methods used to gather the information required by the research questions. It should give information on the sample and provide some justification for gathering the information in the ways proposed. The discussion could also include some arguments about why other methods were not used. This section could also set out the statistical analyses used, but these could also be given in the results chapter.

Chapter 4: Results

What did you find?

This chapter gives the results of the investigation. It may include a commentary on the findings in a separate 'Conclusions' chapter, but usually simply gives the findings of the research questions asked earlier on in the dissertation.

Chapter 5: Conclusion and Discussion

Did you find what you expected, based on the literature? How useful are these results for other researchers?
The final chapter does three things:

1. It compares the results obtained from the study with expectations developed from the literature, and tries to give some explanation where those results differ from expectations.
2. It investigates the strengths and weaknesses of the research methodology adopted.
3. It sets out some further questions for investigation.

Bibliography

This needs to include the sources that you have cited in writing the dissertation and any background reading.

Appendices

The appendices should allow the reader to learn more about your research than you are able to write in the dissertation. The appendices should include your methodology (questionnaire, interview schedule, etc.), details of the sample and the responses, and more detailed statistics than was used in the main text. They might also include your research proposal.

There is no requirement for a research-based dissertation to follow this five-chapter model precisely, and you will need to discuss this with your dissertation supervisor as you start working on this large piece of work.

A Need for Research

The second aspect by which dissertations can differ from essays is that there is often a need for primary research. Not all universities or programmes require students undertaking a dissertation to complete a piece of primary research, but it is a very common requirement to do so. This means that, as a student, you need to have a number of particular skills:

- **Good time management**: No one will be pushing you, so you will need to keep setting milestones in order to get this large piece of work completed on time.
- **Motivation**: To keep working on this for possibly six months or a year.
- **Good understanding of research methodologies and statistics**: The more you know before you start your work, the less time you will need to spend finding this out.
- **Access to information**: Sometimes, including organisations and companies, depending on the nature of your work, will make it difficult to arrange access to busy people in a short space of time, so the more access you have before you begin, the easier your investigation will be.

- **Clear and succinct writing style**: It is a long piece of work, so a clear style will mean that it is easy to follow the ideas and arguments. Such a style also makes a dissertation more pleasant to read.
- **Critical thinking skills**: Essential. You will need to find, read and evaluate journal sources relating to the topic you are investigating. The more descriptive your work, the lower the mark and the less interesting it will be.
- **Ability to learn independently**: Essential. You will need to find your own information, analyse it yourself and come to your own conclusions.
- **Organisational skills**: You will need to organise your information so that you can find and comment on it easily, should the need arise. Your supervisor will also expect you to attend meetings on time, so you will need to be able to manage your diary well (see the first bullet point above).

All of the above are requirements for a student undertaking a dissertation. If you do not have these qualities and you are required to do a dissertation, then you will need to develop them fast.

The Process for Completion

The final areas where essays are slightly different from dissertations relates to the process for completion. In a typical essay, you will look at the question, develop some thoughts about relevant reading, investigate those sources, and add your notes and thinking together to develop a piece of written work which you believe answers the question well.

A dissertation works differently. Firstly, for most dissertations, there are no set questions: you develop your own questions based upon your interests, your career aspirations, and so on. The choice of topic is important: it will signal to an employer your interests; it will need to be completed within the timescale set; it will need to answer questions that you can actually get answers to. Above all, it is highly likely that you will not be able to change the topic suddenly without a full discussion with your supervisor.

Secondly, if you are doing a dissertation, you will be undertaking 'independent learning'. This means that the relationship you have with your supervisor is important here. It is a one-to-one relationship, where you do the work and receive feedback on that work. There is no teaching but there is guidance. Some suggest that the dissertation supervisor has the same role as a sports coach. They are not there to do the work for you, but to give feedback on the content, style, critical thinking, and so on, that you display in your own writing. They may not be an expert on the particular topic that you have chosen, but they can give you guidance on how and where to look for information and on the other criteria that we discussed above in relation to essays. They will also be able to give you advice on how to complete a dissertation, probably reflecting the ideas given in Box 7.3 below.

━━━━━━━━ BOX 7.3 ━━━━━━━━

Completing a Dissertation: Dos and Don'ts

Do

- Start early and get organised.
- Keep in touch and maintain good relations with your supervisor.

(Continued)

- Clarify and follow agreed objectives.
- Have a detailed proposal/project plan - a Gantt chart.
- Make sure you keep the tense the same throughout the dissertation; this is not always easy for a long piece of work.
- Ensure you have ethics approval for your work, where needed.
- Set targets/milestones and deliverables.
- Back up, and then back up your backup.
- Follow any dissertation guidelines given to you by your university or department.
- Critically evaluate theory and research where possible/appropriate.
- Link chapters to each other - develop a narrative.
- Include a methodology.
- Contextualise findings in relevant literature.
- Keep records and reference properly.
- Read the project that you have written.
- Allow time for feedback - particularly at the end.

Don't

- Underestimate the amount of time and work needed.
- Be vague about the project purpose and outcomes.
- Ignore any ethics process your university will require your proposal to adhere to.
- Be vague with respect to methodology.
- Change the proposal or research and not tell the supervisor.
- Ignore relevant key literature.
- Include long, rambling chapters.
- Copy straight from the book or the internet without referencing.
- Leave it to the last minute and rush the writing up.
- Expect instant review and feedback from the supervisor.

Thirdly, on a practical note, dissertations may be undertaken during the summer, as is very commonly the case for Master's degree programmes. If this is the case, then it is your responsibility to ensure that you find out when your supervisor will be available to meet you, when they will be away and how to contact them when they are away. In any event, arranging meetings with your supervisor should be something that is planned in advance. You cannot expect a supervisor to be available just when you want them to be, though, if they are, then that is great. The first meeting with your supervisor is usually when such practicalities are discussed.

In summary, completing a dissertation is unlike most other pieces of work that you will ever do at university. It is usually large in terms of word length, time consuming in terms of the hours of reading and research that will be needed, and challenging in terms of the motivation needed to complete it. Students who ignore the guidance above tend either to do very poorly on their dissertation (because they have not obtained regular feedback or because they could not actually do what they were hoping to do as an investigation or for some other reason) or to get caught plagiarising and cheating. There are no shortcuts to undertaking a dissertation properly, but the skills that you develop and demonstrate during the dissertation will be extremely useful in future careers.

━━━━━━━━━ REFLECTION POINT ━━━━━━━━━

Take some time to think about the following questions and write down some answers.

If you needed to do a dissertation, what would be the first thing that you would do: talk to the tutor, or start reading some relevant literature? Why?

How easy is it to develop your own style of writing?

INTEGRATION AND APPLICATION

You should now have some ideas in your mind about how to write essays and dissertations. Dissertations are very similar to essays in many respects, namely style, need for critical thinking, citations and evidence, but usually students undertake a piece of research as well. Completing a dissertation requires working with a supervisor, while writing essays should be an individual piece of work. However, apart from that, the mechanics tend to be similar.

The most important issues are to:

- Show that you can answer the question intelligently.
- Include evidence that is sufficiently strong.
- Make sure that you include references to others' ideas and work wherever you use them.

Completing a written assessment is not an easy thing to do, but if you have followed the steps outlined in this chapter, then you should do well.

CONCLUSION

By now, you should be able to:

- Develop your own academic style for writing essays and assignments.
- Understand what your tutors mean by the questions they set.
- Evaluate how good your English grammar and spelling are.
- Understand clearly how a tutor approaches the assessment for a piece of written work.
- Express the difference between an essay receiving a pass and one receiving a high mark.

The companion website at https://study.sagepub.com/morgan2e contains a significant amount of material relating to reflective writing and case studies, and gives you the chance to assess three students' examination essays and compare your marks with those of the tutor.

FURTHER READING

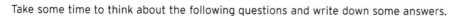

━━━━━━━━━ REFLECTION POINT ━━━━━━━━━

Take some time to think about the following questions and write down some answers.

Based on the content of this chapter, what do you now know about writing essays or dissertations that you did not know before?

(Continued)

What key learning point had the most impact? Why?

Do your answers to either of the above questions have the potential to change your attitude to studies at university? If so, why?

What will you now do differently? (Write this down and put it somewhere where you can see it regularly.)

CHAPTER TASK

Look at the structure and writing style of a research article in a journal. There may be words you do not understand, but in general, how does the journal article:

1) Develop the logic of the paper: why has it decided to investigate a particular topic, what issues does it consider in deciding how to investigate that issue, what do the researchers find, and what might be the next areas for research?
2) Differ in its written style and nature from a serious newspaper article?
3) Provide headings which are similar to or different from the headings in the chapter of a book?
4) Provide evidence for the claims it makes and cite other authors' works?
5) Ensure that the evidence presented (where it gives evidence from others' work) is credible?

Understanding style, structure and the strength of argument are key to being able to provide a credible piece of work.

INTERVIEW QUESTIONS

In Chapters 5 and 6, it was suggested that there would be few interview questions regarding assessment specifically, but that interviewers might ask questions around the topic to find out other things about you (e.g. your ability to think critically or to plan an activity). The same applies to this chapter as well: if you wonder, 'Why would an interviewer want to know about my assignments?', then the only reasonable answer is to understand something more about your personal transferable skills, not the assignments themselves.
    Think about the following questions. What might your answers be?

1. What was the most challenging piece of written work you have worked on? And why? How did you go about ensuring it was a good piece of work?
2. Tell me about your experience with writing reports. Can you briefly tell me about a report you have written?

Chapter 17 gives a lot more information on selection interviews and the online content gives some guidance on these questions.

ADDITIONAL RESOURCES

Want to learn more? Visit https://study.sagepub.com/morgan2e to gain access to a wide range of online resources, including interactive tests, tasks, further reading and downloads.

Website Resources

The following websites offer useful advice on writing assignments.

Sage Study Skills: https://uk.sagepub.com/en-gb/eur/page/study-skills

University of Hull: https://canvas.hull.ac.uk/courses/778

University of Leeds: https://library.leeds.ac.uk/info/1401/academic_skills/83/planning_your_assignment

University of Manchester: www.phrasebank.manchester.ac.uk/about-academic-phrasebank/

Textbook Resources

Bailey, S. (2011) *Academic Writing for International Students of Business*. Abingdon: Routledge.

Burns, T. and Sinfield, S. (2016) *Essential Study Skills* (4th edition). London: Sage (particularly Chapters 11 and 12).

Cottrell, S. (2013) *The Study Skills Handbook* (4th edition). New York: Palgrave (particularly Chapters 11 and 12).

Courtney, M. and Du, X. (2014) *Study Skills for Chinese Students*. London: Sage (see Chapter 5: 'Research and Dissertations').

Furseth, I. and Everett, E. L. (2013) *Doing Your Master's Dissertation*. London: Sage.

Gallagher, K. (2016) *Essential Study and Employment Skills for Business and Management Students* (3rd edition). Oxford: OUP (particularly Chapter 8).

Graff, G. and Birkenstein, C. (2010) *They Say, I Say* (2nd edition). New York: Norton & Company.

Greasely, P. (2016) *Doing Essays and Assignments* (2nd edition). London: Sage.

Hind, D. and Moss, S. (2011) *Employability Skills*. Houghton-le-Spring: Business Education Publishers (particularly Chapter 4).

Horn, R. (2012) *The Business Skills Handbook*. London: CIPD (particularly Chapter 12).

Irwin, D., Jovanovic-Krstic, V. and Watson, M. A. (2013) *So Where's Your Dissertation?* Toronto: Nelson Education.

McMillan, K. and Weyers, J. (2012) *The Study Skills Book* (3rd edition). Harlow: Pearson (particularly Chapters 51 and 52).

Tissington, P., Hasel, M. and Matthiesen, J. (2010) *How to Write Successful Business and Management Essays*. London: Sage.

Walliman, N. (2013) *Your Undergraduate Dissertation*. London: Sage.

8 EXAMINATIONS AT UNIVERSITY

There's an examination for young people to go to university. I failed it three times. I failed a lot.
(Jack Ma, CEO of Alibaba)

CHAPTER STRUCTURE

Figure 8.1

 When you see the 🌐 this means go to the companion website https://study.sagepub.com/morgan2e to do a quiz, complete a task, read further or download a template.

━━ AIMS OF THE CHAPTER ━━

By the end of this chapter, you should be able to:

- Describe the different forms and different meanings of examination questions that are used at university.
- Identify the practical issues you need to know in relation to the examinations that you will be taking.
- Evaluate various mechanisms for improving your revision and memory.
- Avoid some of the common failings when answering university examination questions.

INTRODUCTION

Mention of the word 'examination' tends to fill most people with a sense of dread and fear, but knowing what to expect and what is expected of you will reduce that stress considerably.

Universities will differ from each other in the extent to which they use examinations for assessment, and they will also differ in how they carry out those examinations and in their format. For example, some universities will use much less formal in-class tests in the early stages of a degree, while others will use multiple choice questions in the first year of a degree. We will spend some time looking at how universities conduct examinations and the various formats being used, but we begin with a brief look at what lecturers look for in good examination answers and provide some suggestions regarding issues of preparation, including revision.

WHEN SHOULD YOU READ THIS CHAPTER?

This chapter is designed to help you prepare for your examinations, and so the best time to read this is as you prepare for your first set of university examinations, which in many cases will be at the end of your first semester.

SKILLS SELF-ASSESSMENT

It is not easy to assess your ability to pass an examination successfully unless you have one to take, but you can at least see how prepared you feel and how much you know.

Look at the items below. Complete the brief questionnaire to see how much you know about your examinations at university. Read carefully each of the following descriptions and say how typical you think each statement is of your behaviour or attitude by giving it a score between 1 and 5, where 1 is 'strongly disagree' and 5 is 'strongly agree'. There are right and wrong answers to *some of these*, so be sure to complete the interactive test and compare your answers with those on the companion website at https://study.sagepub.com/morgan2e.

INTERACTIVE TEST

Number	Item	Score
1.	I am really happy to take examinations	
2.	I prefer multiple choice questions because generally I like to guess the answers	
3.	I am not very good at calculations and prefer essay questions	
4.	I revise for examinations by focusing my time or energy on two or three main topics	
5.	I am sure I know what topics will come up in my next examination	
6.	I know how long each of my examinations will last	
7.	I would never cheat in an examination	
8.	If I see others cheating in an examination, I will report it to the person in charge of the examination	
9.	Cheating in an examination is academic misconduct	
10.	Examinations are all about managing your time	
11.	Open book examinations are much easier than closed book examinations	
12.	If I write more in an examination, then I will get a higher mark	
13.	In an examination, I need to include citations and a bibliography	
14.	If there is something in my life which prevents me from doing well, I can just take the examination again	

(Continued)

(Continued)

Number	Item	Score	
15.	Making a plan for an essay during an examination is vital if I am going to get a good mark		
16.	Calculation examinations are easier than essays		
17.	I know where and when all my examinations are going to take place		
18.	Examinations which last a shorter period of time are easier than longer ones		
19.	I always feel anxious before going into an examination		
20.	I always check past papers to see what topics are going to appear in the examination		

With the exception of item 9, there are no right or wrong answers to this exercise (the answer to item 9 is likely to be 'agree' or 'strongly agree', since cheating in an examination is definitely an example of academic misconduct). However, it would be interesting to see whether your view is the same as that of others in your class.

Longer responses to essay questions do not always get higher marks, but there is a stronger possibility of their doing so because you are more likely to include the relevant content. Shorter examinations may expect you to write very succinctly, which can make them harder, and not everyone finds calculations easy. It would be a very useful exercise for you to take your answers to your personal tutor or a module lecturer and discuss them together.

 ━━━━ 'BUT I HAVE A QUESTION ...' ━━━━━━━━

... Why do universities use examinations at all? In the real world, we never have to do things from memory, right? What about assignments?

Yes, assignments can be more interesting and the point about doing things from memory is true, but some tutors want to assess your ability to develop a good argument quickly – and that is also what is needed 'in the real world'. In meetings, you will rarely have time to look up information online, so knowing what you are talking about is crucial.

Some people believe that examinations are used because students cannot plagiarise or cheat in them – or it is at least more difficult. There is some truth in that, but it is never an acceptable reason for using examinations over assignments – and students do still try to cheat. As I have mentioned, it is all about being able to develop a good argument quickly and without reference to external resources.

A third and final reason why universities use examinations is to help others know that the student is able to work calmly and efficiently under pressure. For most people, timed examinations are fairly stressful situations, and while it is not fair to put excessive pressure on students, the ability to work calmly under pressure is a valuable skill.

DIFFERENT QUESTION TYPES AND EXPECTATIONS

Finding out what makes a good answer will depend on the kinds of questions being asked. In some ways, the answer has similarities to those in Chapter 6 and Chapter 7, but there are some subtle differences. There are various types of examination questions, and each will look for slightly different things, as shown in Table 8.1.

Table 8.1 Types of questions

Question type	Example	High marks typically given for
Multiple choice	Which of the following is not a county in the UK? (a) West Yorkshire (b) South Yorkshire (c) East Yorkshire (d) North Yorkshire	Demonstrating understanding and ability to apply course content to the question (Marking can sometimes be negative for wrong answers)
Calculation	If 46% of a company's turnover is profit, and the company had sales of £20,500 three years ago which have risen consistently by 5%, what was the company's profit this year?	Demonstrating the ability to apply concepts covered in the course
Essay	Discuss the advantages and disadvantages of applying Maslow's motivation theory in the workplace	Demonstrating all the requirements of a good essay identified earlier in Chapter 7 – including good structure, relevant knowledge and critical thinking (see Chapter 4)
Case study	Bearing in mind the information given in the case study for the examination, answer the following three questions ...	Demonstrating the ability to analyse information and develop arguments and solutions to problems as given in the case study
Practical exercise	Using the information given in the passage, use Excel to calculate the mean, range and standard deviation ...	Demonstrating the ability to take information and use relevant equipment

The type of question will depend on what the lecturer wishes to assess (i.e. the module's learning outcomes) and on your level of study, but you should have good notice of the type of question that will be used in any examinations you have to undertake. Box 8.1 reflects on whether examination assessment reflects the realities of working life after graduation.

━━━━━━━ BOX 8.1 ━━━━━━━

Do Examinations Assess the Right Things?

We said earlier that university is about 'learning how to think' and, as a result, demonstrating critical thinking skills is important to being able to do well, so the question then is how examinations do this. Some suggest that examinations only really assess a student's ability to remember, but the validity of any assessment criterion can only really be determined in comparison with the needs of employers.

Perhaps there is some truth here, but it is a long way short of the complete picture. At a basic level, examinations assess knowledge, and it is true that the reproduction of knowledge is based on what someone can remember, but there is a separation between knowing something well and knowing it because it is something that someone has revised. Take the example of a student who has thought and read a lot about Maslow's Hierarchy of Needs: they will probably not need to revise it because they will have thought about it (and 'chewed over' the theory). The thinking they have done about the theory means that they know it well.

One other set of skills that examinations assess is related to time management, both in terms of planning for revision and in terms of being able to manage time within the examination itself. There is validity in doing so because being able to complete tasks efficiently is a key aspect of managerial functioning.

(Continued)

There are, however, different forms of examination which can assess other skills. In many cases, the only examinations that students take are those where they sit down, wait a moment or two in silence with just their pens or pencils and then turn over the paper once they are told to 'Begin!'. However, there are some additional formats for examinations used for some courses.

One such variation is the open book examination where students are allowed to take into the examination room any materials they wish. This sounds like an easy examination and reflects one aspect of the real world, since people have access to a wide range of resources to help them in their work and so the argument is that an open book examination best reflects life after university.

'Easy', however, is a word that does not necessarily relate to open book examinations: if a student does not understand some course content or does not have a basic knowledge of the topic, then all the resources available to them will not improve their examination performance. Tutors who offer an open book examination may also have higher expectations and marks may be harder to obtain.

Writing an examination essay is only slightly different from writing an assignment essay and the criteria for assessing an essay will be very similar to those for academic work generally (see Chapter 6). Apart from the fact that an assignment essay is not done under timed conditions, an examiner will generally have fewer expectations when it comes to referencing or providing a bibliography (you need to check the detail of this with your lecturers), but you will still be expected to provide evidence for your arguments and points of view.

There is no ideal length for an examination essay (you could write the same point several times in an essay six sides long!) but a short answer will be unlikely to cover all of the content expected in the depth required for a good answer.

We will now turn to look at some of the preparation issues to consider before an examination.

PREPARING FOR AN EXAMINATION

There are a number of issues here. We will begin by looking at handling nerves (i.e. how we prepare ourselves) and then look at various aids to revision, such as using past examination papers, revision timetables, ideas for memorisation and making notes.

Nerves and Emotions

Most people seem to get nervous before examinations as well as in other contexts, such as when giving a presentation. With group presentations, it often concerns our thoughts about what others might be thinking of us and our expectations about looking at a sea of unfriendly faces (which is hardly ever the reality anyway). With examinations, the issue is often different, but we can still have reactions that we do not always expect – as shown in Box 8.2.

━━━━━━ BOX 8.2 ━━━━━━

Reactions to Examinations

In his 1998 text *Learn How to Study*, Derek Rowntree identified a number of reactions that people can have towards examinations. Have a look at those below. Which ones are closer to your own feelings?

1. I wouldn't say that I take them in my stride, but I wouldn't say that they give me sleepless nights either.
2. No, I won't go bananas. I'll just ration my time out more carefully and think positively.
3. I know I am under a lot more strain when the exams come around, but I just play a lot more squash – that's my way of working off the pressure.
4. I've started smoking again. What more can I say?
5. I get depressed when other students tell me about all the areas they've been looking into and I realise I haven't done anything about them, by how other students seem to have covered so much more of the work than I have and there's no time to catch up.
6. There's so much to remember – I can't believe my memory's good enough to cope with it all.
7. I can get so paralysed with fear that I couldn't think what to revise or get the willpower even if someone told me.
8. I'm that panicky and depressed I feel like going off and never coming back.
9. Of course I'm worried and anxious: who wouldn't be? But I need it. It's the only way I can work up enough steam to get the work done in time.

Examinations generally produce uncertainty about what will be on the paper when we turn it over (i.e. a fear of the unknown). We can minimise this to some extent, but if your lecturers were to remove this fear completely by telling you the questions in advance, then there would be little difference between doing the examination and submitting a piece of coursework. The best that we can do is simply to spend time ensuring that we have completed the practical preparation and have done our best to ensure we can remember the content presented to us during the modules we have taken.

The answer to some of this may rest with the ideas given in the chapter on presentation skills (see Chapter 10), which mentions issues of preparation, and similar ideas apply here. In some ways it can be useful to think of an essay as an oral presentation without the voice and the PowerPoint slides. It might be useful to look at Table 8.2, which provides a checklist of items to find out before the examination.

Table 8.2   Examination preparation checklist

Item	Do I know this? (Yes/No)
1. How long will the examination last?	
2. Will I be given advance notice of topics or questions?	
3. What books and other materials do I need to have with me?	
4. How many questions will I have to answer?	
5. Will any questions contain options within them?	
6. Are some questions likely to be compulsory?	
7. Is the paper split into parts? Do I have to answer questions from each part? Is there a difference between the parts in the paper (i.e. a reason for the split)?	
8. Do some questions carry more marks than others?	
9. Which topics have appeared with more frequency than others?	
10. Are there any areas on which considerable stress has been put (i.e. taken up a lot of time etc.) which have not been examined recently?	
11. What might the questions ask me to do (e.g. discuss, evaluate, etc.)? Do I know what these mean?	

There are some things that we can do to limit nerves and some things we can do to relax. The impact of both will be the same – we will be more relaxed – but the way we address them will be different. In addition to the practical preparation we can do before an examination, we can do some physical and emotional preparation.

Get Some Sleep

Some students believe that spending the whole night revising is the best way to prepare for an examination, but this is rarely true. It might be what some are used to, but the brain is not as alert after a sleepless night as it is after a good night's sleep. If you are used to spending a sleepless night revising for an examination, then you might like to try the next exercise below.

 ══ FOR YOU TO DO ════════════════════════════

This is a test of your memory in some ways, but you will get to see the impact of a lack of sleep on your memory if you complete both parts of this exercise.

Part A

Try the following exercise when you are in your normal state of alertness. Below is a series of numbers. Look at them for about 30 seconds and try to remember them:

1 3 5 7 9 11 12 14 16 18 22 24 19 26 48 27

Now close the book and write down the numbers in the list in the order that they are given.
How many did you get correct?

Part B

Try the same exercise when you have had less sleep.
How long do you have to look at the numbers in order to remember them?

This exercise should have indicated to you that it takes a lot longer and a lot more effort to remember information when we are tired than it does when we are alert.

An issue related to this is that we do not necessarily sleep well when we are stressed or worried or when we don't eat well, and often the times when we don't eat well are those same times when we are anxious, so these two aspects can interact with each other and make life awkward for us. The best way to break this is to have a good meal before relaxing and going to bed.

Talk to Your Tutors

The best preparation for examinations is to learn and remember what you learn as you go through your courses, and for some students, that will be sufficient. However, for most students, there will be an increase in focus and effort – and often stress – closer to the time of the examination. Most tutors will offer revision sessions or office time specifically to assist students with their examination preparation.

They may be frustrated when students ask questions which are already answered elsewhere – especially in a revision lecture – so make sure that any questions are not already answered before meeting your lecturers. But generally, most tutors will be willing to give advice to students who ask for it.

Use Past Examination Papers

There are two ways to use past examination papers in preparing for an examination: 1) as a way to 'question spot', and 2) as a way to practise the kinds of questions which might arise during the examination itself.

Let's look at 'question spotting' for a moment. Of course, if you have an examination paper where you have to answer three questions, then you might be tempted to revise four topics rather than six or eight. It is a lot less work and enables you to focus your reading.

Lecturers will be aware that some of their students may do this, and generally will not approve. In principle, it does not allow you to demonstrate all the knowledge that you should have for passing your courses, and that is something which some academics feel strongly about.

On a more academic note, question spotting does not always work. Multiple choice questions, for example, typically cover the whole syllabus; examination papers might be structured into parts so that you have to answer one question from each part (or a compulsory question and then questions from other parts, or something similar); or questions might link two topics together around a theme common to both. Equally, you might spot the wrong topics or have a question that asks about a topic you have prepared in a way that you did not expect – and that is the risk. Question spotting might sometimes work, but the risks associated with getting this wrong can mean that you waste time trying to question spot, rather than using that time to prepare and revise thoroughly.

QUESTION SPOTTING

If a student attempts to question spot, then they will be trying to work out what topics will appear in the examination. This is often done by looking at patterns of topics in past papers to determine what has and has not been covered more recently.

══════ KEY LEARNING POINT ══════

Question spotting is potentially very risky and failing an examination could put your degree and future job in jeopardy. Some lecturers combine topics in a single examination question.

The second way to use past papers is to prepare answers. The best way to do this is to look at some questions from past papers and get some feedback on how well you are able to answer them. The feedback is crucial: without it, any preparation becomes merely an exercise in how well you can remember what you have revised and in being able to write an essay or answer questions under time constraints. Both of these are helpful in themselves, but the real benefit comes when you know that you can do well under timed conditions. This only really happens when you get feedback on your work.

Note especially that if you are going to use past papers to revise from, you must make sure that the format of the paper and the syllabus of the course have not changed. If the syllabus has changed then the topics examined by the paper in previous years will, of course, be different.

Develop a Revision Timetable

Before we go too far, it is useful to clarify what we mean by 'revision'.

Revision can take a number of forms and different people prefer to use different strategies and techniques to build up that memory.

 REVISION

Revision is the act of building up sufficient memory of a body of knowledge in order to be able to do well in a subsequent examination.

Put simply, a revision timetable is a schedule of what you will revise and when. Different people work in different ways: some prefer to spend a long time on one topic and revise in a block, others prefer to vary things and spend short blocks of time on different topics. You have to work out what is best for you, but most people will need to move between topics and take breaks from time to time.

The challenge, in many cases, is not what to revise and when, or even to build the revision timetable, but usually to keep to it. Most people who make a timetable keep to it for a few days and then lose interest.

Sticking to a timetable requires the same kind of motivation and time management that we referred to in Chapter 3. We need to find motivators and these can come in three forms:

- Incentives that we can link to specific progress in fulfilling our schedule.
- Something that helps us see and record the success we are having in our revision.
- Some mechanism by which we can be accountable.

How we implement each of these will depend on our own motivations and environment, but most of us need to do something around these three issues if we are going to use a revision timetable successfully. Not everyone uses revision timetables and they work better for some people than for others.

━━━ FOR YOU TO DO ━━━━━━━━━━━━

Developing incentives for maintaining a revision timetable

Look at the ideas below in relation to increasing your motivation to keep to a revision timetable. Which ones could be the most effective incentives?

- A bar of chocolate.
- Playing a computer game.
- Chatting with friends on social media.
- Watching TV.
- Buying yourself a present.
- Going out with friends.
- A class of wine/pint of beer.
- A day off for leisure.
- Listening to music.
- Enjoying a hobby.
- Playing football.
- Something else.

Which mechanisms could help you see how much progress you are making in your revision?

- A diary where you tick off each day of revision.
- Testing yourself against the notes you have made to see if you can recall them.
- Talking to a friend about the items you have revised.
- A checklist where you tick off topics that you have revised.
- Writing practice essays under examination conditions for a tutor.
- Studying with a friend to check your progress.
- Other ideas?

Make Revision Notes

Making notes of your notes can sound like a strange idea – if they are notes in the first place, why would you want to make further notes about them? It is a reasonable question. If notes are intended to be a brief summary of larger content, then notes of notes are intended to become a summary of a summary. In effect, notes become easier to remember than larger content, but it is important also to ensure that what we remember has depth to it.

Some students choose to read through an entire module before specialising in certain areas and making notes of those specific topics. That gives them an overview of how all topics within the module link together, enabling them to demonstrate that synthesis referred to earlier.

Prepare Together with Others

There is a saying that 'Together everyone achieves more' – the acronym spells T.E.A.M. – and this is as true when it comes to examination preparation as it is for other activities. Many students study together with those that they live with, or with others who come from the same social/cultural background and that can make the preparation more efficient.

In some cases, students will look at previous examination papers, delegate each question to different members of the group, undertake preparation for the question given to them individually and then come back together to share what they have prepared. This can work well but is subject to the skills, knowledge and academic abilities of the student preparing each question and/or any discussion that follows. It can also mean that all members of the group give very similar answers with little creativity across the group. Finally, the success of such preparation is based on the questions chosen for further preparation: it is risky for any student to try to anticipate examination questions (sometimes students complain that there was 'no question on X so the paper was unfair' – such complaints are usually unsuccessful) but when that 'question spotting' is done in a group, then the risk becomes greater.

It is good to discuss your learning and preparation with others and more can be achieved, but anyone preparing in groups needs to be aware of these issues just as much as they need to be aware of the challenges there may be in preparing more alone.

Use Revision Guides

Various publishers produce summaries of a course syllabus (e.g. business studies). These are very popular and have some use if you are struggling to remember basic information, but the keyword here is basic. The summaries often provide sufficient information to just about pass a module in most universities, but will be unlikely to give enough information to do very well; they cannot provide a brief overall summary and provide evaluative content and detail at the same time. If they did, they would not be providing a summary, they would be repeating the main textbook.

These guides can be useful as an aid to memory, but making your own summary through your own notes is far more useful to learning: it is much easier to remember something that you have written yourself than printed information on a page.

Enhance Your Memory

There are a variety of tools that students use to enhance their ability to remember information in preparation for examinations. Mnemonics, acronyms and acrostics can be very useful for improving your ability to remember key information, but we could also consider how we use and engage with information more broadly.

Mnemonics, Acronyms and Acrostics

Information in lectures is often presented in the form of lists, and these can enable students to develop mnemonics, acronyms and acrostics which help to recall information.

There are also other ways of trying to remember key pieces of information. Marketing has the 4Ps (Price, Product, Place, Promotion), organisational designers have their 7Ss (Skills, Shared Values, Systems, Structures, Strategy, Staff and Style) and strategists have PESTLE (Political, Economic, Social, Technological, Legal, Environmental) to describe the factors which impact on business strategy.

One of the challenges with such lists is to remember what they actually relate to. It is great to remember PESTLE as a framework for making business decisions, but a nightmare when someone cannot remember what PESTLE actually means in practice.

MNEMONICS, ACRONYMS AND ACROSTICS

Mnemonic: Any learning device or tool that improves memory - including acronyms and acrostics.

Acronym: A word made up of the initial letters of other relevant words. Examples are: TEFL (Teaching English as a Foreign Language), AIDS (Acquired Immune Deficiency Syndrome) and BBC (British Broadcasting Corporation).

Acrostic: A sentence constructed from the first letters of words. Example: the colours of the rainbow - Richard Of York Gave Battle In Vain (Red, Orange, Yellow, Green, Blue, Indigo, Violet).

Engage with Information in Different Ways

Table 8.3 indicates a number of ways in which we can handle information. The word 'handle' is probably the wrong word, however, because handling something implies that we are passive with it (i.e. we do nothing with it). We handle a birthday present, but if we simply handle it then we will never find out what is inside. We should really 'engage with' information, and if we follow the analogy of the birthday present, then we would enjoy unwrapping it, opening it and relishing its contents. The figure gives some ideas as to how we might engage with information.

Some of the ideas here may not have been ones that you have thought about, so let's look at each in turn.

- **Writing out information** is better than merely reading it. If we write it out, we are doing something with it, albeit maybe simply repeating it.
- **Turning information into lists** is partially covered above under mnemonics but can refer to any information that is taken from a formalised paragraph and transferred to a bullet list. Again, the act of 'turning information' implies some active engagement with that information.
- **Giving information a sequence** again implies some form of action, and can make information easier to remember. Information that is in a logical order is much easier to remember than random information that has no particular order (in the same way that an essay which has a logical sequence to its argument is much easier to read).

Table 8.3   Ways of engaging with information

Write out by hand

Turn information into lists

Give information a sequence

Use headings

Draw pictures

Personalise the information

Use shape and colour

Repeat, sing or act out the information

Play with information

Active listening and review

- **Using headings** makes information stand out on a page. If you are a visual learner (see Chapter 2), then it will be easier to remember something which stands out than something which is just in normal text.
- **Drawing pictures** can work for some people. Doodles are not particularly helpful to anyone unless they relate perhaps to the content you wish to remember, but diagrams which put the lecture content or your reading into pictures can be useful, especially if you are a visual learner.
- **Personalising information** is about trying to apply the information given to you in a lecture to your own situation. This is clearly not possible in every situation, nor for every subject, but for some subjects (e.g. consumer behaviour, organisational behaviour, marketing) it is very easy to see how the theory relates to your own experience and to business practice.
- **Using shape and colour** is a great idea and works particularly well for those who learn visually. Words can be coloured in your notes (coloured pens can do as well as a coloured font on an iPad) and that makes them stand out on the page when you are revising.
- **Repeating, singing or acting out information** sounds like a strange idea, but does work for auditory learners (see Chapter 2) in particular. Actors often learn their lines by hearing them repeated and repetition can help us to remember information very easily.
- **Playing with information** means that someone looks at it, imagines the information in practice, considers whether it would work in all places and at all times, and generally thinks about it in some depth. The idea of 'playing with' information implies that we can imagine ideas applying to new contexts or subjects.
- **Active listening and review** is the process of thinking about what we hear and trying to enhance the understanding we have of what we are reading. One useful idea might be to rephrase what we hear and put it into our own words.

These are a series of ideas which might help in engaging with information. The more we engage with the information we are given and find for ourselves, the more we are likely to remember it without a huge amount of effort for revision.

Mind-mapping

Mind-maps can be very effective methods of organising information for both memory retention and written work more generally, especially if you are a visual learner (see Chapter 2). As noted in Chapter 5, mind-maps are visual representations of what you have covered. They begin with a central concept and then the ideas are repeatedly subdivided until there is little sense in doing so any more. (See Figure 8.2 for an example of a mind-map for this chapter.)

 MIND-MAP

A mind-map is a visual representation of information.

Mind-maps in real life can be made more complex than this, showing relationships between ideas (see also Chapter 14 on creativity and the reorganisation of information) and showing how certain ideas might be more important than others, where risks for a project might be greater (using colour, thickness of lines, arrows, etc.). At its heart, a mind-map is a graphical way of showing how information and ideas are organised. When it comes to revision, drawing a mind-map and then ticking off the topics as you cover them is a good way to ensure that your revision is organised.

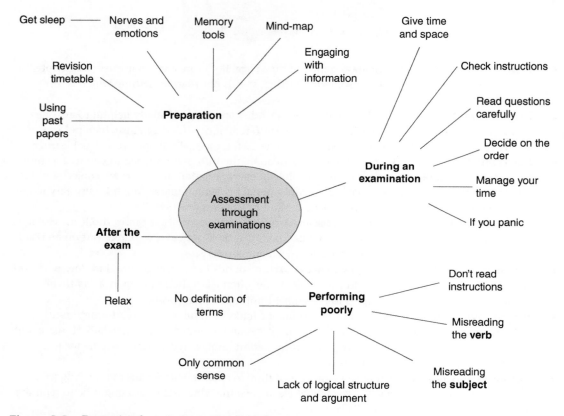

Figure 8.2 Example of a mind-map for this chapter

 KEY LEARNING POINT

Revising is one way to ensure that we can remember information before we go into an examination, but it is much better to learn the key ideas as the course progresses – by reading around such ideas and by trying to apply them to the real world.

Take some time to think about the following questions and write down some answers.

How nervous do you get before an examination? Why?

In your preparation, do you try to spot questions which might come up? Is that a good or a bad idea, do you think?

DURING THE EXAMINATION

Of course, it is during the examination itself that performance becomes vitally important. Having taken time to relax before we go into the room, we need to recognise that there are some fairly simple actions we can take to ensure our performance is as good as it can be.

Give Yourself Time and Space

Arrive early, do *not* rush and do *not* arrive at the last minute. Of course, no one intends to do that (or very few do) but some students always seem to arrive a minute or two either before the start of the examination or after it has started. Some universities do not allow students to enter after the examination starts (it disturbs other students who have already started), so beware!

Make sure that you bring everything you need: Student ID card? Several pens? Calculator? A watch? A drink? Make sure you know what you can and cannot bring into the room, and do *not* take any unauthorised materials to your desk.

Some universities will allocate you a specific desk, so make sure that you know which room (and which desk, if appropriate) to go to.

Finally, make sure that you go to the toilet before you enter the examination room. Once you enter the room, you will probably not be allowed to leave for a particular period of time (depending on the rules for your university).

Carefully Check the Instructions on the Examination Paper

Of course, you should check that the examination paper on your desk is the one you are expecting, but do not turn over the paper until the examination starts and you are told to do so.

Once the examination begins, you should make sure that you follow the instructions. This sounds obvious, but there will be at least one student who answers five questions when they should answer three, or who answers two questions from one part of the paper when they should answer just one. So make sure you know what you are doing.

Also, make sure that you know how long the examination lasts. There may be a warning a few minutes before the end of the examination, but being told 'Please put your pens down now!' should not be a surprise to you.

Read All the Questions Carefully

If you have the chance to select which questions you answer, then take a few moments to think them through. There are some common mistakes which individuals make at this point (see Table 8.4 below).

If a question has two parts, then make sure you answer both parts fully, paying attention to those parts of a question which might carry more marks than other parts.

Decide on the Order in Which you Want to Write Your Answers

If you are asked to write three answers, it is likely that your second answer will be the best. You will typically be more relaxed than you were when you started writing the first answer and have more time than you will have for the final one. Answer the most difficult question first if you can because you will need more time to plan and think through how you will answer the question, and that time can evaporate very easily towards the end of the examination.

 ━━━━━ 'BUT I HAVE A QUESTION' ━━━━━

… What happens if I am unsure about what the examination question means and I write all I know about the topic?

The same principle should apply. If you fail to answer the question well, then you will not receive a good mark. Now, if you write all you know about the broad subject of the question, then you should get some marks, but how many will depend on how well you answer the question – and that will always be the case. Let's imagine that you write two pages in an examination in order to answer a question, and about 25% of that answer is directly focused on the question: the mark is likely to be based solely on that 25%. You may not lose marks for the irrelevant content – it is just irrelevant: neither correct nor incorrect – but you will have wasted the time you took to write the remaining 75% of your answer, and because of that, the 25% will probably not have enough depth.

Manage Your Time

This is very important. It sounds obvious, but if you have two hours to answer three questions, then you need to allocate time according to the marks given for each question. For example, if a paper is two hours long, all questions have the same number of marks and you need to answer three questions, then each question should take no longer than 40 minutes, but if the first question is worth 60 marks and the remaining two are worth 20 marks each, then clearly the first question requires more time and thought.

This time for each question includes the time to think and plan your answer, which should take around 5 to 10 minutes per answer for an essay-based examination (and less for a pure calculation question).

Some questions may have two parts, so make sure that you are careful in the way you use the time given.

Some students write a comment such as 'Ran out of time: Sorry! Please be generous.' Unfortunately, requests like this are not going to result in 'generous' marks. Tutors can only mark what they see and read, and if it is not written down, then no marks will be given.

━━━━━ BOX 8.3 ━━━━━

The Importance of Time Management in Examinations

Before your examination, you are likely to have done your revision, learnt what you have needed to learn and prepared using previous examination papers. You may have done all that has been advised earlier in this chapter and may be confident about your performance. However, all of the above might come to nothing if you are not able to manage your time during the examination.

The way that you manage your time will differ from subject to subject and the format of the examination will of course be a significant influence. However, the following principles apply to any examination:

1) **Check the instructions**: Each year your tutors will receive examination answer booklets where a student has not followed the instructions – for example has answered *all* the questions when they only needed to answer four out of five. (Doing so not only means that a student may find that the fifth question is not considered, but that they have spent less time answering each question than they should have done.) You should know the format of the examination before you sit it, but the first thing you need to do to help your time management is know what you need to do.
2) **Check the weighting**: Is there a question or a section of the paper which is allocated more marks than the others? Then this is where you should spend more time. How much more time will depend on the specific weighting or balance within the paper.
3) **Check the maths**: If all questions are weighted equally, and you have a 2 hour examination and are supposed to answer four questions, then you should allocate 30 minutes (2 hours divided by 4) to each question.
4) **For an essay question**: Give a small amount of time to planning your essay and a small amount of time to reviewing it. For example, if you have 30 minutes for an essay, then 5 minutes at the start to make notes and plan your answer and 5 minutes at the end could really improve the logic, evidence of critical thinking and the structure of your answer, and add between 5% and 10% to your grade.
5) **If you are struggling to answer a question**: Do not panic, but leave the question and come back to it later on. Time and space to think are needed to answer questions but when you are in a state of panic, you remove that opportunity.
6) **Aim to finish writing your answers before the end of the exam**: The examination will have been designed to last a particular time, so you should expect to be writing for most of the time in the examination room, but you should leave around 5 minutes at the end of the examination to check that you have answered everything that you need to, and to do any necessary administration (for example, put your name and student ID on your examination booklet) before the examination booklets are collected up.

'BUT I HAVE A QUESTION ...'

... What should I do if I run out of time? And how much time should I give to reading through my answers at the end?

If you really do run out of time, then the best you can do is to write down what you think is relevant in as short a way as you can. Sometimes this can be with bullet points and brief English. It is better to get something down that you do know, even if there is no detail, than just miss out relevant content entirely.

On the second question, there is less of a simple answer here, because examinations with calculations can take a lot longer to read through than essays. Again, allow 10 minutes or so at the end – though it will depend on your reading speed. Check through and make sure that everything you have written makes sense.

And If You Panic?

Breathe! Take a few long, slow breaths in and a few long, slow breaths out. This can sound very clichéd, but it does work for most people. If you have a drink with you, then take a moment to have a sip.

Many people can react wrongly and think 'If I slow down, I'll have even less time and I'll panic even more,' but in reality 5 minutes of calm thinking can produce much more than 10 minutes of thinking in a panicked state of mind.

If you feel ill during the examination, let the invigilator know. They may give you the option of getting some water or using the bathroom.

UNDERSTANDING WHY PEOPLE DO POORLY IN EXAMINATIONS

This section is intended to examine why people do poorly in examinations, and to answer the question above.

In some ways, the errors made in examination essays may be the same as those made in essays generally, for example, a lack of structure, unconvincing arguments, and so on, but in an examination situation, the urgency of getting something down on paper and a lack of time to prepare can make the probability of errors increase.

Failing to Read the Instructions

Failing to take time to understand how many answers you need to write or from which parts of an examination paper has been covered above, to some extent, but writing more answers than you need to will lower your mark. You will have less time to devote to each answer and so the quality of each will be lower. Your university may or may not have a policy on how to deal with this – some universities will ask tutors to mark the first answers that they see, others may accept the essay with the highest mark – but you should not expect to do better than if you had written the required number.

Similarly, if you write fewer answers than is expected, then it is highly unlikely you will increase the mark of one by a sufficient amount to compensate for the lack of an entire piece of work.

A final scenario relates to a situation where a student is expected to answer one question from part A and one from part B, but instead answers two from part B. In this situation, it is likely that the student will only have one essay answer marked, and will lose a significant number of marks overall.

Misinterpreting the Verb in the Question

The verbs (e.g. analyse, compare, discuss, contrast) in the question will tell you what you need to do: if you do not do it, you will write an answer which does not answer the question and will likely fail. No examination essay will ask you to 'Write all you know about …'. So make sure that your content is relevant, avoids unnecessary content and is focused on the question that is being asked. Answers containing largely irrelevant information are likely to fail.

Read through the verbs listed in Chapter 7 (see Table 7.1) and make sure that you understand what each one means and what you would be expected to do.

Table 8.4   Common errors in examination essays

- Failing to read the instructions
- Misinterpreting the verb in the question
- Misreading the subject of the question
- Lack of logical structure and argument
- Woolly theorising and common sense responses
- Lack of time
- Too much time for description and too little time for critical thinking
- Failing to define key terms

Misreading the Subject of the Question

We can use motivation theory here to give a simple example ('Explain the relevance of Herzberg's hygiene factors to motivational practice in the workplace') and we can imagine a situation where a student writes about 'motivator factors' instead, or a question which asks about Modules but where a student writes about Moodle (an internet-based learning resource). Misreading the subject means that the essay is very likely to fail on the grounds that the answer is not relevant.

Lack of Logical Structure and Argument

There is no real difference here between an examination essay and one which is completed during the semester as an assignment. If an essay is good (contains sufficient critical thinking, evidence for the arguments given, covers sufficient content) then a lack of structure is unlikely to lead an answer to fail, but it could reduce the mark by 10–15%. A lack of logical argument, however, will mean that the essay is likely to fail, since the quality of reasoning is important – as the next point shows.

Woolly Theorising and Common Sense Responses

The kind of answer which ignores any reading, any lecture content and gives a simple response 'This is what I think because it is what I think' is extremely likely to fail. Not only is it likely to irritate the assessor (who will have taken time to give you the lecture content and reading related to the subject), but it also shows a significant lack of engagement on the part of the student towards the course. Universities expect you to do the reading and to present an argument for the view you have; this is what critical thinking is all about, so it is quite reasonable for this kind of answer to fail.

In social science degree courses, this is particularly an issue for subjects related to law. Business students studying law modules can struggle sometimes because they write in a way that might provide a decent argument but does not reference the points made on a case-by-case basis. In a law-based essay, common sense is always insufficient and *will* lead to a failed answer (see Table 8.5).

Table 8.5 Comparison of minimum expectations in business and law essays

Minimum expectations for business essays	Minimum expectations for essays in law-based modules
Reasonable structure Reference to some theory Reasonable argument Covers most of the relevant content	Reasonable structure Points made are supported by reference to law and by reference to specific cases Coherent argument Covers most of the relevant content

Too Much Time for Description and Too Little Time for Critical Thinking

As indicated in the 'But I have a Question …' box above, some students never seem to have enough time to really answer a question in depth. They spend too much time describing a theory before they evaluate it and so run out of time.

The answer to this is to make explicit the assumptions that you are making when you write your answer. For example, if you are assuming that the assessor already understands a particular theory and you feel that you do not need to explain the theory, then it is worth saying so in order to prevent a misunderstanding.

It is true that different tutors will take a slightly different approach to this, and it is a good idea to check before you go near an examination, but most will appreciate the fact that you are spending more time demonstrating your critical thinking skills than merely providing another explanation of a theory that they have read many times. After all, it is not possible to provide evidence of your critical thinking about a theory unless you have a good understanding of that theory first. Simply make explicit the fact that you are doing so within the examination essay. For example, you could probably write something like 'I will not explain Maslow's theory in detail, but will focus on evaluating his ideas' in an examination essay.

Failing to Define Key Terms

In the same way that the introduction to an assignment should clearly indicate the boundaries of the essay (i.e. what the essay will and will not cover), so, too, should the introduction to an examination essay provide the definitions that you are using of the keywords in the question.

Of course, defining a keyword incorrectly at the beginning will raise concerns in the mind of your lecturer about whether you have a sufficient understanding of what you have been taught, but it will at least give the lecturer something clear to feed back to you should you ask for that.

 KEY LEARNING POINT

The criteria for getting a good mark in an examination essay are little different from those for getting a good mark in other forms of assessment: content, critical thinking and coherent structure are expected whatever the nature of assessment.

 REFLECTION POINT

Take some time to think about the following questions and write down some answers.

How often do you take a few moments and write down an essay plan, or do you just start straight away and hope it makes sense to the tutor later? Which is best? Why?

Have you ever had feedback from an examination before? Why or why not? Would you ever consider getting some feedback from your lecturer?

Is there anything you know you usually forget before an examination but that you need during it? What can you do to make sure you do not forget next time?

AFTER THE EXAMINATION

Few people really enjoy examinations and most are happy once they are able to leave the room. In many cases, there is then a process of 'debrief', where students release the built-up tension by talking to each other about the questions they answered, what they included in each answer, and so on.

This is great for releasing tension and is a natural thing to do, but if you find others (and the emphasis here is on several others, rather than just one or two) saying that they included content that you did not, then it is good to remember a few things:

1.   They are not marking your examination – your lecturer is!
2.   Marks usually depend as much on the extent to which you demonstrated your critical thinking as on the content you included – the 'how' you wrote the answer is as important as 'what' you wrote about.
3.   You may have taken an interesting approach to answering the question, an approach that may be more appreciated by the lecturer than by the other students.

If you do feel nervous and anxious about the examination, you might want to speak to a lecturer or someone who can help you think things through in a systematic and logical way. It is always good to learn and be reflective: that reflection can help us improve.

INTEGRATION AND APPLICATION

There is little anyone can do about the tensions and anxieties that people feel before taking an examination, and the pressure to perform can be immense in certain cultures and countries. The steps suggested above should help you limit that tension, so how about trying the following simple ideas?

Firstly, get to know as much information as you can about any forthcoming examinations. Knowledge reduces uncertainty, so the less you do not know, the more you should feel OK.

Secondly, try to practise some past papers and get some feedback from the lecturer. The feedback should help you feel more confident about the things you know and find out what you are not really so sure about.

Thirdly, revise in a way that works for you, so find out what works best. Think about your notes and whether you are a visual learner or learn best from what you experience or hear. If a revision timetable works to schedule your revision, then great, but do not use one simply because everyone else is.

Fourthly, try to get sufficient exercise, sleep and food. When we are stressed, our daily routine tends to stop, so make sure you do all you can to maintain a normal lifestyle.

Fifthly, during the exam, maintain a good sense of time and calm. Plan your time carefully, do not panic, and write whatever you think is helpful in giving a good answer to the question. Remember to look carefully at the verbs and nouns in the question.

Finally, relax after the examination. It is over. You may have others to come, and you will need to concentrate on those, so do not spend a lot of time worrying over your last answer or last examination paper.

CONCLUSION

You should now be able to:

•   Describe the different forms and different meanings of examination questions that are used at university.
•   Identify the practical issues you need to know in relation to the examinations that you will be taking.
•   Evaluate various mechanisms for improving your revision and memory.
•   Avoid some of the common failings when answering university examination questions.

Examinations are stressful for most students, but they do not need to be. Thoughtful revision, sufficient preparation, and careful analysis and planning of the questions once you turn over the paper will all help to ensure you are able to produce answers that are as good as they can be. However, there is no substitute for learning and thinking about what you are being 'taught' as you go through your modules, rather than all at the end. People rarely have time to do sufficient reading and thinking during a stressful revision period, so it is much better to do that reading and thinking during the preceding weeks of a module.

REFLECTION POINT

Take some time to think about the following questions and write down some answers.

Based on the content of this chapter, what do you now know about undertaking an examination that you did not know before?

What key learning point had the most impact? Why?

Do your answers to either of the above questions have the potential to change your attitude to studies at university? If so, why?

What will you now do differently? (Write this down and put it somewhere where you can see it regularly.)

CHAPTER TASK

Different people have different methods and approaches to their preparation for examinations. Look for five or six people who come from a different social/cultural background and ask what methods they use to revise. In particular, do they use any methods that are not listed here? Which methods for examination preparation are used most frequently among other students?

INTERVIEW QUESTIONS

In Chapter 5, it was suggested that there would be few interview questions regarding university studies specifically, but that interviewers might ask questions around the topic to find out about your ability to make decisions or think critically - or to find out more about the way you behave or react to certain situations. The same is true for issues around assessment.

Think about the following questions. What might your answers be?

1. How successful were you at planning your revision?
2. How have you used the feedback from your examinations to improve your performance?

Chapter 17 gives a lot more information on selection interviews and the online content gives some guidance on these questions.

ADDITIONAL RESOURCES

Want to learn more? Visit https://study.sagepub.com/morgan2e to gain access to a wide range of online resources, including interactive tests, tasks, further reading and downloads.

Website Resources

The following websites offer useful advice on examinations.

Guidance from QS – University ranking website: www.topuniversities.com/student-info/health-and-support/exam-preparation-ten-study-tips

University of Hull – library resource: libguides.hull.ac.uk/ld.php?content_id=3166177

University of Leicester: www2.le.ac.uk/offices/ld/resources/study/revision-exam

Textbook Resources

Burns, T. and Sinfield, S. (2016) *Essential Study Skills* (4th edition). London: Sage (particularly Chapter 12.6).
Cottrell, S. (2012) *The Exams Skills Handbook* (2nd edition). Basingstoke: Palgrave Macmillan.
Cottrell, S. (2013) *The Study Skills Handbook* (4th edition). New York: Palgrave (particularly Chapter 14).
Horn, R. (2012) *The Business Skills Handbook*. London: CIPD (particularly Chapter 12).
McMillan, K. and Weyers, J. (2011) *How to Succeed in Examinations and Assessments*. Harlow: Pearson.
Smale, R. and Fowlie, J. (2009) *How to Succeed at University*. London: Sage (particularly Chapter 8).

PART IV
EMPLOYABILITY SKILLS

As we saw in Chapter 2, there is a significant overlap between the skills required for being successful in your studies and those required for the workplace. This is probably what you would expect, otherwise universities would not be producing employable graduates. This part provides this link, *by focusing on the skills that you will develop during your studies but which will have significant relevance to the workplace*. The emphasis here will be on enabling you to behave in a way that will also help you succeed in the workplace.

However, there is a challenge here: every workplace will be different – the importance of the skills will vary and each context may require you to apply them in different ways. Working in a multinational organisation is going to be very different from working in a small startup business with six or seven other people. This text cannot address every possibility, but it will try to give you some guidance for some of the more important and generic aspects of these skills.

In this part, we will cover a number of interpersonal skills: effective communication (Chapter 9), oral presentation skills (Chapter 10), team working (Chapter 11), leadership (Chapter 12) and two areas of intrapersonal skill – cross-cultural awareness (Chapter 13) and problem solving and creativity (Chapter 14). The intention is that this will provide you with sufficient understanding of these areas to be able to apply them well.

GENERAL PRINCIPLES

Whenever we start to discuss human behaviour, there are a number of things we need to bear in mind if certain behaviour is to increase. We could think very simply through the idea of means (do you have the knowledge and ability to demonstrate a particular skill?), motive (are you motivated to do so?) and opportunity (does your course and/or university life in general provide you with the opportunities to demonstrate and develop the skills you need?). The answer to the latter is probably 'yes' – although life is usually a little more complex than that.

As shown in Chapter 2, the development of skills comes through a number of different processes (e.g. taking advantage of opportunities to gain experience, gathering information and knowledge in different ways, reflecting on our experiences, thinking through the possibilities, and so on). No skill can be demonstrated and then developed without such issues being thought through, but it is important to recognise that there is a variety of other factors which can influence behaviour.

We could think about your life and career goals (see also Chapter 3 on time management) and the skills you need to achieve them; we could think about how you get feedback on your abilities (see Chapter 2 and Chapter 5); whether you have the resources and knowledge to demonstrate and develop these skills; and, finally, we could think about the extent to which other personal factors might affect your behaviour and performance.

The chapters that follow in this part will help you to identify where your weaknesses may lie and will go some way to helping you understand what needs to change.

9 COMMUNICATING EFFECTIVELY

The single biggest problem in communication is the illusion that it has taken place. (George Bernard Shaw.)

CHAPTER STRUCTURE

Figure 9.1

When you see the this means go to the companion website https://study.sagepub.com/morgan2e to do a quiz, complete a task, read further or download a template.

━━ AIMS OF THE CHAPTER ━━

By the end of this chapter, you should be able to:

- Describe the communication process and how it can go wrong.
- Identify the various verbal, non-verbal and para-linguistic behaviours that can influence communication.
- Evaluate and develop your communication skills with a particular focus on communicating in difficult situations, giving feedback and active listening.

WHEN SHOULD YOU READ THIS CHAPTER?

You will need to develop and use your communication skills from the beginning of your university career, so it is best to read this within the first year - or earlier if you have a group assignment.

INTRODUCTION

This section of the text deals with some of the important interpersonal skills we need to use when developing and building relations with others. The way we communicate has significant implications in the way that we lead others, work in teams, present information to convince others of a particular message and work cross-culturally. It has links to nearly all that you do in your studies, in your work and in your relationships – and as such on the quality of academic work and the grades you receive.

That is why this chapter is first in this section on employability skills. The aim of this chapter is to give you an awareness of the key things to bear in mind as you communicate.

Understanding human communication is not easy – we could have based this whole book on communication skills. We probably know some people who love to talk, but, on the other hand, there are others who seem to have nothing to say. We could say that both are good communicators if they use their skills appropriately, and in the right situations, but communicating is no more about talking than it is about being quiet all the time. So, we could ask: What does 'use their skills appropriately' mean, and what are the 'right situations'?

In so many situations, the ability to communicate in a way that ensures a message is understood in the way you intend is critical to being able to perform well. Yet it is the one thing that tends to cause the most problems in employment (and personal) relationships. Poor communication with others – or even an unwillingness to communicate (and an awareness of when or why not to communicate) – is important to get right, which is why it is included here.

Finally, much of the content below relates to oral communication, some of which will overlap with Chapter 10 on presentation skills, but there is some content on written communication in Chapter 7. This set of skills – getting grammar and spelling correct, ensuring your academic work is well structured, demonstrating your critical thinking – is also covered in Chapter 7 in relation to academic work. Within employment, however, there is a need to ensure that emails and letters are written in a particular way, so there will be some content covering these areas.

SKILLS SELF-ASSESSMENT

Complete the brief questionnaire below to see how well you communicate with others. Give each item a score between 1 and 5, where 1 is 'not at all like me', and 5 is 'very much like me'.

When I communicate with others, I know that …

Item	Statement	Score
1.	I never interrupt other people in a conversation	
2.	I find myself daydreaming during most conversations because I find what others talk about is quite boring to me	
3.	I want to be the last person to say anything during a discussion	
4.	I think I can reduce tension during an emotional discussion or argument	
5.	I want to think of something funny to say	
6.	I never misinterpret what someone else is saying	

Item	Statement	Score
7.	I vary the intonation (pitch) of my voice	
8.	I smile as much as I can	
9.	I speak very slowly to ensure that I can get my message across	
10.	I am happy to be passionate about a topic if I think it is important	
11.	I speak too loudly	
12.	I use facial expressions (frowns, smiles) to emphasise the message I want to give	
13.	I judge the person who is communicating with me	
14.	I feel nervous about how others will react to what I want to say	
15.	I consider the words I use carefully to ensure that the other person does not react emotionally	
16.	I choose my language and the words that I use so that the other person will understand	
17.	I get impatient with other people if they are taking a long time to say what they want to say	
18.	I am interested in what others have to say	
19.	I do not care how others will react to what I want to say	
20.	I am happy to let others talk if they are saying what I want to say anyway	
21.	I regularly get emotional about what others say	
22.	I always understand exactly what others are trying to say	
23.	I cause problems in my relationships with others, but I do not know why	
24.	I believe that others will interpret my messages in the same way as I intend them	
25.	I enjoy myself	
26.	I struggle to understand different accents when I am talking with or listening to people from different places	
27.	I think carefully about whether I believe what someone is saying	
28.	I reflect on how well I am communicating with others	
29.	I understand when I need to be formal and business-like, rather than informal and friendly	
30.	I recognise how my own personality, perception and past experiences can affect how well I communicate	

━━━━━━ FOR YOU TO DO ━━━━━━

With others you know reasonably well, choose any five of the questions above (maybe randomly) and discuss the following:

1. Do you know others who might have different answers from you for these questions?
2. What might the impact be of working with people whose answers to those questions are different from your own?
3. Why might the questions you have chosen impact on the quality of your communication with others?
4. Do you think there are better and worse answers to these questions?

This questionnaire is longer than that of any other chapter, indicating the complexity and importance to your studies of what we refer to as 'communication skills'. There are few right and wrong answers to this questionnaire, but for most questions the answer we give will have consequences for the quality of our relationships with others – especially those whose answers may be very different to our own.

 'BUT I HAVE A QUESTION ...'

You said that communication skills are linked to grades. How does that work?

Our abilities to communicate have an impact on so many areas of our lives – and academic studies are just one, but even this has many components. Imagine the following scenarios:

1. **Finding the relevant resources** to write an essay without being able to communicate with any other student. This is possible, though not recommended. Others may have a lot of good ideas which can help you.
2. Doing a good **oral presentation**. You struggle to get your message across clearly and within the time given. If you cannot communicate well, then you will find that your audience does not receive the message you want to give.
3. **Working on a group assignment** without being able to communicate. This would be impossible since you need to be able to convey your ideas and thoughts to help the group do better quality work. A failure to communicate will also mean that the **relationships that others have with you** start to disintegrate as distrust and blame for poor group performance start to become more frequent.
4. Being unable to **send an appropriate email**. If you need to make an appointment with any member of staff or seek help to understand a concept in a lecture, you will need to send an email, communicating what you need. Obviously, this is not oral communication, but sending an appropriately worded email is important.
5. **Leading a group** on the group assignment. If you cannot communicate well, then you might find that the group falls apart, no one is motivated for the assignment and completing the work becomes very stressful – and may be done by one or two people, rather than the entire group. Of course, you won't be able to arrange meetings, make sure that everyone in the group is feeling OK and so on. You cannot lead if you cannot communicate well.
6. You are in a **cross-cultural group** but you find you are having arguments with others from other countries in the group all the time. It is something that you find difficult to resolve, but something which could break your group apart before the assignment is finished.
7. You do not know how to **give someone feedback** and how to tell someone that what they do really annoys you. As a result, they do not stop and your life becomes worse and worse. If a flatmate is making too much noise each night, then you get less and less sleep and you cannot concentrate in the lectures.

THE CONTEXT OF COMMUNICATION

Very little communication takes place in isolation. Unless you are a brand-new manager taking over a local business or a new student who has just enrolled on a course, most communication will take place in the context of relationships which already exist.

We will examine most of these processes and technical terms below, but the quality of relationships we have with others tends to be influenced by a number of factors.

The way in which we behave through various media – our words, our facial expressions, tone of voice, and so on – will create impressions of us in the minds of others. Usually, whether we are successful in communicating what we wish to communicate will be influenced by aspects of communication that we can control: our body language (non-verbal behaviour), the way we use our voice (para-linguistic behaviours/cues), the context of and learning from the conversations we have had previously, the ways we communicate (channels, e.g. email or face-to-face) and the words that we use. These issues will all affect the way we 'code' our messages.

However, whether any message will be received and interpreted in the way that we expect will depend on whether those same issues help the recipient of the communication to 'decode' it in the same way.

The ongoing and important challenge is that where communication is not interpreted correctly (i.e. as intended), it will have consequences for the beliefs and attitudes of the recipients, their emotions and then their broader behaviour, which is why many relationship issues in teams, at work and elsewhere tend to arise from poor communication. Resolving where the origins of any poor communication arose can often help to do something to repair relationships, though sometimes this is not possible. The challenge is often that there are no absolutely 'correct' ways to communicate and that every individual has to work out a system (i.e. a set of tools for communicating usefully) that works for them in a variety of situations.

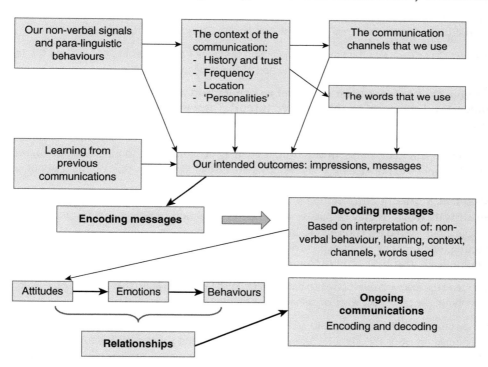

Figure 9.2   The context of communication

The model presented in Figure 9.2 indicates that: 1) the process of communication does not take place in isolation; and 2) there is a definitive process of communication that requires the 'coding' and 'decoding' (or translation) of information. Later sections of the chapter give more details of how these processes of encoding and decoding happen.

Understanding the Process of Communication

Before we get into the details of how different communication skills are best demonstrated, it is important to understand the basics of how all communication processes work. The principles are relatively straightforward to understand; of course, the challenge comes in applying them to our communications. Unless we think about them, all the processes and issues identified below happen unconsciously, but when we do think about them and change what we do as a result, then our communications become much more effective. Let's use an example to illustrate what we mean, and show how things can go wrong.

1. **We have something we want or need to communicate to others and we put it into a form of words (code) that we can send to others in some way**. The experiences we have picked up have gradually expanded from our parents to siblings to friends and then to fellow students and colleagues at work, so the way we have learned to communicate (i.e. the code that we use) as young children will change as we unconsciously learn how to communicate with our expanded 'circle of friends'.

    The information gets coded in our minds in a way that experience tells us is usually interpreted correctly with minimum negative consequences. (I will have 'coded' my words here in this text in a particular way, reflecting my own experiences and ideas about what works.)

Example: I want to check whether someone has done the work I asked them to do, so I use the following question: 'Have you been able to finish that section of the assignment yet?'

2. **We give that information (in code) to others and assume that others will understand the code in the way we intend**. There will be some who understand that code well, namely those with whom we share a 'common language'. The 'language' we use can include technical language or 'jargon' or abbreviations that only those with a particular background or experiences will understand. In addition, there may be words used in a certain way that only certain people will understand correctly. Therefore, the assumption that we make about people always understanding us is rarely true.

3. **We select a 'media channel' as a way of sending a message at a time and place we think will work**. It may be passive and is often a reaction to how a communication was passed on to us, but we have a choice as to how we respond to others' communications. It may be via a meeting, or a reply by email or a corridor conversation, but the channel that we use to communicate does have implications for the way in which that communication is received.

Example: I send the following question as an email: 'Have you been able to finish that section of the assignment yet?' The intention is to find out whether someone has finished their section of the report.

It is certainly quicker and easier to send an email to many people at once, but for many individuals, most of their email communication (including the use of synchronous chat tools, such as WhatsApp, WeChat, Line, Facebook Messenger, etc.) is to individuals. There are times when it is slower to send an email to an individual than it would be to speak to them on the telephone or go to see them (and clear up any communication which is unclear or ambiguous), but the choice of 'best channel to use' will depend on the urgency of the communication, the number of people involved, and the potential for and consequences of any misunderstanding. Box 9.1 explains this in more detail.

━━━━━━━━━━ **BOX 9.1** ━━━━━━━━━━

Understanding Communication Channels

Is there a 'best' communication channel? The answer will depend on a variety of factors. Email and other forms of one-way communication (e.g. newsletters) might be effective for communicating to a lot of people at one time, but are not always the most effective if you want to deal with a sensitive issue that is relevant to just one person and where written communication is likely to lead to misunderstanding.

Written communication is simply *content* and can be interpreted in a number of ways, assuming that the written communication is actually read of course! Someone reading an email at the end of a tiring and stressful day might interpret the email very differently from someone who can take their time, think about what it means and knows how you usually communicate. Communicating with one individual by email may or may not be effective, but if someone does not know you well, then you will need to be very clear about your meaning, using language that most will interpret correctly.

Oral communication over the telephone adds what we call 'para-linguistic cues': small 'behaviours' (some call them 'behavioural tells') which add to the meaning of just giving the words themselves. In written text/chat communication, we have 'emojis', which perform the same function. Although we will cover them in more detail below, these tells – such as speed of speech, pitch, volume and variation in any of these – indicate how important different words and issues might be, and a telephone conversation will give you this extra information in a way that a letter or an email rarely will.

Face-to-face communication is the richest and most complete form of communication. With this, others will be able to see your body language and facial expressions, as well as understand your tone of voice, which means that the chances of your message being interpreted correctly are increased. (This is one of the key reasons why employers use face-to-face selection interviews when selecting their staff.)

One word of caution: the interpretation of your message – even when given face-to-face – is *only as good as the decoding* used by the recipient of your communication, and this is not usually something that is within your control. The additional advantage of face-to-face communication is that you can seek the feedback mentioned above and check instantly whether the message was actually received in the way you intended.

---

4. **Even if the code is understood, there can be a range of issues which distort the reception of the message**. Broadly speaking, communications experts call these 'noise' and 'perceptual filters'. The 'noise' is the external background factors which can impact on the 'hearing' of a message (e.g. the number of tasks we have to deal with, the effort required to decode a message, motivation and interest in relation to the subject content – anything which can affect whether we actually hear parts of a message), while the 'perceptual filters' are internal factors which affect our interpretation of a message (e.g. our own knowledge and previous experience about an issue, trust we have in the individual). Both affect the accuracy of any 'decoding' process that takes place, and therefore the accuracy of the interpretation of any message.

Example: The question '*Have you been able to finish that section of the assignment yet?*' might be received by someone (let's call them 'B') who believes that you do not trust them, and is interpreted as '*I don't think you've finished this part of the report either but I am just checking ...*', indicating impatience.

Such distortions in communication are particularly important when communicating across cultures. Cultural expectations can really distort the way that messages are given since the encoding will usually be very different (see Chapter 13). The point is made clearer when we think of differences between direct translation and interpretation. *Direct translation* from one language to another takes the words and translates them into another language. This is helpful to some extent, but the recipient of that translation still has to give meaning to those words. *Interpretation*, on the other hand, finishes the job, giving meaning to the words and phrases so that the recipient can understand them.

Example: The question 'Have you been able to finish that section of the assignment yet?' is interpreted by someone with poor English as 'Have you found the resources and the ability to finish the section of the report?' Remember: the original intention was to find out if they had finished the section of the report, not really whether they had been able to do so.

5. **We rarely check that others have understood the messages that we give in the way we intend**. To check that this is so takes a lot of time, especially if we are communicating to a large number of people (e.g. by email). That is one reason why large corporate communication events tend to be largely inspirational and thin on detail – the detail will usually need to be discussed in smaller units where clarification is much more possible.

However, even in one-to-one discussions: 1) individuals rarely ask the other person to summarise what has been agreed or to rephrase any instructions given (perhaps because of a fear of seeming to be patronising or worry over whether someone will feel embarrassed because they have not interpreted something correctly); and/or 2) even when they are asked, individuals can simply repeat a phrase or statement without any understanding of what it really means. That feedback is crucial in establishing whether a message has been received in the way it was intended.

'BUT I HAVE A QUESTION ...'

... You say that communicating face-to-face is better than communicating over the telephone or via email. Does this mean that if I give more information about an issue in my emails, the chance that my communication will be understood will increase?

The simple answer is: not necessarily. Let's assume for the moment that this is a communication via email to several people (maybe group members working on a project). If you regularly add increasing detail to the information you give, then you will probably confuse others and it is quite likely that they will just wait for what they think is the final communication. The best thing is often to give as much detail as you think is needed in order to inform the other individual(s) about whatever the issue might be; if they have questions, then be sure to invite them to ask – though the challenge will be with those who *think* they understand, but whose understanding is actually incorrect.

KEY LEARNING POINT

Communication is a complex process which does not always produce the outcomes you intend. Checking that the understanding of your message(s) is the same as you intend with those who receive it is always important.

Communicating on Social Media

Although we probably use social media as if it was water, the history of social media is relatively recent, with the first patents being filed around 2003. We might regularly use Facebook, YouTube, WeChat, WhatsApp or others to find out what people are saying or doing, who's liked our photos and whether there is something that we can share.

Social media has a great role to play in building social relationships and can help us to communicate easily with others, but that same opportunity (like any tool) can bring amazing challenges as well, especially if we comment publicly.

Communicating via social media can take two forms: chatting (one to one, one to many) and commenting on what others say and post, and both can include emojis to enhance the written communication.

We can chat to people who know us and who understand our meaning and can react appropriately. We can joke, share experiences in a virtual world and share specific files and photos privately. Chatting in that way can enhance relationships with others whose values we might share.

The challenges come with comments made or pictures posted publicly, and this is where some individuals find communication on social media difficult, or even dangerous – and it can come as a shock. We get used to communicating with friends who often agree with our way of thinking, but that is not how much of the world thinks. The world – i.e. the general public – will have a wide range of views on every issue (especially those relating to sexual issues, politics, others' behaviour, and religion), and some reactions that you receive might be aggressive, insensitive, rude and so on. The same is true when we post photos or share others' posts.

Those reactions can sometimes be difficult to manage or cope with, so we need to be prepared for that. The same is true for comments that we might post on other websites or on videos posted on YouTube or Youku. Others might not have the same values as us and might disagree violently with our point of view.

How can we prevent this? We can't actually prevent it because people post comments on social media according to their own thoughts, and unless the website or social media platform has strict and very clear rules and monitors those rules carefully, we can do little about what others write. So, we might decide 1) not to comment on an aggressive/abusive post or comment (and this is probably the best option if you don't wish to inflame things further), 2) to comment in a balanced and tactful way ('some people might disagree' rather than 'I think you are wrong!') or 3) to agree that some people might hold their view and some people might not. A fourth and much safer alternative is to only post items relating to things you have done and/or keep your posts private so that only your friends – those who know you reasonably well – can see and comment on them.

One of the difficulties in the way that social media works is that the algorithms which make social media function often send us information based on what we 'like' (i.e. click on the 'like' icon), and that means that the more we like articles with a particular theme or point of view, the more we will see posts and adverts from other people and organisations (and maybe even be sent friend suggestions) which give the same point of view – meaning that people's opinions get reinforced, rather than challenged. In the long term, this erodes individuals' abilities to critically engage in a constructive way.

Take some time to think about the following questions and write down some answers.

Do you ever have emotional arguments with other people, or with someone you know? Why do those arguments begin?

Do you find it easier to communicate with someone you know well, or someone you do not know? What makes the difference?

Do you ever try to find out whether someone has understood your message(s) in the way you wanted them to? Has that ever led to any arguments?

COMPONENTS OF COMMUNICATION

Having examined the way that the communication process works, it is useful to examine the various behavioural 'inputs' into the communication process. These were briefly referred to earlier on as aspects of 'non-verbal behaviours' and 'para-linguistic cues'.

In some ways, it would be wonderful if communication was just made up of the words we use and if everyone interpreted those words in the same way – it would make life much easier and more straight-forward. In other ways, having the extra information can give us more clues as to what someone might be trying to say, as long as we interpret those clues in the way they were meant.

We use non-verbal behaviours and para-linguistic cues all the time, but the way we use them in combination with our words can radically change the meanings. Some individuals are better than others at recognising those meanings.

 PARA-LINGUISTIC CUES

A para-linguistic cue is any type of oral behaviour which adds meaning to the words of a message.

Para-linguistic Cues

There are broadly four areas where we can change our behaviour to have a particular impact. Professional speech coaches will give a great deal of advice on these so that individuals can give speeches that have an impact (some of these areas are covered briefly in Chapter 10), but they also have an impact in everyday conversations:

1. **Speed of speech**: Some people will speak more slowly than others, and some may take more time to speak and contribute than others. This may be a sign of being more thoughtful or of needing a little more time to think something through, but we cannot conclude this from speed of speech alone. However, there is usually a rhythm to our speech which helps others understand when we are about to finish a sentence.
2. **Volume of speech**: In usual conversation, people do not speak loudly enough for others to hear, so a loud conversation is often taken as a sign of heightened emotion, especially if the pitch of voice is also raised (both often occur together). It can, however, be an indication that someone is struggling to hear, so we have to be careful when interpreting behaviour.
3. **Pitch and intonation**: The more monotone our voice, the less interested someone is likely to be in what we are saying. We naturally indicate important issues within a conversation by changing our pitch. There is no better tone – higher pitch is not better than lower pitch – but the pitch we use will probably send a message to others about how calm, emotional or authoritative we are about a particular issue. Higher pitch (and volume) tends to indicate more emotion, but it is not universally the case, and some individuals communicate their negative emotion by using a much lower pitch than normal. With the pitch of our voice, we can indicate scepticism, sarcasm and humour as well as a range of emotions.
4. **Change and modulation in any of the above**: When we continue to use a normal pattern of speech, then the hearer is likely to assume that the information is of 'average' importance compared with other information, but if we suddenly change any of the three aspects above, we signal to the hearer that there is some information that they need to pay careful attention to.

To demonstrate the impact of intonation, consider the example in Box 9.2.

═══════════ BOX 9.2 ═══════════

The Impact of Intonation

Let's take a very simple phrase: 'I want to have a cup of tea'. Which of these five phrases represents the meaning here?

1. I have been waiting ages and I am very impatient to drink my cup of tea.
2. You have brought me a cup of coffee but I really want a cup of tea.
3. Thank you very much for asking: my favourite drink is a cup of tea.
4. I asked for a cup of tea, but you have brought a flask of tea.
5. Everyone wants to have some coffee, but I would like to have a cup of tea.

The simple (and maybe obvious) answer is that we cannot tell. Without knowing where the emphasis was – or whether there was any emphasis at all – we have no idea. So, let's add some emphasis by indicating some intonation:

I want to have a cup of *tea*.

If you say this out loud, then it is clear that the emphasis is on the word 'tea' in order to create a contrast with anything else, so the correct meaning appears to be (b). But if the emphasis is put anywhere else, then the meaning changes considerably. If we add volume of speech and facial expressions as well, then we can determine whether someone is simply making a comment, or whether they appear to be emotional and making a complaint.

Try taking all the alternative answers (1 to 5 above): how would you indicate intonation and volume for each of these possibilities?

BOX 9.3

Punctuation and Para-language

When we read the page of a textbook or a fictional story, we take notice of the punctuation that is there. The punctuation gives us an idea of how we should use para-language to convey the meaning of the words on the page. Consider the following:

A question mark (?) at the end of the sentence means that our tone of voice should go up as we ask a question.

A comma (,) between phrases means that there is a short pause at the end of the statement before moving on to the next statement (or 'clause').

A full stop (.) means that we have finished a particular statement; our intonation should go down at the end of the sentence, indicating the end of that issue. Over recent years, there has been a trend for people to raise their tone, as if they were asking a question; this is not how the 'full stop' or 'period' (US English) should be used.

An exclamation mark (!) usually expresses disgust, surprise, shock or a strong reaction of some kind. As such, the volume and tone of voice usually go up.

This should help us understand more of what someone is trying to communicate, according to their tone of voice.

TIP: A good suggestion for seeing if a written sentence is too long is to see if you can say the sentence in one breath. If you can, then the length is probably reasonably good, but if that is not possible, then the sentence probably needs to be punctuated or broken up.

KEY LEARNING POINT

Para-language is a component of communication that can be used effectively to indicate particular emphases and to differentiate important issues from general 'background communication'.

Non-verbal Behaviour

If the vocal expressions – volume, pitch and speed – say something about our feelings, then other forms of non-verbal behaviour add to the interpretation of the message.

NON-VERBAL BEHAVIOUR

Non-verbal behaviour is any form of behaviour which communicates a message without using speech.

The more information we get about the communication and the more consistent that information is, the more likely we are to interpret a message correctly (assuming that we do actually notice any inconsistencies). However, these signals all add together in terms of the meaning of someone's message. In particular, we can consider facial expressions, body gestures and posture, touch, 'proxemics' and movement.

Facial expressions

Our eyes, the way we move our eyebrows, the amount of eye contact we give and the extent to which we smile all send messages to others. The challenge is to ensure that the message is interpreted in the way we intend. There are around 250,000 different facial expressions, meaning that the brain has to work very quickly to recognise the signals being sent by others.

It is actually difficult not to smile at someone who is smiling at us – it takes some effort and focus – which is why we often interpret smiles as a positive thing. Some people do not seem to smile very much; we could interpret that as a sign of seriousness, though any interpretation needs to be checked carefully. In some Asian cultures, showing the mouth when laughing is not seen as appropriate, so some Asians will cover their mouth when laughing at a joke between friends.

We often move our eyebrows to show curiosity or surprise (raised) and lower them to show concern or scepticism or negative emotion (frowning).

Direct eye contact is a sign of confidence in western cultures (with a lack of direct eye contact being seen as indicating a lack of self-confidence), but used to be considered a sign of a lack of respect in Confucian heritage cultures (e.g. China and Asia). Of course, these two reactions are not exclusive – it is quite possible to show deep respect to others and still have a great deal of self-confidence – but in some places the idea still continues, so we need to be careful when interpreting the behaviour of others where values are represented in ways we might not expect or understand.

We also move our eyes around in different ways. When we remember something, when we are trying to think of something or when we are trying to imagine something, we look in different directions. You may suspect that someone is not telling you the truth because they avoid direct eye contact when they are talking, which is why people often ask others to 'look them in the eyes' when saying something that may not quite be true, but we also need to be aware that they *may simply be thinking about something* or trying to remember something, rather than telling you something that is not true.

━━━━━━━━━━ FOR YOU TO DO ━━━━━━━━━━

Consider the emotions displayed below.

1. As you do so, draw a 'smilie' or 'emoji' (a small face indicating the positions of the eyes, the mouth and the eyebrows) reflecting what you think someone expressing that emotion would show on their face.

    Happy / Sad / Concerned / Confused / Curious / Angry / Laughing / Excited / Amazed / Upset / Sceptical / Uncertain / Joking

2. After you have done this, compare your drawing with that of the person next to you: how similar are your drawings?

3. Take one of these emotions and find someone from a different culture: did they draw something very different from you?

Body gestures

What we do with our head, our arms and our hands adds to others' interpretations of a message that we give. There are those who say that someone with crossed arms is adopting a defensive and potentially aggressive approach to a conversation. In reality, whether this is true will depend on two other factors: 1) whether other non-verbal behaviours are giving out the same signals; and 2) whether this individual normally behaves in that way, even if they are relaxed. We interpret these behaviours instinctively, without thinking too much. It is quite possible for someone to sit in front of you with their arms crossed, to be smiling and to have a relaxed and friendly conversation.

Hand movements are often assumed to be very useful indicators of what is going through another individual's mind at the time they are speaking, though hand (and head) movements when someone is supposed to be just listening can be taken as an indication that they are reacting to something, have stopped listening and are preparing to speak.

Gestures are often used alongside para-linguistic cues to add emphasis to the words that are communicated, especially in formal presentations, but a lack of any hand gestures should not be seen as a lack of emphasis. Some people deliberately hold their hands in a particular way (e.g. behind their back) in order to hide their nerves or to try to avoid distracting their listeners from the actual content (facts and figures) they are trying to deliver.

Of course, the more regularly a particular gesture is made, the more likely it will be that the message conveyed by the gesture will be emphasised.

If we are perfectly content and are thinking of the same thing constantly in the same way, then it is unlikely we will move. Humans move when there is a reason to do so, and that reason can be large and urgent (e.g. people rushing out of a building when there is an earthquake) or small and relatively insignificant (e.g. someone getting up from the sofa when they have been watching TV because they are bored with what they are watching). So when we see people moving, we would naturally assume there is a purpose behind their doing so.

The challenge comes, then, when people do not behave in ways we might expect, either because we expect someone to move or gesture in some way but they do not, or because someone moves when there is no reason for them to do so.

Both the movements we demonstrate and the frequency with which we demonstrate them can be signs of self-confidence. It is assumed that occasional and purposeful movement indicates more self-confidence than erratic movement.

FOR YOU TO DO

Examine the photographs of the gestures given below. What do you think this individual is trying to say with these gestures? Do others agree with your interpretation?

 REFLECTION POINT

Take some time to think about the following questions and write down some answers.

How 'expressive' are you in the way you communicate to other people? Do you use a lot of intonation, or speak in a monotone voice most of the time? What about your facial expressions, or gestures?

Have you ever been told that your use of non-verbal behaviour affects others' reactions to you?

Do others communicate with you in the way you communicate with them? Do those same people communicate differently with others?

BOX 9.4

Can You Tell If Someone Is Lying?

Behavioural psychologists tell us that there are a number of behavioural signs or 'tells' we can look out for when someone is not telling the truth. Most are similar to those occasions when someone is suffering from stress:

1. Having a dry mouth – and needing to drink frequently.
2. Overly frequent 'aggressive gestures' (e.g. forming the hand into a fist).
3. Blink rate – the rate is usually 20 blinks a minute, but is someone blinking faster than that?
4. Hand gestures – does anything appear to represent information being hidden?
5. Covering the mouth with the hand – information is being prevented from 'escaping'.

The key thing for all of these is that, in isolation, it is difficult to conclude that someone is lying. However, if there are many 'tells' occurring at the same time, then perhaps someone is being economical with the truth.

Can you tell if someone you know is lying?

Touch

One type of gesture that some like to give is that of touch.

This is an extremely delicate issue to cover, but it is very important to do so. In some cultures, and for some individuals, touch is something that is unwanted and can cause very serious misunderstandings.

Depending on the kind of touch, it can show compassion, kindness, friendship, love and more. Of course, it is never wrong to show kindness (even if definitions of 'kindness' may vary from situation to situation) and most would say that there is nothing wrong with a hand on the shoulder for encouragement, but *the potential for touch to be misinterpreted is very large* and workplace definitions of sexual harassment often include reference to unwanted physical contact.

In some cultures, it is frowned upon for people to be overly familiar with each other in public. In some cultures (e.g. particularly Arabic cultures), it is very common to see men walking down the street holding hands and greeting each other by kissing on the cheek, but in other cultures this kind of touch could be perceived as inappropriate.

To be safe, do not touch others. A touch can also be seen as a sign of familiarity. Unwanted physical contact can be the start of sexual harassment complaints, so it is better not to touch.

Proxemics

Put simply, proxemics is the study of the impact that location has on communication. The simplest way of demonstrating this is to consider the legend of King Arthur, who was supposed to have reigned in southern England around AD 800. He reputedly had his close followers sit around a round table, rather than one with definite ends, in order to create a discussion among equals, rather than have a clear hierarchy.

A choice to sit at a particular location will have certain consequences. Certain locations will inhibit the number and kind of (supportive or negative) contributions to a discussion – for example, where direct eye contact becomes difficult or where the location seems a long way away from the leader of the discussion. In meetings and other situations, physical distance is often interpreted as reflecting emotional distance, and such an interpretation will have implications for individuals' communication with others. The location someone sits in will have an impact on:

- The number of contributions they are able to make easily without interrupting others.
- The formality or informality of the discussion.
- The sense of support or otherwise for the leader of the discussion.
- The extent to which individuals are engaged in the discussion.

Further online content on the topic of proxemics can be found on the companion website at https://study.sagepub.com/morgan2e.

FURTHER
READING

KEY LEARNING POINT

Non-verbal communication consists of our facial expressions, body gestures and movement, and proxemics. They help us to add meaning to the other signals we receive – the words and the para-language.

'BUT I HAVE A QUESTION ...'

... There is a lot to consider, but how can I possibly pay attention to all of this when I am having a conversation with a friend or with a colleague at work?

This is a good question – and the simple answer is that in most situations you cannot. If you were to think consciously about all of these things then your communication would seem odd, because you would be trying to reconcile their perception of you with their behaviour caused by your behaviour and your tone of voice, and you would be trying to second-guess and assume the impact of all the communication signals you were sending.

The value of the information above comes from three things: firstly, reflecting on conversations that you have had where the other person misinterpreted your meaning and recognising what you might have done differently; secondly, identifying just one or two areas where you could give more clarity in how you say what you have said and working on those; and thirdly, becoming better at making sure that you gather feedback from the other person and checking that they have understood your message as you intended it.

Focusing on a small number of areas will make the challenge of improving your communication skills much more manageable.

Words and Language

So far, we have examined the impact that our para-language, our non-verbal behaviour and proxemics can have on the ways that communication can be interpreted. What we have not yet examined, of course, is the actual language that we use. Examining language is an academic discipline in its own right – a degree in linguistics is offered by many universities – and is extremely complex as an area of study. What we will examine here are four aspects of language: the function that different forms of language can take; power and confidence issues; the ways in which the words we choose may or may not be particularly tactful or diplomatic; and, finally, the use of questions in conversation. There are other components to the study of language, for example the use of what linguistics call 'register' (we will not cover 'register' here, but, in very broad terms, it refers to the technical vocabulary level needed to understand conversations), but we will simply address the four areas highlighted above.

The Function of Language

When we write words as a sentence on a page, it is usually fairly clear what we are trying to do with the sentence. We might be trying to ask a question, give a suggestion or make a statement, and we use punctuation to indicate the functions that our language is trying to represent. As we saw in Box 9.3

above, punctuation is usually represented by our para-linguistic cues and so usually it is clear whether we are asking a question, giving a statement or making a suggestion.

However, there are occasions when things are much less clear. Take the phrase, 'You could always ask the marketing department for their ideas': is this a suggestion – that we *should* ask the marketing department – or an *instruction* that we are expected to/have to ask the marketing department? Alternatively, take the phrase, 'The marketing department usually have some good ideas': is this a *suggestion*, an *instruction* or merely a *statement* of fact which we can ignore if we wish to?

The answer will often relate to the context of the statement (Who said it? Under what circumstances?) and to the non-verbal and para-linguistic signals (tone of voice, volume, eyebrows, eye contact, smile, posture) given while saying it. When we are communicating orally, we take in all these signals and our learning from previous experience gives us an indication of which function the language is playing. When we are communicating by email, however, those signals are not there, and unless there is an exclamation mark (!) we are often left to our own devices to interpret the function that the message is giving us. We do not always get the interpretation correct, but there are occasions when we should probably check.

Box 9.5 examines the various functions that language can play.

 BOX 9.5

Are Questions Always 'Questions'?

We can usually think of questions as being tools for gathering information, and in many situations this is exactly what they are used for. However, questions can be used for a variety of purposes, and not just for gathering information. The examples below show how five fairly similar questions can be used to guide another individual's behaviour and influence decision making:

1. *'Don't you think that would be a really bad idea?'* Leading questions can be used forcefully to push someone to reconsider their actions.
2. *'Do you think there would be any negative consequences to that idea?'* This is a similar but much more gentle way of getting someone to reconsider their actions. Such a question might be used in coaching or counselling situations.
3. *'What do you think senior management might think of this idea?'* This could have a similar function to (2), but might (or might not, depending on who is asking it and how) include a threat – to tell senior management about this.
4. *'Why are you persisting with this really bad idea?'* This shows more about the negative emotion of the person who is asking it than it does in gathering any actual information. When individuals are emotional, they often need to express it in some way.
5. *'Wouldn't that idea cause a problem with X (other issue or individual)?'* This is clearer than (2) but is a leading question and so it achieves the same purpose. Being specific might indicate a desire to learn on the part of the person who is asking, or it might indicate a desire to put some pressure on an individual – more than is represented by (2) but not as much as (1).

The way that an individual would respond to any or all of these questions would give a particular impression of their leadership 'style'.

All of these are questions but have a purpose beyond simply gathering information. The simple information-gathering form of the question would probably be something like 'Can you tell us what you wish to do and why?', but even the interpretation of this would depend on the non-verbal behaviours and intonation used to ask the question.

(Continued)

In formal situations or interviews (disciplinary, selection or performance appraisal interviews), questions are usually asked in the order shown in Figure 9.3, representing a 'funnel', where the first open questions gather a great deal of information, the probing questions gather more detail on one particular issue, the closed question (with a 'yes' or 'no', or a numerical answer) finalises the information gathering and the reflective question checks the information in summary form.

In a more informal setting, there is no need for any such structure and the variety of questions asked can be much broader, but any conversation that consists of mainly closed or reflective questions is likely to be one without a great deal of natural 'flow'.

Chapter 13 covers issues of context in more detail with respect to communicating across cultures, where our interpretations of behaviour *can* be very inaccurate.

 KEY LEARNING POINT

The function of a phrase can have a marked impact on whether we take any subsequent action and on the nature of any action. If there is a lack of clarity, then it helps to *check that our understanding* of the function of what others have said is the same as the person communicating with us.

APPLYING THE COMPONENTS: COMMUNICATING WELL

The way in which we combine all these different elements of communication will vary according to the needs of any given situation, but as we have seen, the communication process is complex and conveying a message whilst building or maintaining a relationship is not easy.

A situation is composed of two (or more) people, a series of messages, a context or goal, why there is a need for communication at all, and perhaps a history. Regardless, we will need to apply verbal communication, non-verbal and para-linguistic elements of communication and other factors together in different ways to achieve different aims: to negotiate, to listen, to persuade, to caution or discipline, to appraise, to interview or maybe to counsel others.

To communicate well in difficult situations takes a great deal of time and effort, but in some instances (e.g. disciplinary or appraisal interviews) it is vital to plan the conversation and be very clear about the issues which need to be raised, as well as the *ways in which* these issues will be raised. This will vary according to the individual you are talking to. Below we look at three areas of communication skill where we can use the above components of communication to enhance the way we relate to others and get our work done effectively – namely, establishing rapport, giving negative feedback, active listening and communicating in a group.

Establishing Rapport

In this chapter, we have covered three elements of communication: para-language, non-verbal behaviour and the language that we use. There is one other area we can note in relation to these three elements, and it concerns the concept of rapport. We say that two people have 'rapport' when they seem to understand each other and enjoy each other's company.

We often know what rapport looks like. If we allow ourselves to enter a social setting, we might expect to be able to recognise individuals who have rapport with those around them and those who do not. Those who have rapport will be smiling at the same time that others smile, will be contributing to the conversation in some way and will be seen as part of a group. If we were to look at dating couples in the same setting, we might be able to see them making eye contact with each other, listening well and not interrupting, and maybe copying each other's gestures (picking up their drinks, putting their hands on their head, etc.) at the same time. We know that rapport has been established when that 'mirroring' of each other's behaviour occurs.

In sales environments, salespeople are trained to copy the language used by the other party, their body language and para-linguistic cues (or, in the case of telephone sales, the tone and speed of speech), until they seem to be 'matching' each other. Once that has occurred, it is believed that rapport has been established and, rather than following the behaviour of the other person, the salesperson can actually lead their behaviour – with the salesperson's body language being reflected in the behaviour of the person they are trying to sell to. In establishing rapport, the salesperson has established a bond of friendship and, by inference, of trust, leading the customer to exactly where the salesperson wants them to be.

RAPPORT

Rapport is a state of being where two or more individuals feel relaxed in each other's company.

Of course, the challenge for all non-verbal behaviour is that we make assumptions about the meanings of others' behaviour based on our own behaviour ('if they do X then they must be thinking Y, because that's what I do when I do X') but we rarely think to actually check our assumptions, and it is this lack of checking (the feedback mentioned in Part III) that can easily lead to misunderstandings in communication.

Active Listening

Of the four communication skills we have at our disposal (the two active ones – speaking and writing – and the two passive ones – reading and listening), listening is one of the most frequent, one of the most important and often is not very well done. In reality, listening well is anything but passive: it takes energy, time and effort if it is to be done well. Your ability to listen well will have an impact on whether others feel respect towards you, whether people continue to communicate openly with you ('I'll not bother – he never listens to a word I say anymore', which can have significant implications on decision making in management) and the broader impression that people will have. Therefore, being good at listening is important and is one of the most valuable communication skills sought by employers.

FOR YOU TO DO

Have a look at the following questions. When you are in a conversation with another person, how often do you ...

- Maintain eye contact with the other person?
- Ask questions to ensure that you actually understand the emotion and facts that are being conveyed?
- Wait until the other person has stopped talking before thinking about what to say next?
- Ensure that you understand what the other person has been saying before they finish their sentence?
- Interrupt the other person because they seem to be saying too much or rambling on for too long?
- Try to summarise what the other person has been saying before the end of the conversation?
- Avoid facial expressions of judgement?
- Ensure that your seating arrangement is appropriate for listening well?

(Continued)

In nearly all cases, the more we do these things, the better our listening skills will be. The exceptions are the fifth and sixth items, which are bad practice when it comes to listening well.

Active listening is not the same as hearing. We talk about 'listening to music', but unless we are processing the words and/or the music in some way, the actual activity we are usually undertaking relates to hearing rather than listening.

Hearing, therefore, is the passive reception of information by the ears, whereas active listening requires far more engagement from the individual, and far more processing of that information.

Active listening is not easy, it requires effort, and typically anything which requires effort tends not to be done particularly well. Tiredness, distractions, accents, active disinterest and making judgements or getting emotional about what is being said can all get in the way of our taking in information, and as soon as we omit information we are likely to miss out on certain parts of that information. Active listening involves ensuring that we take in and use as much information as we can, so not making judgements and trying not to think of what to say next are important.

Because that search is an active one, listening usually involves asking as many questions as it does being silent and gathering information (see Figure 9.3 below).

ACTIVE LISTENING

Active listening is the active search for an accurate understanding of another's message, through the interpretation of verbal and non-verbal messages.

The funnel technique

Open question
'Tell me about ...'

Probing question
'How did you ...?'

Closed question
'When was this?'

Reflective question
'So you ...?'

Figure 9.3   The four key question types

We can often start with an open question which gives us a lot of information about whatever we want to learn about. Then probably several probing questions, asking for more detail about a particular comment that the speaker has made in order to learn more about their opinions. To close a conversation down, the listener may then wish to gather factual information (e.g. yes/no, numerical data) and then finally to check their own understanding of what they have been told, a good listener will summarise what has been said and discussed by asking a reflective question about the situation faced and the actions taken.

Giving Negative Feedback

For managers, being able to give feedback to a strong performer is not difficult, but being able to do so to a poorly performing employee is much less easy. It is an essential communication skill, but one that is not always done well.

Using the definition given here, we can assume that feedback can be non-verbal as well as verbal. A raised eyebrow or a frown can be as useful in communicating a message as what an individual actually says.

Principles of Giving Feedback

Giving negative feedback is one of the most challenging things we can do, especially if we know the other party will not be happy about receiving it. But there are some additional principles we need to bear in mind when giving feedback in order to improve an individual's performance – which is the main goal of giving feedback.

FEEDBACK

Feedback is any communication to a person that gives them information on some aspect of their behaviour.

1. **Check any assumptions**: Ensure that you check any assumptions you have made before starting the conversation. Emotion can sometimes cloud an individual's judgement. This may include the reasons for someone's actions, especially if they are unusual and out of character, as well as the actions themselves. Be clear about the evidence you have for the behaviours you wish to change, and gather evidence from others *if* that will not harm other relationships.

2. **Reframe the purpose of the conversation**: See the conversation as a chance to solve a problem and to change someone's behaviour, rather than as a time to get really tough and make an example of someone. If you take the latter approach, it is likely that the atmosphere will be tense, the language will become aggressive and you will likely create more problems than you solve.

3. **Use passive and active voice appropriately**: Try to keep negative feedback in the 'passive voice', rather than the 'active voice'. For example, 'You did this badly' becomes 'This was done badly'. The identity of the person who performed the action will be implicit anyway, but removing the personal criticism can remove the 'sting' for someone who is lacking in confidence or who is likely to become defensive. The opposite is true for good news or positive feedback (i.e. 'You did this really well'), where personal praise is usually a good thing.

4. **Use a 'praise sandwich'**: In the 'praise sandwich' remove the word 'but' from negative communication. For example, 'You did XXX really well but I wish you had done YYY much better. But I am glad to see that you also did ZZZ well' becomes 'You did XXX really well. We might have to consider further how we move forward with YYY since there seem to be some issues with that, but I am glad to see that you have made some progress with ZZZ'. The word 'but' is almost expected after you praise someone, and it means that the initial praise becomes relatively meaningless, with the only thing that the other person remembers being the negative comment. In the example here, a new sentence removes the conjunction.

5. **Watch your language**: Our input into a conversation will affect someone else's input, so being careful about our language can enable us to achieve our objectives in a way that being very direct will not. For example, refer to 'we' (rather than 'you') as much as possible. Referring to 'we' indicates two people (as a team) working together on improving someone's performance (i.e. they will be supported in the future) and is likely to encourage someone to commit to personal change. Similarly, there are a number of words that will likely increase the emotions of the person hearing the message: for example, 'problem to deal with' can become an 'issue to manage' or a 'challenge', or sometimes even 'an opportunity for improvement'. As mentioned above, try to remove the words 'but', 'however' and (even worse) 'although' from messages about things that have gone wrong. Finally, some people use phrases such as 'less well' to talk about things which went 'badly', or 'not always the best thing to do' or 'unhelpful' to talk about things which would be 'a bad idea'.

FOR YOU TO DO

Think about the phrases given below, all of which seem to arise from frustration with other people in some way. The phrases may all be quite emotive to the person hearing them, so think about how you might rephrase them if you were trying to give the same message in a more neutral manner.

'The English in this work is rubbish. Why don't you get a dictionary? I think you need to do this again.'

'I am so tired of this! No one ever communicates properly with me and I am finding it impossible to continue like this!'

'Guys, can you arrange meetings so that I can actually attend? You know how difficult it is for me with childcare.'

'I like the fact that you email me every day, but it is getting to be too many each day. Can you please stop? Thanks.'

'Why don't you listen properly??! I have already said that same thing at least twice.'

'So, you're saying that my work is no good?' (And maybe think about how you would react to this.)

---

6. **Be clear about consequences**: Do not be afraid of informing someone of the consequences of their future actions. It is unfair to give someone the idea that they can continue to do things poorly without any consequences, if those consequences might well happen: 'But of course, we don't want to see those things happen, do we?' Of course, never try to bluff: if the consequences are not there or cannot be enforced, then do not make them up.

7. **Assume good intentions**: Unless you have information to the contrary, try to assume good intentions. You can always change your view later, but it is very hard to get back to that point if you start off believing that someone had bad intentions or did not care. 'I am sure you did not expect or want XXX to happen. Anyway, it has, so now we have to address it.' Doing so will educate someone to the unintended consequences of their actions.

8. **Avoid emotion during a conversation**: Focus on the evidence throughout the conversation, rather than your reactions to it. Of course, you should show some empathy or identify with the other human being who is struggling in some way, but you need to avoid getting emotional as you will not be in a position to rationally think through any potential solution. Others may already have expressed some emotion to you, but that does not mean that you need to express that emotion to others. After all, your main priority is to solve a performance problem, not to show how tough or angry you can be.

REFLECTION POINT

Take some time to think about the following questions and write down some answers.

How good are you at handling your emotions when someone comes to you upset?

How defensive are you when someone accuses you of making a mistake?

How readily do you apologise when you know you have made a mistake?

---

9. **Ensure that there are no surprises**: There is nothing worse than being told off for something when you did not know that it was wrong – though certain things (bribery, theft, etc.) will be 'known' as wrong anyway. The basic principle here is to ensure that if you need to have a difficult conversation with someone about an issue, then they would be expecting that conversation at some point.

10. **Leave the conversation on a positive note**: If you can, after having agreed some specific goals, put some resources or safeguards in place to prevent the problem from arising again. There is nothing worse than having a conversation which is aimless and does not agree a way forward when there is clearly a problem to be addressed.

11. **Use language which allows for some doubt**: Give the other person 'a way out' without making them feel embarrassed, and, similarly, be prepared for evidence which contradicts your view – you may have got it (your judgement) wrong. If you can, talk about actions which 'might have happened' or 'seem to have' happened, or consequences which 'could have happened' rather than things which definitely did happen. It is a lot easier to recover from a conversation where you have made incorrect judgements before hearing all the evidence if you phrase things as possibilities, rather than from a conversation where you have begun with an incorrect accusation that you later need to apologise for.

12. **Listen well and do not interrupt**: Give someone space to put their own side of the story, even if the evidence you have seems to contradict it. Individuals will often feel very aggrieved if they have not had the chance to share their view. At the end of the conversation, always check that your understanding is the same as those of others involved in the discussion.

13. **Encourage self-reflection**: Give an opportunity for self-reflection early on in the conversation. Some good communicators ask others to comment on what *seems to have happened* first before telling the other person what they think. This gives the conversation a more friendly atmosphere, rather than getting very quickly into a heated argument where neither person is willing to listen to the other.

14. **Do not be afraid of silence**: Silence can give people time to think. If the conversation seems to have stopped, then reminding the other person of the last thing that was being talked about or making an observation about the other person's emotion can be useful for restarting the discussion.

15. **Do not match someone else's 'mood'**: If someone is angry, then one of the worst ways of trying to solve a problem is to become as angry as they are. The same is true for a situation where someone is upset: having two people in tears does not really help anyone. Focus on the issue you are trying to solve – together.

16. **Do not focus on what you cannot change**: Be specific about the behaviour you want to change, but trying to change someone's personality is not going to work (and might be regarded as unethical by some).

17. **Consider whether you need to apologise**: Many people find this hard – and it can be very hard – but giving an apology can be very powerful at healing workplace (or personal) relationships. Often the more specific the apology, the more powerful it will be – and many people will appreciate that you have done so. There may be some who take advantage of it and exploit it to show others that you are not good at what you are supposed to be doing, and so getting some advice from others may be useful sometimes. However, be very wary of apologising for something over which you had no control – something which was not your fault. The next time the same thing happens, the other person will blame you and their trust in you will decrease.

18. **Do say 'Thank you'**: Even if a conversation has been hard or has not achieved any of your objectives, the other person has still given up some of their time for you. They may well have seen the conversation as a waste of time, but it is appropriate to thank people wherever possible and for whatever you can.

Words and Phrases for Communicating Constructively

Communication becomes particularly stressful when we need to say something very important but do not know how to say it because of the personal consequences of doing so, or because of how the individual may react.

This is particularly difficult when we get frustrated with others. In such situations, some people tend to express that emotion very forcefully to those who might be frustrating them. Others might hold things in for a while and then 'explode'. Expressing our frustration emotionally, however, is almost always the worst thing to do.

We know of course that the longer a difficult situation goes on, the worse and more stressful it becomes – and so we do need to develop some tools, ideas and principles for getting our message across. When we communicate with others, there may be some words which are seen as inflammatory – what those exact words are will depend on the individual concerned, but words like 'but' are normally unhelpful. It is in these kinds of situations that we might find some 'tools' or phrases useful, so that we can avoid inflaming a difficult situation.

Look at the examples below, where A is what we might feel like saying, and B might be a more constructive way to get our message across.

A1 *'I liked this but …'*   B1 *'This was good. Perhaps we can make XXX even better'*

B1 emphasizes the positive aspects of what someone did and focuses on increasing all levels of performance, rather than highlighting one area for judgement.

A2 *'You should have …'*   B2 *'I can understand your intention, though perhaps a better way of achieving XXX might have been to …'*

B2 shows some recognition of effort and expertise and the goals, but is phrased as more of a suggestion rather than an instruction.

A3 *'You should have…'*   B3 *'I think next time we can do XXX together so that we can get better results. What do you think?'*

The same phrase as A2, but this time the emphasis is on 'team' and doing things together. 'You' is individual – 'we', 'us' and 'our' can help someone feel they are supported, even if their behaviour was not what was intended. The idea of the question at the end is to open up a conversation and a dialogue so that the individual can feel a sense of ownership of the solution.

A4 *'You did this badly'*   B4 *'I don't think this was done well, to be honest, so let's see how we can improve'*

The active word (did) in A4 has been turned into the passive (was done) so that any personal sense of blame – and therefore emotion – is removed, even though both parties will likely know what happened. The phrase '… to be honest …' makes the communication much less formal, removing emotion further. Finally, the use of 'we' helps someone feel they are supported.

 FOR YOU TO DO

Individuals tend to react negatively to badly delivered messages, so we need to be cautious about how we structure and deliver our messages. Key to this is thinking through how the other person might react, anticipating any negative reaction and preparing to deliver a message that would *work for them* and so *help us*.

Look at the brief situations below. How might you have a conversation (how might you communicate these messages) about the following issues without using the emotive phrases listed above?

1. You are leading a group on a group assignment for a module. Most of their work is good and of a high quality, but this individual has caused a problem by submitting a poor piece of work late.
2. You are living in a student house. One of the people in the house never seems to do any washing up.
3. You want to work in silence in the library, but there is a group at the table opposite who are talking too much and are stopping you from concentrating on your work.
4. You need to say sorry to another student because you still have the library book the other student needs to use, and you did promise to return it.

The way you respond to these situations will be based on your values and learned behaviour, but think about how you might change the way you respond.

KEY LEARNING POINT

Giving feedback to others is something that many people find hard. It requires the use of strong interpersonal skills, especially if we do not have a good relationship with an individual, but the way in which we give feedback is often more important for the outcome than the feedback we give.

REFLECTION POINT

Take some time to think about the following questions and write down some answers.

How easy do you find it to tell someone what you really think about what they did or said?

What was the most difficult message you have ever needed to communicate? Why was it so hard?

How could some of the ideas above help you to convey the message(s) you want to communicate?

'BUT I HAVE A QUESTION ...'

... This is useful, I suppose, but why can't I just be direct and say what I think?

Of course you can – if that is your normal style of communication and you are absolutely confident of what you think, believe and know, then sure. Be direct.

But these ideas are there for those situations when you are unsure about how to handle the conversation, where information might be ambiguous or when you might be dealing with someone whose reaction might be somewhat unpredictable. There are times when less self-confident individuals might find direct

(Continued)

communication threatening, so you need to think about whether being direct is the best way to achieve what you want to achieve.

It is also worth noting that some cultures are more used to using direct forms of communication to get their message across than others (see page 304 on high- and low-context cultures). This has serious implications for business negotiations and other forms of intercultural communication.

Communicating in a Group

Communication, by its very nature, takes place between two or more people, so good communication skills are vital when working with others for the good of the group/team and in order to ensure that the task is completed successfully. There are a number of issues that are important when looking at communication in groups.

Patterns of Communication in Groups

If communicating one to one is difficult, then communicating with multiple individuals – all of whom are constantly sending out messages and signals – at the same time in a conversation that moves from topic to topic and person to person is going to present another layer of complication. Communication patterns can look at three issues: 1) the amount of communication that takes place; 2) the quality of that communication (does it help the group achieve its goal?); and 3) who is communicating with whom (and who is not communicating at all). Look at Figure 9.4.

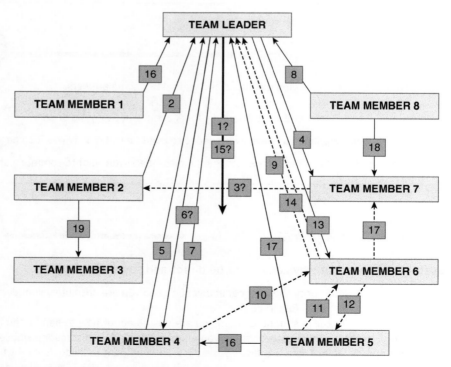

Figure 9.4   Patterns of communicating in a group

We can see that this figure is a representation of 19 different pieces of communication during what was probably the first part of a team discussion. The diagram uses various methods to indicate some detail of the contributions made.

The small numbered boxes indicate the order in which the contributions were made, and those with a question mark indicate where a question has been asked. The thickness of the arrow indicates emotion (the dotted lines indicate negative emotion or annoyance/anger; complete lines indicate positive passion). In reality, it is not easy to represent the detail of communication: even a question can be a statement of opinion; a contribution intended as a positive encouragement can be seen as negative by others; and one statement can be directed to many different selected individuals at a time. Further, the diagram indicates nothing about how long each person was speaking for. What it does indicate is that there are some team members who only speak when asked a question and others who say little.

The preceding paragraph shows that there is a variety of ways we can look at communication. Of course, we know that communication is what builds and destroys relationships and can thus act as an enabler to groups or a hindrance. Getting communication right is imperative, but it is not the only issue that affects how a group or team performs.

Applying Communication Skills in Groups

One question that can take some thinking through is how to use your understanding of the communications process and the issues covered above to communicate in groups. There are a number of levels on which we can answer this question:

1. **The values we display**: This will be determined by what the group puts into something called a group contract (see page 262 of Chapter 11). If you agree to be polite, then anything deemed impolite should not be a part of the group discussion.
2. **The methods of communication**: Are you going to speak by phone, or by Skype, or chat on social media or by email? What methods will you use? As discussed above, the methods you use will affect the frequency and effectiveness of your communication, and the relationships you develop in the group.
3. **How informal the relationships are**: The kind of language you use, the topics you talk about (both informal and formal) and the amount of humour you use will impact on the nature of the relationships you have in the group.

Most student groups will usually have a mix of the above, often determined to a significant amount by the individual leading the group. The most effective groups are those where communication and relationships tend to be a good mix of the informal and formal, and where there is some conversation about personal, irrelevant issues ('How's life? How's your family?') alongside the business that the group wishes to complete ('In this meeting, let's focus on this goal'). However, different cultures will have different approaches to communication at work and cultures with a high 'power-distance' (see Chapter 13 on cross-cultural awareness) may keep the business meeting much more formal and work related.

As with all aspects of group behaviour, it is good sometimes for the group to reflect on the way it is communicating and see what is and is not being communicated effectively. One of the challenges in working in a group is that the communication is fine, but it is incomplete.

Communication and Trust in Groups

Establishing trust among a group is one of the most challenging goals for a group leader, but can be made easier at the formation of the group if the leader manages this well (see Chapter 10). The more informal the communication at the beginning of the task and the more the group learn about each other as human beings (rather than simply group members), the more strong trust-based relationships will be established. Creating a relaxed informal working culture based on mutual respect is important when getting a group to trust each other.

Of course, trust can break down. Individuals can relate to each other as human beings and believe that they are all 'nice people', but if a group member is not doing their work properly or at the right time when they have agreed to do so, then group relationships might come under strain. Some group leaders might decide that this is the time to engage in some informal communication, maybe by holding an informal social activity, but this can sometimes make things worse. A group of individuals sitting (or standing) around but not talking to each other can almost destroy a group.

The best way to address such an issue is probably to talk privately to the specific individuals concerned and find out why they have not done what they promised to do, and to make clear to the group as a whole that there has been an issue but that you hope it has now been resolved. That takes courage and skill (see section below on giving feedback), but the end result will probably be better.

Open and honest communication in such a situation with 1) the individual(s) concerned and 2) the group as a whole is much better than hiding things and hoping that things will improve.

INTEGRATION AND APPLICATION

Learning how to communicate effectively is something that will probably take a very long time. We start at birth when our eyes are taking in all the information they can, and when our brains are trying to develop ideas about what certain facial expressions of our parents mean. Our brains make generalisations about what individuals mean and we learn to communicate with others in a way which we think helps get our messages across. Sometimes these generalisations are correct, sometimes they are nearly correct, but sometimes they are wrong, and we need to revise what we communicate and how we do so. The challenge is that individuals may well have slightly different interpretations of the meaning of the same message because of the perceptual and contextual distortions; we will cover this in more detail in Chapter 13 on cross-cultural awareness.

The most effective solution is to seek feedback from others to ensure that the message we intended to send is the same as the one received. There is an important question here: Should we try to adjust our 'communication style' for each individual we are talking to? The answer is simple and complex at the same time. As leaders, we do need to be consistent in how we communicate what we need to communicate: if we are inconsistent, then our followers may well become confused and their trust in us may start to erode. Our communication is likely to have a formality about it and may be less humorous. As a friend, however, we should probably recognise that our ability to establish rapport and relate to others is based on how well we understand and use similar patterns of communication and language as our friends. We could probably joke with a friend in a way that we might struggle to joke with a manager. Finally, as a colleague in a team, we might wish to use a mixture of informal and formal language but build others' confidence in our ability to do a good job by making definitive commitments and communicating regularly about our own progress. So, to answer the question, it is often less about the personal characteristics of the individual that we are talking to, and more about their own emotional situation and how we relate to them which define how well we work with and/or enjoy the company of others.

CONCLUSION

By now, you should be able to:

*   Describe the communication process and how it can go wrong.
*   Identify the various verbal, non-verbal and para-linguistic behaviours that can influence communication.

- Evaluate and develop your communication skills with a particular focus on communicating in difficult situations, giving feedback and active listening.

In this chapter, we have covered a wide range of issues related to how we communicate with others. We have looked at the context and process of communication and the impressions we create, the impact of using different communication channels, and the verbal, non-verbal and para-linguistic aspects of communication, including the words we use. These components of the communication process were then applied to different scenarios such as communicating tactfully, using questions appropriately and establishing rapport. Finally, the chapter closed with an examination of how we can develop rapport, practise active listening, give feedback to others and communicate effectively with those we work with in groups.

REFLECTION POINT

Take some time to think about the following questions and write down some answers.

Based on the content of this chapter, what do you now know about the processes of communication that you did not know before?

What key learning point had the most impact? Why?

What will you now do differently? (Write this down and put it somewhere where you can see it regularly.)

CHAPTER TASK

Take 30 minutes or so to watch an episode of a weekly soap opera (perhaps in your own language or from your own culture if you are an international student), and particularly pay attention to the ways that the characters communicate with each other. Where there is an argument, how do the characters resolve it – if at all?

Scripts are often written in such a way that arguments and emotions linger, since that gives the script writers the ability to renew the argument in another episode. So, how would you advise them to communicate differently in order to actually resolve the issues in the episode?

INTERVIEW QUESTIONS

Think about the following questions. What might your answers be?

1. Tell me about a time when you tried to communicate an important message, but the message was misunderstood. What went wrong and what did you do afterwards?
2. What have you learnt by watching others around you communicate with each other?
3. Which communication skills do you think are the most important? Why?
4. Imagine that you need to communicate a complex idea to an intelligent audience. How would you go about it? What issues would you need to take into account?
5. From your own experiences, can you give some examples of poor communication?

(Continued)

6. Describe a time when a relationship with a fellow classmate, team member or someone you had to work with went wrong. How did you resolve the issue?

Chapter 17 gives a lot more information on selection interviews and the online content gives some guidance on these questions.

ADDITIONAL RESOURCES

Want to learn more? Visit https://study.sagepub.com/morgan2e to gain access to a wide range of online resources, including interactive tests, tasks, further reading and downloads.

Website Resources

The following websites offer useful advice on communication skills.

Mindtools: www.mindtools.com/pages/article/newCS_99.htm

Open University (MOOC on Communication Skills): www.open.edu/openlearn/ocw/mod/oucontent/view.php?id=19234&section=4

University of Kent: www.kent.ac.uk/ces/student/skills.html?tab=communication

University of Southern California: https://communicationmgmt.usc.edu/improving-communication-developing-effective-communication-skills/

Textbook Resources

Aldag, R. J. and Kuzuhara, L. W. (2015) *Creating High Performance Teams*. New York: Routledge (particularly Chapter 6).
Breakenridge, D. (2018) *Answers for Modern Communicators*. New York: Routledge.
Cameron, S. (2010) *The Business Student's Handbook: Skills for Study and Employment* (5th edition). Harlow: Pearson (particularly Chapter 9).
Dougherty, C. and Thompson, J. E. (2010) *Be a Better Leader*. Oxford: Bookpoint (particularly Chapter 8).
Gallagher, K. (2016) *Essential Study and Employment Skills for Business and Management Students* (3rd edition). Oxford: Oxford University Press (particularly Chapter 4).
Hamilton, C. and Kroll, T. L. (2018) *Communicating for Results* (11th edition). Boston, MA: Cengage.
Hasson, G. (2012) *Brilliant Communication Skills*. Harlow: Pearson.
Hind, D. and Moss, S. (2011) *Employability Skills*. Houghton-le-Spring: Business Education Publishers (particularly Chapter 3).
Malandro, L. (2015) *Speak Up, Show Up and Stand Out*. New York: McGraw-Hill.
Pettinger, R. and Firth, R. (2001) *Mastering Management Skills*. Basingstoke: Palgrave (particularly Chapter 3).
Rees, W. D. and Porter, C. (2008) *Skills of Management*. London: Cengage (particularly Chapter 8).
Robbins, S. P. and Hunsaker, P. L. (2003) *Training in Interpersonal Skills*. Upper Saddle River, NJ: Pearson (particularly Chapters 3, 4 and 5).
Smale, R. and Fowlie, J. (2009) *How to Succeed at University*. London: Sage (particularly Chapter 3).
Smith, M. (2011) *Fundamentals of Management* (2nd edition). Maidenhead: McGraw-Hill (particularly Chapter 11).
Varner, I. and Beamer, L. (2011) *Intercultural Communication in the Workplace* (5th edition). New York: McGraw-Hill.

10 PRESENTATION SKILLS

There are always three speeches for every one that you actually gave. The one you practiced, the one you gave, and the one you wish you gave. (Dale Carnegie)

CHAPTER STRUCTURE

Figure 10.1   Different goals and different delivery styles

When you see the 🌐 this means go to the companion website https://study.sagepub.com/morgan2e to do a quiz, complete a task, read further or download a template.

═══ AIMS OF THE CHAPTER ═══

By the end of this chapter, you should be able to:

- Understand why presentations fail to achieve their objectives.
- Prepare, structure and deliver a good oral presentation.
- Choose and use visual aids relevant to the audience and goals of the presentation.
- Use appropriate strategies for dealing with nerves.

WHEN SHOULD YOU READ THIS CHAPTER?

It is best to read this before you need to do any presentations at university - and that will usually be within the first year of your studies

PRESENTATION

A presentation is the oral delivery of information to achieve (a) particular objective(s).

INTRODUCTION

For many people, giving a presentation in front of others can be scary, for a number of reasons. Sometimes it is fear of the unknown: Who will be looking at me? What will they be thinking? What questions might they ask? Will they be in a bad mood?

The reality is that there are very few occasions when we have much legitimate justification for being nervous about a presentation. In business, the ability to give a good presentation is seen as a fundamental skill – it is impossible to lead without communicating, and presentations are a standard part of business and employment life.

This chapter also is relevant to you as a student – because giving presentations is a key part of business life, your university studies will need to prepare you for doing them.

This definition seems very vague. The reality, however, is that everything you see on TV, hear on the radio or receive in some other way is a type of presentation (see Table 10.1).

Table 10.1   Forms of presentation

• Formal business proposal to senior managers • One-to-one sales presentation to a client • Speech at a family event - e.g. wedding • After dinner speech at a corporate event • Speech to invited guests • Stand-up comedy routine • A theatrical performance	• Classroom presentation • Presentation by a consultant to a client - making recommendations • Presenting a TV show • A YouTube video reviewing or presenting a product • Speech to win a debating competition

It may not be called a presentation, but such situations will 'present' you with some kind of information or will entertain you – or both. There are a large number of ways and situations in which presentations can take place, but there are some common factors that link these activities together. For an academic presentation at university, we can even imagine the presentation as very similar to the spoken version of an academic essay. For the purposes of this book, we will concentrate on those which occur in an academic setting or a typically more formal business setting, though styles and expectations can vary significantly.

We will begin this chapter by giving you the opportunity to reflect on your own abilities. This is a chance to examine your own thinking and behaviour. The chapter will present some issues relating to the identification of presentation goals, give some thoughts on the various skills that are involved in preparing and delivering a presentation, and then move on to consider some issues of presentation structure. The final two areas to be covered in the chapter relate to some suggestions on how individuals might handle their nerves, as well as the variety and appropriate use of visual aids. Finally, in evaluating the impact of a presentation, it is difficult to separate out the impact of the structure, content and delivery methods from each other: all have a significant impact on the ability of a presentation to achieve its goal and so all need to be thought through carefully.

SKILLS SELF-ASSESSMENT

Complete the brief questionnaire below to see how well you prepare and deliver oral presentations. Read carefully each of the following descriptions and say how typical you think each statement is of your behaviour or attitude by giving it a score between 1 and 5, where 1 is 'strongly disagree' and 5 is 'strongly agree'.

Item	Statement	Score
1.	I know my facts	
2.	I am confident in delivering my presentation	
3.	I give a clear introduction to my presentation	
4.	I maintain a logical sequence to the content of the presentation	
5.	I give a clear summary of the content I have presented as a conclusion	
6.	I ensure that the audience can hear everything that I am presenting	
7.	I use eye contact, gestures and other small behaviours to maintain audience engagement	
8.	I use varied pitch, volume, tone of voice and speed of delivery to create impact	
9.	I produce visual aids that are very clear, are relevant and help the presentation achieve its aim	
10.	I do not let nerves affect my delivery	
11.	I have the right amount of content for the length of presentation	
12.	I do not feel nervous	
13.	I ensure that any technology I wish to use will do exactly what I expect it to do	
14.	I go to look at the venue beforehand to ensure that I know what I can and cannot do	
15.	I write out brief notes to use as an aid to memory	
16.	I make sure that I have taken some time to think about my goals	
17.	I take some time to think about the audience – how they will react to what I have to say, how they may be feeling and how big the audience will be	
18.	I move around 'the stage' to try to create interest and engagement	
19.	I start my presentation with a striking comment designed to get the audience's attention	
20.	I think about the possible questions that might be asked after the presentation	

The answers to these questions are personal – they are about you, so there are no right or wrong answers – but you might want to discuss them with a classmate.

The questions will have started you thinking about some of the presentations that you have seen recently. Of course, giving a presentation may or may not be the same as giving a lecture, but a lecture *is* a form of presentation. If we could consider a conversation about a hobby with three others as a presentation, then the idea of 'doing a presentation' might be a lot less daunting than we might otherwise imagine. (Standing up is a decision we make when we think about how to do a presentation, but we do not have to be standing.)

══════ 'BUT I HAVE A QUESTION ...' ══════

... Why do universities assess by presentations, they are so stressful?

It may sound surprising but your lecturers can also find giving lectures and presentations stressful sometimes. If we are teaching a group of people that we have never taught before or a new module or delivering

(Continued)

some new training, then yes, we can get stressed about it as well. If we earn our living through delivering training and education and we are delivering something important to a corporate client, then our income does depend on it.

Regardless, a presentation develops your confidence and your ability to speak and communicate, to lead and to be creative. Everyone who leads has to give some kind of presentation or speech at some time.

The amount of stress you experience will vary from person to person. However, just because you are doing a presentation does not mean you have to get stressed about it. Sometimes it seems people get stressed because almost everyone expects them to. Presentations can be stressful, but nobody ever developed an important skill by doing something that was easy.

In most modules and most universities, you will get lots of chances to practise and develop your presentation skills in front of a tutor and receive their feedback, and, often, these chances will not count towards any grade. So – as I have said before – use the feedback to get better so that when you are assessed, you will know what to do and be able to do it.

PRESENTATION PREPARATION

The way we prepare and deliver a presentation is dependent on our goals, our audience (these two will be linked) and our abilities, which will shape what we feel comfortable with and confident about doing.

The Impact of Goals on Delivery Style

There are expected and unexpected ways of giving a presentation, and there will be appropriate and inappropriate ways of doing so depending on the goal, but there is no one best way. However, there are some principles to consider as shown in Figure 10.2. Different goals relate to differences in delivery

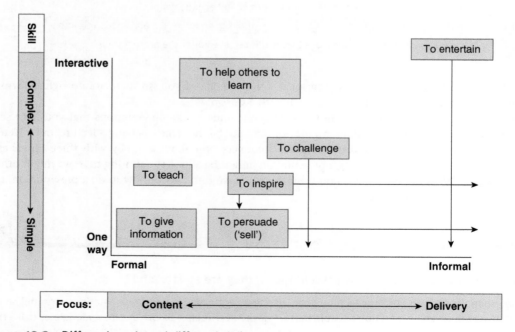

Figure 10.2   Different goals and different delivery styles

method and the formality of the presentation. We may wish to provide stories to inspire, provide jokes to relax and engage others, provide facts and figures to help others make decisions and so on, but how we fit these components together structurally and then add oral delivery to convey our message convincingly is important.

Formality and Informality

It might sound strange that we start a chapter on oral communication and presentation skills by thinking about style before anything else – delivery, structure and so on – but our structure may well be determined by the need for formality, and our delivery certainly will. The purpose of the presentation will have an impact on how we structure and deliver our presentation.

The more formal a presentation is, the more likely it is to be delivered with a script and be one way. Anything more than one way can become a discussion, which by nature is informal, or an argument, which many would say has more formality to it. However, a presentation which is informal can be one way or interactive. A comedian delivering a comedy routine in a local theatre, for example, would be seen as informal, but would largely be one way.

Figure 10.2 indicates that undertaking an interactive presentation will usually require more skill, confidence and creativity. Being able to develop and use exercises well during a presentation typically takes a lot of careful planning (we look at being creative with presentations later). However, a one-way presentation is more common.

 FOR YOU TO DO

Look at the questions below and discuss your answers with another student.

1. Think about the following situations. How formal or informal would you expect each of the following presentations to be?

   ○ Presentation to the executive management board of an international company.
   ○ Sales presentation in a home to three individuals around a table.
   ○ A typical academic lecture on marketing techniques.
   ○ A training session for part-time workers at a chain restaurant.
   ○ A sermon at a local place of worship.
   ○ An assessed presentation by students, undertaken as part of their degree course.
   ○ A drama acted out as part of a presentation in class.
   ○ A speech at a wedding.

2. Why would you expect the above situations to be formal or informal? How much might an audience's expectations impact on someone's style?
3. Is there anything else (other than the goals and/or audience's expectations) that drives the style of the presentation?
4. Which of the above presentation contexts (the list in question 1) would you personally find easier? More difficult?

The Impact of the Audience

A question above asks whether the expectations of the audience have an impact on the delivery style. The answer is that it depends on the goal. If you are trying to sell something or persuade your audience of something, then there is a sense in which you will need to consider their expectations. Not meeting those (and other) expectations will mean that you are likely to be unsuccessful, but if you are trying to teach or merely give information, then you have more control over your success as a presenter.

The audience does impact on presentations in other ways, however:

- **Their knowledge and understanding** – which should dictate what you need to say as background and what you do not.
- **Their emotions about what you are saying** – which can impact on whether they accept what you are saying or not.
- **Their emotions about how you are giving the message** – which can impact on whether they like you or not, and then on whether they accept what you are saying or not.
- **Their general state of alertness (e.g. tiredness)** – which can impact on how effectively you are able to get your message across, how you deliver your presentation and how long the presentation should be.
- **How many people there are** – which can impact on the methods used to deliver the presentation.
- **Where they are sitting in relation to you as presenter** – which can impact on how formal and informal the presentation becomes (a stage or a podium *can* be a significant barrier to being informal).
- **The information is already provided for them** – which impacts on the content you deliver and whether any additional explanation is necessary.

The above points could indicate that giving a presentation is a nearly impossible task since the list of factors to be taken into account is too large to balance effectively. In some cases, this is true (e.g. where a chief executive is addressing the needs of a large and potentially diverse group of shareholders at an annual general meeting) and in those cases it is simply important to use a personal style developed over a long time, but in many situations it is possible to take account of those things in preparing for the presentation, and thinking through what the implications might be.

 KEY LEARNING POINT

Recognising the nature of your audience is a key part of preparing for a presentation, and in developing content and proposed delivery method(s).

Rehearsing

Once we have identified our goals and have thought about our presentation abilities and style, the final part of preparing for a presentation is to rehearse.

Rehearsal is seen by many presenters as vital to the delivery of a good presentation. It is through the rehearsal that presenters identify what they can and cannot remember, are able to practise and perfect their para-linguistic cues (see Chapter 9) and ensure that technically everything works the way that they intend. Rehearsal for some (especially auditory learners – see Chapter 2) will also help memory: the more you hear what it is you are going to say, the better you can remember it. For actors, rehearsal and the repetition of content helps them remember their lines in exactly the same way that repetition of words helps many individuals learn a new language.

There is little substitute for practising in the room where the presentation will take place. You can check, for example, if your PowerPoint presentation works as you intend or whether the room has the internet links you expect, but sometimes this is not possible. Technical preparation can be as important as personal preparation, as the list in Box 10.1 shows.

═══════════ BOX 10.1 ═══════════

Technical Preparation for a Presentation

Preparing yourself is vital if a presentation is to go well, but many forget the requirement to undertake technical preparation or to look at the room beforehand. It has been known for students and senior academics alike to make a series of mistakes like the following:

- Failing to check that there is an internet connection, having saved the presentation at an online location that is not accessible.
- Failing to check that a remote PowerPoint controller has a battery.
- Failing to ensure that there is a power socket for a laptop close to the projector.
- Failing to check that a video inserted into PowerPoint works properly on a different computer.
- Failing to ensure that the USB stick works properly.
- Failing to ensure that the version of PowerPoint (or equivalent) is compatible with that in which the presentation is saved.
- Failing to find out whether someone can hear you at the back of the room.
- Failing to take a printout of the slides with you as an aid to your memory.
- Failing to find the correct room at the right time.
- Failing to ensure that any music or sound can be easily heard.
- Failing to consider questions that you might be asked at the end of the presentation.
- Failing to look at how the room is set up (i.e. locations of chairs etc.).

It is usually not difficult to check all these, but many people are so busy with rehearsal and preparation of delivery that these things can and do get missed.

Why not develop a presentation checklist based on the above and include any other items you might see as relevant?

Rehearsal brings confidence and personal security and helps us deal with nerves, which many individuals suffer from at some point. We will discuss how to deal with nerves later in the chapter.

Making Notes

Only the very best presenters tend not to use notes, and while some will use an autocue or some visual reminders, few people have the ability to remember an entire presentation. As a result, making notes in preparation for a presentation becomes normal for many presenters, even lecturers (some of whom will use bullet points on the PowerPoint slides that you see in exactly the same way as people might use handwritten notes).

Notes tend to be:

- on small pieces of card or paper
- easy to read

- bullet points
- brief.

Notes are intended as a prompt, not as a script.

'BUT I HAVE A QUESTION ...'

... Should I write a script for my presentation?

You will never see individuals at a TED event or giving a high level Toastmasters speech reading from a script (and the same applies to all presentations in business) – and so, if you are doing assessed presentations in your final year or on a postgraduate course, you should try not to do so either. Reading means that 1) you probably won't look at the audience enough, and 2) you will hugely decrease the impact of what it was that you wanted to say. The message might get through, but it will not be because of your delivery.

However, where there is a risk of the audience not understanding an important message, then speakers usually do require scripts, and this is often the case in very formal speeches. It is also a good idea to start off by writing a script – especially if you are not a native speaker in the language of the presentation or if you feel you need to do something rather than just starting to speak – but then practise as much as you can gradually reducing the amount that you are using it.

So then the question changes slightly to, 'At what point should I stop using my script?' The answer is 'When you have practised it enough to be fairly sure that you can deliver the speech without one', and that will vary from person to person.

Technology is making the need for card or paper irrelevant. The smartphone usually has some form of note-making app (e.g. Samsung's 'Note Everything') that can be used. One of the advantages of using a phone is that you can be sure your notes will always stay in the same order, whereas it is possible to get them mixed up when using cards. One of the downsides, of course, is that the phone may run out of power – so beware!

Over-Preparation

Preparation is key to a presentation going well. As Benjamin Franklin, a founding father of the United States, said: 'By failing to prepare you are preparing to fail'. It is a very good feeling to get to a place where you feel confident because of the preparation that has been put in. However, there is a slight risk that you need to be aware of, so balance is important. The risk is that over-preparation can cause problems if something goes wrong.

FOR YOU TO DO

Think about the following two scenarios which relate to occasions when a presenter might be relying too much on their preparation and their notes, rather than on their own knowledge.

Scenario 1

Imagine the situation where you have prepared everything, you are using the PowerPoint slides on the screen as your notes, and you are ready to start speaking, but then the computer crashes and you cannot advance to the next slide. You have two options: to do the remainder of the presentation from memory *or* restart the computer.

Of course, this would never happen to you, but what would you advise the presenter to do?

Scenario 2

Picture yourself in a situation where the script you are reading is the wrong version. You are following what you have written but the slides have been changed since then, and in your group presentation other people are getting nervous because you are taking up their very limited time.

What would you do?

The other issue with too much preparation relates to the following: that in rehearsing too much, the presentation loses its spontaneity and can become less passionate or enthusiastic as a result. Delivering a presentation that has been carefully scripted and memorised word for word may lead to a fairly stale delivery, though confident delivery with extensive eye contact and good memorisation *can* go some way to impressing an audience. One way around this is as follows (it seems embarrassing, but it can work):

- Face a mirror.
- Imagine that you are having a conversation with a friend about something really interesting (or, if it is less embarrassing, ask a friend to use their phone to video you during a real conversation).
- Watch your facial expressions. What do you do during particularly interesting parts of the conversation? What do you do when you want to make a particularly important point?
- Rehearse doing those same facial expressions so that they become part of your presentation.

KEY LEARNING POINT

We can develop the skills required for doing really well in our essays, examinations and other assessed work. The preparation we put in and the way we go about presenting content are crucial to performing well.

REFLECTION POINT

Take some time to think about the following questions and write down some answers.

How much time do you put into preparing for your presentation? Do you feel it is too much, too little or about right?

In your preparation, do you put more effort into the visual aids, considering the audience, rehearsing, or other issues? Is there an optimum balance do you think?

There can be no substitute for good preparation. A presentation that has no preparation can seem unstructured, vague and allows things to go wrong, but, conversely, a presentation that has too much preparation may lack passion and emotion. One of the skills a presenter needs to master is to learn to get the balance right. You can download a useful presentation preparation checklist on the companion website for this book at https://study.sagepub.com/morgan2e.

STRUCTURING A PRESENTATION

Having a clear structure to a presentation fulfils the same purpose as the structure for an essay – it should enable the audience to know exactly what you are discussing, why you are discussing it (i.e. its relevance to the overall message) and what you are going to discuss next. This is important because it will help your audience to feel comfortable and secure as they listen to you. Therefore, like an essay, a formal presentation (for example, to a group of managers more senior than yourself) should have a beginning, a middle and an end. It is worth noting that presentations (and essays) often fail during their introductions and conclusions, and while these may not be the longest parts of the presentation (usually about 10% each of the presentation time), they are almost certainly *the most important*.

The introduction should set out where the work is going and why and stimulate the audience's attention. The introduction can often include phrases such as:

- 'What I'd like to do this afternoon is …'
- 'I'd like to introduce the team who have been working on this project: they are …'
- 'The way we would like to communicate with you about this is through a series of questions on …'
- 'Thank you for inviting me to discuss this with you this afternoon. I have a short amount of time, so …'
- 'We shall be going through the main points which we believe were relevant and, after the presentation, we will be happy to answer any questions, OK?'

 FOR YOU TO DO

Think about the last presentation that you did, and the last one that you watched. Did you hear any of the above (or similar) phrases?

Excluding the phrase introducing the team, are there any occasions when saying any of these could cause a problem? Which ones? Why?

Is it better to keep questions for the end or let your audience ask questions during the presentation? Does it matter who you are presenting to?

BOX 10.2

Grabbing the Imagination: Stimulating Curiosity

Some suggest that there are better ways to start a presentation than to give such a formal introduction. That may be true, but in reality, it depends on the purpose of the presentation. There are times when being more structured and formal is important because you are making a proposal to your tutors or in a business environment. But if that is not the case, then we might want to give the audience some 'bait' and use all our skills at delivery and storytelling to 'reel' them in.

Read the following sentence and consider what is going through your mind:

'The phrases above are good and can give a nervous presenter confidence as well as relax the audience, but they do not grab the imagination: that requires something a little different.'

You might be thinking 'OK, what is coming next? What is it that can grab the imagination? I want to know.' Part of what an author or teacher needs to do is to engage your brain and mind with what they want to deliver next: encouraging your curiosity helps to do that and it is what some people called providing some 'bait'. Have a look at the following phrases. They would not be suitable for every kind of presentation, but corporate speakers and those presenting at events organised by TED or Toastmasters International tend to use them regularly.

'Ladies and Gentlemen, have you ever found yourself in a situation where ...?'

'So, there I was, sitting on a train ...'

'One day, I was realising that I had just been through ...'

'Do you remember how you felt when you were a child? ...'

When you were reading these, how eager were you to know what comes next? If we contrast such phrases with 'Ladies and gentlemen, I want to talk to you today about...' followed by 'I will start by discussing... and then go on to...', then we find that our brain reacts differently, and our level of engagement changes.

Research by Gruber, Gelman and Ranganath (2014) indicates that curiosity stimulates hormones and neurotransmitters such as Dopamine and Serotonin, and these stimulate, among other things, the Hippocampus area of our brain which governs memory. One of the conclusions of their study was that we remember more when we are curious – thus, if we stimulate curiosity in the minds of our audience, then they will remember what they have heard better.

Of course, it is not just the words we use which can stimulate curiosity: the way we use our voice, the use of innovative/unusual visual aids and the combination of contrasting verbal and non-verbal behaviours can all do the same thing (see 'Creativity, Curiosity and Your Presentation' on page 241).

Some of the phrases above apply to team presentations, and others to individual ones, but the principles are the same: the purpose of the introduction is to enable the audience to know: 1) *what* you are going to cover; 2) *why* those issues are important; and 3) *how* you are going to cover them.

Some of the ways in which a presenter can begin their presentation are set out in Table 10.2.

Table 10.2   Beginning your presentation (from Whetten and Cameron, 1996)

Interesting ways to begin a presentation	
Starting fact	Ask rhetorical question
Strong and relevant anecdote	Use an illustration
Striking example	Use a visual aid
Pay the audience a compliment	Refer to a recent incident
Challenging question	Tell a joke

Whichever methods are used, they should gain the interest of the audience and enable them to feel comfortable with where the presentation is going and how you intend to take them there. If you are giving a group presentation, the introduction needs to introduce the group members and preferably indicate what each will speak about.

The middle should enable the audience to understand what you are telling them and why it is important – *to them* more than to you. It should give the message(s) in ways appropriate to the goals of the presentation and should leave the audience in no doubt about what it is that you wish to say.

Finally, **the conclusion** should be a summary of what has been said in the middle. It should be a brief summary, *not a repetition* of what has been said before. It should also thank the audience for listening and invite questions.

The conclusion might contain certain phrases:

- 'Thank you for listening. What I have tried to do is …'
- 'As I come to the end of what I want to present, I would like to reiterate the three main points which I think are important …'
- 'Thank you for your time and attention. We have presented … have indicated why we think … and have given you some ideas about … Now, if you have any questions, we would be very happy to try and answer them.'

Many presentations at university and elsewhere give no conclusion and finish with something similar to: 'That is the end of our presentation, thank you for listening.' For a good presentation, this is usually insufficient as a conclusion. The conclusion should summarise the main issue(s) and any ideas. The presentation should *conclude*, not suddenly *finish*. It is, however, a poor use of time to restate *everything* that has been said previously.

In summary, the introduction should 'Tell the audience what you are going to tell them', the middle should 'Tell them' and the conclusion should 'Tell them what you have just told them'.

 ━━━ KEY LEARNING POINT ━━━━━━━━━━━━━━━━

A presentation that has no clear structure will confuse the audience. The structure of your presentation should be based on the objectives of the presentation.

Having prepared our presentation and given it a structure that enables it to achieve its goals, we will now move on to look at delivery.

DELIVERING A PRESENTATION

The definition of a presentation that we gave earlier stated that there can be a variety of contexts within which a presentation can be given.

When we consider communication, we think about a number of different things, typically based on what we hear and what we see. Those senses drive our thinking, our understanding and then our reactions, so getting our delivery right is, of course, vitally important if we are going to get our message across. The question is, therefore, 'How should we deliver a presentation?'

The answer is less straightforward. It depends on your goals and how the context of the presentation (audience etc.) is likely to impact on the ease with which you can get your message across. However, there are some broad principles that apply.

A presentation without much preparation will likely fail to achieve its objectives. A presentation with poor delivery will tend to do likewise. In technical presentations and where you are communicating in a formal environment, it is often the content that is important, but you can think of delivery as the oil which makes a presentation work well. Even in a technical presentation, get the delivery wrong and people might well be talking about how poor the presentation was, but get the delivery right and folk will be discussing the content.

It is true that most people rarely remember a presentation because of what was said, but more because of how they felt afterwards. It is really interesting to watch (or listen to, if it is on radio) an audience during a political debate, for example. A good presenter will get to their feet and give a speech emphasising one strategy and course of action with passion, excitement and enthusiasm and rising to a crescendo at the end, resulting in a positive audience reaction and perhaps a standing ovation and a smile on everyone's face. Another speaker could do the same, but this time give the opposite message delivered in exactly the same way, yet the same thing happens: everyone smiles and applauds the speaker. The only variable is the way that the speaker delivered their speech. To make the argument even stronger, the same message can be delivered by one speaker with passion and enthusiasm and by another speaker in a logical, factual way, and the reaction will be very different. Human beings like being excited, so if you are trying to inspire or generate passion, then give the audience something which inspires them.

BOX 10.3

Speaking Powerfully: Engaging Emotion

The previous section covered issues around delivery. Our words and delivery of those words will impact on the levels of curiosity experienced by our audience.

Alliteration - the repetition of sounds at the start of words in a phrase, making the phrase easier to remember - is a memory device used by communicators to ensure that their point is clear, succinct and memorable. The more memorable the message, the better the audience will be able to engage with it.

When wanting to engage others' emotions, the words we use are important. Saying that we are 'happy' or 'fine' or that something was 'nice' is probably not going to be as powerful as using an analogy to talking about something. 'It tasted great' has a very different impact from saying, 'It dripped off the tongue like liquid chocolate'. Similarly, 'This was a really painful experience for me' is different from (and much longer than) 'This cut like a knife'. Negative emotions work better when phrases are very short, and positive emotions usually benefit from a longer description. Depending on the audience, we may not want to go that far, but if we are trying to express a particular emotion powerfully, then the words we use are as important as the way we deliver them.

FOR YOU TO DO

Which words and phrases might you use to help someone feel the following emotions? How might you deliver them - Fast/slow? Loud/quiet?

1) Joy

2) Excitement

3) Curiosity

4) Concern/worry

(Continued)

5) Fear

6) Struggle

7) Frustration

Even for presentations that do not attempt to convey a great deal of passion, it is still important to give a competent performance so that you can get your message across. As noted above, the best formal presentations keep things simple, straightforward and clear, and the best presentations to a large number of staff at an annual meeting try to inspire and encourage.

Either way, there are seven important aspects of delivery that we need to get right:

1. **Speed of speech**: People speak at different speeds but usually we speak between 150–160 words a minute. When individuals speak too quickly, we feel that we do not have time to comprehend them properly or to think about the questions we might want to ask, and we can get frustrated. But speak too slowly and the audience will get bored. If you are likely to write out your script, then you have the chance to ensure that you can match the speed to the time limit given. When individuals are nervous, they usually speed up – which can make things worse. By doing so, they forget the other things – the gestures, the intonation, etc. – which are also important parts of delivery.

2. **Intonation/pitch**: Individuals who typically speak in a lower tone are often seen as more credible and authoritative. Margaret Thatcher – British Prime Minister between 1979 and 1990 – was famously known for speaking in a tone that, as the first female UK Prime Minister, gave her credibility among her male colleagues and made her appear more 'masculine'.

3. **Rhythm**: Most of the time we are speaking, we have a form of rhythm. That means it is easy for individuals to work out when we are getting to the end of a sentence or phrase, and when we are going on to the next point. When individuals are writing, they use punctuation to do the same. The tone of voice we use after a 'period' or 'full stop' is different from what we would use after a comma.

 FOR YOU TO DO

Take two passages of writing - one from a piece of research or from one of your textbooks and one from a fictional passage. Look at the punctuation in those passages and read them out loud.

How does the punctuation affect the way you read these passages?

Where do you pause? Stop? Raise your intonation? Speak quickly or slowly? How might you use your intonation to increase the impact of the important parts of what you are reading?

---

4. **Volume**: Just as our speed of speech changes, so too can our volume. We often speak at a volume of 50–65 decibels but in normal speech, we can speak more loudly when we are angry or more quietly when we are upset. (Excitement and happiness tend to show more in speed than in volume.) If we deliver our presentation well in a silent room, we can speak quietly or loudly and the audience will still hear us.

5. **Facial expressions and non-verbal behaviours**: We use our face to communicate our thinking. It is our face that communicates any kind of message before we speak or communicate in any other way, and a simple expression can communicate disapproval, concern, excitement or other emotions. The most obvious issue relating to presentations in this regard is eye contact.

Looking at our audience can make us nervous, but we will lose our audience very fast if we do not look at them. Eye contact is an important sign of respect.

━━━━━ **BOX 10.4** ━━━━━

Understanding the Face: Who are Better Communicators – Males or Females?

The debate around emotional communication has been raging for a long time. It is commonly believed that females are better at picking up human emotion than males, but is this really borne out by research?

A 1986 study by Wagner and colleagues looked at communication accuracy in terms of facial expressions. Communication was deemed to be accurate when the real emotion of the sender was identified correctly by an individual viewing that facial expression. The researchers recorded students' emotional reactions to slides shown during a lecture. Those reactions were then shown to other students – male and female – who were asked to identify which emotions were being displayed.

The findings suggested that, when males and females were asked to identify others' emotions from facial expressions shown by males and females, the female students were generally more accurate for females than the males were for the males, but that neither group were consistently accurate for both groups. Interestingly, the males were more accurate at identifying anger than the females, but otherwise, neither males nor females had more accurate understanding overall.

The key implication of findings such as these is that facial expressions on their own are insufficient to ensure a full comprehension of understanding of another's message – we need the other aspects (words, intonation, volume, etc.) listed here.

6. **Movement and gestures**: Movement is not always possible when we are presenting: a lot will depend on the specific situation. If we are presenting formally in front of a screen to a formal audience, then even if it were possible, a lot of movement could be unhelpful. In some academic situations, presenters often feel the need to stand in one place – typically in front of the computer or to the side of a screen – and speak about what is being shown, but that is not the case in most situations. It is common to watch speakers at TEDx events (independently organised events under the TED umbrella) with no podium or a central location to stand, and those speaking at Toastmasters events rarely do so. In such situations, movement needs to be purposeful rather than random. Regardless of the nature of the presentation, be careful not to rub your hands or move from leg to leg. During a group presentation, stay still if you are not the one speaking.

7. **Contrast**: The previous six areas give us a strong indication of what we should get right when it comes to a presentation. However, if we keep our speed constant, our eye contact constant, our voice monotone and so on, then the presentation will have little interest to the audience and you will not be communicating well: they will not be clear about what is important and what is not and your main point(s) might be lost. So we vary these. We might slow down and/or increase/ decrease our volume, or introduce pauses (see Chapter 9 on para-linguistic communication about adding contrast to your voice), or ask rhetorical questions when we are making important points. Or we might use gestures only occasionally to make clear the main point we want to get across. Regardless, variety means that we can make our point convincingly and enables us to do so in an interesting way.

The key to getting a clear message across is not necessarily whether we keep to some of the statistics given here around words per minute or volume, but rather how we change these dynamics.

Beyond Behaviour

There are some additional practical tips which can help us get our delivery right:

1. **Get feedback**: As we saw in Chapter 2, we can only really improve what we do when we have some form of feedback, either through reflection or through someone else telling us something that we didn't know before. Take time to practise your presentation and to ask someone to watch it – and then use the feedback to improve.
2. **Audibility**: People must be able to hear us. Make sure you can get some idea of whether people can hear you before going too far into the presentation. Try to practise in the same room if you can.
3. **Anticipate audience thinking**: Recognise that the audience may be thinking about what you are saying, which gives you an opportunity to build further rapport by saying something like, 'Some of you might be wondering "why …?" or 'The obvious question from what I have been saying is, "How…?"' and then giving an answer.
4. **Handle information well**: Keep highly detailed information away from any information displayed on the screen. Put it in a document for your audience to read later. Consider carefully when to give out any written information, though. Give it out too early and the audience may spend the whole time reading it rather than attending to you as a speaker; too late and it might be seen as irrelevant.
5. **Dress and appearance**: Dress smartly. This is usually the case for most presentations, and certainly for assessed presentations. Sometimes, you can get away with being just who you are and wearing casual clothes, but for assessed presentations at university, this is not usually the case.
6. **Tell jokes, if you can**: But if you are not good at doing so, then don't. It is OK to use spontaneous humour as well, if you are confident about doing so.
7. **Keep to time**: This is especially important for assessed presentations (or those where you are trying to get a job or sell something to someone). Your audience may be exceptionally busy and may have very limited time for you to get your message across.
8. **Be polite, courteous and respectful at all times**: If you appear arrogant, irritated or unhelpful, your audience will stop giving you their attention. That is why smiling is important.
9. **Say 'thank you' and invite questions**: If your audience has been listening carefully, then they might need to ask for more information or for your opinion on something that you have covered. Dealing with questions that you have not prepared for sometimes feels daunting, but there is little wrong with suggesting that you will get back to someone later with the answer (although make sure you do!).

 ═══ FOR YOU TO DO ═══

Prepare to deliver a presentation entitled 'Why have I come to study at university?' The presentation should be 10 minutes long and you can use whatever visual aids you want.

Deliver the presentation to two or more friends (you can make this a mutual activity if you want, for all of you to do).

Taking each of the seven items listed above under 'Delivery' and the nine areas listed under 'Beyond Behaviour', obtain feedback from those watching you.

What were your personal strengths and weaknesses?

What three things would you improve for next time?

1.

2.

3.

Remember, practising your delivery and receiving feedback is fundamental to getting better at doing presentations. Do not expect your first ever presentation to be perfect: it won't be, but you will get better and better each time.

If you are nervous, start your presentation sitting down with others around a table. As you feel more confident in the message you are giving, stand up and move away from the table.

Creativity, Curiosity and Your Presentation

There was a time when the use of simple PowerPoint graphics would arouse enough awe and wonder as to be sufficiently exciting to maintain our attention, but the use of graphics on TV, or presentation software such as Prezi or interactive tools have raised our expectations significantly.

Box 10.2 discussed the impact of curiosity on memory in terms of the way that you begin your presentation, and the beginning of your presentation will set the level of interest for the remainder of the time that the audience is listening to you. So how might we add interest and stimulate curiosity?

- **Ask questions** (as was done just now): Questions don't need to be answered out loud by the audience but are there for stimulating thought. A good question asked badly – e.g. if tone of voice does not indicate it is a question, or it is too long – will not work, but one that stimulates thought will do well.

- **Tell a story**: Well told stories can release chemicals such as Oxytocin and Adrenalin which create stress or pleasure reactions, and these keep us engaged in the message.

- **Do something unusual**: In his talk to a Toastmasters World Speech Final competition, Mohammed Qahtani started his 2015 winning speech by saying nothing, but to the shock of his audience, started by lighting up a cigarette.

- **Use an appropriate visual aid**: Some thoughts about PowerPoint are given below, but think about physical visual aids. Items which work as simple analogies (see Chapter 14 on creativity and problem solving) can help us explain complex ideas very easily. A rose can be used to symbolise the delicate nature of life, for example.

- **Give a provocative statistic**: Starting with a surprising statement of fact can alert the audience to something they did not previously realise or understand. (Just one word of caution: if that fact is already known to the audience, then it will not have the same impact.)

- **Make it real and personal**: If you are talking about a topic that is relevant to your audience, then why is it relevant to you? Outline the impact of the issue on your life and use your non-verbal behaviours to engage empathy from your audience.

- **Be conversational**: When most people do presentations, they stiffen up, stop being relaxed, stop smiling and use well-rehearsed language – and then get surprised when the audience does the same. If you do rehearse your speech (something that is generally a good idea), try to script it as if you were sitting over a table talking to a friend. Phrases such as 'So, here's what we did: we …' come across a lot more naturally than 'As a result of this, we…'. While it is generally true that formal presentations can require more formal language, relaxing and being more informal once the presentation is progressing will relax the audience as well. TED speakers are particularly good at this and are able to stimulate our curiosity.

The impact of emotions and stories in all presentations can be significant. A well delivered message (such as that of Greta Thunberg to the United Nations in 2019) can galvanise millions of people to action, just as Michael Burke's BBC coverage of the Ethiopian famine did in 1984. Stories move people, which is why understanding how to convey a good story is important.

━━━━━━━━━━━ **BOX 10.5** ━━━━━━━━━━━

Telling Stories Well: Developing your Skills

Over recent years, *Talk Like TED* by Carmine Gallo (2014) has become a major bestseller on the back of the idea that 'TED talks have become the gold standard for public speaking'. The follow up text – *The Storytellers' Secret* – examines what it is that storytellers do that captivates their listeners.

The book – which is as easy to read as good stories are to listen to – provides examples of storytellers who ignite their listener's fire, educate others, motivate their listeners, simplify messages and launch movements. The findings of interviews with some of the best communicators in the world have led Carmine to conclude that the best storytellers are those who: keep ideas simple and succinct, violate expectations, add some humour, are authentic and real, 'paint pictures' for their audience (so that their audience can visualise what they are talking about) and inspire and talk about heroes.

There are other texts on the subject of telling stories. In his book *Storyshowing* (hint: the subject is in the title), Sam Cawthorn (2018) discusses how to engage an audience, not just in the narrative of a story but in its experience as well. Through personal experience and coaching of his own speeches, he identified that the facts can be there but there are ways to bring an audience in to their own experience of those facts through the use of appropriate language. As world champion speakers have done, he noted the role that watching films and reading fiction can play in helping us to develop our storytelling skills. After all, films and books are the epitome of stories.

Another resource of note for storytelling relates to a syndicated radio show called 'The Moth Radio Hour' (https://themoth.org/radio-hour). 'The Moth' gives individuals the chance to practise and learn the art of storytelling: 'A Moth story is a true personal story that you tell live to an audience, without notes. It can be about anything that has happened in your life – big or small, as long as it mattered to you or changed you in some way. It's usually about 5 or 6 minutes long.' Getting practice is key and anyone can get tickets for events across the US, though sometimes in the UK or Australia.

Toastmasters International began in 1924 as a club designed to improve the leadership and communications skills of young men in the US, but now has grown in to a multinational subscription organisation across most continents. Each year, the organisation hosts a major conference which includes an international speech contest – the winners of which can usually be seen on YouTube and elsewhere. Members usually join club meetings to practise their speeches and to improve, and are evaluated by other club members as they do so. The speeches contribute to the completion of projects, and help to build skills around leadership, strategy, innovation, planning and communication, but the best speeches engage the audience in a story where the hero (usually the speaker) has overcome some difficulty and then shares that learning with the audience. Those watching the final of the contest live usually number above 3000 and speeches need to be no longer than 7 minutes and 30 seconds.

Telling stories in our presentations can bring a presentation alive and give it an emotional push. That is not expected in all presentations but doing so where we need to engage the audience is going to significantly enhance the impact of what we, as presenters, can do.

IDENTIFYING AND USING VISUAL AIDS

Probably the most common visual aid used in presentations is the PowerPoint slide, but imagine for a moment that PowerPoint (and the now somewhat obsolete overhead projector) did not exist: what would you use as a visual aid?

This kind of question forces us to be a little creative – and, as the saying goes, 'necessity is the mother of invention'. We are so used to looking at PowerPoint presentations that we could consider that anything that does not use PowerPoint is not a proper presentation. In reality, we could use practically anything as a visual aid, so we do not have to use PowerPoint. Table 10.3 gives some ideas which might be appropriate.

Table 10.3   Ideas for interactions and visual aids

Suggestions for Interaction and Visual Aids	
Video PowerPoint Demonstration Role-play/theatre Quizzes Physical examples Pictures Volunteers from the audience	Stories Handouts Flipchart/OHP/digital media Discussions True/false or multiple choice questions

The list in the figure is not exhaustive and principally anything – and anyone – can be a visual aid. Generally speaking, the more unusual or creative the visual aid, the greater the impact of the presentation. As noted in various places above, the way we do our presentation depends on the goals we have, so we choose the visual aids based on our objectives and presentation style.

Once we have chosen which visual aid(s) we wish to use, the challenge then is to use them correctly. Videos need to have a brief introduction: What do you wish the audience to notice or look out for? Why are you showing the video? Demonstrations need to make sure that everyone can see what you are doing, so you need to use them carefully.

If we are attempting to entertain our audience, then more creative visual aids might be more appropriate. Box 10.6 gives some suggestions that may be useful when trying to enhance the creativity of our presentations. The best presenters often use surprise and excitement to engage the audience (e.g. bringing on a suitcase, so the natural question of what is in the suitcase arises in the mind of the audience, and then only gradually revealing what is actually in the suitcase). Therefore, think not just about what is used as a visual aid, but also how it is used.

BOX 10.6

Creativity and Visual Aids

Creativity is often seen as something which will inspire, grab an audience's attention and make a presentation a lot more interesting than a series of PowerPoint slides. Not all presentations will require a great deal of creativity, but the more an audience is likely to lose interest (perhaps because of the time of day or the length or content of the presentation) then the more creative you may have to be.

The following principles might be helpful:

- **Variety:** If you want to keep your audience guessing about what will come next, then ensure that your presentation includes a variety of activities. Predictability is sometimes unhelpful if you want to keep your audience interested.

(Continued)

- **Planning**: Using activities that you or your audience are not used to will require planning. What could go wrong, and how would you manage that? Will such activities take longer than you have allowed for in your timing?
- **Relevance**: Think through whether the activities really add value to your presentation: Do they help to demonstrate your main point in a different way? What are your audience more likely to take away – their memory of the activity or the message you wanted to convey? Is that a problem?
- **Technology**: Sometimes activities using technology may be great, but what happens if it fails? For example, your tablet or laptop battery fails, or everyone logs on to the same website at the same time: Is the wireless strong enough to handle it? Do you have a backup plan?
- **Regularity**: The more frequently you use a creative activity in a presentation, the less likely an audience is to pay attention to your message, and the more attention to the activities. Infrequent use of activities is likely to be more helpful than constant use of such activities, when a presentation can seem disjointed.
- **Timing**: Think about your most important objectives for the presentation and make sure you give maximum time to their achievement, with less important objectives covered according to the time you have remaining. You should not go over the time allotted to you, and this means you will need to practise what you want to say and work out how long you will need to say it.
- **Ability**: Do not try to do what you cannot. Avoid telling jokes if you are not good at telling them. Magic tricks are a great way to get people interested in a particular topic, but if you have not perfected the trick, then do not try it in front of an important audience. If the ability relates to physical qualities that you do not have, then you might be able to get a volunteer from the audience to do something that you cannot.
- **Overkill**: Too many creative activities in a short space of time for a presentation whose goals do not require creative activities (e.g. presenting a technical report to a management board) can kill a presentation. You do not always need to be creative.

As mentioned above, perhaps the most commonly used tool for presentations is PowerPoint. It is ubiquitous in its availability and use, but it is not always used well and can sometimes be less helpful than intended. Box 10.7 gives some ideas that can enhance how PowerPoint is used.

═══════ BOX 10.7 ═══════

Death by PowerPoint

'Death by PowerPoint' is the popular name for a set of criticisms arising from poor use – and, in some cases, sustained overuse – of Microsoft PowerPoint software. It is simple to use, which is why it is very common among lecturers, but most presenters tend to use the ready-made slide templates and so the software tends to get used in exactly the same way time after time.

The following can be useful in avoiding 'death by PowerPoint':

- **Think about inserting video**: One very useful format is '*.wmv' (Windows Media File), which will play in Windows Media Player as well as enabling a video to play directly in PowerPoint.
- **Using animations and transitions creatively**: Do not over-animate but use them for dramatic effect (which means purposefully).
- **Turn off noises**: Animations and transitions can have sounds associated with them. Rarely should these be turned on; they usually interfere with the audience's concentration.
- **Use colour carefully**: Bright colours do not usually work well and can often distract the audience. Pastel colours tend to work a lot better. Be aware that those suffering from dyslexia can sometimes struggle with 'graduated' coloured backgrounds. Finally, make sure that your audience can read all that is written on the slide; for example, red text on a grey background rarely works.

- **Keep your content succinct**: Write bullet points with as few words as you can. Avoid writing sentences wherever possible. Remember: you should be looking at your audience most of the time, not reading your PPT slides.
- **Check spelling throughout**: There are few things more embarrassing than an incorrect spelling that is highly visible during a presentation. PowerPoint may not indicate a spelling mistake where a legitimate but incorrect word is used, so make sure that you review what you have written.

Developing and using visual aids to enhance the creativity of a presentation requires as much planning as thinking through the content of what it is that you want to say during the presentation. They can make or break a presentation and there are contexts where less creativity creates a better presentation, so their use has to be thought through carefully.

DEALING WITH NERVES

It is not difficult to imagine a situation where all the preparation and rehearsal has been done and the delivery has been 'perfected' as far as possible, only to walk towards the room for the assessed presentation and become nervous. In a group presentation, the good news is that you are probably not alone in feeling nervous, but the bad news is that because everyone else is nervous, they might be too stressed to be able to help each other. Sometimes giving others some encouragement can be good: it takes the focus off yourself and you can feel content to be doing some good for the team.

Nearly everyone gets nervous at some point about giving a presentation. When we get nervous, we show it in a number of ways:

- We speak too quickly.
- We shake – especially when we are holding notes.
- We fidget around – shuffle our feet, play with hair, etc.
- We look down and not at the audience.
- We forget what we are trying to say.
- We struggle to bring our own personality into our delivery.

Therefore, we need to learn to deal with those nerves. Eliminating them completely will take time and experience, but we can manage them.

Think About Why You Might Be Nervous

People get nervous for various reasons, but sometimes those reasons actually do not make a lot of sense. If you have prepared and rehearsed with others and made sure that everything can go as well as it can, then you have controlled as much as you can control and probably should think about relaxing.

Of course, simply telling or pushing yourself to relax is not going to work either – it will actually add to the pressure – so do something totally unconnected to the presentation for a while. Go for a quick walk outside, do the washing up, watch a bit of TV and then go and do the presentation.

Deal with the Reasons

If you have controlled everything that you can control, then the only things which can make you nervous are the things you cannot control – and some of them are unknown. It is often the unknown that challenges us, especially if we are used to being in control of everything.

━━━━━ ■ BOX 10.8 ■ ━━━━━

True or False?

What do you really think of the statements listed below? These beliefs have the power to determine a lot of what we think about and do, but are they really true?

- 'Things that go wrong will affect the whole of our life …'
- 'People will be judging us – our self-image …'
- 'Other's opinions of us really matter hugely …'

Interestingly, none of the sentences in Box 10.8 need to be true. Some individuals make them true for themselves, but that is their choice. Generally, things that go wrong will not be huge in terms of their life impact, and it is much better to make mistakes and learn from them than to believe that we will never make mistakes.

Strategies for Handling Nerves

Even the best lecturers get nervous sometimes – perhaps when facing an important client or when delivering a new course, so they are not immune to nerves. But learning how to handle and use the anxiety is really important. Consequently, some of the strategies below might be useful:

- **Give yourself some 'breathing space'**: After introducing yourself, ask the audience to discuss something relevant to the topic you are going to discuss. This is not always possible but works really well for an informal presentation to a large number of people when having such a large number of people looking at you can seem daunting. Having started the discussion, you can then take a few moments to look around and relax.
- **Appear confident**: Enter the room very deliberately, look down if you need to (although it is better to look up if you feel able to) and walk as if you are walking to someone else's dorm room.
- **It is a conversation**: Try to remember that what you are there to do is to give some information. You are the only one who knows what you are going to say and you are the only person who can say it. Imagine that you are talking to three or four people: one or two at the back, two somewhere in the middle and a couple of people in the front. Do not stare at them, but if you find a friendly face then do smile and try to get them to smile back.
- **Do not rely on memory alone**: If you are new to giving presentations, then do not just rely on memory. Established presenters can do it, but they have had a lot of practice. Unless you are used to presenting without memory aids or do not have a problem with nerves, it is best to practise to ensure you can remember the content of the presentation.
- **Be yourself**: You will have seen a large number of other presentations at university by your lecturers and possibly other students. Do not try to do what others can do so much better than you can, but, over time, learn to develop your own style. This can mean trying out different styles and experimenting, but it is perhaps better to do this in practice sessions than to do it when being assessed.
- **Keep your hands still**: If you have a tendency to move around or your hands shake when nervous, then actively do something to prevent such behaviour from affecting the presentation. If you move around, then sit down when someone else is presenting and stand (if you need to) only for your part of the presentation. If you move your hands a lot, then hold your hands behind your

back or hold on to the podium, or try something to make sure that your hands do not distract from the delivery.

Above all else, there is no substitute for thorough preparation. Prepare yourself, the room, the content, the visual aids and your behaviour as a presenter (which means getting feedback from others), and all should go well.

Some students do not enjoy giving presentations, while others do. In many cases, those who do not enjoy presentations are those who experience anxiety about doing them. Whichever you are, presentations will likely form a part of your course assessment somewhere, and it is better to get practice in doing them at university than to make some significant mistakes when in the workplace.

KEY LEARNING POINT

Getting the preparation, structure and delivery of a presentation right is crucial to the credibility of the message.

REFLECTION POINT

Take some time to think about the following questions and write down some answers.

After giving a presentation, do you ever evaluate your own presentation skills? Or do you get someone else to evaluate your presentation?

Have you ever given a poor presentation? Why did it go wrong?

INTEGRATION AND APPLICATION

The chapter has consistently shown that the success or otherwise of any presentation will depend on the extent to which the goals of the presentation drive the structure, content and delivery of the presentation. In both business and academic life as a student, having unclear goals is likely to lead to failure, regardless of how much preparation is undertaken.

Bearing this in mind, we can develop a step-by-step process which will help you compile and deliver a competent presentation:

Step 1: Identify the goals of the presentation. If you need to do the presentation simply because it is part of the assessment for a course, then the goal will be, 'To answer the question set in a convincing manner', and this will be explained in more detail through the criteria by which the presentation is to be assessed. If you are doing a business presentation, then you need to ask, 'What am I aiming to achieve? What do I want those listening to learn that they did not know before?'

Step 2: Do your research and gather appropriate content. Sketch out what you *want* to cover to answer the question, and then identify what you *need* to cover in order to answer the goal(s) of the presentation. Less relevant or very detailed information can be given in a handout.

Step 3: Identify how best to structure and organise that content. Identify a logical flow where possible, with examples and evidence.

Step 4: Consider how best to deliver the message(s) that you have selected. Use visual aids and other activities to add value and avoid unnecessary items which might act as distractions.

Step 5: Rehearse your presentation and get feedback if possible. Think about how your audience is likely to react to what you are saying. Where necessary, edit and restructure what you have presented until you have something which matches what is expected and will achieve your goal(s).

Step 6: Develop your introduction and conclusion. There is little point in finalising the introduction and conclusion until the main body of the presentation has been written.

Step 7: Rehearse again until you are confident with what you have put together, and then deliver.

If you struggle with nerves, then just remember that every presentation you do is likely to make the next presentation easier.

CONCLUSION

By now, you should be able to:

- Understand why presentations fail to achieve their objectives.
- Prepare, structure and deliver a good oral presentation.
- Choose and use visual aids relevant to the audience and goals of the presentation.
- Use appropriate strategies for dealing with nerves.

Throughout this chapter, we have noted that giving presentations is not easy and there is more than one way to deliver a message successfully. As noted, identification of the goals is essential in delivering a good presentation, but even having done so there can be issues in terms of how we prepare, structure and then give the presentation. As with all skills, there is a need for feedback and motivation to ensure that we get better at it, and the more practice we have, the more confident we become – and the more feedback we receive, the better we become.

We will often learn a lot about presentations from those we watch others give, and from those we are involved with ourselves. There is no one definitive style and you may find that you are better giving some kinds of presentations than others, so over time you will need to develop your own particular style.

 CHAPTER TASK

Watch two speeches (either TED/TEDx talks or Toastmasters International speeches). Did these speeches have a message? How did they deliver that message in terms of:

1) Structure

2) Delivery

3) Visual aids (for TED talks).

What did you learn by watching them?

INTERVIEW QUESTIONS

In some interview situations, you may be required to give a brief presentation to answer a particular question. If so, the interviewer will be looking in your presentation for all the qualities described above, but even if they do not ask you to do so, they will be looking at how you communicate through the answers that you give and the way that you give them.

Therefore, it is unlikely that you will be asked to talk about your presentation skills in an interview where they can be evaluated in other ways and where time is very limited. Any questions which might be asked about presentations will more likely be asked in order to determine your ability to plan and deliver a piece of work – either individually or in a group. But your interviewer might want to check that you have had experience of presentations if it is relevant to the job you will be asked to do, and so might ask you some short, closed questions such as:

1. Thinking of an example of a presentation that you had to give, how did you go about preparing and giving the presentation?
2. What do you find are the most difficult issues with preparing and giving a presentation?

Chapter 17 gives a lot more information on selection interviews and the online content gives some guidance on these questions.

ADDITIONAL RESOURCES

Want to learn more? Visit https://study.sagepub.com/morgan2e to gain access to a wide range of online resources, including interactive tests, tasks, further reading and downloads.

Website Resources

The following websites offer useful advice on presentation skills.

Algonquin College: algonquincollege.libguides.com/studyskills/presentation-skills

Encyclopaedia Britannica Digital Learning – resources to help with preparing for and delivering presentations: http://school.eb.com/resources/pdf/BSW_Oral_Presentation.pdf

Mindtools: www.mindtools.com/pages/article/newCS_96.htm

University of Leicester: www2.le.ac.uk/offices/ld/all-resources/presentations

Textbook Resources

Duarte, N. (2012) *HBR Guide to Persuasive Presentations*. Boston, MA: Harvard Business Review Press.
Matthews, A. (2013) *The Successful Presenter's Handbook*. Strensall: HLS Publishing.
McCarthy, P. and Hatcher, C. (2010) *Presentation Skills: The Essential Guide for Students*. Crows Nest, Australia: Sage.
McMillan, K. and Weyers, J. (2012) *The Study Skills Book* (3rd edition). Harlow: Pearson (particularly Chapter 57).

11 TEAM WORKING

Great things in business are never done by one person; they're done by a team of people. (Steve Jobs)

CHAPTER STRUCTURE

| Characteristics of Groups and Teams | → | Team Composition and Personality Theory | → | Team Development | → | Coursework Groups | → | Additional Group-Working Challenges |

Figure 11.1

When you see the this means go to the companion website https://study.sagepub.com/morgan2e to do a quiz, complete a task, read further or download a template.

■■■ AIMS OF THE CHAPTER ■■■

By the end of this chapter, you should be able to:

- Understand why people in groups behave as they do.
- Work more effectively with others.
- Understand how teams in the workplace are different from those at university.

INTRODUCTION

There are different ways to describe the way that we 'work with others'. Universities tend to talk about 'group working' (e.g. group work assignments) while employers discuss 'team working'. There are some important differences, and also some significant overlap in terms of human behaviour, hence the use of 'work(ing) with others', which is intended to cover that overlap.

A brief look at the shelves of bookstores will show you that team working is the subject of a large number of books. It is also true that, while you can and should use resources such as books and research articles on teams, the essence of your team-working skills is your behaviour. The way you behave with others as you work with them will have consequences for you and for them, and no textbook can change your behaviour on its own. So, the aims of this chapter are relatively modest: to give you some insights, to show you the consequences of certain actions, and to give you some resources to help you work better in teams.

We will also examine the relationships between attitudes and behaviours, and the ways that certain attitudes can affect behaviour. The chapter will also examine some of the reasons why teams can sometimes be ineffective and will give some answers which will help to solve these issues.

Finally, when we look at team working in this chapter, there will be significant links between this topic and that of leadership considered in Chapter 12. The two topics involve different ways of working with – or relating to – others, and each has a distinct contribution to make to the effective completion of a task. However, the role of leader involves a distinct set of activities and is examined in some detail in Chapter 12.

WHEN SHOULD YOU READ THIS CHAPTER?

This chapter gives you some ideas around how to work with others, particularly in group assignments, and so it is best to read this during your first semester at university.

SKILLS SELF-ASSESSMENT

Complete the brief questionnaire below to see how well you work with others. You can think of an academic university situation (e.g. assessed coursework) or your activities within a student society or working in a team in the workplace. Give each item a score between 1 and 5, where 1 is 'not at all like me', and 5 is 'very much like me'.

When I begin to work with others, I am likely to …

Item	Statement	Score
1.	Really enjoy the experience	
2.	Feel anxious about whether others will accept me	
3.	Want to get started on any activity we are given straight away	
4.	Worry about whether others will do their work properly	
5.	Think about which parts of the activity are best suited to me and which are better for others to do	
6.	Check my understanding of what we have to do with that of other people	
7.	Have some very clear ideas about how the task should be done	
8.	Write down my thinking about what the next step is	

(Continued)

(Continued)

Item	Statement	Score	
9.	Think about how I can show others that I can make a better contribution to the activity than them		
10.	Think about how the activity relates to other work I have done before		
11.	Get bored very easily		
12.	Consider how I can get others to like me		
13.	Worry about whether my English and/or accent is going to be good enough for me to help the group		
14.	Think about whether others are going to easily accept my opinions and points of view		
15.	Get excited about the potential for working with others on a project		
16.	Be really happy about starting 'a new thing'		
17.	Make a plan for who should do what		
18.	Think carefully about how I can encourage others within the group		
19.	Deal with people who don't cooperate with the group's activities		
20.	Make sure that everyone has the contact details of everyone else in the group		

Most of these questions do not have right or wrong answers, but nearly all of the answers will have consequences for how we interact with others, whether the group or team is working together for a long time (e.g. a department within an organisation) as a business function (e.g. marketing or accounting), or whether it has a specific and time-defined purpose (e.g. to complete a project within two months).

You can complete an interactive version of this test and find answers and guidance on the questions at https://study.sagepub.com/morgan2e.

Our feelings, emotions and behaviours – and others' perceptions of our behaviours – will impact on how well we are able to work with others. If any of the answers (particularly those which start with 'Worry about …') are likely to affect your natural behaviour too much, then maybe there is a need for you to consider whether these worries are real or just built up from other experiences which may not reflect the reality of the situation you are currently in. In general, many of the things we worry about are unlikely to become reality, but the more we think about them, the more we are likely to create a self-fulfilling prophecy.

CHARACTERISTICS OF GROUPS AND TEAMS

There are two important terms to define here – groups and teams – and there is no shortage of discussion in the academic literature as to what constitutes each one. In some situations, it might not matter greatly as to whether you think you are working in a group or in a team, but if other people have a different view, then their behaviour will be different.

Some (e.g. Muchinsky, 2003) have argued that groups and teams are actually nearly the same thing. Both consist of individuals working together to accomplish something. These individuals will likely have some differences in terms of their interests, personality, demographics and perhaps abilities, but there is something that brings them together. In terms of groups and teams, this is probably where the similarities between groups and teams end.

A group might be a social group (e.g. a club or a number of folk who like to meet after work). A team, on the other hand, can be quite different.

Teams possess the same characteristics as groups, but with some notable and important additions. Katzenbach and Smith (2005) looked at teams which were performing well and those which were performing badly, and identified a number of key factors that made the difference between low- and high-performing teams:

GROUP

A group is usually defined as a number of people sharing something in common and meeting together in relation to their shared characteristics.

- **Small**: You need a reasonably sized team in order to ensure you have all the knowledge and skills that you need, but a team that is too large will likely become dysfunctional. It will be difficult to coordinate diaries, to arrange meetings and then for folk to communicate at those meetings if the team is too large. A team of between five and seven is seen as ideal.
- **Complementary skills**: A team of five people undertaking a task which requires eight different types of knowledge and/or expertise is probably going to work if team members are selected carefully, but if all those five people possess exactly the same skills, then the team will not be effective. The skills and knowledge possessed by the team should complement rather than replicate those of other team members.
- **Common purpose**: The team members should be committed to the team's aims. This commitment could show itself in their willingness to make sacrifices for the team – an effort which is then repaid by others willing to give up their own ideas and activities to support each other. The purpose of the team drives the emotional effort put in by members.
- **Specific goals**: Where goals are unclear, then the level of performance required and the outcomes sought are also unclear. The outcomes sought from the team – and from any members of the team contributing particular work – need to be specific. A lack of clarity could well lead to frustration as members then feel a need to edit other members' work.
- **Common approach**: It is fine to share the goals, but the team needs to be in agreement about how it will achieve those goals. Without agreement, the team is likely to suffer from division.
- **Mutual accountability**: A team has a sense of 'togetherness', with each member supporting every other member. This has the potential to create a strong bond, which means that there is great strength in the team, but it also means that the team needs to stick together and assist each other when things do not go according to plan, and 'act as one' if the results are not good. It also means that the relationships formed within the team are maintained a long time after the team has finished what it was formed to do.

Working in a high-performing team can be an extremely rewarding experience. All those in the team understand each other, practically support each other and encourage each other as the task progresses. They put their egos aside for the good of the team.

Teams are typically built for particular projects where particular skills and expertise are needed (e.g. to solve a problem or develop a product). Once those activities are complete, the team will often be disbanded.

TEAM

A team is a number of individuals working as one to achieve a particular goal to which they are all mutually committed.

'BUT I HAVE A QUESTION ...'

... Why do universities set students assignments to do in groups? Groups in the workplace are so different.

That is true to some extent. People can be sacked from teams at work or demoted if they do not do their work properly, whereas that doesn't happen at university. But the authority for sanctions or some form of

(Continued)

punishment is usually there in academic life as well: just talk to your tutor if things go wrong, but do so before they become a crisis.

But the other thing (and this is common with many of the skills you develop during your studies) is that university is a good place to practise and develop these skills. Employers will probably ask you about your experience working in teams because this forms part of the requirements for the job, and so they want to know how good you are at working with others. If you have had no experience doing so, then this will be a problem for you later on. Working in teams is as difficult at work as it is at university – though probably for different reasons. But that does not mean that you should run away from such experiences, just because they are tough.

 REFLECTION POINT

Take some time to think about the following questions and write down some answers, first on your own, and then with others you might be working with.

Is the way that a team is formed in business any different from the way you would form a team to work on an assignment or group project? Why, or why not? What are the consequences of those differences?

When you are working with others on an assignment, are you working as a group or as a team? Does it make a difference?

According to the definition and ideas given earlier, everyone in a team working on coursework is supposed to support each other and to be mutually accountable for what the team does. Is this your experience when working with others on a piece of coursework? What helps or hinders this? What can be done about any hindrances?

It is common when working on an assignment with others to delegate responsibility for different parts of the task to certain members of the group or team, and then one final person will edit the work. Is this the best way to do a group assignment, or is there a better way?

Assignments where you have to work with others are often used by universities to develop your skills and abilities to work with others in preparation for employment. Do you like working with others or prefer to do your own work? Why or why not?

What differences and similarities are there between working on a group assignment at university and working with others on a team assignment in the workplace?

TEAM COMPOSITION AND PERSONALITY THEORY

The way the team is put together is key to its success. Teams can be put together in various ways – for example, according to personal knowledge, according to the importance of having certain connections outside the team, according to members' abilities and according to individuals' access to financial and other resources.

Two personality models related to team performance are frequently discussed. In the 1920s, a system known as DISC personality profiling was developed by William M. Marston to identify the different roles that individuals play in teams. Research carried out by Meredith Belbin and his team in the 1970s and 1980s at Henley Management College resulted in what has become known as 'Team Role Theory'.

We will now briefly look at both. Both models are based on an understanding of individual personality – and both have roles which are more adventurous and roles which are more conservative.

━━━━━ ■ BOX 11.1 ■ ━━━━━

Personality Theory

Since Hippocrates developed a view of personality types in ancient Greece, the ideas he introduced have continued to engage individuals, though some attribute the ideas to another Greek: Aelius Galenus. By examining the four fluids in the body, Hippocrates developed four personality types based on three issues – extraversion, task or people orientation and speed of action:

- Choleric: An extrovert personality task-oriented type that tends to act quickly.
- Phlegmatic: A more patient or reserved people-oriented personality type that is slow to act.
- Sanguine: An extrovert people-oriented personality type that is quick to act.
- Melancholic: A reserved task-oriented personality type that is slow to act.

These ideas have become popular in recent times in terms of TED talks, careers guidance tools and books. Rarely will any individual be just one of these personalities, but rather we will have a variety of personality types, and may be stronger in some of them than others. Carl Jung took ideas similar to those of Hippocrates and used them to develop four main dimensions of personality theory – namely, Extroversion and Introversion, Thinking and Feeling, Sensing and Intuition, and finally Judgement and Perceiving. This model lead to the development of the Myers-Briggs Type Inventory, which classifies individuals into one of 16 four-lettered personality 'types' based on their scores on each of the four dimensions. For example, someone classified as 'ENTJ' would be someone whose score would represent an '**E**xtrovert', scoring highly on '**IN**tuition' and so can see the big picture rather than the detail, is a '**T**hinker' focused on making decisions through logic, and who is higher on '**J**udging' and thus is decisive and likes to follow rules.

The model has been used extensively in understanding team performance and behaviours, and in careers guidance and relationship counselling. The most common personality types for men tend to be ISTJ and ENTJ, while for women they are ISFJ and ESFJ. The corresponding rare types are INFJ and ENFJ for men and INTJ and ENTJ for women.

Other theories based around five personality traits – Openness, Conscientiousness, Extraversion, Agreeableness and Neuroticism (known as the Five Fold Factor Model of personality or FFFM) – have been supported by extensive research into performance at work. This model has shown that Conscientiousness is the factor most strongly related to higher levels of performance at work, while Agreeableness can sometimes be a disadvantage in more competitive careers such as the law profession.

Belbin's Team Roles

Research by Belbin and others in the 1970s (Belbin, 1981) indicated that two factors were important: 1) the knowledge that a person has in order to contribute to a group – their occupational function; but, more importantly, 2) the skills and abilities that individuals bring to a task.

By analysing the performance of teams on simulations and investigating the personalities of members of the team in relation to that performance, Belbin and others argued that the combined personalities of the individuals in a team – or the combination of individual 'team roles' – could significantly enhance or detract from the ability of that team to complete particular tasks. These are not functional roles that someone asks you to perform, but rather emerge very naturally from your personality as you engage in team activities, and from your strengths and weaknesses will emerge particular functional roles and activities for you to do. Box 11.2 provides a brief summary of the nine team roles that emerged from the research. There were originally eight team roles, but further investigation gave rise to a ninth – that of 'specialist' – which emerged when the nature of the simulation was changed.

━━━━━ BOX 11.2 ━━━━━

Belbin's Nine Team Roles

The team roles listed below arose from the research carried out by Belbin and his associates (Belbin, 1981). Look at the brief descriptions given below: these describe the respective contributions to the team and the allowable weaknesses respectively. The two-letter abbreviations are commonly used when employing this model.

Team role (and abbreviation)	Strengths	Allowable weaknesses
Coordinator (CO)	Mature, confident and identifies talent	Can be seen as manipulative Offloads own share of the work
Implementer (IMP)	Practical, reliable and efficient Turns ideas into actions and organises work that needs to be done	Somewhat inflexible Slow to respond to new possibilities
Shaper (SH)	Challenging, dynamic, thrives on pressure Has the courage and the drive to overcome obstacles	Prone to provocation Offends people's feelings
Completer-Finisher (CF)	Painstaking, conscientious, anxious Searches out errors, polishes and perfects	Inclined to worry unduly Reluctant to delegate
Resource Investigator (RI)	Outgoing, enthusiastic and communicative Explores opportunities and develops contacts	Over-optimistic Loses interest once initial enthusiasm has passed
Specialist (SP)	Single-minded, self-starting, dedicated Provides knowledge and skills in rare supply	Contributes only on a narrow front Dwells on technicalities
Monitor-Evaluator (ME)	Sober, strategic and discerning Sees all options and judges accurately	Lacks drive and ability to inspire others Can be overly critical

Team role (and abbreviation)	Strengths	Allowable weaknesses
Plant (PL)	Creative, imaginative, free thinking Generates ideas and solves difficult problems	Ignores incidentals Too preoccupied to communicate effectively
Team worker (TW)	Cooperative, perceptive and diplomatic Listens and averts friction	Indecisive in crunch situations Avoids confrontation

Belbin suggests that we usually have primary roles – ones that are closest to our personality – and secondary roles – ones that we are very similar to and can perform if we need to.

The identification of individuals' team roles (their primary role and secondary role, reflecting what individuals would naturally do and what they could do if they needed to, respectively) emerges from an analysis of an individual's own responses to items on a personality questionnaire (Belbin Team Role Self-Perception Inventory) and observations made by trained observers watching individuals complete the simulation. The research carried out by Belbin and others suggests that the more the team is 'Balanced' and reflects all the team roles, the better the team's performance on the simulation is likely to be. The team can still be kept small, since all the team roles can be found through individuals' primary and secondary roles. The task of those putting the team together is simply to ensure that all the roles identified above are represented in the team, according to the needs of the task.

Not every task will require every role, and certain team roles might be more or less important at different stages of the task. Table 11.1 indicates at what stages certain roles might be particularly important.

There are a number of issues that some people have with this model. The questionnaire (Belbin Team Role Self-Perception Inventory) is not always seen as the easiest to complete, it is unclear why changing the simulation would allow a previously unknown role to emerge, and some claim that other internal and external contextual factors (e.g. individuals' attitudes, organisational politics or policies) can undermine the effectiveness of the team.

Table 11.1   Task requirements and relevant roles

Stages and roles of task completion

Task stages	Roles seen as important
Identifying needs	SH and CO
Finding ideas	PL and RI
Formulating plans	ME and SP
Making contacts	RI and TW
Establishing the organisation	IMP and CO
Following through	CF and IMP

KEY LEARNING POINT

The balance of a team in terms of personalities and Belbin's team roles is crucial to the performance of that team.

FOR YOU TO DO

Consider for a moment that you have been asked to work in a group of five for a presentation in one of your subjects. You have decided to work with these individuals because you get on well together and broadly share the same characteristics. As you look through the personalities listed above and the members of your group, you believe that you can recognise the personalities of six of the nine team roles in your team, but there are others which you think are missing.

If the following roles are missing:

- Resource Investigator
- Coordinator
- Shaper
- Plant
- Completer-Finisher

1. What might the impact be on your presentation preparation and your team meetings?
2. How might you ensure that you can complete the task successfully?
3. How would you work together if you have two or more individuals who share the same primary roles?

BOX 11.3

Critique of Belbin's Team Role Theory

Research on Belbin's ideas has not always been supportive, and it was not until the late 1990s that Vic Dulewicz and others who worked with Belbin revealed their original research methodologies. The Henley team began by using various personality questionnaires – including a well-known personality assessment tool known as the 16PF – and examining team performance. Their initial studies had eight team roles, some of which were named differently, so the Chairman became the 'Coordinator' and the 'Specialist' did not exist as a role. It was not until the team exercise – on which the Henley team was basing their work – was changed that the role of 'Specialist' was introduced.

The lack of openness and change in task during the research has led some to criticise Belbin's research. The research has also been criticised in relation to the way that the questionnaire has been developed and the kinds of data that it generates. Most questionnaires used in research ask respondents to respond on a 1 to 5 scale, giving data on questions that can be easily correlated with each other and producing easily understandable statistics. However, Belbin's original questionnaire asked individuals to allocate 10 marks across nine statements, making the analysis much more problematic and less conclusive.

These criticisms, however, have not stopped Belbin's work from being used widely in business and from the model being seen as very popular. That would not happen without some evidence to support the ideas in Belbin's model.

REFLECTION POINT

Take some time to think about the following questions and write down some answers.

Thinking about yourself, which of the descriptions of the team roles seems closest to your own personality?

Is there a secondary team role that you could perform?

To what extent are the allowable weaknesses really allowable?

Finding a team with all the team roles may not be the first issue on your mind when trying to form a group for a coursework assignment. The first question is usually, 'Are my friends doing this module?', with a second being, 'Are they already in a group?' Choosing to work with our friends, however, may not always be the best thing.

=== 'BUT I HAVE A QUESTION ...?' ===

... I can choose my team-mates for an assignment, but should I work with my friends or not?

You may not always get the chance to choose your team-mates for a piece of group coursework: there are times when you might not know your group mates well, or when tutors believe that in the real business world, that is not going to be the case, so it should not be the case at university. However, there might be other occasions – particularly when the impact of the individuals you work with is greater on your academic grades – when you get to choose those you work with. So, when working as a university student, is it better to work on coursework with others who are your friends, or to be put in a team by your tutor? What are the consequences of either?

It is very natural – and very frequent – to find you have a group work assignment to do and suddenly decide to work with your friends. You know them reasonably well, presumably you have something in common, you might have a similar sense of humour and might live close together, but are these the best reasons to work with them?

Actually, some of these are good reasons to avoid working with friends, since they tend to ignore some of the best practice identified above. Having good relationships does not mean that you have the right skills, motivation or academic abilities to do well on a piece of coursework. If we take the view that everyone is equally and strongly motivated to do the project that you have been set, then the worst situation would be a group which just happens not to have the right skills. The best situation is that your friends are highly motivated, have strong bonds with each other and have all the skills needed for a particular project.

But, if we take the view that one or some members of the group are not motivated to do the task, then there is a problem. We either ignore the lack of effort from our friends and get on with the work ourselves (and keep the friendship, albeit at a reduced level of commitment), or we start to damage the friendship by criticising our friends. It is very hard to work with friends when we have different levels of motivation and commitment to a task.

So, should you work with your friends? The answer is simple: it depends. You need to consider the impact on your work and your friendship, should things turn out badly.

TEAM DEVELOPMENT

Having looked at how we put teams together, it is also appropriate to look at how teams work over time. Research carried out in the 1960s by Tuckman (1965) indicated that the development of the team will occur in a number of stages, each of which can affect interactions between members of the team. The terms used in brackets are those given by Tuckman.

Stage 1: Formation (Forming)

The formation of the team does not solely mean the putting together of team members. The composition of a team based on function and skill does not guarantee that it will instantly work well. As they are put together, individuals usually have questions such as: What am I doing here? How do I relate to others in the team? How well will I perform? The 'formation stage' is designed to help members feel relaxed and comfortable working with each other, and to start undertaking the task. Much of the team leader's role at this stage is to ensure that members get to know each other, to ensure that roles and contributions are clear, and to start the task; this can be done very easily through social and informal events (e.g. meals, going out together).

Stage 2: Disagreeing (Storming)

As the task gets underway, different team members will contribute in different ways, of course. As they do so, a number of difficulties are likely to emerge. It is quite possible that team members will start to find out that other members might have strong ideas, might not appear to listen properly or respect others enough, or may not be contributing enough to the task. The natural reaction to any of these issues is to feel resentful and start to argue, hence the name 'storming' given to this stage. In some ways, the open expression of emotion could be taken as a measure of how open the relationships within the team might be, but this could be a generous way of looking at it.

The challenge for the leader is to allow such disagreements to occur. The alternative is to close down communication, which could stop some members contributing altogether, although it is out of disagreement that creativity can emerge – but not so far as to break the team. Thus a great deal of skill and wisdom is required: knowing when to intervene to calm discussions down, and when to allow and enable free discussion, is not easy. Handling emotional conversations was discussed in Chapter 9 ('Communicating Effectively').

Stage 3: Developing Ways of Working (Norming)

In order to emerge from a time of disagreement and discussion and ensure that members do not damage group processes, both the team and the team leader will need to consider how to prevent damaging conflict, or rather, how to manage it. The process of doing so – which may be quite brief – means that rules and procedures get developed and the team acquires values or 'norms' (e.g. only one person to speak at a time) by which it operates. These processes may change a little over time and may be added to as new issues emerge.

 ━━ REFLECTION POINT ━━━━━━━━━━━━━━

Think about a time when you were in a group where there were rules to help the group perform better.

Did you agree to them? If not, did you follow them?

Thinking back, do you think the rules were at all useful? Did they help or hinder your ability (as a team) to work better?

Would you advise others working in teams to have rules to ensure that the goal could be accomplished?

━━━━━━ BOX 11.4 ━━━━━━

The Dangers of Group-Think

The 'norming' process is designed to limit conflict and argument in a group, and most groups which are suffering from continuous argument and emotional and personal dispute would be seen as dysfunctional. The constructive discussion of ideas can have two effects: if managed well, it can enhance creativity (see section on brainstorming in Chapter 14, and particularly the case of IDEO) but well-managed discussions can also limit the impact of a significant problem when working with others called 'group-think'.

GROUP-THINK

In 1986, 73 seconds after lift-off, the Challenger shuttle exploded and disintegrated with the loss of all seven astronauts on board. In reviewing the disaster, Irving Janis (1982) noted that a group of intelligent and expert individuals had ignored or not shared the concerns they had. What emerged was a recognition that strong group cohesion (where an unwillingness to provide a dissenting voice in favour of group cohesion) can cause problems. The challenge of group-think is that it stops open discussion of issues that should be discussed.

Group-think is defined as 'a mode of thinking that people engage in when they are deeply involved in a cohesive in-group, when the members' strivings for unanimity override their motivation to realistically appraise alternative courses of action' (Janis, 1982: 9)

Another scenario – taken from a BBC episode of 'The Apprentice' in 2007 – describes a team working together with one team member (courageously perhaps) dissenting from the broader group view. In the final event, it turns out that this team member is absolutely right in what she has been saying, and her team lose – partially as a result of the apparent group-think. A telling comment is given during the discussion when one team member says, '*The team* is making that decision, so how can it be wrong?' and again when another says (paraphrased), 'You have to show that you are 100% behind the team decision': a less persistent member of the team might have kept quiet.

Group-think is seen as inherently unhelpful, with a number of consequences for the team:

* Excessive optimism – 'We can do this, we should not be negative'.
* Discrediting of negative feedback – 'That can't be true: we can overcome this'.
* Belief in the inherent morality of the group – 'How can this be wrong, if the team are saying this?'
* Negative stereotyping of 'opponents' – 'They are always unhelpful in the team'.
* Pressure to conform and reach consensus – 'Unanimous agreement: that's what we should push for'.
* Self-censorship – Thinking 'I'd prefer to stay quiet: I am sure the others in the group know better than me'.
* Illusion of unanimity – 'No one thinks any differently, right?'
* Mind guards – 'We cannot allow ourselves to get distracted with thinking negatively about this idea'.

As a result of group-think, at best, teams may perform less effectively than they might do, and at worst, make poor decisions resulting in a loss of life.

Stage 4: Performing

The fourth stage is a result of the previous three: having developed some rules on how to work, and an understanding of the personalities and roles within the team, and feeling comfortable enough to disagree in a respectful manner, there is little to prevent motivated individuals from performing together well as a team. As a result, the task gets completed.

Stage 5: Completion and Finish (Adjourning)

As mentioned earlier, teams are often created for a particular task and usually disband after finishing that task. In a team that has developed good relationships over a period of time, this process can be emotional, so the leader needs to ensure that the ending of the team is respectful and smooth. Just as social and informal events can be used to form the team, some form of celebration and/or a more formal 'thank you for your contribution' can work well to maintain team relationships.

There has been some debate as to whether teams do go through these five stages in the order listed. In reality, teams may well disagree about different things at different times. It is usual for the group to move between the storming and performing stages several times before a task is completed. It is also common practice in many teams for rules (norms) to be made explicit early on in the team's development, during the 'forming' stage, though of course these might be renegotiated as the team progresses with its task.

COURSEWORK GROUPS

It is not uncommon for students to need to find a number of other individuals and to complete a group assignment in just 10 weeks. This is faster than many teams need to work in business, and so it is important for such teams to make sure that they develop and work together well.

When it comes to looking at the stages of team development, academic group work is usually something of a challenge. Forming a group with friends (see previous 'But I Have a Question' box) can be easier in some respects as you do not need to go through the first 'Forming' stage in the same way. You will already have the relationships with others and will already be able to arrange who is going to do what in terms of getting the assignment completed. However, if you are not familiar with the others in your group (which means that others may be in the same position), then maybe the group needs some social activities to get to know each other, and in particular, what makes each of you work in the way you do, your motives, skills, abilities and interests. In that way, you can start to develop really useful relationships.

The challenge of working in academic coursework groups (see 'Additional Group-Working Challenges' below) is that working with friends can mean that conflict within the group gets hidden as the implications of dealing with conflicts between friends can make life complicated. That means that the 'Storming' phase noted above never gets experienced, but the group (or members of the group) then 'copes' with the situation being unresolved: it is not unheard of for the work of some groups to be done by one or two people who are frustrated but who take no action to resolve the situation.

The easiest way of dealing with potential disputes is to be proactive and to pre-empt them: such conflicts may not occur, but to have procedures in place for dealing with them is better than getting frustrated. Team members need to agree to a set of values and procedures – termed a 'Group Agreement' or 'Group Contract' – aimed at reducing the potential for any disagreement.

Such a contract should be discussed at the first meeting, and should cover the following:

- **What is the objective of the group?** This may sound very simple, but ... Be clear about what you have agreed to achieve. This needs to state the quality (what grade are you after?) of the work, in terms of consistent writing style (if it is a piece of written work) or presentation style (e.g. formatting of slides, if it is a presentation), and should give as clear guidance as possible to *all* in the group.
- **What are the timescales and project milestones?** When are you going to meet? By when should group members have done their work (*both* drafts and final versions)? Plan the project carefully so that you give yourself enough time to do what is needed, including any final editing before submission.

- **How will you communicate?** You need to have at least one set of contact details from each individual in the group and share these across the team. Be clear about what methods you will use to communicate. Not everyone will necessarily feel happy about giving their phone numbers, so consider using social media tools to communicate, but you *must* have agreement to communicate using one tool *and* to ensure that group members access this regularly. It is all too easy for group members to miss a meeting or an instruction because they are not checking the tool used or because group members suddenly start to use a different tool. Make sure that you have the relevant contact details of everyone else in the group.

- **When and how often will you meet?** Group members need to be clear about what they are expected to have done by when, and in the cases of those students who have jobs or family responsibilities, they will need to plan for group meetings, so be clear about when and how meetings will be arranged and take place. Be open to the possibility of using internet tools (e.g. Skype, Zoom or Starleaf) and holding a virtual meeting if some group members cannot attend for some reason.

- **What values will guide your group?** Of course, at the start of a piece of group work, everyone in the group will commit to doing a good job, but life can sometimes change people and their situations. So, you need to have procedures in place for handling group members who do not do their work or who do it at the last minute, so what sanctions can you have? These processes might already be given to you by the course tutor, so check with them first, but make sure that you agree these within the group *and* with the course tutor. In your contract, you might also want to talk about turning up to meetings on time, how you communicate politely (e.g. not interrupting others when talking in meetings, who will record the minutes of meetings) and other behaviours which foster respect within the group and can ensure that good relationships are helping to get the work done well.

- **How will you share your work?** Group assignments are living documents and grow as the group members complete their work. In addition, it is really useful for group members to be able to see how the writing style and presentation etc. of the assignment is looking as the assignment is compiled, so how are you going to ensure that this happens? Putting documents onto a website such as 'googledocs' or something similar can really help to give universal access, and at a basic level, emails within the group can help in a minimal way. This can also prevent the situation where someone loses their work half way through (either because a computer breaks down or worse), or a team member withdraws from the group. Have a process for storing and sharing your work.

- **How and when will work be shared and feedback provided?** You need to have agreed clear processes for ensuring that all work is reviewed and feedback from the group is given. When members submit work, there is nothing worse than submitting and hearing nothing until the end of the project, when everyone is in a panic and emotions are running high, when feedback comes without the calm respect that it should have. So agree timescales: 'all submitted work will receive feedback from group members in three days', for example.

- **Who is doing what?** You need to be clear about who is doing what within the group in relation to the assignment or required work. More complex practical tasks may take more time to plan and execute, so consider how these might get done. In particular, consider who might lead the group, who might arrange meetings, take notes, organise the group (these do not all need to be the same person).

Each member of the group needs to sign this contract at the beginning of the group project, and in some cases, a tutor might ask you to submit this for their information. You need to agree within the group what will happen if group members do not follow what they have agreed, and discuss this with the course tutor so that the implementation of any sanction has the authority of course lecturers.

KEY LEARNING POINT

It is not reasonable simply to put a team together and expect it to perform from the outset. A team needs time to form and learn how to work together, and the team leader needs to ensure that this happens.

REFLECTION POINT

Take some time to think about the following questions and write down some answers.
    Consider a group or a team that you have worked with. To what extent:

*   Was the task a definite task, with a particular goal to be achieved?
*   Did your progress reflect all of the stages detailed above? Why or why not?
*   Was there conflict and disagreement within the team? How well did the team leader handle it?
*   Did the team have rules? Were these rules applied well?

Why Coursework Groups Sometimes Struggle

We have noted the need for groups at university to work together well, but business teams do not always work well either: after all, they are made up of imperfect human beings. In their text *Why Teams Don't Work*, Robins and Finley (1998) laid out a number of reasons why teams might fail. Some of their ideas relate to team composition in the first place, but other issues relate to factors external to the team.

FOR YOU TO DO

*   Private agendas & mismatched needs
*   Confused & cluttered goals
*   Confused roles
*   Right decisions, wrong process
*   Bad policies, stupid procedures
*   Bad leadership

*   Bleary vision
*   Teams are not part of [my] thinking
*   Lack of feedback
*   Lack of incentives
*   Lack of trust
*   Unwillingness to change
*   Lack of tools &/or support
*   [Unresolved] personality conflicts

Figure 11.2   Why teams might fail

Source: Robins and Finley, 1998

    Have a look through the issues identified by Robins and Finley (1998) (see Figure 11.2) around workplace teams and answer the questions below.

1. How would you feel if you were in a coursework group experiencing the above issues? What would go through your mind?

2. If you were leading a group experiencing these issues, how might you go about solving them?
3. Are there any other issues which affect the way that groups working on university assignments might perform?

An interactive task and some suggestions are provided on the companion website at **https://study.sagepub. com/morgan2e**, although each individual and leader will have a different way of dealing with these issues.

INTERACTIVE TEST

ADDITIONAL GROUP-WORKING CHALLENGES

We have already addressed the characteristics of an effective team (see pages 252) and these relate to academic coursework groups as much as any other groups in terms of size, commitment to a common goal, mutual accountability and so on. We have also discussed the nature of a group contract and the need to set rules and processes in place before starting a project, as well as some issues around arranging meetings and developing group agreements, but there are three further issues which need addressing: 1) developing a cohesive group, 2) handing arguments in the group, and 3) developing group leadership.

Developing a Cohesive Group

Much of the way that we develop a cohesive group relates to issues we have already covered, including developing a set of rules, but cohesion goes beyond mere obedience to rules. A cohesive group is one where there is a strong sense of mutual support, of 'togetherness' and where there is strong identification as a member of the team. There are a number of ways that team leaders can create cohesion and a sense of identity within a team, meaning that people will be willing to commit effort even when there is no external reward for doing so. These include:

- **Experience of success**: A team which has never been successful will struggle to get a sense of excitement about success. Part of this is about establishing a vision for success ('What would it be like if …') and a team that can understand success is likely to go over and above the minimum effort required to reach that success.
- **Challenge of a common enemy**: A team which has one enemy to fight against can focus its energy more effectively. If members of the team have different 'enemies', then it will be more difficult to create the idea that the team is trying to achieve one thing. A common enemy focuses energy outside of the team.
- **High status**: A team which everyone wants to be part of because of its position in an organisational hierarchy is likely to maintain its cohesion. People will want to be members of the team because of its organisational influence, and that will motivate the team members. If you – as a team and as a leader of the team – are able to put in the effort to create a group that others wish they had joined, then you are more than half way to creating a highly effective team.

Handling Conflict within a Group

Handling conflict requires the possession of a set of skills and one or two really important attitudes, and the wisdom to apply the content already provided in this chapter in a way which alleviates tension and facilitates constructive discussion. Understanding two key principles can help tremendously:

1. People become agitated when they are afraid, feel threatened or do not feel respected – or some combination of the above. Respecting everyone in the team means that everyone has an equal chance to get their voice heard. If people do not feel that they will have a good chance to give their views (especially when it is their work that is being discussed), then they will get agitated. So, if you are leading the group, try to remove that fear, or sense of threat, and make sure that everyone has a clear chance to contribute, and that everyone *knows explicitly* that they will be able to do so.

2. People are rarely emotional and logical at the same time. This has two implications – firstly, that emotional individuals will not be likely to clearly hear the message you want them to receive, and secondly, that we have an opportunity to calm someone down by getting them to think, and the way we do that is by asking simple questions – what, how, when, *but never* why? This also means that we are engaging with them and that adds to their sense of being respected.

There are some other simple tools we can use to calm situations down:

*   **Keep your voice calm and stable**: Raising volume or pitch will only make situations worse.
*   **Consider whether you need to stop a discussion and take a break**: This can diffuse tension and give the group leader a chance to talk one to one to provide whatever reassurance is needed or to ask questions to calm the other person down.
*   **Smile to put the other person at their ease**: They may just be having a very hard day in some way, so a reassuring smile can help someone to relax.
*   **Ask others in the group to listen to this individual**: They may or may not be correct in what they are saying, but ensure that they have the opportunity to do so.
*   **Remember that the aim of the group is to get a job done**: Avoid a big argument by treating a disagreement as *a problem to be solved*, rather than as a massive issue that is the fault of someone in the group.
*   **Try not to respond to comments from others in an angry or emotional manner**: You may have misunderstood the issue and/or need time to consider what someone else has said in an environment which gives you the chance to interrogate your thoughts properly.
*   **Avoid voting wherever possible**: Voting rarely solves conflicts in a group and instead often creates an impression of ignoring someone's views in favour of a majority decision – even if that is not the intent. Getting agreement by consensus is significantly better.
*   **Listen to everyone**: Give everyone an opportunity to talk to the group leader once any conflict has been solved. Individuals may still be feeling awkward afterwards, so giving others that time and space to talk can improve their effectiveness.

All of the above ideas apply regardless of whether or not individuals are from our own cultures. Indeed, we may not understand why someone is getting emotional about something (and sometimes nor might they), but learning to respect and communicate well with them is going to make life so much easier than having arguments. It is one reason why the group contracts (discussed above) are so important.

Developing Leadership

Ensuring that the above two elements – developing a cohesive team and handing conflict in a team – are done well usually requires some careful leadership. A leadership role is often something that people want for the profile and skills it will give them, but individuals can be much less excited about taking the responsibility when things do not go as planned.

Regardless, a group leader has the responsibility for ensuring that the group works well – and for acting promptly to stop problems in the group from becoming crises. If they do what has been suggested throughout this chapter, then they should do a good job and enable the group to achieve its goals.

'BUT I HAVE A QUESTION...'

... How do we handle the situation where a group member does not do their work?

It's a good question – though in some ways, it is more a question about leadership. It is useful to recognise that what is seen is not necessarily the complete picture. For example, a group member may genuinely have been unable to do the work because of illness, or sudden and important commitments. Maybe they were clear on what they needed to do or by when, or did not have the resources (including books) to do what they were asked to do. Sometimes these issues might be used as excuses, but a good analytical approach will identify whether the issue is actually more than just motivation. A good leader will do some investigating before arriving at a judgement.

If the issue is about motivation, then a good leader will hold individuals accountable, and will ensure that the individuals do what is required between meetings. If it looks as if a group member is not doing what they were asked to do, then they will closely monitor the progress of particular group members to ensure that they are doing the work. If that is still not happening, then the group leader will talk to the individual concerned to find out why outside of the meeting. If the problem continues, then the group leader might consider addressing it publicly in the next group meeting. Not addressing this publicly when everyone is aware of a lack of effort on the part of a group member means that such behaviour is tolerated – and what is tolerated can become acceptable.

Another possible solution may lie in any formal mechanism set up by the lecturer. Peer evaluation is sometimes one such idea, where students confidentially rate other students in their group according to the amount of effort others have given – and where such ratings make a difference in the tutor's mark. In some longer courses, it is possible for the lecturer to build in the possibility of group members being 'sacked' from the group at some stage in the group work.

The worst possible solution would be where the individuals receive the mark for work to which they have made no contribution. If group members are not doing anything, and there is no mechanism to make a complaint to the lecturers (or no desire to do so), then there are times when all the work is done by one or two members of the group. This is wholly unacceptable, but it happens.

It is also a sign of bad leadership, in the sense that usually, good leadership would have meant doing something about the problem before the hand-in date approached. A good leader would also have ensured that the group was very clear about the rules for completing the work – including what would happen if an individual decided that they didn't want to do any work (or considered themselves too important to do so!). If rules are set and agreed at the beginning of the group work, then it is not difficult to push group members to abide by them. However, without any power or authority, the role of a group leader for a piece of coursework is always likely to be less than it would be in a working situation.

In some situations, approaching the lecturer about the problem may be necessary, but see what ideas you can apply before doing so if possible.

FOR YOU TO DO

Have a look at the scenarios given below. What would you do to deal with the situation? What advice would you offer the groups involved?

(Continued)

If you were the leader for each of the six teams listed below, how would you go about handling these situations? What would your first action be? What possible reasons might the 'problematic individual(s)' give for their behaviour? And how would you address them?

1. You are concerned about Asif. He has been causing problems by criticising others in the team. Julie is quite upset because Asif told her that her spreadsheet charts were not very good and were unclear. She spent ages doing those charts.
2. Sarah, whom you don't know very well, is in your team. She seems very bored when she comes to meetings and keeps apologising that she has forgotten to do her actions. She got very defensive when you mentioned that this is holding up the team and now seems quite distant with you. Aisha tells you Sarah has been telling other people that you bully her.
3. The team had a meeting last week and you thought everyone had agreed to do something. This week nobody seems to have done anything at all. The team seems to have forgotten what was agreed and spends most of the meeting discussing the same things as last time. This is really frustrating.
4. Ika and Roman have just had a huge bust-up in a meeting. Ika has accused Roman of not doing what he agreed to do and called him lazy. Roman called Ika a control freak and stormed out of the meeting. Each of them is refusing to come to the next meeting if the other is there.
5. Simon and John don't seem to want to work with Michelle, Keisha and Thomas. They often don't turn up to meetings and are hard to contact. Michelle and Keisha are worried because they are high-achieving students and are concerned about their grades, especially as the group mark is shared and Simon and John are supposed to do a certain part of the project.
6. The team has just found out that Robert has gone into hospital. He was supposed to complete the images for the presentation and is the only one with copies.

(Above scenarios written by Martin Sedgley at the University of Bradford.)

 KEY LEARNING POINT

Working in a group can sometimes be challenging, but rarely are problems insurmountable or permanent. Group contracts and the development of good communications are hallmarks of great groups, and of competent leadership.

BOX 11.5

Working in Intercultural Teams

Some individuals might struggle to work in intercultural teams. They might find it challenging to accept differences in cultural values and standards as to what is acceptable behaviour and what is not (see Chapter 13).

Of course, every individual is slightly different from every other individual anyway, but it is the extent to which diversity of values shows itself in a multicultural team that can cause particular problems.

So, have a look at the behaviours below. Which would you find difficult to accept from others in your intercultural team? Which would make you feel embarrassed to be in the group?

1. An individual constantly interrupts another individual.
2. The group always meets in a pub and others in the group tend to drink a lot.
3. The group always seems to be laughing and joking around.
4. Other members of the group arrive late to meetings.
5. Some members of the group seem to argue aggressively with each other.
6. The group has meals regularly but the food is always spicy and the leader never asks other members what they would like.
7. The leader seems to be weak – they never make a decision on their own, but always ask other people what they think.
8. Everybody seems quite selfish – the group never has any meals together.
9. The group always speaks in a language other than your own.
10. No one seems to care enough for each other: there is no friendly conversation in the group and everything is directed to the task.

The reaction that we might have may be based around our cultural values, but if those are different from others' values, then we may face a challenge in working easily with others. Chapter 13 gives a lot more information on working with people from other cultures, but if you find that you do not respect the group, then the quickest and easiest way to manage such situations is to ask your tutor for some anonymous help available for all international students in the class.

INTEGRATION AND APPLICATION

This chapter has tried to present both theory and some practical ideas in relation to working in teams, but there are no specific steps to working in teams. 'Team working' is a set of skills that you will need to develop throughout your university career, and employers will be looking for cooperative and insightful team members, but more importantly team leaders.

Teams need to be composed and put together well. Moving from the 'Forming' stage of a team to being able to 'Perform' well will require the team to interact informally before it develops sub-goals, norms and processes to enable it to accomplish what it was set up to do. As we have seen, understanding how the various roles operate together and contribute at the different stages in solving the task requires that we have a clear sense of the skills and abilities of each team member – and the demands of the task.

CONCLUSION

By now, you should be able to:

- Understand why people in groups behave as they do.
- Work more effectively with others.
- Understand how teams in the workplace are different from those at university.

It is important to work as part of a team as much as possible throughout your university career. The experience you have will depend hugely on who is in your team, how good the team leader is at balancing team, task and individual priorities, and how available the required skills are within those teams.

As noted in the introduction to this chapter, working in teams is about relationships, character, action and communication. Over time, it is also about learning and adapting. Two team situations can be very different, and leading two different groups of people can also be very different, but both sets of situations will reveal a great deal about who you are as an individual and your strengths and weaknesses to others.

REFLECTION POINT

Take some time to think about the following questions and write down some answers.

Based on the content of this chapter, what do you now know about teams that you did not know before?

What key learning point had the most impact? Why?

Do your answers to either of the above questions have the potential to change your ability to work in a team? To lead others? Why?

What will you now do differently? (Write this down and put it somewhere where you can see it regularly.)

CHAPTER TASK

Look at a group you know well – maybe another team doing the same assignment as your group, or maybe a group from another course. What challenges have they had? How – if at all – have they overcome those challenges? What might you do differently? And finally, what can you learn from how other groups around you function?

INTERVIEW QUESTIONS

The areas covered in this chapter are both very broad and very important to nearly every organisation. As a result, it might well be that up to half of an interview could be devoted to these skills, so there are a large number of questions an employer might ask.

Think about the following questions. What might your answers be?

1. What do you think makes a good team worker?
2. Tell me about a time when you needed to work with others to accomplish a difficult task. What did you do and how successful was your group?
3. Can you tell me about a time when you have had to work with others to complete a challenging task with limited resources? What did you do? What was the impact of your actions?

With nearly all the questions given above, you can answer from any experience you have had – during your course or in a student society.

Chapter 17 gives a lot more information on selection interviews and the online content gives some guidance on these questions.

ADDITIONAL RESOURCES

Want to learn more? Visit https://study.sagepub.com/morgan2e to gain access to a wide range of online resources, including interactive tests, tasks, further reading and downloads.

Website Resources

The following websites offer useful advice on working in groups.

Belbin website: www.belbin.com/about/belbin-team-roles/

Mindtools: www.mindtools.com/pages/main/newMN_TMM.htm

University of Leeds: https://library.leeds.ac.uk/info/1401/academic_skills/110/group_work

University of Reading: https://libguides.reading.ac.uk/groups

Textbook Resources

Aldag, R. J. and Kuzuhara, L. W. (2015) *Creating High Performance Teams*. New York: Routledge.

Barrett, D. J. (2011) *Leadership Communication* (3rd edition). New York: McGraw-Hill (particularly Chapter 10).

Belbin, R. M. (2003) *Team Roles at Work*. Oxford: Elsevier.

Burns, T. and Sinfield, S. (2016) *Essential Study Skills* (4th edition). London: Sage (particularly Chapter 9).

Cameron, S. (2016) *The Business Student's Handbook: Skills for Study and Employment* (6th edition). Harlow: Pearson (particularly Chapter 9).

Cottrell, S. (2013) *The Study Skills Handbook* (4th edition). New York: Palgrave (particularly Chapter 10).

Dougherty, C. and Thompson, J. E. (2010) *Be a Better Leader*. Oxford: Bookpoint (particularly Chapter 9).

Flint, M. and Hearn, E. V. (2015) *Leading Teams: 10 Challenges and 10 Solutions*. Harlow: Pearson.

Gallagher, K. (2016) *Essential Study and Employment Skills for Business and Management Students* (3rd edition). Oxford: Oxford University Press (particularly Chapter 11).

Hamilton, C. and Kroll, T. L. (2018) *Communicating for Results* (11th edition). Boston, MA: Cengage (particularly Chapter 10).

Harvard Business Review (2011) *Building Better Teams*. Boston, MA: Harvard Business Review.

Hawkins, P. (2017) *Leadership Team Coaching* (3rd edition). London: Kogan-Page (particularly Chapters 2, 3, 7 and 11).

Hind, D. and Moss, S. (2011) *Employability Skills*. Houghton-le-Spring: Business Education Publishers (particularly Chapter 9).

Horn, R. (2012) *The Business Skills Handbook*. London: CIPD (particularly Chapter 5).

Katzenbach, J. R. and Smith, D. K. (2001) *The Discipline of Teams*. New York: Wiley.

Lamberg, T. (2018) *Leaders Who Lead Successfully*. Lanham, MD: Rowman and Littlefield.

Tissington, P. and Orthodoxou, C. (2014) *Study Skills for Business and Management*. London: Sage (particularly Chapter 8 on working in groups).

West, M. A. (2012) *Effective Teamwork* (3rd edition). New York: Wiley.

12 UNDERSTANDING LEADERSHIP

If your actions inspire others to dream more, learn more, do more and become more, you are a leader. (John Quincy Adams)

CHAPTER STRUCTURE

| Leadership and Management Compared | Defining and Understanding Leadership | Leadership, Power and Influence | The Skills of Leadership | Leadership, Coursework and the 'Poor Contributor' | Models of Leadership | Leadership in the Future |

Figure 12.1

 When you see the 🌐 this means go to the companion website https://study.sagepub.com/morgan2e to do a quiz, complete a task, read further or download a template.

━━ AIMS OF THE CHAPTER ━━

By the end of this chapter, you should be able to:

- Develop different styles of leadership.
- Distinguish effective leadership from ineffective leadership.
- Let who you are influence the way you lead.

INTRODUCTION

Leaders are paid more than others, have more responsibility, are often believed to have a higher profile and are generally seen as 'more successful' than others. Of course, these various qualities tend to go together – and for good reason. As we will see, leading is not easy: for some individuals, it is an exciting and rewarding activity, though for others it is seen as too risky and difficult. Individuals are different and not everyone will want to be a leader, but, in reality, leadership can come in many forms, While there are some common qualities, leadership is usually about developing a vision for yourself and others, and then setting up and monitoring processes related to the achievement of this vision. How that is done can vary significantly: given the right motivation and opportunity for development, leadership is something that anyone *can* develop.

WHEN SHOULD YOU READ THIS CHAPTER?

This chapter is about how to lead effectively, and so it is best to read this before you need to do any group work, and probably during your first year at university.

There is a great deal that has been written about leadership. Trying to summarise this writing in a brief chapter such as this is not easy, but we will cover a number of pertinent issues. We will begin by providing a definition of leadership, looking at what good leadership is and is not in terms of values and skills. We will look at issues of power in leadership, how – as leaders – we might go about handling issues of group coursework where individual(s) are not contributing as they should, as well as examining a number of models of leadership, before closing by looking at leadership in the future.

Understanding and developing leadership skills is something that can take a lifetime, but the quicker we begin the process and develop our understanding of what leadership actually is, the more likely it is that we will be able to demonstrate leadership when it comes to getting a leadership role after graduation.

SKILLS SELF-ASSESSMENT

Complete the brief questionnaire below to see how well you work with others. You can think of an academic university situation (e.g. assessed coursework) or your activities within a student society or working in a team in the workplace. Give each item a score between 1 and 5, where 1 is 'not at all like me', and 5 is 'very much like me'.

When I begin to lead others, I am likely to …

Item	Statement	Score
1.	Really enjoy the experience	
2.	Feel anxious about whether others will accept me as their leader	
3.	Develop a sense of vision of what I want the team to achieve	
4.	Watch what other teams doing the same activity are doing, and then motivate my team to follow the same ideas	
5.	Set the standard as high as I think is needed	
6.	Sit back and carefully think about how I am going to lead the team	
7.	Get more information on what different team members are able to do	
8.	Ensure that I personally fulfil my team members' needs above everything else	

(Continued)

(Continued)

Item	Statement	Score	
9.	See what I want to do and identify things that I can delegate to others within the team		
10.	Ensure that my team does everything expected of it through identifying appropriate punishments		
11.	Tell others outside of the team that I am the team leader		
12.	Consider how I can get others to like me		
13.	Learn about leadership from books and journal articles		
14.	Make sure that I am the one people come to in order to solve the problems within the team		
15.	Learn to understand why people do and say what they do and say		
16.	Ensure that I very clearly tell my team what they need to do		
17.	Encourage the people in my team as much as I can		
18.	Think carefully about how I can encourage others within the group		
19.	Deal with people who do not cooperate with the group's activities		
20.	Make sure that everyone has the contact details of everyone in the group		

Some of these overlap with those in the equivalent questionnaire for Chapter 11, so you might wish to discuss with someone else whether they are tasks for the leader to do, or tasks for other team members to undertake.

One role for the leader, of course, is to create an environment where individuals are willing to support rather than blame each other, but this is not an easy thing to do. It is useful, finally, to develop and review the conceptions and definitions of leadership. To do so, it is helpful to provide a brief comparison between two frequently discussed ideas – leadership and management.

LEADERSHIP AND MANAGEMENT COMPARED

There has been a great deal written about the differences between these two ideas. The commentary below summarises the main points.

Management

Management is usually seen as the poor cousin to leadership, and usually involves *working to expectations* – nothing more, nothing less. Being a manager is often about *keeping things going*. In some ways, management has been seen as *reducing risk* and *enhancing predictability*. In the mid-1900s, Frenchman Henri Fayol established the idea that management was about planning, organising, staffing, directing and controlling. Much that is written about management is reflective of a broadly unimaginative and stable function which is characterised by *processes*, *systems* and *procedures*.

Leadership

Leadership on the other hand has not been defined clearly, other than to note that a simple and common definition is that 'a leader is someone who has followers'. But there are some common ideas which come through from an examination of the literature. Scherr and Jensen (2007) argue that in its most exciting form, leadership is about dreaming, dealing with the unknown, creating visions of the impossible out of what is known to be currently possible. More commonly, thoughts on leadership talk about archetypal leaders as those who question the status quo and push for things to change in order to realise a particular vision. They create commitment in the lives of those they lead, act as a role model throughout their relationships and are talked about long after they have left the organisation because of their remarkable achievements.

When we compare the two, we can clearly see that the potential for a leader to add value to a business is much greater than that of a manager, hence the fact that employers often seek those who have been in leadership positions previously.

━━━━━━━━ 'BUT I HAVE A QUESTION ...?' ━━━━

... Is it true that everyone is a leader in some sense – that we lead ourselves all the time?

There are a number of views and discussions around leadership – leaders are borne, not made, everyone is a leader, leaders are charismatic and so on. The idea that everyone *is* a leader is probably not as true as the idea that everyone *can be* a leader: it is more a question of understanding what leadership is, and realising that attitude – a belief that you can be a leader – is a key part of changing and engaging in our own leadership-like behaviour. Confidence is another element of leadership – it is easier to follow someone who seems to know what they are doing than one who doesn't – but others will need to follow you somewhere and so you need to have a sense of vision for your own situation – career, life, goals. Leaders are not always what we might call charismatic, but we do hear more about those who are. So, is everyone a leader? Probably not, but developing a sense of vision and confidence and understanding the tools to ensure that others follow are things we can usually change.

The other part of this discussion is that some are quite happy to follow, and if that is where those individuals are at, then putting them into positions where they are required to lead but are not ready to do so will not be helpful. Individuals need to be able to make informed decisions and to be in control of those decisions.

DEFINING AND UNDERSTANDING LEADERSHIP

Leadership is similar to some other concepts that are used in common language: it is easy to recognise when we see it but less easy to define. Someone who is a leader is seen as possessing certain qualities and abilities (see Table 12.1).

Table 12.1   List of qualities frequently cited in definitions of leadership

- Vision – developing an idea of the future that is different from the current situation
- Persuasion/influence – motivating others to create that different situation
- Direction – putting energy into achieving certain goals
- Challenging – not accepting the status quo
- Communicating – be able to listen, negotiate, persuade and communicate in a way that builds commitment from others

A great deal of leadership research is conducted with individuals who are in leadership roles. They may have been given such positions for a variety of reasons, and may be reluctant leaders at times (leadership is not easy), or they may not actually be leading at all in the way discussed above.

There may be leaders who are doing the items listed in Table 12.1 with some people but not with others. They may be in leadership roles but not actually leading, which brings us to a useful definition.

LEADER

A leader is someone who has followers.

How they lead may vary, but a leader without any followers is not leading anyone. Other definitions give particular ways in which leaders ensure that they have people following them, and mention issues of influence, vision, direction and persuasion.

'BUT I HAVE A QUESTION …'

… Can a team have more than one leader?

If you take the definition above as being reasonably comprehensive, then you would say 'no', simply because a team that has members following two or more individuals will struggle to stay united and support each other. However, this does not mean that there will not be more than one person demonstrating leadership within the group, and people will do that in different ways, but if there is a power struggle within the group because there is more than one leader, then things may not go well.

There are slight exceptions to this – where there are sub-teams within the team generally, where the leader of the sub-team is accountable to the main team leader (in which case you might argue that there was more than one team, anyway) or where there is a deputy leader, who should share the same goals and ways of achieving those goals with the main leader.

There are also some situations where the tasks of a leader are split around the team, which then operates in a democratic manner. In such situations, the whole team has shared responsibility for undertaking the tasks that a leader would undertake, with the explicit agreement of all those working in the team. Undertaking the leadership role in such a way is not easy and requires a high degree of cooperation across the team, but it can work.

FURTHER
READING

The question remains, however, about what to do when there is more than one person trying to lead the group and where there are distinct differences in opinion, or a desire for power. You can find additional online content on the companion website at **https://study.sagepub.com/morgan2e**, including a highly relevant section looking at 'power in teams'.

Understanding the Qualities of Good Leadership

As we have already seen, a leader is 'someone who has followers', but even with a shared definition, the way that an individual's leadership is perceived and accepted will depend on our own view of what leadership is about and understanding the extent to which this reflects the behaviour of the individual in that particular role.

FOR YOU TO DO

Good and Bad Leaders

When the words 'good' and 'bad' are used to describe leadership, we need to be clear about what they mean. Different people will have different values, particularly in different cultures. For example, leadership is often seen as doing the right thing at the right time with the right people in the right way, but people – especially those who are followers – will have very different ideas of what the *right ways* are.

Which of the following do you think are 'good' and 'bad' leaders? Why?

- Michelle Obama
- Richard Branson
- Jack Ma
- Queen Elizabeth II
- Imran Khan
- The Pope
- Nancy Pelosi
- Donald Trump
- Adolf Hitler
- Vladimir Putin
- Melinda Gates
- Steve Jobs
- Elon Musk
- Greta Thunberg
- Jamie Oliver

Which of the following are a requirement for someone being called a 'good' leader?
A good leader is someone who:

- Achieves the goals set out for the organisation or team.
- Shows integrity and 'does what they say they will do'.
- Is very effective at generating followers.
- Acts ethically and fairly in line with others' values.
- Has a great profile on LinkedIn and Facebook.
- Can be trusted with confidential information.
- Is easy to contact to arrange a meeting.

If you discuss your ideas with others, you will start to develop your own ideas about what you consider good leadership to be.

What Leadership Is About

However you might conceptualise leadership, there do tend to be some ideas that appear regularly. Leadership is about:

- **Creating the correct atmosphere/culture** for action to happen.
- **Inspiring others** to increase emotional and practical effort towards a particular goal.
- **Having a vision** – and communicating that vision effectively – for how things can be different, and having a commitment to realise that vision.
- **Building effective relationships** with followers to ensure that they can follow you in tough times as well as easy times.
- **Communicating effectively** and regularly, so that followers understand where action and effort are needed.
- **Doing things differently** and creating a profile/brand for the team or organisation.

Are you ready to lead?

A leadership position is something that many graduates aspire to achieve, and certainly many employers want to see something special when they take on someone who has been through university – after all, they will pay more for those with leadership potential. However, it is something that carries a number of challenges for many students, bearing in mind the different ideas that come together. The questions that you need to answer over the time of your studies are these: Are you ready to lead others? What challenges do you think you will face as you do so?

Think about the following issues, which might help you to answer these questions.

1. How courageous are you? How ready are you for people not to like you, or what you do?
2. Are you a determined and persistent individual, or do you give up fairly easily when things get hard?
3. How would you deal with a situation where you have made a mistake that negatively affects other people?
4. How do you respond to criticism?
5. Think of a good leader you know well. How do you demonstrate the skills that they show in their leadership role?
6. What do you do/have you done to improve the situation around you?
7. One individual's personal value statement is 'Work hard. Be nice. Dream big.' What would yours be? How have you implemented such ideas in your situation?

These are similar to some typical interview questions designed to help organisations identify those who have had leadership roles or have leadership potential, but they are very good to consider before you get anywhere near a selection interview.

What Leadership Is Not About

Leadership does take courage and determination and an ability to implement actions leading to sustained change. Having a leadership position can be fantastic if you have the right abilities, and there are certainly rewards spread across a career for those who are good at it, but unless we are leading an organisation we ourselves own, we are likely to be there on a temporary basis. In a university team or a task team in an organisation, this will be just for the duration of the task. For more senior leadership roles, we are leading on behalf of others (shareholders, owners, etc.). From an ethical point of view, this will put limits on what we have the right to do. The implication of this is that we may be expected to act in particular ways.

Some believe that leadership is not about the following:

• **It is not about being popular at the expense of everything else**: If you go into leadership because you think that it is about being popular, you will never be able to make decisions that have negative consequences for some people but good consequences for others – or the organisation. In addition, you cannot always provide all the resources or make all the decisions that everyone wants or needs all the time, so you will disappoint some of your followers some of the time.

- **It is not about delegating *everything* to other people** so that you do not have to do any work. If you do this, you will find that people will stop taking on tasks or will leave your team/organisation because they do not respect you.
- **It is not about gaining power** for the sake of gaining power. Those who seek leadership positions solely for the purposes of gaining power will likely be the ones who use power inappropriately – to push and bully others into doing what they want them to do. There may be times when power does need to be used strongly, but that should never be the reason for someone wanting a leadership role.
- **It is not about getting emotionally close to lots of followers**: There may be a time when followers need a little emotional support, but building strong emotional relationships with many people is difficult. And there will probably be times when you have to disappoint those with whom you have a good relationship, which can then be very difficult.
- **It is not about doing nothing**: A leader who changes nothing is probably not leading, and when there is no vision for any change, then that becomes reflected in others' emotional commitment to their roles, and individual motivation will decrease.
- **It is not about your ego**: Some people become leaders because it will give them self-esteem and status when talking to others. The best leaders usually show some humility, since it is rarely they alone who have had the vision, developed action plans and implemented that vision – they have usually had a significant team of well-qualified others to help them do so, and since maintaining 'followership' is key for a leader, recognising that effort publicly is often important.

'BUT I HAVE A QUESTION ...'

... I want to be a leader because I want to change a small part of the world around me. So, how can I do that?

There is a range of levels at which people can consider the idea of leadership. Obviously, working on a team project at university is one way and leading a student society is another, but think about the following questions to begin with:

1. Why did you decide to study at university? Were you just following others, or was it a conscious choice with a good reason behind it? Why are you studying the subject you are studying at the university you are at?
2. Think about your life after university. How do you see your life in the future as different from your life now? How do you think you will have benefited from a university degree?

The first question is about making decisions that are right for you, regardless of what other people do: if you are just following the decisions that other people make, then how do you know it is right for you?

The second question is about vision for your own life (and is not really intended for you to discuss how better – or worse – off you will be financially). If you do not have a vision for your own life, then it is quite possible that you might struggle to enrol others in a vision for things which are going to affect their work and their lives.

If you want to change a small part of the world around you, then it might be an idea to consider: 1) how you would like your life to be different, and 2) how you might improve the experience of other students around you and then seek to make the necessary changes. This might mean some emotional challenge somewhere, but you will almost certainly develop and demonstrate persistence. Making changes to your situation and those of others is key to demonstrating effective leadership.

Leadership is a complex skill or, in reality, a series of skills: communicating appropriately, managing relationships, decision making, handling emotions, dealing with uncertainty and complexity, influencing and persuading, demonstrating self-awareness and emotional intelligence, and developing and implementing vision. Each situation will require a slightly different approach, and research has come to the conclusion that there is no one way of leading all of the people all of the time.

LEADERSHIP, POWER AND INFLUENCE

We have indicated above (see Table 12.1) that leadership is about creating influence, and that influence needs to come from somewhere. When it comes to leadership, there are a number of ways to influence others and that means being aware of why we have come to be in a position of leadership in the first place – or rather what are the factors (sources of power) that helped us to get there and now are keeping us in a leadership role. For some, the use of 'power bases' to maintain influence means talking about the abuses of power and manipulating situations in order to hold on to power: that is sometimes seen in the lives of those we regard as leaders, but is not really what we are referring to here.

In the late 1950s, French and Raven (1959) examined the ways in which leaders use and maintain sources of power, and they identified six sources of power.

1. **Legitimate power**: Where an individual has power or influence because of the position they hold. At a university, a lecturer has the authority to control their classroom by virtue of their position or job title.
2. **Reward power**: Individuals like to receive encouragement for a job done well or rewarded for good work. The ability to do so brings respect from others, and a desire to follow.
3. **Expert power**: Where individuals have particular expertise or knowledge around a specific topic, then they are seen as very useful to those who need to use that expertise.
4. **Referent power**: Individuals will have followers who like to be around the leader, simply because they are good to be around. They might have a great sense of humour or be able to tell stories.
5. **Coercive power**: Under certain conditions, leaders might need to force others to do certain things or punish those who fail to comply. This is rarely the most effective source of power for building a long-term body of followers, but it is usually there with relevant job descriptions.
6. **Informational power**: Individuals who have the ability to control information sometimes have the ability to control others. Information can be released or held back in a way that manipulates others, and so to gain cooperation, individuals can use information as a currency with which to 'buy' what they want.

Leaders will use all or some of these sources of power to maintain their base of followers (since any leader has to have followers) and to influence others. Using power is not the only way to influence others – and many in leadership roles would say that in most cases, the use of explicit 'power' over and above good argument is actually very rare – but it is there in many cases with the roles and authority that individuals in leadership have.

In many cases, influence and persuasion come from good relationship management as well as 1) good communication skills, 2) the ability to construct good quality arguments and 3) the ability to deliver good quality arguments. These three latter factors are skills that universities will be trying to help you develop during your studies.

=========== 'BUT I HAVE A QUESTION ...' ===========

... The word 'power' is one I am uncomfortable about using. How should I use my power if I am a leader?

In reality, good leaders rarely need to use their power explicitly; instead they influence others to do what needs to be done. Sometimes, this is through negotiation: 'I need you to do this, so I will provide you with this to motivate you' (the motivator could be something tangible, or merely be some respect); but, sometimes, it will be through the authority they carry as a leader: 'I'm asking you to do this because it needs to be done, and I want you to do it.'

Which strategy a leader employs to get things done will depend either on the specific individual they are talking to, or on their own philosophy of leadership more generally. Some individuals will readily do what their leader asks (simply because they are the leader), while others will need something in exchange.

Using power openly can cause problems. If, as a leader, you use your authority to get things done that others do not want to do, then you will likely face resistance. Some leaders are perfectly happy to meet that resistance (i.e. have a 'fight for power') in order to establish and increase their power, or to remove individuals from the team, but that can cause ill feeling within the team more broadly, so it is usually more effective to influence and persuade. A leader who regularly uses their power on the basis of 'I am the leader so you need to obey me' is likely to be highly ineffective in many cultures.

=========== KEY LEARNING POINT ===========

A leader has followers because they have some power given to them, either by the organisation or by their followers. How they use that power is important to their effectiveness as a leader.

THE SKILLS OF LEADERSHIP

Guirdham (2001) lists a range of qualities sought by followers in order to influence them to follow:

- Institutional knowledge: A leader ranked hierarchically would be expected to possess a great deal of institutional knowledge.
- Competence in both keeping a group well managed and using their expertise to contribute to a task.
- Status, as defined by their expertise and activities outside of the group.
- Loyalty to the group: A leader who shows their loyalty to the group will have the group's respect, and then 'followership' becomes easy to expect and it is easier to influence the group.
- A leader's motivation must be sincere and not about undertaking tasks selfishly.
- A leader must be seen to be undertaking tasks which support the group.
- A leader must communicate in a way and using language which is appropriate for the team.

Some of these qualities are about situations in which a leader finds themselves, but when a leader shows all of these characteristics, they will be able to influence their followers more easily. But if the definitions of leadership that we provided above are true, then we should see that a number of communication skills become important.

Smith (2011) cited research suggesting that leaders need to be:

- Energetic and tenacious.
- Motivated by the act of leading others.
- Honest, trustworthy.
- Able to organise.
- Intelligent and verbally fluent.
- Self-confident and interpersonally skilled.
- Commercially astute.

This is an interesting list, but some of these points are more perceptual qualities than real skills or behaviours. Whether others see you as honest and trustworthy is not always within a leader's control; there are times when an energetic leader operating with a team of people who are not energetic might find themselves struggling; and the list does not seem to be exhaustive. However, it is true that a leader without the ability to understand the importance of characteristics or apply them where necessary is likely to find life as a leader less than the motivating experience they had hoped for.

Sternberg (2007) has suggested that a simple acronym, WIC (Wisdom, Intelligence – in a practical sense – and Creativity), is sufficient, although these three words actually break down into a much wider set of skills. For example, wisdom includes personal values, tacit organisational knowledge and the ability to determine the right skills at the right time. Intelligence means the ability to deliver solutions by applying previous experience and knowledge.

 KEY LEARNING POINT

Asking individuals how someone should lead (i.e. 'what to do as a leader') is unlikely to get one universal answer, but asking them what characteristics good and bad leaders 'possess' is more likely to get a more coherent response. Personal qualities are more important as a leader than prescriptive actions.

 REFLECTION POINT

Take some time to think about the following questions and write down some answers.

How might the information given above change the way that you think about leadership and leading others?

How confident would you feel about taking on a leadership role in one of your groups for coursework?

What would make you more confident? Why?

LEADERSHIP, COURSEWORK AND THE 'POOR CONTRIBUTOR'

One of the main challenges in leading a team at university is when it comes to dealing with individuals who present challenges. They might be 'free-riding' (doing little while benefitting from the effort and work of others), not turning up to meetings, not communicating, doing poorer quality work than desired or creating problems in the group when their ideas are not listened or agreed to. Leading such a team is not easy at all – it is more challenging than when you *do* have a position of authority and *can* implement sanctions against individuals, which is why being able to lead a successful team in a course-work project for university can be such a strong indicator of leadership success, especially if those in your team were chosen for you.

Such situations demand two kinds of skills: the problem-solving skills to be able to identify the issue(s); and the communication and conflict resolution skills to be able to implement the interpersonal issues that occur.

FOR YOU TO DO

Some suggest that the mark of good leadership is to be able to solve conflicts and resolve difficulties. It is certainly true that, in the mind of some, this ability is key to leading a team. Have a look at the brief scenario given below about how a leader intended to assist a team to work on a piece of group coursework, and think about the three questions that follow.

In a group-working situation at university, the group had hit a stalemate about a critical decision for our project. The views of the group were mixed although there were - broadly speaking - two distinct options. It appeared that neither side wanted to compromise their position, as they all believed that a compromise or decision to take the alternative action would seriously affect their grades.

As a previously neutral and passive member of the group, I could see both sides of the argument. In my opinion, this made me the most qualified to take charge of the situation and lead the group to an amicable decision. The situation then quickly escalated and it was essential at this point to bring in rational thought in order to maintain group cohesion. At this point, I entered into the discussion and calmed matters down by suggesting that the group took a break. This gave each member time to collect their thoughts and consider each other's positions. It was no surprise that, during the break, two distinct sub-groups formed, as was shown after the break in terms of seating arrangements.

Questions:

1. Do you think that this was a good solution?
2. Is there anything that the team leader could have done differently?
3. What should the group leader do next?

Some of your modules might be developed in a way that enables the team leader (and sometimes team members) to implement penalties against those not working well, but, as a team leader, dealing with performance issues is part of the job. Often this means having a private discussion with team members, but also means dealing with things carefully, as laid out in the steps below (see also Chapter 14 on problem solving).

Step 1: Find out what the issue seems to be.

It is very tempting in a very busy world to accept what members of the team are saying without finding out more details – finding out information takes time, and leaders and team members rarely seem to have time. We can imagine a situation where a team member complains about other team members but we make the following mistakes:

- We might hear something from one team member and assume that their view is held by everyone; in reality, this might not actually be the case.
- The team members report what is happening with this person, but their judgements are merely guesswork.
- We can assume that everything is the fault of the individual who is not engaging with the task, but in reality:
    - The team might actually not be communicating in the right way for the other person to be involved sufficiently in the task.
    - The expectations might not be clear enough for the other team member to understand.
    - The 'reluctant' team member might be a non-native speaker of English and cannot contribute as other members speak too quickly.
    - Relationships between some team members might already be established and the other team member is excluded.
    - Most team members live on campus, while this other team member lives some distance away.

This step involves gathering information: What is happening/not happening? How often? When is it happening/not happening? How many people are involved? Asking detailed questions with factual answers and examples is important for step 2.

Step 2: Discuss the issue with the 'problematic team member'.

If a problem is to be solved then the leader needs to have a conversation with the problematic team member as quickly as possible after the discussion with others from the team. (For more on how to have a difficult conversation see Chapter 9 on communicating effectively (the section on handling emotional conversations) and Chapter 14 on problem solving.) Ironically, the purpose of the discussion needs to be almost exactly the same as step 1, that is to gather information, except this time you, as the leader, will be checking information already gathered as well. It is important here to:

- Withhold judgement until you have sufficient and comprehensive information from both parties.
- Try to explore why certain things might be happening. There might be very good reasons relating to personal or practical issues that are a problem, or a lack of:
    - Clear goals by which to define expectations.
    - Feedback from other members of the team.
    - Motivation to do the task.
    - Cooperation and engagement by other members of the team.
    - Resources to do the tasks given to them.
    - Confidence to communicate with other members of the team in another language.
    - Ability to do what they have been asked to do.
- Examine possible solutions – which may include some penalties, or may simply be ways of solving the problem. These would usually include phrases such as, 'If this situation arises again …' (and such phrases could be used as advice to the 'problematic' individual, as to what action to take if they find themselves in similar situations in the future).

For example, someone might not be attending meetings because they have a part-time job, but all the other team members can only attend at that particular time. This is not an easy issue to resolve, but it does not stop the team leader consulting the member with the job about the things they will discuss before the meeting and then talking to them after the meeting to convey decisions. In other situations (e.g. domestic commitments at home), technology (Skype etc.) can be used to enable participation in discussions, for example. Problem solving often takes some imagination and creativity, and there are usually ways around most team issues.

Step 3: Give feedback about your decision to the team and monitor what happens next.

As a team leader, you have the 'legitimate authority' (see the content below on legitimate power) to implement solutions.

Leading a team when there are few sanctions or motivators available is never going to be easy: you have to rely on others' willingness to help and on the more intrinsic motivators (sense of value, excitement, passion and interest in the job, etc.), but some people are not necessarily that willing to help. This is one of the biggest challenges of leadership. Try as far as possible not to take the issue to the module leader. It is not wrong to do so but sometimes it is necessary; however, try to solve the problem on your own first. An employer at an interview will want to see that you are likely to be able to solve difficult problems without needing to get advice as soon as there is any kind of problem.

Step 4: Work with the team to develop norms and an agreement governing how the team works in solving problems generally.

Problems should never be left unaddressed, otherwise they will just remain and eventually either the team will complete its work/coursework and adjourn, or team members might struggle with the emotional pressure that other individual(s) bring and show extreme annoyance at some point.

KEY LEARNING POINT

How *you* deal with each of the issues above is going to be based on a mixture of your own attitudes, learning from other situations and learning from others' mistakes. Leaders rarely do things right all the time, but they usually have a reason for doing what they do in the way that they do it.

MODELS OF LEADERSHIP

We will look at three models of leadership. There are similarities, and differences, in each approach.

Hersey and Blanchard's (1977) Situational Leadership Theory

Paul Hersey and Ken Blanchard (1977) developed their model of situational leadership as a way to help answer part of the question, 'What leadership style is the most effective?'. Their model matched specific leadership styles against the maturity and readiness of others to be led in particular ways, but still referred to the two dimensions of 'Task Behaviour' (provision of guidance) and 'Relationship Behaviour' (provision of support) incorporated into their model, giving rise to four 'situations'. There were four leadership styles (Telling, Selling, Participating and Delegating) and four ways to describe follower-readiness (see Table 12.2).

Table 12.2   Aspects of situational leadership theory

Styles of leadership:

Telling – Provide specific instructions and supervise closely
Selling – Explain decisions and give opportunities for clarification
Participating – Share ideas and facilitate decision making
Delegating – Turn over responsibility for decisions and implementation

Follower-readiness:

Leader needs to direct:
R1: The follower is unable and unwilling (or insecure) to do what is needed
R2: The follower is unable but willing to do what is needed

Follower directs:
R3: The follower is able but unwilling (or insecure) to do what is needed
R4: The follower is able and willing to do what is needed

Situations and appropriate leadership style:

S1/R1: Low relationship (no supportive behaviour needed) and high task-centred (guidance on task needed) leadership style needed, i.e. *Telling*
S2/R2: High relationship (little supportive behaviour needed) and high task-centred leadership (guidance on task needed) style needed, i.e. *Selling*
S3/R3: High relationship (little supportive behaviour needed) and low task-centred leadership (guidance on task needed) style needed, i.e. *Participating*
S4/R4: Low relationship (little supportive behaviour needed) and low task-centred leadership style needed, i.e. *Delegating*

The model began to help leaders understand why no one leadership style was always going to be effective all of the time, and gave them a rationale by which to evaluate and then adopt different styles.

Robbins and Hunsaker (2003) have suggested a number of additional situational variables which affect the suitability of different leadership styles:

Follower trust: Enabling others to trust you is about establishing integrity (being honest and truthful), competence, consistency, loyalty and truthfulness. A leader cannot establish trust unless there is integrity, and particularly honesty.

Clear goals: Establishing clear goals is vital for any team leader, but teams will vary according to the extent to which they are ready to aim for certain goals. If the goals are too ambitious, then the teams will feel that they are being pushed too far, but make them too easy and the goals will not inspire the team.

Task characteristics: A structured task will probably not need a leader to intervene in the task very much, but one that is unstructured 'might require leaders to help clarify and structure the work' (Robins and Hunsaker, 2003: 146) somewhat. This builds on Fred Fiedler's work (Fiedler, 1967) looking at the ways in which leaders and team members interact (or exchange) with each other (commonly referred to as Leader-Member Exchange, or 'LMX').

Rewards: A leader can engage with different members of the team by offering different kinds of rewards, according to individuals' preferences (and organisational policies). Offering the same rewards to all can be seen as fair, but may not produce the engagement from every team member that the leader might seek.

Time: Making decisions in very short timescales can be problematic for those who like to see their leaders consulting other team members more. In a situation where there is less time, decisions may not be made in a particularly consultative manner. (We will look more at this when we look at leadership decision making.)

Adair's (1973) Action-Centred Leadership

John Adair's model of action-centred leadership (Adair, 1973) is conceptually similar to situational leadership, in that it still contains issues related to task and issues related to relationships. However, as a model of leadership, it has the advantage of being simple to remember.

The principal idea is that effective team leadership is demonstrated when leaders recognise and act on the interplay between paying attention to the tasks being undertaken, the well-being of the individuals within the team, and the 'togetherness' of the team itself (see Figure 12.2).

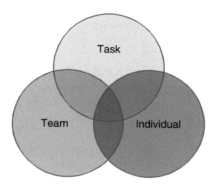

Figure 12.2   Adair's model of action-centred leadership © John Adair, 1973

The model emphasises that a leader needs to have some way to monitor and then improve each of the three areas as a team develops and progresses. The leader might have a style, but their behaviour is intended to be flexible and address the three issues on a regular basis. There is a body of literature which discusses what is known as 'Servant Leadership' – the following section provides more details on what this approach really means.

SERVANT LEADERSHIP

In 1970, Robert Greenleaf – as a senior executive working in AT&T – published some ideas relating to the role of the leader as a servant to others in the organisation. At the heart of his ideas were the following:

> The servant-leader is servant first ... It begins with the natural feeling that one wants to serve, to serve first. Then conscious choice brings one to aspire to lead. That person is sharply different from one who is leader first ... The leader-first and the servant-first are two extreme types.

> The best test [of effective leadership], and difficult to administer, is: Do those served grow as persons? Do they, while being served, become healthier, wiser, freer, more autonomous, more likely themselves to become servants? And, what is the effect on the least privileged in society? Will they benefit or at least not be further deprived? (Greenleaf, 1970: 6)

This view of leadership is often at odds with the impression that is given of good leadership in western media and in professional publications, yet those ideas have received significant support from such researchers as Peter Senge, John Kotter and Ken Blanchard, among others.

Scherr and Jensen (2007): A New Model of Leadership

A 2007 paper by Allan Scherr and Michael Jensen set out some pertinent ideas about how leaders need to have courage in order to succeed beyond the mistakes that each human being makes and to inspire those they lead to push through and beyond such issues to achieve the extraordinary: their view of leadership certainly enhances the idea of transformational leadership into the arena of inspiration. Even their definition of leadership – 'We define a leader as an *ordinary* human being with both a commitment to produce a result whose realisation would be *extraordinary* given the current circumstances as seen by the participants, and the *integrity* to see this commitment through to its realization' (2007: 5) – goes beyond allowing some leaders to act more like managers perhaps, and instead emphasises the unusual and brave.

Under their ideas around leadership, Scherr and Jensen (2007) argue that a successful leader will do four things:

- Create a new vision for an uncertain future, even making declarations where reality is behind the vision.
- Enrol sufficient people in that vision to realise the vision.
- Identify problems and breakdowns – and do so publicly so that a solution will be found quickly.
- Resolve problems, or *achieve despite them.*

They explain that establishing a vision is about making declarations – statements that change a state of being – rather than assertions which may describe how something 'is' at that particular moment in time. The leader must be fully committed to the vision in order to lead others towards it. Enrolling others in that vision requires a leader's ability to reflect their own personal commitment to that vision in a way which excites others to the extent that they too commit to that vision. That, then, creates a team of committed individuals responsible for delivering on their own area of the broader vision as well as including those who might adopt a sceptical approach.

The next element of their ideas relates to dealing with issues that are likely to affect the ability of the team to realise the vision they have committed to, using the notion that unexpected issues will push a team to be more innovative than they might otherwise have been. By acknowledging that difficulties may arise, breakdowns can be prevented before they occur. The idea of publicising breakdowns is unusual, but makes sense in terms of creating or finding ways to deal with them, and it can also be used to generate a sense of re-commitment to the team by the members. Scherr and Jensen (2007) note that backing away from a previously made commitment due to difficulty can lead to everyone abandoning the earlier stated vision.

The model is an exciting one because it establishes the idea that leaders demonstrate their strong and on-going commitment to a very clear and challenging vision, despite experiencing difficulty on the way. In many cases, individuals would prefer an easier view of leadership which involves establishing a vision and leading others towards that vision without any breakdowns – but that may be much rarer than many students might think.

 KEY LEARNING POINT ══════════════════════

There is no one way to lead, but there are basic principles to bear in mind, and it is the appropriate use of those principles that will lead to effective leadership.

'BUT I HAVE A QUESTION ...'

... If leadership is so straightforward, then why are so few good at it?

The simple reason is that to do these things is not straightforward, and being a good leader involves a complex set of skills. What has been discussed above is a very simple way of ensuring that leaders pay attention to a number of factors, but how leaders do so with a wide number of different people is not straightforward. For example, if we try to apply the Hersey and Blanchard model to just one individual, then it is not difficult to determine how ready and able a team member might be, but if there are different team members with different skills and different ability levels, then the best we can do is to adopt different approaches towards different people at the same time.

Developing trust and integrity, being able to offer appropriate rewards, communicating appropriately, behaving consistently for how you would like to do things differently, having a vision and the other qualities identified by Robbins and Hunsaker actually make life more complex.

Look back at the possible interview questions about whether you want to and are ready to lead. It is a set of skills developed over a long time in a variety of situations.

KEY LEARNING POINT

There are different ways to conceptualise and to theorise about leadership. Leadership research will continue to grow and develop, but it is unlikely that we will develop one easily applicable theory that explains all leadership successes and failures.

REFLECTION POINT

Take some time to think about the following questions and write down some answers.

What model(s) of leadership (given above and from other reading perhaps) do you find easiest to understand?

How easily could you apply any of these ideas to any leadership role you might have?

LEADING AND MAKING DECISIONS FROM A POINT OF STRENGTH: KNOWING YOURSELF

When you are leading, you have to have a good understanding of the individuals you are leading. Every decision you make, every problem-solving process (see Chapter 14) and every opportunity for communication (see Chapter 9) you take require you have some kind of understanding of those you lead directly and

(Continued)

how they might react. You need to consider whether this is really going to change *what* you do, though it might have an impact on *how* you do what you do. It may seem strange, therefore, that there is a section here on knowing yourself.

However, those you are leading will look to you for solutions to challenging situations, for a sense of vision and an ability to bring others together; leading effectively will mean that you will need to have a sense of vision and the self-confidence to see that vision become reality, and this means bringing your personality into how you lead. Much of the time, organisational leaders do not seem to connect with those they are leading – they seem to remain distant and somewhat aloof, maybe because it is what others have thought of them which has led to their getting promoted, so those who follow them tend to follow what they see or mimic their behaviour. They are taught to perform, but not to relate, yet it is often their values that have caught the eye of those promoting them.

What does this mean in practice? That we should not be nervous about allowing our personality to show, to let our values guide what we decide to do and not to do, and that we should be sufficiently confident to be spontaneous and to let who we are show to others. Brittain (2012) puts it like this:

- **Trust in our unique gift set**: We are unique in who we are. We should allow our intuition, faith and creativity to guide us, rather than feeling as if we need to perform to a particular role model we have seen in the movies or in our employment.
- **There is no perfect decision**: We live in a world full of unpredictability, volatility, complexity and ambiguity, so a decision can often be outdated or made imperfect as quickly as it is made. The challenge is not to make perfect decisions, but in how we respond as individuals.

Allowing our own personality to show will enable others to feel relaxed about letting themselves be themselves as well. This will tend to produce a group of followers who are less stressed, more confident and more agile in making decisions.

Just as there is no perfect human, so too is there no perfect leader for every individual in every situation, which leads to the question 'Why try to be what we are not?'

 REFLECTION POINT

Take some time to think about the following questions and write down some answers.

What reaction do you have to the view that we should not try to be perfect?

To what extent do you find your own behaviour driven by others' expectations of you, rather than who you are?

Are there times when you think you know what to do or say, but do not say it because you are nervous about what others will think?

How much does nervousness about 'making the *right* decision' affect your ability to make decisions?

Is there ever one right decision?

LEADERSHIP IN THE FUTURE

It is difficult to know what leadership might look like in years to come. Generally in society, we are seeing economic, social and technical changes far more rapidly than has happened previously. When we realise that the internet only started to be widely used in the mid-1990s and that smartphones and iPads have only been around since the early 2000s, and that the ability of social media to impact on our lives has been relatively recent, then we start to understand that predicting what will happen in a world of big data, self-driving cars and artificial intelligence is going to be challenging.

It is likely that some skills required for good leadership will not change. Leaders will still need a sense of vision, will still need to communicate well to maintain their followers and will need to have the resilience to see those visions achieved. However, they will likely need to be much more flexible as the pace of change increases, be more able to communicate and establish trust using new tools and understand the importance of ethics as society's values change regularly. Their ethical stance on controversial issues will mean that the successful leaders of the future will lose some followers, but will gain others: no one ever said that leadership is easy.

Learning is going to become more important than ever – not in terms of sitting in lectures but in terms of an ability to quickly analyse difficulties, failures and problems and being able to reflect on previous performance. The ability to recall and learn from mistakes – and the importance of being honest about those mistakes – is likely going to increase. Similarly, it is possible that the role of confidence will change. Leaders are required to have a sense of confidence, but confidence without the humility to learn from changing situations (or arrogance) will be a disadvantage when individuals are put in new or unstructured situations where listening to others is vital.

INTEGRATION AND APPLICATION

The challenge in leading well is that it is complex, and your behaviour and values will be unique to you. There is no one model which will explain all that you can do in terms of being a leader, just as there is no one style which can make you successful all of the time, but there are some common ideas:

Idea 1: Be assured that who you are – rather than others' views of who you are – is what is going to carry you through. People judge leaders and their decisions more harshly than they judge others, but if you know that you made the right decisions for the right reasons, then no one can really criticise you for that.

Idea 2: Engage with your followers, otherwise you are not going to lead anyone. Let your personality – your sense of humour, your interpersonal skills – help you build relationships. There is no reason why the skills that you have developed throughout your life should be any less useful when you become a leader.

Idea 3: Monitor what is really happening – you need to be able to see what is likely to happen in the future with regards to external issues outside your team, as well as what is happening inside your team.

Idea 4: Think of those you lead as a group of individuals who are as imperfect as you, but who are willing and capable. If they are not willing, then you might need to find the reasons for this, but ultimately you might want them out of the team. If they are not capable, then they should first be given training before any discussion of whether they should leave the team. If you expect them to be perfect, then you will find that they will always disappoint you, and that will frustrate you and demotivate them.

Idea 5: Be sure to have a vision of where you are going to lead people – and why. People engage with a clear statement of where they are being led. Having such a statement will enable them to feel confident about their journey, even if the journey might be a bit tough at times. Not having that vision will mean that people might enjoy the journey while it is easy, but will be more likely to dismiss the leadership when things are hard.

CONCLUSION

By now, you should be able to:

- Develop different styles of leadership.
- Distinguish effective leadership from ineffective leadership.
- Let who you are influence the way you lead.

It is important to take as much leadership responsibility as possible throughout your university career. The experience you have will sharpen your leadership abilities in a situation (being at university) that will give you 'safe' opportunities to show an employer what you can do before you actually get into a situation where poor leadership can have 'live' risks in the workplace.

As noted in the introduction to this chapter (and that of the Chapter 11 on working with others), leadership is about relationships, character, action and communication. However, there is always going to be a balance between how committed a leader is to a particular vision and understanding where flexibility with that vision becomes necessary. Leading two different groups of people can also be very different, of course, but doing so without a sense of vision or by using inappropriate styles of communication is going to test all your strength and determination.

 REFLECTION POINT

Take some time to think about the following questions and write down some answers.

Based on the content of this chapter, what do you now know about leading others that you did not know before?

What key learning point had the most impact? Why?

Do your answers to either of the above questions have the potential to change your ability to lead others? Why?

What will you now do differently? (Write this down and put it somewhere where you can see it regularly.)

 CHAPTER TASK

Examine the biographies of five leaders that you respect. What were their attitudes to the situations they met and might have struggled with? How did they show integrity, trust and persistence? What can you learn from them?

 INTERVIEW QUESTIONS

The areas covered in this chapter are both very broad and very important to nearly every organisation. As a result, it might well be that up to half of an interview could be devoted to these skills, so there are a large number of questions an employer might ask.

Think about the following questions. What might your answers be?

1. Can you tell me about a time when you felt that you needed to take the initiative to achieve a goal? What did you do, and how successful were you in achieving your goal?
2. Tell me about a time when you needed to persuade someone to change their mind.
3. Tell me about a leader that you admire. Why do you admire them?
4. How would you describe your personal leadership approach?
5. How would you go about leading a team member who seemed not to be producing the work they needed to? Can you give an example of a time when you have had to do so?
6. What is the most pioneering activity that you have undertaken?
7. Can you describe how you have gone about setting goals for a team you have worked with?

With nearly all the questions given above, you can answer from any experience you have had – during your course or in a student society.

Chapter 17 gives a lot more information on selection interviews and the online content gives some guidance on these questions.

ADDITIONAL RESOURCES

Want to learn more? Visit https://study.sagepub.com/morgan2e to gain access to a wide range of online resources, including interactive tests, tasks, further reading and downloads.

Website Resources

The following websites offer useful advice on leadership skills.

About Leaders – website dedicated to development of leadership skills at university: https://aboutleaders.com/leadership-skills-university/#gs.azityy

MindTools – a comprehensive series of resources around leadership development: www.mindtools.com/pages/main/newMN_LDR.htm

Open University – online MOOC for development of leadership skills: www.open.edu/openlearn/ocw/mod/oucontent/view.php?id=68669

SkillsYouNeed: www.skillsyouneed.com/leadership-skills.html

Textbook Resources

Barrett, D. J. (2011) *Leadership Communication* (3rd edition). New York: McGraw-Hill.
Byham, T. M. and Wellins, R. S. (2015) *Your First Leadership Job*. Hoboken, NJ: Wiley.
Cameron, S. (2010) *The Business Student's Handbook: Skills for Study and Employment* (5th edition). Harlow: Pearson (particularly Chapter 10).
Dougherty, C. and Thompson, J. E. (2010) *Be a Better Leader*. Oxford: Bookpoint.
Flint, M. and Hearn, E. V. (2015) *Leading Teams: 10 Challenges and 10 Solutions*. Harlow: Pearson.
Hamilton, C. and Kroll, T. L. (2018) *Communicating for Results* (11th edition). Boston, MA: Cengage (particularly Chapter 10).
Hawkins, P. (2017) *Leadership Team Coaching* (3rd edition). London: Kogan-Page.

Horn, R. (2012) *The Business Skills Handbook*. London: CIPD (particularly Chapter 18).

Lamberg, T. (2018) *Leaders Who Lead Successfully*. Lanham, MD: Rowman and Littlefield.

Owen, J. (2011) *How to Manage* (3rd edition). Harlow: Pearson.

Puccio, G. J., Mance, M. and Murdock, M. C. (2011) *Creative Leadership: Skills that Drive Change* (2nd edition). Thousand Oaks, CA: Sage.

Radcliffe, S. (2010) *Leadership Plain and Simple*. Harlow: FT-Prentice-Hall.

Smith, M. (2011) *Fundamentals of Management* (2nd edition). Maidenhead: McGraw-Hill (particularly Chapter 8).

West, M. A. (2012) *Effective Teamwork* (3rd edition). New York: Wiley (particularly Chapters 4 and 9).

13 DEVELOPING CROSS-CULTURAL AWARENESS

> To effectively communicate, we must realize that we are all different in the way that we perceive the world and use this understanding as a guide to our communication with others. (Anthony Robbins)

CHAPTER STRUCTURE

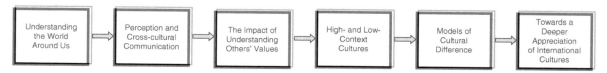

Figure 13.1

When you see the this means go to the companion website https://study.sagepub.com/morgan2e to do a quiz, complete a task, read further or download a template.

━━━ AIMS OF THE CHAPTER ━━━

By the end of this chapter, you should be able to:

- Analyse your own and others' world views.
- Overcome perceptual and other cultural barriers in order to develop a good understanding of others' communication.
- Develop your insight into other cultures.
- Become more of a global citizen, able to operate with understanding in other cultures.

🧩 WHEN SHOULD YOU READ THIS CHAPTER?

You will almost certainly need to work with individuals who are different from yourself and who might come from overseas, and so it is best to read this chapter during your first year at university.

INTRODUCTION

We live in a global world which is changing fast – technologically, legally, politically, economically and environmentally. We can travel pretty much anywhere nowadays, we can see strange and amazing things, we can interact with people who are vastly different from ourselves and we can enjoy some of the most wonderful places that nature can provide. We can travel to countries with little more than our phone and passport, with our tickets and money accessible through smartphones and no need of paper documentation. Yet there are places where power cuts are a daily occurrence and where the price of accessing the internet by phone is so expensive that many cannot afford it. And, of course, there are places in the world where people need food and shelter much more than they need to access Facebook, WeChat or Skype. Very often, our interaction with this international world in which we live does not help us to understand the people who live in it or the impact that they might have on us in our home country. Whether we like it or not, international economics and global trade affect the value of a house and the amount of tax we pay, as well as the exchange rate when we go on holiday. Those same pressures affect some of the social issues we experience and which we see played out on the international news – immigration, battles and wars, education, and so on – and yet the issues affecting us in our home country – an aging population, unemployment, international diplomacy – are likely to be exactly the same as those affecting millions of others in countries we can now travel to.

Even if we do not live in another country during our lifetime, we will almost certainly interact with individuals who look and speak differently from us, who eat different food and who have different world views, values, attitudes and behaviours. Societies are becoming much more diverse as global movement and travel becomes easier, yet typically we make little effort to learn another language, to learn about others' values and to understanding how others think, behave and communicate – and that level of effort will not help us in the longer term. In reality, as human beings (or even as animals), we tend to protect ourselves from and fight against that which we do not understand; this is natural, but there is a great deal more value in developing that understanding than in being defensive.

If we are open to learning about others' values, then we can start to change perceptions. Of course, sharing a common language makes life easier, but sharing a common language does not mean that we share the same values, in the same way that looking similar does not mean that we share the same outlook on life. The globalised world that we now live in requires culturally literate managers and leaders who understand what it means to recognise that others might be thinking in very different ways from them. Being able to communicate effectively and understand how others from diverse backgrounds might react will enable us to operate far more cross-culturally than those competing for the same jobs, something that is very much needed in this international world.

━━━━━━━━━━ **BOX 13.1** ━━━━━━━━━━

If you are an international student (and even if you are not), you should read this

If you are an international student and have come to study in a country which is not your own – or are perhaps a student in your own country but studying in a language which is not your own – then you are probably already one or two steps ahead of many of the students in your classroom. You will likely have come to the university through a foundation programme or have achieved IELTS results of 6.0 or 6.5 or above. To become so good in a second language that you can study for a degree in that language is a great achievement, so well done! You may not understand everything that is being said and may struggle some-times with different accents, different kinds of food, or the weather, and so on, but you are doing something that the home students might not understand, but should appreciate. They might not have left their family, their familiar surroundings and their community to spend a considerable time in a city and culture which may or may not appear welcoming.

Being an international student is not easy but can be a great adventure, and if you can learn more about the culture, people and language in which you are studying, then the experience can be a fantastic one. Learn how the transport system works, get to visit some of the key places, make friends with local students and improve your language skills.

Above all, try to break out of your own community. Try to spend some time with home students, because it is one of the best ways to learn about the culture. What is the value of an education in another country if all you do is spend time with those from your own culture, visit some tourist spots and struggle with your English? You may not feel confident in your own English language abilities (even though you have every right to be confident if the university has accepted you onto the degree programme), but you will never develop that confidence or learn about others' cultures if you never break out of your own cultural group.

Finally, do try the local food! While international food is widely available, if you are in the UK, potatoes feature in many meals, fish and chips can seem pretty tasteless without salt and vinegar, each person will probably order their own meal, and there are distinct 'stages' in a meal (starter or appetiser, main course and then dessert with coffee) rather than all the dishes coming at the same time.

This chapter will examine the ways in which perceptual processes can impact helpfully and unhelp-fully on building cross-cultural awareness. We will also spend time looking at how individual cultures might differ, how communication works differently in different cultures and what individuals can do to give themselves a competitive advantage in developing an international career.

We will begin with a skills assessment, looking at our awareness of other cultures, our attitudes and values, and our engagement with the international environment.

There may well be very different responses to the questions posed. While the world has become more global in terms of trade, and while we have a much better understanding of the world than we might have done some years ago thanks to the internet, much of the world does not seem to want to under-stand how to operate with what some call 'global literacy' – and that is what the remainder of this chapter is about.

SKILLS SELF-ASSESSMENT

Complete the brief questionnaire below to see how well you could do when it comes to developing a global career. Read carefully each of the following descriptions and say how typical you think each statement is of your behaviour or attitude by giving it a score between 1 and 5, where 1 is 'strongly disagree' and 5 is 'strongly agree'.

Item	Statement	Score
1.	As a human being, humility is an important quality for me to possess	
2.	I enjoy travelling to other countries	
3.	I love trying international and unusual food	
4.	I find it easier to talk to someone who looks like me than someone who does not	
5.	I think most other cultures are friendly	

(Continued)

(Continued)

Item	Statement	Score	
6.	From what I hear on the news and read online, I do not think I really want to live in another country		
7.	Learning another language is something that I will never need or want to do		
8.	I believe that if people speak the same language - grammar, vocabulary - then they can easily understand each other		
9.	I am likely to find living in another country really stressful		
10.	The national and online media have a significant influence on my attitudes towards those from other countries		
11.	I do not really believe this chapter is an important one for me; I am never going to interact with those from other cultures		
12.	I know what a passport is, and I know (in very broad terms) what I need to do, practically, to get a visa		
13.	I have a good number of friends who come from a culture which is not the same as mine		
14.	I only really see the value in communicating with others who come from the same culture as me		
15.	My values and attitudes are more important and useful than those of people from other cultures		
16.	If you do not agree with me, then I am likely to think you are a bit weird or strange		
17.	I have a passport [Answer should be either 0 or 5 for 'yes' or 'no' respectively.]		
18.	I use my passport regularly to travel to countries which are quite different from my own		
19.	I have never spoken to someone who disagrees with my view of how the world operates		
20.	If I lived in another country, I know what I would find difficult		
21.	Going on holiday is one of the best ways to find out about others' cultures		
22.	Being at university has exposed me to many people who come from cultures which are different to mine		
23.	I interact regularly with individuals who do not speak my language		
24.	I am more likely to meet up with people who are from my culture than from other cultures		
25.	I know something about the history and culture of other countries		

UNDERSTANDING THE WORLD AROUND US

Viewing the world around us can be done on so many levels at any one time. At one end of the scale, perhaps you have been on holiday or perhaps you have actually lived in another country. Maybe you are an overseas student who is trying desperately to make sense of both living in another country and simultaneously trying to adapt to a university system which can seem somewhat strange. Whatever your level of engagement, developing an understanding of how the world operates is something that we build up over our lifetime, most of the time wholly unconsciously. We call it our 'world view'.

The view we have of how the world operates comprises a range of thinking on a number of levels (see Figure 13.2). Usually, we do not think about what our world view is. We simply carry around with us a series of assumptions about how the world operates. That view will be based on our beliefs.

The best way of explaining how this works is to illustrate it with a couple of contrasting examples. This might be according to religious or philosophical belief. For example, an eastern viewpoint will indicate that life carries us along and it is for us to make the best of it that we can. This differs considerably from a typical western viewpoint which 'empowers' the individual to 'go out and change the world to make it a better place' in some way.

WORLD VIEW

Our world view is our view of how the world operates.

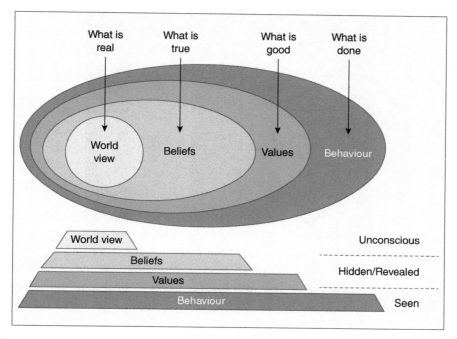

Figure 13.2 Components of a world view

Those beliefs often influence our view of what is good and what is bad – our values. Some cultures might suggest that modesty, respect for elders, filial piety and hard work are espoused. In a western culture, it would be very unusual to see a statement of values, since there is tolerance for a wide range of views about what is good and what is bad – often referred to as 'post-modernist' philosophy. The state-

CULTURE

Culture is the overarching system of rules and guidelines which determine what is and what is not acceptable.

ment in the photograph in Image 13.1 – outside a department store in China – encourages adherence to a particular set of views. Cultural values play a significant role in creating a cohesive society, but are not always straightforward to understand or apply, as shown in Box 13.2.

REFLECTION POINT

Take some time to think about the following questions and write down some answers.

Thinking about your own country, what changes have been happening – socially, economically, politically, in terms of technology?

(Continued)

How easy is it to identify your own country's culture?

How could any changes your country is facing impact on your own national culture?

Image 13.1   Basic standards of citizenry: values of one city in northeast China

While your own view of what is real, true and good is generally hidden, your own behaviour – what is done – is seen and is visible. Similarly, you will see the behaviour of those from other cultures. Our behaviour is the outworking of our reaction to what we see and experience, and that reaction is based on our perception.

As we have indicated, others' behaviour is a result of their reaction to events based on their own world view, just as our behaviour is a reflection of our world view. Because we do not usually talk about our 'world views' (even in conversations with those who are different!), we can arrive at an incomplete understanding of why people behave as they do, and this can cause us problems in accepting others.

 KEY LEARNING POINT

Understanding another person's 'world view' is crucial for understanding how that person is behaving and what they are thinking – and why. This implies that we need to have increased conversations with those who are different from ourselves, to find out what they really think.

PERCEPTION AND CROSS-CULTURAL COMMUNICATION

The impression(s) that others have of you will determine how they communicate with you. For example, if they have the impression that you are lazy, then they might be somewhat more aggressive towards you than if that were not the case. Alternatively, if they think you are a hard worker and that you put more effort into your activities than others, then they will probably be more likely to believe you if you say you are overworked and too busy. This does not mean that we should do all we can 'to get people to like us' – going into a managerial career because we want people to 'like us' is a recipe for disaster, simply because we will always face conflicting priorities – but it does mean that we should communicate well enough for people to understand why we do what we do. Doing so in a world of uncertain perceptions is not easy, but if we understand how perception works, then we can probably minimise the impact of poor perception by controlling how and what we communicate.

The process of 'attending to' information refers in the definition to the fact that we do not pay attention to all that happens around us at any one time, but only to that which is within our perceptual 'field of vision', because it is going to have a strong and/or immediate impact on our situation, because it relates to something we are interested in, or because it will have a clear impact on others around us. We 'interpret' information according to our previous experiences and ideas about likely meanings. If we cannot easily interpret what we see, then we will likely investigate further, but if we think we have interpreted something correctly, that is much less likely – even if we are not correct in our interpretation. This becomes a particularly challenging issue when we are communicating across cultures. The final unconscious element involves 'organising' information and categorising it so as to ensure our brain can find the information next time we need it. Any mistakes in any of these three unconscious processes can lead to difficulties on our part and on the part of the recipients in the way our communication is delivered or interpreted.

There are several reasons for what we call 'perceptual errors':

PERCEPTION

Perception is the unconscious process of attending to, interpreting and organising information so as to develop an understanding of the world around us.

1. **We form impressions and make judgements and decisions about people on very little information**: Our brain likes to take as little time as possible to reach judgements on others and, as a result, fills in any gaps in information itself from what it thinks is likely to be true.
2. **Underlying this is a need for meaning**: We try to categorise experiences/situations/people so as to achieve stability. This stability helps us to believe that our view of the world is the correct one, but, in doing so, we unconsciously introduce bias and distortion.
3. **We may attribute behaviour incorrectly**: If we believe that someone is highly capable and intelligent, we may believe that their poor behaviour on a particular occasion was due to factors outside of their control. This supports our stable world view and concurs with the 'information gaps' that our brain has already 'filled in' for us.
4. **Such processes are unconscious**: Rarely do we challenge or think about our judgements, preferring to believe that our original understanding is correct. As a result, we become reluctant to change our views. We are likely to do so only if we are challenged to support our original judgement with hard evidence, or if something significant happens that forces us to re-evaluate our original assessments.
5. **What seems similar in some aspects, is probably similar in all aspects**: Relating this to point 1 above, if there are two things that seem similar, then they probably are similar. When we are perceiving people, we can believe that two people who act in a similar way are probably demonstrating not only the same behaviours, but also the same attitudes and values. This leads to stereotyping and to incorrect approaches to communicating with two people who may display the same behaviour but for very different reasons.
6. **We feel personally more secure with those who are like us, and have a preference for those who seem similar to, not different from, us**: This is not dissimilar to point 5: we believe that those who look like us will probably act like us, think like us and enjoy the same things that we enjoy. Of course, the reality is not usually so simple, but believing this means that

the brain has to do a lot less work. In practice, what all of this means is that what we understand of the world around us and how it works is not necessarily the reality, and that means that we can get things badly wrong when we are planning how to communicate with others from different cultural backgrounds.

 FOR YOU TO DO

Have a look at the picture below. It is a very simple picture featuring three people and has been used regularly in management training.

When you look at the picture, try to answer the following questions and give a summary of what you see – first on your own, then with a friend, and then perhaps with someone from a different cultural background.

1. Where are these people?
2. What do you think their jobs might be?
3. Do you think they know each other? If so, how?
4. Why do you think they are together?
5. Is there anything else you can interpret from what you see?

Be as creative as you can – that will make this exercise more interesting – but also try to analyse carefully what you see to develop an accurate interpretation.

BOX 13.2

Interpretation of cultural norms

Some time ago, I had a friend who was working in another country. After he had been there for some time, I asked him how it was going. His answer surprised me: 'I am finding it OK, but I am not sure if the locals like me very much.' On hearing this, I asked why he had said that. He replied, 'Because they are often spitting at me.'

We react to what we interpret of others' behaviour. People in his own country did not spit in public. In his culture, spitting was something that was seen as rude and impolite. That was his perception and he was reacting to it. In other cultures, particularly some tribal cultures in Africa where water is scarce, spitting is seen as a sign of respect.

Some months later, I met him again and asked how things were going and whether people were still spitting at him. His response this time was much more accepting of others' behaviour: 'Oh yes, but I've learnt that the spitting was nothing to do with me – they were simply clearing their throats of phlegm.'

His perception had changed based on a lot more experience of that culture – and on many conversations he had with local individuals much more familiar with this culture.

We interpret others' behaviour in the light of our own experiences, but when we move to another culture, *those experiences and interpretations become less relevant.*

One of the best ways to prevent inaccurate perceptions from affecting how we engage and communicate with others is to challenge ourselves and ask ourselves questions about our earlier assessments of others. This typically involves deciding to try to collect information which actually contradicts our original assessment. If we cannot find any having made an honest and definite attempt to do so, then we can be reasonably sure that our assessment is probably correct, but, of course, once we have *gathered* the information, we need to be very careful to ensure that we *interpret* the evidence accurately as well.

Of course, it is not just us that are affected by those perceptual processes – those receiving our communication are just as subject to these processes as we are, though they may not be aware of it. Some people like to discuss this with others that they communicate with on an ongoing basis, so that any misperceptions can be addressed easily. Some organisations will engage in what is known as '360° feedback', where information from others is used as part of a performance review process. This may not necessarily change *what* is done, but may change *how* it is done and *how* the individual communicates with others.

The final note here is that all the forms and components of communication covered below will generate perceptions in others. Our non-verbal behaviour, our para-language, our movements and gestures, and our appearance will all have an impact. Some of these we will be able to control, and others we might struggle to control, but it is important to recognise that the perceptions that others have of our communications will be affected by the way they interpret the ways we have communicated previously.

════════════ FOR YOU TO DO ════════════

This is a perceptual activity and a private one for you to do on your own. Think of one individual that you are struggling to work with or get on with, and then ask yourself the following questions:

1. What is it that they did which originally generated your impression of them?
2. Why do you believe they did what they did?
3. What evidence do you have for that assumption (in question 2)?
4. Is there any other possible interpretation of that evidence? Could there have been anything externally which influenced them to do what they did?
5. Have they done the same thing, before or since?
6. If not, what set of factors might have led them to do what they have done? Will you change your perception? If so, what can you do to prevent it from happening again to you? To others?

Whether your original perception was correct or incorrect, it may still not be possible to work with them. We do not all have the same values or attitudes and sometimes this can cause conflicts, but *if we have perceived someone incorrectly*, then at least we can start exploring those other issues with a little more objectivity.

KEY LEARNING POINT

Other people's perceptions of us will have a significant impact on how the messages we communicate are received and acted on.

THE IMPACT OF UNDERSTANDING OTHERS' VALUES

Chapter 9 showed us that accurate communication processes require that messages encoded in one way should be interpreted or decoded in the same way, enabling both parties to understand the meaning. It also indicated that there should be a feedback loop to ensure that all parties were clear on whether or not the message had been understood well.

Communication across cultures causes problems in both these processes. Firstly, the encoding and decoding processes might work completely differently in different cultures (depending on how different the cultures are in terms of their world view). Secondly, the feedback loop might not yield the information expected for a variety of reasons, including that some cultures might even find the need for such a feedback loop quite offensive.

Resolving these challenges sometimes requires a good degree of knowledge of how different cultures might use and interpret the communication processes. In cultures where individuals say exactly what they mean and this is clearly understood, there may not be a big challenge. However, other cultures might require a reasonable understanding of cultural values in order to interpret others' communication accurately and, in doing so, we start to talk about high-context and low-context cultures.

HIGH- AND LOW-CONTEXT CULTURES

Since we try to derive meaning from our communications with others, one of the key challenges with communicating cross-culturally is that we assume that items and behaviours we see as familiar may have very different meanings from our understanding. This becomes problematic when we are operating in what we call 'high-context cultures', where we may not accurately understand others' communications with us.

HIGH- AND LOW-CONTEXT CULTURES

High-context cultures are those where, to communicate well, a deep understanding of the culture is needed.

Low-context cultures are those where little understanding of the culture is needed.

Understanding the culture is sometimes vital to understanding the underlying meaning of what someone is trying to communicate. In a low-context culture, individuals will be clear and direct about what they mean, and communicating in low-context cultures is relatively straightforward.

FOR YOU TO DO

Look at the statements below. Assume that they are given with a pleasant facial expression and little in the way of para-linguistic or non-verbal cues. Without knowing anything about the culture of the speaker, which of the three ideas below each expression do you think is being communicated by the speaker?

1. 'Thank you for your presentation. Very informative. Let me discuss your findings with my colleagues. We've no questions at this stage. Thank you again.'

a. 'It was a really great presentation which answered everything I think we need to know.'

b. 'I think your presentation told us some things, but it didn't really inspire us. It wasn't really what we are looking for.'

c. 'We're confident that you have given us what we are looking for, but if we agreed to everything you said right now, then we would look a bit foolish. No one ever agrees to everything right away without checking their information.'

2. 'We are concerned about the delays in this project. We were hoping that we can work with you more effectively than this, so if there is anything we can do to help you, please let us know.'

a. 'We want to continue to work with you to resolve these delays.'

b. 'We are not really satisfied with how this project is progressing. You shouldn't really ask us for any help, but we are offering it in order to maintain the relationship.'

c. 'We want to stop the contract and offer it to someone else who we think can do a better job.'

3. 'The analysis of our own data tells us beyond any doubt that customers do not approve of the technology we are using for this product. We cannot go on like this!'

a. 'In order to avoid a problem, we will have to work as a team to change what we do.'

b. 'The person who thought this up must have been stupid. I hope he's no longer part of the organisation.'

c. 'I believe that the organisation's Chief Technical Engineer has the answer.'

In reality, there are no right or wrong answers to any of the above statements, but an understanding of an individual's values and attitudes might have a significant impact on how you interpret their statements. If we take two countries – the Netherlands (which is a low-context culture) and Japan (which is a high-context culture) – we can see these differences very clearly. The messages given in high-context cultures can be very difficult to understand accurately. Box 13.3 provides some examples.

═══ BOX 13.3 ═══

Expressing Messages in Different Cultures

Below are a number of statements indicating how individuals in high- and low-context cultures may express similar kinds of messages.

Expressing dislike about someone

Direct, low-context culture: 'I don't like them.'

Indirect, high-context culture: 'I am sure they have some significant strengths.'

Refusing hospitality

Direct, low-context culture: 'Thank you, but I really don't want any more.'

Indirect, high-context culture: 'It is very kind, but my partner needs me to be back at home.'

Offering hospitality

Direct, low-context culture: 'Can you come to the restaurant tonight?'

Indirect, high-context culture: 'My colleagues and I would be honoured if you could join us.'

(Continued)

Giving negative feedback

Direct, low-context culture: 'This was not done well.'

Indirect, high-context culture: 'The effort you made was very welcome. We have asked someone else to continue your wonderful beginning.'

Asking for more time to complete your work

Direct, low-context culture: 'I need some more time. Is that possible?'

Indirect, high-context culture: 'We are becoming more and more confident that we will be finished around the deadline that you gave us.'

The messages given in a high-context culture may seem contradictory to the message that is intended, but that is because there is little understanding of the values underlying the communication. If we take the examples above and assume they are given by a Confucian Heritage Culture (CHC) where traditional Confucian values have been important, such as China, Korea or Japan, then we might recognise that:

1. Preservation of the other party's dignity is extremely important.
2. It is vital that the other person's confidence in us is not damaged.
3. The collective 'we' guides a lot of what is done: 'if you wish to work with us, then you will need to become part of the collective team'.
4. Hierarchy is really important, so that offers made by senior individuals should be received with a significant amount of respect.

These attitudes will govern the phrasing of the above messages. Other cultures will have their own attitudes, often around such issues as time, the speed at which good relationships can be built up, the extent to which hierarchy is important, how hard-headed (or, alternatively, empathetic) someone is allowed to be, how much risk is acceptable when undertaking new activities (or engaging in new relationships), and how strongly they are expected to sacrifice personal activities and goals for the good of society.

 'BUT I HAVE A QUESTION ...'

... If this is the case, how can I be sure that I understand what anyone from another culture is really saying? And how do I know if someone comes from a high-context or a low-context culture?

These are good questions. There are various ways of getting to know a culture, though some are less beneficial than others. Visiting a place as a tourist is perhaps the most superficial action anyone can take. Apart from visiting or living in a second country, the best way to get to know another culture is by making friends and asking lots of honest questions. Learn from those friends and find out what their attitudes and values might be, and the extent to which these values affect styles of communication.

Doing those things – along with some background reading – will help you understand more about the cultures with which you are interacting.

In all of these things, the most effective approach is often a cautious one, which means not expressing yourself directly. It is not difficult to become direct subsequently, but to be direct and then to become more cautious is much more difficult.

═══════════ KEY LEARNING POINT ═══════════

Communication with individuals from cultures other than our own means that messages may well be misunderstood. We need to recognise that this is the case and ensure that we gather feedback on our own communication and check the meanings of others' messages wherever possible.

MODELS OF CULTURAL DIFFERENCE

Stating that any country has one culture is likely to ignore subtle variations. Firstly, countries change: cultures and values evolve over time. Secondly, assuming that everyone in a particular culture shares the same values or behaves in the same way is likely to be inaccurate. Individuals from the same countries do differ. Research published in 2014 indicates that the United States and Canada have distinct regional cultures (Dheer, Lenatowicz and Peterson, 2014). However, while there is a variety of models accessible to researchers, two frameworks for identifying and explaining differences in behaviour have become accepted knowledge, and it would be inappropriate to ignore them completely.

Hofstede's Dimensions of Culture

The best-known framework was developed by Geert Hofstede, a Dutch researcher, in the 1970s. Hofstede undertook research for IBM across its national subsidiaries in various countries and then produced his findings in a book called *Culture's Consequences*. Hofstede's model is one of the easiest to remember and the website that bears his name is well regarded by practitioners in the field.

The most recent version of Hofstede's model contains six dimensions:

- **Masculinity vs femininity**: How hard-headed and 'tough' is the national culture? Does it show much mercy, or is it intolerant of failure? How much pride is shown in the country by individuals living in that culture? Does the national culture seek harmony or show readiness to enter a conflict if pushed a little? As with many labels given to dimensions, some might disagree with these characterisations, but the dimension has nothing to do with whether a culture's population is male or female.
- **Power-distance (high <> low)**: How accessible to the general public are organisational and national leaders of the country? Are leaders and managers expected to be aloof and deeply respected, or is the general attitude one of friendliness? Are organisations likely to be very hierarchical, or relatively flat in terms of structure?
- **Uncertainty avoidance (high <> low)**: How readily do individuals in the country accept (or even embrace) risk? Is there an entrepreneurial spirit, or do individuals prefer a cautious approach? How quickly would decisions be made if things were uncertain?
- **Individualism vs collectivism**: How readily do individuals put the national interest above their own? Is there a noticeable desire to serve others, or are people generally competitive and/or selfish? How is wealth regarded in the country – as a personal asset or as something to be shared?
- **Long-term outlook vs short-term outlook**: To what extent are individuals interested in closing the single deal or in a much longer-term relationship? How will parties react if one party

breaks the agreement in a minor way? Will countries be interested in talking to solve a problem, or will they resort to more 'para-legal' means?

- **Indulgence vs self-restraint**: To what extent does society allow individuals to freely express emotions of excitement and joy? Is there societal pressure not to express such feelings? How freely can individuals enjoy having 'fun'? Societies which are free to have more fun tend to believe that they are in control of their own destiny.

The questions given here are not exhaustive, but should give you enough information to understand the dimensions of the model.

Hofstede's original research has been criticised by some on the grounds that it committed a fatal flaw in undertaking the research in the way that it did. When we are examining what we see and trying to make deductions based on what we see, we are in serious danger of interpreting behaviour based on our own understanding, and that may well be inaccurate. Some have criticised Hofstede for carrying out research in just this way: that interpretations of culture were originally based not on reality but on perceptions and interpretations of reality by individuals who did not necessarily understand whether those interpretations were accurate, or did not take time to check. As time has moved on, the model has received a great deal of acceptance internationally and research methods for Hofstede's recent work have become somewhat more refined.

 'BUT I HAVE A QUESTION ...'

... You mentioned earlier that it is dangerous to generalise, so presumably it is really dangerous to stereotype and generalise at a national level? If so, what can we do about it?

Yes, you are correct on both issues. It is dangerous and unlikely to be wholly accurate to generalise or to say that everyone from a certain culture will be high on 'power-distance', low on 'masculinity', and so on. In some ways, this addresses a fundamental issue about the application of research. Research can only model what it sees, and what research sees is always measured in terms of probabilities. It hardly ever produces absolute certainty, and the same is true for cross-cultural research: it produces a model or a series of hypotheses which need to be tested every time we meet others.

So, to answer your second question, on what we can do about uncertainty, we need to test those hypotheses – it is as simple as that. So, we use as many opportunities as we can to find out about people, to learn what is important to them, how they deal with certain issues and how they determine what is important and what is not important. As we will see later on in the chapter, learning about others' attitudes and cultures from individuals themselves – often called 'ethnography' – is one of the most important steps to understanding another's culture.

Having said that, the models given above do give us a set of thoughts from which we might start asking questions, and in some business settings, groups of individuals in some countries are more inclined to follow a national culture than to follow their own individual values. This is going to be particularly true in more collectivist/communitarian societies, of course.

 FOR YOU TO DO

Think about your own national culture. Your own culture (world view, beliefs and values) will have an impact on how you see other cultures and how you behave towards them. Try to answer the following questions:

1. Looking at the dimensions listed above, how high or low on the dimensions given would you place your own culture?
2. How easy was it to answer question 1? How clearly defined is your own national culture?
3. Can you readily think of individuals from your country who do not fit your own national culture?
4. What would be the dangers of ignoring the cultural differences between you and someone else in (a) a group coursework situation and (b) a business meeting?
5. What could you do to get to know international students studying at your university?

=========== KEY LEARNING POINT ===========

Describing individual, group and national cultures is not easy, and unless we are dealing with individuals there will always be a degree of generalisation taking place. We can, however, begin with our own analyses of individuals we know by using the models as a framework – to be tested and proved or disproved as appropriate.

TOWARDS A DEEPER APPRECIATION OF INTERNATIONAL CULTURES

As a student, you are likely to be exposed to a large number of students from international backgrounds. In the early 1990s, there were very few international students in the UK, but as political systems around the world changed and as countries began realising the cultural and other benefits of inviting international students into their classrooms, those numbers have grown considerably.

This brings certain challenges – to nations, groups, institutions and individuals – but also opportunities to learn about the world around us, which have never before been so easy to find out. As mentioned in the introduction, the world has become global and to ignore others' cultures is something we do at our peril.

The questions therefore are: 'What skills and qualities do we need to develop in order to become culturally aware?' and 'What can we do practically to develop such awareness?'

There are a number of answers to these questions. For the former question, Box 13.4 outlines some of the qualities leading to 'intercultural competence' identified in research, and the content below (based on Figure 13.3) identifies some relevant actions, some of which give us a fairly superficial view and some of which help us understand other cultures in considerably more depth.

========== BOX 13.4 ==========

What Is 'Intercultural Competence'?

Sheridan (2005) identified a number of characteristics – the 7Cs – of what was called 'intercultural competence', relating to the extent to which an individual:

- possesses knowledge about being 'cross-cultural' (Capability).
- considers all stakeholders – including international customers and employers – in making decisions (Care).
- is used to engaging with diverse and international communities (Connection).

(Continued)

- is humble enough to be aware of their own strengths and weaknesses in relation to cross-cultural operations (Context).
- understands situations without making any judgements (Contrasts).
- develops followers according to their cultural backgrounds (Consciousness).
- has experience of living abroad (Cultural immersion).

Questions

1. When you look at these 7Cs, to what extent do you possess these qualities?
2. How could you develop those qualities you do not possess?

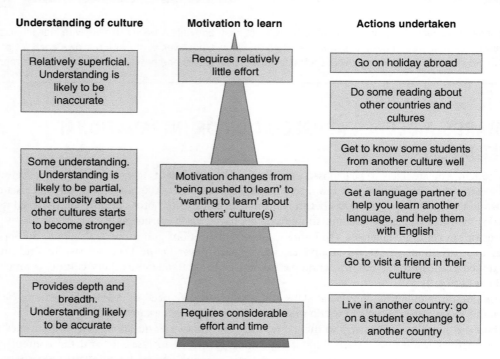

Figure 13.3   Developing an awareness of others' cultures

Figure 13.3 shows some ideas for how to develop cultural awareness. Let us look at how each of these actions can give you some benefit when it comes to developing intercultural competence.

- **Visiting new places**: This can help us to understand the more obvious differences between cultures, for example the language or the history of a particular place, but we are unlikely to develop any kind of detailed understanding of the culture simply by seeing things which are different. In fact, the more things we see that are different without trying to understand them, the more we will be in danger of developing stereotypes based on very limited knowledge of the culture. Perceptual theory tells us that we are then more likely to find evidence to support that inaccurate understanding, rather than evidence which contradicts it. However, it is better to realise that cultures are different than stay at home and wonder why other 'strange' cultures do not understand you.
- **Doing some reading about other cultures**: This still has a sense of superficiality about it in some ways since you are relying on what you read (and reading comments on Facebook is not

going to be helpful), but you will learn things. Reading develops your knowledge about a country and, without knowledge, your understanding will be very limited.

- **Getting to know some students from another culture well**: While we do need to be very aware that not everyone from one particular culture is the same, the better we can get to know other individuals and their cultures – their behaviours, their values and beliefs, and their world view – the better we can engage in constructive relationships with others from that culture. A great deal of learning can be developed through discussion. The easiest way of doing this is to work with international students on group coursework.

══════════ 'BUT I HAVE A QUESTION ...' ══════════

... We are a group of students from a variety of different cultures working together on coursework, which can sometimes present certain challenges. Are there ways to make this easier?

Working with those who have different values and cultures from our own can sometimes present challenges, and in some cases can even produce conflicts within the group. Of course, the solution is to identify exactly where the problem might lie. Some students:

- may not seem to speak as much in the group. This does *not* mean that they do not wish to contribute to the group, only that they may not understand as much as native speakers, or that they need more time to process the information. The solution is to find out informally what the issue is, to reassure those students that their contribution is valuable, and then to give time and space to ensure that their contributions are heard.
- may do their work in a different way or on a different timescale from others. This may be related to their values and experience in their own culture. The solution is often to ensure that the group develops some standardised rules and values (including procedures for communicating effectively) and then to ensure that everyone understands the values and norms of the group before getting too far into the work (see section on storming in Chapter 11.
- may want to stick together with other students from their own culture. If you were living in another country, you would probably want to do the same. It is a lot easier to understand and communicate with those who naturally eat the same kind of food, share your cultural values and speak your language.
- may not want to do the same social activities as other members of the group. Certain social events might be very common in some cultures, but may be disapproved of by certain cultural values or contradict religious values. The group needs to ensure that social events can be accessible to all students; it would not take too much imagination to organise such activities.

There may be other challenges that you face. As in working with anyone with a slightly different lifestyle or background to your own, solutions usually relate to addressing concerns from *all* individuals in the group, rather than just the leader, or the loudest.

- **Getting a language partner to help you learn another language, and help them learn to speak your language**: Being willing to lean a language is a great way of showing how committed you are to developing an international mindset. In the UK, we (in general) are very lazy about learning languages, partially because we think: 'So many people around the world speak English, so why bother?'

    o   The answer is very simple: It shows commitment and engagement with that culture, and more often than not, it will be a significant advantage to being able to do business in that culture.

- o   Doing so with a language partner rather than in a class will enable you to ask questions which occur to you about that culture as you progress, and will also help the international student to develop their English skills in an informal situation.

- **Visiting a friend in their culture**: Spending time with people you know in their own culture is probably one of the best ways to learn about that culture. Because they are a friend, you can ask them nearly anything you wish about their culture, you can see what they do, how they act and how they relate to others and the world around them. You can never buy that kind of experience from a book (even this one!).

  - o   Some cultures would be very happy for you to ask whether you can do this, while others would not react well to such a request and would expect you to wait to be invited. So you need to take time to develop the friendship first so that you can understand which is most acceptable. You also need to be very clear on who will pay for what. Assume at the outset that you will need to pay for everything, including a gift for your host. Misunderstandings can damage friendships and it would be a big shame if you got this wrong.

- **Living in another country or going on a student exchange**: Long-term exposure to another country cannot fail to enhance your understanding of other cultures, and so a semester abroad – either on an exchange programme or, if not, as part of a study abroad programme – would be a great place to start. Your university will usually have a number of 'partner universities' where students can go and study for a semester or a year, and where their students will come to your own university. If you do go abroad, make sure you ask questions about health insurance, bank accounts (including getting access to your own money while abroad) and visa requirements; these can take some time to set up.

CULTURE SHOCK

Culture shock is the emotional reaction to recognising that your experience, knowledge and understanding of a different culture are incomplete or inaccurate, but knowing that you cannot isolate yourself from that culture.

- o   Student exchange programmes are usually free in terms of course fees, will contribute to your degree in the same way as if you were studying in your own university, and will usually give you a good 'study experience' in the other culture. Study abroad programmes will vary in these areas, but will usually require you to pay extra. You must also check whether such programmes will contribute to your degree, or whether they are going to mean that you just add a year onto your degree.

- o   You also need to be prepared to experience culture shock as you immerse yourself in that second country (see section below on overcoming culture shock). The best way of reducing culture shock is to get to know as many people as you can from that country and talk to them about what you might expect to experience, or go to that country on holiday, where things may still seem strange, but where you will be able to escape 'the strangeness' relatively quickly and insulate yourself against it temporarily by staying with other foreigners. (This latter strategy will *not* work if you are genuinely trying to become culturally competent, but it can serve as a short-term coping strategy.)

Overcoming Culture Shock

The graph in Figure 13.4 – based on the Kubler-Ross Transition Curve – was developed to explain individuals' reactions to situations where they were being subjected to changes in their environment over which they have no control, and thus it could apply to any student coming to university for the

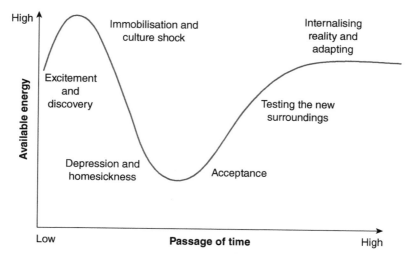

Figure 13.4   Emotional reactions to culture shock: 'Kubler-Ross Transition Curve'

first time (see Chapter 1) as much as to someone going to live abroad.

At its heart, the model works like this. An individual going abroad might be expected to have an initial sense of excitement regarding their new situation. Everything seems different and those differences make life interesting and exciting. Just as we might enjoy becoming like children again and learning (see the relevant content in Chapter 14 on physical and practical 'play'), so too we now enjoy learning from our new situation by trying to make sense of it. After a time, however, we recognise that the sense of fun starts to decrease as we struggle to get basic things done.

We might struggle and feel some confusion with some or all of the following:

- **Understanding jokes and the other culture's sense of humour**: Smiling and laughter help us to build relationships, but if we find that we don't understand what makes people laugh, then building and keeping relationships with others from what we might term a 'host culture' can seem challenging.
- **Knowing how to address people and avoid cultural 'faux pas'**: Many high context cultures do not readily show their small 'rights and wrongs' when it comes to ways of offending others, so we might feel nervous about making such mistakes, especially when meeting important individuals (e.g. at a business meeting).
- **Understanding how to engage in general day-to-day conversation**: There are cultural taboos – topics we should not discuss – in every culture, but unless we have discussed those with local individuals, we may not know what they are. We also need to learn how (or if) to approach strangers, and what ways might be considered offensive.
- **Understanding day-to-day habits**: There are a number of other areas of behaviour we may not understand well. The ways that people drive, the typical daily schedule (when people wake and sleep), the kinds of food people enjoy, attitudes towards a range of social issues such as marriage, poverty and wealth, the purposes and behaviours around physical contact: these can all be very different from our own situation. When put together, these small differences can make us feel uncomfortable.
- **Understanding how and when to develop trust with others**: Just as our behaviour is affected by our own culture, the way that we approach others can affect their desire to trust

us. Trust is not always easy to develop across cultures, but the more we engage with others and learn to adapt our behaviour, the less difficulty we will have in doing so.

As a result of any or all of the above, we can feel lost. We can feel that we are struggling to unpick the attitudes and behaviours that we have come to regard as useful and second nature when living in our own culture in order to re-learn them for a new situation. Homesickness and distress can be a natural result of these issues, and we might need some emotional support at times.

 FOR YOU TO DO

Watch a movie

The number of times one of your lecturers is going to ask you to watch a movie may not be large, but there are a large number of movies which discuss individuals' experiences of cultures other than their own, or which are set in an unfamiliar culture. Maybe one of the best known movies to do this of recent times is *The Best Exotic Marigold Hotel* (2011) featuring the stories of a number of individuals who travel to India and have various experiences as they do so – good and bad. Similarly, *Slumdog Millionaire* (2008) gives us a glimpse into one viewpoint of Indian culture – but it is one viewpoint, and there will be many others. The 2008 film *Gran Torino* shows Clint Eastwood's character empathising with some local Chinese immigrants who are having a tough time dealing with a local gang and, of course, the *Lord of the Rings* trilogy shows the hobbits dealing with a range of different types of creatures and cultures.

1. **Find a movie** which shows something of others' experiences dealing with being in a cross-cultural situation. It does not need to be about different countries – often several cultures will exist within the same country – but it is about interacting with individuals who are different from yourself.
2. **Look at the issues**: What problems do the characters face when interacting with each other? Sometimes if we can see those in a well-acted movie, we can imagine how we might feel.
3. **Identify solutions**: How do the characters deal with these situations? Do those solutions work? Would you deal with those situations any differently?

Recognising that we need help with our language skills and cannot do what we would find second nature in our own country raises some serious issues for us. We may for a while try to deny that we find certain things hard, but eventually come to accept that we need help. Having found sources of help, we learn to experiment within our new environment and test out ways of doing what we need to do. Eventually, we find ways to cope and adapt and we get used to living in the new culture. This does not mean that we never have any more issues in getting used to the culture: there may still be surprises – some exciting and some depressing – that we experience, but it does mean that we can relax and be more content.

Questions

1. If you have always lived in one country, how would you feel about living abroad? What would be the main challenges you would face – cooking, travelling, finding friends?
2. How would you cope with these issues?

Overcoming these emotional reactions is important and can take more or less time according to a number of issues related to personal attitude – are we used to learning about others and others' cultures? – and experience – have we travelled much in our lives? The longer we spend in one culture and the more emotionally attached we are to that culture, the more challenges we might find in overcoming culture shock.

But there are some things which will help us overcome these challenges:

- **Ask questions**: Any relationship is usually based on mutual understanding, so find someone and ask them questions. Usually people will be very happy to talk about their own background and culture, so ask someone if they would be happy to help you understand the environment in which you live.
- **Be patient**: Adopting a patient attitude will help us enormously. We will be able to relax and see the situations we face from different perspectives. The challenge is, of course, that this is easier said than done, but the more we try to do this and the more we remind ourselves of the need to be patient, then the more we are likely to accept what we see – even if we don't understand it.
- **Make compromises**: When we go to another culture, the natural instinct is to criticise what is not familiar to us, or that which seems to contradict our values. The second instinct is then to fight against what seems wrong. In reality, we are very unlikely to change the culture we are experiencing, and so the only option is to adapt to it. That usually involves compromising somehow; not doing so is likely to make our cross-cultural experience more painful.
- **Practise empathy**: When we go into another culture, we bring our own experiences, values and history, some of them good and some of them less good perhaps. Those things help to make us who we are. When we go into that other culture, we enter a world that has its own history, challenges and influences. But we also need to learn to deal with individuals who have their own histories and challenges and influences, some good and some painful perhaps. It is no different from how we might deal with anyone even in our own culture, but it becomes particularly important when we are in another culture, where emotions are going to be heightened and there are more challenges to deal with. Learning to understand and show empathy for another's situation can help to focus our attention on others.
- **Build hypotheses, not facts**: Throughout your time in another culture, you will be making very quick judgements about what you see. These judgements will be based on interpretations you have learned to make throughout the previous years of your life, and you will have refined those interpretations so that your brain can very quickly understand what is going on without collecting additional information. However, when you move to a different culture, you will find that many of those interpretations are no longer correct, and as a result, the best that you can do is to treat the interpretation of what you see as a hypothesis, not as a statement of truth. The more different the culture is from your own, the less accurate your interpretation of what you see and experience.
- **Make friends**: There is nothing more helpful in a strange place (where maybe you cannot speak the language) than making friends – especially if they can help you with the practical things you need to do, with the language and with understanding others' behaviour. A great thing to do *before you go* to another culture is to find individuals from that culture who might be living close to you (in your own country) and start to learn more about their culture from them (assuming that they moved relatively recently: speaking to someone about the country that they left 20 years ago is probably only going to give you a very partial picture of the culture there now).

KEY LEARNING POINT

Overcoming culture shock is a process and can take some time. Different people will struggle with different things in different ways, and some will take more time than others, but with time, overcoming culture shock is not difficult.

REFLECTION POINT

Take some time to think about the following questions and write down some answers.

How important do you think it is to develop your own sense of awareness of the world around you?

Do you study with (attend lectures, do group work, live in the same accommodation, etc.) people from a different cultural background? What have you done to find out about their culture?

Do you think you can use any of the ideas in this section to develop more cross-cultural awareness?

INTEGRATION AND APPLICATION

Living in a global world requires that we engage with the world around us. To do so, we need a number of personal qualities:

1. Humility – to admit that there may be other and better ways of doing things.
2. Open-mindedness – to accept that others can have a different way of doing things.
3. Acceptance – to allow others to continue doing things their way if they actually work well for them and have no impact on the organisation.
4. Understanding – of the idea that others have a point of view which may be different from yours.

In developing our cross-cultural skills and our readiness for a world that is unquestionably global, we need to possess knowledge about other cultures, but knowledge is not going to be sufficient – the ability to apply our skills to use that knowledge is crucial.

In all that we do, we need to have motive, means and opportunity. In seeking to develop cultural literacy, we can consider the following:

- **The motive for being global**: We look at the world around us and see changes happening on a scale that limits the effectiveness of unilateral action, and we wish to position ourselves strategically (see issues related to personal branding for job applications in Chapter 16) to ensure we can take advantage of such opportunities.
- **The means**: We can look at the ways in which our skills (or lack of them sometimes) can be enhanced so as to demonstrate to employers that we can work in a global world, and take action to do so. This can sometimes take us on journeys – including real physical journeys – during our studies which can appear scary, or alternatively as adventures.
- **The opportunities**: There are now numerous ways in which we can take advantage of opportunities to interact with other cultures. From examining the diverse communities in which we live (including student accommodation) to spending time with individuals we know in an environment which is unfamiliar, we would be foolish not to seek to understand those with whom we interact – and will interact – on a daily basis.

CONCLUSION

You should now have a good idea of how to:

- Analyse your own and others' world views.
- Overcome perceptual and other cultural barriers in order to develop a good understanding of others' communication.
- Develop your insight into other cultures.
- Become more of a global citizen, able to operate with understanding in other cultures.

This chapter has sought to establish an awareness of what it means to interact in a global world. We have covered what we mean by a world view and discussed issues relating to our beliefs, values and behaviours. We have discussed what it means to have a global mindset. We have discussed how perceptual processes can present challenges in understanding others and how communication processes can become difficult, particularly in high-context cultures. The chapter has also presented a brief discussion regarding theoretical models of culture – useful for comparing cultures with each other – and provided some practical steps that individuals can take to develop an increasingly important ability, namely cross-cultural literacy.

CHAPTER TASK

Find an international student (or if you are an international student, find someone from the country that you are studying in). Without judging their country or their values, chat to them for an hour about:

- Important points in their country's history.
- What they value in life.
- What is the greatest pressure and greatest joy they have experienced in life.
- What it is like to live in their country.

Asking questions is the best way to find out about others' lives and cultures. You might like to extend this exercise and do this with a group of other students from different countries to find out more about their cultures.

INTERVIEW QUESTIONS

In nearly all cases, the questions in previous chapters have only been about determining your skills and abilities in certain areas. However, being a global citizen involves knowledge as well as skill, and so some of the questions which might be asked in this area could try to find out how much you know as well as what you are able to do.

Think about the following questions. What might your answers be?

1. What do you think are the biggest issues currently facing international organisations?
2. What difficulties would you expect to face if you were offered a role in another country?
3. Imagine a situation where you – as a departmental manager – needed quickly to resolve a conflict between two individuals of different cultural backgrounds about an issue where both held very strong and opposing views. How would you handle such a situation?

Chapter 17 gives a lot more information on selection interviews and the online content gives some guidance on these questions.

ADDITIONAL RESOURCES

 Want to learn more? Visit https://study.sagepub.com/morgan2e to gain access to a wide range of online resources, including interactive tests, tasks, further reading and downloads.

Website Resources

The following websites offer useful advice on cross-cultural awareness.

Oregon State University student blog: http://blogs.oregonstate.edu/dorrespblog/cssa-competencies/4-multicultural-awareness-knowledge-skills-and-ability/

INSEAD Knowledge: http://knowledge.insead.edu/career/the-rise-of-multicultural-managers-2552

MindTools – cross-cultural communication: www.mindtools.com/CommSkll/Cross-Cultural-communication.htm

MindTools – working with diverse groups: www.mindtools.com/pages/article/cultural-intelligence.htm

Study.com: study.com/academy/lesson/cross-cultural-communication-definition-strategies-examples.html#lesson

Textbook Resources

Barrett, D. J. (2011) *Leadership Communication* (3rd edition). New York: McGraw-Hill (particularly Chapter 8).

Christopher, E. (2012) *Communication Across Cultures*. Basingstoke: Palgrave.

Connerly, M. L. and Pederson, P. B. (2005) *Leadership in a Diverse and Multicultural Environment*. Thousand Oaks, CA: Sage.

Harvard Business Review (2011) *Building Better Teams*. Boston, MA: Harvard Business Review (particularly pages 103–24).

Hind, D. and Moss, S. (2011) *Employability Skills*. Houghton-le-Spring: Business Education Publishers (particularly Chapter 15).

Schneider, S. C., Barsoux, J.-L. and Stahl, G. (2014) *Managing Across Cultures* (3rd edition). Harlow: Pearson (particularly Chapters 7 and 8).

Varner, I. and Beamer, L. (2011) *Intercultural Communication in the Workplace* (5th edition). New York: McGraw-Hill.

14 PROBLEM SOLVING AND CREATIVITY

Creativity is intelligence having fun. (Albert Einstein)

CHAPTER STRUCTURE

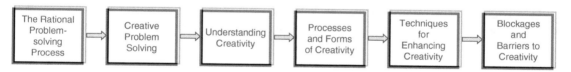

Figure 14.1

When you see the this means go to the companion website https://study.sagepub.com/morgan2e to do a quiz, complete a task, read further or download a template.

━━ AIMS OF THE CHAPTER ━━

By the end of this chapter, you should be able to:

- Follow both rational and creative problem-solving processes.
- Describe the key components of creativity.
- Develop and enhance your creativity.
- Recognise blockages to creativity in yourself and in others.

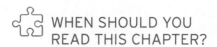

WHEN SHOULD YOU READ THIS CHAPTER?

Increasing your creativity and ability to solve problems is something that you will need to work on regularly throughout your time at university, and so it is best to read this and practise your creativity throughout your first year at university and beyond.

INTRODUCTION

Before we go too far into this topic, let's look at two quick questions:

'What is the maximum number of dates a guy or girl could have in a month?'

'The adrenalin suddenly kicked in. He heard the gun and ran. As fast as he could, away from the others. Fast, and with speed, pushing forward in case they reached him. For what was two kilometres, he ran. He didn't try to stop. He didn't try to hide. He saw the guy with the gun and went past him five times. How can you explain why he ran past the guy with the gun five times?'

We will have a quick discussion of the answers in the conclusion to this chapter.

Developing novel solutions to complex problems is something that many managers have to do (especially those in highly competitive markets where innovation is the main source of competitive advantage).

There are discussions about whether individuals are naturally creative or are more comfortable following rules and solving structured problems by using solutions which have worked before. In reality, most individuals can be helped to add more creativity to their thinking. This creativity relates not just to solving problems – although that is often an area where creativity plays an important part – but also to establishing an innovative vision for an organisation, where capturing individuals' imagination can be a powerful motivator, or to giving a speech where presenting a unique view of something can enable individuals to see things in a totally different way.

This chapter will set out some of the ways that this can be done and will first look at standard models for solving problems before moving on to examine some of the issues involved with understanding creativity and applying tools to enhance our creativity, but as usual it begins with a skills assessment.

SKILLS SELF-ASSESSMENT

Complete the brief questionnaire below to see how well you are able to solve problems. Give each item a score between 1 and 5, where 1 is 'not at all like me', and 5 is 'very much like me'. Some of the questions here may seem the same as others, but there are some subtle differences.

When I am faced with a challenging problem, I usually …

Item	Statement	Score
1.	Try to seek help from others around me	
2.	Look to see whether there are any answers in the books I have	
3.	Try to fix it	
4.	Wait until the problem has passed	
5.	Ask someone else to solve the problem for me	
6.	Try to find a parallel situation which helps me to find a solution	
7	Look to see what others do	
8.	Adopt a very structured and analytic approach to solving the problem	

Item	Statement	Score
9.	Watch how others have solved similar problems	
10.	Work on the problem for hours and hours to show how committed I am to finding a solution	
11.	Try to use my understanding of relationships between relevant concepts to build up solutions	
12.	Feel sure that I can develop a solution	
13.	Feel able to evaluate potential solutions recommended by others	
14.	Feel comfortable accepting untested ideas from others	
15.	Enjoy doing new things without being able to fully evaluate their impact	

You can find an interactive version of this test, along with answers, comments and thoughts about these questions, on the companion website for this book at https://study.sagepub.com/morgan2e.

INTERACTIVE
TEST

FOR YOU TO DO

Creativity 101

In order to use your creativity, let's set a few challenges for you – feel free to work with others on these. All creativity is based – to a smaller or greater extent – on the knowledge you have about the issues involved. If we don't understand what something is or how it works, we usually have to ask – so don't be afraid of doing so from others around you. The first set of challenges are ones that many students face so you should know enough yourself to develop some potential ideas to solve them. The second set – labelled team challenges – are on a bigger scale and might require much more thought, but give them a go anyway.

Challenges as a University Student

The way we cope with difficulties is important, but so too are the resources we use to help us overcome them. Universities will have given some resources to help you with these things, but is there anything new or innovative you can develop that others may not have thought about? How might you help yourself and your fellow students to:

1. Prepare better for your examinations?
2. Develop cross-cultural skills?
3. Deliver a better presentation?
4. Use more sustainable products/processes while you study?
5. Identify opportunities to help provide emotional support for other students?

Team Challenges

These challenges are taken from those set for teams in previous competitions for the Hult Prize, funded by Bill Clinton, former president of the USA, and run in conjunction with Hult International Business School (see www.hultprize.org). They are intended to be set for teams working together for some time and the winners need to produce a realistic business proposal, which is then funded with up to $1 million to address the particular issue set. Without thinking of the detail at this stage, just think conceptually around some general ideas which may not have been tried before. How would you build a sustainable and scalable social enterprise to:

(Continued)

1. Address issues of non-communicable diseases in slums.
2. Address the early childhood education gap in kids aged 0–6 years old.
3. Double the income of 10 million people residing in crowded urban spaces by better connecting people, goods, services, and capital?

Further online content on the Hult Prize can be found on the companion website at **https://study.sagepub. com/morgan2e.**

THE RATIONAL PROBLEM-SOLVING PROCESS

FURTHER READING

The frameworks for solving a structured problem can seem relatively straightforward and typically follow a set of stages: clarifying the problem, establishing causes, developing options and making a choice. You can find a lot more about the stages of problem solving by going to the companion website at https://study.sagepub.com/morgan2e.

Stage 1: Clarify the objective – what do you really wish to achieve (what is the problem you really want to solve)?

In some organisations, there can be tension between what is said and what is believed, or between what is said and what the underlying issues really are. Here personality really does play a part. If you are nervous about upsetting others or want to please other people, then it is possible that any disagreements between people will not be addressed and any solution will not really help the organisation move forward. Instead, you will likely end up with a solution that maintains the present situations.

The challenge for solving any problems in this case is that the way you 'frame' the problem (i.e. the way you describe what the problem is) will have significant repercussions on the solutions proposed and chosen. If the real objective is not clarified at the beginning of the process, then it is unlikely that the problem will be solved, and the same is true if the problem is not identified correctly.

Stage 2: Establishing the cause(s) of the problem

In the 1950s, two British individuals, Charles Kepner and Ben Tregoe, identified a decision-making process which became a well-established framework for problem solving (Kepner and Tregoe, 2013). This rational and scientific approach helps to identify and verify the cause of a problem by seeking to identify where, when and with whom problems are occurring, are not occurring, and any changes or differences in situation which might explain why they do and do not occur – see Table 14.1.

Table 14.1   Defining, describing and establishing possible causes for a problem

	Is	Could be but is not	Differs in the situations	Changes over time
What the problem ...	You hear reports that a team member is not engaged with the activity	You hear that other team members are able to complete their own work	The issue seems to be with this team member	Up until three months ago, the team member worked as hard as the others
Where the problem ...	This individual is located in the sales team	This individual also works in the project management team, but it has not reported any issues	The sales team is smaller and has a larger budget and task to undertake	Similar problems were reported in the data collection team a year ago, but stopped three months ago

	Is	Could be but is not	Differs in the situations	Changes over time
			This individual came from an IT company whereas others rose through the organisation to join the sales team	This individual has become less and less engaged with the task
When the problem ...	This happens every time the team meets	This does not happen in any of the other activities the individual is involved with	The team is different The demands on the team have increased	The problem has become more pronounced over the past three months
Extent of the problem ...	Limited to just this individual	Could be that no other team members seem to feel engaged, but this is not the case	The individual is not behaving in the same way as the other members of the team	Gradual apparent decline in effort over the last three months

The above analysis can lead us to a very different hypothesis according to the questions we ask.

 ## 'BUT I HAVE A QUESTION ...'

... What do you do if you do not know and cannot get data about where problems are or are not occurring?

Sometimes we cannot get all of the details to follow the Kepner-Tregoe approach as fully as we might want. In such situations, we sometimes have to investigate the causes of problems as far as we can, implement a solution and see whether that solves the issue. If not, then we simply need to start again.

There are times when we simply do not know what the cause may be. Sometimes, the issue can be one of life and death. If we take something like the discovery of AIDS in the 1980s, then all that seemed to be happening was that people were getting colds and pneumonia and had a much lower immunity to certain conditions than they should have had. It was not until some investigation revealed linkages with other situations that the AIDS virus was discovered. It was then that the search for a treatment could begin.

Of particular relevance was the way that researchers made these linkages - identifying where the condition was and was not - as a means to discovering what was really going on.

An alternative – and many think better – way of establishing the cause of any issue is simple: ask the question 'why?' until you arrive at what you think is the most likely answer, based on any data you get.

Figure 14.2 gives an example of this process, around the following situation: there is a procedure for submitting invoices to ensure that the organisation can do its accounting correctly. However, not enough people follow the procedure correctly.

By asking 'why?' a sufficient number of times (seven is good ...) we can usually identify the most likely cause of an issue.

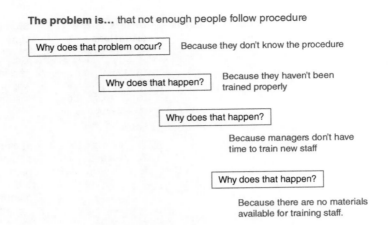

The problem is... that not enough people follow procedure

| Why does that problem occur? | Because they don't know the procedure |

| Why does that happen? | Because they haven't been trained properly |

Why does that happen?

Because managers don't have time to train new staff

Why does that happen?

Because there are no materials available for training staff.

Figure 14.2

Stage 3: Generate the options for solving the problem

Once the main problem has been identified, the next step is to generate options which might help to solve the problem, and often this is where creativity becomes an essential part of the process. Ideas on how to use different techniques to produce creative results are presented on pages 328–339.

Stage 4: Make a balanced choice

Once a small number of appropriate solutions have been identified, the next step is to choose which to implement, and how, when and with which people. A decision about the choice of solution would usually be based on a number of criteria related to the problem we are trying to solve. We would usually score each solution according to those criteria. For some decisions, the criteria would need to be weighted to indicate relative importance. Making mathematical calculations then becomes relatively easy and the best decision would then be the one with the highest score.

Making and/or implementing the decision is likely going to rest with the relevant team or committee, which in turn needs to be provided with appropriate resources over a particular timescale.

Whatever is chosen, it needs to be capable of addressing the relevant problem without creating bigger problems. A large organisational change project will almost certainly create other issues (e.g. staff morale, people being made redundant or even internal sabotage) but in the longer term, the benefits have to outweigh the costs.

In some form or another, we are conditioned to solve problems using this rational problem-solving process outlined above. Time, effort, social convention and other constraints force us to have a logic explaining why we do what we do, and ensure that we have the facts and figures to support our point of view. Such processes are even at the very heart of academic life, where critical thinking demands that we support our case with logic and ideas based on good research and published theory.

Given the right circumstances, we can often be more creative than we are conditioned to be. The next section will examine how creative individuals construct processes to assist them in developing innovative ideas and solutions.

KEY LEARNING POINT

Following a systematic process can be helpful and useful when solving certain kinds of problems.

====== REFLECTION POINT ======

Take some time to think about the following questions and write down some answers.

How confident are you that you can solve problems that you come across in your life?

Do you think others have the same problems to overcome as you?

How often do you ask others how they have gone about solving a particular problem – that is, do you ask for advice or do you prefer to solve the problem on your own?

CREATIVE PROBLEM SOLVING

As mentioned above, we are typically 'programmed' to engage in rational, common sense decision making. However, given the right circumstances, we can often be more creative than we are conditioned to be. At Harvard Business School (see Box 14.1), the teaching is universally done through the use of reality-based business problems which are discussed in class, with the aim of enabling students and managers to see things from different perspectives.

====== BOX 14.1 ======

Case Studies in Class

Since problem solving is an important skill for students to develop, lecturers sometimes use what is known as the 'Harvard case method' (Harvard Business School, n.d.). This involves using detailed and extensive information about scenarios, often about 15-20 pages in length. Students are asked to identify what they think are the 'real issues', and then develop potential solutions.

Case studies are an excellent way of developing your problem-solving skills. The issues are usually complex and the case material is often full of information which is distracting and unhelpful. This can be seen as problematic, but it reflects real life where the issues are unclear and vague, and where different people will be giving you different pieces of information.

At Harvard Business School, students are graded on their engagement with each other in class as well as in more formal ways. These discussions will develop individuals' self-confidence and their ability to defend a particular point of view.

By the end of the class, the board will be full of the relevant concepts and theoretical models written by the course tutor as the discussion has gone on. The world is not straightforward, and as much as we try to construct a world that is simple so we can adopt and apply solutions easily, the use of case studies goes a lot further than many teaching tools to show that believing in a simple world without ambiguity is likely to be unproductive.

UNDERSTANDING CREATIVITY

Creativity in terms of problem solving means that we can see a problem in a new way and/or we can identify new possibilities that have the potential to change something around us in some way. In order to understand how to use it, we need to understand more about what is involved in 'being creative'.

We recognise creative ideas when they make us sit back and think 'I wish I had thought of that', but understanding what creativity is can potentially be more problematic. In fact, we can examine creativity on a number of levels. We can think about the outcomes of creative processes, we can think about what people call the 'creative arts' (where representations of reality are shown in different forms – dance, poetry, artistic painting, drama), we can think about biological functioning and how hormones and our brains function, and we can think about the psychology of creativity and how mental functioning can impact on how creative we are.

The definition of creativity, therefore, might also vary accordingly, so we might need to take a very broad view.

 CREATIVITY

Creativity is a personal quality shown through the production of innovative ideas.

Amabile (1998) indicates that the ability to be creative has three components: technical knowledge, creative abilities and motivation. As we will see below, undertaking tasks creatively can be a great deal of fun, though it does require an ability to enjoy 'fun'.

Knowledge

Knowledge and expertise come in very different forms and may be used by different people in different ways. Creative individuals use knowledge not simply by applying it to situations based on previous experience, but by identifying relationships between different concepts and ideas. The mental manipulation of those relationships enables creative individuals to develop innovative ideas that others will not have thought about. Knowledge can also apply to processes as much as to facts and ideas, so changing relationships between concepts and then understanding how those changes can lead to changes in process can radically alter the view an individual might have of any one particular problem.

We might expect that the greater someone's knowledge from their experience, the more creative they would be. In reality, the longer someone has been in a role, the more fixed their ideas become – perhaps based on thinking that they 'have seen it all before'.

Creative Abilities

Solving a novel or unstructured problem will require the ability to see the problem in relation to ideas and knowledge gained from elsewhere, but in a way that others are unable to do. It seems that successful scientists spend a great deal more time defining a problem than those who are less successful (Mumford, 2000). However, it also seems that more creative individuals will spend more time playing around with visual representations of problems to identify relevant concepts and possibilities than those who are less creative. Constructing and manipulating a visual representation of a problem requires an understanding of the relevant ideas, concepts and processes, but research indicates that developing a creative definition of a problem is more successful when the individual concentrates on processes and concepts, rather than on goals (Mumford, 2000).

Motivation

As noted above, creativity requires the use of technical expertise, problem-solving skills and motivation. Sometimes that motivation comes through the intrinsic sense of fun that developing new ideas can give us, but sometimes it comes from external pressures that we can face in business.

================ BOX 14.2 ================

When Is a 'Problem' Not a Problem?

The obvious answer to this comes from one of those situations where something might be a 'nice problem to have' – e.g. you have too many customers rather than too few – though even this will lead to other issues. However, there is a sense in which things might need to change even when there is no obvious problem, and there are some obvious situations in which this is important.

1. **Keeping ahead of competition**: In business situations, managers find themselves needing to compete with other organisations and stay ahead of the game. Internally, there may be no significant issue, but externally, there is pressure to drive for continuous improvement. Hape toys (based in Germany but largely manufacturing in China) is aware that others may try to copy their toys, so their strategy for addressing this is to make sure that they are continually innovative, ahead of the competition.
2. **There is no issue now, but** … The external environment – including competitors, but also government, technological changes, economic changes and so on – might be changing and pushing your business to adopt new ideas that it had never needed before.
3. **Cultural values**: There may be (and in many organisations should be) a need to drive for ongoing continuous improvement. The closer an organisation is to performing at what it thinks is good enough, the more chance there might be of something going wrong, and a chance that targets might be missed. A culture of continuous improvement keeps everyone contributing to improving what they do. Dell computers' vision statement used to be 'To be the next Dell' as a way of emphasising this.

A 'problem' may not be a 'problem' which currently exists, but seeking continuous improvements and innovations can ensure that problems actually occur less than would otherwise be the case.

Understanding how to be creative is about understanding how to build hypothetical possibilities – without restrictions – and then working out how those hypothetical possibilities can be brought into reality. Solving a problem that others cannot solve often involves seeing the problem (to conceptualise it) differently from others. Typically this means that we conceptualise the issue differently, come up with solutions that others have not developed and/or implement a solution in a way and at a time that others have not thought about.

================ KEY LEARNING POINT ================

Allowing our mind to be flexible and to play around mentally with ideas, knowledge and concepts is much more likely to lead to the development of innovative ideas and solutions to problems.

================ REFLECTION POINT ================

Take some time to think about the following questions and write down some answers.

What is going through your mind as we start to look at creativity? Do you think you are creative? Do you love being creative, but feel that you cannot be for some reason?

(Continued)

Were you creative as a child? Did you enjoy painting, drama, writing poetry? Did that ever stop? If so, why?

Do you ever 'see', in your mind, the ways that ideas could relate to each other? Do you ever ask yourself the question, 'If this changed, what would happen?

PROCESSES AND FORMS OF CREATIVITY

As a process, creativity comes in stages and in different forms. Whetten and Cameron (2011) indicate that there are four stages in a creative problem-solving process:

Stage 1: Preparation (which involves problem definition and gathering information).

Stage 2: Incubation (largely unconscious, where ideas are combined in an attempt to find a solution).

Stage 3: Illumination (a conscious 'Eureka!' moment, where an insight is recognised).

Stage 4: Verification (where evaluation of the proposed solution is undertaken).

The development of innovative ideas can take place at any stage, but the conscious enhancement of ideas typically takes place in the preparatory stage.

As indicated above, there are different forms of creativity (Whetten and Cameron, 2011):

- **Imagination** – where creation is seen in terms of the creation of new and radical ideas (e.g. Google Glass).
- **Improvement** – taking an idea and making it better in ways that others had not thought about (e.g. development of flat screen TVs).
- **Investment** – taking a competitive approach to achieve results faster than others (e.g. the 'battle' between Samsung and Apple to develop similar but different products).
- **Incubation** – where networks of individuals are brought physically together and lively discussion of new possibilities can take place (e.g. businesses in Silicon Valley).

These forms of creativity are complements and suitable for different circumstances, depending on the magnitude of the change and the speed with which any change needs to be implemented. Each of these four forms of creativity can take various forms, reflecting different techniques for enhancing and demonstrating our creativity, but, in reality, most individuals can demonstrate at least one of them.

TECHNIQUES FOR ENHANCING CREATIVITY

Maybe you consider yourself to be creative or maybe not. However, most people are creative to some extent (as indicated above in terms of the four forms of creativity), though it is true that some need more encouragement to feel free to demonstrate that creativity and, for others, a little insight into various tools and techniques may be useful.

Brainstorming

This very frequently used word describes an activity where individuals contribute to a discussion in order to solve a problem. It can be used at any stage of a problem-solving process (including identifying the nature of a problem), but is most often used when trying to develop solutions to problems. A record is usually taken of these contributions in a way that others can see (e.g. flipchart) and a discussion can be very energetic, but there may be problems.

- Group-think may mean that no one feels able to contradict what others have said: Perhaps this is because they might be made to feel that their ideas had no value or are intimidated in some way. Having unity within a team is very important for a team to be able to function well (see page 253 on the characteristics of an effective team) but developing a sense of unity which does not allow for disagreement is not helpful.
- Not everyone has the chance to talk: If a discussion is progressing at a fast pace, then there will probably be little chance to ensure that everyone has a chance to contribute and the group may get to a decision too quickly for others to voice any disagreement. Those chairing such discussions need to be sure that everyone has the chance to say exactly what they think.
- The written record is not accurate: There may be occasions when individuals unconsciously filter out and do not record aspects of the discussion which might later prove to be really valuable. Those omissions may mean that certain pieces of information are never followed up.
- The discussion is based on assumptions: It is very tempting to believe everything that everyone says, but often (and particularly in a single fast-moving conversation) statements can be made based on subjective opinion, rather than on the more objective evidence. There are times when assumptions can be correct, but trying to develop solutions to a problem means that we need to be sure that those solutions will actually solve the problem, rather than generate a set of brand-new and more challenging problems.
- The wrong objective: It is very encouraging to have a discussion where the objective is to reach a decision – or even gather a number of ideas – but brainstorming is not about making decisions, it is about gathering ideas. There are often times when gathering ideas needs much more consideration than one meeting will allow. Extending the process over more than one meeting may mean that accurate information can be collected and people can have time and space to think about other ideas.

━━━━━━━━ BOX 14.3 ━━━━━━━━

Brainstorming at IDEO: Sutton and Hargadon (1996)

The process of brainstorming was first developed by Osborn in 1957 in a text called 'Applied Imagination', and involved adherence to four 'rules':

1. Come up with as many ideas as you can.
2. Do not criticise one another's ideas.
3. Free-wheel and share wild ideas.
4. Expand and elaborate on existing ideas.

Over time, many have criticised the idea of brainstorming as ineffective and inefficient. Researchers have argued that on their own and outside of meetings, individuals have developed more ideas than has ever been the case when discussions have taken place in groups. One suggestion is that designers and others can develop more ideas - or contributions to ideas - without being hindered by the complex psychology that can affect individuals' generation of ideas in a face-to-face meeting, and research has been done looking at

(Continued)

electronic brainstorming, where communication is less personal and where people can 'talk over each other' (i.e. send messages at the same time) without feeling that they are being disrespectful. There are also views around brainstorming being ineffective because individuals are apprehensive about giving 'weird' ideas, and that individuals can be seen as free-riding.

However, two researchers at Stanford - Sutton and Hargadon (1996) - spent time looking at how one of the world's leading creative design consultancies, IDEO, has been so successful in using brainstorming as a technique for developing creative design solutions. Their central argument was that counting the number of ideas generated through brainstorming as a measure of efficiency is too narrow a perspective, and that it can be used very effectively.

The case study evidence seemed to suggest that earlier research into brainstorming did not look at: 1) how teams were developed, 2) what training was given to those engaging in this activity, 3) the knowledge base of participants (and therefore the composition of teams), and 4) how teams were facilitated. It is likely that change in just one of these things is unlikely to suddenly change the productivity of a brainstorming meeting, but in their research the two authors suggested that IDEO seemed to operate brainstorming processes a little differently from conventional wisdom:

1. Most designers were involved in between 4-80 brainstorm meetings a year, lasting between 45 and 120 minutes.
2. The emphasis on the meetings was fun, with practical examples being played with and, in one case, designers being taken onto the roof of a building to experience what it was like to cast a fishing rod.
3. Members of a brainstorm meeting would often come from different, unrelated projects, bringing fresh ideas.
4. Facilitation would be based on inspiration and positive comments from both members of the team and any clients who would attend the meetings.
5. Selection processes for designers would be based on the extent to which they were 'like-minded' in their enjoyment of the creative processes (and those who joined few brainstorm meetings would be likely to leave).
6. The benefits of the brainstorming process went far beyond measuring the 'number of ideas', and extended into examining company culture, revenue related to client satisfaction, the development of wisdom and a need to seek more knowledge, internal competitiveness among staff, and a growth in personal skill and well-being.

Ultimately, if the way that creative companies such as IDEO can do brainstorming leads to increased revenue, then there must be something of benefit in the process: they would not do it if it did not help the organisation. The challenge is probably that IDEO sees the process as integral to the future of the company and puts significant effort into developing the facilitation and team-based skills that make this process work: that is not always the case in every organisation.

 'BUT I HAVE A QUESTION ...'

... If brainstorming has so many faults and problems and only seems to work in organisations that provide a lot of support, then how can I use this in my life as a student when a team I am working with only has one semester to do its work?

It is a good question. The time pressure can make brainstorming less effective and can also affect creativity generally. So here are some tips to improve the quality of your brainstorming:

1. Make a commitment as a group to accept all ideas, but to acknowledge that those of any one individual - including yourself - might not be the best. This requires some maturity and the ability to think above your own interests, however tough this might be.

2. Any feedback you give should look to 'take ideas' forward. That means that any feedback is constructively given and should look at how poorer ideas might be worked on more, rather than discounted completely.

3. Ensure that someone is skilled at expressing emotional ideas in a non-confrontational way, summarising comments and ideas, and that you have someone who can keep your ideas focused on the problem you are trying to address. It would also be good to have someone who can reflect comments such as 'What X means is ...' in a way that builds rather than damages relationships in the group.

4. Record all ideas on a flipchart or online equivalent (such as Padlet). Note the challenges with each idea as well as giving sufficient detail around the ideas that have potential. Challenges can be overcome with thought and effort and sometimes the ideas that do not work best initially can become those that eventually work with a bit of effort.

It does not take a long time to establish an atmosphere of cooperation and sometimes even excitement about a task, so brainstorming can be done without some of the pitfalls noted above.

Examining Past Experience

The great thing about some problems is that either we have solved the same issue previously, or someone else has probably experienced the same problem before and has found a way of solving it. It is extremely tempting to assume immediately that a solution tried and tested previously is going to work for you – or that what worked last time will work again. There is often a sense of 'Yes! That will work ...' when we find that someone else has developed a solution for the same problem that we are examining, but we do need to exercise a little caution and perhaps ask questions such as these:

- Is our situation exactly the same as the one experienced before?
- Has anything changed in terms of the timing of our problem compared with that previously?
- Are the people involved this time likely to react in the same way?
- Are the resources we have access to the same as those we had before?

Adopting others' solutions – or adapting them to fit our own circumstances – is a common approach. It is why managers seek to learn from others. There is little wrong in learning and trying a solution that others have found works for them. The list of potential resources includes professional magazines and academic journals (e.g. *Harvard Business Review, Administrative Science Quarterly*), case study information, attending public training courses and conferences, networking events, news articles and senior staff who have some institutional memory. The pace of change – certainly technological change – has meant that solutions that others have adopted may have a limited lifespan, and simply uncritically adopting any of these without thinking through what they can and cannot contribute will likely cause problems.

De Bono's Thinking Hats

In discussing solutions to a particular issue, we might struggle to find a way both to identify innovative solutions (if indeed innovative solutions are needed) or to evaluate those ideas we have previously developed. In the early 1970s, Edward De Bono (1971) developed a technique using six different ways to engage individuals with solutions to issues, and to assist them to develop new ideas. One stimulus to the development of this model was the lack of satisfaction with a binary (agree or disagree) model of evaluating ideas – something which changed considerably with the development of the 'six hats', with each hat representing a different approach to ideas, where individuals put on and take off different hats in order to indicate the role that they wish to undertake during a discussion.

White Hat: Gives facts, information and logical argument. The wearer might say, 'Let's look at the facts/data'.

Red Hat: Allows for the expression of emotion and intuition. It allows the wearer to be open about their feelings. The wearer might say, 'I feel that this is a really bad idea' or 'I am uncomfortable with this possibility'.

Black Hat: Enables the wearer to discuss the disadvantages of ideas but only in a logical manner, based on policy, resources or experience. The wearer might say, 'I can't see this working because it would use too many resources'.

Yellow Hat: This hat is all about encouragement and finding reasons why a suggestion will work, or adding value to an idea already presented. It looks forward to the results of actions already proposed. The wearer might say, 'I think this is a really good idea: it fits all the requirements we need'.

Green Hat: Encourages the individual to look at things in a different way, ignoring assumptions and developing creative and lateral ideas. The wearer might say, 'This is not working for me. Maybe we should look at this from a different perspective'.

Blue Hat: Looks at the general management of the overall thinking and discussing process. The wearer might say, 'I think we have done well so far. I think we need more time for green hat thinking'.

No one person should wear one hat all the time, and if the blue hat wearer (or anyone else) suggests it, then someone can be asked to wear a different hat. Alternatively, an entire group might be asked to wear a particular hat for a period of time – or none. There is no prescribed sequence of wearing the hats and the tool is not designed to produce creativity, but rather to give time and space in which individuals might produce more creative ideas.

 'BUT I HAVE A QUESTION ...'

... I have read that some people are just naturally more open to ideas than others – a personality attribute called 'Openness' – so doesn't that make some people more creative than others or make it difficult for some people to wear different hats?

Well, some people have strengths in terms of their logic and other people have strengths in terms of their ability to develop new ways of thinking, but that does not mean that people cannot develop certain skills and cannot change the way they are used to behaving. In some cases, we have different levels of different abilities, and that can help us to facilitate discussion in other ways. What De Bono's method brings us is an ability to be part of a discussion which develops ideas in what is arguably a more interesting way than methods discussed elsewhere.

Analogies and Metaphors

What you know of how the world operates can be used very effectively to develop analogies and representations of problems from very different angles – some refer to this as a process where we make the 'strange familiar' or the 'unfamiliar strange'. These analogies may come from nature, from other activities we undertake, from other forms of relationship, from sport, and so on, but the idea is that we take the situation we are facing and use an analogy to see the problem in a different way, without the constraints of one view of the problem. The better analogies are those where there is no close relationship between the real situation and the picture we are creating in our mind, but they are also used more effectively where we are very familiar with both situations and are clear about the elements – verbs and items (or nouns) – present in our pictorial representations of the real situation.

Let's imagine for a moment that we have a problem in our organisation. We need to increase the amount of creativity we are seeing, but we are uncertain of how we can do that, so we think about the assumptions we are making and ask ourselves a number of questions. We could assume, for example, that everyone has some creative talent that they wish to use and, therefore, the issue is how to *release* that talent.

So, let's take an analogy with the following elements: a pan with a lid being heated on a gas stove, where we are boiling some water to cook some vegetables, and we wish to let the steam escape (to *release* the steam).

What might those elements represent? The pan could be the individual, the boiling water could be the ability to be creative, the steam could be the explicit demonstration of that creativity, the lid could be the constraints and the heated gas under the pan could be the motivation and incentives (we can forget about the vegetables for now).

Bearing in mind this analogy, *how are we representing the problem?* We would like to see how we can heat the water faster so as to allow more steam to escape from the pan more easily.

At this point, we can ask one more question about the analogy as a way of facilitating the generation of ideas. If we wanted to heat the water so that we had more steam escaping more quickly, what could we change? Some ideas that we would naturally think of might be to:

- Add some salt so that the water heats up more quickly.
- Remove the lid to allow more steam to escape.
- Stir the water to ensure that the gas is heating all the water equally.
- Turn up the heat under the pan.
- Put less water in the pan so that the water heats up more quickly.

The final step here is to reinterpret these solutions in the real situation – to 'de-analogise' the situation, if you like – and, in doing so, we may find that the ideas do not always fit. This is fine, because an analogy is just that – it is not intended to be a 100% accurate representation of the real situation – and, in fact, in presenting representations that do not reflect reality, we may find additional ideas that we would not have otherwise identified. (The only thing that can be 100% accurate is the situation itself.) Looking at the example above, we could reinterpret the five ideas above as follows:

Add some salt so that the water heats up more quickly	Add something - training, mentoring, incentives, conferences - to the organisation or the individual to increase their creativity
Remove the lid to allow more steam to escape	Try to identify and remove any barriers to creativity
Stir the water to ensure that the gas is heating all the water equally	Create situations where individuals are mixing - or are being mixed - with other individuals to create more creativity The additional question then becomes: 'What are we using to stir the water? Would stirring the water with different items - spoon, fork, large spoon, small spoon, etc. - make this idea more or less effective?
Turn up the heat under the pan	Stimulate creativity, in different ways. Perhaps, create different or more incentives for individuals to be creative, perhaps make creativity more explicit as an organisational objective
Put less water in the pan so that the water heats up more quickly	This would work for the analogy (pan heating water), but would not work in a situation where we represent individuals with less creativity (i.e. less water) producing more creative outcomes (i.e. more steam), so the analogy falls down here, but that is OK

As in the example above, some solutions do not seem to work, but most people would argue that it is better to have more ideas than less, and we can always discard them later on when deciding which solution(s) to implement. However, if an analogy does not work or 're-translate' well back into the specifics of the real-life situation, then we could always ask the question, 'Is there a way of making the solution in the analogy work better?' Using the last solution proposed in the analogy above, this might mean *replacing* the water with something else which heats up faster and produces more steam than water, or, translating this back, *replacing* the individuals in the team or the organisation with more creative individuals.

Note that the verb used here, namely 'replace', is used in both the analogy *and* the real-life example. One of the great things about using an analogy to manipulate (or 'reorganise') the imaginary situation is that you can change the verbs *and* the nouns in the analogy, or vice versa. Taking the example above, our thoughts might go like this:

> We might decide that we can stir the water – i.e. stir up or stimulate creativity – in various ways, but could we replace the word 'stir' with something else – e.g. 'divide'? Well, we can't 'divide water', so is there a better analogy that we could use? Maybe we should use something other than a pan holding water as an analogy? Translating this back: of course, our knowledge about creativity would tell us that division rarely enhances creativity (or indeed many things), so maybe the analogy we are using is fine.

 REFLECTION POINT

Take some time to think about the following questions and write down some answers.

If you were to use any of the above processes for increasing creativity, which would you be most likely to use first – or not at all?

If you did use such methods to identify potential solutions, what would be your criteria for evaluating success?

Analogies and metaphors represent a progressive series of thoughts and questions which can arise when we start to use the familiar to represent unfamiliar problems we are struggling to solve. We can see that by following the process above – thinking of an analogy, identifying the different items in the analogy and then manipulating the analogy – we can start to define problems in very different ways, and by 're-translating' the example, we can actually identify further questions which might help us further. It is the *ability and freedom to ask questions* which can lead us to develop some solutions we might not have thought about before. Having a *working knowledge of the issues* is vital for the re-interpretation of the analogy: without that knowledge, it is not possible to play around with mental images of relevant concepts and issues (nor would we know what is and is not relevant).

 FOR YOU TO DO

Look at the problems given below. What kinds of analogies might be used to represent them?

1. The production line keeps slowing down because the operators work at different times. Is there a way of enabling the production line to move at a constant pace?

2. There is a series of personal arguments going on between two senior managers, both of whom have the same amount of power and neither of whom are being entirely truthful. How might you stop this conflict?
3. An individual in your company is very traditional and feels more comfortable with old processes than new ones, even if the individual knows that the old ones are inefficient. How might you convince this individual to try the new ones?

There are no right or wrong analogies for any of these, but as you explore how they might be used, you might find that you change your analogies to fit the situation more closely.

Reverse the Definition

Understanding how all the elements in an issue come together to form a problem can help us to expand our range of potential solutions, but by deconstructing the problem and recognising those linked but separate elements, we can often develop solutions which seem insightful and original. Key to being able to do so is the recognition of the verbs, adjectives and nouns we are using. The clearest example of this kind of situation was when one well-known car producer needed to increase car production greatly in order to keep up with demand in the United States in the early 1900s. Cars were made by teams of employees working together and each car took a while to build. Once one was built, the team moved around the factory to build the next one.

We can state that the problem was, 'How to get the teams to work faster to meet demand by moving from one car to the next more effectively?' Immediately, some clear solutions come to mind:

1. Increase efficiency by decreasing rejection rates and increasing quality.
2. Decrease the size of factory so that the teams do not have to move too far.
3. Subcontract production to other car producers.
4. Improve the training given to the teams.
5. Increase the number of teams working in any one factory.

All of these might well have the impact of increasing car production, but of course there would be a cost to pay. Buying a new factory would incur significant financial investment and ongoing rental payments, increased numbers of employees would need training in complex skills quickly, and efficiency could only be increased so much: the stronger the demand for faster production, the more likely efficiency would decrease, not increase.

Examining the nouns and verbs used in the definition of the problem above gives us:

- Teams
- Work
- Faster
- Move
- Car

The words 'meet' and 'demand' might also have some impact here, except that they refer to the outcome of the problem, not the problem itself. In the same way, it is not helpful to consider adverbs (e.g. 'more effectively') since they describe how well something might be done, and again refer to the intended outcome rather than the inputs to produce such outcomes and so cannot really be changed.

Using the idea of 'reverse definition', we could ask, 'How might we view the problem if we changed any of these words?' If we changed the word 'team' to 'individual', how might that impact on our perception of the problem – likewise, for 'fast' and 'to work'? 'How might limiting the 'movement' of the teams in some way help us to deliver our outcome? Are there parts of the 'car' that we can change or remove so that we can speed up the process?'

Asking such questions might suggest to us that maybe the words 'more effectively' are better than 'faster', and perhaps we might develop proposals that refer to improving the team work rather than anything else. Alternatively, we might consider the nature of the 'work' itself, and enable the teams to work in a different way, or not at all.

In this real-life example, the problem was viewed as simplistically as this: 'The team built and then moved the car before starting on the next one'. Instead, the production process could be done by individuals working on small elements of the work and the car could be moved rather than the team. As a result, Henry Ford developed the world's first production line, and the car production revolution began.

Physical and Practical 'Play'

Being creative can be great fun, but enabling senior managers to play with ideas can sometimes be a challenge. Senior managers can sometimes appear to believe that they are expected to keep their sense of fun hidden. With the right encouragement or facilitation, however, most people can be encouraged to let the more child-like side of their personality emerge for others to see.

Our ability to play with ideas and allow ourselves to see possibilities that we had not thought about before can be enhanced by aspects of physical play, especially in terms of using our hands to create new representations of reality. Two tools that are used in childhood have perhaps surprising applications in management, namely Lego® and Playdough®. Both come in different colours, and blocks of Lego come in different sizes, shapes and configurations. Each characteristic (size, shape, colour) can be used to represent different aspects of mental concepts and physical realities, so creating and recreating those realities can enable new possibilities to be established. In the same way, Playdough can be used in a very flexible way to allow individuals to create items which are not constrained by being forced into particular shapes (perhaps representing organisational rules).

Management consultants can sometimes use such tools to enable individuals to come up with ideas that they had not thought about before. In the same way that analogies and metaphors can enable certain aspects of life to represent particular elements of managerial problems, so, too, can 'physical analogies' such as Lego be used to represent particular aspects of organisational life (Image 14.1). They have the advantage that they can be used in different ways, without any processes limiting what would otherwise be seen as difficult or challenging, so that an innovative solution can be developed and further problem solving can be done subsequently to reduce any implementation difficulties.

A typical session using Lego or Playdough would begin with a warm-up exercise, to enable participants to feel comfortable about engaging in something playful. In many cases (unless participants have children who enjoy playing with such toys), it will have been quite a long time since these adults engaged in something considered playful. Some individuals will relish the experience, while others will struggle to relax and reveal that aspect of their behaviour which is more child-like.

Once participants are comfortable with the idea of engaging in some playful activity, the facilitator will usually explain how the 'toys' can be used to represent certain aspects of whatever problem or issue is being dealt with. This may require a little demonstration, but the facilitator will need to consider carefully how much they use the toys themselves to demonstrate the process: too much and the participants may limit the extent to which they allow themselves to think freely about the issue; too little and the exercise might not work because the participants may not understand how the toys could be used to represent reality.

The third stage is to give sufficient space and time for the participants to play with the toys, to discuss with each other the potential consequences and outcomes of constructing realities in various ways, and then finally – as the fourth stage – participants may have some fun looking at each other's creations (animals, structures, buildings, etc.) while someone explains how they went about creating what they have created and why.

Enabling a sense of play is an important aspect of facilitating creativity. Most people enjoy being a little child-like and having some fun, and if that enjoyment can lead to the development of innovative solutions, then the activity will have served a number of purposes.

Image 14.1   Managers on a training course using Lego® to build representations of their organisation

═══════ FOR YOU TO DO ═══════

Make a list of all the simple games and exercises you have ever done which you might consider 'play'.

Students from some cultures might find it easier to build this list than others, but here are some simple suggestions to start you going:

- Scavenger hunt.
- Two truths and a lie.
- Move from one side of the room to the other without using the same method that anyone else has used.
- Go around the circle remembering everyone else's names (or some other information) by repeating them every time.

Establishing a sense of play does not in itself produce creativity, but it enables everyone to be relaxed and that may produce the creativity you are seeking.

Concept Mapping

This method of developing creative ideas and solutions derives from activities undertaken to define the problem. By clarifying the characteristics of the problem, the range of potential solutions can be increased considerably.

Let's take a brief example. We wish to increase the efficiency of a manufacturing process. Without breaking down the problem, we might seek to reduce waste, change the machinery or train the employees. However, by examining each aspect of the manufacturing process, we can identify many more alternatives. At a more abstract level, we could ask individuals to find as many uses as possible for a paper clip. Suggestions might be a hook, an earring or a pendant for a necklace, but if we were to recognise explicitly the qualities of the issue at hand – that the paper clip is metal, extremely flexible, small and easy to carry – then it might remind those trying to find ideas of other items which have some of the same characteristics.

We could do this by a process known as concept mapping. Concept mapping is a way of representing knowledge which gradually develops understanding. In a group, this can be seen as a similar process to that of brainstorming, but it enables individuals to address issues and ideas in turn. Relationships between the ideas and concepts discussed are seen as 'relating to' other concepts in terms of items which:

- cause
- require, or
- contribute to

other processes and concepts. The key difference between this form of brainstorming and that of mind-mapping is in terms of the focus on relationships between different concepts. We have previously identified that one aspect of creativity relates to reorganising information and relationships between concepts and ideas. Concept mapping provides a way to do so which can be shared beyond the single individual by using others' knowledge to extend gradually the number of ideas involved in building a model of how 'things work'. Figure 14.3 provides an incomplete representation of a number of ideas relating to human performance in the workplace, and the next 'For You to Do' section below asks you to consider some questions to complete the concept map.

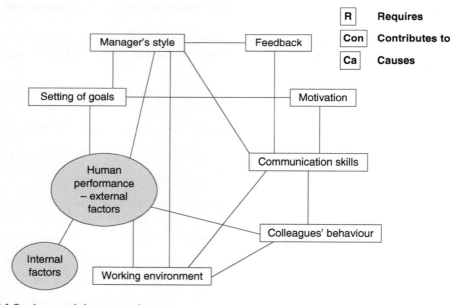

Figure 14.3   Incomplete concept map

 FOR YOU TO DO

The concept map in the figure was constructed in order to help a manager improve the performance of one of their employees. It shows how some ideas relate to each other and to understanding human performance. You need to complete the diagram and help the manager identify potential solutions, by:

1. Identifying the relationships (requires - R, causes - CA, contributes to - Con) between the ideas shown by writing 'R', 'Ca' and 'Con' respectively along the line between the two items which have some relationship.
2. Extending the diagram to include internal (e.g. personality, intelligence, etc.) factors which might affect performance.
3. Rearranging the diagram to indicate which relationships are close/strong and which are distant/weak; those which are close should represent items that are physically close in the diagram.

Question 3 should help prioritise the likely solutions to the problem.

The above example shows the importance of knowledge in the creativity process. It would be nearly impossible to complete the diagram without an understanding of how the various ideas might link together.

Enhancing Our Own Creative Abilities

There may be times when we do not necessarily have a problem that we need to solve creatively and so we may be tempted to ignore our natural creative abilities, but the more we get used to using them on a day-to-day basis, the more likely we will be to recognise the abilities we have and use them when we really need to.

Whetten and Cameron (2011) provide some useful ideas that we can use to enhance our own creativity on an ongoing basis:

1. **Discuss ideas with others**: Clearly, if two or more individuals share the same knowledge, abilities and motivation to be creative, then discussing a problem with others can lead to a larger number of creative ideas.
2. **Give ourselves time**: Being busy is the enemy of creativity: to be creative and just to think without worrying about any restrictions is also important. Relaxation time can lead to daydreaming, and while in lectures daydreaming is not encouraged, doing so when thinking about problems or issues that you are facing can enhance the chance of coming up with a new solution or idea.
3. **Seek a relaxing place**: Finding a place to think is important for a similar reason: it removes us from the pressures and busy-ness of life and enables us to reconceptualise or reorganise the relevant ideas and facts.
4. **Read something new**: Reading something interesting and outside of your own area(s) of interest can build up knowledge of how different processes work, and can help in two ways: 1) it can enable the development of different metaphors and analogies around the new topics; and 2) it can stimulate interest in new topics and new ideas.
5. **Remove yourself from barriers**: Examining how creativity can be blocked can help us to recognise where those barriers might be affecting our own creativity. The implication is that, where possible, we remove ourselves from those barriers. This might include giving ourselves time to think and removing ourselves from others who restrict our creativity with comments such as 'That will never work' or 'I'm not sure why you're really bothering – we've tried that before and it will never work.'

There are many ways in which we can 'become' more creative. In reality, some of these ideas are about releasing our latent abilities, which are rarely used for a variety of reasons. Learning to play with information and concepts, having fun and releasing ourselves to enjoy developing creative ideas are key parts of most jobs, even if we do not realise it.

— KEY LEARNING POINT ▬▬▬▬▬▬▬

We can learn to apply our creativity to problem solving by using various tools and techniques. Not all tools can be used by all people, but most people can demonstrate creativity in some way, if they are given the chance.

BLOCKAGES AND BARRIERS TO CREATIVITY

When we think about our behaviour, there are always a number of issues which can influence our ability to do, or feel like doing, certain things. Some issues will prevent us from undertaking what we wish or need to at the quality we would like, while other issues will act as enablers. When it comes to creativity, the same principle applies: there are certain factors – some within ourselves (e.g. attitudes, abilities, etc.) and some imposed on us by others – which can help or hinder the development and demonstration of our creativeness. In reality, we may well have the ability to be far more creative than we believe – we just need to 'let it out'. The content below is intended to help us understand more about how to do that.

We can think systematically about blockages in terms of the three elements needed for creative activity to take place, which we identified at the start of the chapter, namely knowledge, creative ability and motivation.

Pressure

Pushing people to be creative in ways that they are not skilled at doing is not going to produce creative outcomes. (In fact, pushing people to demonstrate any skill that they are not able to do is not going to produce a positive outcome.) Winstanley (2005: 62) stated that: 'The more you try to think about solving a problem, the less likely you will be to develop a solution.' The issue is particularly pertinent, however, with *requiring* people to be creative (rather than selecting people who naturally *are* creative) since giving people time and space to think is one of the ways in which creativity can be enhanced. Removing that time and space but requiring people to be more creative are typically very contradictory intentions.

Conceptual Blocks

Conceptual blocks can come in a great many forms, but they all share one outcome: that thinking becomes constrained. At one level, we could argue that someone's openness to something or someone new could be limited simply by their stereotyped impressions of that situation or individual, or their bias against a particular department's 'apparently' political agenda.

🧩 CONCEPTUAL BLOCK

A conceptual block is any way of thinking that prevents us from being open to new possibilities.

When it comes to problem solving, we have also recognised that the way we define a problem has a significant impact on our ability to generate creative solutions. We could think about a failure to ask questions, assuming that present problems are very similar to past problems, or anything that constrains us from having an open mind. Nowhere does this become more apparent than in police investigations, where having a closed mind in relation to searching for evidence or lines of enquiry can mean that homicides are not solved as quickly as they could be.

Take some time to think about the following questions and write down some answers.

In the problems you have to solve, do you ever constrain your own thinking, or that of other people, by making certain assumptions?

Do others do this to you?

How willing are you to challenge your own and others' conceptual blocks?

One conceptual block that does limit individuals on occasion is the belief that they are not, and cannot be, creative. Few researchers in this area would agree, suggesting that individuals do not get much opportunity to exhibit creativity or to play around with ideas. What does seem to be apparent, of course, is that people are creative in different ways, and that the different forms of creativity are equally important.

Motivation, Emotions and Behaviour

There may be any number of reasons why someone does not want to be creative. They may not feel comfortable playing and take the view that anything which is 'fun' cannot be seen as 'work'.

There are others who may just not want to be creative and are more content with situations as they are, rather than changing anything. This can occasionally be satisfactory in the situation where nothing in the external or internal environment is changing, but rapid changes in technology, politics and society in general mean that such situations are now very rare.

Lack of Appropriate Knowledge

Knowledge, as we have seen earlier, is required for solving problems creatively. It therefore follows that a lack of expertise in particular subject domains can significantly impact on an individual's ability to generate creative options, or to ensure that the definition of the problem is sufficiently broad to allow for a variety of views. Imagine a car mechanic trying to determine why a car will not start without having an understanding of how a car engine works.

The good news on this issue is that knowledge is not that difficult to obtain, and while there is an obvious need to ensure a good awareness of how particular knowledge might fit a particular situation, a willingness to search for knowledge is usually a good thing anyway.

Many people have blockages to creativity, but they can be overcome. Those who develop creative ideas have often worked out ways of overcoming these blockages.

INTEGRATION AND APPLICATION

As we have seen, most problem solving can be broken down into a series of relevant questions.

1. **Is this a new problem?** Problems that we have encountered before and where solutions are relatively easy to develop and identify can be said to need less creativity than those that are new, so the first question that managers need to be able to answer is whether it is a new problem or a problem that has been faced previously. In making such a decision, any manager will need to take care to ensure that they are actually facing the same problem: the question is not always an easy one to answer.

2. **If this is a new problem, what can we do to solve it?** If it seems to be a new problem, then the first two stages of the problem-solving process (defining the problem and generating alternatives) can become very different. A sense of fun, creativity and the use of a range of techniques can be employed to solve the issue in an innovative way.

3. **What can we do to ensure there are no blockages to enabling individuals' creativity?** We need to be careful that we are not limiting the creativity of ourselves and others by putting up or maintaining inappropriate barriers. Make sure you keep an open mind and maintain it in others.

CONCLUSION

You should now have a good idea of how to:

*   Follow both rational and creative problem-solving processes.
*   Describe the key components of creativity.
*   Develop and enhance your creativity.
*   Recognise blockages to creativity in yourself and in others.

Becoming more creative is often as much about allowing yourself the freedom to come up with strange and weird ideas as it is about actually having the appropriate abilities in the first place. This chapter should have gone some way towards helping you to engage in creative activities and creative problem solving, and to see how such activities can be fun.

We still need to address the questions asked at the beginning of this chapter.

The first question, 'What is the maximum number of dates a guy or girl could have in a month?' can be answered in three ways. Some people will interpret 'date' as a meeting between two people who are attracted to each other, others as an event on a calendar, and finally a third would be the fruit, typically from the Middle East. The second is probably the most likely interpretation – i.e. the maximum dates in a month (1st, 2nd, 3rd, 4th and so on) – so the answer is 31 or 30, though February has 28 or 29, of course. This is the only really quantifiable number here, but the wording of the question uses a homonym (like 'desert' or letter') and has several meanings, and the use of 'guy' and 'girl' in the question might lead a reader to assume the meaning is of two people meeting up.

The second question was a riddle, where the idea is the same – using language to create assumptions that then become contradictory or challenging to make sense of: 'The adrenalin suddenly kicked in. He heard the gun and ran. As fast as he could, away from the others. Fast, and with speed, pushing forward in case they reached him. For what was two kilometres, he ran. He didn't try to stop. He didn't try to hide. He saw the guy with the gun and went past him five times. How can you explain this?' The answer is that the guy was in a running race, and the gun was the starting gun, fired at the start of the race – 2000 meters means that the runners on a 400m track would go past the starting point five times. However, the style of writing implied a criminal activity was underway and so our interpretations are all based around that idea. Did you get it right?

CHAPTER TASK

Look at the ideas given in this chapter about enhancing your creativity and ability to solve problems, even if they are not current problems. Next, look at the business and popular press to find stories about how organisations and individuals have been creative and innovative in what they have done.

Which of the ideas given in this chapter seem to have been used most often? Why?

INTERVIEW QUESTIONS

In nearly all cases, the questions in previous chapters have only been about determining your skills and abilities in certain areas. Being creative is something most people enjoy a great deal and can enhance your problem-solving skills, which are necessary in the workplace. So showing you can be creative is something that will get you ahead in the chance to get that job.

Think about the following questions. What might your answers be?

1. Tell me about a time when you solved a problem that others were struggling to solve.
2. How would you go about finding a new way of delivering one of our services? (Or 'a new use for one of our products?', if the company is a manufacturing company.)
3. Imagine a situation where you – as a departmental manager – needed to resolve a cash flow problem quickly. How might you go about it?

Chapter 17 gives a lot more information on selection interviews and the online content gives some guidance on these questions.

ADDITIONAL RESOURCES

Want to learn more? Visit https://study.sagepub.com/morgan2e to gain access to a wide range of online resources, including interactive tests, tasks, further reading and downloads.

Website Resources

The following websites offer useful advice on problem solving and creativity.

Creative Education Foundation: www.creativeeducationfoundation.org/creative-problem-solving/

TED Talks – Creativity: www.ted.com/topics/creativity

University of Kent – IDEAL model of problem-solving: www.kent.ac.uk/ces/student/skills.html?tab=problemsolving-and-analytical-skills

Textbook Resources

Cameron, S. (2016) *The Business Student's Handbook: Skills for Study and Employment* (6th edition). Harlow: Pearson (particularly Chapter 12).

Cottrell, S. (2010) *Skills for Success* (2nd edition). New York: Palgrave (particularly Chapter 7).

Gallagher, K. (2016) *Essential Study and Employment Skills for Business and Management Students* (3rd edition). Oxford: Oxford University Press (particularly Chapter 12).

Hamilton, C. and Kroll, T. L. (2018) *Communicating for Results* (11th edition). Boston, MA: Cengage (particularly Chapter 9).

Puccio, G. J., Mance, M. and Murdock, M. C. (2011) *Creative Leadership: Skills that Drive Change* (2nd edition). Thousand Oaks, CA: Sage.

PART V

UNDERSTANDING EMPLOYEE SELECTION

If you can hire people whose passion intersects with the job, they won't require any supervision at all. They will manage themselves better than anyone could ever manage them. Their fire comes from within, not from without. Their motivation is internal, not external. (Stephen Covey)

THE FIRST DAY ... OF THE REST OF YOUR LIFE

It is common to believe that your career begins when you leave university and enter employment for the first time. But as we have discussed in this book, throughout your time at university, you will have been learning skills and developing your ideas on how the world operates. So whether you enter employment using the knowledge you have learned, and/or the skills you have developed, you will have started your career on the first day of university. If you are studying a postgraduate course, then you will already be well on your way. You start learning knowledge and developing your skills through the experiences you gain from your degree programme. It is too late to start doing that in your final year when you are thinking about the jobs that you could apply for, but it is towards the end of your time at university that the importance of the skills you have developed becomes very clear.

This final part of the book is somewhat different from Parts I–III, which were largely about university study, and Part IV, which was about developing skills for employability (and life in general). This part is not so much about developing skills as it is about developing awareness – an awareness of the selection processes used by employers and an understanding of what lies ahead of you after graduation. If a graduate job is not something you are sure you wish to commit to just yet, then this part also addresses other options for you to consider.

This part will largely focus on selection methods used at graduate level (i.e. what you need to know when applying for jobs with some responsibility) but the same principles will probably apply for voluntary internships, part-time work and work placements undertaken as part of a degree course. The main differences between these areas will be the extent to which resources are devoted to the selection process, since the status of the job will usually be linked to the resources applied to finding the 'best' candidate.

Chapter 15 will begin by taking a look at how employers select their graduates, and then cover a range of components of the process in the order that they would typically occur in a graduate selection process. Chapter 16 examines applications, that is CVs, covering letters and application forms, and then, if successful at the application, a candidate would then expect to attend a selection interview (Chapter 17). The final chapter (Chapter 18) provides a conclusion to the book, giving some ways in which others have developed and used their university experiences and skills to develop their own careers and life.

There are two additional chapters available on the companion website which could prove very useful. The first concerns psychometric tests and assessment centres, and finally, the second provides some ideas for additional options after graduation, such as setting up your own business, taking a gap year and further study (MSc or PhD studies).

The chapters will focus on giving specific guidance, taking the view that you might be either applying for jobs or considering what to do after graduation. Each chapter will set out specific ideas, provide you with reflective questions and exercises to work through and include answers to questions which might occur to you; there are no skills assessments in these chapters.

It is true to say that there is a wealth of information and guidance available from AGCAS (Association of Graduate Careers Services, Prospects) and from a very wide range of other organisations, including your own university. You will almost certainly be able to make an appointment at your own careers service to help you find your way through what is available.

It would be good, however, to deal with some limitations of a text like this.

WILL YOU HELP ME CHOOSE MY CAREER?

The simple answer is 'no'. What these chapters will not do – as much as you might wish them to – is to cover in detail the important issue of 'What should I do? What kind of job should I go for?' There are some principles to consider and to some extent your degree title *could* limit your options, but this is unusual. Choosing a career is as much about you and your personality and motivation as it is about the skills you have, and this needs careful discussion with someone at your careers services. The earlier you do this in your university career, the better.

Degree subjects (and your university school or department) are generally classified into groups or faculties. You might be studying business or politics or sociology. If so, then you are studying what is called a 'social science', designed to develop interpersonal (interacting with others) and intrapersonal (making yourself more effective) skills, a broad range of knowledge relevant to your subject and critical thinking skills. If you contrast these with someone studying engineering or medicine, then technical knowledge becomes the priority (most people would rather have a doctor with poor interpersonal skills but a great knowledge of medical treatment than the other way around, although both would be helpful of course). Someone studying law needs to have an excellent background in whatever area of law they practise, but someone studying a social science could move into any one of a number of career areas. In other words, a social science degree (politics, history, sociology, psychology, marketing, business, HRM, economics and other subjects) gives you the critical thinking skills you need to take you into a leadership role and your specific knowledge becomes less important. The subject you are studying at university does *not* need to limit your choice of career.

This does not mean, however, that the knowledge that you learn is not important: it is very important. In times of economic recession or when companies are selecting fewer graduates, companies do use the degree subject as a way of 'screening out' applicants that they would need to train as opposed to those who already possess the relevant knowledge.

Having noted that the degree subject is not always the main issue in choosing a career, you might need to think about what you are interested in. Your careers services will have access to a number of tools designed to help you identify the characteristics of things that you are interested in. At a basic level, this might be something as simple as 'Do you prefer logical and structured activities and hobbies or unstructured ones where you can be more creative?', and they will match those to what is known about certain career and job types.

There is one thing that is vitally important and which has been stressed throughout the earlier chapters: academic success in your degree is going to be a very significant factor in your being able to get the future you want, but it is not the only factor. To an employer, a student who has a first-class degree in philosophy but no leadership or work experience or no involvement in social activities is more likely to be overlooked for a graduate role than one who has a lesser degree (e.g. 2:1 or 2:2, more rarely a 3rd class), but leadership experience in a student society and some work experience. It is about balance, and employers are looking for competent and able individuals who are critical thinkers, analytical and able to use their communication and interpersonal skills to work well with others. This means that your working career starts on day one of your university studies – and your choices made during the start of your time at university *can have* a significant impact on your employability at the end of it.

In previous parts of this text, the chapters have included interview questions relating to the abilities covered in each chapter. Of course, this is not relevant to the chapters in this part of the book, but Chapter 17 does present a review of each of these questions and gives some guidance. Regardless, each of the following chapters should enable you to develop some understanding of how to give yourself a good chance of at least getting through to an interview.

15 UNDERSTANDING EMPLOYEE SELECTION

Hiring the right people takes time, the right questions and a healthy dose of curiosity. What do you think is the most important factor when building your team? For us, it's personality. (Richard Branson)

CHAPTER STRUCTURE

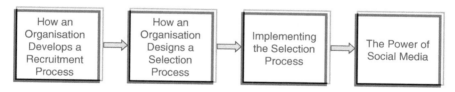

Figure 15.1

When you see the this means go to the companion website https://study.sagepub.com/morgan2e to do a quiz, complete a task, read further or download a template.

━━ AIMS OF THE CHAPTER ━━

By the end of this chapter, you should be able to:

- Understand how employers view the recruitment and selection processes.
- Describe how employers select and use different selection tools.
- Identify the qualities needed in different kinds of roles.
- Understand how your studies and other experiences have helped you to develop these qualities.
- Use social media appropriately to enhance your image to employers.

WHEN SHOULD YOU READ THIS CHAPTER?

This chapter addresses the basics of graduate selection, and so it is best to read this during the first four or five weeks of your final year at university.

RECRUITMENT

Recruitment is the process of identifying a number of applicants who are willing to apply for a particular job or training programme.

SELECTION

Selection is the process of comparing information from the applicants with the requirements as specified in the advertisement, and selecting those who meet the essential requirements to move forward in the selection process.

INTRODUCTION

Developing an understanding of recruitment and selection is key to understanding how employers develop a selection process and how and why they use certain tools. Human resources management (HRM) or the personnel department is usually responsible for the development and administration of the process, and while it is usually senior and middle-level managers who will be involved in its operation, the HRM or personnel literature is usually a good place to start reading more. Occupational psychologists will usually help to design the process in a scientific manner, but the process will vary in nature and in the order of certain activities according to what the organisation can invest in the process and what it sees as important.

This chapter sets out how the processes of recruitment and selection work and will give you an idea of the experiences you could expect at different stages, if you were successful. However, it is useful to give some definitions of the two processes here.

It is important to note that nothing further can happen unless there are applicants willing to apply for the job. Once they have submitted their applications, then the process of selection can begin.

These two processes can work differently depending on the situation:

- A job vacancy that is advertised because the previous job holder has left the organisation will be developed in one particular way.
- A vacancy that is advertised as a new job role may have a little more uncertainty about it, but will be broadly similar.
- A vacancy on a graduate training scheme will be developed around some core skills and values possessed by the desired candidate, making them suitable for the organisation generally, while their suitability for a specific role in the organisation will be identified during the scheme.

Each of the above will have a slightly different emphasis on how the process is conducted and what employers will be looking for. There is one additional scenario: that is, employers will recruit internally. This is carried out in a different way, but is less relevant for most graduate applications, so we will not be examining it further.

HOW AN ORGANISATION DEVELOPS A RECRUITMENT PROCESS

The recruitment process itself has a number of elements to it, some of which are more straightforward than others, but when you see a job advertisement or an invitation to apply for a graduate training scheme, the organisation will usually have undertaken some kind of job analysis and developed some way of identifying and describing what it is after.

Job Analysis

A job analysis is the process of identifying what tasks the job will involve. This is useful for you, so that you know whether you might like the job, and useful to employers, who can use it to identify the kinds of qualities they are looking for. There is a variety of ways that employers might undertake this role – interviews, questionnaires, discussions, diaries of those doing similar jobs – and all have strengths and weaknesses, but employers will have taken some time to assess the job.

An analysis of the tasks involved in doing the job itself, however, is not going to produce a rounded picture of the 'ideal' candidate. Employers also need to consider the organisation and whether a candidate is going to be a good fit to the values and culture there, so these areas need to be considered as well. At a basic level, it is fine to have someone who can do the job, but if they are going to behave unethically, then that is going to be problematic. Employers call an ability to conform to the values of an organisation 'person–organisation fit' and an ability to do the job 'person–job fit'.

If the job is a general one (i.e. for a training scheme), the requirements are less important than 'person–organisation fit', although organisations will usually have some 'core competencies' – that is, essential qualities required for most or all jobs operating at a particular level.

COMPETENCY

A competency is a quality (skill, behaviour, attitude or personality trait) that helps an individual to perform a job well.

CORE COMPETENCY

A core competency is a quality that is an essential requirement for all employees operating in similar job roles.

Developing a Person Specification

The organisation will have taken the job description and other information (e.g. organisational core competencies, organisational values) and will have developed an idea of the qualities required from the successful candidate. These are usually referred to in terms of the 'knowledge', 'skills', 'abilities' and 'other' qualities (or KSAOs) that are sought. In this context, 'other' can refer to attitudes and values, educational attainments and experience.

For graduate-level jobs, the KSAOs will usually relate to some or all the following, with some key defining questions given alongside to assist you to understand these more:

- **Leadership and team-working skills**: Are you able to communicate, manage information, make good decisions and inspire others to follow what you would like them to do? Are you able to encourage others and manage tasks successfully? (See Chapter 12.)
- **Reasoning and critical thinking abilities**: Can you understand information that is given to you and draw accurate conclusions based on that information? Are you good at accurately analysing and interpreting evidence quickly without making incorrect assumptions? Are you able to quickly see what information is not given to you but is needed for a conclusion? Are you able to identify which information given to you is relevant and important and which is not? (See online chapter on psychometric tests.)
- **Numeracy**: Can you undertake relatively simple calculations quickly in order to make decisions? Are you able to understand how different pieces of numerical information may impact on conclusions you draw? Do you need to use your calculator or phone for every basic calculation you do, or can you do calculations quickly in your head? (See online chapter on psychometric tests.)
- **Interpersonal and communication skills**: Can you communicate clearly, rationally and using appropriate techniques in order to achieve a particular goal (e.g. helping others'

understanding, negotiating, gathering information by listening, influencing, etc.)? Can you do so in a way which shows the ability to understand others who may think in very different ways from you? (See Chapter 9 on communication skills)

- **Self-confidence**: Can you present your ideas to others regardless of their potential reactions? Do you have the resilience to persist in the development and implementation of your ideas in situations where not everyone will agree with you?

- **IT literacy** (proficient in use of MS Teams, Zoom, Skype, Project Excel, Access, etc.): Are you able to use such tools as relevant in order to achieve your goals efficiently, using IT to save time where needed? Are you nervous about using new software?

- **Presentation skills**: Can you communicate to both large and small audiences in both formal and informal settings in a way that achieves the purposes of the presentation and enables the audience to engage with you and hear/believe your message(s)? Are you able to use tools and to be creative – where relevant – which assist you in doing so? Can you give a presentation without reading from a script? (See Chapter 10 on presentation skills.)

- **Self-awareness**: Are you aware of your personal strengths and weaknesses, and are you able to find additional resources (including people) to assist where you do not have the relevant skills? Do you understand what causes you stress and how you behave under stressful situations? Are you aware of the impact you have on others and the activities/issues you find difficult to address? Can you accurately answer all the questions listed here? (See Chapter 2.)

- **Ability to learn**: Are you enthusiastic about and interested in learning new skills, behaviours, technologies? Do you take time to understand other people and to think about how they react under different circumstances? Can you identify who might know what you need to learn, and where such information might be? Do you reflect regularly on what you do and do not do, and identify better ways of doing what is needed? (See Chapter 2.)

- **Resilience**: Do you have the determination to do what you need to do? How likely are you to give up when it becomes challenging to implement what you want to do? Are you willing to push through barriers of frustration and see success in your activities? Are you likely to give up the search for jobs or internships if you don't get what you want, or to keep going and try a different approach?

- **Ethical values and honesty**: Are you likely to stick to what you think is right, even when your boss suggests an idea that is more possible but is ethically more compromising? Are you clear on what is acceptable and unacceptable? Do you have a clear understanding around showing mercy and punishing where needed? Can you identify issues and circumstances which might lead you to give a view or information that is untruthful?

- **Problem solving and creative abilities**: Are you able to quickly analyse problems and identify potential options? Can you quickly solve issues and challenges which seem illogical? Are you able to identify and use additional resources which can assist you and others to solve problems? Can you foresee challenges in completing a project or a piece of work in advance, and then implement appropriate solutions? (See Chapter 14.)

- **Organisational abilities**: Do you have a clear method for dealing with significant amounts of information, sometimes arriving in a tight time span? Are you able to differentiate between information which is of some but limited use, and that which could have a significant impact on the decisions you make?

- **Knowledge gained during the degree course**: Are you aware of what you have learned? Do you/have you tried to understand how the different subjects you are studying link to each other? Are you clear on how the various theories and ideas you have studied get implemented in practice?

- **Attitudes** (towards others, studying, etc.): Can you hypothetically demonstrate to an employer (who might observe you in an assessment centre) that you are hard working and very strongly motivated to succeed in your studies and in life? Can you show that you value others and recognise their abilities alongside your own? Can you demonstrate that you show respect to those around you, regardless of their job, social status, education, income, etc.?

The organisation will separate the list of competencies (or KSAOs) into 'essential' qualities ('the candidate selected must possess ...') and 'desirable' ('the candidate selected should also ...') qualities. The lists are separated according to whether a particular skill can be trained or not, and then how important it is to the job. Although rare in graduate recruitment, an organisation might also mention 'undesirable' qualities and those qualities which would disqualify someone from working in a particular kind of organisation (e.g. fraud conviction for a position in a bank or 'fear of flying' for an airline steward). The qualities being sought will establish the criteria against which each candidate is assessed.

 **FOR YOU TO DO**

Which KSAOs have you developed through:

- Student societies?
- Part-time employment?
- Family life?

(You can add to the list of KSAOs if you think you have extra qualities to offer.)

BOX 15.1

Looking to the Future

It seems to be a very human thing to do – to want to know the future – and of course, the more we explore, the more we can feel prepared for what we are about to face. Things are changing faster than we know and some argue that many of the jobs that graduates will apply for when they finish their courses did not exist when they started. The argument also goes that we will need new skills for a far more modern workforce and that some skill areas (e.g. handling complexity) will be needed in the future far more than they have been needed in the past.

The reality is that all of these views are truer in some areas of work than in others, with the other perspective being that we will be doing the same things that we have always done, but just in new ways. The changes that have come and are coming are a mixture of what we need to do and how we will need to do it. Let's consider three areas which have affected the nature of work and management over the past three years.

Understanding 'Blockchain'

Blockchain is not an easy concept to understand, because – rather than being one process or activity – it is a philosophy about enabling processes to become more efficient through the sharing of data. You might have heard about Bitcoin, but Bitcoin uses Blockchain technology to move data around money. For example, if a person wants to move money from A to B, then a third trusted party is usually used. Blockchain removes

(Continued)

the third party and enables transfer to happen quicker and more cheaply and enables every stakeholder to see what is happening with the data. Blockchain began with financial data.

It works according to the principles of:

A. Openness and transparency – which enables the checking of transactions
B. The data is held by all stakeholders (nodes) – so that there is no centralised data, but there is synchronisation of all data across all stakeholders, so ...
C. Some of the stakeholders ('miners' = nodes who CAN authorise any changes) are able to have the authorisation to say that when data is changed, the change is authorised, and they do so by randomly finding the key which will change the data for everyone, and then lock that change into place so that everyone shares. (The 'miners' are paid for taking on this task.)

The above is taken from a YouTube video (Rubin, 2016) and is a very simplistic overview as to how Blockchain technology works in principle.

Big Data

Seven years ago, few had heard of the concept of 'big data' yet now it is a core part of most business degrees and is certainly a focus of degrees teaching computational finance and statistics. Big data gets its name from the sheer volume of information that is gathered – some of it with our permission and some without our knowledge. Each time, for example, that we take our smartphone into town, it sends a signal to a mobile mast which could – if desired – collect that data to see where the thousands of people living within a city usually travel, and that can assist with designing bus routes or identifying difficulties with road layout.

Or every time we access a website, we often authorise that website to install a cookie, which mines into our computer and sends data back to the server about who is accessing that site, and so the server and owner of the website can understand a lot more about how the website is working.

In reality, big data goes a lot further than that. Data is collected from our computer about our health, every search we make on an e-commerce site such as Amazon so forth, and matched with computer held data about our age, location, interests, etc. That data can then be combined with that from all the others who access that website and analysed using artificial intelligence to give us similar options, so when we click on Amazon, we get a 'You might also be interested in ...' set of products, or when we click on YouTube, we get suggestions for similar videos.

Deriving meaning from all the data collected from all the thousands of individuals undertaking particular activities (hence the name 'big data') requires programming languages, and the most frequently talked about is 'Python'. The software will 'mine' through the data as instructed and will identify trends from thousands of records, but the accuracy of that search will be dependent on the instructions it is given. A search for candidates for a job through LinkedIn searches will be successful if the terms it looks for are correct, but there have been examples of companies looking for a candidate who has a particular job title only to find that the title in question is unique to that same company. The use of the analysis is also up to the human being at the end of the process.

Artificial Intelligence

Artificial intelligence (AI) is very likely to transform the workplace landscape significantly in the next 10-15 years if not before. When we chat/type to someone on the end of a helpline on a corporate website, it is becoming very difficult to know whether we are chatting to a human being or a piece of very well written software programmed to answer us as if it were a human. AI is also being used to screen candidates for jobs, and, in some exceptionally rare cases, to mark students' essays according to phrases and keywords. Whether AI will be used to give lectures in due course is unclear.

AI takes on the task of making decisions based on information it receives. The more complex that information and the more serious the implications, the less easy it will be to adapt AI to do the job, but that does not mean it will be impossible.

Human beings are by nature 'intelligent', and while learning can be undertaken by a machine (as many science fiction films have shown), that learning can be very subtle, and engaging emotions into rational decision making is something that will take time to develop. But at the same time, we will need to be aware of how to use AI well to do things that we need to do.

These three changes mean that we will need to develop our understanding of new skills and be able to apply them in a world where technology is having a significant impact on what we do and how we do it.

'BUT I HAVE A QUESTION ...'

... There is a list of skills and abilities graduates generally need given earlier, but how do I know what skills and abilities any one particular company is looking for?

Well, usually the company will tell you in the advertisement. Remember that what the company is looking for is evidence that you have the appropriate KSAOs for the job. Organisations will be looking for two things: firstly, job-person fit and, secondly, person-organisation fit.

The issue in relation to the question is that the first one is usually spelt out quite clearly, but the second is far more implicit. There are times when you can guess what the culture of the organisation might be like (i.e. what it is like to work there) by the language used on the company website or in a company brochure, but at other times you will have to be yourself and if the company is different from you, then it is obviously not going to work out in the long term anyway.

One of the broader qualities that graduate employers look for is work experience. This could be part-time work in a student bar, but the best kind of experience is from working in a professional role for a year as part of a placement programme. Many universities actually assess your performance during a work placement in some way (e.g. behaviour in the job, reflective assignment done while on a job placement, etc.) as a way of encouraging you to obtain that work experience. In reality, there are few substitutes for obtaining relevant work experience in a professional environment, either as part of a sandwich degree or in an internship. Having such experience alongside leadership responsibilities in a student society will put you ahead of other candidates when you are applying for jobs.

KEY LEARNING POINT

Employers and their organisations usually have a number of personal characteristics (KSAOs) that they are looking for in a new employee, and it is up to candidates to apply for jobs where they think they can match the essential (and hopefully also the desirable) qualities sought.

HOW AN ORGANISATION DESIGNS A SELECTION PROCESS

The selection process is a series of stages, but the first activity for an employer is to remove from the pile of applications those that do not possess sufficient evidence of the essential abilities the employer is seeking – that is, the screening process.

Screening

The process of screening refers to the process of examining the applications and deciding which candidates are the most appropriate for inviting to interview. Most vacancies for graduate trainee positions that are well advertised will likely attract several hundred applicants, and that can either be discouraging ('Why should they pick me?') or give you a sense of determination ('Someone has to get the job, so why shouldn't it be me?'). Your attitude will be important in life generally and will show itself especially when things do not go well.

 ### SELECTION METHODS

1. A *selection interview* is a conversation designed to determine whether someone has the appropriate abilities to do the job.
2. A *psychometric test* is a test of an individual's mental abilities, developed using scientific methods to ensure consistency and accuracy.
3. An *in-basket exercise* is a timed exercise involving candidates that deals with a range of issues in different email/memo messages.
4. A *personality questionnaire* is a questionnaire designed to elicit information regarding an individual's behaviour and personality.
5. A *work sample* is an example of someone's work.
6. An *assessment centre* is a structured programme of selection exercises, designed to enable selectors to see an individual in a simulated work environment. This method of selection can include a wide range of other methods carried out over a day or longer.

The process of screening can be relatively fast and brutal: a CV can be dismissed in as little as 10 to 30 seconds – or even be electronically scanned by relevant software for keywords so that it is never actually seen by a selector. This means that your application needs to be eye-catching and relevant, and you will need to learn how to market yourself. Selectors will be looking for significant evidence relating to the requirements of the job, which is why engagement with responsibilities in student societies, part-time work or voluntary experience is so important.

 **FOR YOU TO DO**

What makes you different?

Being different and special in a way that is useful to an organisation is one of the things that you will need to convey in order to get your application noticed. In marketing terms, those selling services or products usually emphasise their USP (Unique Selling Proposition, namely their unique qualities) to their customers. Bearing in mind that employers are your customers in this instance and will be looking for candidates who possess the relevant KSAOs, what are your USPs?

Think about:

1. Your skills and abilities.
2. Your knowledge.
3. Your other qualities – attitudes, values, character.

'BUT I HAVE A QUESTION ...'

... I have found my dream job, what do I do next?

The answer will depend on 1) how long you have before you need to submit an application, and 2) how far the requirements of the job are from your list of current skills. In other words, while you would love to get the job, you also need to be realistic about your chances of success. If you do get the job but do not have the right skills, then your 'dream' job could turn into a 'nightmare' as that gap starts to cause significant stress.

Imagine the following (very extreme) scenario. You want to be a pilot and somehow (maybe because there were no other candidates at all) you get the job, but you do not know how to land the plane, so landing it will be a nightmare for you. More realistically, you get a job as a manager, but you are unable to confidently make or communicate decisions, so you either ask someone else to advise you to give you self-confidence, or you delay making decisions, neither of which will be particularly impressive as far as your boss is concerned.

We need to aim high but how high will depend on that gap between what the job involves and the skills we have, and on the time we have to get to where we want to go to. There's nothing wrong in progressing steadily in our skills, but applying for jobs we cannot get is not a good idea: it will waste our time and damage our self-confidence. So one of the best things to do when applying for a job is to identify the skills required in that job and then identify how we can demonstrate to ourselves and another human being that we have those skills based on our previous experience.

Just one serious word of caution needed here. As mentioned above, taking on a job that you cannot do is not sensible, but applying for a job and *pretending* that you have all the relevant skills is even more dangerous. Firstly, you will be found out – through references asking about your previous experience or student activities, through a selection interview where you will be asked detailed questions about what you did and how, and if you are very lucky and able to get the job, through your performance rating in the job itself (and the resulting stress you suffer).

There is hardly ever any such thing as the perfect candidate: but in the shortlisted set of candidates there is usually a number of people who have significant strengths and allowable weaknesses. So you should not try to convince an employer that you are going to be the perfect candidate. If you were, then you would already be doing the job. Be honest: no one can criticise you for that.

Having identified the skills required for a job, the organisation will then examine the best methods for determining whether a candidate possesses the skills required. Because employing graduates has an element of risk to it (they might have some relevant experience, but it is unproven in the commercial or 'real' world) and because organisations might be taking on a large number of trainees all at once, the investment that organisations put into the selection process is considerable.

Selection Methods

Once the screening process is complete, the process then moves on to selecting the right person for the advertised post. This involves consideration of two things:

1.   Will they fit the values and culture of the organisation (person–organisation fit)?
2.   Will they have the motivation and ability to do the job well (person–job fit)?

The first asks whether the personality and attitudes/values of the individual will relate well to those of the organisation. For example, a very informal and relaxed organisation will probably not want some-one who is very formal and gives a lot of importance to rules, and similarly a very entrepreneurial organisation will probably not want someone who does not like to take risks. In such cases, individuals who do not share organisational values will probably find it quite difficult and possibly stressful to work in those environments, *whatever their abilities and skills might be*. Someone who does not fit is unlikely to proceed very far in the selection process. Identifying whether someone will fit could be done through asking candidates to upload a quick video illustrating what is important to them or a brief informal conversation with a current employee.

The second question here really follows on from the first, and is why employers and organisations use the methods that they do. Two organisations might use the same selection tools quite differently – use them in a different order in the selection process and/or for different purposes – but the tools are there to assess whether someone has 1) the correct abilities, 2) appropriate attitudes, and 3) motivation to do the job. They are also used, of course, to determine who would be the best individual to do the job where several candidates possess the relevant qualities.

Table 15.1 Selection methods

Selection tool	Description	Typically used for	Key considerations
Application Form (see Chapter 16)	• Candidate responding to questions to assess suitability and experience • Standardised questions to all candidates	• Screening of candidates • Assessing candidates' ability to meet essential requirements of job	• Well-written form takes time to complete • Often screened using AI software to identify key words • Be clear, honest and succinct
CV (see Chapter 16)	• Candidate constructs own story • Lack of standardisation	• Screening of candidates • Assessing candidates' ability to meet essential requirements of job	• Good CV takes considerable time to compile • Keep to 2 sides max • Should be accompanied by a covering letter
Selection Interview (see Chapter 17)	• Series of job-relevant questions asked to a job candidate • Typically lasts between 30 and 45 minutes • A conversation, enabling the employer to find out about the candidate and the candidate to find out about the employer	• Assessing candidates' ability to meet all requirements of job through examining ability and experience, motivation and potential. • Assessing motivation and personal style of candidate	• Prepare thoroughly • If online, be very clear about technical connection issues
Psychometric Tests (see online chapters)	• Tests of candidates' abilities to understand and use information (verbal, numerical, pictorial, etc.) appropriately • Right and wrong answers • Usually administered and scored online • Time-based, with tight time limits	• Assess the abilities possessed by job candidates in relation to relevant requirements • Sometimes used for screening candidates out on essential requirements regarding use of information	• Don't panic if you do not finish • Your score will usually be the number of correct answers, with no penalty for wrong answers • Don't need to take anything with you • Your careers service may provide some examples or some training, so ask
Personality Inventories (see online chapters)	A series of questions: • Asking how you would usually respond to certain situations • Asking which responses to situations would be most and least like you	• Identifying person–organisation and person–job fit in terms of values, attitudes and motivations	• Answer honestly: these tools often have a way to identify whether candidates are simply saying something they believe is 'desirable' or are being honest • Usually followed up by an interview giving you a chance to correct any misunderstood questions and to give examples of when you have behaved in a particular way

Selection tool	Description	Typically used for	Key considerations
Assessment Centre: Group Exercises (see Chapter 11)	• Usually a residential event taking place over a day and a half, in a hotel or a training facility • Candidates complete a task with others in a particular time • A leader might be selected from among the group in advance, or may not (leaderless) • Assessors (usually more than one) will watch how individuals behave in the group and will provide a commentary to other selectors later on • Different group exercises in one assessment centre will probably not involve candidates working with the same people • A single exercise may have several components – e.g. a negotiation followed by a presentation • An assessment centre may have several group exercises	• For evaluating the interpersonal (e.g. leadership, communication, project management, time management, persuasion, negotiation, presentation, etc.) skills of candidates • For evaluating how individual candidates are likely to work with others in the workplace • For gathering detailed and behavioural evidence from multiple sources on the above	• Act naturally • Relax and try to enjoy the event, but work hard: they are watching you to see how you would behave in the workplace • Find out as much as you can about how this company runs its assessment centres in advance – maybe from your careers service, or maybe online
Presentations (see Chapter 10)	• Candidates are asked to present on a topic that they either 1) don't know but have time to prepare, or 2) should know about • This can be something that is unprepared or something candidates are told to prepare in advance • This may be with or without PowerPoint, and candidates may or may not be required to stand up to do the presentation	• Evaluating candidates' presentation skills • If the presentation is unprepared, then the employer may be evaluating candidates' ability to research, design and undertake a presentation in a short time span • Possibly evaluating candidates' ability to present complex ideas in a simple way (i.e. using analogies and examples) and to be creative with limited resources	• Stay calm and focus on the objectives of the presentation • Plan your time appropriately: do not over-run • Where possible, learn as much as you can about what you will be asked to do in advance of the presentation
Assessment Centre: In-Basket Exercise (see online chapters)	• Candidates will be asked to make a number of decisions on how they would deal with some complex circumstances in a very tight timeframe • There will probably be a follow up interview to find out why candidates made the decisions they did • Candidates will probably be presented with a number of emails, reports and/or notes from meetings 'they' (as the candidate) are supposed to have attended, and which might be typical of what the job holder will need to deal with • Some of the decisions will be time/calendar based (i.e. Are you free to do certain activities on a certain date?), others will be people based (Who to ask to do xxx? How will you manage yyy?) • Candidates will need to record their decisions in a report form and/or a diary • Likely to be computer-based	• Evaluating candidates' personal administrative, decision making and informational skills • Identifying how candidates make decisions and why • Evaluating candidates' ability to use very limited time and sometimes deal with conflicting pieces of information efficiently	• Stay calm • Take some time to think carefully: do not always jump to conclusions, so think about whether you have the information you need to make a decision, and what further information you might need • Watch your time carefully: you will not have a great deal of time, so keep an eye on the clock • Some issues will take longer to think through than others: that is usual and reflects working life • Make notes about your actions as much as you can • Get used to managing a complex diary • Don't worry about getting all the answers 'correct': some issues will not have correct answers

The most common selection methods are detailed in the following chapters, but it is helpful to give a quick overview (see Table 15.1). Some – e.g. graphology (the deduction of personality from handwriting analysis), and astrology (the use of star signs to determine personality) are not generally used much because of issues around scientific validity and so are not listed here. The actual tools used in any one situation will depend, of course, on the requirements for the job.

These are not the only tools which might be used. Assessment centres, for example, often include the chance to meet with the people who are assessing you over a meal, but you will be observed to see how you interact with others, even during such 'informal' occasions.

It is also true that some tools are much better than others: assessment centres gather a lot of extra information than could be gained from a simple interview, for example, and whenever there is a lot more information gathered, the selection tool is seen as having much stronger validity or fitness for purpose. Similarly, structured interviews – with well-designed questions asked to all candidates and where questions are related clearly to job requirements – are generally seen as having much more usefulness. Unstructured interviews – merely informal conversations – might be good at determining organisational fit, but are much less good at identifying those who will perform well in the workplace.

Never drink or smoke before meeting people from the organisations to whom you are applying, and try to keep some emotional composure during the selection process.

More on each of these and other selection tools is available in the chapters below and on the companion website for this book at https://study.sagepub.com/morgan2e.

FOR YOU TO DO

Do you understand the brief definitions and information given above? Look at the descriptions below and match them to the selection methods listed in Table 15.1.

- 'I needed to indicate which of the answers (A to D) was most like me and least like me. One of the guys from the company then spent some time with me discussing my results and asking me for examples of my typical behaviour. It was quite interesting really – no one had ever done that before – but I am not sure if I was convincing in the answers I gave.'
- 'I think this exercise was about my administrative and organisational skills, but also my communication skills. Each of the pieces of information I needed to deal with required me to do something – either add something into my diary or respond to a particular message from an employee or customer. It was tough: there wasn't really enough time and I needed to think very quickly.'
- 'The questions were quite hard and both of the managers I was talking to looked really strict. I needed to give examples of times when I had done something particularly special or difficult. At the end, I did get the chance to ask questions, but there didn't seem to be a great deal of time to answer the questions. I never really knew who I should look at.'
- 'This was a large event, actually. There were around 20 people there, and we met in a hotel. During the day, we had to do some reasoning tests, we had an 'inbox exercise' to complete, I had to read a case study and do a presentation and then at the end we had an interview. Lunch was good, but I couldn't really relax, as I was sitting next to one of the guys from the organisation.'
- 'It was a difficult thing to do and I didn't finish in the 30 minutes they gave us. I had a calculator and made some notes for the questions as I went along, which was a really useful thing to do because they were then useful for other questions. But it was tough and I don't think anyone finished. I think I guessed some of the answers, because the questions were multiple choice.'
- 'I had to do a presentation before my interview and then they asked me questions about it. I was nervous, a bit shaky and I am not sure if I did what I was really capable of doing or had done before, but I did it.'

Not all companies will use all of these methods, and even when they do, they might use them in a different order or vary the specific methods (e.g. telephone interview vs face-to-face interview) or the people involved. Some companies use psychometric tests or personality inventories/questionnaires to screen out candidates *before* they get to the interview stage. The order in which companies use the selection methods is usually determined by how important those qualities are. There is little point in engaging with a candidate to the end of the process through some expensive selection methods only to find that they do not possess one of the basic requirements of the job, see Box 15.2 below.

════ REFLECTION POINT ════

Take some time to think about the following questions and write down some answers.

Are any of the selection methods listed above ones which you have experienced before?

From the descriptions above, which methods might be the most and least stressful for you? Why?

In using these methods, employers are just trying to find out if you have the KSAOs they are looking for, so do you ever feel that you should 'put on an act' and pretend to be someone you are not? Or do you just try to be yourself? Which is better, do you think?

════ BOX 15.2 ════

The Police Helicopter Crew

The role of the police helicopter is to oversee police activity and criminal behaviour, and to assist police officers on the ground to apprehend those alleged to have committed some crime. Within the team in the helicopter there is a pilot, an observer and a rear crew member. The rear crew member's job is to ensure that the helicopter is where it needs to be and to plan where the helicopter needs to be. As such, it is quite a complex job.

The skills required for the job relate to the following:

- Accurate and timely communication skills.
- Excellent geographical/navigation skills.
- An ability to multi-task and use multiple resources at the same time.
- An ability to fly in a helicopter while using navigational aids without feeling airsick.
- Good team-working skills.
- An awareness of relevant laws.
- Good strategic planning skills.

If you were to put these in order, which would you consider the most critical and therefore would look for first?

During the selection exercise for a rear crew member, one police force used more theoretical exercises (including a paper exercise where candidates needed to draw the route being taken by the helicopter on a map in order to prove their navigation skills) early on in the process. This would save costs in that only a small number of candidates making it through to the end of the process would need to be given a simulated exercise in the helicopter, rather than taking all candidates up in the sky and making a large number of expensive trips. In the end, however, one of the three finalists let slip that they had a fear of flying and was denied the job.

Bearing in mind the reasons for their decision, would you have done anything differently? Why?

As noted above, the choice of selection methods is made according to the skills sought. As an obvious example, you cannot reliably examine someone's presentation skills merely by asking if they are good at presentations during an interview, or even by asking for an example of when they have given a presentation. The best way to assess someone's presentation skills is to ask them to do a presentation. This is why graduate employers often use a variety of different methods to select candidates – because they will be looking for slightly different things.

 **FOR YOU TO DO**

You are a manager who needs to recruit a new staff member. Look at the hypothetical job advertisement below.

Trainee Client Relationship Manager

This is an exciting opportunity to make a major contribution to the operation of a new but quickly growing advertising consultancy. BWK was established three years ago with an office of six staff and has now grown to 32 individuals, each of whom plays a significant role in the development of their own business within the BWK family, which now has an annual turnover of around £3 million. We aim to expand to set up other offices around the UK and to have a turnover of around £18 million within the next five years – and you will be making a contribution to that success.

You will be a self-starter, able to establish teams and work with clients, and excited about the possibility of working for BWK. It will be hard work and will be challenging – the expectations will be high – but you will be working with an excellent and growing technical and customer support team who have recently won regional awards for their expertise and assistance. Your excellent organisational skills will complement your IT skills and enable you to liaise promptly with clients and write/analyse reports regarding your progress, while your excellent interpersonal skills will help you develop client relationships with customers who will stay with BWK for the long term.

In return, BWK will provide you with a salary and appropriate transport commensurate with this exciting role, and training opportunities relevant to your own development needs. We see this as a long-term relationship with you as well, and while we are not perfect, we do take a great deal of pride in the team work atmosphere we have at¸BWK.

If you think you are who we are looking for and/or want to know more, then please contact us at madeupjob@bwk.co.uk.

Questions for you to consider

1. What qualities are the company looking for in the successful employee?
2. Would this job fit your abilities and qualities? Why, or why not?
3. What kind of person would do well in this organisation? Are there any qualities which might be important but which are not stated explicitly?
4. Would this organisation be one that you could work for? Why, or why not?
5. Take your list of the qualities the company is seeking and then establish whether those skills are desirable or essential.
6. Look at the list of selection methods used by organisations in Table 15.1. Which method(s) would the company be likely to use to establish whether a candidate has the necessary qualities to do the job?

When thinking about applying for a job (and in order to identify how realistic your chances might be of getting the job), it is a good idea to identify the skills required and apply them to your own experience (see Table 15.2). You might like to do this based on the job description given above.

Table 15.2   Examples of application of required skills

Skills required	Evidence and examples of when I have done this
Self-starter	I responded to a need and began a club at my university so that people could play table tennis more effectively ...
Able to establish teams	I had to work in a group on XXX module. I knew I needed someone who was really good at managing meetings and someone else who could get us some information and data so I asked A and B to work with me and a couple of other students ...
Able to work well (with clients)	As a member of the student representatives committee, I needed to work with other students and with my professors in order to improve the student experience ...

(You may not have direct experience of *working with clients*, but you might have some experience that is similar and can show that you are able to establish good communications with other stakeholders.)

 **'BUT I HAVE A QUESTION ...'**

... This selection process seems really lengthy. Do companies really do all of this?

Not all companies, no – and even those that do will not do it for every vacancy. At the end of the day, an organisation has to decide whether a lengthy selection process is worth the expense (and risk) to do so. A job role carrying a high salary will usually carry a fair degree of risk – the responsibility will be greater – so the higher the salary, the more likely it is that the organisation will invest more in the selection process.

But it is lengthy – yes. Some selection processes can last as little as 45 minutes (e.g. interviews) while others can take a day and a half (e.g. an assessment centre). Employers will want to see as much evidence of your personality and skills as possible, and that means seeing evidence of those skills in several situations. It can make people nervous, but the best advice for any selection process is to be yourself.

KEY LEARNING POINT

Selection processes for graduate-level jobs rarely involve a single selection method, but are more commonly a combination of various methods to ensure that the candidate is the best possible fit for the organisation and job role.

IMPLEMENTING THE SELECTION PROCESS

Having carried out the screening process and identified those candidates an employer is interested in, the next stages in the process are relatively straightforward. Candidates will receive an invitation to attend for whatever selection methods are used and the selectors make a decision having seen all the candidates.

Most selection for graduate-level roles involves at least two stages, typically an interview and then an assessment centre. More details on how both processes work are given in the chapters that follow.

There is very little difference between the three types of jobs: for general trainee jobs, for specific jobs and for jobs which are new to the organisation. The process as described above – and as given in Table 15.3 – is almost identical.

Table 15.3   Overview of the recruitment and selection process

- Person specification
  - o Analysing the job
  - o Writing the job description
  - o Detailing the skills needed
- Recruitment
  - o Advertising
- Screening
  - o 'Topping and tailing'
- Selection
  - o Using predictors to make decisions

THE POWER OF SOCIAL MEDIA

One area that has changed in the last 15 or so years has been the prevalence and then use by employers of what used to be called 'social networking sites' and more recently has been termed 'social media'. The term 'social' has various meanings and the way that professionals socialise for work purposes is generally not the same as the way that you might do this with your peers at university. There are a variety of social media apps and websites which enable people to network, and the ways that we post content varies from site to site. However, employers are now regularly using networking sites to find and evaluate their candidates, and they do so in different ways at different stages of the recruitment and selection processes.

How are employers using social media for selection?

According to a survey carried out by CareerBuilder (2018), 48% of companies use social media to check on the behaviour of their employees (whether they post provocative images, use drink or drugs, comment inappropriately on others' race or religion, etc.), but from a recruitment and selection perspective, that same survey also revealed that, depending on the industry sector, the vast majority of employers now use social media to gather information on job candidates. The figure is higher for IT related (74%) and manufacturing related (73%) jobs, but is still significant for those in sales related positions (59%). This means that you need to be careful about what you post.

 ———— 'BUT I HAVE A QUESTION ...' ━━━━━━

... Why should employers want to snoop around into my private life? I mean my personal life is my personal life. Isn't this unfair?

Yes, that is true, but it is less true in more recent times when our interaction with colleagues and customers can continue online outside of the physical workplace, and when colleagues and customers can learn about us and come to some judgement about how much they should trust us based on what we post. This parallels ideas about how well defined or blurred the boundaries of work really are (should we take a phone call from our boss if it is outside of the 9–5 traditional working day? Does the answer to that vary if we happen to be on a business trip in a different time zone, or if we are working in a sales role and a client wants a decision on something quickly?), and as a future employee, you will need to develop some initial thoughts around such issues – even if priorities will change due to your personal circumstances.

And to some extent, the issue goes beyond just what we post. Imagine the following scenario: you arrive late at an interview at a college campus. Your answers are poor, you look untidy and you fail to proceed any further. That bad impression rarely stays just within that one company. The managers involved in such interviews will often meet each other at conferences, industry meetings and so on, and employers have been known to swap the names of those who have made a poor impression. And that was happening before any social media was around. Now it is a lot easier for information to be found.

There are some ways to keep a social media page away from the eyes of employers, but the best way of making a 'good' impression is not to make a bad impression. Keep your profile clean, professional and try not to post too many pictures and stories about getting drunk, swearing, having lots of inappropriate relationships or comments about past or potential future employers. You should never share confidential information from a current or past employer online.

At the moment, employers can legally access and use what you post and can use this for selection (and workplace management) decisions, so until that changes a cautious and intelligent approach to what you post on social media is needed.

It is helpful to examine what employers look for when they look at social media profiles, and where they look. The CareerBuilder survey (2018) indicated that employers tended to get favourable impressions of candidates from social media when their posts:

- Supported their professional qualifications for the job: 37%
- Indicated creativity: 34%
- Conveyed a professional image: 33%
- Showed a broad education and a wide range of interests: 31%
- Indicated a good fit within the company culture: 31%
- Showed great communications skills: 28%
- Referred to receiving awards and accolades: 26%
- Others made complementary comments about the job candidate: 23%
- Showed awareness of and interaction with company's social media accounts: 22%
- Included compelling video or other content: 21%

Whether a candidate has a large number of followers or subscribers is less important to employers (less than 20% of employers saw this issue as important), though for marketing or sales roles, having a large network of a particular target group would be a distinct advantage. It is now not unheard of for some users of YouTube (YouTubers) to make significant sums by posting content around sponsors' products to a large audience on a regular basis.

However, the other side of the coin is that some content can cause you problems moving forward in the hiring process. Employers tended to view the following content negatively:

- Provocative or inappropriate photographs, videos or information: 40%
- Information about candidates drinking or using drugs: 36%
- Discriminatory comments related to race, gender, religion, etc.: 31%
- Content indicating links to criminal behaviour: 30%
- Content indicating that the candidate lied about qualifications: 27%
- Poor communication skills: 27%
- Bad-mouthing previous employers or fellow employees: 25%
- An unprofessional screen name: 22%
- Sharing confidential information from previous employers: 20%
- Lying about an absence: 16%

According to the survey, it does not seem to matter whether people post regularly or rarely, but posting something relating to any of the above is going to be problematic. Generally, employers viewed social media posts as giving information about a candidate's all-round personality, their communication skills and whether they saw a candidate as a good fit for the company overall.

Which social media are used the most?

There are broadly two categories of 'social' media – professional and social – with Facebook straddling both groups, and both are used differently by different groups (recruiters and students). Figure 15.2 provides some ideas as to where commonly used social media might fit along the continuum.

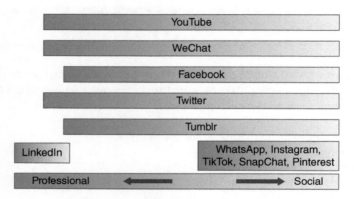

Figure 15.2   Social media: From professional to social

LinkedIn is the best known professional networking site and is used extensively by employers looking for job candidates. By paying a monthly premium fee, they can easily search for keywords on your profile, learn about your job history, chat to those who work with you and find out about your previous experience. In the same way, a monthly subscription will show you who has been viewing your profile and enables you to see what keywords they used to search for their next employee. Whether it is worth getting a subscription is up to you, but not having a reasonable profile on LinkedIn may impact on whether you are invited to apply for a post.

Like Facebook, LinkedIn gives the facility for you to show what you know, to link to relevant articles in the media or to published research, and to ask questions of users using hashtags (#). Again, that raises your profile.

Facebook, YouTube and Twitter may all also be used to check for the characteristics listed above, but the time an employer spends checking a networking site may depend on the risk associated with employing the wrong person, the availability of other methods of collecting the desired information and the time and resources they – or headhunters using social media – will have available to do so.

FOR YOU TO DO

There are three tasks here for you to do. Neither will take a lot of time and neither will cost you any money.

1. Look at Figure 15.2. Are there any social networking sites listed here that you don't know? Could they or other sites be useful to you in terms of your future employment?

Undertake some research into these and other sites (https://influencermarketinghub.com/top-social-media-sites/ lists around 50 social media sites) that could be useful to you.

2. Review your own social media profiles. Is there publicly available content (pictures, comments) that an employer might consider to be very unhelpful or unfavourable if you were applying for a job?

Have a look at the above list of issues that employers see negatively and make a decision about what you will and will not post in the future.

3. If you do not have a LinkedIn profile, then undertake some research to determine whether this is something you need to do.

LinkedIn does not need to cost anything and is something that many students worldwide use to publicise who they are, and employers use to find candidates. If you want to go into a career in marketing or sales in particular where you have to promote products, then one thing an employer will want to see is how you promote yourself.

CONCLUSION

You should now be able to:

* Understand how employers view the recruitment and selection processes.
* Describe how employers select and use different selection tools.
* Identify the qualities needed in different kinds of roles.
* Understand how your studies and other experiences have helped you to develop these qualities.

The recruitment and selection processes have a degree of subjective judgement about them. However, the greater the investment in the individual who is successful, the more detailed and careful managers tend to be to ensure they get it 'right'. Organisations do need to be careful about taking on an employee who says all the right things but cannot deliver when it comes to performance.

For you as a candidate, this means that you need to be clear in your mind about what you have done previously and the impact of those actions. The first step is selling yourself to an employer; we will look at application forms and CVs in the next chapter.

━━━━━━━━━━━━━ CHAPTER TASK ━━━━━━━━

Go to your Careers Advice Centre – online or physically – and have a look at a vacancy that might interest you (either now or in the future).

List the qualities you think they might be looking for.

How do you think they might learn whether you or other candidates possess such qualities? What selection tools do you think they might use?

Talk to a careers adviser to find out what they know about how the selection process might work for this vacancy and which selection tools (interview, online tests, etc.) might work.

Review the online chapter about the use of psychometric tests and assessment centres to learn more about these important aspects of many graduate selection processes.

ADDITIONAL RESOURCES

Want to learn more? Visit https://study.sagepub.com/morgan2e to gain access to a wide range of online resources, including interactive tests, tasks, further reading and downloads.

Website Resources

The following websites offer useful advice on employee selection.

Changingminds.org – job analysis: http://changingminds.org/disciplines/hr/job_analysis/job_analysis.htm

Graduate Recruitment Bureau: http://employers.grb.uk.com/selection-methods

KPMG – overview of the KPMG recruitment and selection process: www.kpmg.com/PT/en/careers/graduates/Pages/recruitmentselection.aspx

Real Prospects 2010 – The Best Graduate Employers as Rated by Graduates? www.hecsu.ac.uk/assets/assets/documents/Real_Prospects_2010_-_Main_Report.pdf

Textbook Resources

Arnold, J. and Randall, R. (2010) *Work Psychology: Understanding Human Behaviour in the Workplace* (5th edition). Harlow: FT/Prentice-Hall (particularly Chapter 4).

Burns, T. and Sinfield, S. (2016) *Essential Study Skills* (4th edition). London: Sage (particularly Chapter 13.2).

Cottrell, S. (2010) *Skills for Success* (2nd edition). New York: Palgrave (particularly Chapter 10).

Smale, B. and Fowlie, J. (2009) *How to Succeed at University: An Essential Guide to Academic Skills, Personal Development & Employability*. London: Sage (particularly Chapter 9).

Smith, M. (2011) *Fundamentals of Management* (2nd edition). Maidenhead: McGraw-Hill (particularly Chapter 7).

16

CVs AND APPLICATION FORMS

I have not failed, I have just found 10,000 ways that don't work. (Thomas Edison)

CHAPTER STRUCTURE

Figure 16.1

When you see the this means go to the companion website https://study.sagepub.com/morgan2e to do a quiz, complete a task, read further or download a template.

▬ AIMS OF THE CHAPTER ▬▬▬▬▬

By the end of this chapter, you should be able to:

- Understand how employers use CVs, covering letters and application forms in the selection process.
- Identify the qualities of good applications.
- Write and compile CVs, covering letters and application forms.
- Develop speculative applications.

WHEN SHOULD YOU READ THIS CHAPTER?

Making job applications for graduate vacancies is something you will need to do towards the end of your studies, so it is best to read this in the summer before starting your final academic year at university.

CV (CURRICULUM VITAE)

A CV is a document aimed at convincing an employer that who you are, your qualifications, work experience and your skills makes it worthwhile for them to offer you either work experience or a chance to move forward in a formal selection process.

COVERING LETTER

A covering letter is a professional business letter which provides an employer with an introduction to an accompanying CV.

APPLICATION FORM

An application form is a document completed by a job applicant (usually completed online) aimed at gathering information about the applicant's experience, skills and abilities.

INTRODUCTION

The previous chapter examined the recruitment and selection process, and indicated that while there may be some common qualities that graduate employers are looking for, it is rare to find a large number of jobs that are identical, in organisations that are identical. Most organisations will be looking for slightly different combinations of skills, education and experience. Therefore, CVs, covering letters and application forms have one important characteristic in common: you *must* adapt your application – namely, these three items – to the qualities being sought in order to be successful. When developing your CV, you *must* make it relevant to the job being advertised: if it is not, the application will be ignored. (It is no different from writing essays: you have to fulfil the criteria to get a good mark.)

This chapter will give advice on building up your profile, CV structure, content and presentation, and then on completing application forms in a way that helps you to stand out. The information here should give you a solid basis on which to begin and then refine your application, but you should also refer to your university careers advice service to get their perspective.

The Basics

Completing a job application or writing a CV is something that nearly everyone who wants to work for someone else will need to do at some point in their life. Many people start by believing that this is an easy process, which they can probably complete using an online 'CV Wizard' (a simple template) in a very short space of time. Another thing that people believe about a CV is that it is a simple list of everything that you have ever done. Finally, there is a belief that once you have done a CV, you can use it for every job you apply for.

None of these ideas is true!

Any CV is expected to be accompanied by a covering letter. If you have never written a professional business letter before, then the first experience of doing so can be daunting.

The covering letter gives the employer a formal introduction to what is contained in the CV. More details are given below, but key to writing a successful covering letter is your ability to write succinctly and clearly in a way that makes the employer interested in you.

Application forms tend to be more structured documents, again aimed at giving employers specific information about you so that they can assess your suitability for moving forward in the selection process. They tend to be completed online.

KEY LEARNING POINT

Any job application *must* be matched to the criteria being sought by the organisation in order to be successful. A single application cannot simply be sent out for lots of different jobs: it must be adapted appropriately.

In this chapter, we need to be very clear on the purpose of the application: it is submitted in order to help an employer know more about your suitability for the job, and to feel confident enough to invite you to an interview. In some cases, the application becomes less relevant after the interview stage. Examples will be given of how each area *might* look, but there is no one best style and your application needs to reflect who *you* are, so you will need to personalise any application that you make.

It is worth noting that 81% of companies use online application forms for graduate jobs, while only 14% of graduate recruiters ask for CVs (Institute of Student Employers, 2019). This enables companies to compare candidates easily, and where there are a large number of applications, it enables computers to scan the applications for useful and significant words. If you submit a CV when the company asks for an application form, you are unlikely to get through the first stage, and your application may be dismissed in less than three seconds, so do follow instructions. The reason for putting the CV content first is a simple one: constructing your CV will help you to collect enough examples of the relevant activities that you have been involved in to be able to answer specific questions on the application form.

BEFORE APPLYING

It is really tempting simply to apply for every vacancy you find. You look in your careers services or a national newspaper or a profession-related magazine or on LinkedIn, find all the jobs you can and submit a CV and letter that you had prepared for a previous vacancy for those jobs. This might seem a bit of a 'lucky dip' approach, and in reality it is, so this section will explore what you – as an applicant – should do before applying. One or two of the ideas here need to be considered a long time before you start thinking about applying for jobs.

Find Out About the Organisation

You need to know about the organisation before thinking about applying. The best way of finding out about the organisation is to talk to it – or at least do some investigating. Do you know anyone who works there, or who can give you some guidance? Is there information online (YouTube, *Financial Times*, etc.) which can give you some idea as to what the organisation is like? Larger organisations will often attend graduate job fairs or are usually happy to respond to politely and professionally worded emails sent to the graduate recruitment department. Gently developing contacts within the organisation on LinkedIn in order to ask relevant questions can also work (Facebook might be more difficult in this regard). It might help you to decide whether you really want to work for an organisation if you find out the following:

- What is the organisation's strategy for doing what it wishes to do? (This may be challenging to find out since it is commercially sensitive, but it will show you where the opportunities might be within the organisation in a couple of years. An annual review on a company website may contain a vision or strategy section.)
- How does the organisation train and develop its staff?
- What is it like to work there – are individuals friendly, or are lower level employees not treated well?
- Are there many rules and procedures to follow, or are people fairly free to get on with their work in their own way?

At this stage in the process, you will want to find out whether you want to work for the organisation and whether you and the organisation make a good match. However, at interview, companies will also want to see evidence that you know what they do, where they are located, how they work and the impact of any external factors (e.g. government regulation) on the way they do what they do.

Finding Out About the Vacancy

The range of methods you can use to find jobs is now considerable. Some time ago, employers used to go round to universities and recruit students through presentations and do interviews on campuses. That still happens but is less and less the case, and now students are able to access job vacancies through:

- Prospects, the UK graduate jobs website.
- Careers service advertisements and mailings.
- Job and CV sites online (e.g. Monster.co.uk).
- Professional networking sites (e.g. LinkedIn).
- Other CV hosting and job application sites.
- Company websites, if you know what kind of company you want to work in.
- Search engines.
- Friends and family through Facebook.

Or there is always the option of writing to a company in the hope that they have a vacancy and will let you apply.

Having taken some time to examine the organisation and your personal qualities, the final part of the process is to identify what the organisation is looking for in terms of KSAOs. This information can come from two sources: your analysis of the organisation (which should help to determine how well your values, ideas and behaviour might fit) and information given on the job vacancy. The information you collected earlier in the chapter, where you analysed an organisation, will apply to any vacancy within the organisation, but the knowledge and skills that it is looking for may either be spelt out or be inferred from content in the advertisement. In some industries, employers may also expect you to know about the industry as well.

If the information is clearly stated, then the key issue is to ensure that you address the skills required. A simple table can help, such as Table 16.1 (or see Table 15.2 in the previous chapter).

Table 16.1 Providing evidence of relevant skills

Skills/qualities sought	Evidence
• Good organisational skills	I organised the student society party …
• Proficient at using MS Word and Excel	I needed to use MS Word to write my assignments, and Excel to analyse complex data in writing my dissertation
• Demonstrable leadership ability	I lead others in two coursework groups, as well as taking significant leadership roles in a student union society

If the skills are less clear, then you may have to use your analytical skills and do some 'intelligent guesswork'. Figure 16.2 shows an example of an advert for a generic training programme.

We are seeking highly competent individuals to join as graduate trainees. As such, you will be expected to analyse data produced by other team members, to lead project teams and to present your findings both orally and in writing to middle management on a regular basis.

Figure 16.2 Brief job advert for graduate training programme

We can see that the job requires individuals who are:

- Competent – that is, have some record of success in their academic and non-academic activities.
- Analytical – able to use analytical skills.
- Able to lead.
- Experienced in project management – it is difficult to lead a project team unless you have project management skills.
- Skilled in presentations – 'orally'.
- Skilled in writing reports – 'and in writing'.

Therefore, any application needs to address the skills required and, where possible, show that the organisational values match those of the candidate. The application will need to give evidence to show how these skills have been demonstrated and developed. In themselves, all job applications require a significant level of analytical ability. Whatever you write, it must be relevant and directly appropriate for the job. The clearer you show this to the recruiting employer, the better.

It is worth noting two further pieces of information. Firstly, the information you receive about the graduate vacancy or training scheme may or may not give an indication of salary. Average salaries for those graduating in the UK in 2019 were around £29,000 (Institute of Student Employers, 2019), but if salary is not given, it does not mean that it will be low. Many graduate recruiters do not reveal their graduate starting salaries for reasons of commercial confidentiality – and because different graduates working in different areas of the business with different qualifications (in different locations) may be paid differently.

Secondly, there may be a very limited time window for you to apply for the job. Most graduate employers are able to select their employees within an eleven-week window from application to offer (Institute of Student Employers, 2019), which means that timescales are tight.

KEY LEARNING POINT

An analysis of the organisation, of your capabilities and of the skills required for a general vacancy is the starting point for the development of any application, and is likely to take some time to complete.

DEVELOPING AND WRITING YOUR CV

If you have never written a CV before, then it can seem daunting, but if you have compiled a list of all you have done and any significant or interesting projects, then developing your CV is not going to be too difficult. The challenge comes in ensuring that your CV is targeted towards a job vacancy. The structure and content of a CV is challenging, but getting the presentation right is also vitally important.

Note that the examples given here are *simply illustrative*: they are presented to give you an idea of what your content *could* look like and *could* include, but are meant solely to be a guide; not every employer will like the way these are presented. The section of this chapter on the presentation of your CV gives you a lot more information to consider in terms of presentation style.

CV Content and Structure

It is vital to recognise that there is no such thing as the ideal CV in terms of structure or presentation, but one that does not demonstrate relevance to the requirements of the organisation or of the job will not get through, however well structured and presented it may be. In addition, the later you are in your career, the longer your CV will usually be.

Good CVs will usually include the following content.

Personal contact details

These should include any university and personal email addresses and an up-to-date telephone number. Including your Skype details is also a good idea (see e.g. Table 16.2), but you do not have to give your date of birth, though many people do. Some might suggest that you should also include a photo, but there is no requirement to do so. Some people also give a LinkedIn username. This can be useful if an application is taken further to interview stage, but an employer will likely struggle to find time to look at this at the screening stage. Giving a Facebook account is not usually a good idea: not only is it a little informal, but also people often have content on there that business professionals might find inappropriate. If you are going to be away from your accommodation during university holidays then you need to give an alternative address as well, and the dates that you will be there.

Table 16.2   An example of contact details

Personal contact details

Name:	Mr Mike Smith
Email:	Mike.smith@anyoneemail.com
Telephone:	07777 777 7777
Address:	59 Madeup Street Townsville Nice Place XX12 3ZZ
Skype username:	Mrsmith98

It is worth checking your email address and, if necessary, setting up a new one. An email address which sounds silly or immature (e.g. littleredridinghood@yahoo.com or muscleman2@gmail.com) will show more of your personality than you might want. If you need to get a more professional email address, then do so. The importance of creating the right impression at this early stage cannot be understated, and while some information will be briefly scanned, the email address is one small piece of information which should not draw the wrong kind of attention.

Personal statement

This is not something that all applicants or CVs contain, but it has become more common recently. A brief personal statement should be no longer than three lines, or maybe two to three sentences. An example is given in Table 16.3.

Table 16.3   Example of a personal statement

Personal statement

I am a highly successful individual who is likely to obtain a **first class honours** degree in Business Studies. I have strong **leadership abilities**, enjoy **working in teams** and am able to **present well**.

Writing this brief statement (two to three brief sentences; no more than 50–80 words) enables you to give an employer a very rapid and focused idea of who you are – your skills, your personality and your character. It should sum up what makes you different and relevant and should reflect the brand you want to create (see page 381 on creating a personal brand). The list of your achievements can help here, but if you do decide to include a character statement within your CV, then its purpose should be to entice the reader to read more about the skills and achievements that you can offer.

If you do use one, then be sure that you have the evidence to support what you say. Some people advise refocusing this on your career goals. At the start of your career, this may be a good thing to do, but as with many aspects of CVs, there is no one correct way to do this.

═══════ 'BUT I HAVE A QUESTION ...' ═══════

... Do I have to include a personal statement? I cannot think of anything to write.

No, there is no necessity to include a personal statement, but it can bring the qualities and strengths that you have to the attention of the selectors very easily, and give them a clear idea of what you can offer.

On the second issue – that you cannot think of anything to write – the suggestion would be that you need to consider some of what was written in Chapter 2 about knowing yourself very well. You will have certain strengths and weaknesses: the personal statement is not the place to discuss your weaknesses, but you will have knowledge, skills, motivation and experiences that you can mention here. The example given above is just an example – you could instead talk about what motivates you or particular achievements, but it *must* be kept short.

It *must* also be relevant. Including a personal statement which is not relevant will mean that your CV will be rejected very quickly: in professional terms, it is the equivalent of writing a letter and sending it to the wrong person.

Education and qualifications

When writing a CV, some students omit the necessary details here. Employers will be looking for someone who pays attention to detail, so it is important to get this correct. You need to indicate:

1. Your qualification title: BSc (Hons) Business Studies/A-Level/AS-Level/GCSEs/Gaokao/ International Baccalaureate or other internationally accepted and relevant qualification.
2. The dates (month and year) when you started and then received each of your qualifications.
3. Your result – or, in the case of your degree, your anticipated result (e.g. 2:1) and three to four results from relevant modules (make sure that the results are good and from relatively recent modules).

You should always list the most recent qualifications and studies first; most people write this in table form (e.g. Table 16.4). If you have not yet graduated, you will need to indicate your expected outcome.

Table 16.4   An example of results

Qualification	Dates (from/to)	Institution	Outcome (or expected outcome)
BSc (Hons) Business Studies	September 2015-July 2018	University of Macclesfield	2:1 Hons (expected to graduate: July 2018)

(Continued)

Table 16.4 (Continued)

Qualification	Dates (from/to)	Institution	Outcome (or expected outcome)
A-Levels: Geography English Biology	August 2015	General High School	A B B
GCSEs: 10, including: Maths English Literature English Language Biology	August 2013	General High School	A A C B

'BUT I HAVE A QUESTION …'

… I have heard something about a 'HEAR' or 'GPA'. What are they?

Universities in the UK are trying out more ways to be fairer to students who are very skilled at what they do, but may not get the best results academically. The result of discussions on how to do this has resulted in the *Higher Education Achievement Report* (HEAR), a document which provides information about academic and non-academic activities undertaken during your time at university.

It is broken down into eight sections:

1. Data about the individual – name, date of birth, etc.
2. Confirms the qualification title.
3. Confirms how the qualification fits with others (MSc is higher than a BSc, for example).
4. Qualification details – module and qualification results, mode of study, etc.
5. What the qualification is intended to help an individual to do (e.g. enter a career in …).
6. Extra-curricular activities, awards, particular achievements and prizes.
7. Authentication of the HEAR.
8. Web-link to the relevant national university system of the institution.

The intention of the UK government is to increase the availability of the HEAR across universities (Universities UK, 2012) and to increase its use by employers. The expectation is that employers will engage with it more.

Details are available at the HEAR website: www.hear.ac.uk/

Some UK universities are also considering the use of Grade Point Average (GPA), a cumulative marking system used more in the United States and internationally than in Europe. Students in the United States, where a fail mark is anything less than 60, receive one of five grades: 0.0, 1.0, 2.0, 3.0 or 4.0 (or 4.33, representing an A+ grade). Graduation or passing is usually dependent on achieving 2.0 or sometimes 2.75, depending on the university.

There may be some qualifications that you took some time ago or qualifications that are not educational (e.g. Duke of Edinburgh Award scheme). These do not fit here, but should be mentioned under a section on personal achievements, or in your brief personal statement (e.g. 'I demonstrated leadership skills when I was …'). Sports certificates are not usually relevant for management roles, but might be included within your 'Hobbies and Interests' section.

International qualifications are always helpful, though sometimes an international employer will need a little help to understand their significance. Similarly, terms such as 'BSc' and 'MSc' translate to 'MS' and BS' in the US system.

Work experience

As in education and qualifications, start with the most recent work experience, give the dates (month and year) of each period of work, the job title and two or three points (10–15 words) outlining what you did and/or your key achievements (Table 16.5). If you have had responsibility for some aspect of management while in that role, then you need to state clearly what you were doing and what you achieved.

Table 16.5   An example of work experience

Work experience

Smith & Sons (Accountancy firm): Trainee Accountant (July–September 2015)

- Responsible for auditing receipts from clients
- Customer service duties: arranging appointments, responding to emails
- Communicating with managers, customers and other stakeholders to ensure smooth operation of customer service

=========== 'BUT I HAVE A QUESTION ...' ===========

... If I worked for just two weeks on a voluntary basis, should I include that?

The simple answer is that it depends what it adds to the impression an employer might have of you. If your longer-term work experience was working in a bar serving customers (which could have led to your developing your communication skills and 'customer orientation') but the two-week experience was work shadowing a senior CEO from a major multinational, then it would make sense to include both.

On the other hand, if that two-week voluntary internship was making the coffee and photocopying reports, then it is probably less useful to mention it.

Anything you put into the CV needs to add evidence of your credibility as a candidate, either by demonstrating a certain skill which has already been presented, or a new skill. Try not to be repetitive.

Additional responsibilities and activities

This important section tells an employer what you have done outside of your studies. For example, you may have reasonable grades, but if you have been president of a student society or had some responsibility for managing the budget of an athletics club, then this is something that a prospective employer would be extremely interested in (Table 16.6).

If you are successful in the application process and are taken on by the organisation, you will likely be leading others in some management role, so if you can demonstrate that you have already done so while at university (when you can make mistakes that will not affect businesses and public organisations), then you will have a much better chance of getting to the interview stage than without such experience.

Table 16.6   An example of key responsibilities

Key responsibilities

President, University Canoeing Society (September 2015-November 2016)

- Leading canoeing committee: setting agendas, scheduling meetings, leading team, setting goals, delegating event duties, responsible for increasing club profile
- Liaising with student union: dealing with queries, report writing, negotiating club budget
- Communicating with society members: established members' newsletter, developed club recruitment video (through leadership team), established club competition

Whatever you have done, you need to demonstrate to an employer that you have gained relevant skills and understanding from those activities. When it comes to activities that you have undertaken as part of a group (and hopefully in a position of some leadership or responsibility), you also need to be clear about your contribution to the achievement of the team's goals. What specifically did you do which helped the team achieve its goal?

Hobbies, interests and achievements

It may not seem the most relevant part of who you are, but including these can reveal a great deal about your abilities (Table 16.7). You might have organised a trip for a group of people during your time at university (showing organisational skills), or be good at a second language or musical instrument (showing persistence and determination), or be responsible for the finances in your student house (showing administrative and leadership skills). This section is your opportunity to indicate to an employer that you are an interesting individual who does more than just study, and tells the employer more about what motivates you and what you enjoy.

Table 16.7   An example of hobbies, interests and achievements

Hobbies, interests and achievements

Photography: I have been interested in photography for about five years and have had my photographs printed in two local magazines and a national newspaper. I have also organised my own exhibitions locally and have sold prints to clients.

Sailing: I have been taking sailing lessons every month for the past two years and have reached Level 3 in the National Sailing Standards Certificate.

References

You will normally need to indicate two referees who can provide an employer with a reference. You should give a minimum of one academic referee – often a personal tutor or a lecturer you know well – and one other, who can be a previous employer or another academic tutor. *Referees should always be asked before their name and contact details are given* and should never be:

- A relative.
- A personal friend.
- Another student (even if they have worked with you on group projects).
- Anyone who does not know you well enough to comment on your strengths and weaknesses.

Academic tutors are very used to writing references, but if they have no formal responsibility to do so for you, then be very polite in how you ask them to do it. Do not give them a short time limit.

When giving references, you need to give the referee's:

- Formal title (including Dr or Professor as appropriate – be sure to get it right) and name.
- Job title (Personal Tutor, Academic Lecturer, Associate Dean, etc.).
- Place of work.
- Postal and email addresses, and telephone numbers.

Some applicants choose not to give references and that is acceptable (particularly if you have no space left on the page), but if you decide not to give any names, then you do need to indicate that you are willing to do so, should the need arise, by saying 'References available on request.'

Understanding Your Experience

It may not seem like it, but you will have done a lot, either as part of your degree or via experience at school or part-time employment. If you are a postgraduate student, then the range of your activities should be even greater. The best way to prepare your applications is to make a list of anything that you have done or achieved that is significant to you or which had a positive impact on others around you. The following kinds of activities might be a good place to start, but will not be exhaustive:

- Activities and learning that you undertook at school before you came to university – employability and work experience sessions.
- Any leadership responsibilities you have had in student clubs or societies.
- Any unusual or interesting projects that you did as part of your degree. Did you go to visit any companies and write reports about them? Did you do a consultancy project of any sort?
- Anything you have done that was not part of a module or a degree course, but was connected to your university – teacher-led voluntary activity or skill development programme.
- Any leadership that you have done at work or during an internship which might have changed the way the organisation worked.
- Any high marks, university or regional awards or scholarships that you have received.
- Any dissertations or projects which show your interest and motivation in a particular area.
- Anything that you have been able to change in your role as a student representative.
- Any activities and responsibilities that you have had outside of your life at university – including at your previous school or college.

You may not have a great deal of work experience or involvement in student clubs, so you need to think about some other areas as well:

- Have you ever organised a family holiday, or one with friends? That requires management of resources, good communication, planning skills, sometimes conflict management, etc.
- Do you have any hobbies that require you to use or develop any leadership or management skills? Think about sports or other hobbies that you might do with other people.
- Are you responsible for managing your household – managing budgets? Keeping a calendar of everyone's appointments? Managing transport for the family? Decision making – or leading family discussions, or delegating decisions to others? Coordinating complicated and unpredictable schedules?

- What activities did you do through your course? Did you lead or take part in a group discussion, or give any team or individual presentations? Did you plan a schedule to complete your coursework? Did any of your coursework assignments require you to analyse and solve any challenging problems?
- Did you take part in any business competitions during your course? Maybe a case competition or developing and trying to sell a new product? What was the most interesting aspect of your course – did you demonstrate or develop any skills during that? What did you learn from this about your own motivation?

These are questions to consider carefully if you are struggling to find some student activities or work experience, even from your everyday life you can usually think of some way to identify and evidence the skills you say you have.

Make the list as comprehensive as you can, put dates by the activities and keep updating it regularly. As time moves on, you will probably forget many of the things that you have done and, for an employer, the more recent activities might be more useful.

This document does not need to be well formatted or include any personal details, it is solely a record of achievements and activities which will: 1) serve as a reminder of what you have done (which should be an encouraging thing to read); and 2) give you some content, which you can later use as a resource (not as the CV itself!) to compile your CV or complete an application form.

If you find yourself struggling to think of activities and leadership actions that you have undertaken, then try asking tutors, friends and/or family for some ideas of what you have done.

Skills-Based Structure

The above structure is a common way of developing your CV, but it is not the only way. Some people like to use a skills-based structure, as follows:

1. Personal and contact details.
2. Education and qualifications.
3. Brief list of work and social activities completed.
4. Details of how each of a number of relevant skills have been developed and demonstrated (see the example in Table 16.8).
5. References.

Table 16.8 An example of skills content

Skill 1: Communication skills – developed through:
• Social activities as president of the university abseiling club
• Academic modules requiring me to undertake presentations as part of a group
• Internship with PWC, where I needed to undertake presentations on management issues
Skill 2: Team-working skills – developed through:
• Group activities (e.g. marketing assignment) undertaken as part of my university studies

This structure is a good way to indicate clearly to an employer the skills you have and how you have developed them. Some applicants find it easier to write according to chronology (i.e. in the order that they have developed the experience) and some employers find it easier to see how someone has progressed in their studies and experience if the CV is done according to the detail presented above. For those with more life experience, a CV that is ordered chronologically will show more clearly any gaps in either employment or studies – employers are often very interested in such gaps.

Put simply, there is no one way of structuring a CV, nor should you ask an employer what their preferences are, of course – an employer will expect you to make up your own mind.

──────────── KEY LEARNING POINT ────────────

There is no one ideal CV structure, but employers will look to see if they have sufficient information on which to base a decision to select or reject.

CV PRESENTATION AND FORMATTING

Getting the presentation of a CV correct is very important, but we can talk about two areas here: spelling and grammar, and visual appearance. The former clearly have some right or wrong practices, but when it comes to visual presentation, there is no right and wrong, only personal preferences. Chapter 7 covered issues of spelling and grammar, and included a short exercise to work through; we will not repeat it here, but we can look at issues of visual presentation. One piece of advice, however, is to try to develop your own style rather than use a 'CV Wizard' available online. These tend to produce very standard applications that do not always stand out as much as they need to.

We need to look at three aspects of 'presentation': firstly, identifying what makes you different – your 'personal brand'. Secondly, the way we create a professional impression to enhance that 'brand' through the way we present content. And finally, the visual layout of the CV, which should be clear, uncluttered and useful.

Creating Your Personal Brand

During the academic year 2018–19, the average firm received more than 2000 applications for graduate jobs. Graduate employers typically received around 50 applications per vacancy (Institute of Student Employers, 2019). Financial services organisations seemed to attract around 51 applications per vacancy, while those dealing in fast-moving consumer goods received around 67 per vacancy. However, there is scope for finding a graduate job if you are prepared to look hard – and if you are able to make your application *stand out* in some way. This means that you need to think about what makes you special – and make sure that the employers get to see it, for the right reasons.

──────────── FOR YOU TO DO ════════════

Consider the following companies and places. What makes the brand stand out? When you think of these brands, what qualities or images come to mind?

1. Apple
2. Mercedes-Benz
3. Iceland (country)

4. Sony
5. Gucci
6. Emirates (airline)
7. United States
8. Virgin Atlantic
9. Latin America
10. Hello Kitty

These items will usually bring some image to people's minds that makes them different from other companies or places, so when you sell yourself to employers, you need to think about what it is that makes you different.

There are three aspects to generating a personal brand or your Unique Selling Proposition (USP): 1) what you have done; 2) who you are as an individual; and 3) making sure that the world – particularly employers (your 'target market', as it were) – knows about it, and the fastest way to ensure that the world knows about your personal achievements is to develop a professional online profile.

You can use your list of achievements (see the section above on understanding your experience) to write a personal profile, a succinct summary of yourself that highlights your USP for a prospective employer.

Over time, who you are, what you have done and how you sell yourself need to give an employer the same message. For example, it makes little sense trying to persuade an employer that you wish to have an international career when you have never been abroad, do not speak a foreign language and have no international friends. Instead, if you really wanted such an international career, you would have put effort into doing things – like going on a student exchange, organising potentially adventurous trips for you and your friends to unusual places, making friends from various places to find out more about their culture, and so on. These would show an employer your curiosity, sense of adventure and willingness to put effort into something that was not going to be easy.

 REFLECTION POINT

Take some time to think about the following questions and write down some answers.

What makes you different from others around you? Think about your character, your skills, your education and your experience.

As an individual, would there be some kinds of organisations that you would prefer to work for, and others you would not? Why?

If you were leading others in an organisation, what words might describe your leadership style?

These questions (and others you can think of) should help you to identify your 'brand' – which, in turn, should help you use the right kinds of words when writing your CV and covering letter.

If you spend a little time comparing your brand to the culture of the organisation, then you might be able to decide whether the organisation would be a good one to work for.

Creating a Favourable Impression

Creating a favourable impression is about the way we express ourselves in detailing what we have done (i.e. the nature of the job and responsibilities in student societies etc. during our studies), learned and achieved. Many times, students and recent graduates discuss what they have been doing but don't always present anything about the skills they have developed, the learning they have gained or the achievements that they have accomplished: employers are looking for exactly these things.

When you present your work experience or responsibilities during your studies, identify clearly and succinctly:

*   The **nature** of the job/activity: I was responsible for …
*   What you **learned**: I developed my skills in … I learned how to …
*   What you **achieved**: I changed the way we … I was able to save £xxx … I grew my sales by xxx%

━━━━━━━━━━ FOR YOU TO DO ━━━━━━

Earlier in the chapter, we examined how to use a brief job description (see Figure 16.2) to identify the skills required for a job application.

Using that job description, we could look at the 'Work Experience' section of two CVs given below. Each one has three sets of work experience, including placements or internships, and the jobs are the same. Which do you think is going to go forward and get the job interview?

Example 1

Dates	Organisation and Job Title	Nature of Work
June 2016-Sept 2016	Nextquik Drinks and Beverages: Drink Vendor Assistant	• I was responsible for delivering drinks and beverages to local shops - I had 24 stores around the city to deliver to and did so well • Driving around the city as efficiently as possible, and making sure I did not obstruct other traffic when parking • Taking 10 minutes to complete a detailed report sheet each day
August 2017-May 2018	Supersam Accounting: Accounting Assistant	• Completing daily checking of receipts • Discussing with manager plans for the next day • Reviewing information on income and outgoings
June 2019-Sept 2019	Morden City Bank: Bank Teller	• Dealing with customer queries • Assisting with the opening of accounts • Checking cash deposits

(Continued)

Example 2

Dates	Organisation and Job Title	Nature of Work
June 2016-Sept 2016	Nextquik Drinks and Beverages: Drink Vendor Assistant	• Successfully organised drinks deliveries • Established and negotiated personal delivery schedule in order to deliver drinks to customers on time • Analysed issues and problems to improve service to customers • Developed my analytical and customer service skills • Was able to reduce length of delivery trips by 25%
August 2017-May 2018	Supersam Accounting: Accounting Assistant	• Provided accounting advice service to three large clients • Provided monthly oral report to accounting team relating to those clients • Wrote monthly reports for clients to assist in improving accounting procedures • Developed my skills in Excel and report writing
June 2019-Sept 2019	Morden City Bank: Bank Teller	• Led short project with other members of banking team to enhance layout of customer service areas • Worked independently to organise own workload • Achieved 'Outstanding Customer Service Award' in August 2019 • Trained my replacement in how to undertake the role with a focus on customer service • Developed leadership and communication skills

Which candidate would you put forward for the interview?

When we look at these two example CV sections, we can see that while the jobs listed were identical in both cases, the way that the candidates have presented themselves is very different. For reference, it is the second example that is most likely to go forward to get an interview because:

1. They have given content that is more relevant to the job description. There is mention of oral communication, written reports and analysing information. The comment about leadership with the second candidate in the final part of their work experience would instantly stand out to a recruiter.
2. The first example gives a very broad impression of what someone has done and while we must keep that accurate and truthful, there is no real focus or thought given to how the content might be understood. The way we phrase what we have done is important in creating the impression of someone who is focused on how they work.
3. The second example gives more clarity about what they have learnt and achieved during the three parts of their work experience. The words 'developed', 'achieved' and 'analysed' are what are called 'power words' (see Table 16.9 below) and help to give a more professional impression of what someone has done.
4. The way that the candidate in example 1 has phrased some of their comments suggests someone who saw very little value in what they were doing. There are no comments about what they have learned or achieved, and some small irrelevant details are included ('and making sure I did not obstruct other traffic when parking') which actually give a very poor impression. Overall, the comments here are either so brief and unfocused as to be useless to a recruiting employer or are overly long and irrelevant and give a very poor impression.

Use of 'power words'

Those who provide careers guidance often talk about 'power words'. These are words that can enhance the significance of what you have done. Table 16.9 gives some examples of the kinds of words which help create more of an impact.

Table 16.9 Power words for use in a CV or covering letter

• Advised	• Discovered	• Performed
• Analysed	• Distributed	• Planned
• Arranged	• Edited	• Prepared
• Assembled	• Evaluated	• Prescribed
• Assisted	• Examined	• Presented
• Audited	• Expanded	• Processed
• Calculated	• Identified	• Produced
• Charted	• Implemented	• Promoted
• Collected	• Improved	• Provided
• Completed	• Increased	• Recorded
• Conducted	• Installed	• Referred
• Consolidated	• Instituted	• Represented
• Consulted	• Instructed	• Researched
• Coordinated	• Interpreted	• Reviewed
• Corresponded	• Interviewed	• Served
• Counselled	• Invented	• Sold
• Created	• Lectured	• Solved
• Delivered	• Maintained	• Studied
• Designed	• Managed	• Supervised
• Determined	• Negotiated	• Supplied
• Developed	• Networked	• Trained
• Devised	• Observed	• Translated
• Diagnosed	• Obtained	• Wrote
• Directed	• Operated	
	• Ordered	
	• Organised	

Spelling and Grammar

Getting the spelling correct in your CV is a must. The spelling exercise in Chapter 7 (page 153) gives you a chance to examine and practise some common words that are spelt incorrectly, but even our typing can get in the way sometimes. If you have not already completed that exercise, now might be a good time to do so.

══════ BOX 16.1 ══════

A Common Spelling Error in CVs

How do you spell CV properly? People simply write 'CV' at the top of their submission, but it is also common to write out the words in full. Getting that very first heading wrong can mean your CV never gets looked at.

The correct spelling is 'Curriculum Vitae', but it is not uncommon for employers to see variations such as:

(Continued)

'Curiculum Vitae'

'Curirculum Vita' or

'Curriclum Viate'

Of course, this is not the only kind of spelling mistake that can occur. The most disastrous spelling mistake would be getting your email address (or that of your referees) wrong, and this happens from time to time as well. Other spelling mistakes in section headings, like 'personel details' or 'work experience', are surprisingly common. Employers' names should always be spelt correctly, of course, and make sure you spell the name of your institution correctly: it should be 'university', not 'univeristy'. If you need to, check your spelling against the words in Table 16.9 above.

Getting your spelling (and in a covering letter or application form where you are writing in full sentences, your grammar) correct is important for a variety of reasons, not least because poor spelling or grammar implies a lack of attention to detail, especially in a situation where you are trying to make a good impression.

 FOR YOU TO DO

Have a look at the sample 'Student Activities' section below. How would you succinctly write this part of the CV, maybe using bullet points? What would you include, and leave out? Once you have done so, compare your answers with other students.

> I was membership secretary for the Student Hiking Association between Dec 2018 and May 2019. I was responsible for everything to do with the membership of the club, from making sure that we had enough leaflets to give out to making sure that membership fees were paid. I also had to create forms to ensure that we were insured for every member, and for getting students to complete and submit those forms before we went on any hiking activity. I also needed to make sure that everyone paid their membership fees on time and send a report back to the Student Union.
>
> Being a senior leader in this organisation was a tough challenge for me. I wasn't used to pushing students to do what they needed to do, or to make sure that bureaucratic forms were completed on time when people didn't understand why (and when I was just a member, that included me as well). But I learned why they were important and then I thought about how I needed to communicate that so that others would understand.
>
> I worked with a couple of other students in a team and helped them to organise the activities for the students. As part of the leadership committee for the SHA, I enjoyed being a member of the team. The club president needed us to give a brief oral report at each of the monthly meetings we had and we discussed our achievements and areas to develop. During the time I was membership secretary, we increased club membership by 15% and I helped to significantly improve our income by slightly raising both the number of members and the fees. At the same time, the other members of my own team increased the number of events we held from 8 during the year to 11, making the club more attractive to join.

 KEY LEARNING POINT

Your CV is an advertisement for yourself. There is no perfect or universally ideal way of writing a CV, but a poorly written one will be very memorable.

'BUT I HAVE A QUESTION ...'

... I struggle to get started and this all seems to be so complicated, and then when I have done my CV it never seems perfect. What should I do?

Well, firstly, there is no such thing as a perfect CV, as we have said before. A CV is always going to be a living document. You add to it as you take on new responsibilities or have accomplished more achievements, and that means it is constantly changing as your life and career grows and changes. The CV you put together now will not be the CV you use for jobs in three years' time. Of course, even now, you might list everything you are doing but that list will be edited and you will need to delete things that do not seem relevant to the jobs that you are applying for.

If getting started is the challenge, then how about making a list of what you have done - your key modules and grades, your student society activities and responsibilities, your work experience (including your internships) and other things. Start with these headings and begin to make a list, OK?

Once you have that list, then you can start to:

1. Edit out content that is not relevant for the job.
2. Check spelling and grammar.
3. Rewrite what you have written to ensure the content is succinct.
4. Rephrase and edit, using any relevant and truthful 'power words'.

And then you will have something that might be good to submit, once you have adapted this to make sure that the visual layout is good - and that is what we are going to look at next.

Visual Layout

When it comes to establishing a good visual impression of your application, you are looking to ensure that the recipient can easily see what you want them to see (which presumably is what is required for the job). This might mean a little variety in how you present certain information and how you colour, format and present your CV. It does not mean, however, that you need to use expensive paper or fancy and elegant fonts, or that you need to have a CV 10 pages long.

Length

Your CV should be no longer than two sides. Some recommend developing a CV that is one side long, but that is going to be a challenge if you have sufficient information to match all the required skills for the role. There is no word count, but write succinctly. CVs that are two sides long are fine.

Using bold text

Bold text – or *italics* or <u>underlining</u> – is a great way of ensuring that certain words in your CV stand out, but use bold formatting sparingly. A sentence that has every other word in bold will obviously not have the desired effect.

Using bullet points

These are used a great deal in CVs and can be useful for ensuring that the recipient knows that they are getting outline notes, rather than complete sentences (e.g. 'I spent three years working as a hotel receptionist during my time at university' can become 'Three years' experience as hotel receptionist during my studies'). General advice is not to have absolutely everything in bullet points – the danger is that it becomes a little repetitive and unappealing to the eye.

Colour

Using colour in your CV is usually not necessary. For many graduate positions, it is highly likely that your CV will be photocopied in black and white, and circulated to a variety of people, so colour in your CV becomes fairly irrelevant. However, a controlled and purposeful use of shading can be quite useful, either for headings or to highlight occasional and important words. If you do use shading, ensure that it is dark enough to be photocopied, but not too dark so as to obscure any writing.

'Clutter'

It is not easy to define what is meant here, but a balance is needed between something which looks 'very busy' (lots of information, untidily crammed into a small space, where it is not easy to distinguish relevant words from less relevant ones) and something that is so neat and tidy that it looks very sparse, as if you have hardly anything to say about yourself. A CV which has so much information that it needs to use a font smaller than Calibri size 11 (font and size) is probably going to be too cluttered; the suggestion would be to reduce the information on the page.

The best way to see if your CV looks cluttered is to hold it at arm's length and see whether it appears 'neat but not empty' to you.

Care and attention to detail

The following need to be **avoided**:

- Careless spelling mistakes (watch out for using the wrong words: a spell-checker will *not* identify these for you!). Make sure that you spell headings, the names of previous employers and referees correctly.
- Sentences, paragraphs or tables which go over the page break.
- Informality and being too chatty: keep the CV succinct and focused.
- Text that uses different fonts, or fonts of different sizes. Be consistent throughout.
- *Any* dishonesty: if you are dishonest, you will almost certainly be found out, and if that happens then you will either be fired (if the truth comes out after the job offer has been made) or you will not progress. Be aware that employers and HR professionals do talk to each other, even if they are from different organisations, so lying on one application may mean you do not get considered for others as well.

 KEY LEARNING POINT

What you do include is usually as important as what you do not include. Before submitting your CV and covering letter, you need to check through carefully to ensure that everything is as you want it to be. Try to get someone else who can give you some good advice to go through it as well.

COVERING LETTERS

A covering letter introduces you to a prospective employer. If the CV is the bones of who you are and what you have done, then the covering letter provides the linkages and the muscle. The CV should be written in note style (it does not need to be in full sentences), but the letter is a piece of business writing, written in good English and formatted in a particular way.

However, in the same way that a CV should not reflect literally everything you have done, so too the covering letter should summarise why you are suitable for the job. It must not be a list of everything that you have done and should supplement rather than repeat the information in the CV, but each of the main paragraphs should relate to a different aspect of your suitability. It must establish the contribution that you can make in a way which does not appear arrogant, and it should say more about what you can do for the company rather than what the company can do for you or your career.

Understanding Business Writing

Before we go into detail on writing a covering letter specifically, it would be helpful to address some aspects of writing a formal business letter. Business letters tend to be laid out in a fairly standard format.

═══════════════ FOR YOU TO DO ═══════════════

Have a look at a formal business letter that you have received. It might be from your bank, from a university or from another organisation that you have contact with.

1. Look at the formatting. On the letter, where is your address? Where is the address of the sending organisation? Where on the page is the date?
2. Look at the kind of language used. If a friend was writing this to you, how would their language and words differ from those in the letter in front of you?
3. How does the letter end?

Noticing the layout and the language used in the letter will help significantly in ensuring that your own covering letter meets a minimum professional standard. A possible layout is given in Table 16.10.

If you can find out the name of the individual who might be dealing with graduate applications, then that could be useful, but applications to a graduate training scheme may go to departmental managers. Try to find a name if you can (it will make the application seem a lot more personal), but be cautious about using a name if you are unsure.

Always refer back to the CV as much as you can, using phrases such as 'As shown in my CV ...' or 'The CV also indicates that ...'. Do not forget that the purpose of the covering letter is to direct the prospective employer to the important parts of your CV, but the covering letter should *not* repeat the CV.

Have a strong, positive ending, including information on how and when you will follow up, and inform about availability for interviews if applicable.

Table 16.10   An example of a covering letter

Your address and postcode
Your email address(es)

Recipient's address and postcode

Date

Dear Sir/Madam,

Re: Job Application for Vacancy Ref: XXX

I am writing to express my interest and to submit an application for the role of … I enclose my CV, which gives details of my degree, my work experience and my involvement in university clubs and societies. I would like to use this opportunity to explain why I think I am suitable for this role.

[Paragraph explaining your education and why it is relevant. What relevant knowledge and skills have you developed during your degree?]

[One or two paragraphs explaining how your experiences have contributed to who you are and the skills you have.]

[Paragraph explaining your education and why it is relevant. What relevant knowledge and skills have you developed during your degree?]

[Brief paragraph explaining your motivation for a particular career.]

Thank you for taking the time to read my application: I hope you will find that I have the skills and abilities to be able to take the application further, but please do not hesitate to contact me if you should need any additional information.

I look forward to being able to discuss my application with you in the near future.

Yours faithfully,

[Signature]
[Print your name]

Writing in a Business Style

In the earlier chapters, we covered how to write in an academic style. Writing in a business style is somewhat different. Some tips are as follows:

1. Keep your sentences short and focused on evidence for the skills that employers are looking for.
2. Be unemotional and keep your letter factual: words like 'amazing', 'wonderful', 'really' and 'fantastic' are not appropriate.
3. Be specific about your contribution to any team activities.
4. Be polite and try not to overdo things. Phrases such as 'My magnificent achievement …' are a little excessive.
5. Do not tell employers everything, but give them enough about your KSAOs (your knowledge, skills, abilities and other qualities) to make them interested; they can always follow up with questions at an interview.
6. Remember that your reader will have lots of such letters to read, so make yours stand out.

Business letters usually end 'Yours sincerely' or 'Yours faithfully' (notice small 's' and small 'f'). They both have a very specific use:

- 'Yours faithfully' is used when you are writing to someone *you do not know*, in which case you will have started the letter with 'Dear Sir/Madam'.
- 'Yours sincerely' is used when you are writing to someone *you do know*, in which case you will have started the letter with 'Dear Mr XXX'.

COMPLETING APPLICATION FORMS

The principles which govern good CV writing also apply to completing an application form well: both require you to demonstrate to an employer that you have the skills to do the job they are recruiting for. However, an application form has more in common with a selection interview than it does with a CV. The use of an application form gives the employer the opportunity to ask those questions that they want to ask.

Understanding the Application Form

In one sense, application forms are fairly straightforward and standardised. All application forms will ask for your contact details, your educational qualifications and your work experience, and will ask you to give the names of referees who can testify to what you have done and how well you have done it. However, this is probably where the similarities between application forms from different employers will stop.

Most graduate application forms will give you an opportunity to talk about how you have developed and demonstrated specific skills that the employer is seeking. If you have undertaken little extra-curricular activity during your time as a student, then you might struggle with some of the questions which appear on application forms.

Most also give you a tight word limit (often 200–300 words) in which to give your answers.

 FOR YOU TO DO

Look at the following questions. How would you respond?

1. Give an example of a time when you had to make a difficult decision without complete information. How did you go about it and what was the result?
2. Discuss an occasion when you contributed to the learning and development of others. How did your input change their behaviour?
3. Describe a time when you had to inspire and motivate others. How did you go about it, and what impact did you have?
4. How have you used your creativity to solve a difficult problem? Briefly outline the situation and indicate how successful you were.
5. Outline a situation in which you had to prioritise conflicting demands on your time. How did you go about deciding on your priorities?
6. Describe a situation in which you realised that you had made a serious mistake in your work. What action did you take after you realised you had made the mistake? Why did you take such action?

Each of the questions given above is designed to assess your previous experience in demonstrating the skills employers are looking for. Looking at each question in turn, it is not difficult to see the skills that they are seeking:

1. Decision making.
2. Management of others' learning.
3. Inspiration and leadership.
4. Creativity.
5. Time management.
6. Ability to deal with a mistake.

At one level, these are obvious, but each of the questions will have been designed to assess your competence in other ways as well:

- Q1 is also about how you respond to uncertainty. In management, many decisions need to be made quickly, with incomplete information. How confident you might be in doing so could be a key success factor in the job.
- Q2 could also be about how you give feedback to others. 'Contributing to others' learning' is often more about one-to-one management than it is about standing up and giving a training seminar. If you have done this in a student society or at work, then you have a story to tell.
- Q3 is about leadership, but the question asks, 'How did you go about it?', so there is a less obvious 'planning' aspect to this. The question also asks about the impact of what you did, so your answer should indicate that you know how to evaluate the impact of actions, whether those are your own actions or those of others who might be working for you.
- Q4 is perhaps more obvious, but the more difficult the problem, the more excited an employer is going to be when they read that you were able to solve it successfully. What is important, however, is that you have actually tried to solve difficult problems, rather than give them to someone else to solve.
- Q5 is probably not difficult for many students to write about. You have probably had two assignments due at the same time, or job hunting and assignments taking place together, but the more unusual and challenging the situations you give, the more impressive will be the fact that you have had success.
- Q6 is somewhat different, because this question has no apparent right or wrong answer. The question is about your values, rather than your skills. When employers are looking at the responses to a question like this, they will determine whether someone's actions would be desirable or undesirable for their own organisation. The 'correctness' of an answer depends on the culture and values of the organisation, but it is clear that an employer will expect you to be honest.

 FOR YOU TO DO

Look at the three answers given below for the first question above, repeated here:

1. Give an example of a time when you had to make a difficult decision without complete information. How did you go about it and what was the result? (200 words max)

   a. 'I needed to decide how to complete a coursework assignment but the criteria were not clearly described in the course documents. I was able to talk to other classmates and find out about their ideas and that helped me get the assignment completed. In the end, I got a mark of 65%.' (52 words)

b. 'I was on the committee of the canoeing club and we were holding a social event to attract new members. As part of that social event, we wanted to ensure that we had good catering for the event and we had two possibilities but neither could commit to supplying food and drink without knowing whether they could really supply what was needed (which was based on how many people would be coming), which we could not confirm at the time. The price of one supplier was cheaper than the other only if there were more than 65 people at the event. I made the decision to choose that supplier based on numbers who had attended a similar event at the same time last year. We finally had 120 students turn up for the event and we made a profit by choosing the cheaper supplier.' (144 words)

c. 'I was working as part of a group and we had to interview three local firms as part of our coursework. The intention was that we interviewed individuals in these firms to find out about their strategy and whether there were any difficulties in their trying to achieve their strategy, but the course materials didn't give much guidance so we decided to find just anyone who was working in those companies. We interviewed six people and so our strategy was quite successful.' (82 words)

Questions

1. What do you think makes a strong and a weak answer?
2. What weaknesses do these answers show about their other qualities? Is there anything that was mentioned which did not give a good impression of any of the candidates?
3. Does length make a difference to the strength of the answer?
4. Which do you think is the stronger and weaker answers? Why?
5. Bearing in mind your thinking about weak and strong answers, try to provide your own strong answers to the remaining five questions above (questions 2 to 6).

In all the questions above (and probably others that you will find in application forms), there are some commonalities. They all expect you to give an example ('of a time when you …'), to communicate succinctly and clearly, and to evaluate the outcomes of your actions.

Employers are also looking to see your breadth of experience. If you have part-time work experience and have taken a leadership role in a student society or led a coursework team, then you will probably have enough experience to answer the questions well, but make sure as far as possible that *your answer to each question uses an example of a different situation.* (One situation which involves all the challenges and difficulties asked for is either likely to be stressful or has been managed very badly by yourself and/or others in your team.)

Always talk about what *you* did: Chapter 9 talked about using 'we' in your communication, but when you are applying for a job, using 'we' makes it somewhat unclear as to what your own contribution was.

Completing an application form is not easy, so take time to practise your answers. Online application forms will usually ask you to enter text into webpages, but will usually enable you to prepare an answer offline. Such forms may give you an option to download and save your form, and might be scanned by a computer for keywords, but you *must* keep a copy of what you send – employers will almost certainly want to know more once you get to an interview.

It is also worth noting that if the process is facilitated online, then you will not be able to apply after the closing date, so you will need to get your application in *on time*.

=== KEY LEARNING POINT ===

Targeting your application is more difficult with a CV than with an application form, but completing an application form for a graduate job can take a great deal of time and skill.

SPECULATIVE APPLICATIONS

The above sections work well when you are applying for a specific vacancy, or a specific training programme. Some people will select particular companies that they wish to work for on the basis of accurate and good information they have about what it is like to work there (e.g. 'employer of the year' awards etc.), and will write to them asking whether they would have any vacancies in the near future.

There is a significant difference between the principles outlined above and those identified here. In the traditional process, an application will need to be focused on the criteria required to be able to do the job well. However, a speculative application would (by definition) approach a particular individual asking for consideration in relation to any forthcoming vacancies.

The internet has considerably impacted on the need for speculative applications. There is a great deal of information publicly available that was not available previously. Websites such as LinkedIn and Monster.co.uk enable individuals to upload their CV and vacancies are posted on organisation websites, so if you have a particular company in mind, you *must* check its website before making a speculative application – if you do not, then you might give the impression that you cannot be bothered to do so.

A speculative application needs to be approached with caution. A CV needs to be no longer than two pages, so you need to consider carefully what goes into the CV and what you leave out, but, without having a particular role in mind, it can sometimes be difficult to know what to include and what to leave out. Including skills that are not relevant for any vacancy a company might have – or leaving out ones that are – can mean that your application does not get the attention you might want it to receive.

The letter that would accompany a speculative CV also needs to be worded very carefully. If you wish to make a speculative application, then you need to ensure that the impression you create is neither of someone who is desperate, nor of someone who can do any job that might exist in that organisation. Box 16.2 gives more information.

■■■■■■■■■■ **BOX 16.2** ■■■■■■■■■■

Phrases to Use in Speculative Application Letters

Getting the phrasing right in a speculative application is important for the impression you want to create. Again, many of the 'power words' given earlier can assist in this, but here are some additional phrases and their meanings which might prove useful:

'I am [intending to work in/seeking] a marketing role.'

'After some careful thought, I have decided that I [would prefer/am extremely keen] to work in a [multinational/small/public] organisation like your own because ...'

'I would like to work for [name of organisation] because ...'

'I believe that my skills, knowledge and experience are suitable for this kind of a role because ...'

'My education [indicate your degree] has given me ...'

'I am a confident and innovative individual who ...'

'I understand that you may not be able to give me a reply, but would be grateful if you could keep my application on file for any forthcoming vacancies.'

One perceived advantage of speculative applications is that you can apparently send the same – or very similar – applications to many different organisations with relatively little effort. In effect it is like direct marketing of yourself to the 'customer', but just as a great deal of direct mail is put into the bin, it can take a fair amount of luck to catch the right organisation at the right time.

However, there are some ideas which can help to increase your chances of success:

1. Look in the financial and business news for companies and industries which are expanding and which are exploring new markets, especially if you have knowledge or skills (languages) in those new markets.
2. Look in the personnel magazines for vacancies related to graduate recruitment. If new graduate recruitment staff are being taken on in an organisation, it might mean that they are expecting to recruit more graduates.
3. Consider carefully whether to apply to organisations that are making lots of people redundant or to ones that are merging: organisations which merge often do so to save costs, though such mergers might give some interesting opportunities. You might decide, however, that organisations which are going through such changes provide less certainty than those which are more stable.
4. Think about applying to smaller companies, especially those which have only recently started up. Such businesses often need expertise quickly, but because they are not well known, many graduates may not apply to their vacancies. They rarely have significant resources to devote to graduate recruitment, so might well welcome speculative applications. They can be great places to work as their small size and hopefully rapid growth can give you early responsibility and breadth of experience very quickly.

Speculative applications rarely succeed, but if they are targeted and constructed carefully (which means finding out about the organisation, understanding the culture and then reflecting those same values in your application), then they can sometimes be successful.

 KEY LEARNING POINT

A well-targeted speculative application will usually take as much work and time to complete as an application for an advertised position.

SELF-CONFIDENCE AND APPLICATIONS

For some, this might have been a really tough and frightening chapter. Maybe you are approaching the end of your degree and have come to realise that you have not had much work experience and you have not really got involved in student clubs or societies or taken any responsibilities within those – and maybe that is making you have doubts about your ability to get a job. There are two areas to think about here – the nature of our previous experience, and the self-confidence we have.

The Nature of Our Experience

If we are going to be successful at applying for jobs and start our careers, then the more evidence we have and the stronger the proof of that evidence, then the higher chance we will have of getting that job. But not having a part-time job or not being involved in student societies does not mean that we do not have these skills – and sometimes, even having that experience does not necessarily mean we develop or demonstrate any skills!

In this way, CVs and application forms are different. CVs give you the control over the skills and experiences you talk about, whereas an application takes that control from you and asks you specific questions: 'Tell me about a time when you …'. That means that sometimes CVs can be more difficult because we do not typically think of things we do in life that are outside of working or student clubs. See the section above on understanding our experience for some additional ideas.

The Nature of Our Self-Confidence

The second issue relates to our levels of self-confidence in putting together and submitting an application. There are typically two approaches here: either we think that we will get the job anyway because our degree is a high class degree or because our previous experience and background tells us that there is never going to be an issue. The truth is that getting a job after university is a competitive process: depending on the subject of your degree, you may or may not find that competition very strong and your degree alone is hardly ever going to be enough.

In order to get through to an interview, you need to demonstrate that you have evidence of most (90%) if not all of the skills required for the job, and where the job is rare and competition is going to be strong, that you have stronger (multiple sources) and clearer evidence of all skills than most others. In most cases, the competition for graduate jobs *is* going to be extremely strong.

There is a balance to be struck between self-confidence and self-doubt – and the need to be realistic – and these things are not easy to balance. You may well have better evidence for the skills than you think you have, so seek advice on your application and the vacancy from a careers adviser or maybe a friend who works in a professional role.

INTEGRATION AND APPLICATION

Covering letters, CVs and job applications all require you to know about yourself and your experience, so one of the first steps to take in making a job application is to find out about yourself.

Step 1: Make a list of all the significant activities you have done and what you have achieved through them.

Step 2: Next to each one, identify the skills that you have developed and demonstrated through those activities. Each activity will probably have more than one skill.

You now have a list of your skills, and evidence for each of them.

Step 3: Review and discover what skills are needed for each vacancy that you are applying for and select those events/activities that are relevant.

This should now give you a focused list of activities, ready for emphasising on an application form, and for mentioning in your CV.

Step 4 (for the CV/covering letter): Prepare a standard structure and format for your CV and covering letter so that you can 'slot' the information into that structure, using appropriate 'power words' (as long as they are truthful).

Step 4 (for the application form): Review the questions and draft your answers carefully in a document. This gives you time to edit, use appropriate 'power words' and ensure that, as far as possible, each question deals with a different situation you have faced.

Step 5: Check your spelling, check relevance and re-read your application carefully.

Step 6: Give your application to someone else who can give you some expert advice – maybe a careers guidance counsellor. You could give it to a friend who works in a managerial role, but they will need to reflect carefully on what the recruiter is looking for, rather than on their own judgement.

Step 7: If you are happy with your application, make sure you submit it *before* the closing date! A late application will not usually be considered, unless there is a shortage of applicants.

The Link with Your Studies

The skills needed to complete a good job application are similar to those needed to do well in your studies. A CV will require you to write succinctly; application forms will require you to provide a relevant and direct answer to any question; both will need you to present evidence for the points that you raise; both will need you to demonstrate your analytical skills; and the work you need to do to find out about the organisation is little different from what you might need to do for an academic assignment.

There are some limits to this parallel, of course: you should never include paragraphs of text in your CV; you should not be citing research; and while your letter should have some sort of structure, it should not start with the same sort of introduction or end with the same sort of conclusion as a traditional academic essay. However, it is useful to recognise that the skills you use for your academic work are going to be useful in other contexts as well.

CONCLUSION

By the end of this chapter, you should be able to:

- Understand how employers view the recruitment and selection processes.
- Describe how employers select and use different selection tools.
- Identify the qualities needed in different kinds of roles.
- Write and compile CVs, covering letters and application forms.
- Develop speculative applications.

Submitting good applications takes a great deal of time and effort. You will need to analyse the vacancy (if there is one), determine the skills being sought and then provide evidence to the recruiters that you have exactly those skills. Further, you also need to suggest to them that you have the knowledge and education that will help their organisation to progress and achieve its goals.

This evidence needs to address sufficiently all the essential requirements and some of the desirable ones as well.

ADDITIONAL RESOURCES

Want to learn more? Visit https://study.sagepub.com/morgan2e to gain access to a wide range of online resources, including interactive tests, tasks, further reading and downloads.

Website Resources

The following websites offer useful advice on writing CVs, application forms and covering letters.

Prospects: www.prospects.ac.uk/careers-advice/cvs-and-cover-letters

Purdue University: https://owl.purdue.edu/owl/job_search_writing/resumes_and_vitas/index.html

University of Kent: www.kent.ac.uk/ces/student/cvs.html

University of Leicester: www2.le.ac.uk/offices/careers-new/applications-and-cvs

University of Sheffield: www.sheffield.ac.uk/careers/applications

Textbook Resources

Bailey, S. (2011) *Academic Writing for International Students of Business*. Abingdon: Routledge (particularly Part 4.2).

Cameron, S. (2010) *The Business Student's Handbook: Skills for Study and Employment* (5th edition). Harlow: Pearson (particularly Chapter 17).

Gallagher, K. (2016) *Essential Study and Employment Skills for Business and Management Students* (3rd edition). Oxford: Oxford University Press (particularly Chapter 13).

Harwood, L., Owens, L. M. D. and Kadakia, C. (2017) *Your Career: How to Make it Happen* (9th edition). Boston, MA: Cengage (particularly Chapters 4, 5 and 6).

Hind, D. and Moss, S. (2011) *Employability Skills*. Houghton-le-Spring: Business Education Publishers (particularly Chapter 6).

Neugebauer, J. and Evans-Brain, J. (2016) London: Sage (particularly Chapter 4).

Rook, S. (2013) *The Graduate Career Guidebook*. New York: Palgrave (particularly Chapters 10, 11 and 12).

Smale, R. and Fowlie, J. (2009) *How to Succeed at University*. London: Sage (particularly Chapter 10).

17

SELECTION INTERVIEWS

If opportunity doesn't knock, build a door. (Milton Berle)

CHAPTER STRUCTURE

Figure 17.1

When you see the this means go to the companion website https://study.sagepub.com/morgan2e to do a quiz, complete a task, read further or download a template.

AIMS OF THE CHAPTER

By the end of this chapter, you should be able to:

- Identify potential questions you might be asked in advance of an interview.
- Understand some basic dos and don'ts.
- Identify questions to ask the potential employer.
- Evaluate the impact of your non-verbal behaviour as well as the content of the answers that you give.

WHEN SHOULD YOU READ THIS CHAPTER?

The best time to read this chapter is before you have your first graduate job interview, so you should be reading this during the first semester of your final year as a university student.

INTRODUCTION

Undergoing a selection interview is often seen as one of the most nerve-wracking and challenging experiences that an individual is likely to face. In the perception of many, the stress of the experience is not dissimilar to taking your driving test or giving a professional presentation for the first time, but the reality is that it does not need to be. This chapter aims to dispel some of the myths surrounding the selection interview, and to present some ideas about how employers assess individuals' responses. The chapter will examine how employers construct selection interviews, what goes through their minds when undertaking interviews and how they develop a structure and questions. It will also examine how employers make judgements after a selection interview and will give you the chance to be in the interviewer's shoes and evaluate different answers.

One of the assumptions in being invited for a selection interview is that any decision making is one way: that if the organisation decides you are the individual for the role (or for a general training scheme), you will accept it. While reading this chapter it is important to recognise that the interview is probably one of the few chances you will have to find out about the organisation before you commit to working for it, if you are given the chance to do so.

The principal communication skills required for doing 'well' at an interview are likely to be similar to those used in a good conversation. Establishing a sense of rapport, smiling and speaking clearly are generally important, but being skilled at engaging in conversation is not going to be sufficient for performing 'well' at a selection interview.

The chapter will begin by looking at what 'performing *well*' means in practice and will establish what the selectors' objectives are. It will then look at the various stages of a selection interview and give some views from those who are used to conducting selection interviews, and who have seen the mistakes that candidates often make. The chapter will move on to examine some issues that you might like to think about when considering whether it is a job role that you want, and will give some advice for when things do not go the way you had hoped.

PERFORMING WELL: THE EMPLOYER'S OBJECTIVES

It might seem strange to put the two sides of the interview – the candidate and the employer – together at the start of this chapter, but it is important to define clearly what we mean by 'performing well', and the only way we can do that is by considering what the employer is seeking to gain from the encounter. (In this way, it is no different from considering how to write a good essay by defining what a lecturer is seeking.)

An employer will likely be seeking the answer to one or more of the following questions:

1. Is this candidate likely to be able to perform well in the role?
2. Is this candidate likely to be able to perform at an acceptable level within the organisation?
3. Is this candidate likely to fit into the culture of the organisation?

The first question will certainly apply where there is a specific job on offer, whereas both the other questions address the two requisite qualities for performing well in an organisation: namely, person–job fit and person–organisation fit. The second question might be more important for a selection interview where successful individuals will the join a general training scheme of some kind.

If the objective is to identify whether a candidate is likely to be able to perform well in the role, then, as we saw in Chapter 15, the questions asked will be designed around the job role. A skilled interviewer will want to ask questions based on the job role that they have in mind, will do so in a structured and systematic manner, and will always be seeking information to enable them to answer one of these two questions. They will, therefore, reject candidates who fail to give sufficient information, who give information that fails to answer the question asked or who give an answer that would be considered inappropriate or 'incorrect' in some way.

SELECTION INTERVIEW

A selection interview is a conversation with the purpose of deciding whether a candidate has the ability and sufficient experience to perform well in a job role.

The time given to any first stage interview is limited. A final-year undergraduate will need to convince an employer within 30 or 45 minutes that they are worth taking to the next stage. If the interviewer is seeking convincing evidence that the candidate possesses five qualities (usually it is more) and allows the candidate to ask questions as well, then they would have five minutes or less to gather evidence about each quality; if it is seven or eight qualities, then the time drops to about two or three minutes. This means that candidates need to give sufficient answers that are succinct and convincing.

In order to gather the convincing evidence that they are seeking, employers will be seeking specific examples of when the candidate has done particular activities or demonstrated particular skills relevant to the job role.

 KEY LEARNING POINT

In a selection interview, employers have limited time to seek examples and gather convincing evidence of the skills and attitudes they require for the job role.

PREPARING FOR A JOB INTERVIEW

It is possible to consider a job interview in the same way as we might think of an academic examination: we do not know exactly what the questions are going to be but we do know how long it will last and we should know where and when it will take place. We might also have a reasonable idea of what the employer (or in the latter case, examiner) might be looking for, but the unpredictability in both situations comes from uncertainty regarding the questions.

Review Your Application

Therefore, the preparation for both situations is very similar. For an examination, we do revision, usually over a long period of time. We could think of a selection interview as an examination where the topic is 'yourself', so the revision you need to do is to go back over your application and remind yourself of what you have described and the experiences you have had. More broadly, however, it would be a good idea to go back over all that you have done during your time at university which might be relevant, so you can recall events and situations in the interview.

Review the Job Specification

When interviewers are preparing to conduct a selection interview, they will have a look at the KSAOs (Knowledge, Skills, Attitudes and Other factors) listed in the person specification. Time will be limited in a first-stage selection interview, so, first of all, employers will want to concentrate on identifying evidence for those skills deemed essential, and, secondly, those deemed desirable if there is time left. As a candidate, it makes perfect sense to do the same.

Sometimes, those qualities will be very clearly stated, but where the application is for a graduate training scheme, the qualities will probably be far more general and might relate more to your suitability for the organisation than for a specific job role. The advert for such a scheme might be very clear, but the values, motives and attitudes that the employers are seeking may or may not be explicitly listed in any advertising.

Selection is always a two-way process, and the better the fit between your personality and that of the organisation, the more likely you will be to stay.

Dress Appropriately

Identifying what is meant by 'appropriate' is hard, but the best advice is always to adopt a more conservative and formal perspective than a relaxed one. In most cases, something smart in dark or pastel colours will be expected.

Whatever you wear, your dress should be comfortable. The interview should not be the first time you have worn the clothes: you need to concentrate on answering the questions, rather than trying to deal with any pain or unease caused by ill-fitting shoes or trousers which are too tight. If you are not sure what to wear, then ask a friend or a careers adviser what impression a certain combination of clothes will create. There is nothing wrong in wearing something that makes an impression and gives an indication of an extrovert and confident individual – if that is what you are *and* if you are sure it fits with the culture of the organisation. However, most organisations will expect interviewees to wear something quite conservative.

Consider the Questions You Might be Asked

There is less science than you might expect in developing good interview questions. While occupational psychologists are correct in trying to ensure that the questions asked have maximum predictive validity (i.e. they predict behaviour on the job), in many cases managers use their intelligence and a bit of common sense.

However, it is also true that managers are trained to ask good questions, and 'good' questions are not designed to trick candidates, but to separate those who have the potential to do the job from those who do not. Examples of different types of good questions are given on pages 406–8, but, as you look through them, try to imagine why some of the qualities sought are important and then consider a question you might be asked to see if you have each particular quality.

Be aware that they almost certainly will not ask you, 'Are you good at handling people?' (to which the answer would probably be 'Yes, I am very good at handling people'), but more likely to seek an example: 'Can you give an example of when you think you handled a difficult person very well?'

Finally, once you have identified some potential questions, develop some good answers for them; see pages 411–416 for what constitutes a good answer. There is nothing worse than sitting in an interview and thinking, 'Yes, I came up with this question when I was preparing, but I have no idea now how to answer it!' Remember that some questions might appear regularly, but each job will be a little different, so the questions you prepare for each interview will need to be different.

Role-play the Interview with a 'Critical Friend'

If you have done your preparation and identified some potential questions, then there can be nothing better than to go through these questions with someone. Often your careers services will be able to give some time to do this if you give them sufficient notice. The advantages of using your careers services are: 1) they usually have some professional experience and can find good additional questions to ask (or can rephrase the questions you have developed); and 2) they can be objective when it comes to giving you feedback.

If possible, role-play the whole interview from when you enter the room to when the interview comes to a conclusion. It is not just the answers that you give that will make the difference, it is how you give them and the broader impression you create while answering them. Feedback on all of these aspects will help you improve your interview performance.

=== KEY LEARNING POINT ===

Preparation is going to be very important to your performance at interview and to reducing your nervousness in the interview room.

Find Out as Much Information as You Can about the Interview

Often, the first indication that you have been successful in your job application is an email or a letter inviting you for a job interview. The letter will state where and when the interview will take place and it may tell you how long the interview will be and sometimes who will be interviewing you. If there is information that you would like to know which is not given in the invitation, then contact the relevant graduate recruitment department or individual who is arranging the interviews – either by phone or by email.

Contacting a professional organisation by phone and speaking to someone is something that some individuals find challenging. If you have never done this before, then there can appear to be something 'special' about individuals who are working in a particular business, but such individuals are just human beings and there really is nothing to be worried about, even if English is not your first language. In addition, you will be speaking to managers from the organisation in the near future anyway, so it may help to get some practice over the phone.

=== REFLECTION POINT ===

Take some time to think about the following questions and write down some answers, first on your own and then with others that you might be working with.

How much time do you think you will need to spend preparing for a selection interview?

Would you feel nervous before a selection interview? What could you do to help you to reduce your nerves?

You need to look professional for the interview. What would you wear? Do you have smart business-like clothes?

AT THE INTERVIEW
The Interview Process

Interviews are always seen as occasions when we feel nervous. We can feel that someone is judging us and that there is nothing we can do about it. In some ways, this is true – we are being assessed – but the assessment is about whether we can do the job, rather than whether we are a 'good human being'.

Our value as an individual is not determined by whether or not we can get through a job interview, it is about far more than that, but the more we can give convincing answers to show we can do the job, the better our chances of getting the job. Therefore, the less nervous we are, the better our answers should be.

Our nervousness can be reduced when we:

- Believe that the interview is really just a conversation to find out if we can do the job.
- Believe that the interviewers are interested in us and want to find out more about us, because there is something in our application that has caught their eye.
- Have prepared as much as we can – both practically (travel arrangements etc.) and in terms of the questions we might be asked.
- Eat well and get a good night's sleep the day before the interview.
- Understand that the worst that can happen is that we do not get the job – and whether you believe it or not, there are much worse things that can happen to us in life.
- Know roughly what is going to happen during the interview.

It is this last point that the next section is designed to deal with.

Interview Structure

An interview is usually composed of four sections: in a 45-minute interview, the structure and length of each section will be similar to those described in Box 17.1.

=== BOX 17.1 ===

Typical Graduate Selection Interview Structure (timings are based on a 45 minute graduate interview)

1. **Welcome and introduction** (1–2 mins): You will be given the name of the interviewer. If it is a panel interview, the chair of the interview panel will introduce each member of the panel, and usually for a graduate-level job there would be no more than two people interviewing you. The interviewer would also outline the structure of the interview, give an indication of the length of the interview and check that you are ready to start the interview.
2. **Questions to you** (25–35 mins): These questions will relate to the qualities being sought from the successful candidate. You will be asked to respond to questions about your skills, attitudes, experiences and/or motivation in order to determine your suitability for the job. As mentioned elsewhere in this chapter, the answers you give and the way that you give them will determine whether you move through to the next part of the selection process.
3. **Your questions** (approximately 5 mins): You will be invited to ask the interviewer(s) any questions you might have about working at the organisation. You will need to ask some questions, or have engaged with the interviewers beforehand, to find out the information you wish to know.
4. **Thank you and summary of next steps** (1–2 mins): Unless you have already asked, the interviewer(s) will outline what will happen next and indicate how quickly you might expect to hear whether or not you have been successful. The interviewers will thank you for attending and will usually shake your hand as you leave.

Every interview may be slightly different, but knowing what to expect is important if you have never been to a job interview before.

Entrance and First Impression

The idea that many interviewers make very quick assessments of a candidate's suitability for the job has some truth to it. Research seems to indicate that the first 30 seconds is key, but good interviewers (i.e. those who gather accurate information and make a judgement about the relevance, breadth and significance of that information after the interview) will withhold judgement until after the interview.

Regardless, a 'weak' entrance will not be seen as a good start and you may find yourself with an uphill battle to convince an interviewer afterwards. It is also important, however, not to enter in a way which is overly enthusiastic, so try to get the balance right. This means the following:

- **Shake hands**: Firmly, but do not crush their fingers! You do need to create an impression of 'friendly professionalism' so try shaking hands with a friend and get their feedback. Hold your hand firmly but not stiffly. Make sure that your hands are clean and dry.
- **Smile**: You need to smile as you enter. If you do not naturally smile, this may take some practice, but you should avoid having a smile which is so big and sustained as to appear artificial. If this is not easy for you, then perhaps try taking some 'selfies' and get some feedback from friends in order to develop a smile which others like.
- **Eye contact**: Look at the interviewers in the room. You may have only one or two interviewers, but as you enter the room make sure that you make eye contact. Imagine that this is a business meeting and you are trying to sell something to the people in the room: you want to be friendly and confident, even if that is not how you feel.
- **Move purposefully**: When you move from the door to the chair, do so in a way that demonstrates confidence (i.e. be deliberate). Walk towards the chair and the interviewer(s) in a calm but confident manner. Practise this with a friend if you feel you need to. Avoid having too much with you: coats and bags can make your entrance less smooth than desired.

As was stated above (see the 'Dress Appropriately' section), you must pay attention to your appearance. You want to demonstrate to an employer what they might expect from you if you were to go to a business meeting.

DEALING WITH INTERVIEW QUESTIONS

Being able to give 'good answers' to the questions you are asked is what is going to help you get further in the selection process. There are some very common interview questions that you should prepare for, regardless of the nature of the job.

══════════ FOR YOU TO DO ══════════

Have a look at the questions listed below. What would your answers be?

1. Why did you choose this university and your degree course?

(Continued)

2. Why do you want this job?
3. Why do you want to work in finance, marketing, HR, etc.?
4. What are your strengths and weaknesses?
5. What has been your biggest achievement?
6. What makes you suitable for this graduate training scheme?
7. What can you bring to this role?

During a selection interview, the interviewer(s) will be following a strict structure or 'interview schedule', asking each candidate the same questions in the same order in the same way. The aim is to ensure that the validity of the interview (i.e. whether it collects accurate and truthful information) is high.

The questions asked above should not be difficult to answer: if they are, then you might struggle with some of the others, but there is no need to panic. Think carefully about your answers before you give them.

Question Types

Questions asked at interviews can take a number of different forms, but regardless of the type of question, the interviewers' objective is simply to gather enough information to help them identify whether they think that you can do the job and/or fit the organisation.

Open questions

Open questions invite you to tell the interviewer as much information about a particular subject (often yourself) as you wish to: for example, 'Tell me something about yourself'. These are usually asked at the start of the interview and are designed to help you relax: talking about yourself is something most people should have little problem doing. It is true, however, that employers might expect you to give an answer which is relevant in some way to the job, or to give information that you consider important in your answer first. Open questions will usually be followed by probing questions.

 OPEN QUESTION

A question designed to begin a conversation where the questioner has little or no information about the respondent.

Probing questions

These are designed to get more detail about a relevant aspect of the information that you have given. For example, if you talked about 'leading others' in your first answer, then you might expect to be asked something like, 'So what was the most difficult part of your leadership role there?' On occasions, interviewers may ask probing questions to find out if you are really telling the truth. Answers which are vague or unclear are often seen as indicators of something that may not be completely true or may be exaggerated in some way.

Closed questions

Closed questions are designed to check the information that you have given and make sure that the interviewers have accurately interpreted what you have said: for example, 'And was he satisfied with that action?' One of the issues that interviewers often face is a lack of time. If you have seven or eight qualities that you are seeking and 45 minutes or an hour to conduct the interview, then your time for each quality (which usually relates to one question) will be very short and the use of closed questions will be limited.

Leading questions

The advice given to most interviewers is not to use leading questions, since a candidate can be led to answer a particular question in a certain way. If you are asked a leading question and you want the job, then you will likely give the answer that is closest to what you think the interviewer is looking for. Interviewers' facial expressions and tone of voice can also have the same effect when reacting to an answer or asking a follow-up probing question, even if the question is not designed to lead a candidate.

However, leading questions can be useful in terms of seeing whether a candidate holds a particular view strongly and is able to develop their own ideas independently of others, or is likely to be easily led towards a particular answer. For example, 'Don't you think that it is important to protect an organisation from employees who are likely to make significant mistakes?' The leading answer to this is, 'Of course it is', but rarely are situations so black and white, so the interviewer may be expecting you to debate the question a little more.

It may also be that the answer you give is not important, but the evidence you give for your answer and the passion with which you defend your point of view are always going to be important.

Hypothetical questions

Hypothetical questions broadly ask 'What would you do if ...?', so you need to consider carefully how you might react in various situations faced by managers at work (Table 17.1). In technical terms, interviewing using this kind of question is termed 'situational interviewing'.

Table 17.1   Examples of hypothetical questions

1. What would you do if two of the employees in your business started fighting in the office?
2. If you were the manager of a footballer who had suddenly become uncharacteristically aggressive towards another player on the pitch, what would you say to them?
3. If your part of the business was suddenly losing money after a period of sustained profit, what action would you take?
4. How would you handle a well-liked member of staff whom you knew was lying to others on a regular basis about important issues?
5. If one of your managers made a mistake which cost the organisation up to 5% of its revenue, what would you do?

The best type of answer to a hypothetical question is to refer to an occasion when you actually have faced the situation, and that is why gaining leadership experience before you graduate cannot be underestimated in terms of its importance. If you are unable to think about a real situation when you have faced these kinds of issues, then consider quickly how you might handle them. The truth is that there are rarely purely right or wrong answers – every action might be right in some organisation – but there are answers which would fit with the culture of the organisation and others which would not: that is, there are answers which are 'better' and answers which are 'worse'. The situations described in these kinds of questions may be rare, but they often make the difference between a successful and an unsuccessful manager. Not having an opinion is not going to be an option.

Behavioural questions

In some ways, these are very similar to hypothetical questions, but they ask about a time when you have actually done something. Their main purpose is to find out what you have actually done, and they do so based on the idea that the best predictor of your behaviour in a future situation is your behaviour in a previous one. The technical term is 'behavioural interviewing'.

Behavioural questions tend to request examples of what you have done, how you have done it, and so on. Some examples are given in Table 17.2.

Table 17.2 Examples of behavioural questions

1. Tell us about a time when you needed to manage conflicting priorities. What did you do and how successful were you?
2. Give an example of when you have had to give negative feedback to someone you believed was creating problems for others.
3. Provide an example of an occasion when you have had to persuade somebody to change a view that they had previously held strongly.
4. Can you describe a situation when you have had to analyse uncertain information quickly in order to make an important decision?
5. Have you had any experience of working in a team? What role did you play? What was your contribution?

The questions given above all ask for an example. Again, if you cannot think of any examples, then you will struggle with the interview. However, there are hidden subtleties in these questions. The first is about breadth and the second is about significance.

Breadth refers to the number of situations you have experienced, so if you have only had one leadership position for a very short time, any questions you are asked about leadership are going to refer to the same situation. Employers will look for as much breadth as possible in the scenarios you describe.

Significance refers to the importance of the situations, and usually the risks involved in getting something wrong. For example, leading a student club of 50 people is seen as more significant than leading a team of four working on a small piece of group coursework.

If you can provide answers demonstrating significance and breadth of experience, then you are more likely to be rated highly by the interviewers.

For both hypothetical and behavioural questions, interviewers will usually have a scoring system with which they score each answer, according to whether certain issues are covered.

Sample Interview Questions

Throughout the previous chapters, we have looked at some typical questions that you might be asked at the selection interview, with the aim of encouraging you to consider succeeding at the selection process as one of the key goals of your university career. Remember that interviewers are looking for evidence that you can do the job well, that you want to do the job and that you could fit into the organisation.

FOR YOU TO DO

1. If you have not already done so, have a look at the interview questions from the previous chapters of the text. Prepare some answers and, with a friend, review whether they seem to give the interviewers the evidence that they need.
2. You can find an interactive version of these questions along with helpful guidance on answering them on the companion website for this book at **https://study.sagepub.com/morgan2e**. Does that guidance make sense? How might it confirm (or change) the relevance and nature of the answers you give?

INTERACTIVE
QUESTIONS

Chapter 1

1. Why did you choose the university, and the course you have been studying?
2. How successful have you been at achieving the goals you set out to achieve by studying at university?

━━━━━━━━━ **FOR YOU TO DO** ━━━━━

Have a look at the four answers that follow, two for question 1 and two for question 2. For each question, which answer do you think is better (A or B), and why?

Question	Answer A	Answer B
Question 1	I chose the university because it was closer to home and that would enable me to maintain my previous social activities and my friends. It is known locally as quite a good university and I didn't want to go to the local college, even if the college was closer. I chose the course - Business Studies - because I wasn't sure what I wanted to do and I thought it would give me a general grounding in subjects that would help me to start my career.	I chose the university because it had the right grades for me and because it was far enough from home for me to escape my parents and develop an independent life. It also had a good reputation nationally for environmental sustainability and those sorts of things are hugely important for me. I chose Business Studies because I wanted to go into HR. But I have found that HR is much more about policy and procedures than it is about people, so I am wanting to pursue a general business career for now and wait to see what I enjoy in practice.
Question 2	I think it is difficult to say. When I started my degree, I wasn't sure what my goals would be. No one in my family or close community had been to university before and so I was not really sure what to expect. But I knew I wanted to make my family proud and to get a job which would expand my horizons, and since I began university, I have really wanted to stretch myself - which is why I have got involved in leadership roles in my student organisations, and I have really enjoyed that. So, my goals have probably developed and changed a lot since I started, but I am certainly on course to get a good degree and a good job.	I am pleased to say that I have achieved all my goals, as far as I am concerned. When I started university, I was very clear: I wanted to get a good quality degree, develop my social network, learn skills that would be relevant in the workplace and become interested in the world around me. At the beginning, I set these as SMART objectives and wanted to achieve these by the beginning of my final year - which is exactly what has happened. And so now, I am sitting in front of you feeling very satisfied and hungry for the next step.

As you read these, assume that these are four answers given by four different students:

1. Which of the answers for Q1 seems the best to you?
2. Which of the answers for Q2 seems the best to you?
3. If one student had answered both with A, and another student had answered both with B, which one do you think would be the most likely to get the job?
4. Discuss your answer for these questions with other students, if you are able to.

If you struggled to answer these questions, then you might need to think very carefully about what examples you can give for what you have done. You may need to revisit the suggestions for how these questions might be answered given in the interactive test on the companion website at https://study. sagepub.com/morgan2e.

KEY LEARNING POINT

The clearer the answers to your interview questions, the more likely it will be that you will be successful in moving further through the selection process.

REFLECTION POINT

Take some time to think about the following questions and write down some answers, first on your own and then with others that you might be working with.

Which of these interview questions would you find difficult to answer? Which would be the easiest? Why?

Are there any questions – relating to your abilities – that you would not like to be asked? If you did get asked them, how would you reply?

'BUT I HAVE A QUESTION ...'

... I've heard that many employers will ask about my strengths and weaknesses, so how should I answer that?

It is a good question, and yes they do – and it is expected that you will have a very good answer ready. They ask for a couple of reasons. Firstly, they like to know what you know about the job. A personal 'strength' is only a strength if you are good at a particular skill *and* the situation is likely to require it. If the situation does not require it, then being particularly good at that skill does not make it a strength (e.g. being a fantastic presenter when the job does not require any presentation skills), and the same is true for a personal 'weakness'. The best advice here is to do your preparation and a good analysis of how your skills and abilities match up with those required for the post.

The second reason an employer will ask is genuinely to find out about your abilities, and to gather evidence to help them understand whether you should be taken any further in the selection process. Your skills will have various qualities but some skills – often those which are clearly evident from observable behaviour – are easier to train than others. So, in addition to the advice given in the paragraph above, think about weaknesses that you could be trained in quite easily, and wherever you talk about your strengths, you *must* give evidence to support your comments.

In answering this question, try to respond in a way which is confident, but not arrogant. You might have all the right strengths, but many employers would prefer to have someone that they can mentor and develop a little, rather than someone who thinks they have nothing to learn and that they will be CEO in two years' time. Give some examples of where you have demonstrated your strengths, but importantly some examples of when you have developed yourself in areas where you were previously weak. It is OK to have a weakness, but knowing that you have a personal weakness and apparently doing nothing about it is not going to get you the job.

The final comment here is that how you demonstrate your skills in one setting may not relate exactly to how you might demonstrate your skills in another. The situation and context will change how you go about working with others or doing a presentation, for example, so be aware of this in how you prepare your answer to this question - one single bad presentation does not mean that you will always be bad at giving presentations.

So:

- Consider your relevant strengths and weaknesses carefully, based on the job you are applying for.
- Discuss examples of when you have used your strengths.
- Identify weaknesses that you can develop, and give examples of when you have developed those skills.
- Answer honestly, but in a manner which shows some humility. Even if you are graduating with an MBA, you will still have something to learn.

Giving Good Answers

Understanding the kinds of questions that will be asked at a selection interview is important, but so too is the ability to give a good answer.

═══ 'BUT I HAVE A QUESTION ...' ═══

... What do you mean by a 'good answer'?

This is an important question, so let's look at it from the perspective of an interviewer. Each candidate will be asked the same questions, but the answers may vary significantly. So let's examine two hypothetical situations where an interviewer asks the question, 'Tell us about a time when you have had to solve a challenging problem within a short timescale', and evaluate the two answers below.

Candidate A replies: 'I needed to persuade all my group mates to work harder on a piece of group coursework. We were getting closer to the deadline and I felt that people weren't working hard enough to get the work finished.'

Candidate B replies: 'I needed to persuade the Dean to allow my student society to use an academic facility that had not been available for students to use before, and to give us a budget for refreshments. Once I presented the case, he let us use the room and agreed to sponsor the event.'

Answer B is the *stronger* answer, even though there are lots of important details missing from both answers, which would usually be expected. Persuading the Dean to provide a venue and some sponsorship takes more effort than persuading some classmates to complete their coursework faster. In addition, answer B talks about specifics - a venue and finance - whereas answer A is quite general.

Finally, answer A gives an answer which shows as much about the respondent as it does about those the respondent was trying to influence. Answer A seems to be quite judgemental and critical, and actually shows that the respondent was not very successful at either planning the completion of the coursework or motivating other group members earlier on. But neither answer is particularly strong or detailed, and there seems to be a lot of information missing.

Understanding the information that is missing in the above two answers requires thinking through an approach that careers advisers typically refer to as the 'STAR framework' – Situation, Task, Action, Result. A good interviewer will be seeking answers to behavioural questions that conform to this model.

Let's illustrate this with the same question: 'Tell us about a time when you have had to solve a challenging problem within a short timescale' and use an extended version of answer B. The model is based around the need for information regarding: the **S**ituation; the **T**ask that needed to be done; the **A**ction taken; the **R**esult or impact of that action.

 A GOOD ANSWER

A good answer is one which provides convincing evidence to an interviewer that you have the capability and potential to do what is needed in the job.

The situation

You need to begin your answers by briefly describing the situation you were facing. You need to be as complete as you can, but remember that they can ask follow-up questions if they need to, so give the most important information.

In using the example above, the candidate might have responded:

> It was the end of the semester and we – the Student Management Society – had just been told that the venue we were hoping to use for a social event was not going to be available since it had been booked by another group the week before. The only other venue was out of bounds for undergraduate students – it was the MBA facility – and the costs of hiring that privately (as a non-MBA organisation) were too high for us to bear. So, I needed to persuade the Dean of the Business School not only to give us permission to use it, but also to help in paying some of the fees.

This part of the answer gives us the context for the action that was taken. It indicates how easy or difficult the task was, and thus gives the interviewers an indication of the candidate's abilities.

For this particular answer, it also shows a number of other things:

- The candidate uses the word 'we', implying someone who is usually a good team worker. In outlining the actions taken, *the candidate will need to talk about what they did as an individual*, but 'we' usually shows a predisposition to work well with others.
- It might imply some creativity and an ability to think creatively when resources were not readily available, but it can only *imply* that here. We do not know whether the problem solving that was done was the candidate's or whether the solution was developed by others in the team.
- Use of 'not only … but also' adds to the impression that this was not going to be an easy thing to do.

The task that needed to be done

Having described the situation, there is then a need to start beginning to talk about what you needed to do to solve the problem. You need to let the interviewer(s) know why the task was significant, why it was difficult and what would have happened if you had not taken any action. Consider the following response:

> We needed to have the party since it was the highlight of the undergraduate year at our university. We could have cancelled it, but that would have meant that the main social reason for people joining the society would have been ignored, which would have decreased the motivation for students to join next year. So as president of the society, I needed to find an alternative venue, and for that I needed to persuade the Dean.

The answer given above provides a succinct and relatively comprehensive view of what was happening, but it also shows:

- An ability to analyse information and reflect on the consequences of various alternatives, including doing nothing, an option often implicitly ignored.
- An understanding of human motivation and behaviour.
- An acceptance of responsibility for the position this candidate has in the society.

The action taken

The third part of the answer is then to outline what action you took. It is vital that the information in this part of the answer is accurate and relates to the behaviour of the candidate and no one else:

> I made an appointment with the Dean. I wanted him to help with the event, so in order to give him something in return, I decided I would ask him to present some of the society prizes and to give a brief speech. As an undergraduate society, I thought he might be more reluctant to sponsor us than the postgraduate students (who pay a great deal more for their studies) but I wanted us to draw as many students to the event as possible – and the presence of the Dean and the use of the MBA venue could help to do that.

> I met with the Dean who asked me how we had found ourselves in this situation and what we planned to do about it. When I asked for his help, he listened carefully and then asked for some suggestions as to how we could limit the impact on the MBA students who might be around the venue at the time of the event. We had a discussion about those, and the meeting ended after about 35 minutes.

The answer above details the specific actions that the candidate took and gives full details on the candidate's planning and preparation. It shows:

- Insightful awareness of the situation faced by the other party in this event.
- A willingness to be proactive in carefully thinking about how they might get the Dean and others involved.
- Careful consideration of the thinking, planning and preparation which went into the discussion with other individuals involved.
- Creativity in developing incentives for someone who might be difficult to persuade – and the recognition that incentives were necessary.

In demonstrating these issues, the candidate is giving the interviewer(s) sufficient evidence for them to conclude that the candidate is a highly competent and credible individual.

The result of the action

The final part of the answer to a behavioural question should succinctly indicate the result of the actions taken: were the intended objectives achieved? If the answer did not previously give or imply the intended objectives, then there was something missing, but those can be given here. In our example, the candidate might say:

> As a result of my discussions with the Dean, we were able to use the MBA venue and we were given a budget of £500 to order some refreshments from the school canteen for those attending. I organised

some prizes, suggested some things that the Dean might want to say and set up a small team to work with him to identify what the prizes might relate to and who should be awarded those prizes by the Dean. In the end, we were able to confirm that the event was going ahead with enough time to spare to sell tickets to students who had been told that the event had been put on hold. We had 370 people attend the event – an increase on the 230 the previous year – which more than covered the costs of the event, and the Dean attended with two other senior members of staff.

Because we made a small profit, I returned some of that to cover the costs of the other student group who had not been able to use the venue. They had been wanting to hold a relatively small activity there and had been able to move their date relatively easily, but we made the donation as a good-will gesture.

You need to make this part of the answer the strongest – i.e. give a lot of detail and refer back to the objectives you had set yourself as a result of the situation you faced. Interviewers can be forgiving when objectives were not achieved, but would be less forgiving if there was no information given of why that was the case.

In reviewing the four parts to the answer above, what do you notice about the relative length of the four sections? Usually the latter parts (Action and Result) are much longer than the first two sections, and the longest of all needs to be the Results:

Situation	Task	Action	Result
10%	20%	30%	40%

FOR YOU TO DO

Look at the following three answers to the question, 'Tell me about a time when you have needed to overcome a problem in a team in which you were working. What was the problem, and how did you overcome the problem?' and then answer the four questions below.

Answer A

I needed to overcome the issue of a group member who was not doing his work for a piece of written group coursework. I was the group leader.

He needed to complete the introduction to the assignment and had not done so, despite the fact that we gave him two extra days to do the work.

I talked to the other group members about the issue and we agreed that I tell him that he had one more day to complete the work before his name was removed from the assignment.

Answer B

We were working in a budget committee for a student society, but we were finding it really difficult to arrange a time to meet in order to discuss the budget for the society.

Between us, we agreed that we needed to make some compromises for our time. One team member could only make two nights a week, but both of those were inconvenient for the other team members.

So we thought we could either have a vote on which night we would have all of our meetings, or we could rotate the time and day of our meetings so that everyone could be involved in at least one meeting.

Answer C

I was leading a team where we needed to complete a project for an international business competition. We needed to find a potential solution to youth unemployment, and if we won, our solution would be chosen to receive $1 million for use across the world.

I discussed these ideas with some other students who had heard about this competition and who I trusted to work with me to develop an excellent proposal. I also wanted the team to be international because I thought this would give a better impression to an international team of judges. We had about three weeks to develop an idea.

Answer A	Answer B	Answer C
He did not do so and did not respond to any emails about this issue so we spread his work between us and successfully completed and submitted the assignment. In the end, we were very happy to receive an A for our work.	In the end, we decided to rotate the night of the meeting which worked for most members, and we gave a verbal report of the meeting and any actions we discussed to anyone who could not attend. In addition, we could invite comments on proposals electronically ahead of the meeting. The result of this was that we were able to decide on a budget within the time limit we had, and everyone agreed with the budget and felt happy to be a part of the team.	We came up with the idea of a website which could enable young people to sell their own products and services to others – maybe even globally – and to benefit from the advice of business leaders who would provide some free comment and guidance. We presented this idea to one of the tutors at our university who was involved in the local heat of the competition, and he gave us some feedback. When I led the team into the university round of the competition, I was nervous about how our slightly adapted proposal would be received, but I knew that it could work and had concrete ideas to put it into action. At our university, the judges believed that our idea was the best and we went through to present as an international team in the next round in Dubai. I made sure we practised and improved our presentation and knew what we were talking about. We were not successful in going further, but the experience was an amazing and encouraging one, and we are now working with some potential investors to make this a reality.

There are four questions here for you to answer – both on your own, and/or in discussion with other students:

1. Which of the answers do you think presents the STAR framework the best?
2. Which of the answers do you think would present the strongest answer to the question? (It may be different from the answer to Q1).

(Please note: The length of an answer never directly indicates the quality, so do not disregard the shorter answers here.)

3. If you were the interviewer and you could ask a follow-up question, what would you ask?
4. How would *you* answer this question?

Overall

The STAR framework should be used when answering behavioural questions; however, when answering any questions:

- Keep answers as comprehensive but as brief as possible. If you read aloud the answers above in order, then it would take around two and a half minutes, excluding any time given for thinking about the answer initially.

- Watch your speed of speech: when we are nervous, we might typically speak more quickly than usual.
- Imagine the issues you might face in doing the job, and prepare examples of how you have demonstrated, or might demonstrate, your skills in handling those issues well.
- Focus on *your* contribution and activities – the interviewer is after evidence of *your* skills. If you refer to 'we' all the time, then your own contribution will be blurred.
- Be honest: even if you do get through the interview and get the job, you will need to demonstrate your skills anyway.

 'BUT I HAVE A QUESTION ...'

... What do you do if you cannot think of an answer to a question they asked, or if you do not understand a question?

This happens fairly frequently in graduate interviews, so the first thing to say is, 'Don't panic!' Of course, it is easy to say that, but it is perfectly OK to:

- Ask for a little time to develop an answer, as long as the silence in the interview does not last for an uncomfortably long period of time.
- Ask the interviewer to repeat the question; they will probably not rephrase it, but they can repeat it.

If they are asking about a situation you have never faced, or where you are not sure how you would deal with it, then the best thing is to be honest and say so. That will probably not help you get further in the selection process, but it might be that the quality they are asking about is not an 'essential' criterion, or that all the candidates might struggle to answer it. It is not appropriate to make up an answer since that will come through in a number of ways and will mean that the interviewer(s) will not trust any of your other answers either.

Above all, be sure to give a relevant answer to the question. There is nothing worse than giving what you think is a really great answer only for the interviewers to conclude that they have insufficient information to make a decision. Have a look at the next 'For You to Do' section below.

 FOR YOU TO DO

Look at the two answers below to the question: 'Can you give us an example of a time when you have had to work with others, and tell us how you worked together?'

Answer A: 'I had to work with others in a student society. We had a party to organise and after we had decided how we wanted to separate the tasks, my role was to obtain funding from sponsors, and there was one other person doing the same thing. I went about identifying potential sponsors but I kept the team and the other person informed of what I was doing. We met every week and I needed to give an update on my progress.'

Answer B: 'I had to work with others as part of a coursework assignment. It was a case study for a module on strategic management. I was leading a group of five people and I had to decide what we were going to do and how. I did the part of the work that related to gathering the literature, which was actually quite hard because the library is not really well equipped and does not have enough books.'

Which of the two answers do you think is more *relevant*?

The strength of an answer is measured by the extent that it helps the interviewer believe or otherwise that you have the potential to fulfil the requirements of a role in a way that matches the expectations of the organisation.

'BUT I HAVE A QUESTION ...'

... How should I answer questions – should I be passionate or should I keep my emotions out of my answers?

This is not an easy question to answer, but the best answer is to be passionate about those things that you are passionate about, and to be calm when that is appropriate. The best advice is not to be too extreme in the way you answer the questions. Use hand gestures purposefully and to emphasise what you say, but the key is usually moderation.

Showing no passion or conviction during the interview will probably mean that your interviewers are not going to be passionate about your answers, or you as a candidate. At a basic level, a lack of passion or emotion will be interpreted as a lack of interest in the job – and that will disqualify you very quickly.

KEY LEARNING POINT

Remember that the objective for the interviewer is to gather sufficient evidence to be able to say with some confidence: 'Yes, we think this person can do a good job for us'.

QUESTIONS TO ASK AT THE END OF AN INTERVIEW

At the end of an interview, you will be invited to ask the interviewer(s) questions. These could be questions about the organisation or about the job role. Selection is always a two-way process and the best candidates might have more than one job offer, so this is an opportunity to determine what working in the organisation is going to be like. Not having any questions is going to indicate a lack of interest in the vacancy (or vacancies) and asking inappropriate questions is also going to send the wrong signals. You should never ask about salary (or any other terms and conditions) until you have a job offer.

The best questions are those which reveal that you have thought carefully about what it will mean to work in this role. Consider the following:

- What kind of training might I receive?
- What assistance is available for me in terms of finding accommodation?
- What is it like to work for this organisation?
- Would I be working with a team or largely independently?
- How formal are relationships between junior and senior management?
- How resistant are people to change in your organisation?
- How would my performance in the job be evaluated?
- ... and any other issues that might affect whether you would enjoy working there.

When thinking about the questions you ask, you need to be honest in asking what you want to know. There are some questions which appear 'clever', but which could count against you, for example: 'What is the company's view on 'dress-down Fridays'?' or 'What are the company's plans for increasing annual turnover?' These would not be relevant for your decision about whether or not you take the job, and would just be seen as a potential sign of arrogance or 'being clever for the sake of being clever'. Such questions should be avoided. ('Dress-down Fridays' are those days when an organisation's formal dress code would be relaxed, but not every office has a dress code.)

What you do need to know is whether you might enjoy working there, so any questions that would honestly help you make this decision are to be encouraged. However, it is not wise to ask any questions that are already on the company website (e.g. 'How many employees do you have?', 'How many offices do you have and where are they?'). This will show a lack of preparation and/or a lack of real interest in the company.

You probably need to have two or three questions ready and they should not be closed questions giving you a 'yes' or 'no' answer. Remember that the interview is a conversation with a purpose, and a conversation which has just yes or no answers is not going to last very long.

 KEY LEARNING POINT ═══════════

The interviewer needs to get as much information from you as possible to determine whether you are suitable for the job. Giving full and complete answers to their questions is essential to enabling the interviewer to make that decision.

 REFLECTION POINT ═══════════

Take some time to think about the following questions and write down some answers, first on your own, and then with others that you might be working with.

In a nervous situation, it is our emotion which usually takes over rather than rational thought. How could you become so used to using the STAR framework that it becomes instinctive?

How good is your memory about the activities you have done? Is there anything you can do to improve the range of examples you could give?

GENERAL BEHAVIOUR AT INTERVIEWS

If you have never had an interview before, or have never worked in a professional office before, then you might have questions about what is appropriate and what is not. Understanding professional values in terms of day-to-day behaviour is something that you will have to do when it comes to working in a professional environment if you are to work well with others. Those values can vary significantly from organisation to organisation, but they are not always written down; the only times that individuals pick up on them is when they or someone else acts in a way which contravenes them. For the graduate selection interview, however, there are some basic expectations which are less hidden (Table 17.3).

Table 17.3 Some do's and don'ts during an interview

Do	Don't
Dress smartly, and make sure that you look in the mirror before going to the interview	Have a cigarette or drink alcohol immediately before an interview
Go to the bathroom before the interview starts	Be late or leave yourself with too little time to get to the interview
Use formal language	Be too friendly or overly familiar with the interviewers
Maintain eye contact with the interviewer(s) as much as possible	Blame others for mistakes or errors – it creates a negative impression
Use facial expressions, hand gestures and tone of voice appropriately (i.e. only when you want to emphasise something) – using them all the time will be seen as a little odd	Use humour to denigrate others (even if you think it is funny)
Respond appropriately to non-verbal signals from the interviewer(s) indicating that they have heard enough of an answer to a question	Use slang or jargon
Sit upright and lean forward when answering questions	Slouch in the chair, look disinterested or excessively fiddle with your hands or hair
Prepare some questions to ask at the end of the interview	Use the interviewers' time to answer questions they have not asked or show them evidence of something they have not wanted to see
Turn your phone off	Finish the interview by asking when you will start the job
	Don't panic! If you cannot think of an example to discuss, then be honest

=== 'BUT I HAVE A QUESTION ...' ===

... I have heard that some people have telephone or Skype interviews. If I have an interview like this, should anything I do change at all?

Yes, this is an increasing trend. According to data cited by TARGETjobs (n.d.), the Institute of Student Employers 2019 survey found that 47% of employers had started using video interviews, up from around 21% in 2014. The impact of the Covid-19 pandemic is likely to increase this significantly in the years to come, of course.

To answer your question, the simple answer is 'not really', but do make sure that your technology works well and that your interviewers have contingency plans (e.g. a landline telephone number) in case the internet or the phone does not work. It may sound strange, but your intonation will give an impression of your facial expression – so smiling while you are talking works as well for a telephone interview as it would for a face-to-face interview. If you have a Skype interview (or equivalent on Gotomeeting.com or Zoom), then you need to dress appropriately as well.

If you are applying for a job in a country which is not your own, then make sure you are aware of any time zone issues – and particularly changes with BST (British Summer Time).

Other than ensuring that the technology works and that you are well prepared, nothing else should really be different. You should think about the questions that you may be asked, use the same tone of voice and give the answers in the same way.

AFTER THE INTERVIEW

What you do after the interview will depend to some extent on the nature of the interview, and on what you have been told about the individuals who will have been interviewing you. If you have their names and email addresses (e.g. you might be applying for a specific vacancy), then a very brief email thanking those individuals and saying that you are 'looking forward to hearing from them soon' would be very appropriate. After an interview like this, you will probably be told whether you are being taken forward to the next stage of the selection process (if there is one) fairly quickly. Asking for feedback on such interviews might be quite helpful.

Where you are applying for a graduate training scheme, however, you will not have the interviewers' information, and an email to a generic graduate admissions email address is likely to have very little impact. (Such email addresses will probably be handling several thousand emails.) It may be some time before you hear of the outcome, unless you are given an indication during the interview, which can happen on very rare occasions, since, theoretically, all the first-round interviews will need to be completed first. It is also true to say that the feedback given from a generic graduate training scheme first-round interview is likely to be very brief, if it is available at all. The number of interviews being carried out makes the provision of detailed feedback challenging for employers, but there is no reason why you should not ask for it.

It is very tempting to reflect on your performance immediately after the interview – and in some ways, it is a good idea to think about the questions and whether you made a good impression and gave answers which were sufficiently detailed. Ultimately, you will not have any definitive information until you are told about the outcome, but some initial thoughts could be useful.

INTEGRATION AND APPLICATION

There are a number of steps involved in performing well at selection interviews:

Step 1: Prepare well. Think about the job that you have applied for, identify potential questions you might be asked and role-play the interview with a critical friend. You also need to review your application carefully to remember what you have done in order to identify examples that you can draw on when answering questions.

Step 2: Behave professionally. Watch what you say, how you say it and how you behave generally. It is important that this starts from the moment you enter the building until the time you leave it. Be professional and mature.

Step 3: Answer the question well. The answer needs to be:

- Relevant.
- Complete. If it is a behavioural question (asking for an example), use the STAR framework.
- Delivered in a calm and professional manner (criticising others is not a good idea).

Step 4: Have some questions to ask. Make sure you prepare some questions which would affect your decision to accept a job, if you were offered it. The questions should not ask for information that is already available on the website.

Step 5: Write a brief email to thank the individual who set up the interview. The email should be short – that you thank them for arranging the interview, that you enjoyed the opportunity to get to meet those working for the organisation and the chance to learn more about the job and/or the company (assuming that you asked some questions and got some answers) and that you look forward to hearing about any 'further outcomes in due course', and should close with 'Yours 'sincerely' (since you met them at the interview). It is a basic sign of respect and is noted.

Step 6: Review and evaluate. Think about whether you did or said anything that might have been interpreted in a way which might prevent you moving further in the selection process.

CONCLUSION

Throughout this chapter, we have reviewed how interviews work, what employers are looking for in a good answer and have identified the kinds of questions that may be asked as well as suggesting some questions that candidates might like to ask.

There are some behavioural suggestions about what you should and should not do in the interview itself in Table 17.3, but it would also be good to provide a summary of the various 'Dos and Don'ts' we have covered throughout the interview process more broadly; see Table 17.4 below.

Table 17.4   Summary of do's and don'ts during the interview process

Do	Don't
• Prepare, by reviewing your application, reviewing the job specification, dressing appropriately and finding out as much information as you can in advance • Act and dress so as to look and behave professionally throughout the interview process • Practise some relevant questions with someone else – if you cannot think of any, use those at the end of each chapter • Answer questions using a STAR framework where questions ask you about something you have done, with the emphasis on the outcomes of your actions (R) • Make sure you have some questions to ask at the end of the interview	• Be late or dress inappropriately • Rush, panic or excessively show your nervousness – that can include laughing inappropriately • Bad-mouth your current or previous employer: you may want to leave because of them, but that does not normally create a positive impression • Be defensive if they challenge you about something you have said: they may simply need clarification, or they might want to see how you respond to negative feedback • Ask for feedback on the interview at the end of the interview

You should now be able to:

* Identify potential questions you might be asked in advance of an interview.
* Understand some basic dos and don'ts.
* Identify questions to ask the potential employer.
* Evaluate the impact of your non-verbal behaviour as well as the content of the answers that you give.

ADDITIONAL RESOURCES

Want to learn more? Visit https://study.sagepub.com/morgan2e to gain access to a wide range of online resources, including interactive tests, tasks, further reading and downloads.

Website Resources

The following websites offer useful advice on selection interviews.

American Psychological Society – on what to say and not say at internship interviews: www.apa.org/gradpsych/2010/01/missteps.aspx

Businessballs.com – background information on selection interviews and tips for interviewees: www.businessballs.com/interviews.htm

Changingminds.org – information on different forms of interview: http://changingminds.org/disciplines/hr/selection/interview.htm

Graduate Recruitment Bureau: www.grb.uk.com/graduate-interview-techniques

Newcastle University: www.ncl.ac.uk/careers/interviews/

Prospects: www.prospects.ac.uk/careers-advice/interview-tips

TARGETjobs: https://targetjobs.co.uk/careers-advice/interview-techniques

The Guardian – a good source of advice for job-seekers around interviews: https://jobs.theguardian.com/careers/interview-advice/

Textbook Resources

Cameron, S. (2010) *The Business Student's Handbook: Skills for Study and Employment* (5th edition). Harlow: Pearson (particularly Chapter 17).

Hamilton, C. and Kroll, T. L. (2018) *Communicating for Results* (11th edition). Boston, MA: Cengage (particularly Chapters 7 and 8).

Harwood, L., Owens, L. M. D. and Kadakia, C. (2017) *Your Career: How to Make it Happen* (9th edition). Boston, MA: Cengage (particularly Chapters 9, 10 and 11).

Hind, D. and Moss, S. (2011) *Employability Skills*. Houghton-le-Spring: Business Education Publishers (particularly Chapter 6).

Rook, S. (2013) *The Graduate Career Guidebook*. New York: Palgrave (particularly Chapter 13).

18

CONCLUSION: SKILLS AND EMPLOYABILITY

When you see the this means go to the companion website https://study.sagepub.com/morgan2e to do a quiz, complete a task, read further or download a template.

INTRODUCTION

We began this book with a welcome message in Chapter 1: 'Welcome to the rest of your life!' You are now several years on from when you first read that chapter, or perhaps you are reading this chapter now in order to get some kind of perspective on some of the issues you will be facing in the future. Whichever it is, this chapter is intended to be quite different from the others in its content, style and structure.

This chapter is something of a conclusion, but could also be read at the start of your university studies, so that you can see some of the issues that might go through your mind in times to come. If this is the case, then recognise that you will change a great deal during your degree – you won't necessarily see that, as the changes in any week or month are usually fairly small, but you will change and grow in maturity and your thinking – and please don't feel that the views being expressed are views you need to have now: when you have climbed to the top of a mountain, the view you have from the summit is very different from the view at the bottom, and it is one step at a time. As we have seen when we were talking about writing essays (see Chapter 7), a conclusion is really intended to bring the previous material together in a brief summary. The first part of this conclusion will do that, through a review of the text, and the second part will offer some reflections on careers, with comments from graduates who have become successful in their own careers.

REVIEW OF THE TEXT

Overall, this book has been about preparation and learning – from learning how to make the most of your time at university and understanding how university works, to preparing to begin the next major stage of your life: post-graduation 'work' (which might also include voluntary activity, setting up your own business, taking a postgraduate course or other activities). Let's recap the book chapter by chapter, just to make sure that you have not missed anything.

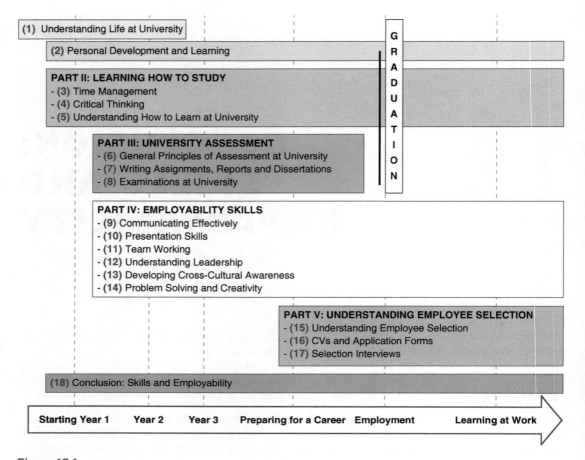

Figure 18.1

Each chapter has been designed to have relevance to different stages of your life, and some chapters – particularly those around personal development and learning, employability skills and employee selection – will have relevance throughout your life and career. The further we progress in our career, the more we operate at the boundaries of our skills and the more we need to learn new ways of thinking.

Part I: Life at University

Chapter 1: Understanding Life at University

The first chapter was designed to be very specific: to introduce you to the new world of university with all its processes, procedures, opportunities and challenges. The chapter was intended to help you to understand what you were getting yourself into – and managing to survive and hopefully enjoy it. If you are reading this at the end of your studies, then those days will seem a long time ago now and you might have wondered why it was so difficult to get used to your new life (if it was difficult).

Some find the challenge of living in a new place, learning to manage finances and become independent pretty difficult, but it is necessary to learn how to do things for yourself. Maybe, when you started your degree, you were used to your parents doing everything for you – organising your life, cleaning your clothes, etc., and if you have been living at home, then that won't have changed – but for many, you will have now learned to do those things. From a personal perspective, living in another country brings additional challenges and if you have come from another country, then making friends with others from the country in which you have studied will have helped enormously, while developing friendships with others from your own country will have given you a means of finding out how to do things together.

Chapter 2: Personal Development and Learning

The second chapter provided some ideas about how we learn. Learning never stops – or should never stop. There are many quotes about the power of learning throughout our lives ('When we stop learning, we stop living' etc.) and it is easy to become cynical or lazy about pushing ourselves to learn new things. The exciting thing is that there are now so many ways to learn and so many resources online to help us to do so – whether we are talking about skills or knowledge. Technology and software have come to be powerful tools in our lives and universities and institutes are thriving, not with degree programmes as such but by providing tools and resources – apps, videos, discussions – to help us learn whatever we wish. If we want to learn about Blockchain or programming in Python or how to use the latest version of Photoshop or whatever, we can go on YouTube or elsewhere and watch someone explaining it. As noted in Chapter 15, life is changing quickly, and if we stop learning then we will have a problem.

Part II: Learning How to Study

The next part of the text – Part II – brought together three chapters designed to help you to develop the skills needed for studying at university, but it is vital to realise that the university has always been intended as a gateway for your career, so all the modules and the skills and knowledge you gain at university has been designed to help you develop skills that are important for the life ahead of you. That is why such skills are usually referred to as 'transferable': they are designed to be taken with you from your life at university to a new life in a career. (The slight exception to this idea is Chapter 5, 'Understanding How to Learn at University', which is more relevant to university life than elsewhere, but we will look at that below.)

Chapter 3: Time Management

Time management is one of *the* most important skills you will develop. In the years after you begin your career, you might be fortunate enough to have a personal assistant (and in your personal life, a spouse might assist in managing your time) but until that happens, you are responsible for identifying and allocating sufficient time to those things which are important to you and/or your role at work. There is no difference between this and your life at university: at university, you (and no one else) are responsible for identifying and allocating sufficient time to those things which are important to you and/or your role as a student.

So we spent time looking at goals, techniques, the development of priorities and some ideas as to how this can work for you. The importance of time management in your life is all pervasive, and without good time management, you could suffer from stress, get defensive and irritable, suffer from depression and guilt, and harm relationships with those around you – your group members, your lecturers, your family sometimes – as you realise that you can't do what is needed in the given time. The chapter is there as a guide to assist you in this, but most of us can always improve how we manage ourselves, so there's no reason to stop reviewing what we do and how we do it.

Chapter 4: Critical Thinking

This chapter is intended to help you understand what your lecturers are looking for as you develop your assignments and essays, but can be applied to many other parts of life as well. Imagine watching a news report and simply accepting it, or a social media post and just believing that it is true. It is not that we should be sceptical about everything we believe, but rather that we should be able to analyse information well and spot inappropriate conclusions or the use of information from dubious sources. In these days of fake news and leaders who do not always believe scientific conclusions, we need to be able to consider information carefully.

There are times of course when scientific research has it wrong. There are research papers that get withdrawn and sometimes even if the results are correct, the conclusions are not correct, but research papers published in journals go through a review process using two or three other senior academics whose role is to examine whether the conclusions and findings are sound. Using good sources of information, checking their conclusions and making sure we are not making assumptions are key to good critical thinking and are important skills for using any information.

Chapter 5: Understanding How to Learn at University

We looked at how university – with the seminars, case studies, lectures, online learning and so on – is different from learning at school. Learning in the workplace is slightly different again, though training programmes, online courses and development projects (which can really enhance leadership skills) take this learning to a very practical level in terms of their workplace relevance. Fail to engage with the learning at university and you may fail some courses (which is not pleasant and you should never aspire to do this, of course!) but fail to engage with the learning at work and your performance may suffer and you may not get the opportunities you hope to get as you progress in your career – assuming you don't do something which will lead to you losing your job on the way, of course.

Training sessions in the workplace should have a lot more direct relevance to you than some of your modules. As explained in the first chapter, the QAA sets the framework for what you should learn in a business degree, but at work, the agenda is set by your job description and development needs moving forward. But the skills of recording, analysing and applying information remain relevant throughout our lives.

Part III: University Assessment

The third part of the text looked at how we might do well in the assessments that universities ask their students to complete. The section looked at assignments, reports, dissertations and examinations. (Chapter 10 on presentations also has some relevance here.) However, the section began with some general principles where we looked in more detail at issues around the application of critical thinking to written work, academic misconduct and how to get referencing style right.

Chapter 6: General Principles of Assessment at University

The critical thinking section of the chapter used Maslow's theory of motivation to apply a theory of learning developed by Bloom (Bloom et al., 1956). We didn't examine Maslow as a theory – that was not the purpose of this text which is about study skills rather than specific business theories – but we did use the hierarchy of needs to show how Bloom's ideas around critical thinking might apply to a theory such as the one discussed.

The second part of the chapter concerned plagiarism. As we saw, plagiarism is not primarily about referencing, though referencing is the medium through which this offence is evidenced: plagiarism is about taking someone else's ideas and submitting them as your own – and it is this that is the offence. It is different from poor academic practice, which means a lack of your own contribution in an essay which is almost entirely taken from others' work, but referenced well (and for which you are likely to get a 0).

Chapter 7: Writing Assignments, Reports and Dissertations

The next chapter in this section covered written assignments, reports and dissertations. Reports are regularly used in the workplace, so universities use them to develop your skills so that you will be able to produce something professional at work. Assignments and essays tend to perform a different function – to determine the extent to which you can think critically and structure/develop an argument in a way which convinces those reading it (or in the case of a presentation, watching it). Dissertations fulfil a different purpose still and because they are significantly larger pieces of work, develop additional skills such as project planning, research skills and the determination and motivation to work on a significant piece of work over a longer time span.

In terms of assignments and essays, we looked at how we might apply a writing process, how we might ensure we can spell and write correctly (which is important, even though there are many tools and resources available now to assist with this), how you might develop a good argument (which is important in many meetings and discussions at work) and the importance of understanding the audience in any communication. We also looked at how the structure of a report differs from that of a traditional essay and some practical ideas for how we might go about writing a dissertation.

Chapter 8: Examinations at University

Chapter 8 looked at how we might prepare for – and do well in – academic examinations. Examinations are used in the workplace as well, though not in every kind of occupation. In order to get promoted in work, qualifications matter. They are taken as a measure of the knowledge you have and the ability to apply that knowledge, and examinations at university do exactly the same (which is why employers usually look for a good degree outcome as a measure of your learning from university). So professional qualifications from the Chartered Institute of Marketing (CIM), the Chartered Institute of Personnel and Development (CIPD), the Association of Chartered Certified Accountants (ACCA) and so on are taken seriously at work. Learning how to do well in examinations is therefore important.

In the chapter, we looked at the nature of different question types, preparing for examinations, how to do well in examinations and planning revision. We also looked at some ways of improving our ability to remember information – something that we need to do on a day-to-day basis anyway – and what we need to do during an examination to ensure we do as well as we can – including managing our time well. Failing is not something any of your lecturers want you to do, so there are some ideas given about why people fail, to help you avoid those mistakes.

PART IV: Employability Skills

Part IV of this text shifted focus to some extent on to skills that are important in the workplace for general overall interaction with others (interpersonal skills – communicating effectively, leadership, working in groups and presentation skills) and performance in specific contexts (problem solving/creativity and cross-cultural awareness). All the skills already covered have application both at university *and* in the workplace and so maybe the term 'employability skills' is not helpful, but these tend to be skills specifically and explicitly looked for by graduate employers, over and above those needed to do well at university.

Chapter 9: Communicating Effectively

It is difficult to separate out the importance of communication from the other skills covered in this section – particularly leadership, group working and cross-cultural awareness: all three areas rely heavily on getting communication right. Of course, getting communication wrong in the workplace can have significant consequences: many talented individuals have not been promoted because they have not been able to communicate sufficiently well with others in order to maintain relationships. Sometimes that is about managing our own reactions and emotions to others' actions and behaviours, but sometimes it is simply about taking a bit of time to think and carefully practise how we communicate what we want to say.

In the chapter, we spent time looking at communication channels, the different components – verbal and non-verbal – of communication, and communication in teams, which is so often where things go wrong. The importance of getting communication right in teams and when we lead means that it underpins many other aspects of work performance. We looked specifically at how we might give negative feedback to others, the use of questions in communication, and the importance of building rapport in the relationships we have.

Chapter 10: Presentation Skills

Following on from the chapter on communication skills was one on presentation skills, which uses many of the behaviours covered in Chapter 9 and applies them to the context of a stand-up presentation. Whether you like or dislike giving presentations, you must be able to do them – no one ever gets a graduate job without both needing to show they can present information during an employee selection process *and* being able to give a presentation to colleagues, superiors and customers. It is one of the most predictable requirements for all graduate level jobs – though of course the nature of the audience and the objectives of the presentation might vary from situation to situation.

During the chapter, we spent time looking at the preparation necessary to succeed at a presentation, and with that the importance of considering the nature of the audience and the objectives of the presentation. We looked at some of the technical issues involved in giving a presentation, the need for a clear structure which supported the objectives and some ways of really engaging an audience through non-verbal communication and the appropriate (and inappropriate) use of tools and visual aids. Of course, some people get very nervous before a presentation and so we looked at some ideas for how to deal with nerves. Getting nervous is OK and we need to be honest about that, but letting our nerves prevent us from delivering a message clearly is not good.

Chapter 11: Team Working

Very few employees spend their lives working apart from others, though admittedly, working with others is not the same as working in a team: you could work in proximity to others but be doing a very different job, but that was not the focus of this chapter. This chapter focused on the challenges individuals face when working in conjunction with others to get a task completed, and depending on the size of the project, sometimes that might be through delegation or sometimes by working in smaller teams. Teams often rise or fall on the basis of the quality of the relationships within that team (hence the importance of good communication skills), but it is important to recognise the skills, personalities and the roles that individuals bring to the teams they join. Not paying attention to such issues in the workplace could mean that companies never see products they invest in launch successfully, information and knowledge possessed by employees never gets applied, and companies fall apart over poorly managed relationships where arrogance, distrust and politics get in the way of making good, bold, strategic decisions. So the importance of these issues has guided the content of this chapter.

In Chapter 11, we spent some time reviewing the qualities of good teams, the composition of teams and the personalities of team members, and gave some thoughts around the application of these issues to working on group-based assignments at university. We looked at the processes of group development at work, why groups at university sometimes struggle – and some ways of dealing with those struggles – and finally, the impact of working in a diverse and international team. There is little more painful at work or at university than needing to work in a team with others that you do not get on with, but that is sometimes unavoidable and we need to be willing to cooperate with others in various situations in life, even if we do not get on with them.

Chapter 12: Understanding Leadership

It is as difficult to cover issues of working with others in groups or teams and not cover issues of leadership within those groups as it is to cover working in groups and not look at communication. Graduate employers want to see leadership from all those that they employ – individuals who will develop and implement new ideas and add value to the business. They want to make sure that there are sufficient individuals with sufficient leadership skills to maintain and grow the organisation, so they put a great deal of resources into selecting those individuals with leadership skills and giving them projects and tasks to work on in order to enhance and develop those skills. That is why Chapter 12 talks about student societies so much, because it is a 'safe' environment (you are not going to bankrupt anyone) to practise and develop those skills.

As with many of the skills in this section (or even in this book), you are not going to develop leadership skills by reading a chapter of a book – or even a whole book – on leadership: there is absolutely no substitute for going out and doing it, but books can give us some ideas on what to do when things do not go according to plan, and can bring into our minds some issues to consider in order to make sure we have got things right. So the chapter spent some time looking at the differences between leadership and management and defining leadership – though it is sometimes easier to talk about what leadership seems to be 'about' rather than giving clear definitions. The chapter looked at workplace power and influence and leadership skills, but also looked at the challenges of leading a coursework group where others are causing difficulties. We also looked at some models of leadership and some ideas about how leadership might work in the future as those we lead change.

Leadership is never easy: it is about managing relationships, and while it would be great (i.e. give us a simple life) if everyone thought like we did and simply obeyed what we wanted them to do, that is very rarely the case in the real world. Leadership is based on relationships and so is messy, complicated and challenging – so be prepared.

Chapter 13: Developing Cross-Cultural Awareness

This is not a chapter solely for those individuals who want to go and work abroad – 'abroad' is coming to us, wherever we are. Even if you have no intention of working in another country, it is almost certain that you will be working with people from different backgrounds to yourself. In fact, some of the issues addressed in this chapter apply not only to issues of culture, but class, gender, geographical location, sometimes disability and other aspects of diversity. Whether we like it or not, we will need to learn to work with people who are different from us and who communicate in different ways from us wherever we work – so get used to it. Similarly, if you have come from overseas to study in the UK then this section is important for you too.

Adapting what we do to those from other cultures is something that is not easy. We started the chapter by looking at perception and perceptual processes. Understanding that our perception may be different from others' perceptions – and thus what is real to us may not be real to others – is really important when working with others (including those from our own cultures/backgrounds). We looked at world view, others' values and how communication and behaviour works in high and low context cultures. The chapter presented some well-discussed ideas from Geert Hofstede about how cultures differ and presented some ideas for how we might develop 'intercultural competence', and as students, you might have found the section on working with other students from different cultures interesting as well.

Finally, the chapter looked at dealing with culture shock and suggested ways of thinking about how we overcome our emotional reactions to situations and cultures we are not naturally comfortable with.

Some people talk about 'becoming a global citizen': sometimes we are not that experienced or familiar with other cultures, but they are all around us, so employers will be looking for graduates who are adaptable and able to understand those around them.

Chapter 14: Problem Solving and Creativity

While being 'the one' who managed to solve an unanswerable question might lead to admiration from others, respect from strangers and featuring in magazines and articles, in reality, solving problems happens in business every day – from small issues about how to work with a difficult person to establishing processes that help others work more efficiently. Employers look for people who can analyse issues and have sufficient insight to manage processes and solve problems, though it is often done by a team working together. Problem solving is easy when we are familiar with a problem from another context, but doing so when the problem is unfamiliar is a whole new challenge – employers want individuals who can look at things from unusual perspectives and draw on their own and others' knowledge to be able to see ways forward.

Being creative can be a lot of fun. In Chapter 14 we looked at a typical problem solving process (also called a 'rational approach'): that works well for structured issues that we are familiar with, but we also spent considerable time looking at some other issues in the context of more challenging problems. We looked at what creativity is, different forms that creativity might take, tools and techniques for enhancing our own and others' creativity (including analogies and the importance of 'play'), and blockages that can hinder our creativity from time to time. Applying these techniques systematically is not easy at first and takes practice, but when we can do so, then many more things become possible than we might have originally expected.

Part V: Understanding Employee Selection

This section is an unusual one to find in a text about study skills and personal transferable (termed 'employability') skills: most advice in this area is given through university careers advisory services, but there is little point in having a text directed at helping you develop skills for your career without then giving you some guidance on how to make the goal of your education – to begin a successful career – a reality. So the chapters here are intended to be very practical. Of course, the specifics of how employers select their graduates will change (e.g. online versus face-to-face interviews) but generally, the chapters here aim to give some useful advice.

Chapter 15: Understanding Employee Selection

This chapter aimed to provide you with a general overview of how selection processes work and how they are designed. We looked at how employers analyse jobs to better understand the nature of the person they are looking for, and provided some indication of the generic qualities expected from graduates. We examined the process of screening, looked at how different selection tools are used and how individuals might consider providing evidence of their skills and abilities. There was also some powerful comment on the use of social media by recruiters.

Chapter 16: CVs and Application Forms

This chapter again aimed to be very practical and as interactive as possible, bearing in mind the importance of the topic. It began by setting out issues around impression management, content and structure.

The chapter noted that there is no one best way to compile a CV, but any successful CV will give clear evidence that a candidate meets the criteria. It discussed the development of a 'personal brand', suggested some useful 'power words' which can be used as long as they are accurate, and noted that a CV which is suitable for one job may not necessarily be suitable for others. The chapter also covered issues around writing a covering letter and gave guidance on layout and content – including identifying when to use 'Yours faithfully' and when to use 'Yours sincerely'. Finally, the chapter gave some advice on completing application forms and on submitting speculative applications.

Chapter 17: Selection Interviews

The final chapter in this section covered a number of issues related to those stressful and important occasions – selection interviews. It examined issues around preparation and gave some thoughts about how to answer some typical interview questions, as well as giving some opportunity for you to evaluate others' answers from an interviewer's perspective. Importantly, the chapter set out the characteristics of a good answer to behavioural questions based around the STAR framework, and gave some examples. Finally, it gave some suggestions about questions which could be asked by a candidate at a job interview.

Online Chapters

There are two additional chapters available online which are relevant to this section of the book. The first deals with psychometric tests and assessment centres, and the second provides some information about alternative options after graduation.

Psychometric Tests and Assessment Centres

This online chapter is intended as a guide for those students who are faced with these selection processes as part of their search for a graduate job. It provides examples of the kinds of activities – ability tests, group exercises, personality questionnaires, etc. – that students might be faced with during the selection process and some ideas of what to do and what not to do.

Alternative Options after Graduation

Getting a graduate job is not the only option for students leaving university. This chapter covers issues relevant to the following:

- Voluntary experience.
- Internships.
- Further studies – professional and postgraduate (including Teaching and/or Teaching English as a Foreign Language, and PhD).
- Starting your own business.

It provides details of some things to consider in order to help you decide whether any of these options might be suitable for you, though practical issues will also play a significant part of course.

REFLECTIONS ON CAREERS

The content which follows comes from five individuals who have become successful in their own careers. Some of them were contacts from LinkedIn, some were previous students. They were asked two questions, one broad question about the lessons they had learnt from their life and career so far, and a second question which asked them to give their thoughts on the particular skills that we have covered in the preceding chapters. They have all given their permission to use this material.

Making Sense of These Views

There is a reasonable variety of individuals who gave their thoughts. With that diversity, however, comes contradiction. These are individuals who have various levels of experience, but even with that experience they offered advice as different individuals – with different attitudes, personalities, world views (see Chapter 13) and learning. Perhaps if we were to add a 'key learning point' here, it would be that there is no one definitive way to lead or manage others, or work in a team, or communicate with others, or become globally aware, etc. Instead, each person needs to find what works for them.

Each action and decision will have consequences, however, and you will need to consider those in the decisions you make and the way that you implement and communicate them. Hopefully, these consequences will be ones you can live with and will not affect the motivated and able staff you will have around you – but even if they are not, then it is a mistake you will need to learn from and not make again.

Contributions from Others

It is time to let those working in 'the real world' speak. The comments below are largely unedited and I prefer not to give too much comment – even though that is very tempting. Some key highlights from their comments are given above each person's contributions.

 **FOR YOU TO DO**

1. As you read the comments below from professionals with several years of experience, think about how they might help you to do what you want to do better than you might have done it before.
2. As you read the comments below, make note of anything which seems to be a recurring theme for you, or which is interesting. Some ideas are repeated regularly, others may be suggested just once or twice, but you need to think about what is being said here.
3. If you have been in employment previously, then think about whether you agree with what has been written here.
4. If you disagree, then think about why you disagree.
5. Is there anything you might need to change in your behaviour now?

In each case, a little background information is given so that you can contextualise the comments made. These descriptions are those given by the individuals themselves but the names given here are fictional.

John

John graduated two years ago and has been working in a small but successful startup organisation based in Kuala Lumpur, Malaysia.

Highlights: Think about your goals; build character; cross-cultural communication is important.

Little things matter – in life there are many times we feel that we're just doing 'small things' and we always want to achieve the '*big*' thing'. What I learned is that the pursuit of excellence in doing even the little things is how you achieve, how you achieve your '*big*' thing'. Never underestimate how doing little things well can build your character. Transparency and openness is one very crucial practice that allows better communication and understanding. Sometimes it might be a simple sentence but different people with different personalities and cultural backgrounds will interpret it very differently. It is good to always explain the reasons for anything you say in a discussion.

Mark

Mark has had several years' experience working in an organisation in the engineering industry in the UK. His work often takes him overseas to source materials and items for use in manufacturing.

Highlights: Care about others; relationships count, so solve problems rather than threaten.

A couple of things I've learned working in the private sector in 'modern' times: 1) If you want people to care about what you know, they need to know that you care. Even in 'hard-nosed' business, people matter, and you'll get more from your team if they know you care about them personally. 2) Business doesn't have to work on a linear scale, so that the more one party 'wins', the more the other party has to 'lose'. People can paint themselves into a corner whereby they have to fight their way out. Often, there is a solution that avoids one person having to win at the other's expense. For example, under pressure to recover costs for weekend work 'required' to support above-contracted-capacity demand, I was coming into conflict with the customer's purchasing team, who weren't set up to support claims. Under pressure to get something, you start making subtle references to threats (to hold shipments, refuse to support future spikes, etc.) which never go well. I learned that by: (a) working with Operations to plan further ahead, (b) finding a dedicated team at the customer who could handle such claims, when made in advance, and (c) communicating clearly and logically the basis for the claim, I was able to recover the costs without damaging relationships.

Sarah

Sarah worked as a corporate lawyer in private practice for seven and a half years and has been a compliance officer in a financial institution for almost four years.

Highlights: Pace yourself; be consistent; respect others.

Three lessons I have learnt over the years. 1) Pace yourself. Your career is a marathon not a sprint. Burn out is a very real thing. I learnt that, where possible and necessary, do not be afraid to ask for a time extension or turn down a time-sensitive project if you are working at full capacity. 2) You are only as good as your last piece of work. People do not always remember the good you have done but they will definitely remember when you screw up, so be consistent and do your best each time. 3) Respect and be nice to everyone. From your boss to the tea lady who looks after the pantry. Spend a few minutes when you can getting to know the administrative staff and the secretaries better. This will set you apart from the majority of your peers. I cannot count the number of times that my boss's secretary saved me by putting my work at the top of his review pile and squeezing me into his appointment schedule ahead of others when I needed to see him.

I think that the attribute that stands out for me is communication skills. I'm in a role where I tell people what they can and cannot do under the law. It is not a job that will make me popular in the company any time soon. My colleagues are, however, less resistant when it comes to following the rules if I let them know that I am not out to make life difficult for them but to help them succeed. I am still telling them what they can and cannot do but how I communicate it to them makes all the difference.

Phillipa

Philippa is a Wall Street investment banker turned knowledge management practitioner in a professional services firm. She has spent more than half her life schooling, working and living away from her Singapore home in the US, UK and China. She counts her husband and three children as her greatest blessings in life.

Highlights: Prioritise your life carefully; be good at cross-cultural management; lead with humility.

Prioritise what is important to you in life. As much of a cliché as it is, money isn't really the most important thing in our lives, so don't have your head buried in your work, never lifting it up to appreciate everything else around you. Invest in your family, your friends and yourself. Find a hobby, spend time with your spouse and children, seek fulfilment in things that truly matter. No one will ever say on their death beds that they wished they had spent more time at work, but rather, wish they had spent more time with the people they love. Make your life count.

Being truly cross-culturally aware requires us to clear our minds of any pre-conceived notions of what we *think* we know of others' cultures and norms. When in doubt, ask. You will probably find most people happy to share about their cultures and work norms which may be vastly differently from what you thought they were. A good one is to stop referring to time periods as winter or summer since this means something different to an American than to an Australian!

A real leader needs to set aside her title, rank and pride and truly lead by example with humility and kindness. Listen and provide counsel with sincerity and honesty. Most of all, recognise each team member as an individual with many facets to their lives which involve more than just work.

Lisa

Lisa is a Chinese MBA student at a graduate college in Boston, MA. Previously, she had worked for a Business School Dean in China, and had completed a Master's degree in the UK. She writes about leadership.

Highlights: Don't be too aggressive in leadership.

Leadership is nothing to do with power. All power is transient, and the more you use power directly the more likely [you are] to lose it. But the problem is while those of us who know the truth of leadership, such as [being] quietly confident, working hard, and staying focused on our strategy, the aggressive ones around us often perceive us as being weak. And, even if we will win through our wisdom, the aggressive ones can make our life miserable in the meantime.

REFLECTION POINT

Take some time to think about the following questions and write down some answers.

How did you react to the ideas given above? Were there any which struck you as unexpected or unusual?

Make a list of the key themes which came through to you as you read. Which ideas and themes do you think are going to be most important? Rank them in order of importance.

Talk to your personal tutor or a careers adviser about your ranking. Do they agree with you?

Concluding Comments

Some of the comments here are more specific and detailed than others, and some include a reason for saying what they have said, but all are from individuals who believe that they have something to contribute to help you understand what you will face in the world of work.

And that is where I hope this book will take you next, after graduation. Assuming that you have done well in your degree studies and assuming that you know what will happen after your graduation, then the chapters on personal development and learning employability skills will help you as you build on your experiences at university, while those on assessment and teaching styles and life at university are now less relevant to you. Keep it, use it and may it help you as you develop your career.

BIBLIOGRAPHY

Adair, J. (1973) *Action-Centered Leadership*. New York: McGraw-Hill.

Adebakin, A.B. Ajadi, O. T. and Tayo, S. S. (2015) 'Required and possessed university graduate employability skills: Perceptions of the Nigerian employers', *World Journal of Education*, 5 (2), doi: 10.5430/wje.v5n2p115.

Aldag, R. J. and Kuzuhara, L. W. (2015) *Creating High Performance Teams*. New York: Routledge.

Amabile, T. M. (1998) 'How to kill creativity', *Harvard Business Review*, September–October, 77–87.

Anderson, L. W. and Krathwohl, D. R. (eds) (2001) *A Taxonomy for Learning, Teaching, and Assessing: A Revision of Bloom's Taxonomy of Educational Objectives*. New York: Longman.

Arnold, J. and Randall, R. (2010) *Work Psychology: Understanding Human Behaviour in the Workplace* (5th edition). Harlow: FT/Prentice-Hall.

Association of Graduate Recruiters (2014) *The AGR Graduate Recruitment Survey 2014: Summer Review*. Available at: www.agr.org.uk/CoreCode/Admin/ContentManagement/MediaHub/Assets/ FileDownload.ashx?-fid=125071andpid=11533andloc=en-GBandfd=False (accessed 14 April 2016).

Association of Graduate Recruiters (2015) *The AGR Graduate Recruitment Survey 2015: Winter Review*. Available at: www.abdn.ac.uk/careers/documents/AGR_Winter_Survey_2015_Results.pdf (accessed 11 April 2016).

Azmi, I. A. G., Hashim, R. C. and Yusoff, Y. M. (2018) 'The employability skills of Malaysian university students', *International Journal of Modern Trends in Social Sciences*, 1 (3), 1–14.

Bailey, S. (2011) *Academic Writing for International Students of Business*. Abingdon: Routledge.

Barrett, D. J. (2011) *Leadership Communication* (3rd edition). New York: McGraw-Hill.

Belbin, R. M. (1981) *Management Teams: Why They Succeed or Fail*. London: Heinemann.

Belbin, R. M. (2003) *Team Roles at Work*. Oxford: Elsevier.

Bloom, B. S., Engelhart, M. D., Furst, E. J., Hill, W. H. and Krathwohl, D. R. (1956) 'Taxonomy of educational objectives: The classification of educational goals', *Handbook 1: The Cognitive Domain*. New York: David McKay.

Breakenridge, D. (2018) *Answers for Modern Communicators*. New York: Routledge.

Brittain, B. (2012) 'Leadership perfected: Leading from the whole you', *Ivey Business Journal*, September–October. Available at: https://iveybusinessjournal.com/publication/leadership-perfected-leading-from-the-whole-you/ (accessed 23 July 2020).

Burns, T. and Sinfield, S. (2016) *Essential Study Skills* (4th edition). London: Sage.

Byham, T. M. and Wellins, R. S. (2015) *Your First Leadership Job*. Hoboken, NJ: Wiley.

Cameron, S. (2016) *The Business Student's Handbook: Skills for Study and Employment* (6th edition). Harlow: Pearson.

Cameron, K. S., Whetten, D. A. and Woods, M. (1996) *Developing Management Skills for Europe*. Addison-Wesley.

CareerBuilder (2018) 'More than half of employers have found content on social media that caused them NOT to hire a candidate, according to recent CareerBuilder survey', press release. Available at: http://press.careerbuilder.com/2018-08-09-More-Than-Half-of-Employers-Have-Found-Content-on-Social-Media-That-Caused-Them-NOT-to-Hire-a-Candidate-According-to-Recent-CareerBuilder-Survey (accessed 18 July 2020).

Cawthorn, S. (2018) *Storyshowing*. Melbourne: J. Wiley & Sons.

CBI-Pearson (2017) *Helping the UK Thrive: Education and Skills Survey 2017*. London: Pearson. Available at: www.cbi.org.uk/media/1341/helping-the-uk-to-thrive-tess-2017.pdf (accessed 6 July 2020).

Christopher, E. (2012) *Communication Across Cultures*. Basingstoke: Palgrave.

Cottrell, S. (2013) *The Study Skills Handbook* (4th edition). New York: Palgrave.

Courtney, M. and Du, X. (2014) *Study Skills for Chinese Students*. London: Sage.

Covey, S. R. (1989) *The Seven Habits of Highly Effective People*. New York: Simon & Schuster.

Deane, M. (2010) *Academic Research, Writing and Referencing*. Harlow: Pearson.

De Bono, E. (1971) *Lateral Thinking for Management: A Handbook of Creativity*. New York: American Management Association.

Denicolo, P. and Reeves, J. (2014) *Developing Transferable Skills*. London: Sage.

Dheer, R., Lenatowicz, T. and Peterson, M. F. (2014) 'Cultural regions of Canada and United States: Implications for international management research', *International Journal of Cross-cultural Management*, 14, 343–84.

Dougherty, C. and Thompson, J. E. (2010) *Be a Better Leader*. Oxford: Bookpoint.

Duarte, N. (2012) *HBR Guide to Persuasive Presentations*. Boston, MA: Harvard Business Review Press.

Fernbach, P. (2017) 'Why do we believe things that aren't true?' TEDxMileHigh; available online at: https://www.youtube.com/watch?v=jobYTQTgeUE&list=PLCJxQIIsdezGHgyouwaLpbX2Wyt2Yxszv&index-=4&t=0s (uploaded 13 September 2017).

Fiedler, F. E. (1967) *A Theory of Leadership Effectiveness*. New York: McGraw-Hill.

Fisher, A. (2011) *Critical Thinking: An Introduction* (2nd edition). Cambridge: Cambridge University Press.

Fleming, N. and Baume, D. (2006) 'Learning styles again: VARKing up the right tree!', *Educational Developments*, 7(4), 4–7.

Fleming, N. D. and Mills, C. (1992) 'Not another inventory, rather a catalyst for reflection', *To Improve the Academy*, 11 (1), 137–55.

Flint, M. and Hearn, E. V. (2015) *Leading Teams: 10 Challenges and 10 Solutions*. Harlow: Pearson.

French, J. P. and Raven, B. (1959) 'The bases of social power', in D. Cartwright (ed.), *Studies in Social Power*. Ann-Arbor, MI: Institute for Social Research. pp. 150–67.

Furseth, I. and Everett, E. L. (2013) *Doing Your Master's Dissertation*. London: Sage.

Gallagher, K. (2016) *Essential Study and Employment Skills for Business and Management Students* (3rd edition). Oxford: Oxford University Press.

Gallo, C. (2014) *Talk Like TED*. London: Macmillan.

Gallo, C. (2016) *The Storyteller's Secret*. London: Macmillan.

George, D., Dixon, S., Stansal, E., Gelb, S. L. and Pheri, T. (2008) 'Time diary and questionnaire assessment of factors associated with academic and personal success among university undergraduates', *Journal of American College Health*, 56, 706–15.

Graff, G. and Birkenstein, C. (2010) *They Say, I Say* (2nd edition). New York: Norton & Company.

Greenleaf, R. K. (1970) *The Servant as Leader*. Indianapolis, IN: Robert K. Greenleaf Centre for Servant Leadership.

Greenleaf, R. K. (2002) 'Essentials of servant-leadership', in L. C. Spears and M. Lawrence (eds), *Focus on Leadership: Servant-Leadership for the Twenty-first Century*. New York: Wiley. pp. 19–26.

Gruber, M. J., Gelman, B. D. and Ranganath, C. (2014) 'States of curiosity modulate hippocampus-dependent learning via the dopaminergic circuit', *Neuron*, 84 (2): 486–96, doi: 10.1016/j.neuron.2014.08.060.

Guirdham, M. (2001) *Interactive Behaviour at Work* (3rd edition). Harlow: Pearson Education.

Hamilton, C. and Kroll, T. L. (2018) *Communicating for Results* (11th edition). Boston, MA: Cengage.

Harvard Business School (n.d.) 'The HBS case method'. Available at: www.hbs.edu/mba/academic-experience/Pages/the-hbs-case-method.aspx (accessed 8 July 2020).

Harwood, L., Owens, L. M. D. and Kadakia, C. (2017) *Your Career: How to Make it Happen* (9th edition). Boston, MA: Cengage.

Hasson, G. (2012) *Brilliant Communication Skills*. Harlow: Pearson.

Hawkins, P. (2017) *Leadership Team Coaching* (3rd edition). London: Kogan-Page.

Hersey, P. and Blanchard, K. H. (1977) *Management of Organizational Behavior: Utilizing Human Resources* (3rd edition). Englewood Cliffs, NJ: Prentice Hall.

Hind, D. W. G. and Moss, S. (2011) *Employability Skills*. Tyne and Wear: Business Education Publishers.

Hodges, D. and Burchell, N. (2003) 'Business graduate competencies: Employers' views on importance and performance', *Asia-Pacific Journal of Cooperative Education*, 4 (2): 16–22.

Hofstede, G. (2010) *Culture's Consequences: Software of the Mind* (3rd edition). New York: McGraw-Hill.

Honey, P. and Mumford, A. (1992) *The Manual of Learning Styles* (3rd edition). Maidenhead: Peter Honey.

Horn, R. (2012) *The Business Skills Handbook*. London: CIPD.

Institute of Student Employers (2019) *Inside Student Recruitment 2019: Findings of the ISE Recruitment Survey*. London: ISE.

Institute of Student Employers (2020) *Student Development Survey 2020: Supporting the Learning and Development of Entry-level Hires.* London: ISE.

Irwin, D., Jovanovic-Krstic, V. and Watson, M. A. (2013) *So Where's Your Dissertation?* Toronto: Nelson Education.

Janis, I. L. (1982) *Groupthink* (2nd edition). Boston, MA: Houghton Mifflin.

Jobs.ac.uk (n.d.) 'Employability: What are employers looking for?' Available at: www.jobs.ac.uk/careers-advice/interview-tips/1515/employability-what-are-employers-looking-for (accessed 22 July 2020).

Katzenbach, J. R. and Smith, D. K. (2001) *The Discipline of Teams.* New York: Wiley.

Katzenbach, J. R. and Smith, D. K. (2005) 'The discipline of teams', *Harvard Business Review*, 83 (7–8), 162–71.

Kaye, S. M. (2012) *Critical Thinking.* Oxford: Oneworld.

Kepner, C. H. and Tregoe, B. B. (2013) *The New Rational Manager.* Princeton, NJ: Princeton Research Press.

Kolb, D. A. (2015) *Experiential Learning: Experience as the Source of Learning and Development* (2nd edition). New York: Pearson Education, Inc.

Kubler-Ross, E. (1969) *On Death and Dying.* USA: Scribner.

Lachman, S. J. (1997) 'Learning is a process: toward an improved definition of learning' *Journal of Psychology*, 131 (5), 477–480.

Lamberg, T. (2018) *Leaders Who Lead Successfully.* Lanham, MD: Rowman and Littlefield.

Luft, J. and Ingham, H. (1955) 'The Johari Window: A graphic model of awareness in interpersonal relations', University of California Western Training Lab.

Malandro, L. (2015) *Speak Up, Show Up and Stand Out.* New York: McGraw-Hill.

Marshall, L. A. and Rowland, F. (1998) *A Guide to Learning Independently* (3rd edition). Maidenhead: Open University Press.

Martin, R., Villeneuve-Smith, F., Marshall L. and Mckenzie, E. (2008) *Employability Skills Explored.* London: Learning and Skills Network.

Marton, F. and Säljö, R. (1976) 'On qualitative differences in learning: I – Outcome and process', *British Journal of Educational Psychology*, 46, 4–11.

Maslow, A. H. (1943) 'A theory of human motivation', *Psychological Review*, 50 (4), 370–96.

Matthews, A. (2013) *The Successful Presenter's Handbook.* Strensall: HLS Publishing.

McCarthy, P. and Hatcher, C. (2010) *Presentation Skills: The Essential Guide for Students.* Crows Nest: Sage.

McMillan, K. and Weyers, J. (2012) *The Study Skills Book* (3rd edition). Harlow: Pearson.

McMillan, K. and Weyers, J. (2013) *How to Improve Your Critical Thinking and Reflective Skills.* Harlow: Pearson.

Muchinsky, P. (2003) *Psychology Applied to Work* (7th edition). Pacific Grove, CA: Brooks-Cole.

Mumford, M. D. (2000) 'Managing creative people: Strategies and tactics for innovation', *Human Resource Management Review*, 20 (3), 313–51.

Neugebauer, J. and Evans-Brain, J. (2016) *Employability: Making the Most of your Career Development.* London: Sage.

Nielsen, J. A., Zielinski, B. A., Ferguson, M. A., Lainhart, J. E. and Anderson, J. S. (2013) 'An evaluation of the left-brain vs. right-brain hypothesis with resting state functional connectivity magnetic resonance imaging', *PLoS ONE*, 8 (8): e71275. Available at: http://journals.plos.org/plosone/article?id=10.1371/journal.pone.0071275 (accessed 18 April 2016).

Novotney, A. (2013) 'No such thing as "right-brained" or "left-brained", new research finds', *Monitor on Psychology*, 44 (10), 10.

Omar, N. H., Manaf, A. A., Mohammed, R. H., Kassim, A. C. and Aziz, K. A. (2012) 'Graduates employability skills based on current job demand through electronic advertisement', *Asian Social Science*, 8 (9), 103–10, doi: http://dx.doi.org/10.5539/ass.v8n9p103.

Osborn, A. F. (1957) *Applied Imagination.* New York: Scribner.

Owen, J. (2011) *How to Manage* (3rd edition). Harlow: Pearson.

Pauk, W. and Owens, R. J. Q. (2014) *How to Study in College* (11th edition). Boston, MA: Cengage.

Payne, E. and Whittaker, L. (2006) *Developing Essential Study Skills* (2nd edition). Harlow: FT/Prentice Hall.

Pettinger, R. and Firth, R. (2001) *Mastering Management Skills.* Basingstoke: Palgrave.

Prospects (2010) *Real Prospects 2010 – The Best Graduate Employers as Rated by Graduates?* Available at: www. hecsu.ac.uk/assets/assets/documents/Real_Prospects_2010_-_Main_Report.pdf (accessed 22 July 2020).

Prospects (2019) '7 skills for a successful management career'. Available at: www.prospects.ac.uk/jobs-and-work-experience/job-sectors/business-consulting-and-management/7-skills-for-a-successful-management-career (accessed 22 July 2020).

Puccio, G. J., Mance, M. and Murdock, M. C. (2011) *Creative Leadership: Skills that Drive Change* (2nd edition). Thousand Oaks, CA: Sage.

Purdue Online Writing Lab (2020) *APA Formatting and Styleguide* (7th edition). Available at: https://owl.purdue.edu/owl/research_and_citation/apa_style/apa_formatting_and_style_guide/general_format.html (accessed 7 July 2020).

Quality Assurance Agency (2015) *Student Benchmark Statement: Business and Management.* Available online at: www.qaa.ac.uk/docs/qaa/subject-benchmark-statements/subject-benchmark-statement-business-and-management.pdf?sfvrsn=db39c881_5 (accessed 6 July 2020).

Rabin, L., Fogel, J. and Nutter-Upham, K. E. (2011) 'Academic procrastination in college students: The role of self-reported executive function', *Journal of Clinical and Experimental Neuropsychology*, 33, 344–57.

Radcliffe, S. (2010) *Leadership Plain and Simple.* Harlow: FT-Prentice-Hall.

Raven, B. H. (1965) 'Social influence and power', in I. D. Steiner and M. Fishbein (eds), *Current Studies in Social Psychology.* New York: Holt, Rinehart, Winston. pp. 371–82.

Rees, W. D. and Porter, C. (2008) *Skills of Management.* London: Cengage.

Robins, S. and Finley, M. (1998) *Why Teams Don't Work.* London: Orion.

Robbins, S. P. and Hunsaker, P. L. (2003) *Training in Interpersonal Skills.* Upper Saddle River, NJ: Pearson.

Robinson, W. L. (1974) 'Conscious competency: The mark of a competent instructor', *The Personnel Journal* (Baltimore), 53, 538–9.

Rook, S. (2013) *The Graduate Career Guidebook.* New York: Palgrave.

Rossi, B. (2012) 'Open University to launch new online learning platform', *Information Age*, 14 December. Available at: www.information-age.com/open-university-to-launch-new-online-learning-platform-2137308/ (accessed 7 July 2020).

Rowntree, D. (1998) *Learn How to Study* (4th edition). Exeter: Warner Books.

Rubin, S. (2016) 'What is Blockchain', YouTube, 8 June. Available at: www.youtube.com/watch?v=93E_GzvpMA0 (accessed 8 July 2020).

Scherr, A. L. and Jensen, M. C. (2007) *A New Model of Leadership.* Harvard NOM Working Paper No. 920623. Available at: http://papers.ssrn.com/abstract=920623 (accessed 8 July 2020).

Schneider, S. C., Barsoux J.-L. and Stahl, G. (2014) *Managing Across Cultures* (3rd edition). Harlow: Pearson.

Sheldon, J. L. (1997) 'Learning is a process: Toward an improved definition of learning', *The Journal of Psychology*, 131 (5), 477–80.

Sheridan, E. (2005) 'Intercultural leadership competencies for US leaders in the era of globalization', PhD Dissertation. University of Phoenix Online. Available at: www.dialogin.com/fileadmin/Files/User_uploads/executive_summary_delphi_study_results_sheridan_june_2005.pdf (accessed 15 July 2016).

Shivoro, R. S., Shalyefu, R. K. and Kadhila, N. (2018) 'Perspectives on graduate employability attributes for management sciences graduates', *South African Journal of Higher Education*, 32 (1), 216–32, doi: http://dx.doi.org/10.20853/32-1-1578.

Smale, B. and Fowlie, J. (2009) *How to Succeed at University: An Essential Guide to Academic Skills, Personal Development and Employability.* London: Sage.

Smith, M. (2011) *Fundamentals of Management* (2nd edition). Maidenhead: McGraw-Hill.

Sternberg, R. J. (2007) 'A systems model of leadership: WICS', *American Psychologist*, 62 (1), 32–4.

Sutton, R. I. and Hargadon, A. (1996) 'Brainstorming groups in context: Effectiveness in a product design firm', *Administrative Science Quarterly*, 41 (4), 685–718.

Tanna, M. (2011) *Think You Can Think?* London: Oxbridge Applications.

TARGETjobs (n.d.) 'Expert performance tips for Skype and video interviews'. Available at: https://targetjobs.co.uk/careers-advice/interview-types/323749-expert-performance-tips-for-skype-and-video-interviews (accessed 22 July 2020).

Tissington, P., Hasel, M. and Matthiesen, J. (2010) *How to Write Successful Business and Management Essays*. London: Sage.

Tuckman, B. W. (1965) 'Developmental sequence in small groups', *Psychological Bulletin*, 63 (6), 384–99.

Universities UK (2012) 'Bringing it all together: Introducing the HEAR', *Higher Education Achievement Report*. Available at: www.hear.ac.uk/tools/bringing-it-all-together (accessed 10 January 2016).

Varner, I. and Beamer, L. (2011) *Intercultural Communication in the Workplace* (5th edition). New York: McGraw-Hill.

Wagner, H. L., MacDonald, C. J. and Manstead, A. S. (1986) 'Communication of individual emotions by spontaneous facial expressions', *Journal of Personality and Social Psychology*, 50 (4), 737–43.

Walliman, N. (2013) *Your Undergraduate Dissertation*. London: Sage.

West, M. A. (2012) *Effective Teamwork* (3rd edition). New York: Wiley.

Wheebox/Confederation of Indian Industry (2019) *India Skills Report 2019*. Available at: www.aicte-india.org/sites/default/files/India%20Skill%20Report-2019.pdf (accessed 10 March 2019).

Whetten, D. A. and Cameron, K. (1996) *Developing Management Skills for Europe*. Harlow: FT/Prentice Hall.

Whetten, D. A. and Cameron, K. S. (2011) *Developing Management Skills* (8th edition). Upper Saddle River, NJ: Prentice Hall.

Winstanley, D. (2005) *Personal Effectiveness*. London: Chartered Institute of Personnel and Development (CIPD).

Wong, L. (2012) *Essential Study Skills* (7th edition). Boston, MA: Cengage.

World Economic Forum (2016) 'What skills do graduates need to get a job?' Available at: www.weforum.org/agenda/2016/02/what-skills-do-graduates-need-to-get-a-job/ (accessed 10 March 2019).

INDEX